THE DIARY OF
SAMUEL PEPYS

THE DIARY
OF
SAMUEL PEPYS

A new and complete
transcription edited by

ROBERT LATHAM
AND
WILLIAM MATTHEWS

VOLUME XI · INDEX

Compiled by
ROBERT LATHAM

UNIVERSITY OF CALIFORNIA PRESS
BERKELEY AND LOS ANGELES
1983

ISBN 0-520-02098-7

Library of Congress Catalogue No. 70-96950

Set in Monotype Bembo by
Richard Clay (The Chaucer Press) Ltd, Bungay, Suffolk
Printed in Great Britain by Fletcher & Son Ltd, Norwich
Bound by Hunter & Foulis Ltd, Edinburgh

CONTENTS

PUBLISHER'S NOTE

The publication of Volumes X (the *Companion*) and XI (the *Index*) marks the completion of the eleven-volume edition edited by Mr Robert Latham and the late Professor William Matthews.

Professor Matthews' main work as Joint Editor was the transcription of the original manuscript of the *Diary* in the Pepys Library at Magdalene College, Cambridge. He had arrived at the end of this immense task shortly before his death in 1976 but sadly did not live to see the completion of publication.

Mr Latham has borne the responsibility alone for the *Companion* and *Index* volumes. He started work on this eleven-volume edition in 1950. Since that time he has held academic posts in England, the USA and Canada, and from 1972 until 1982 has been Fellow and Pepys Librarian at Magdalene College, Cambridge. Throughout these years he has spent an enormous amount of time on the research required for this edition and the publishers are deeply grateful to him for the scholarly dedication and skill he has brought to this massive undertaking.

The publishers are particularly pleased that it has been possible to complete this new edition for publication in 1983, the 350th anniversary of the birth of Samuel Pepys.

PREFACE

In this volume an index is provided to the text of the diary, the principal footnotes and the editorial introduction. It does not cover the *Companion* (volume X) which is designed to be in most respects self-indexing.

References to everyday or recurrent events, such as attendance at the office or at church, are not indexed if Pepys makes no more than a passing mention of them. Other omissions are indicated in the head-notes to the entries, and in this preface under *Places*.

An attempt has been made to avoid excessive use of that bane of indexes – the unbroken run of numerals. In avoiding that extreme I may have been guilty of using more words than is usual in an index. This has often been necessary for the sake of clarity. It has also been due to an attempt to catch something of the diary's flavour – hence the use of Pepys's own phrases where briefer ones could easily have been substituted. Here and there, as in the entry on the diary itself, it is hoped there are passages which will not only serve the reader who is looking for references but may also give pleasure to the reader who wants to browse.

Persons

Where the diary is the only authority for the spelling of a surname it appears in that form. In other cases it is spelt in the form used, or used most often, by its owner (if that is known), or in the standard books of reference, with Pepys's spelling (if substantially different) added in brackets. Occasionally, as with Will Hewer, all Pepys's variants are recorded.

Brief identifications are added in many cases, and are always given – if the information is available – in those cases where no identification is given either in the footnotes to the text or in the *Companion*.

The longer entries are divided into sections and sub-sections arranged in logical rather than alphabetical order. Thus the section 'misc[ellaneous]' may come last, and that on 'public affairs' may precede that on 'private life'. Within the sections and sub-sections the order in which the references are given is usually that of the diary, though occasionally a thematic order has seemed preferable. 'Social' is a subject-category borrowed from Dr de Beer's index to Evelyn – a model to all indexers. Pepys's sociability gives the category a special value, but it should be added that its use is limited to those occasions about which he reports nothing beyond the social encounter itself. If he has at those points a statement about any other subject, the reference is omitted from 'social' and entered under another heading such as 'news from' or 'business with'. Where he records, as he so often does, what was eaten or drunk on those occasions the reference is repeated in the entries 'Food' and 'Drink'.

The treatment of Pepys and his wife has called for special measures. A small number of references to Pepys has been gathered under his name, covering events before the diary period. For the rest it has been taken for granted that the diarist is himself the subject of his diary. References to him are therefore distributed throughout the index. Some entries (e.g. 'Clerk of the Acts') are devoted exclusively to him; others such as 'Dress' include references to him which are signalled by a prefatory '(P)'; while certain large subjects have two distinct entries – e.g. 'Tangier' and 'Tangier (P)'. A list of the principal entries relating directly to Pepys is given below at page xiii.

A different policy has suggested itself for his wife. She is indexed for the most part under her name, but other references to her (marked 'EP') are entered elsewhere, principally under the subjects to which cross-references are given in the headnote to her entry.

It is probable that the index, like the diary itself, is unfair to Elizabeth. There are many occasions when Pepys takes his wife's presence for granted and does not accord her a mention.

Places

London and Westminster are treated similarly to Pepys, since – almost as much as Pepys himself – they may be assumed to be omnipresent in the text. Streets, buildings and other places within the two cities are indexed under their names except for those grouped as taverns or theatres. The entries 'London' and 'Westminster' are confined to listing events and corporate affairs.

No attempt is made to include passing references to well-known streets such as the Strand.

Subjects

Many subjects are dealt with under group headings rather than individually. Animals for instance are impounded in a single entry. Similarly with other topics – books, naval stores, pictures, plays, sermons and so on. The longer lists of items are usually arranged alphabetically; the shorter ones in the order of their appearance in the diary. In the case of certain subjects (books, prices, plays, ships, taverns) some editorial information (specified in the headnotes) has been added.

Extensive use has been made of subject-entries in order to make accessible the mass of information which the diary contains, even though in many instances this involves the repetition of material to be found elsewhere in the index under other entries. 'Parliament' and 'Privy Council' for instance carry many of the references given in 'Navy' and 'Navy Board'.

Format

The form of reference to volume- and page-numbers, different from that used elsewhere in this edition, has been chosen as the most convenient for note-taking.

Asterisks and daggers are occasionally added to the references to convey editorial information. Their meaning is explained in the headnotes.

The sub-heading 'also' is used for minor but substantive references, and is distinct from 'alluded to' which introduces passing mentions only.

The tilde ($\sim$) indicates material tangential to the main subject of the entry – in the case of persons, often a servant or relative.

PRINCIPAL INDEX ENTRIES CONCERNING PEPYS

ACKNOWLEDGEMENTS

My wife Linnet has shared in the making of this Index. I laid down the ground plan, but she involved herself in every process of its construction. She read aloud the entire text of the diary while I took notes – discussing with me, as we went along, exactly what words might best introduce the successive groups of references, and thus converting what might have been a chore into a paper-game. At later stages she undertook innumerable investigations into detail, and checked from the text every reference in the typescript.

My thanks are also due to David and Susan Yaxley who, once the ground plan had been established, read the whole of the diary text and compiled index slips in draft which I found useful as a basis for my own slip-notes.

Various scholars have contributed to parts of the Index. There are several subjects which it would have been impossible to index adequately without the information which only experts can provide. The entry 'Health', for instance, is at some points organised around diagnoses made by Dr C. E. Newman. Similarly Professor W. A. Armstrong helped with 'Theatre', Professor Kerry Downes with 'Whitehall Palace', Professor A. Rupert Hall with 'Science', Dr Richard Luckett with 'Music' and Mr J. L. Nevinson with 'Dress'. The entry 'Prices' is based on a study made by Hugh Walton. I thank them all.

My publisher's editor, Mary Butler, and her assistant Elizabeth Brooke-Smith, have been a tower of strength in the preparation of the book for the press, and have been quick to lighten my task in every way they could.

Once again I express my warmest thanks to Mary Coleman who has typed the manuscript and (with her colleague Aude Fitzsimons) has undertaken much of the checking. I cannot believe that there are many as fortunate as I in having secretarial help of such quality.

Robert Latham

'A man may think a place is missing, when it is only put in another place.'

PEPYS, 8 JUNE 1663 (on Newman's *A Concordance to the Holy Scriptures*)

INDEX

ABBOT, George, Archbishop of Canterbury 1611–33: his hospital and tomb at Guildford, 9/273 & n. 3

ABEBURY: see Avebury

ABERGAVENNY, Lady: see Nevill

ABINGDON, Berks: custard fair, 9/227 & n. 2; P visits Christ's Hospital, 9/227–8 & n.; MSS at, ib. & nn.

ABLESON, Capt. [James], naval officer: killed in action, 6/122

ABRAHALL, [Thomas], ship's chandler: gift to EP, 4/415

ABRAHAM, [John], bo'sun: acquitted of murder, 4/76 & n. 3

ACTON, Mdx: 7/240

ACWORTH, [Elizabeth], wife of William: her good looks, 1/147; 2/13; 4/20; rock, 4/20; balsam, 4/64; P tries to 'begin acquaintance' with, 4/241; refrains from making advances to, 5/155; illness, 9/484–5

ACWORTH, [William], storekeeper, Woolwich: at The Hague, 1/147; his pretty house, 2/13; incompetent accountant, 3/136; consulted about masts, 4/50; reports malpractices, 4/241; 5/181 & n. 1; his malpractices, 5/130 & n. 2, 156, 181; 9/123–4 & n.; case against, 9/145, 258, 281, 291, 382 & n. 3; consulted on history of naval administration, 9/484; social: 4/20; 5/306; his Dutch clerk, 6/216–17

ADAMS, Henry, of Axe Yard: marriage, 1/190; social: 1/21, 77, 287; 2/228; alluded to: 1/270

ADAMS, Ald. Sir Thomas, Bt; Lord Mayor 1645–6: M.P. London 1654–5, 1656–8: death, 9/136 & n. 2; kidney stone shown to P, ib.

ADDIS, [?John], navy victualler: gives fish dinner, 1/287; gift to P, 3/28

ADMIRAL, the LORD HIGH: see James, Duke of York

ADMIRALTY [see also Coventry, W.; James, Duke of York; Justice, administration of; Wren, M.]: COMMISSION OF: report of commission

of 1618, 4/96 & n. 4; rumoured proposal to create (1668), 9/278, 279; P's career in (1673–9) vol. i, pp. xxxvi–viii

PREMISES: moved from Derby House to Whitehall, 1/174 & n. 4, 229; P does business, 1/87, 89, 90, 174, 226–7; writes letters, 1/176; and diary, 1/204; Navy Board meets, 1/229, 241

ADMIRALTY AND NAVY, COMMISSIONERS of the, Feb.–April 1660: replace Treasurers at War, 1/82; to reduce fleet, 1/102–3 & n.

AFONSO VI, King of Portugal 1656–83 [see also Luisa Maria, Queen-Mother and Regent]: simple-minded, 2/197; 3/91; deposed, 8/578 & n. 3; alluded to: 3/252

AFRICAN (Guinea) HOUSE, [Old] Broad St: P visits, 4/395, 437; 5/48, 52, 66, 124; 7/323

AGAR, [Thomas], Chancery clerk: 2/222; 6/79

AGRICULTURE: P's observations on harvest, 4/220; and calf-rearing, 6/179; fall in rents, 7/355; 8/84, 158 & n. 1, 199; 9/1, 44; cultivation of tobacco, 8/442 & n. 2; flax, 9/496; failure of gentry to export corn, 9/1

AILESBURY, Earl of: see Bruce

AIX-LA-CHAPELLE, TREATY OF (1668): alluded to: 9/281–2

ALBEMARLE, Duke and Duchess of: see Monck

[ALBRICI], Vicenzo (Vincentio), composer: 8/56 & n. 6, 64–5

ALCOCK, Harry, P's cousin: goes to Ireland, 1/260; asks for place, 3/119; 9/208; social: 3/132

ALCOCK, [Stephen], of Rochester, Kent: social: 2/68 & n. 1, 70, 72; 3/31

ALCOCK, Tom, P's schoolfellow at Huntingdon: 1/87, 90

ALDEBURGH (Alborough, Albrough) Bay, Suff.: Sandwich's fleet in, 6/35; also, 7/142, 143

ALDERSGATE: regicides' corpses displayed on, 1/269–70

& n. 3; his ships aground off Gibraltar, 6/8 & n. 3, 12; attacks Dutch fleet off Cadiz, 6/13–14 & n., 19; returns to Portland, 6/62 & n. 4; made Rear-Admiral, 6/147; on *Royal James*, 6/287; dispute about pay, 7/93–4 & n.; and about chaplain's groats, 7/97 & n. 1; neglected by Albemarle, 7/178; captures Dutch merchantman, 7/249, 255; complains of Rupert's misgovernment of fleet, 7/332; presses men for winter voyage, 7/355; elected Elder Brother, Trinity House, 7/382; ill, ib.; to be 'land-admiral' at Plymouth, 8/149; engagement with La Roche, 9/96–7 & n.; low reputation in Mediterranean, 9/137; Tangier voyage, 9/272, 274, 427–8 & n.; victuals sent to, 9/382; concludes peace with Algiers Feb. 1669, 9/473 & n. 1; returns, 9/508, 510 & n. 3; to be sent back, 9/513 & n. 2; discusses policy towards Algiers, 9/516; said to be P's enemy, 9/529
SOCIAL: 4/4, 53, 340; 8/140; 9/544, 563
MISC.: house, 4/405; coach, 8/479
ALLUDED TO: 9/276
ALPS, the: 9/206
ALSOP, [Josias], Rector of St Clement Eastcheap 1660–6: preaches, 2/219
ALSOP, [Timothy], brewer to the King: anecdote by, 4/156; court gossip from, 5/56–61 & nn.; victualling contract, 5/196, 199, 204, 210; illness and death, 5/217–18, 221, 223, 224; social: 5/195
AMEIXIAL, battle of: 4/198 & n. 2, 202–3, 215 & n. 1, 220
AMERICA: see New England, New Netherland
AMSTERDAM: city gives yacht to Charles II, 1/222 & n. 1; plague in, 4/340 & n. 2, 358; 5/142; quarantine on ships from, 4/399 & n. 2; comet reported, 5/134 & n. 1; bank, 7/252 & n. 4; burgomaster, 8/68; propose cession, 8/108
ANABAPTISTS [*see also* Fanatics]: dismissed from fleet, 1/101, 109 & n. 2; elected to Parliament for London, 2/57 & n. 1 [error]
ANDERSON, Charles, physician, P's contemporary at Magdalene: 1/149–

50; 2/103; ~ his brother, 1/90
ANDREW(S), John, steward to Lord Crew: transactions with P, 1/4, 32, 43, 64, 95; alluded to: 1/313
ANDREWS, John, timber-merchant, Bow: pessimistic about public affairs, 8/377; musical: 6/324–5; 7/422; social: 7/421; 8/483
ANDREWS, ——, wife of the foregoing: expecting child, 6/325; social: 7/421–2; 8/483
ANDREWS, Matt, coachman to Lord Crew: social, 1/18
ANDREWS, [Thomas], merchant, of St Olave's parish: contract for Tangier victualling, 5/223, 226, 236, 263; 6/37, 85, 86, 139, 193, 337; discusses Tangier business with P/Povey, 6/38, 97–8, 105, 130, 185, 201(2); gifts to P, 6/57, 202, 251, 337; accounts, 6/201, 202; in country during Plague, 6/185; P's regard, 6/201–4 passim; to resign victualling to Gauden, 6/203–4, 226–7, 251; receives sacrament, 6/210; also, 8/205; musical: sings, 5/120, 194, 199, 209, 217, 226, 325, 332, 337, 342, 349; 6/24, 27, 32, 39, 44, 55, 73, 80, 88, 98, 125, 131, 219; social: 6/62, 86, 210; 7/413; 8/64, 377; 9/220, 404; ~ his wife [Hester], 5/342; 9/220, 404; his son, 9/404
ANGEL, [Edward], actor: 9/85 & n. 5
ANGIER, John, sen., tailor, P's cousin, of Cambridge: drinks King's health, 1/67; EP visits, 2/180; asks for place, 4/363–4, 409; bankrupt, 4/439; social: 1/69; 2/89; 3/217, 218; alluded to: 2/136; 4/409; ~ his wife, 2/89; 4/430
ANGIER, John, jun.: asks for place, 4/178, 363; to be sent to sea, 4/409; a rogue, 4/439; death, 5/291
ANGIER, Percival, P's cousin, of London: at East India House, 4/384 & n. 4; burial, 6/16; social: 4/364
ANGLESEY, Earl of: see Annesley
ANIMALS [For domestic animals and household pets, *see* Household etc.; and under names of owners. Horses are principally indexed under Travel (road). *See also* Entertainments; Games etc.]:
GENERAL: menagerie at Tower, ?1/15 & n. 2; 3/76 & n. 2; noises made by

animals in Rochester, 8/313; P's dislike of cruelty to, 9/154, 203; theories of generation, 2/105 & n. 4, 160
PARTICULAR: baboon [?chimpanzee; gorilla]: from Guinea, 2/160 & n. 3; bears: in Baltic, 4/413; boars: in Baltic, 4/413; bulls: 2/209 & n. 2; 7/245–6; cat(s): P/EP's, 1/325; 8/553; experiments on, 6/95–6; survives Fire, 7/277; colt: allegedly mistaken for sturgeon, 8/232–3 & n.; cows and calves: 3/221 & n. 2; 6/179; deer: in Baltic, 4/413; hunting terms, 8/475; dogs: P tempted to steal, 2/149; kill child, 3/205; P chased/frightened by, 4/131; 7/26; experiments on, 5/151; 6/57, 84; 7/370–1 & n., 373, 389; 9/263 & n. 1; guard dogs, 7/133 & n. 1; sheepdog, 8/339; elephant: hunting of in Siam, 7/251; foxes: hunting of in Baltic, 4/413; frogs: 2/105; horses: manège, 4/120; kidney stones, 4/146; staggers, 8/390; Royal Mews, 5/70–1; performing, 9/297, 301; kitten: experiment on, 6/64; lions: ?1/15 & n. 2; monkeys: performing, 2/166; 4/298; snakes: story of, 3/22 & n. 2; sow, Hamburg: alluded to, 9/420; toad: in drink, 7/290; whale: skeletal remains of, 1/150 & n. 2; fished off Greenland, 4/125; wolves: in Baltic, 4/413
ANJOU, Duc d': see Philippe
ANNE of Austria, wife of Louis XIII of France (d. 1666): Bristol's intrigues with, against Mazarin, 4/212 & n. 1
ANNE (b. Hyde), Duchess of York (d. 1671):
PERSONAL: plain, 2/80; proud and extravagant, 3/64; 8/286–7; 9/38; dress, 6/172; portraits by Lely, 3/112–13 & n.; 7/82 & n. 1; her 'silly devotions', 9/164
CHRON. SERIES: birthplace, 6/198 & n. 1; to visit Portsmouth, 4/24; jealous of Monmouth, 4/138; Western progress, 4/321; ill, 4/436, 439; 5/4; to visit Harwich, 6/104; effect of Clarendon's fall on, 8/424, 506; 9/11, 153; reconciled to Coventry, 9/336, 342; receives French ambassador, 9/284; favours French alliance, 9/536;

friendly with Lady Castlemaine, 9/417
MARRIAGE AND FAMILY: marriage, 2/40–1 & n.; also, 1/275, 315, 319, 320; 2/1; 7/261, 354; birth of son, Charles, Duke of Cambridge, 1/260–1, 273; his death, 2/95; death of daughter Princess Mary, 3/75; of son, James, Duke of Cambridge, 4/229; about to lie in, 6/19; birth of son, Charles, Duke of Kendal, 7/201 & n. 2; of son, Edgar, Duke of Cambridge, 8/436 & n. 2; death of grandmother, 2/213; and of mother, 8/570; jealousy, 3/248; dalliance with husband, 4/4; love affairs, 6/302 & n. 1; 7/8, 323; said to have poisoned Lady Denham, 8/8; and (with children) to have pox, 9/154–5 & n.; domineers over husband, 9/342
HOUSEHOLD: maids of honour, 6/41
SOCIAL: at theatre, 2/80, 164; 7/347; 8/167; gives play at court, 7/325; attends Feast at Inner Temple, 2/155; at Durdans, 3/184; Whitehall chapel, 3/42; 9/163–4; Somerset House, 3/191; 5/300; ball at Whitehall, 3/300–1; 7/372; dines in public, 4/407; 8/161; at court lottery, 5/214; in state at Whitehall, 8/33; plays cards on Sunday, 8/70; at Hinchingbrooke's wedding, 9/51; at Deptford party, 9/468–9
ALLUDED TO: 9/344, 407
ANNESLEY (Anslow), Arthur, cr. Earl of Anglesey 1661, politician and Treasurer of the Navy:
CHARACTER: 5/336; 8/301, 327
CHRON. SERIES: appointed to Privy Council, 1/171; opposes motion in Commons to reward Sandwich, 1/178; chairs Council's Admiralty Committee, 5/319; 6/45; at Fishery Committee, 5/336; at Privy Council/ Council committees, 8/278, 291; pessimistic about war, 8/288, 291; (untrue) rumour of appointment to Treasury commission, 8/367; manager of conference between Houses, 8/551 & n. 4, 561; rumoured dismissal from Council, 8/571, 596, 600; views on issues in Skinner v. E. India Company, 9/196 & nn.
AS TREASURER OF THE NAVY: appoint-

ment, 8/295 & n. 3, 297, 301, 322; attends Board, 8/327; 9/39, 196; anxious to learn from P, 8/334; his allowance, 8/334–5 & n., 378; proposals for paying-off fleet, 8/397, 456, 567, 571; active in sale of prize ships, 8/484; rumoured dismissal, 9/10; promises reforms, ib.; annoys Duke of York, 9/253, 256, 310; criticises P, 9/244, 295, 306 & n. 1, 308; 'suspended and discharged', 9/340–1 & n., 346 & n. 3, 357; resists order, 9/341, 342–3, 344–5, 416; petitions King, 9/351, 362 & n. 1; Board's complaints of, 9/428; unspecified business, 8/462; also, 9/42, 67 & n. 3
POLITICAL NEWS FROM: 8/375, 555, 561, 565; 9/8–9, 25, 323
ALLUDED TO: 1/66; 9/145, 209
ANNIS, [Robert], workman, Woolwich yard: to be tried for embezzlement, 3/137 & n. 2
ANSLEY (Annesley), Capt. [Abraham]: appointed Master-Attendant, Deptford, 9/441 & n. 1
ANSLOW: see Annesley
ANTIGUA, Leeward Is.: captured by French, 8/38 & n. 1
ANTRIM, Earl of: see Macdonell
ANTWERP: 9/396
APPLEYARD, ——, of Huntingdon: 9/224
APPRENTICES: riots/demonstrations, 1/39 & n. 1, 54; 5/99–100 & n., 101; 9/129–30 & n., 132, 133, 152 & n. 2; church attendance, 3/194; in good seats at theatre, 9/2; affray in Moorfields between Weavers and Butchers, 5/222–3 & n.; hard life of apprentice fisher-boy, 6/241–2
APSLEY, Sir Allen, M.P. Thetford, Norf.: reports news of battle of Ameixial, 4/215 & n. 1; drunken speech in Parliament, 7/416; establishment as Master-Falconer reduced, 8/394–5 & n.; alluded to: 7/73
APSLEY, Sir Anthony [recte Sir Allen]: 7/73
APSLEY (Appesley), Col. [John]: accused of forgery, 3/43–4
ARCHANGEL: hemp from, 4/175, 394; map of river, 4/390

ARCHER, Betty, sister of Mary: admired by P as undergraduate, 2/220
ARCHER, Mary, of Bourn, Cambs., later wife of Clement Sankey: at theatre, 2/220 & n. 4, 226; her portion, 2/220; alluded to: 2/225; ∼ her uncle's house, 2/220
ARCHES, Court of: see Justice, administration of
ARCHITECTURE, P's taste in [asterisks denote the occasions when he makes a descriptive comment]: admires Audley End House, 1/69–70★; 8/467–8★; disappointed with alterations at Hinchingbrooke, 3/220★; with Old Wanstead House, 6/102★ & n. 4; and Wilton, 9/230★; admires Gauden's house at Clapham, 4/244★; Wricklemarsh, 6/94★ & n. 3; Swakeleys, 6/215★; Dagnams, 6/159; Clarendon House, 7/32★ & n. 2, 42★; Sir P. Warwick's new house, 7/64; Bridewell, 8/6; Belasyse's new house, 9/202; and Goring House, 9/276
ARGIER(S): see Algiers
ARITHMETIC: see Science and mathematics
ARMADA, Spanish [see also Navy, Royal]: 3/187; alluded to: 8/293
ARMIGER, [William], relation of P: in pre-coronation procession, 2/82; attempts to court EP, 2/208; lodges with Tom P, 3/6; 4/183; social: 1/54, 88; 2/43, 53, 60; ∼ his son, 5/71
ARMORER, ——, [? the following]: claims to have enjoyed favours of Duchess of York, 4/138
ARMOURER, [?Sir Nicholas], Equerry of the Great Horse to the King: in drunken frolic, 8/446–7 & n.
ARMY [For P's service in, see Mountagu, E., 1st Earl of Sandwich. See also Commonwealth; Militia; Tangier]:
CHRON. SERIES: Lifeguards routed in Venner's rising, 2/10; troops sent to Portugal, 3/48, 63; their conduct in campaign, 4/215 & nn.; Guards quell riots by seamen, 7/416; 8/28; by apprentices, 9/129, 130, 132; blow up houses in Fire, 7/269; regiments raised against invasion threats, 7/395; 8/265; troops moved to Portsmouth and

Sheerness, 8/98; deployed against Dutch raids, 8/276; conduct in Medway crisis, 8/308, 309; numbers reduced by disbandment, 8/476; 9/32; soldiers man ship, 8/147, 153; Lifeguards stop tobacco-growing, 8/442 CEREMONIES: Lifeguards escort Russian envoy, 3/267–8; Horseguards at Whitehall and Somerset House, 5/56 FINANCES [*see also* Fox, Sir S.]: Guards paid from excise, 8/572, 576; 9/197; Albemarle gives precedence to payment of, 8/591 OFFICERS: attempts to dismiss Catholic officers, 7/354, 378 & n. 2 QUARTERS: at inn, 6/245 REGIMENTS: alleged corruption and cowardice of Lifeguards, 4/377; Admiral's regiment, 8/334 & n. 5 REVIEWS: in Hyde Park, 4/216; 9/308, 557 STANDING ARMY: parliament's distrust, 3/15; 8/324, 352–3, 355; and city's, 8/260; fear of Duke of York raising new army in north, 6/277 & n. 2, 302; 7/395; and of King's intention to rule by, 7/307; 8/332 & n. 1, 366 & n. 3; 9/32; King's denial, 8/360–1

ARRAN, Earl of: *see* Butler, Lord R.

ARTHUR, [?Robert], of Ashtead, Surrey: 4/245

ARTILLERY GROUND, Spitalfields: 9/528

ARUNDEL HOUSE, Strand: gardens and gallery, 2/110; sculptures, ib. & n. 2; Royal Society /its council meets, 8/7, 11, 17, 242–3, 528, 540–1, 553–4; 9/113, 263, 334, 379; alluded to: 9/353

ARUNDEL STAIRS: 2/110

ARUNDELL, ——, organist: 4/283

ARZILL: *see* Azila

ASCENSION DAY: beating the parish boundaries, 2/106 & n. 1; 9/179 & n. 2; parish dinner, 9/179; Navy Board holiday, 4/162

ASCUE: *see* Ayscue

ASHBURNHAM, John, Groom of the Bedchamber to the King: part in Charles I's escape from Hampton Court (1647), 6/316–17 & nn.; said to have sold viscountcy (1646), 8/126 & n. 1; anger at shortages in King's

household, 8/417–18; also, 7/383; 8/419

ASHBURNHAM, William, Cofferer of the King's Household: business concerning money for Household, 7/92, 133, 134; 8/112, 193, 198; 9/269, 280, 306; P's regard, 7/383, 407; court news from, 7/384, 385; congratulates P on parliamentary speech, 9/105; admires P's shorthand, 9/269; house, 7/160; 8/198–9 & n.; social: 6/300; 7/160, 335, 406; 9/280, 320

[ASHBY, Capt. Arthur], naval officer: killed in action, 7/231 & n. 4

ASHE, Simeon, Presbyterian minister (d. 1662): sermons mimicked, 1/280

ASHFIELD, [Sutton], of Brampton: 8/220; ~ his wife [Lucy], 8/117

ASHLEY, Lord: *see* Cooper, A. A.

ASHMOLE, Elias, savant (d. 1692): P sings with, 1/274 & n. 1; his views on generation, 2/105 & n. 4

ASHTEAD (Asted), Surrey: P's boyhood memories, 3/152 & n. 1; P and Creed lodge at, 4/245 & n. 3; visit church (St Giles), 4/247

ASH WEDNESDAY: Exchequer open, 8/73

ASHWELL, Mary, companion to EP: CHRON. SERIES: engaged, 3/298; 4/14, 16, 19, 21, 32, 40, 49, 72; at Chelsea school, 4/45 & n. 2, 59; pleases P, 4/74, 79, 81, 88, 90; EP jealous, 4/122, 165, 180; accused of stealing, 4/171; neglected, 4/175; visits Brampton with EP, 4/183, 184, 205; quarrels with EP, 4/210, 262, 274, 276; dismissed, 4/278, 279–80, 287; to resume teaching, 4/280; informs P about Sandwich's liaison, 4/392; revisits Seething Lane, 5/18; also, 4/84, 96, 97, 107, 128, 155, 162, 285; 5/10 MUSICAL: plays harpsichord, 4/75; virginals, 4/79, 87, 93, 99, 103, 120; P buys music for, 4/76; P teaches, 4/122 SOCIAL: accompanies EP on visits etc., 4/73, 74, 82, 99, 108, 141, 142, 149, 154; visits parents, 4/83, 173, 284; dances, 4/106, 109, 141, 179; plays cards well, 4/107; entertains P and EP with recitations, 4/112 ALLUDED TO: 4/92, 113, 118, 133, 150 ~ her uncle, 5/10

ASHWELL, Samuel: 1/272
ASHWELL, Mr ——, of the Exchequer: daughter proposed as EP's companion, 4/16, 21, 32(2); musical: 1/5; social: 1/33, 272; 2/31, 227; alluded to: 4/83, 173, 274, 278 ~ his wife, 4/32, 83; sister, 3/286
ASIA: stories (unspecified) of travels in, 5/34
ASKEW, Askue: *see* Ayscue
ASSHETON, family of: at Great Lever Hall, Lancs., 3/254
ASTED: *see* Ashtead
ASTROLOGY: *see* Popular beliefs etc.
ASTRONOMY: *see* Royal Society; Science etc.; Scientific and Mathematical Instruments
ATHENS: proposers of new laws in [error], 9/60 & n. 2
ATKINS, Col. [Samuel], merchant: news from, 7/348; supplies coal to Tangier, 7/381 & n. 3; 9/249; house, 9/345; also, 6/46; 7/44
ATKINSON, [Thomas], goldsmith: 1/7
AUBIGNY, Lord d': *see* Stuart, L.
AUCTIONS (by inch of candle): of ships, 1/284 & n. 2; and naval stores, 2/45, 69; bidding described, 3/185–6
AUDLEY, [Hugh], scrivener, Fleet St: death and estate, 3/264 & n. 2; biography, 4/22 & n. 5; alluded to: 8/497
AUDLEY END HOUSE, Essex: described, 1/69–70 & nn.; 8/467–8 & nn.; pictures, 1/70; 8/467 & n. 4; garden, 8/468; King and Duke of York visit, 7/68, 71; 9/325; King buys, 7/68 & n. 2; alluded to: 8/470
AUSTIN (Augustine) FRIARS, Old Broad St: 5/282–3; alluded to: 7/44
AUSTIN, Godfrey, scrivener, King St, Westminster: 1/34
AUSTRIA: *see* Empire, Holy Roman; Germany
AVEBURY (Abebury): P visits, 9/240 & n. 2
AXE YARD, Westminster: P takes up residence in, vol. i, p. xxiii; 1/1 & n. 2; pays rent, 1/87, 88; returns after Dutch voyage, 1/179, 182; expenditure, 1/213; sells lease, 1/213,

218, 219, 235, 244, 245, 247; removes papers, 1/248; ~ coronation bonfires in, 2/87
AXTEL, Col. Daniel, regicide: executed, 1/268 & n. 1, 269
AYLESBURY, Anne, Lady Aylesbury, widow of Sir Thomas: Duke of York in mourning for, 2/213 & n. 1
AYLESFORD, Kent: P visits Sir J. Banks's house, 9/495–6 & n.; and Kit's Coty House, 9/496–7 & n.
AYLETT, Capt. [John], naval officer: dismissed for cowardice, 7/174 & n. 1
AYNSWORTH, [Elizabeth], prostitute: at Reindeer, Bishop's Stortford, 8/466, 467; 9/209; expelled from Cambridge, 8/466 & n. 1; bawdy song, ib. & n. 3; to move to London, 9/210
AYRES: *see* Eyres
AYSCUE (Ascue, Askew, Askue), Sir George, naval commander: opposes sending convoy to Turkey, 6/10 & n. 4, 11; serves under Sandwich, 6/147; refuses share of prize-goods, 6/260–1; taken prisoner by Dutch 7/153, 169; 8/426; portrait by Lely, 7/102 & n. 3; also, 2/173, 185; 5/27, 149, 186, 288, 317; 6/241
AZILA (Arzill), N. Africa: offered to England, 8/347–8 & n.

BABER, Sir John, royal physician, Covent Garden: 7/14, 71–2
BACKWELL, Ald. Edward, goldsmith-banker, Lombard St:
CHARACTER: industry, 4/396; pride, 9/517
BUSINESS WITH P: Tangier: 5/339; 6/274; 9/152, 249; unwilling to lend money, 6/85, 109; provides money/credit for garrison, 8/528(2); 9/253, 315, 316, 328, 415; Navy Board: informs P about marine insurance, 4/394, 395; and difficulties with Navy Treasury, 7/214–15 & n.; refuses further credit, 7/330–1; private: changes foreign money, 1/183; sells plate etc. to, 1/322, 323, 324; 2/4; 5/47; P deposits cash with, 2/76; 5/269 & n. 1; accounts, 7/34
BUSINESS WITH SANDWICH: sells plate, 1/185, 192; loan, 2/120, 122; changes

BALLOW (Ballard), [Stephen], leather
seller: 4/265 & n. 1; ~ his wife, ib.
BALTIC, the (the Sound): convoys,
1/102; 6/328, 331; Sandwich in
(1659), 1/141, 180, 285; 4/69 & n. 2;
P in (1659), 1/285; 2/185 & n. 5;
fishing through ice, 4/412; ships from,
6/202, 248
BALUE, Cardinal [Jean], (d. 1491):
death, 9/256 & n. 2
BANBURY, Oxon.: Tom P visits,
3/176, 213; Coventry to take waters,
9/258 & n. 2
BANCKERT, Adriaen, Dutch naval
commander: sails north, 6/133 &
n. 2; brings fleet home, 6/146; ship
burnt in action, 7/229 & n. 5
BANES, [J.]: see Baines
BANES, [? Robert]: on *Naseby*, 1/99
& n. 1
BANISTER, John, court musician: to
play at Mitre, 1/25 & n. 4; airs by,
7/171; replaced at court, 8/73 & n. 3;
plays theorbo, 9/138; teaches song to
Knepp, 9/189; writes out song for P,
ib.; also, 9/134, 175
BANISTER, ——: 7/246
BANKER(T): see Banckert
BANKS, Sir John, merchant: his
wisdom, 7/24; praises Cromwell,
5/52 & n. 1; advises P on victualling,
6/265; (unspecified) Tangier business,
7/24, 132; report on Dutch raid,
7/162; views on Exchequer as bank,
8/132; complains of Navy Board's
debts, 9/149 & n. 2; political views,
9/399; house near Aylesford, 9/495–6
& n.; also, 9/497, 562
BANKS and bankers [*see also* Amsterdam; Backwell, E.; Colvill, J.;
Finances (P); Vyner, Sir R.]: loans to
government, 3/297 & n. 2; 4/17;
King controlled by, 4/176; P's business with, 6/193, 332; 7/195, 196; at
risk under monarchy, 7/252; reluctant to lend to government, 6/133, 311;
8/143, 591; Exchequer as bank,
8/131–2 & n.; Treasury's/Downing's
hostility, 8/230, 240 & n. 2; run on
during invasion scare, 8/263, 270,
275–6, 285, 450; proclamation in their
support, 8/285 & n. 3
BANKSIDE [*see also* Taverns etc.:

Falcon]: plague burials at, 6/213;
alluded to: 2/114; 7/271
BANNESTER, Bannister: see Banister
BANSTEAD DOWNS, Surrey: horse
races and footraces, 4/160 & n. 5, 243,
255
BANTAM, Java: 6/36 & n. 1
BAPTISTA: see Draghi
BAPTISTE: *see* Musical Compositions:
Lully, J.-B.
BARBADOS, W. Indies: attack on St
Kitt's from, 7/390 & n. 3, 391; naval
action off, 8/430; fire at Bridgetown,
9/243 & n. 2; also, 8/275, 374
BARBARY COMPANY: *see* Royal
African Company
BARBER, [John], purser: 2/207
BARBER: *see* Barbour
BARBER-SURGEONS'   COM-
PANY: *see* London: livery com-
panies
BARBER-SURGEONS'   HALL,
Monkwell St: rebuilding after Fire,
9/292 & n. 5
BARBON (Barebone), Praisegod, re-
publican: petitions Parliament, 1/51 &
n. 3; windows broken, 1/54 & n. 4, 65
BARBOUR, [William], clerk in the
Navy Office: asks for place, 7/345–6
& n.; news from, 8/280
BARCKMANN, Sir Johan, Baron
Leijonbergh, Swedish Resident 1661–
72, Envoy 1672–91 (d. 1691): dispute
about prizes, 8/21–2 & n., 23, 123 &
n. 1, 135–6; his house, 8/22 & n. 1;
perspective painting, 9/352; ~ his
wife, 7/372; his secretary, 8/23
BARCROFT, [John], Serjeant-at-
Arms: 8/86 & n. 3, 92–3 & n.
BARDSEY: *see* Bawdsey
BAREBONE: *see* Barbon
BARKELY: *see* Berkeley
BARKER: *see* Baker
BARKER, Ald. [William], Baltic
merchant: hemp recommended by
Batten, 3/155, 157; stories of Baltic,
4/413; at Apposition Day, St Paul's
School, 5/37; on hemp trade, 5/63;
dispute with Ormond, 8/404, 407,
420 & n. 2; 9/119
BARKER, ——, companion to EP:
kinswoman to Fauconberg, 6/235 &
n. 4; homely appearance, 6/235;

wharf, 4/284; ~ almost drowned near Portsmouth, 3/253–4
FINANCIAL BUSINESS: at pays at Treasury Office, 2/227; 4/2, 291–2 & n.; 7/332; works on Treasurer's accounts, 3/240; 5/318; and Creed's, 3/279; 4/11; on commanders' pay, 4/7; also, 6/72; 7/314, 374; 8/20, 200, 274, 510
JUDICIAL BUSINESS: in Field's case, 3/280–1; 4/171, 172, 350, 421–2; at Court of Admiralty, 4/76
OTHER BUSINESS: visits wrecks, 1/313; 6/54; attends launches, 4/102–3; 5/307; visits ships, 4/203–4 & n.; 6/193–4; 7/352; arranges weighing-up of, 8/266, 325; buys Common-wealth arms, 2/69 & n. 2; has Com-monwealth figurehead burnt, 4/418 & n. 2, 420–1; angered by pacifist sermon, 2/37; assaulted by seamen, 6/288; abused by seaman's wife, 8/268; part in Carkesse's dismissal, 8/60, 76, 100, 109, 146, 213, 215, 238, 385; unspecified: 1/239, 243, 253; 2/40, 206; 3/21, 22, 24, 62, 101, 146, 203, 229, 272; 4/4, 31, 43, 61, 177, 222, 243, 278, 322, 338; 5/138, 156, 156–7, 274, 299, 342; 6/13, 19, 98, 145, 222; 7/12, 105, 107–8, 115, 162; 8/25, 142, 181, 186, 278
PERQUISITES AND PROFITS [*see also* Reputation]: chest of drawers from ropemaker, 3/197; granted lighthouse patent, 5/314; 6/3 & n. 4; fails to obtain place in Prize Office, 5/322, 327, 328, 333; buys ketch, 7/105–6; given share in privateer (*Flying Greyhound*), 7/299, 300–1 & n.; her voyages and prizes, 7/316, 418, 424; 8/1, 8, 17, 180, 344, 349, 351–2, 369, 441–2; dispute with Swedish Resident about prizes, 8/21–2, 23, 27, 128, 130, 135, 135–6, 169; to become sole owner, 8/112; buys out P, 8/341, 385, 462; 9/119; alleged favour to crew, 9/99
RELATIONS WITH COLLEAGUES AND ASSOCIATES: with P: mutually critical, 3/59, 64, 145; 6/92; quarrel about warrants, 3/163–4; mate's appoint-ment, 4/110; contracts, 5/115–16; 7/358–9; supplies, 5/157, 238; un-

specified quarrels, 5/118; 7/232; ally in Field's case, 4/51–4 passim; and in Carkesse affair, 8/101–2, 105; high opinion of P, 8/419; also, 5/45, 341; 7/36; with others: mutual recrimina-tion over Interregnum careers, 2/65; complains of colleagues' malice, 3/171; relations with Pett, 1/240; 4/53–4; 8/100; Warren, 2/78; 4/437; 5/318; Slingsby, 2/202; Waith and officers of Navy Treasury, 3/29; Carteret, 3/59; Mennes, 3/14, 227; 4/194; 5/235, 293; 6/233, 234; Cox, 4/149; Hewer, 4/337; Commissioner Taylor, 5/326, 350; 6/295; Penn, 6/66; 8/217; Brouncker, 7/410; 8/78, 80, 97, 126
REPUTATION: criticised by P for cor-ruption, 3/145; 4/205, 325; 5/120, 121, 131, 143, 182; 6/298; for corrupt collusion: with hemp merchants, 3/101–2 & n.; flagmakers, 3/148 & n. 3; ropemaker, 3/155 & n. 3, 157; tar merchant, 4/182; Cocke, 4/194, 241, 284; Wood, 4/201; 5/117; Castle, 5/83 & n. 3; and Dr Walker, 8/123; criticised by P for inefficie-ency, 3/59; 4/2, 97, 98, 113; 5/120; 6/284, 330; 7/359; 8/12, 582; said to be more diligent, 3/174; corrup-tion/inefficiency criticised: by Warren, 3/131; 5/131, 143; Capt. J. Allen, 3/155, 157; Coventry, 4/17, 194–5, 196, 341, 397; 5/169; 7/409; 8/570, 571; Carteret, 4/97; 6/74; P. Pett, 4/98; Barrow, 4/134; Hempson, 5/140–1; C. Pett, 5/109; Waith, 5/155; Gilsthorpe, 8/560, and in 'libel', 7/388
OTHER PUBLIC OFFICES: as M.P.: elected for Rochester, 2/55, 57, 58; attends Commons, 4/58; 6/274–5; Trinity House: defeated in election to Mastership, 3/93; elected, 4/185; rebuilds almshouses, 5/116–17 & n.; claims members' exemption from militia, 6/24–5 & n.; power in, 6/107, 298; unspecified business, 2/26; 3/29; dinners at, 2/4; 3/103, 187, 190; 4/209, 343; at Trinity Monday service, 5/172
NEWS FROM: naval: 6/115, 119; 7/151, 156, 225, 228, 395, 415, 416; 8/350;

BEE, [Cornelius], stationer: dispute over *Critici Sacri*, 9/259 & n. 2
BEECHAM: *see* Beauchamp
BEESTON, [William], actor: in ?*The damoiselles à la mode*, 9/307 & n. 1; reads part in *The Heiress*, 9/436 & n. 1
BELASYSE, Sir Henry, son of the 1st Baron Belasyse; M.P. Grimsby, Lincs, kted 1661: on *Naseby*, 1/130; arrested for manslaughter, 3/34 & n. 2; defence printed, 3/35–6 & n.; in brawl at Lord Oxford's, 4/136; killed in duel, 8/363–4 & n., 377, 384; alluded to: 8/454–5 & n.
BELASYSE (Bella(s)es, Bellassis), John, 1st Baron Belasyse, Governor of Tangier 1665–7; Lord-Lieutenant of E. Riding, Yorks., and Governor of Hull:
AS GOVERNOR OF TANGIER: P's low opinion, 7/130; 8/100, 155; appointed, 6/6–7 & n.; asks for P's support, 6/9; supported by committee, 6/18; instructed in duties, 6/22, 25; attempts to reorganise victualling, 6/105; concerned for own profit, 6/306; 7/99; complains of shortage of money, 7/4; returns from Tangier, 7/129; profits 7/130 & n. 2, 265; anxious to increase garrison, 7/130; bills, 7/174, 264; professes friendship for P, 7/185, 320; dislikes Creed, 7/185; meets Excise Commissioners, 7/190, 191; cheated by Vernatti, 7/264 & n. 2, 338; proposal for payment of garrison, 7/320, 321; accounts, 7/330, 338; 8/22, 32, 52–3, 63, 103; passed by committee, 9/199; examined by Exchequer, 9/202, 429, 529; profits in currency exchange, 9/205; tricks Cholmley, 8/45, 100, 127; criticised in committee, 8/61; to resign or be dismissed, 8/103, 111, 117, 127; resigns to become Captain of Pensioners, 8/154, 160; to purchase navy treasurership (rumour), 8/222; supports P in dispute over paymastership, 9/417; unspecified business, 6/13, 27; 7/164, 417, 423; 9/272
MILITARY CAREER IN YORKSHIRE: stories of Civil War, 6/30–1 & nn.; visits Hull to prepare garrison, 7/185 & n. 1, 193, 266; to go to Yorkshire on militia

business, 8/154–5 & n.; offers P help concerning prize ship, 8/345–6 & n.
POLITICAL/COURT NEWS FROM: 7/342–3; 8/74–5, 155; 9/462, 467–8, 472
PRIVATE AFFAIRS ETC.: lodging in Lincoln's Inn Fields, 6/9, 28; new house [? in Bloomsbury Square], 9/202 & n. 2; pictures, 9/202 & n. 4, 434–5; ~ his wife [Anne], 7/171; 9/537; his daughter, 7/171
BELASYSE, John, son of the 1st Baron Belasyse: arrested for manslaughter, 3/34 & n. 2; defence printed, 3/35–6 & n.
BELASYSE, Mary, Lady Fauconberg, (b. Cromwell),wife of the 2nd Viscount: 2/83 & n. 1; 4/181
BELASYSE, Thomas, 2nd Viscount Fauconberg: at theatre, 4/181
BELL, Capt.: *see* Ball, Capt. [?Naphthali]
BELL (Aunt Bell), Edith, sister of P's father: birth-date, 5/360 & n. 1; dies of plague, 6/314, 342; social: 1/205; 2/141, 172; 4/272; alluded to: 1/11
[BELL, William], Rector of St Sepulchre, Holborn: sermon, 5/347 & n. 4
BELL ALLEY, Westminster: plague deaths, 6/132
BELLAMY, [Robert and Thomas], relatives of P and petty-warrant victuallers: debt owed by Navy Board, 4/374 & n. 2; 6/54, 59, 111
BELLAS(S)ES, Bellassis: *see* Belasyse
BELLS, ringing of [*see also* Music: church]: for Monck, 1/52; arrival of Queen, 3/83; peace with Dutch, 8/399
BELLWOOD, Mr ――, formerly clerk to John Turner, lawyer: conceit, 9/463; news from, 9/465
BELL YARD, Lincoln's Inn Fields: gaming house, 2/211–12
BENCE, Ald. [John]: (untrue) story of wife's death of plague, 6/187
BENCE (Bens), ――, [? the foregoing]: 1/323; 2/220
BENDISH, ――, son of Sir Thomas, distant connection of P: 1/259 & n. 1
BENDY, Mrs ――: 5/130
BENIER (Beneere), Tom, barber: shaves P, 3/108, 233; theatre gossip from, 3/233
BENNET, Sir Henry, cr. Baron

[BERE], forest of, Hants.: 3/69
BERGEN, Norway: Teddeman's attack on Dutch fleet, 6/193, 195–6 & n., 197, 213, 218 & n. 2, 229; 7/13, 17, 55; official account, 7/335 & n. 2; parliamentary enquiry, 8/494, 538, 549–50
BERGEN-OP-ZOOM, Netherlands: 8/80
BERKELEY, Sir Charles, cr. Viscount Fitzharding 1663, Earl of Falmouth 1664: low reputation, 4/331; 6/71, 123–4 & n.; Coventry's praise, 9/294; appointed Keeper of Privy Purse, 3/227 & n. 2; rumoured promotion to marquessate, 5/232; ambitious to become Captain-General, 5/345; enjoys King's favour, 3/303, 4/25, 137, 138, 256; 5/168; services to King as pimp, 3/282; gifts from King, 5/40 & n. 3, 50, 56; relations with Lady Castlemaine, 3/289; 4/38; 5/21; Duke of York's confidence in, 4/138; enmity to Clarendon, 5/345; and Rupert, 6/12; patronage of Fitzgerald, 4/116; 5/344–5 & n.; of H. Brouncker, 6/59–60, 61–2; and of Creed, 6/71; at Tangier committee, 5/61–2; 6/58, 61; claims to have enjoyed favours of Anne Hyde, 1/315; 4/138; offers Elizabeth Pearse £300 p.a., 3/227; death at Battle of Lowestoft, 6/123–4 & n.; 9/294
BERKELEY, Sir Charles, son of the 9th Baron Berkeley: 8/338 & n. 1
BERKELEY, [Elizabeth], daughter of the 9th Baron: at court ball, 7/372; admired by Louis XIV, 8/338 & n. 1
BERKELEY (Barkley, Bartlet), George, 9th Baron Berkeley (of Berkeley Castle), cr. Earl 1679 [usually Lord George Berkeley]: dines with Manchester, 1/75; on *Royal Charles*, 1/156; entertains royal party at Durdans, 3/184 & n. 2; at meeting of E. India Company, 5/76; and of Royal Society, 8/243; house in Piccadilly, 6/39 & n. 2; experiment in cart design, 9/328–9 & n.; alluded to in error, 6/316 & n. 4; ~ his wife, 8/338
BERKELEY, Sir John, 1st Baron

Berkeley of Stratton; Navy Commissioner 1660–4; Ordnance Commissioner 1664–70:
CHARACTER: 6/118, 316
AS NAVY COMMISSIONER: appointed, 1/191, n. 2; relations with Sandwich, 3/122; 6/54; and with Coventry, 6/16, 118; examines Creed's accounts, 4/216; defends Warren's mast contract, 4/421; disagrees with P about flag supplies, 5/178; hostile to Hayter, 6/118; demands prize-money for navy, 8/144; part in *Lindenbaum* case, 8/181, 231; supports Carkesse in dispute with Board, 8/189; sells his place to Sir T. Hervey, 8/294 & n. 1; also, 4/331; 5/301, 333; ~ his clerk, Davis, 4/408
HOUSES: Navy Office lodgings, 1/197; chamber at St James's, 5/220
MILITARY CAREER: appointed Ordnance Commissioner, 5/316 & n. 1; boasts of prowess, 6/38 & n. 1; attends Privy Council, 8/112; to take charge of Suffolk militia, 8/255; defends work on Medway fortifications, 8/496
AS STEWARD TO DUKE OF YORK'S HOUSEHOLD: boasts of profits, 4/331; and financial acumen, 8/149; arranges for Milles's appointment as chaplain, 8/241; dishonest handling of Duke's revenues, 9/319 & n. 1
TANGIER BUSINESS: appointed to committee, 6/7; criticises Povey's accounts, 6/13, 38, 79; 9/371; friendly to P, 6/69, 118; proposals for victualling, 6/171; attends meetings/discusses business, 6/58, 61; 9/272, 316
SOCIAL: 4/155, 340, 341, 487–8; 5/11
MISC.: praises Louis XIV's government, 4/416; and discipline of Commonwealth, 6/45; P consults about case in Lords, 5/110; serves on commission for repair of St Paul's, 5/220; attends meetings of Royal Fishery, 5/336; 6/53; views on taxation, 6/69; praises P's parliamentary speech, 9/105 ~ his wife, 8/487
BERKELEY, Mary, Countess of Falmouth, widow of the 1st Earl: her beauty, 7/178 & n. 2; to marry H. Jermyn (rumour), 8/366, 368; social: 9/468

BERKELEY, Capt. William, kted 1665, naval commander: emissary in negotiations with Turks, 4/369–70 & nn.; account of Algiers, 4/386; accused of avoiding action in Battle of Lowestoft, 6/129 & n. 5; serves under Penn, 6/147; offers marriage to Lawson's daughter, 6/150; illegally takes prize-goods from Dutch E. Indiaman, 6/263; portrait by Lely, 7/102 & n. 3; killed in action, 7/169; body displayed in The Hague, ib. & n. 3; alluded to: 6/132

BERKENHEAD (Birkenhead), Sir John (1617–69): P consults about tax assessment, 3/283 & n. 5

BERKSHIRE HOUSE, Westminster: occupied by Clarendon (1666–7), 7/375 & n. 1; 8/93; and by Lady Castlemaine, 9/190 & n. 3

BERMONDSEY: Jamaica House, 8/167

BERNARD, Sir John, son of the following; succ. bt. 1666; lawyer, of Brampton Park, Hunts.: family's electoral interest in Huntingdon, 1/86–7 & n.; elected M.P., 1/87, n. 1, 99; at Brampton church, 3/220; at Brampton manorial court, 4/309; arbitrates in dispute about Robert P's will, 3/265; influence in Brampton resented, 8/220 & n. 2; ~ his wife [Elizabeth], 3/220 & n. 1

BERNARD, Sir Robert, Bt, Serjeant-at-law, Huntingdon: advises P about Robert P's will, 2/137, 194–5, 205; 3/220–1; presides over Brampton manorial court, 3/222–3; 4/308–9; attends arbitration meeting, 3/276; distrusted by Sandwich, 3/281; retained by P in dispute with Thomas P, 4/28; arranges disposal of P's reversionary interest, 5/36, 44; arranges part-payment of Piggot's debt, 5/149, 158; dismissed from recorder-ship of Huntingdon, 4/30, 62; interest in Brampton manor, 4/343; ~ his wife (Lady Digby), 2/137 & n. 5

BERNARD, William, son of Sir Robert: social: 2/208, 210, 213–14

BERNARDISTON: see Barnardiston

BERNARD'S INN GATE: see Barnard's Inn Gate

BERTIE (Bertus), [Edward]: on *Naseby*, 1/134 & n. 5

BERTIE, Montague, 2nd Earl of Lindsey (d. 1666): in brawl, 4/136

BERTIE (Bertus), [Robert]: on *Naseby*, 1/134 & n. 5

BEST, Mrs —— (Goody Best), of Gravesend: 8/313

BETHEL, Capt. [?Slingsby], army officer: given new commission, 8/265; social: 2/13

BETHNAL GREEN: P visits, 4/200; 5/132; Sir W. Rider's house, 4/200; 7/272, 282, 283; story of blind beggar, 4/200 & n. 6; naval guns heard, 8/254

BETTERTON, Mary ('Ianthe') (b. Saunderson); actress, wife of Thomas: P admires in *The Bondman*, 3/58 & n. 3; 5/224 & n. 2; *The Duchess of Malfi*, 3/209 & n. 1; Orrery's *Henry V*, 5/240 & n. 3; and *The Rivals*, 5/335 & n. 1; marriage to Betterton denied, 3/233 & n. 1; her voice, 5/34; acts in *The valiant Cid*, 3/273 & n. 1; 'ordinary' performance in *Mustapha*, 6/73; alluded to: 7/347

BETTERTON (Baterton), Thomas, actor and dramatist: P admires in *The Bondman*, 2/47 & n. 2, 56, 207; *Hamlet*, 2/161 & n. 3; 4/162; 9/296; *The Duchess of Malfi*, 3/209 & n. 1; Orrery's *Henry V*, 5/240 & n. 3; 9/256–7; *The Rivals*, 5/335 & n. 1; and *The mad lover*, 9/453 & n. 2; 'the best actor in the world', 2/207; sobriety, 3/233; marriage to Mary Saunderson denied, ib. & n. 1; in *The valiant Cid*, 3/273; compared with Harris, 4/239; in *Mustapha*, 6/73; laughs in serious part, 8/421; illness, 8/482, 499, 521; 9/63; returns to stage, 9/256; alluded to: 7/347

BETTON(S), Mrs ——: 7/110

BEVERSHAM, [Robert], grocer, Fen-church St: P orders sugar from, 6/149; dies of plague, 6/298; ~ his pretty wife, 6/149, 298

BICKER, family of, Amsterdam: quarrel with House of Orange, 6/147 & n. 1

BICKERSTAFFE [Charles, later kted], clerk in the Privy Seal Office: in dispute about clerkship, 1/207 & n. 2, 208, 235, 236; alluded to: 9/474

BIDDLE, ——: 1/85

BIDDULPH, Ald. Sir Theophilus, merchant of Westcombe, Kent: consulted about site for mast-dock, 5/353; and prevention of plague at Greenwich, 6/206, 211 & n. 5; social: 6/208, 338

BIDE, Ald. [John], brewer, Shoreditch: his ale, 8/389 & n. 2, 399, 443, 485

BIGGLESWADE (Bigglesworth), Beds.: P buys stockings, 2/138; P/EP at, 4/313; 5/233

BIGGS, [Thomas], Fellow of Trinity College, Cambridge: chosen taxor, 3/218 & n. 3

BIGGS, [Abraham], Clerk of the Kitchen to the Duke of York: dismissed, 3/214 & n. 1

BILBAO (Bilbo): convoy to, 1/185

BILL (Bills), Lady [Diana]: 7/329

BILLING, [Edward], Quaker: abused by soldiers, 1/44 & n. 2; denounces Hesilrige, 1/50; criticises clergy, 1/279 & n. 1; warns P of parliamentary critics, 8/349

BILLINGSGATE [see also Taverns etc.: Salutation]: 3/150; 8/39; 9/124

BILLINGSLY, [?Richard]: 1/15

BILLITER LANE [see also Taverns etc.: Ship]: 8/156, 345, 443

BILLOP, [Thomas], clerk to Matthew Wren: 9/287, 370

BIRCH, Jane: see Edwards

BIRCH, Col. John, M.P. 1660–91:

CHRON. SERIES: on parliamentary commission for paying off armed forces (1660–1), 1/227, 228, 229; methods criticised, 1/247 & n. 3, 249, 254; at pays, 1/253–4, 255, 262; proposal for reorganisation of naval administration, 7/304; examines Navy Board accounts, 7/305; distrusted by Coventry, 7/310; proposal for rebuilding city, 8/81; to be given regiment, 8/265; on Committee on Miscarriages, 8/502; opinion of P, 9/44, 76–7, 83; lobbied by officers of Navy Board, 9/83, 86–7; praises Cromwell's secret service, 9/70–1 & n.; defends Board, 9/95–6; also, 8/559–60; 9/162

MISC.: stories of fall in land values, 9/44 & nn. 3, 4; proposed purchase of bishops' land, 9/44–5 & n.; views on episcopacy etc., 9/45–6 & n.

BIRCH, Wayneman (Wayneman, the boy), brother of Jane and servant to P:

CHRON. SERIES: enters P's service, 1/250 & n. 3; P beats for lying, 2/206–7; 4/7–8; fighting, 4/12–13; and general misbehaviour, 3/37–8, 66, 116; 4/109, 193; P angry with, 2/239, 295; 4/186; sent to Brampton, 3/141, 145, 151, 200; EP complains of, 3/184, 199, 206–7; P's father refuses to have again, 4/180; to be dismissed, 3/295, 301–2; 4/67, 113; runs away, 4/193, 194, 202, 205; recaptured and dismissed, 4/220; P refuses to take back, 4/252; to go to Barbados, 4/382 & n. 2

AS SERVANT: learns how to put P to bed, 1/251; escorts P/EP in London etc., 1/270, 278, 304; 2/36, 188; 3/289, 292, 293; carries links, 1/290; 2/214; 3/216; 4/30; runs errands etc., 1/325; 3/103, 241; 4/172–3; livery, 3/47, 50, 54, 77; also, 2/79, 174, 241; 3/105, 260–1, 273; 4/15, 71, 171, 177

SOCIAL: sees pre-coronation procession, 2/83; at Vauxhall, 3/95; on country walks, 3/108; 4/112

BIRCH, William, groom, brother of Wayneman: sent for by P, 3/295; attempts to prevent Wayneman's dismissal, 4/67, 202, 252; dies, 8/340 & n. 2; alluded to: 4/113, 194

BIRCHENSHA (Berchenshaw), [John] musician [see also Books]: gives P lessons in composition, 3/8–9 & n., 10, 16, 19, 34, 35; his 'rules', 3/35 & n. 1, 36–7; 5/174–5 & n.; 6/266, 282–3; helps P to compose songs, 3/27, 34–5, 36, 46; his instrumental music, 5/238; house at Southwark, 3/35

BIRCHIN (Burchin) Lane: 5/105

BIRD, [Theophilus], actor: injured during performance, 3/204

BIRD, Thomas, Rector of Great Munden, Herts.: inscription to, 1/70 & n. 4

BIRD: see Beard

BIRDS [omitting those indexed under

proposed as EP's companion, 5/107, 224, 229(2), 230, 236, 242
BLAKE (Blacke), Gen. Robert, military and naval commander (d. 1657): courage, 5/169 & n. 3
BLAKE, Capt. Robert, naval officer (d. 1661): made captain of *Worcester*, 1/109; given command of squadron, 1/119 & n. 3; death and burial, 2/73, 74; also, 1/324; 2/15, 16, 17
BLANCH APPLETON (Blanche Chapiton), Aldgate: 5/18
BLAND, John, merchant, first Mayor of Tangier: P's opinion, 5/266; 9/430; writings on trade and Tangier, 3/157–8 & n.; informs P about mercantile practices, 3/255; 4/10; attends Tangier committee, 4/21, 23; 5/105; foreign news from, 4/198 & n. 2; P acts for in freightage dispute, 4/398, 404 & n. 2, 424, 426; 5/19, 23, 26, 36, 139; provides pieces-of-eight for Tangier, 5/15, 226; in dispute about Portuguese customs dues, 5/43 & n. 2; interest in Tangier victualling, 5/212; anxious for post there, 5/226; at Tangier, 5/265, 270, 287–8, 291; 7/109; dispute with Norwood, 9/392 & n. 1, 430–1 & n.; proposals for civil government of Tangier, 9/430–1; unspecified business, 3/300; 4/13, 14, 18, 198; 5/232; social: 3/188; 4/41, 81, 85, 242; 5/265, 270; ~ his son [Giles], 6/65; his kinswoman: musical, 4/242; 6/28
BLAND, [Sarah], wife of John: her grasp of business, 3/300 & n. 2; 5/266; goes to Tangier, 6/28, 42, 43, 44
BLAND, 'one': 9/175
BLAND, ——, waterman: 9/313
BLANQUEFORT (Blancford, Blancfort, Blanfort): *see* Duras
BLAYNEY, Edward, 3rd Baron Blayney (d. 1669): commends Montaigne, 9/120
BLAYNEY, [Robert], secretary to Lord Ashley: 9/152
BLAYTON (Payton), [Thomas]: accompanies P to Audley End and Cambridge, 1/66, 68, 69, 71; gift to P on appointment as purser, ?6/190–1; social: 1/210
BLEAU: *see* Balue

BLENKINSOP, ——: 3/44
BLINKEHORNE, ——, miller, nr Wisbech, Cambs.: 4/311–12
BLIRTON: *see* Blurton
BLONDEAU, [Pierre], Engineer to the Mint (d. 1672): to introduce improvements, 2/38–9 & n.; stamps for new coinage, 3/265 & n. 2; secret process, 4/70, 147
BLOUNT (Blunt), Sir [Henry], traveller: talks about Egypt etc., 5/274 & n. 1
BLOUNT (Blunt), Col. [Thomas], inventor, Fellow of the Royal Society, of Wricklemarsh, Kent: experiments with chariot design, 6/94 & n. 2, 213; 7/20 & n. 2; house and garden, 6/94 & n. 3
BLOW (Blaeu), John, composer (d. 1708): 8/393–4 & n.
BLOWBLADDER (Blowblather) St: 8/371
BLOYS: *see* Boys, Sir J.
BLUDWORTH (Bluddell), Sir Thomas, Lord Mayor 1665–6: appointed sheriff, 3/162; presses seamen, 7/187, 190; incompetence, 7/190, 269(2), 280 & n. 4, 393 & n. 2
BLUNT: *see* Blount
BLURTON (Blirton), Mr ——: tells bawdy anecdote, 2/43; social: 2/125, 193; 3/48
BOATE, Mrs ——: 2/54
BOCKET (BOCHETT), Mrs ——: courted by Dr Child, 1/301 & n. 3; at Sandwich's 1/309; ~ her dirty children, 8/193
BODDILY, Bodilaw: *see* Badiley
BODHAM, [William], Clerk of the Ropeyard, Woolwich: Penn's clerk, 3/69, 75; clerk to Chatham Chest, 5/122; appointment to Woolwich, 5/231; complains of its cost, 5/231, 248; his stores, 5/325; story of Tom of the Wood, 8/270; inspects batteries with P, 8/284; alluded to: 3/156; 6/189
BODVILE (Brodvill), [John]: case in Lords, 5/140 & n. 1
BOEVE (Bovy), [James], merchant: 9/206 & n. 6
BOIS: *see* Boys
BOIS-LE-DUC (The Boysse), Netherlands: 8/80

BOLES: see Bowles, [J.]
BOLLEN, [James], Groom of the Privy Chamber: 2/234 & n. 2
BOLTELE: see Bulteel
BOLTON, [Richard], cornet: preaches mock-sermon, 9/554 & n. 3
BOLTON, Sir William, Lord Mayor 1666–7: sworn in, 7/346 & n. 2; suspended from Court of Aldermen, 8/562 & n. 1
BOMBAY (Bombaim): naval expedition to, 4/139 & n. 2, 204 & n. 1, 210, 291–2, 299; decay of Dutch trade, 4/139; English government deceived about, 4/299 & n. 2
BOND, [Henry], teacher of mathematics (d. 1678): instructs P on timber measurement, 3/105 & n. 2; 5/115
BOND, Sir Thomas, Bt, Comptroller of the Household to the Queen-Mother (d. 1685): 1/322 & n. 3
BONFIRES: in celebration of: Monck's action against Rump ('the Burning of the Rump'), 1/52 & n. 4, 53; 3/95; 7/136; readmission of secluded M.P.s, 1/63; Restoration, 1/89, 122, 163; 7/136; arrival of Henrietta Maria, 1/281–2; Gunpowder Plot, 1/283; 7/358; coronation, 2/87, 88; Queen's arrival, 3/83, 87; King's birthday, 3/95; anniversary of the coronation, 4/109; 7/109; 9/172; Queen's birthday, 4/382; Battle of Lowestoft, 6/123 (at Navy Office); 6/129 (by Dutch at Dunkirk); Four Days Fight, 7/152, 344; Holmes's attack on Dutch in Vlie, 7/249; P's comments: bonfires few for King's birthday, 3/95; few in city, 7/136, 358; none lit for peace, 8/399
BOOKBINDER, P's [see also Books]: 5/199; 9/32
BOOKER, [John], astrologer (d. 1667): criticises Lilly, 1/274 & n. 2
BOOKS [see also Booksellers (P); Languages; Musical Compositions]:
 P'S COLLECTION:
  GENERAL: history, vol. i, pp. xxxix, lxxi–lxxiv; removed from Sandwich's lodgings to Axe Yard, 1/59; French books bequeathed to EP, 1/90; collection moved to Seething Lane

and rearranged, 1/232, 241, 268, 302; dusted, 5/358; put in order, 7/37, 311, 316, 322; 9/24(2); removed to and from Deptford in Fire, 7/?273, ?276, ?278, ?285, 290–1; missing books found, 7/290 & n. 3, 292; to be limited to two bookcases, 9/18, 48; shown to guests, 9/411, 424; P consults Naudé's book on collecting, 6/252 & n. 1; books acquired from Holland, 1/140 & nn., 260; and France, 9/431–2 & n.
  BINDING [see also Nott, [W.]; and Richardson, [W.]: ordered, 5/199 & n. 2; 7/41; to be made uniforms, 6/14, 24, 31–2, 33; gilded, 7/243, 266, 303–4, 306, 307, 311; of maps, 5/55; of plays, 7/104–5; books bought ready bound, 1/140 & nn., 260; cost, 1/281; 4/240; 6/28; 9/166
  BOOKCASES (presses): made by Simpson, 7/214 & n. 4, 242, 243; delivered, 7/251, 252, 258
  CATALOGUES: books numbered and listed, 7/412 & n. 2, 416, 417, 419, 421; 8/8, 40(2), 45; 'titled', 9/49 & n. 2, 72; catalogued, 9/72, 559–60
 OTHER COLLECTIONS: Earl of Peterborough's, 4/270; Wisbech parish, 4/311 & n. 3; Earl of Arundel's, 8/6–7 & n.; Capuchin friary's, 8/26; Fouquet's, 9/173 & n. 3; Clarendon's, 9/480
 BOOKS AND PAMPHLETS MENTIONED IN THE TEXT [a single asterisk denotes that P read or 'looked over' a book, or part of a book; a second that he comments on it]:
[ALLESTRY, R.], The causes of the decay of Christian piety: 9/10–11 & n. 2
ALSTED, J.H., Encyclopaedia: 1/275 & n. 4
ARETINO, PIETRO: 4/136–7 & n.
ARISTOTLE: 4/267(2)
[ASHLEY, A., The mariner's mirrour]: 4/240 & n. 1
BACON, F., Sermones Fideles (Faber Fortunae): 2/102** & n. 1; 5/39**; 7/72**, 129**, 242**, 346; Novum Organum: 1/140 & n. 4
BARCLAY, J., Argenis: 1/231 & n. 1; 4/369*
BARTAS, DU (trans. Sylvester), Divine weekes and workes: 3/247** & n. 1

BARTHOLINUS, T., *Anatomia*: 1/243 & n. 2

BATE, G., *Elenchi Motuum*, pt i: 1/67 & n. 3; pt ii: 4/42 & n. 1

[BAYLY, T.], *Herba Parietis*: 3/96★★ & n. 1

BEAUMONT AND FLETCHER, [*Fifty comedies and tragedies*]: 4/410 & n. 4

[BESONGNE, N.], *L'etat de la France*: 9/428 & n. 2

Bible: 1/42★, 206★ & n. 2, 270★, 281–2★ & n. 2; 4/174★ & n. 5 (concordance), 254–5 & n. 1, 269, 383★; 8/237–8 & n.

Bills of mortality: *see below*, General bill; *see also* Plague

BIRCHENSHA, J., *Templum Musicum*: 8/96★★ & n. 3

[BIRKENHEAD, SIR J. (attrib.)], *Cabala, or An impartial account of the nonconformists' private design* . . . : 4/257★★ & n.2

[?] [BLAEU, J., *Theatrum civitatum* . . . *Italiae*]: 5/38★ & n. 5

[?] BLAND, J., [*To the King's most excellent majesty, the humble remonstrance of John Bland*]: 3/157–8★ & n.

?BLAND, J., [*Trade Revived*]: 3/157–8★ & n. 1, 291★ & n. 7, 293

BOOKER, J., [*Telescopium Uranicum for MDCLVII*], (1666), 8/42 & n. 2

BOYLE, R., *Experiments and considerations touching colours*: 8/188★ & n. 2, 236–7★★ & n., 247★★ & n. 2; *Hydrostatical Paradoxes*: 8/250★ & n. 2, 258★★, 351★★, 400★★; *The origin of forms and qualities*, 9/144 & n. 2, 431(2)★★; *Some consideration touching the Holy Scriptures*, 8/438★★ & n. 1

[BROWN, J., *Description and use of the carpenter's rule*]: 4/104★ & n. 2; *The use of the line of numbers* . . . : 4/85★ & n. 1, 180 & n. 1

BROWNE, A., [*Ars Pictoria*]: 9/561 & n. 5

[BROWNE, SIR T.], *Religio Medici*: 5/27 & n. 2

[BUSSY, COMTE DE], *L'histoire amoureuse des Gaules*: 7/114 & n. 3

[BUTLER, S.], *Hudibras*: 3/294★★ & n. 2; 4/35 & n. 2, 400★ & n. 1, 411★ & n. 1; 5/27; 6/262★

BUXTORF, J., *Thesaurus grammaticus linguae sanctae Hebraeae*: 1/28 & n. 5

Cabala, sive scrinia sacra, Mysteries of state and government in letters of . . . *the reigns of King Henry the Eighth, Q. Elizabeth, K. James, and K. Charles*: 4/410–11 & n. 1; 8/313★ & n. 3

CAMDEN, W., *Britannia*: 2/217 & n. 4

[CAVENDISH, G.], *The life and death of Thomas Woolsey, Cardinal* . . . *written by one of his own servants, being his gentleman usher*: 8/248★ & n. 3

[CERVANTES, M. DE], *Don Quixote*, cited: 8/553 & n. 1

[CHAMBERLAYNE, E.], *Angliae Notitia; or The present state of England*: 9/432★★ & n. 3

[CHAPMAN, G.], *Bussy D'Ambois*: 3/259★★ & n. 2

CHARLES I, Βασιλκα; *The workes of King Charles the Martyr* . . . : 3/105–6 & n. 1; 6/101 & n. 3, 204★; 9/213★ & n. 2

CHARLES II, [*His Majestie's gracious speech, together with the Lord Chancellor's to both houses of parliament; on* . . . *the 29th day of December 1660*]: 2/4 & n. 1; [*His Majesties gracious speech to both Houses of Parliament on Wednesday, February the 18th 1662*]: 4/50★ & n. 2; [*His Majesties* . . . *speech to both Houses of Parliament on Friday the 8th of February* . . . *at their prorogation*]: 8/52 & n. 4

[CHARLETON, W., *Chorea Gigantum*]: 9/226 & n. 1

CHAUCER, *Works*: 4/410 & n. 4; 5/199, 200★; 7/378★★ & n. 4

CICERO, *Offices*: 2/6 & n. 4; *Second oracion against Catiline*: 3/107★★ & n. 4, 112★

COKE, SIR E., [*Institutes of the laws of England*]: 6/70 & n. 3; 8/284★★ & n. 3, 531★★; 9/480★★ & n. 3, 482★★

[CORDEMOY, L. G. DE, (trans.), *A philosophicall discourse concerning speech*]: 9/385–6★★; n. 5

[CORNEILLE, P.], (trans.), *Pompey the Great*: 7/176★★ & n. 2

[CORRARO, A., *Rome exactly described* . . . *in two curious discourses*]: 4/425★ & n. 3

COTGRAVE, R., [*A French and English dictionary*]: 2/43 & n. 1

[COTTON, C.], *Scarronides, or Virgile Travesty*: 5/72* & n. 2

COTTON, SIR R., [*An answer to such motives as were offer'd by certain military-men to Prince Henry . . .*]: 8/547** & n. 1, 564**, 568**

COWLEY, A., *Naufragium Joculare*: 2/39* & n. 3; 4/218 & n. 1; [*Verses lately written upon several occasions*]: 4/386* & n. 3; 6/186* [*Critici Sacri*]: 9/259 & n. 2

DANIEL, S., *The collection of the historie of England*: 5/247 & n. 2

[DAUNCEY, J., *The history of the thrice illustrious Princess Henrietta Maria de Bourbon, Queen of England*]: 1/275* & n. 2

[DAVENANT, SIR W.], [*The first day's entertainment at Rutland House*]: 5/40** & n. 2; *The Siege of Rhodes*: 5/278* & n. 4; 6/247**, 248*; 7/235**; 9/396*

[DAVIES, J.], *The history of Algiers and its slavery*: 8/582** & n. 3, 585**

DAVILA, E. C. (trans. Aylesbury), [*Storia delle guerre civile di Francia*]: 7/206** & n. 4

A Declaration and vindication of the Lord Mayor, aldermen and commons of the city of London in common-councell assembled: 1/122 & n. 3

DENHAM, SIR J., [*Poems and translations*]: 8/380 & n. 2

DESCARTES, R., [*Discours de la méthode*]: 4/263 & n. 2; [*Géométrie*]: 4/263 & n. 2; [*Musicae Compendium*]: 9/148 & n. 4, 167 & n. 3, 400–1** & n. 1 [*A Dialogue concerning the rights of His Most Christian Majesty*]: 8/253–4** & n. 1

[DOLEMAN, R. (Robert Parsons), *A conference about the next succession to the crown of Ingland*]: 9/480 & n. 2

DRYDEN, J., [*Annus Mirabilis*]: 8/40** & n. 3; *Essay of dramatic poesy*: 9/311** & n. 2; *The Indian Emperor*: 8/508 & n. 2; *The mayden queene*: 9/29* & n. 1; *The rival ladys*: 7/210** & n. 3, 233**

DUGDALE, SIR W., *History of St Paul's cathedral*: 1/163 & nn.; 4/410 & n. 4; *Originales Juridiciales*, 7/297 & n. 7; 8/168 & n. 3, 170(2)**

[EDMONDS, C., *The commentaries of C. Julius Caesar*]: 9/400* & n. 1 [*Ephemeris Parliamentaria*]: 8/10** & n. 2

ERASMUS, *De conscribendis epistolis*: 8/32** & n. 4

ESTIENNE, H., *Thesaurus Graecae linguae*: 2/239 & n. 3; 3/3, 290 & n.3; 4/33 [*Evangelium Armatum*]: 4/111* & n. 4

EVELYN, J., [*Elysium Britannicum*]: 6/289* & n. 4; *Hortus Hyemalis*: 6/289** & n. 6; [*Publick employment and an active life . . . preferr'd to solitude*]: 8/236(2)* & n. 2; [*Thersander*]: 6/289** & n. 5 [*An exact and most impartial accompt of the . . . trial . . . of nine and twenty regicides*]: 1/284* & n. 4, 286 [*Fair warning: the second part*]: 4/111* & n. 2

FARNABY, T., *Index Rhetoricus*: 1/140 & n. 5

FISHER, P., [*Epinicion vel elogium Lodovici XIIIIti*]: 1/200 & n. 2; panegyric on Charles II: 1/209 & n. 1

[?FLECKNOE, R., *A letter from a gentleman to the Hon. Ed. Howard, Esq.*]: 9/311** & n. 2

[FLETCHER, J.], *The madd lovers*: 5/280** & n. 1; *A wife for a month*: 3/286** & n. 1

[FLETCHER, J. AND MASSINGER, P.], *The custome of the country*: 5/280** & n. 2

FOURNIER, PÈRE G., [*Hydrographie*]: 9/17 & n. 5

[FOXE, J.], *Book of Martyrs*: 9/284 & n. 5, 327

[?FRANCO, N.], *La puttana errante*: 9/22 & n. 1

[FRANZINI, G.], *Las cosas maravillosas . . . de Roma*: 1/49* & n. 4

FULLER, T., *Andronicus*: 9/543 & n. 2; *The church-history of Britain*: 1/56* & n. 6, 261*, 308*, 312*, 321*, 322*, 325*; 4/329–30** & n., 369*; 7/302*; 8/94**, 535*, 537*; *The historie of the holy warre*: 2/207* & n. 1; *History of the worthies of England*: 2/21 & n. 1; 3/26–7* & n., 34*; 4/410, 411, n. 1; 5/118* & n. 1; 8/94**

and signal success of a part of His Majesty's fleet]: 7/252 & n. 2

The tryal of Sir Henry Vane, Kt., at the Kings Bench, Westminster, June the 2nd and 6th, 1662 . . .: 4/40** & n. 2

[TUKE, SIR S.], *The adventures of five houres*: 4/165, 167*; 7/248–9** & n., 250** & n. 2, 255*

? [*Urbium praecipuarum mundi theatrum quintum*]: 5/38* & n. 5

USHER, J., *A body of divinitie*: 4/127** & n. 4

[*The victory over the fleet of the States General* . . . *begun the 25 of July inst.* . . .]: 7/229* & n. 1, 230*, 234* [*A vindication of the degree of gentry in opposition to titular honours, and the humour of riches being the measure of honours. Done by a Person of Quality*]: 4/151** & n. 2

[VORAGINE, J. DE, (trans.), *Legenda Aurea*]: 9/161 & n. 1

[*Vox et lacrimae Anglorum*]: 9/65 & n. 2

WAGENAER, L. J., [*Spieghel der zeevaerdt* (trans. Ashley, *Mariner's Mirrour*)]: 4/240 & n. 1; 7/290 & n. 3

WALLER, E., [*Poems etc. written upon several occasions*]: 7/369* & n. 2

WALSINGHAM, E., [*Arcana Aulica: or Walsingham's manual of prudential maxims* . . .]: 5/10 & n. 2*; 7/161–2** [WALTON, I., *Life of Richard Hooker*]: 8/223(2)** & n. 2

The way to be rich, according to the practice of the great Audley . . .: 4/22* & n. 5

[WEBSTER, J.], *The Duchess of Malfi*: 7/352** & n. 3, 358**

[WELDON, SIR A.], *The court and character of King James* . . .: 6/33 & n. 3, 102** & n. 8

WILD, R., *Iter Boreale*: 4/285** & n. 2; 8/589 & n. 3

WILKINS, J., *Essay towards a real character, and a philosophical language*: 7/12 & n. 6, 148; 8/554; 9/200, 202*, 215** & n. 4, 255(2)*, 331 & n. 3, 381**, 382**

[WILSON, J., *Andronicus Comnenius, a tragedy*]: 7/181 & n. 2

[WINSTANLEY, W., *The honour of Merchant-Taylors*]: 9/277** & n. 2

WREN, M., [*Considerations on Mr*

Harrington's Oceana, or Monarchy Asserted]: 8/414 & n. 3

[WRIGHT, A.], *Five sermons in five several styles*: 9/300** & n. 5

BOOKS INSUFFICIENTLY IDENTIFIED: merry pamphlets against Rump, 1/56 & n. 4; P's French books, 1/90; 'little French romances', 2/35*; Spanish books, 2/131; book on improvement of trade, 4/160* & n. 1; cookery book, 4/272–3**; French verse, 5/58; little book of law, 5/202; two or three good plays, 5/220; collection of modern plays, 7/103, 104–5, 117; French book on navigation, 9/432* & n. 1

BOOKSELLERS: losses in Fire, 7/297 & n. 3, 309–10 & n.

BOOKSELLERS (P) [*see also* Allestry, [J.]; Herringman, [H.]; Kirton, J.; Martin, [J.]; Mitchell, Mrs [A.]; Morden, [W.]; Playford, [J.]; Shrewsbury, [W.]; Starkey, [J.]]: parliamentary news at, 8/576–7; foreign booksellers, 4/87; also, 9/309

BOONE, [Christopher], merchant: arraigned before House of Lords, 9/193 & n. 1

BOONE, Col. [?Thomas], cr. Baron Delamere 1661 (d. 1684): 2/60

BOOTH, Sir George: released by Parliament, 1/63 & n. 2, 74

BOOTH, Mr ——: 1/230

[BORDEAUX, Antoine de], French ambassador 1652–60: 1/10 & n. 7

BORDEAUX: Dutch Bordeaux fleet taken, 5/326, 348–9, 354; wine merchants' trick, 7/256; also, 6/177–8; 7/200

[BOREEL, Jan], Dutch ambassador 1667–72: King dines with, 9/451

BOREMAN, [George], Keeper of the Wardrobe, Greenwich Palace: Mennes and Batten lodge with in Plague, 6/208 & n. 1; political news from, 8/401; social: entertains Navy Board and others, 6/208, 233, 237, 275, 280, 285, 288, 293; 7/4; gives music party, 7/15, 16; also, 7/1; ~ his son, 6/299

BOREMAN, ——: account of Vane's execution, 3/109

BOREMAN, Dr [Robert], Rector of St Giles-in-the-Fields: sermon, 8/99

BOREMAN, Sir William, Clerk Comptroller of the Household: consulted about mast-dock, 5/353; measures against plague, 6/211 & n. 5; social: 6/208

BORFETT (Burfett), [Samuel], chaplain to Sandwich: social: 1/210, 285; 8/99

BOSCAWEN, [Edward], M.P. Cornwall: examines Navy Board accounts, 7/305 & n. 2; praises P's parliamentary speech, 9/109

BOSSE, [?A.], painter: copy of P's portrait, 9/261 & n. 4

BOSTOCK, ——, formerly clerk in the Exchequer: social: ?1/319; 2/162–3; 5/30

BOSTON, —— [?the foregoing]: 1/319

BOTELER: see Butler

BOTTOMRY (bummary): risky investment, 4/398 & n. 2; fraudulent claim concerning, 4/401 & n. 3

BOUGHTON, Northants.: Sandwich at, 4/307–8

BOULOGNE (Bullen, Bulloigne): storm near, 3/143; Dutch fleet off, 7/279, 281; alluded to: 8/380 & n. 2

[BOURBON, Henri de, Duc de Verneuil], French ambassador-extraordinary Apr.-Dec. 1665: arrives incognito, 6/76 & n. 1

BOURBON-L'ARCHAMBAULT (Bourbon): Henrietta-Maria takes waters, 6/142 & n. 3

BOURNE, Maj. [Nehemiah], Navy Commissioner 1653–60: 1/197 & n. 1

BOVY: see Boeve

BOW: P/EP visit(s), 1/280; 5/175; 7/113, 117, 120, 124, 151, 208, 240; 8/326, 377, 443, 447; 9/470, 528, 546; dancing meeting, 7/238; girls' school, 8/448, 451; King's Head, 3/169; Queen's Head, 8/112

BOW CHURCH: see St Mary-le-Bow

BOWCOCKE (Brecocke), [Richard], landlord of the Swan, Stevenage: 'the best Host I know', 8/475 & n. 1

BOWES, Sir Jerome, envoy to Muscovy 1583–4: anecdotes of, 3/188–9 & n.

BOWES (? Bewes), ——, shopkeeper: 3/52

BOWLES (Boles), [John], grocer: death and burial, 7/256; ~ ?his wife, 5/166; 7/394

BOWLES, John, of Brampton, servant to Sandwich: accompanies P to London, 8/474–5; explains hunting terms, 8/475; social: 2/105, 108, 138, 183; 8/477, 478, 481; 9/224

BOWLING ALLEY, Westminster: 7/123 & n. 3

BOWMAN, Mr —— [?Edward or Francis, Gentlemen-Ushers to the King]: 2/80 & n. 2

BOWRY, Capt. [John]: ship hired, 4/52–3 & n.

BOW ST: alluded to: 6/1; 9/62

BOWYER, [Elizabeth], wife of Robert: her remedy for cold, 1/85; social: 1/317; 2/21, 113; 3/61; alluded to: 1/166

BOWYER, Mary, daughter of Robert: sends maid to EP, 2/218 & n. 3

BOWYER, [Robert], ('father Bowyer') Usher of the Receipt in the Exchequer: EP stays with at Huntsmoor during P's absence in Holland, 1/84, 85, 131, 166; drowned in riding accident, 5/34; social: 1/229, 286; 2/21, 49, 86, 87, 113, 215, 241; 3/65; alluded to: 1/249, 251, 314, 323; ~ his daughters, 1/317; 2/113; 3/61, 258

BOWYER, William, son of Robert; doorkeeper in the Exchequer: escorts EP to Huntsmoor, 1/89; her valentine, 3/29; simple discourse, 3/145, 299; youthful appearance, 6/235; social: 1/88, 176, 192, 201, 244, 320; 2/232; 3/174; 5/262; alluded to: 1/209; 5/34

BOWYER, [William], tar merchant: supplies, 4/182, 187; gift, 4/182

BOYLE, Lady Anne: see Mountagu, Anne, wife of Edward, 2nd Earl of Sandwich

BOYLE, Lady Henrietta: see Hyde, Lady Henrietta, wife of Laurence Hyde

BOYLE, Richard, succ. as 2nd Earl of Cork 1643; cr. Earl of Burlington 1664: travels to Flushing, 1/?106,

?112; as Lord Treasurer of Ireland, 8/301 & n. 1; house in Piccadilly, 9/321 & n. 1; social: 8/498; 9/131 ~ his wife [Elizabeth]: 8/498; 9/322

BOYLE, Richard, son of the foregoing: killed in action, 6/122

BOYLE, Robert, scientist [see also Books]: at Royal Society, 6/36 & n. 5; recommends oculist, 9/248

BOYLE, Roger, Baron Broghill, cr. Earl of Orrery 1660, politician and dramatist [see also Plays]: influence with Richard Cromwell, 1/180; and King, 6/301 & n. 2; supports Sandwich, 6/301; 7/54; opposes Ormond, 9/185; as dramatist, 9/522; also, 1/260; 9/276

BOYLE, ——, [?Charles or Richard]: 1/106 & n. 3, 112

BOYNTON, [Katherine], Maid of Honour to the Queen: seasick, 5/306

BOYS (Bloys), Sir John: on Naseby, 1/106 & n. 4; supports King, 1/112 & n. 3; carries letters between King and Sandwich, 1/125; also, 1/136

BOYS, [John], wholesaler at the Three Crowns, Cheapside: marriage, 3/163; house burnt in Fire, 5/247–8; ~ his wife: 3/163

BRADFORD, [Martha], housekeeper, Hill House, Chatham 1661–9: P complains to about accommodation, 4/225 & n. 3

BRADLY, ——: at Graveley manorial court, 2/182

BRADSHAW, [John], regicide (d. 1659): Westminster lodgings, 1/13 & n. 4; body exhumed and displayed, 1/309; 2/24, 27, 31

BRAEMS (Brames, Breames), Sir Arnold, merchant: social: 1/293, 323; 2/192; 9/57

[BRAGG, Thomas], chaplain, Portsmouth dockyard: sermon 'full of nonsense and false Latin', 3/72 & n. 1

BRAHAM (Brames, Breame), Sir Richard, merchant: 3/43

BRAHE, Nils Nillsson, Graf, Swedish ambassador-extraordinary 1661: in dispute about striking flag, 2/212 & n. 3; 3/14; state entry, 2/187, 188, 189

BRA(I)NFORD: see Brentford

BRAMES, Breame(s): see Braems/ Braham

BRAMPTON, Hunts. [see also Ball, Sir P.; Barton, [J.]; Bernard, Sir R.; Day, [J.]; Dickinford, ——; Gorham, [M.]; Pepys, Robert; Pigott, [R.]; Prior, ——; Stankes, W.; Taylor, ——]:

P'S ESTATE [for his inheritance from Robert P and the subsequent disputes, see principally Pepys, R.; Trice, T.]: attempts to buy Norbury's house and land, 2/124 & n. 5; fails to unite scattered holdings, 8/282–3; income, 4/119 & n. 2, 121; 5/36, 44, 354, 360; his 'Brampton book', 3/48; 'Brampton papers', 4/121, 122; 5/31, 39, 195(3); 8/264

P'S HOUSE: alterations, 2/182–3; 3/94, 97, 219; Sandwich's plans, 3/206, 210; further alterations planned, 8/237, 471; parlour, 8/469; garden and summer-houses, ib.; P sends gold to in Medway crisis, 8/263–4, 272, 273; recovers gold, 8/472–5, 539; thinks of retiring to, 7/315, 332; 8/237, 469; 9/293; to be let, 9/212; also, 7/340

MANOR: sold to Sandwich, 3/102, 176; also, 4/343

MANORIAL COURT: P attends, 3/222, 223; 4/308–9; 5/281, 282, 298; his speech at, 4/308–9; also, 3/48, 199, 206, 208, 209–10, 211, 213, 219, 221; 4/300, 303, 305

PLACES IN: Bull inn, 4/309; church [St Mary's], 3/220; Green, 8/471; Portholme meadow, 2/135; 5/158; 9/210; river, 4/312; woods, ib.

P'S VISITS [for visits by other members of family, see under names]: 2/133–9, 180–4; 3/216–25; 4/307–14; 5/294–9; 8/453, 457, 460, 464, 465–75; 9/209–12, 223, 224; cost, 8/479; also, 3/127

MISC.: storm, 3/35, 42; parish feast, 3/144; 4/237

BRAYBROOKE, Robert, Bishop of London 1381–1404: tomb etc., 7/367–8 & n.

BREAD ST: 4/181

BRECOCKE: see Bowcocke

BREDA, Netherlands: Charles II at, 1/117; alluded to: 1/129

BREDA, DECLARATION OF: read

in Parliament, 1/118 & n. 2, 122; to Sandwich's Council of War, 1/123–4 & n.; welcomed by fleet, 1/124, 131; invoked by King, 4/58 & n. 3; alluded to: 1/127

BREDA, PEACE OF: see War, Second Dutch

BREDHEMSON: see Brighton

BREKINGTON: see Beckington

BRENTFORD (Branford, Brainford), Mdx: P visits Povey's house, 6/198, 214, 266, 267; market day, 1/20; plague, 6/225; church [St Lawrence], 6/199 & n. 1; inns, 6/199 & n. 1; 7/26; alluded to: 6/216; 7/54; 9/509

BRENTWOOD (Burntwood), Essex: plague at, 6/181

BRERETON, William, 3rd Baron Brereton: appointed to Brooke House Committee, 8/577 & n. 3; his manner, 9/10 & n. 1; plays organ, 9/11

BREST: French troops at, 8/1 & n. 3; engravings, 9/437

BRETT, Sir Edward, soldier: 1/264

BRETTON (Britton), Dr [Robert], Vicar of Deptford: P's opinion, 4/175; 6/107; preaches to Trinity House, 4/185; 5/172; 6/107

BREVINT (Brevin), Daniel, Canon of Durham (d. 1695): 3/85 & n. 1

BREWER, Capt. [William], painter: 4/15, 187

BREWER'S YARD, Westminster: 1/175; 5/212

BRIAN, Mr ——: 3/217

BRIDE LANE, Westminster: see Taverns etc.: Black Spread Eagle

BRIDEWELL [see also New Bridewell]: the house of correction, ?1/167; pressed men in, 7/187, 190, 191; building described, 8/6; the precinct: ?1/167; 2/116

BRIDGEMAN, John, Bishop of Chester 1619–52: armorial glass, 3/254 & n. 3

BRIDGEMAN, Sir Orlando, Lord Chief Baron of the Exchequer 1660; Lord Chief Justice of Common Pleas 1660–7; Lord Keeper 1667–72: charge to jury at regicides' trial, 1/263 & n. 2; appointed Lord Keeper, 8/410–11 & n.; popularity, 8/410; 9/375; P admires, 8/421; speech to Parliament,

8/476 & n. 2, 480 & n. 2; opinion on charge against Clarendon, 8/541; member of Cabal, 8/585; 9/425; friendly with Coventry, 9/41; opposes dissolution of Parliament, 9/360, 375; attempts reorganisation of Navy Board, 9/290, 291–2 & n., 321, 503, 550; illness, 9/425 & n. 4; his part in Coventry's petition for release, 9/475, 491; also, 8/412; 9/106; social: 9/352; alluded to: 3/254

BRIDGES, [Richard], linen-draper, Cornhill: calico contract, 5/292 & n. 1, 295, 351

BRIDGES, Sir Toby, soldier: praised by Albemarle, 5/310 & n. 1

BRIDGEWATER, Lord: see Egerton

BRIEFS (Chancery): frequency, 2/128 & n. 3

BRIGDEN, Dick, haberdasher, Fleet St: sells sword to P, 1/94; 2/24, 28; made captain of auxiliaries 2/24; house damaged in storm, 3/32; social: 3/165

BRIGGS, [Timothy], scrivener: gift to P, 6/83, 100, 101

BRIGHAM, [Thomas], royal coachmaker: complains of Duchess of Albemarle, 1/181 & n. 4

BRIGHTON (Bredhemson, Brighthemson), Sussex: Charles II's escape from (1651), 1/156 & n. 1; 8/74; alluded to: 7/288 & n. 2

BRISBANE (Brisband, Brisbanke), [John], naval official: P admires, 6/176–7; talks of spells etc., 6/177–8; takes P to gambling at court, 9/2–3, 4; news from: 9/66, 86, 179; social: 6/179, 182; 7/326, 388; 8/164; 9/35, 87, 126, 188; alluded to: 7/387

BRISTOL, Earl of: see Digby

BRISTOL (Bristow), Som.: story of mayor, 3/180; Rupert surrenders (1645), 5/170 & n. 2; 6/30; ships built, 8/47 & n., 270 & n. 4; 9/235 & n. 1; P and family visit, 9/234–6 & nn.; dog-carts, 9/234 & n. 4; Bristol milk, 9/235–6 & n.; Cross, 9/236 & n. 3; Custom House, 9/235 & n. 3; Horse Shoe Inn, 9/234 & n. 2, 236; Marsh St, 9/235; Quay, 9/235; Sun Inn, 9/234 & n. 6, 235; Tolzey, 9/236 & n. 2; Three Cranes tavern, 9/234 & n. 5

BRITTON: see Bretton

BROAD ST [see also African House; Navy Treasury; Taverns etc.: Glasshouse]: dancing meeting, 1/253; Plague, 6/128; Fire, 7/289
BRODRICK, Sir Allen, M.P. Orford, Suff.: witty, 6/313; drunken speech in parliament, 7/416 & n. 3
BRODVILL: see Bodvile
BROGHILL, Lord: see Boyle, Roger
BROGRAVE, ——: 2/31
BROMBRIGE: see Bromwich
BROME (Broome), Alexander, poet: wit and conceit, 4/100 & n. 3; death, 7/193; social: 7/12 & n. 1
[BROME, ——], daughter of [Richard Brome], landlord of the Ship tavern, Billiter Lane: admired by P, 8/156, 345, 443; 9/51, 284, 485–6; marriage, 8/345, 346
BROMFIELD, Mary: see Harman
[BROMFIELD, Thomas], Common Councilman: 1/24 & n. 6
BROMWICH (Brombrige), [Francis], Capt.: murdered, 9/412 & n. 2
[BROOKE, Francis]: history of Abingdon hospital, 9/227 & n. 3
BROOKE, Lord: see Greville
BROOKE(S), Sir Robert, M.P. Aldeburgh, Suff.: ability, 8/493, 572; house at Wanstead, 6/102 & n. 4; 8/172, 197; appoints Milles rector, 8/241 & n. 1; proposes recall of Sandwich, 8/486; chairman of Committee on Miscarriages, 8/493, 537–8, 546, 560; 9/88, 142; praises P's parliamentary speech, 9/110; also, 8/540, 544, 572
BROOKE HOUSE, Holborn: Commission of Accounts at, 8/559 & n. 2; 9/254, 394 & n. 2, 562
[BROOKE HOUSE COMMITTEE]: see Brooke House, Holborn; Parliament (the Cavalier): seventh session
BROOKES, Capt. [John], Master-Attendant Chatham: grounds ship, 8/310 & n. 1; gives evidence against Commissioner Pett, 8/461 & n. 3; suspended, 9/258 & n. 3
BROOME: see Brome, A.
BROUNCKER (Brunkard), Henry, Groom of the Bedchamber to the Duke of York; M.P. New Romney, Kent, 1665–8; succ. as 3rd Viscount

1684: character, 8/69 & n. 3, 406 & n. 4; claims treasurership of Tangier, 6/59–60 & n., 61; pimp to Duke of York, 7/159; 8/286; supports Carkesse against Navy Board, 8/169, 178; dismissed by Duke of York, 8/406, 416, 447; misconduct at Battle of Lowestoft, 8/489–90 & n., 491–2; blamed by Committee on Miscarriages, 9/142; flees to France, 9/169 & n. 2, 170; expelled and impeached by Commons, 9/170; appeals to King, 9/178; returns to court, 9/348; duel, 9/470 & n. 1
BROUNCKER, Sir William, 1st Viscount Brouncker (d. 1645): anecdote of, 8/126 & n. 1
BROUNCKER (Brunkard, Brunker (d)), William, 2nd Viscount, Navy Commissioner:
CHARACTER: 5/341; 6/193; 7/96–7, 237; 8/311, 312;
AS NAVY COMMISSIONER:
  GENERAL: appointment, 5/324 & n. 3, 341; ignorant of naval affairs, 5/341; instructed by P, 5/343; studies ship's drawing, 6/7; chairs Board, 9/365; neglects office for mathematics, 9/501; clerks, 8/104
  CHRON. SERIES: visits fleet, 6/228; in charge of Dutch prize goods, 6/234, 236, 237, 242, 262, 263, 280, 300; 8/446; complains of pillage, 6/249; examines suspected pilferer, 6/309, 329, 333, 334; 7/22; to despatch fireships, 7/258; defends Carkesse, 8/76(2), 78, 80, 83, 97, 100–1, 103, 104, 105, 109(2), 126, 146, 178, 189, 203, 204, 213, 215–16, 217, 531; at Chatham in Medway crisis, 8/259, 268, 271, 296, 350; at Rochester, 8/306, 307; blamed for discharging ships by ticket, 8/271, 273; examined about tickets by Committee on Miscarriages, 8/504, 508, 509, 510, 538; 9/62, 69, 77; lobbies M.P.s, 9/79, 80, 83, 84; his defence, 9/100, 102, 103, 107; examined by Committee on Miscarriages about Chatham defences, 8/496, 501, 508; proposes reform of Board, 9/287–8, 341, 400; suspects P of writing Duke's letter criticising Board, 9/295; his reply, 9/305; resents powers of joint-Treasurers, 9/408;

7/105; friary, 8/25–6; godfather to Carkesse's child, 8/111; at theatre, 8/395, 509; 9/57, 148, 157, 166, 178, 310; Teddeman's funeral, 9/200; Bartholomew Fair, 9/301; parish dinner, 9/559; at houses/lodgings of naval associates in Greenwich and London: 6/186, 187, 191, 212, 220–1, 222, 228, 334; 7/18, 34, 38, 68, 279, 364; 8/3, 4, 77, 394, 482, 525; 9/34, 214, 283, 410–11, 505; at his house in Covent Garden, 6/2; 7/36, 40; 8/431; 9/104, 161; his lodgings in Greenwich, 6/204, 213, 217, 226, 227, 232–3, 332, 338, 339; 7/1, 3, 4; Madam Williams's lodgings, 6/302, 303; 7/77, 92–3, 341; 9/199; taverns etc., 6/38, 119; 7/43, 63, 74, 329; 8/49; 9/82, 115; elsewhere, 5/238; 7/253, 320; 8/180; 9/183, 198
ALLUDED TO: 9/309
~ his kinswoman, 9/146
BROWNE, [Alexander], drawing master: gives lessons to EP, 6/98 (2) & n. 1, 205, 282; to Peg Penn, 6/210; P jealous of, 6/246; objects to his presence at table, 7/116, 117; his painting, 9/261; his *Ars Pictoria*, 9/561 & n. 5; social: 7/134
BROWNE, Sir Anthony, of Weald Hall, nr Brentwood, Essex: 6/181 & n. 2 ~ his brother, ib.
BROWNE, Capt. [Arnold], naval officer: 5/30
[BROWNE, Frances], of the White Horse, Lombard St: her beauty, 7/68; commits suicide, 8/82 & n. 1; ~ her husband [Abraham], 7/68 & n. 3
BROWNE, John, Clerk of the Parliaments: social: 3/89; 9/1; ~ his wife [Elizabeth], 1/177 & n. 1; 2/15, 16; 3/89; his mother, 3/89
BROWNE, John, Deputy-Storekeeper of the Ordnance, Chatham: 4/260 & n. 3, 261; 5/30
BROWN(E), [John], mathematical-instrument maker, the Minories: sells P 'White's ruler', 4/84 & n. 2; pocket-ruler, 4/266, 267; slide-rule, 5/17 & n. 3, 237; Wren's drawing instrument, 9/537–8 & n., 548; also, 4/434; 5/14
BROWN(E) Capt. [John], naval

officer: to sail to Jamaica, 3/150 & n. 3; quarrels with purser, 3/284 & n. 1; accidentally killed, 4/113; social: 2/36, 53; ~ his wife, 2/53; 4/113; his son baptised, 2/107, 109, 110, 146; his children, 4/113
BROWNE, [John], Storekeeper, Harwich: 1/196
BROWNE, Sir Richard, Clerk of the Privy Council: opposes new dock at Deptford, 3/18 & n. 1; explains quarantine order, 4/399 & n. 2; discusses freight charges, 4/430; clerk to Council's Committee for Retrenchments, 8/405, 406; his council work alluded to, 8/176, 278, 279; 9/350; political news from, 8/317; social: at Lord Mayor's dinner, 6/126; also, 8/552; 9/206, 502
BROWNE, Maj.-Gen. Ald. Sir Richard, kted May 1660, bt July 1660, M.P. London 1660, Ludgershall, Wilts. 1661–9; colonel in city militia; Lord Mayor 1660–1: resumes seat in parliament, 1/64 & n. 2; proclamation against repealed, 1/65; at ship's pay, 1/253–4; house, 1/275 & n. 3; his Lord Mayor's Day, 1/276–7; measures against Venner's rising, 2/8, 11; against riots, 5/99; 9/466 & n. 1; consulted about militia assessment, 3/283; sued for arbitrary arrests, 6/126; to pull down houses in Fire, 7/271; also, 5/114; social: attends Lord Mayor's dinner, 6/126; also, 2/105, 232
BROWNE, Sir Richard, son of the foregoing: at Lord Mayor's dinner with father Richard and son Richard, 6/126
BROWNE, Capt. —, of the Victualling Office: takes oath, 3/135
BROWNE, ——, nicknamed Colonel, of Brampton: 9/212
BROWNE, Mr —, of St Malo: 7/133
BROWNLOW, [William], P's schoolfellow: 9/153 & n. 3
BRUANT: see Culan de
BRUCE, Robert, styled Lord Bruce, M.P. Bedfordshire 1661–3, cr. Earl of Ailesbury 1664: introduces test bill, 4/136; returns from Flanders, 7/142

BRUMFIELD: see Bromfield
BRUNKARD, Brunker(d): see Brouncker
BRYAN, Jacob, purser: 8/271-2
BRYDGES, William, 7th Baron Chandos (d. 1677): 3/288 & n. 1
BUAT, van: see Culan de
BUCK, [James], Rector of St James Garlickhithe Dec. 1661-86: preaches at St Gregory-by-Paul's, 2/192 & n. 5, 211
BUCK(E), Sir Peter, Clerk of the Acts 1600-25: P's pride in his knighthood, 1/318 & n. 2
BUCKDEN, Hunts.: Robert P's property, 2/183 & n. 3; EP at, 3/148; 7/93; Bishop of Lincoln's house, 9/35 & n. 3
BUCKHURST, Lord: see Sackville, Charles
BUCKINGHAM, Dukes of: see Villiers
BUCKINGHAM, Bucks.: P visits, 9/224-5; church and school, 9/225 & n. 1; bridge, ib. & n. 2
BUCKLERSBURY (Butlersbury): 1/210; 4/182
BUCKNELL, Ald. [William], kted 1670: 9/507 & n. 4
BUCKWORTH, Sir [John], merchant, Crutched Friars: P's regard, 6/145-6 & n.; ~ his wife [Hester], 5/259 & n. 4; 7/273; his son, 7/273, 419-20; his daughters, 9/533
BUCKWORTH, Hunts.: Backwell's estate, 9/185 & n. 2
BUDD, [David], Admiralty lawyer: 8/27
BUGDEN: see Buckden
BUGGINS, [John], of Stukeley, Hunts.: 3/176 & n. 2
BUGGINS, Mrs ——: 5/27, 94
[BULL, Nathaniel], Surmaster, St Paul's School: 2/238 & n. 2
BULLEN: see Boulogne
BULTEEL (Boltele), [John], secretary to Clarendon (d. 1669): social: 7/38, 68; 8/394
BUN(N), Capt. [Thomas], naval officer: gift to P, 1/231; helps to design Tangier jetty, 3/238 & n. 2; social: 2/120
BUNCE (Bunch), Sir James: recounts

Cavaliers' grievances, 6/329-30 & n.
BUNTINGFORD, Herts.: P visits, 4/307
BURCHIN LANE: see Birchin Lane
BURFETT: see Borfett
BURFORD, Mr ——: social: 8/465-8 passim
BURGBY, Mr ——, writing-clerk to the Privy Council: news from, 5/72-3
BURGESS, [William], Exchequer clerk: P visits on Tangier business, 6/235; 8/295, 326, 329, 341, 377, 383, 440; 9/477
BURGLARY, robbery and theft [see also Law and Order etc.]:
GENERAL: increase allegedly due to disbanded soldiers, 1/256 & n. 3; Rotherhithe notoriously dangerous, 3/201; and road between Westminster and Kensington, 5/180; thefts by servants, 4/294 & n. 3; by disbanded Cavaliers, 4/374 & n. 1
PARTICULAR CASES: thefts from dockyards and ships: 1/316; 3/137 & n. 2; 4/76-7, 236; 6/184; attempted burglary, 1/305; tankard and cloak stolen from P's house, 2/140; EP's new waistcoat from coach, 4/28; horse stolen, 4/310; looting in Fire, 7/282; shoplifting, 9/285; also, 4/260; 5/10-11, 13; 8/316 & n. 2, 319, 321; 9/51
P'S FEAR OF BURGLARY AND LOOTING: leaves lighted candle in dining room, 3/101; fears looting in Fire, 7/285, 286; and by rioting seamen, 7/415; fears burglars, 1/305; 2/4; 5/201, 281, 282, 296; 6/25; 7/197-8; 8/552, 555
P'S FEAR OF ROBBERY AND THEFT: 2/158; 6/106, 200, 232, 235, 236; meets men with cudgels, 5/193; 9/172; fears attack in ruined streets after Fire, 8/60, 62, 371; 9/4, 8, 55; fears for EP's necklace at theatre, 7/412; fears pickpockets at Queen's Chapel, 8/588; and Bartholomew Fair, 9/313; armed guard on coach, 3/201; carries drawn sword in coach, 8/60, 62
POLICE MEASURES AGAINST: watch warns P of open door, 4/304; also, 7/363-4; 8/589; 9/134(2)
BURLINGTON, Earl of: see Boyle, Richard
BURNET, Dr Alexander, P's physician,

1/22, n. 1; attends Mossom's congregation, 1/58, 76, 173, 183; drinks King's health, 1/58; goes to Ireland, 1/209, 214, 308; social: at dancing school, 1/253; also, 1/21–2, 45, 60, 83, 178, 192, 200, 207; alluded to: 3/299; ~ his father, 1/207, 217; his mother, 1/207

BUTLER, ——: witness against Field, 4/71; also, 4/110

BUTLER, —— [? the foregoing]: accuses Coventry of selling places, 4/170

BUTLER, Mrs ——, of Banbury, Oxon: daughter's proposed match with Tom P, 3/201, 208, 226, 227, 228, 231, 232–3

BUTLERSBURY: see Bucklersbury

BUTTOLPH'S WHARF: see St Botolph's Wharf

BUTT(S), [William], merchant, of Bristol, Deb Willet's uncle: shows Bristol to P, 9/234–6 passim; visits Bath with P and others, 9/238, 239

BYROM, John, poet and teacher of shorthand (d. 1763): vol. i, pp. lxxii–lxxiii

BYRON, Lady: see Gordon

CABINET: see Privy Council

CADBURY, [Humphrey], mast-maker: 4/266

CADE, [John], stationer, Cornhill: a Presbyterian, 7/420; fears French alliance, ib.; P shops at, 1/296, 298; 3/1, 286; 4/434; 5/41; 7/34; 8/238; has MS. bound, 3/286; and wins books in Cade's lottery, 7/47–8; also, 6/114; 7/4, 184; 8/573–4; 9/31

CADE, [Thomas], royal chaplain: 1/143, 144

CADIZ (Cales): sherry from, 3/14; Allin attacks Dutch fleet at, 6/14, 19; de Ruyter's fleet off, 5/181; English fleet at, 7/46, 71; 9/382; alluded to: 9/392, 430

CAESAR, musician: see Smegergill

CAIUS, Dr [John], physician (d. 1573): his diet, 8/543 & n. 2

CAKEHOUSES: 7/70, 93; 8/169

CALAIS: Sandwich at, 3/146; P plans pleasure trip to, 4/399 & n. 4; Hinchingbrooke at, 6/169 & n. 3;

invasion from feared, 7/186; Clarendon's flight to, 8/566, 568; also, 3/262

CALAMY, Edmund, sen., Rector of St Mary Aldermanbury 1639–62: alleged to have worn surplice, 1/170 & n. 2; sermon at Whitehall, 1/220; preaches at extrusion, 3/162; imprisoned, 4/5–6 & n.; contribution to *Evangelium Armatum*, 4/111 & n. 4

CALES: see Cadiz

CALLENDAR, Hugh L., physicist and writer on shorthand (d. 1930): transcribes parts of P's diary, vol. i, pp. xcii–xciii

CALLIGRAPHY: P admires, 1/132–3; 6/339; engraved, 4/270; 5/237

CALTHORPE (Calthrop), [Edward], grocer: 1/37, 43

CALTHORPE (Calthrop), Sir James, of Ampton, Suff.: 1/6 & n. 3; ~ his widow, 1/6

CALTHORPE (Calthrop), [Lestrange], barrister: pays debt to Sandwich, 1/4, 5, 6 & n. 3, 24, 36, 37; arbitrator in dispute over Robert P's will, 3/270, 274; alluded to: 1/38; 3/276; ~ his man, 1/37, 38

CALVIN, John: sermon against, 4/93; praised by Hollier, 4/386

CAMBRIDGE [see also Fairs etc.: Sturbridge; Pepys, Samuel: university]:

VISITS BY P/EP: 1/60, 66–70; 2/135–6, 146–9, 180, 181; 3/217–18; 8/468–9; 9/210, 212–13, 306

BOROUGH: Roger P chosen M.P., 2/56; assizes, 2/145, 146; 8/484 & n. 2; Plague, 7/219 & n. 2; town waits, 8/469, 474; buildings: Bear [Black Bear] inn, 2/181 & n. 2; 3/217, 223; Falcon inn, 1/66 & n. 4, 67, 68, 69; Rose inn, 1/68 & n. 3, 69; 2/136, 146; 9/210, 212, 213; Dryden's reference to in play, 8/468; St Botolph's church, 1/68; Three Tuns, 1/67 & n. 4

UNIVERSITY: general: quarrels in at Restoration, 2/146–7 & n.; drunken scholars, 9/210; P defends against Oxford, 9/545; buildings: the schools, 3/217; Regent House, 3/218 & n. 1; degrees: P pays for M.A., 1/222; Monmouth receives honorary M.A., 4/99 & n. 3; officers etc.: tripos, 1/68 &

n. 1; election of proctors and taxors, 3/217–18 & n.; praevaricator, 5/278 & n. 1; parliamentary election: 1/108–9 & n.

COLLEGES: Christ's: factions, 1/63–4 & n.; P visits, 2/135, 180; Jesus: 9/213; manorial court, 2/182; King's: P walks in grounds, 1/68; visits chapel, 2/135–6 & n.; 3/224; 8/468; Magdalene: P visits, 1/67, 68; 9/212; remarks on 'old preciseness', 1/67; recalls undergraduate days, 1/67; 3/31, 54 & n. 1; 5/203, 361; 8/466, 468; 9/212; W. Penn, jun. to be entered for, 3/17 & n. 4, 21; gateposts, 8/469 & n. 1; buttery, 9/212; college beer, ib.; St John's: P visits library, 3/224 & n. 1; 8/468; Trinity: P visits, 3/224; 8/468; celebration of Monmouth's visit, 4/99; Trinity Hall: P entered at (1650), vol. i, p. xxi; visits, 2/146; 3/218; alluded to (in error): 8/133

CAMBRIDGESHIRE: parliamentary elections, 1/112 & n. 2; 8/85–6 & n.; Roger P's estate, 4/159; P's proposed purchase of land, 5/196; prestmoney, 8/85 & n. 2

CAM(P)DEN, Lord: see Hickes

CANARY COMPANY, the: patent criticised in parliament, 7/314 & n. 2, 342, 414; 8/2 & n. 5, 70; cancelled, 8/297 & n. 4

CANNON ROW, WESTMINSTER: 3/285

CANNON (Canning) ST: road widened, 4/77 & n. 3; Fire, 7/269, 270; subsidence, 9/288

CANTERBURY, Kent: King visits, 1/161; P visits cathedral, 1/172; remains of Becket's tomb, ib. & n. 3; list of archbishops in, 6/339 & n. 4; alluded to: 2/32; 4/25

CAPEL, Arthur, cr. Earl of Essex (d. 1683): 9/418

CAPEL, Sir Henry, M.P. Tewkesbury, Glos.: 9/418, 527–8

CARACENA, Don Luis de Benavides, Marques de, Governor of the Spanish Netherlands 1658–64: unpopularity, 9/396 & n. 3; confessor, 9/396–7

CARCASSE: see Carkesse

CAREW, [John], regicide: executed, 1/266 & n. 1

CARISSIMI, Giacomo, composer: songs, 5/217 & n. 2; alluded to: 8/56

CARKESSE (Carcasse), [James], clerk in the Ticket Office:
CHARACTER: 6/193; 7/366; 8/78, 94, 146
CHRON. SERIES: Brouncker's clerk, 6/193; servant to Marquess of Dorchester, 7/366; work in Ticket Office, 7/366, 418; injured in riot, 8/60(2); charged with malpractices, 8/63–4 & n., 76, 83–4, 97, 100–1, 103, 109; championed by Brouncker, 8/83, 97, 100–1, 103, 104, 178, 189, 203, 215, 217; dismissed, 8/103; case referred back to Board, 8/146; appeals to P, 8/109, 150, 169, 200, 204, 238(2), 302; Pett's attitude, 8/166, 200; case discussed, 8/178, 186, 198, 343–4; report on, 8/204–5, 212–18 passim, 343–4; referred to Council, 8/376, 379, 385, 386, 388; Carkesse reinstated, 8/555; gives evidence against Board to Committee on Miscarriages, 8/523, 524, 531; appears before Brooke House Committee, 9/43; hostility to P, 8/392; asks forgiveness, 8/555; makes allegations against, 9/99; P's MS. account of case, 8/186; case alluded to: 8/101–2, 105, 260
SOCIAL: watches Fire, 7/271; at parish dinner, 8/218
~ his wife, 7/67; his brother, 7/271; his child, 8/111

CARLETON, ——, coachman: 4/155

CARLINGFORD, Lord: see Taafe

CARLISLE, Earl of: see Howard, Charles

CARNEGIE, Anne, Countess of Southesk: Duke of York's mistress, 9/154; gives him pox, 6/60 & n. 2; 9/154–5 & n.; at theatre, 9/383

CARNEGIE, Robert, 3rd Earl of Southesk: revenge for wife's infidelity, 9/154–5 & n.

CARPENTER, [Richard]: preaches at St Bride's, 3/162 & n. 2

CARR, Sir Robert, M.P. Lincolnshire: attacks Sandwich in Commons, 9/174 & n. 5; social: 8/363

CARR, [William]: petitions Commons

against Gerard, 8/581 & n. 1; punished by Lords, 8/583, 587; 9/32; tried for desertion, 9/55, 57

CARRICK, Mrs ——: 1/27

CARTER, Charles, Rector of Irthlingborough, Northants., 1664–75: gift to P, 1/321 & n. 4; chaplain to Bishop of Carlisle, 8/51 & n. 2; news of Magdalene friends, ib.; social: 1/45, 287; 2/123

CARTER, Mr —— [?the foregoing]: visits P, 1/203

CARTER, Mrs ——: servant to Lady Wright, 1/41, 288; 6/160; wants a husband, ib.; social: 7/17

CARTERET, [Anne], daughter of Sir George: marriage, 4/254 & n. 3

CARTERET, [Benjamin], son of Sir George; naval officer: 4/433

CARTERET, Betty, daughter of Sir George (mentioned in error): 4/254 & n. 1

CARTERET, [Carolina], daughter of Sir George: marriage, 4/254 & n. 1; alluded to: 5/15

CARTERET, Sir Edward, Gentleman-Usher to the King: 8/115

CARTERET, Elizabeth, Lady Carteret, wife of Sir George:
CHARACTER: P's regard, 3/60; 7/88, 295; 8/48
CHRON. SERIES: portrait by Lely, 5/104; pleased at son's match with Jemima Mountagu, 6/138, 153; kindness to P/EP, 6/152–3, 156; fears Plague, 6/156; gifts to Jemima, 6/157, 158; wedding visit to Dagnams, 6/167, 168, 173, 175–6, 179; gratitude to P as matchmaker, 6/178, 182; fears for husband's position at Court, 7/57, 88; 8/165; 9/339; laments state of nation, 7/325; 8/113; pleased at husband's resigning Treasurership, 8/299; also, 6/161, 163, 212; 7/291; 8/149, 480
SOCIAL: in Hyde Park coach parade, 3/78; visits Lady Sandwich, 5/179; at Sheriff Waterman's dinner, 6/79; P and EP visit at Cranbourne, 7/54–7; also, 3/85, 126, 179, 197; 5/105; 6/112; 7/89, 335; 8/42–3, 163, 450, 596; 9/10

CARTERET (Cartrite), Sir George, Treasurer of the Navy 1660–7; Vice-

Chamberlain of the Household 1660–70; Vice-Treasurer of Ireland 1667–73; M.P. Portsmouth 1661–9:
CHARACTER: said to be diligent but grasping, 5/73; P's view: incompetent, 4/132, 192, 233; 6/72, 95; 7/293; good-natured, 1/296; 5/104; likeable, 8/117; honest, 8/165; Coventry's view: able but lazy, 3/243; 8/47, 140, 164–5, 179, 290
AS TREASURER OF THE NAVY:
CHRON. SERIES: appointed, 1/191, n. 2; his salary, 1/194, n. 4; 7/313 & n. 2; his poundage, 3/106–7 & n., 107–8, 174, 243; 4/302; reduced by Additional Aid Act, 6/292 & n. 3, 311(2), 312–13, 323; 7/4, 5, 24; by payment in course, 6/304; and by Poll Tax, 8/30 & n. 3, 67; too powerful, 3/177; rarely attends Board, 8/162, 252; colleagues criticise his officials, 3/28, 29–30; methods of payment, 6/75, 83, 95; accounts, 7/43, 64, 77; and dilatoriness in raising credit, 8/47, 140, 164–5, 179, 290, 327; accounts examined by parliament, 7/260–1, 262, 287, 291, 292, 294 & n. 1, 295, 313, 319, 321–2, 356; attacked by 'libel', 7/342; in danger of dismissal, 7/319; 8/304; to sell office, 7/334; 8/222, 277; defends himself, 8/2, 18, 247, 251, 295, 301; accounts examined by Brooke House Committee, 9/117, 179, 214, 562; exchanges offices with Vice-Treasurer of Ireland, 8/295 & n. 3, 297, 299, 301 & n. 1, 322; to retire, 8/597; also, 9/67
FINANCIAL BUSINESS: general: accounts examined/passed by Board, 3/14, 240; 4/96–7, 99; 5/104, 105, 318, 329; 6/119(2), 257; 7/289; 8/141, 169–70, 449, 458, 460, 497, 598; 9/222, 250; complains of lack of money, 3/104, 108; 6/293(2); 7/284, 331; 8/41, 73, 205; applies to Lord Treasurer, 3/278, 279; 6/74, 78; 7/48; surplus, 4/305, 317; cash supplied from customs, 7/11; to obtain cash from Prize Office, 8/58, 144; opposes loan from city, 7/160; uses officials' credit, 8/48, 327; and his own, 8/180, 290; successful in raising loans, 8/140; 9/448; complains of bankers' refusal

to lend, 8/143, 149; to pay in course, 4/75 & n. 2; pays with own money, 6/150; particular items: scheme for paying seamen, 1/308; cashes/certifies bills, 2/61, 62, 96; 4/283, 414; 6/24; at pays, 3/58, 66, 69–75 passim, 193, 203, 290; 7/132–3, 196, 308; victuallers' accounts, 3/62; 4/389; Creed's, 4/192, 197, 198, 204, 207, 215–16, 219; Dunkirk money, 3/269 & n. 3; customs dispute, 5/54–5, 76; purchase of tar, 5/134; estimates for parliament, 5/329; pay tickets, 6/72, 74; 8/110; Board's expenses, 6/74; marine insurance, 6/112; Warren's bills, 7/354; method of paying bills, 8/89

OTHER BUSINESS: Navy Office premises, 1/194; sale of stores, 2/45; appointment of ships' masters, 2/108, 111; projected dock, 2/198; shipping, 2/202; 3/40, 59–60, 81, 85; trial of yarn, 3/102; contracts, 4/241, 327, 383; 9/542; mast-dock, 5/202, 353; appointment of Commissioner Taylor, 5/350; surveyorship of victualling, 6/266; enquiry into victualling, 7/260; Board's report to Duke of York, 7/375–6; Carkesse case, 8/102, 103, 215; also, 1/192, 242; 4/314; 5/7; 6/149; 7/319; 8/153, 154, 155; unspecified: 3/22, 48, 51, 53, 101, 106, 148, 192, 280, 284; 4/4, 12, 81, 105, 106, 152, 175, 258, 322; 5/333; 6/105, 324; 7/291, 312, 369; 8/131, 141, 189, 277, 281, 355, 405–6, 429, 524

RELATIONS WITH COLLEAGUES AND OTHERS: tries to get colleagues appointed prize commissioners, 5/327, 333; supports P's appointment as Clerk, 1/192; P helps him set office in order, 1/194; cultivates his goodwill, 3/75, 79, 210; 6/75; 7/57, 61–2, 66, 67; his esteem for P, 3/81, 108, 171, 172; 7/334; supports P over contracts etc., 3/100; 4/327, 380, 383; 6/116(2), 138; they exchange confidences, 3/59; 4/397; 7/78, 131; P supports him in dispute with Coventry, 3/107; advises P on prize-goods, 7/219; angry with him, 8/69; distrusts Batten, 3/59, 157; 4/182; 6/74; annoyed with Penn, 3/79; his complaints/accusations against Coventry,

3/79, 104 & n. 3, 107–8; 4/170, 330–1 & n.; Coventry's hostility, 7/27, 41, 42, 43, 83; they are reconciled, 6/147; 7/196, 325; also, 3/5; 9/339

OTHER APPOINTMENTS: Governor of Jersey 1643–51: 3/243 & n. 2; alleged malpractices, 4/195 & n. 1, 305–6; 8/161 & n. 4; on Tangier commission: 3/238; displeased at P's appointment as Treasurer, 6/60; signs bills, 6/191–2; attends meetings, 4/335; 5/308; 6/58; 7/156; Master of Trinity House: 5/172, 5/210; on appeal tribunal for prizes: 8/181, 231

NEWS FROM: political/parliamentary/ court news, 3/79; 4/103, 212; 6/291; 7/172, 303, 308–9, 370; 8/126, 207, 229–30, 277, 355, 416, 418, 479–80, 525, 573, 596–7; 9/9, 67; naval, 3/79; 5/275, 352, 353; 6/198; 7/143, 159–60; 8/41–2; foreign, 4/198; 7/250

AS POLITICIAN: deplores court's immorality, 6/167; 8/355; believes in 'show of religion', 8/355; comments on approach of war, 5/175, 353; despairs of war and state of nation, 7/24, 62, 83, 131, 160, 196, 281, 307, 334, 370, 383; 8/161, 222–3, 573, 596–7; 9/67; visits fleet, 7/124, 159–60; 8/514; criticises naval tactics, 7/143, 159–60, 188; 8/148; and naval unpreparedness, 8/117; dislikes Treasury commission, 8/244; his influence, 6/190, 323; 7/6, 8; 8/18, 69, 166–7; supports Clarendon, 4/195; 5/205, 212, 213, 218–19; 8/406, 418; envious of Sandwich, 4/117, 219; allies with, 6/277, 313, 323; 7/54; 8/462(2); supports in prize-goods affair, 7/262; 9/87, 96; attends Cabinet/Council, 5/317; 8/117, 278; also, 2/82; 3/240; 8/18, 217

FAMILY: pleasure in son's marriage, 6/137, 138, 141, 153, 161, 167, 168, 173, 178, 179, 182, 200; reports approval of King and Duke of York, 6/144–5, 148; marriage settlement, 6/148, 180 & n. 3, 191; attends wedding, 6/175–6, 179, 182; wedding gifts, 7/358; 8/207, 221; arranges Hinchingbrooke's match, 8/190 & n. 4, 208, 216; 9/28; daughter Poppet, 8/155; daughters (unidentified), 3/197;

9/116–17; at Whitehall chapel, 8/145; also, 7/356, 383; 8/598
ALLUDED TO: 7/17
CARTERET, Lieut. [Philip], naval officer: 3/153
CARTRITE: *see* Carteret
CARTWRIGHT, [William], actor: as Falstaff, 8/516
CARY, [John], Master of the King's Buckhounds: 4/260
~ ?his wife: 1/157
CARY HOUSE, Strand: Mossom's congregation at, 1/60; P dines at, 8/553–4; ?Royal Society at, 8/555
CASE, Thomas, Presbyterian divine (d. 1682): at Scheveningen, 1/140 & n. 6; sermons mimicked, 1/280 & n. 3; printed sermons, 4/111 & n. 4; Presbyterian manner, 9/31, 190
CASE, [?Thomas], clergyman: preaches at Brampton, 2/183 & n. 5
CASE, ——, of the Rolls Office: 9/483
CASTEL-RODRIGO, Emmanuel de Moura-Cortereal, Governor of the Spanish Netherlands 1664–8: 9/176 & n. 3
CASTELL (Castle), [John], clergyman: sermon, 2/52 & n. 2
CASTLE, Dr [John], Clerk of the Privy Seal: business with P, 1/245 & n. 2; 2/63, 64; 3/61, 80; social: 1/208; ~ his clerk, 3/61
CASTLE, Martha (b. Batten), wife of William: P's dislike, 2/161; 3/28; 4/177; in Navy Board pew, 3/40, 55; marriage, 4/177 & n. 3, 217–18, 236–7; social: P's valentine, 2/36 & n. 2, 42, 44, 192; visits Rotherhithe, 2/45; Dartford, 2/57–8; and Deptford, 3/198; at Dolphin tavern, 2/61, 175, 218; 3/31; sees pre-coronation procession, 2/82; at theatre, 2/193; at Penn's wedding anniversary, 3/4; also, ?1/317; 2/?19, 21, 22, 39, 59, 78, 204, 232; 4/5, 253
CASTLE, [William], shipbuilder, Deptford: marriage, 4/177 & n. 3, 217–18; leagues with Batten, 5/83; hostile to J. Taylor, ib.; to Ford and Rider, 6/170; and to Deane, 7/127–8;

slanders P, 5/131; P's low opinion, 5/312; 6/170; masts unsatisfactory, 5/123; and timber, 5/312, 347; builds *Defiance*, 6/7 & n. 2, 169; 7/69, 119; and *Monmouth* yacht, 7/38 & n. 3; social: 2/69, 78; 4/236–7, 253, 284; 7/115; 8/188–9; 9/26–7; alluded to: 5/116, 337
CASTLE, ——, ?of Huntingdon: Brampton business, 9/451, 452; social: 9/212
CASTLE: *see* Castell
CASTLEHAVEN, Lord: *see* Touchet
CASTLEMAINE, Earl and Countess of: *see* Palmer
CATHERINE OF VALOIS (d. 1437), wife of Henry V: P kisses corpse, 9/457 & n. 1
CATHERINE OF BRAGANZA, wife of Charles II:
APPEARANCE, DRESS etc.: handsome, 3/89, 97 & n. 1, 100; 4/229–30; P's opinion, 3/277; broken English, 5/4; dress, 4/229–30; 9/557; sets fashion, 7/335; portrait by Huysmans, 5/254 & n. 4
CHARACTER: modesty and tact, 3/191, 289; 5/40; pleasant humour, 4/174, 177; piety, 7/384
CHRON. SERIES: marriage, 2/52 & n. 1, 65; dowry, 3/90–1, 99, 100; income/jointure, 4/127 & n. 1; 5/40, 50; her court at Lisbon, 2/185, 189, 197; prayed for in London, 2/211; voyage to England, 2/129, 242; 3/15, 51, 62, 79, 90; preparations for arrival at Portsmouth, 3/64, 68, 70, 71, 78, 80; arrives, 3/83, 87; gifts to, 3/72 & n. 2, 74, 100 & n. 4; at Hampton Court, 3/81–2, 89, 95, 97, 100, 146; at Whitehall, 3/175 & n. 2; attends St James's chapel, 3/202; 5/188; 7/384; 8/588–9; said to be pregnant, 3/217 & n. 2, 290, 303; 4/177 & n. 4; miscarries, 7/48–9 & n.; 9/191, 552, 560 & n. 3; inability to have children, 5/56; 8/269 & n. 2; relations with King affectionate, 3/282; 4/222, 272; 5/4; 8/356; 9/205; worsen, 4/112; 5/20, 56; 8/558; rumours of separation/divorce, 8/422 & n. 3, 438, 518; relations with Lady Castlemaine, 3/147, 234; 4/216, 431; 7/159; with Frances Stuart, 5/40; with

Moll Davis, 9/219; seriously ill of fever, 4/337, 339, 342, 344, 347, 348, 352, 356, 358, 363, 378, 407, 439; 5/4; looks ill, 5/107; takes physic, 7/87; visits Tunbridge Wells, 4/240, 251; 7/214; Bath, 4/292; Oxford, 4/315, 321; movements in Plague: at Salisbury, 6/172; Wilton, 6/189; Hampton Court, 7/46; returns to Whitehall, ib.
HOUSEHOLD: her Maids of Honour: their beauty, 4/230; 7/347; dress, 3/92 & n. 2; 5/188; 7/162, 325; complain of drinking water, 3/92 & n. 3; stories of, 3/177 & n. 1; 4/37 & n. 4, 37–8; some return to Portugal, 3/234–5; attend launch, 5/306; play cards, 7/48; 8/70; visit Tunbridge Wells, 7/214; also, 3/299; 4/142; 5/107; court ill-attended, 3/197, 299; 4/49; physician(s), 3/235; 4/345; closet, 5/188 & n. 3; council, 7/303
SOCIAL AND CEREMONIAL: listens to music, 3/90; 8/534; 9/322–3; entertained by Lord Berkeley, 3/184; Lord Mayor, 4/193–4; Buckingham, 4/238; at court ball, 3/300, 301; 7/371–3; at ambassador's audience, 3/297; banquet at Windsor, 4/113; military review, 4/216; her birthday, 4/382; 7/341 (error), 371–3; at opening of parliamentary session, 5/93; visits fleet, 5/193, 196; at launch, 5/306; 9/101; court lottery, 5/214, 215; plays cards, 7/48; 8/70; dines in public, 8/161, 404, 428; 9/320; receives Duchess of Newcastle, 8/163; also, 4/229–30; 5/163, 348; 8/551, 570; 9/294, 323, 331
AT THEATRE: at Cockpit, 3/260, 273; Whitehall, 7/325, 347; 9/219, 456; Theatre Royal, 8/167; 9/203
ALLUDED TO: 8/464; 9/276
CAVALIERS: alleged plots against Commonwealth, 2/204, 225; 5/264; unjust treatment, 3/42–3 & n.; act for relief of, 3/199 & n. 2; cause indiscipline in fleet, 4/169; unfit for employment, 4/196; importune King, 4/373; danger to law and order, 4/374 & n. 1; grievances, 6/303, 329–30 & n.; manners, 9/478
CAVE, [John], Gentleman of the

Chapel Royal: killed in street quarrel, 5/32 & n. 3
CAVE, ——, of St Bride's parish: boards Tom P's child, 5/114; imprisoned, 5/114, 252–3; demands money, 5/82, 154, 158, 167–8
CAVENDISH, Margaret, Duchess of Newcastle (b. Lucas, d. 1673), wife of the 1st Duke [see also Plays]: eccentric dress and behaviour, 8/163–4 & n., 186–7, 196, 243; attracts crowds, 8/163–4, 196, 197, 209; visits Royal Society, 8/243 & n. 3; house at Clerkenwell, 8/209; Life of husband, 9/123 & n. 3
CAVENDISH, William, styled Lord Cavendish, 4th Earl (1684), and 1st Duke (1694) of Devonshire (d. 1707): on Naseby, 1/134
CAYUS: see Caius
CECIL, Robert, 1st Earl of Salisbury (d. 1612): tomb, 8/381 & n. 5
CECIL, William, 1st Baron Burghley (d. 1598): letters, 8/313 & n. 3
CECIL, William, 2nd Earl of Salisbury (d. 1668): 'simple', 5/298–9 & n.; report of expulsion from Lords, 1/127 & n. 1; ~ his gardener, 1/59; 2/139
CENTEN (Seaton), Capt. Bastiaan, Dutch naval officer: killed in action, 6/122 & n. 5
CERVINGTON (Servington), [Charles], tally-cutter in the Exchequer: 2/241
CHAMBERLAIN, Mr and Mrs ——: their singing, 6/316, 338
CHAMBERLAYNE (Chamberlin), Sir Thomas, Governor of the E. India Company: news of Dutch in India, 5/49–50 & n.; supports war, 5/108–9
CHANCERY [see also Justice, administration of]: Rolls Chapel: P hears case, 1/50 & n. 2; orders stationery from, 1/88–9 & n.; hears sermon, 6/80; examines patents in, 9/480, 483; Six Clerks' Office: P visits for patent as Clerk of Acts, 1/197; about agreement with Barlow, 1/205; and dispute with Trice, 2/210; 4/221, 242, 345, 346, 351
CHANCERY LANE [for buildings,

see Chancery; Taverns etc.: King's Head; Pope's Head; Sun]

CHANCERY ROW, Westminster Hall: 1/61

CHANDLER, [?William]: 2/148

CHANDOS, Lord: *see* Brydges

CHANNELL, Luke, dancing master: 1/253

CHAPLIN, [Francis], provision merchant, Sheriff 1668–9: 7/25, n. 2; P's regard, 9/34; wealth, 7/25; political news from, 8/95–6; nominated Sheriff, 8/432; 9/34; social: 1/187, 249, 250, 268, 287

CHAPMAN, ——, periwig maker: 4/362, 378, 380

CHAPPELL, ——, clergyman: preaches to Mossom's congregation, 1/176

CHAPPELL, ——, son of the preceding: page to Oliver Cromwell, 1/176, 3/5; ~ his mother, 3/5

CHARACTERS: *see* Ciphers

CHARCOAL: 4/14

CHARD, Adam, shop-keeper, Pope's Head Alley: 1/80; marriage, 2/35; social: 1/87

CHARETT (Cherrett), Madame, shopkeeper, Covent Garden: 5/28

CHARING CROSS [*see also* Royal Mews; Taverns etc.: Chequer; Goat; Golden Lion; King's Head; Three Tuns; Triumph]: execution of regicide, 1/266 & n. 1; roadworks, 2/184–5; EP lives at during 'differences' with P, 4/277 & n. 1; puppet plays, 3/254; 8/121, 500; giants on show, 5/242–3; 8/326, 500; posthouses, 6/197; rails, 3/80; Royal Mews, 2/184

CHARING CROSS (STAIRS): 8/412; 9/75, 92, 185

CHARLES I:

CHARACTER: 5/73

PUBLIC AFFAIRS: coinage, 4/148; naval administration, 8/374 & n. 2; seizes Spanish bullion (1640), 7/253 & n. 1; privy purse, 8/324, 331 & n. 2; court, 6/127; quells mutiny at Newark (1645), 6/30–1 & nn.; flight to Scottish army (1646), 6/30 & n. 1; escape to Isle of Wight (1647), 6/316–17 & nn.; treaty of Newport

(1648), 4/373 & n. 2; betrayed by Cromwell (1648–9), 5/335 & n. 2; execution witnessed by P, 1/265; and recalled, 1/33; anniversary of execution proclaimed a fast, 2/24 & n. 2 [for its observance, *see* Church of England: special services]; anniversary of sentence, 3/19

PORTRAITS ETC.: statue at Royal Exchange, 1/89 & n. 3, 99 & n. 3, 113; bust at Swakeleys, 6/215 & n. 1; tomb at Windsor, 7/58 & n. 6; portrait by Van Dyck, 8/181 & n. 3

MISC.: *Workes*, 3/105–6 & n.; 6/101, 204; *Eikon Basilike*, 9/213 & n. 2; W. Sanderson's *Life*, 1/132 & n. 4; attitude to theatre, 8/56; taste in pears, 8/417

CHARLES II [biographical; omitting references to the King by which P clearly means the state]:

CHARACTER ETC.: reputation, 2/1; 3/85; 7/407 & n. 4; P's first impressions, 1/144; compassion, 1/296; extravagance, 2/189; 7/404; 8/507, 534; 9/7; love of pleasure/sexual indulgence/neglect of business, 3/127; 4/30, 136–7; 5/21; 6/210, 267, 342; 7/57, 197, 323, 349, 350, 371, 400, 406; 8/68, 179, 181, 207, 249, 275, 282, 286, 288, 342(2), 355, 356, 361, 377, 378, 525, 571; 9/20, 182, 257, 375, 536; would save nation if industrious, 7/197, 350, 371, 400, 406; 8/37; too easily influenced, 5/73; witticisms, 5/12–13; 7/105–6; lampooned in *Second advice to a painter*, 7/407 & n. 4; foolish, 8/449

PORTRAITS: [Luttichuys], 1/292–3 & n.; 2/59; Lely, 3/113 & n. 2; head, on coins (Blondeau), 3/265 & n.2

CHRON. SERIES:

BEFORE 1660: governess, 6/316 & n. 3; story of naval encounter (1648), 5/169 & n. 1; stories of escape after Worcester (1651), 1/155–6 & nn.; 8/74, 526; quarrel with Duke of York (1656), 8/431 & n. 1; stories of Franco-Spanish war (1657–8), 9/6 & n. 2

RESTORATION: diary's evidence, vol. i, pp. cxxxiii–cxxxiv; growing support for, 1/74, 79, 89, 92, 101, 106,

Braganza. For his mistresses *see* Davis, Moll; Gordon, Eleanor, Lady Byron; Gwyn, Nell; Haslerigg, Mrs; Stuart, Frances, Duchess of Richmond; Villiers, Barbara, Countess of Castlemaine, Walters, Lucy; Weaver, [Elizabeth]]: story of proposed match with Frances Cromwell (1654),5/296–7 & n.; speculations about choice of bride, 2/37–40 passim & nn., 45, 52 & n. 1; Dutch oppose Portuguese match, 2/65 & n. 3; letters from Catherine of Braganza, 3/51; her arrival, 3/83, 87, 97; quarrels with over Lady Castlemaine's appointment to Household, 3/147 & n. 2; neglects her, 3/234–5; 4/439; 5/56; 8/558; grieved by her illness, 4/339, 342; 9/204–5; gives away part of dowry, 5/50 & n. 4

MUSICAL: guitar, 1/172; comments on anthems, 1/220, 265; beats time to, 4/394; liking for French music, 1/297–8 & n.; 8/73 & n. 3

NAVY BOARD AND ADMIRALTY BUSINESS ETC.: visits Woolwich, 3/265; 4/103; helps design *Henrietta*, 4/123 & n. 1; derides Petty's double-keeled ship, 4/334; 5/32–3 & n.; at launches, 5/306, 353; 9/101; commends A. Deane's *Rupert*, 7/127; patronises van Heemskerck's design, 9/171; visits Dutch E. Indiaman, 4/204; inspects fleet, 5/156, 193, 196; 6/170; 7/168; appoints prize commissioners, 5/333; orders about sale of prize goods etc., 8/16, 446; attends Navy Board meetings, 6/55; 7/201; 8/126; appoints commanders, 6/148; orders Board to Greenwich, 6/195 & n. 1; issues merchantmen's passes too freely, 7/349; orders money for fleet, 8/57–8, 68; inspects Sheerness, 8/84, 126–7; plans for campaign (1667), 8/97–8; action in Medway raid, 8/260, 263; plans criticised, 8/306; blames Board, 8/315; consulted by Board about ticket controversy, 9/101; with Duke of York adjudicates dispute between commanders, 9/107 & n. 3; and makes appointments, 9/128, 131; with Duke authorises payment of navy creditors, 9/149, 150, 152, 153; overrides Duke in replacement of Penn, 9/349–50,

551; orders Duke to suspend Anglesey, 9/340–1, 351, 362; orders fitting out of fleet, 9/425–6; and report on Board's constitution, 9/444 & n. 2, 519, 551; reassured about navy debts, 9/447; also, 4/360; 5/291; 8/477–8, 515

PARLIAMENT [omitting formal occasions]: sends message about Catholic priests, 4/92 & n. 3; holds conference with Commons on supply, 4/183 & n. 1; condemns attempted impeachment of Clarendon, 4/229 & n. 3; obtains repeal of Triennial Act of 1641, 5/93, 112 & n. 4; promotes merchants' complaints against Dutch, 5/105, 137; appeals for war effort, 6/270 & n. 1; power reduced by scrutiny of accounts, 7/307, 308; libel against circulated in Commons, 7/342; orders M.P.s from theatres etc. to vote, 7/399–400; threatens dissolution, 7/404; appoints commissioners to examine accounts, 8/2 & n. 3, 6, 193–5 & n., 251–2 & n.; quarrels with Commons over dispensing powers, 8/6, 9–10 & n., 18–20 passim; relations strained, 8/38, 125; to recall parliament, 8/292–4 passim; against recall, 8/362; allows enquiry into miscarriages of war, 8/424–5, 485; thanked for Clarendon's dismissal, 8/479, 480; to hold elections (rumour), 9/71; to meet parliament about religion, 9/104; attends Lords' debate on precedence, 9/106–7; urges Commons to vote supply, 9/141 & n. 2; message about adjournment, 9/174

ENCOUNTERS WITH P: calls P by name, 6/82, 104–5; high opinion of, 6/91, 292; 7/26, 27, 28, 31; grants him *Maybolt*, 8/477–8; appealed to on Hayter's behalf, 6/115–16; and on A. Joyce's, 9/33; congratulates on parliamentary speech, 9/105, 122; grants leave of absence, 9/558, 560; also, 3/191; 8/365–6

PICTURES: collection, 1/257–8 & n.; 3/82 & n. 2, 292; 4/319, 393 & n. 1; 7/97, 102 & n. 3

POLITICAL FAVOURITES [for appointment and dismissal of ministers, *see* under names]: Clarendon, 2/142; 'old

and Doll Common, 9/415; courtiers despondent about war, 7/153, 155, 197, 213–14; anxious for peace, 8/62; dislike its terms, 8/399; underestimate Dutch, 8/283
MISC.: in mourning, 7/39 & n. 2; 8/154 & n. 1; fails to help during Fire, 7/298; at launch, 9/101
CHARLES II, King of Spain 1665–7: plain dress, 8/79 & n. 3; Louis XIV's negotiations, 8/107
CHARLES X, King of Sweden 1654–60: gift to Sandwich, 1659, 1/238 & n. 1; 2/49; death, 1/76, 83; ~ his son (Gustaf), 7/289 & n. 2
CHARLES, Duke of Cambridge: see Stuart
CHARLETON, Dr Walter, royal physician (d. 1707): on vegetarianism, 7/223–4 & n.; social: 7/92
CHARL(E)TON, Sir Job, M.P. Ludlow, Salop, 1659–78; Justice Common Pleas 1680–6 (d. 1697): 9/93
CHARMS: see Popular Beliefs etc.
CHARNOCK, [Roger], clerk to Sir P. Warwick: 6/154
CHARTERHOUSE YARD: 2/58
[CHASE, John], royal apothecary: eye-lotion, 9/507 & n. 5
CHATELIN'S: see Taverns etc.
CHATHAM, Kent:
TOWN: Charles II's reception, 1/240; oysters, 3/41; St Mary's church, 3/153, 154; 4/227, 259; plague, 7/42 & n. 1, 253
DOCKYARD [see also Allen, J.; Barrow, P.; Cox, J.; Gregory, E.; Pett, Peter]:
CHRON. SERIES: guard, 2/11; squadron at, 2/62; proposed wet dock, 3/154; 4/225–6 & nn., 259; disputes among officers, 3/155–6; 4/149 & n. 2; 5/47; strikes etc., 8/271–2, 291 & n. 1, 307; launch, 4/225; King/Duke of York at, 5/156; 8/298; use of horses, 6/248; standing officers retained, 7/140; yard fortified, 8/125 & n. 2, 256, 260; Dutch raid, 8/259, 261–8, 271–3 passim, 327, 343, 490, 492, 506, 515; 9/524; discharge of ships by ticket, 8/497, 504, 507, 545; 9/69; proposal for surveyor, 8/391; administration criticised by Duke of York, 9/253 & n. 2; master-attendants

suspended, 9/258 & n. 3; dispute about methods of pay, 9/412
VISITS: by P, 1/172 & n. 4; 2/16, 67–73; 3/152–6; 4/222, 225–8, 258–61; 6/182–3, 194–5, 248; 8/305–11; 9/494, 495, 497, 499, 501; by other officers of Navy Board, 2/112, 116; 3/205, 227; 4/314; 6/83, 144, 197; 7/408; 8/350
HILL HOUSE: said to be haunted, 2/68; 4/227; lease, 4/260 & n. 2; housekeeper, 4/225; Treasurer's chamber, 2/68; 4/258; Comptroller's, 4/258; garden, 3/154; P visits/stays at, 2/68–72; 3/153, 155; 4/225–6, 228, 258–60; 6/182, 194, 249; 9/495; also, 8/309
MISC.: musters, 3/155 & n. 2; 4/228, 259; pays, 1/255; 3/215, 290; 4/222, 225; 8/257; 9/495; sales: of stores, 2/68–9; surveys, 1/204; 2/?112, ?116; ?3/68; 4/118; officers' houses, 2/69; 3/155–6; new ropehouse, 6/182 & n. 3; also, 3/163
CHATHAM CHEST: commission of enquiry into, 3/130 & n. 5, 158, 172 & n. 3, 174 & n. 5, 179, 257, 273; 7/109 & n. 2, 110; abuses in management by Commissioner Pett, 3/274; 5/76, 122; and Batten, 5/122, 141, 196, 301; 6/68, 183; 8/277, n. 2; 9/149–50 & n.; pay advertised in *Gazette*, 7/116 & n. 2; insolvency, 8/277; pays, 8/292, 309–10; alluded to: 2/100
CHATTERIS, Cambs.: P overnight at, 4/312
CHAUCER: P's admiration, 4/184 & n. 1; his copy of the *Workes* bound, 5/199 & n. 2; quoted, 5/237 & n. 4
CHEAPSIDE [see also Taverns etc.: Mitre; Star]: gibbet, 1/28; bonfires, 1/52; Lord Mayor's show, 1/277; 4/356; great laceman, 4/332; riot, 5/99, 100, 101; fire, 5/247–8; Great Fire, 7/275, 277; P visits ruins, 7/289; Three Crowns (shop), 3/163
CHEFFINS: see Chiffinch
CHELSEA [see also Taverns etc.: Swan]: P visits, 4/82, 114–17, 160; 7/235, 240; 8/371; 9/216, 563; Plague, 7/95; places in: church [All Saints'], 4/82; girls' school, 4/45, 59, 82, 112; neat-houses, 2/158 & n. 2; 5/268; 7/235; 8/371; 9/216; ~ Little Chelsea, 4/160

CHELSEA COLLEGE: proposed grant of, to Royal Society, 8/537 & n. 3
CHESHIRE: antiquity of families, 9/280 & n. 2
CHESTERFIELD, Lord: *see* Stanhope
CHESTERTON, Cambs.: P's old walk, 9/212; church (St Andrew's), ib.; ferry, ib.
CHESWICKE, ——, musician: 5/194
CHETWIND (Chetwin, Chetwynd), [James], Chancery clerk: P's regard, 3/275; his office, 1/50; P consults on Garter fees, 1/162; his pictures and lute, 1/182–3; chews tobacco, 2/128; his dog, 3/3; dies rich, 3/275 & n. 2; news from, 1/61; social: at old club in Bull Head, 2/127; 7/375; also, 1/50–3 *passim*, 74, 80, 92, 95, 244, 248; 3/49
CHEVERTON: *see* Chiverton
CHEVINS: *see* Chiffinch
CHICHELE, Henry, Archbishop of Canterbury 1414–43: portrait, 9/226 & n. 2
CHICHELEY, Sir Henry, of Wimpole, Cambs.: on *Naseby*, 1/130
CHICHELEY, Sir John, naval officer: begs prize-ship from King, 8/508; to give evidence to Committee on Miscarriages, 8/527, 549; social: 7/401; 8/433, 575; 9/281
CHICHELEY, Thomas, kted 1670; Ordnance Commissioner and M.P. Cambridgeshire:
PUBLIC CAREER: appointed to Ordnance Board, 5/316; attends Navy Board, 7/104; 8/215 ['Cholmley' ed.'s error]; attends Privy Council committee, 8/112; reports on gun-trials, 7/183 & n. 1; disappointed of Comptrollership of Household, 8/185 & n. 1; a 'high-flyer' in Parliament, 8/85–6; opposes comprehension bill, 9/112; praises P's parliamentary speech, 9/105; parliamentary news from, 8/501, 527
PRIVATE AFFAIRS ETC.: house in Great Queen St, 9/112 & n. 1; high style of living, ib.; social: plays tennis with King, 8/418–19; also, 5/330; 9/281
[CHIDLEY, Samuel], scrivener: 4/344, 345 & n. 1, 351
CHIFFINCH (Cheffins), Thomas,

Keeper of the Private Closet to the King: death, 7/94
CHIFFINCH (Chevins), William, page of the Bedchamber to the King: shows P King's pictures, 8/403; his lodgings, 9/557–8; social: 9/198, 507, 560; alluded to: 7/374
CHILD, Josiah, merchant, cr. bt 1678: P's regard, 6/255 & n. 1; declines Tangier victualling, ib.; bids for navy victualling, 9/287, 288, 316, 323; proposed appointment as Navy Commissioner, 9/507, 509, 550; complaints of, 9/549, 551; social: 9/543
CHILD, [William], organist: suitor to Mrs Bockett, 1/301 & n. 3; to be made doctor of music, 4/199 & n. 1; plays organ, 1/292 & n. 3, 297; 4/428; 8/145; sets music for P, 1/302, 324; 3/33; 7/227; 8/167; plays lute, 1/324; and viol, 2/39; takes P to rehearsal, 2/41; takes P and EP to service, 7/57–8; social: 1/234, 276, 285; 2/96–7; 7/59–60
CHILDREN, P's attitude to [for his foot-boys, *see* Birch, W.; Edwards, T.; Servants]:
HIS CHILDLESSNESS: disappointed of hopes of children, 1/1; finds new use for nursery, 2/127; considers possibility of childlessness, 3/16; 4/365; 5/277, 281; sorry to have no heir, 8/49; given advice on curing infertility, 5/222; asked to adopt child, 6/37; wishes cousin's boy were his own, 8/442
HIS AFFECTION FOR/INTEREST IN: jokes with, 2/72; enjoys company of Mountagu boys, 2/158; takes children to zoo, 3/76; pleased to see Bridewell children at work, 5/289; children dance to his singing, 9/196; admires child at Lamberts', 2/123; Cocke's boy, 2/218; Sir T. Crew's children, 3/76; Gauden's, 4/244; 'stout witty' Dick Penn, 6/35; roguish wit of young J. Pearse, 6/317–18; 7/70, 100; 8/103, 188; pretty boy in church, 7/169; Buckworth's children, 7/273, 419–20; 9/533; the seven children of Sir S. Fox, 7/406; pretty daughter of Mrs Knepp, 8/57; quick wit of boys on trial, 8/319; 'false tone' of shepherd-

boy reading Bible aloud, 8/338; intelligence of Mountagu twins, 8/472; Princess Mary's dancing, 9/507
CHILLENDEN (Chillington), Capt. [Edmund], soldier: 1/7 & n. 4
CHITTERNE, Wilts.: P visits, 9/231
CHIVERTON, Ald. [Sir Richard]: his hemp, 6/77
CHOLMLEY, Hugh, succ. to baronetcy 1665, engineer, Gentleman-man-Usher to the Queen 1662–c. 79:
PERSONAL: duel, 3/157; 4/47; house in Pall Mall, 8/99 & n. 4; ill, 9/95, 99, 122
TANGIER: appointed to committee, 3/238; attends committee, 5/154; 7/321; distrusts Irish, 5/302; hopes to become Governor, 7/99; 8/45, 103–4, 111, 116–17, 127; victualling business, 6/101–2; 7/121; 8/445, 461, 491; mole business: contracts for construction, 4/13 & n. 1, 26–7, 35–6, 45, 88 & n. 3; his gifts to contractors, 8/592–3; to be appointed Surveyor-General, 9/199 & n. 2, 364; accounts/money for, 5/344; 6/103; 7/18–19, 98–9, 323, 403; 8/63, 77, 205, 212–13, 298, 344, 377, 440–1, 482, 518–19, 522, 592–3, 596; 9/197, 199, 214, 388; also, 9/455; unspecified business: 7/132; 8/106, 205, 449; 9/492
COURT/PARLIAMENTARY NEWS FROM: 5/153; 7/163, 336–7, 403; 8/61–2, 93–4, 100, 106–8, 167, 244, 282, 292, 329–30, 412, 438, 446–7, 478, 482, 518–19; 9/53, 185, 530
OPINIONS: of court, 8/331; government by army, ib.; monarchy's prospects, 8/378; Anglesey, 8/301; Coventry, 8/518
RELATIONS WITH P: P's regard, 8/99–100, 331; 9/326; P opposes him over Tangier mole, 5/303; P's annual retainer from, 6/306; 8/593; also, 7/407 & n. 4
RELATIONS WITH SANDWICH: 5/343; 9/326; gift to, 8/592–3
SOCIAL: 5/215; 7/308, 375; 8/557; 9/22, 328–9, 465, 518
CHRIST CHURCH, Newgate St: P attends service, 7/169; Fire, 7/309
CHRISTENINGS: P/EP godparent(s) at private ceremonies: 2/109(2), 216; 5/176; 6/152; 7/49, 128, 129, 329–30;

8/202, 404–5, 540; 9/260; also, 1/42; 2/171, 230; 4/82–3; 5/265; 6/102; 7/129, 394; 8/438; 9/84; public service, at French church, 3/296; Roman Catholic, 7/329–30; customs: 2/109–10, 216; 4/82–3; 5/200, 211; 7/49, 329–30; 8/202, 405
CHRISTIAN, Prince of Denmark, later King Christian V 1670–99: installed as Knight of Garter, 4/108 & n. 3
CHRISTIANIA, Norway: timber from, 3/118 & n. 3
[CHRISTINA OF BOURBON], Dowager-Duchess of Savoy: court mourning for, 5/18 & n. 3
CHRISTINA, Queen of Sweden 1644–54: 8/164 & n. 1
CHRISTMAS, Mr ——, P's schoolfellow: remembers P as 'a great Roundhead', 1/280; mimics preachers, ib.; social: 2/62
CHRISTMAS [see also Drink; Food; Twelfth Night]: wassail bowl, 2/239; boxes, 4/426; 7/422; 8/589; 9/403; gifts (to P's father), 5/344, 346; wedding, 6/338; Catholic ceremonies, 8/588–9; gambling during, 9/2, 4
CHRIST'S HOSPITAL, Newgate St: P buys fairings at, 2/166; Spital sermon, 3/57–8 & n.; children boarded out after Fire, 7/17 & n. 7
CHURCHILL, Arabella, Maid of Honour to the Duchess of York and mistress of the Duke (d. 1730): 9/413 & n. 2
CHURCH OF ENGLAND [see also Christenings; Funerals; Nonconformists; Presbyterians; Religion (P); Sermons; Weddings]:
CHRON. SERIES:
RESTORATION 1660–2: disputes between Presbyterian and Episcopalian clergy, 1/204 & n. 2; consecration of bishops, 1/276 & n. 2; Worcester House Conference, 1/271 & n. 3, 278 & n. 2, 282–3; bishops restored to Lords, 2/82 & n. 7, 111, 216; Savoy Conference, 2/141; restoration of lands, 1/152; restoration of services: 1/190 & n. 1; at Westminster Abbey, 1/190, 261, 283, 324; Whitehall, 1/176, 195, 210; St Margaret,

Westminster, 1/215; St Olave, Hart St, 1/282, 289; 3/213, 235, 247; Rochester Cathedral, 2/70; King's College, Cambridge, 2/135–6; Brampton, 2/183; St Paul's Cathedral, 2/215; St Bride, Fleet St, 3/30
1662–9: Act of Uniformity: 3/161 & n. 4, 166; its reception and effects in London, 3/166 & n. 1, 169, 178 & n. 2, 190, 210 & n. 1; 4/372 & n. 3; 5/190 & n. 1; difficulties of enforcement, 4/243; proposed schemes of comprehension and toleration: Clarendon's proviso to bill of uniformity, 3/49 & n. 1; proposed council order (Oct. 1662), 3/186 & n. 2; King's declaration (Dec. 1662), 4/5 & n. 3, 44 & n. 2, 50, 57 & n. 4, 58 & nn., 62, 63, 65, 82; bill (1668), 9/31 & n. 4, 35, 45–6 & n., 51–2, 60, 96, 104, 111, 112; rumoured plans to confiscate church lands, 9/45 & n. 1, 347 & n. 3, 360, 473
CLERGY:
GENERAL: arrogance/unpopularity, 2/167 & n. 1; 4/372; marriage deplored, 8/67; exempt from poll tax, 9/120–1 & n.
BISHOPS: arrogance/unpopularity, 1/259; 2/57; 3/255, 271, 303; libels against, 8/585; oppose toleration, 4/5; 9/45; lose influence through support of Clarendon, 8/532 & n. 3, 584, 596; 9/1–2, 73; power to be reduced, 9/45 & n. 1, 73, 485
COURTS: Prerogative Court of Canterbury, 2/160; Court of Arches, 4/33; 9/45; excommunications, 4/372 & n. 4; 9/45 & n. 2; public penance, 6/159–60 & n.
FEASTS AND FASTS: All Hallows Day, 8/515; Ascension Day, 8/218 & n. 1; 9/559; Candlemas Day, 5/35; Easter Day, 1/113; 2/74; 3/54; 4/105; 5/118; 6/66; 7/99; 8/154; 9/126, 514; Lent [for P's observance, see Religion (P)]: plays in, 4/57; 8/90, 122; observed by Mediterranean fleet, 4/415; wedding, 9/493; St Peter's Day, 9/251; weekly fast, 1/58
SPECIAL SERVICES: of thanksgiving: for restoration of Charles II, 1/186 & n. 5; his birthday and restoration, 2/109 & n. 2; 3/95; 4/163; 5/159; 6/111; 7/135;

9/563; for weather, 2/119 & n. 4; Battle of Lowestoft, 6/132 & n. 1; cessation of Plague, 7/376; of commemoration: for execution of Charles I, 2/24 & n. 2, 26 & n. 1; 3/20; 4/29; 5/31; 6/25; 7/30, 325; 8/37; 9/42, 431; of intercession: against unseasonable weather, 2/119 & n. 4; 3/10 & n. 2; and Plague, 6/155 & n. 4, 179, 294, 320; 7/37, 68, 91, 150–1, 193, 231, 306, 359(2); for naval success, 6/73; 7/138, 140; against the Fire, 7/316 & n. 3; 8/413; 9/297; for women in childbed, 3/91; churching of women, 2/185; 3/259; 9/137; lectures: 3/70
CHURCHYARD STAIRS: 6/192
CHYRURGEON'S-HALL: see Barber-Surgeons' Hall
CINQUE PORTS: parliamentary elections, 1660, 1/93 & n. 2, 96, 97; Barons at coronation, 2/85, 86 & n. 3; Duke of York as Lord Warden, 9/280 & n. 4
CIPHERS: P writes for Downing, 1/30, 31; for Sandwich, 1/115; correspondence in cipher between Sandwich and P, 1/22, 44; between Sandwich and Carteret, 7/354
[?CISII, Pietro]: at court, 9/17 & n. 3
CIVIL WAR, the:
GENERAL: origins, 7/343; meetings of Eastern Association, 3/224 & n. 3; Treaty of Uxbridge (1645), 4/212 & n. 1; King's escape from Hampton Court (1647), 6/316–17 & nn.
MILITARY EVENTS: defence of Lyme Regis (1644) and Taunton (1644–5), 5/169 & n. 3; surrender of Bristol (1645), 5/169–70 & n.; 6/30; mutiny at Newark (1645), 6/30–1 & n.; siege of (1646), ib.
NAVAL EVENTS: attempted mutiny in parliamentary navy (1642), 4/124 & n. 1; encounter in Thames (1648), 5/169 & n. 1; 8/306
CLAPHAM, [John], of the Ticket Office: 8/263 & n. 4
CLAPHAM, Surrey: P visits, 4/244; 6/172–3
[CLARE MARKET, Lincoln's Inn Fields]: 1/5 & n. 4
CLARENDON, Earl of: see Hyde, E.

CLARENDON PARK, Wilts.: sold
by Albemarle to Clarendon, 5/61 &
n. 1; dispute over timber, 5/203–6
passim, 210, 212–14 passim, 216, 218,
219, 238, 318, 321; alluded to: 9/321
CLARGES (Clerges), Sir Thomas;
Muster-Master General; M.P. Westminster 1660; Southwark 1666; kted
1660: Sandwich's low opinion, 1/129;
army's envoy to King, 1/128 & n. 2,
129; report on navy's debts, 1/288 &
n. 1; criticises Navy Board, 8/510;
9/62; alluded to: 1/184
CLARKE: see Clerke
CLARKE, [Frances], wife of Timothy:
P admires, 1/214; 3/75–6, 99; witty
but conceited, 3/299; 4/14; 5/197; a
poor housewife, 4/142; 8/58–9;
proud, 7/100; 8/157; slanderous anecdote of, 7/100; painted, 8/58; social:
4/88 89, 97; 5/245, 291; 8/101, 421;
alluded to: 3/298; 4/42; ~ her
cousin, 4/14; her kinswoman,
5/197
CLARKE, [Julian] (Aunt Kite): fatally
ill, 2/172 & n. 2; disposes of property,
2/173 & n. 1; burial, 2/178, 179; P as
executor, 2/179; goods valued, 2/190
CLARKE (Clerke), Capt. Robert,
naval officer: arrests Cavalier, 1/99;
gift to P, 1/104; kindness to P, 1/257;
serves on *Antelope*, 6/19; and *Gloucester*, 7/148; conduct in Dutch raid
criticised, 8/310; criticises sinking of
Monmouth, 8/327–8; social: 1/115;
2/74, 210
CLARKE, [Timothy], royal physician:
CHRON. SERIES: P's regard, 1/134;
5/245; on Dutch voyage ('the Doctor'), 1/134, 135, 136, 145, 153–4,
156, 157; tells P story, *The fruitless
precaution*, 1/135 & n. 2, 266; at The
Hague, 1/138; discusses nature of
tragedy, 1/236 & n. 3; visits Portsmouth, 3/69–72; tells bawdy stories,
3/69; to nominate P as Fellow of
Royal Society, 3/72 & n. 3; at Royal
Society club, 6/36; part in P. Carteret's marriage negotiations, 6/136,
137; criticism of Davenant, 8/59;
writes play, 8/59–60; also, 8/159
AS PHYSICIAN: attends Capt. Ferrers,
2/103; Sandwich, 4/17; and King,

5/197; dissects cadavers before King,
4/132; prescribes for P, 4/407, 441;
experiment with opium, 5/151; discusses arrangements for war wounded, 5/332 & n. 5; also, 7/177; 9/254
COURT NEWS FROM: 1/143; 3/282; 4/19;
7/48–9; 8/35, 47
SOCIAL: entertains P to poor dinner,
8/58–9; also, 1/173, 211, 214; 3/73,
74, 230, 299; 4/14, 142; 8/157; 9/200,
413; ~ house, 3/76
ALLUDED TO: 1/159; 4/10, 97
CLARKE (Clerke), Sir William, kted
1661, Secretary at War 1661–6:
orders troop movements, 1/86; P
asks favour from, 6/169; news from,
6/280–1 & n.; a 'brisk blade', 7/84;
Sandwich's low opinion, 7/203; fatally wounded in action, 7/147, 149,
154; alluded to: 6/121 & n. 2, 122–3;
9/317
CLAXTON, [Hammond], of Booton,
Norf., P's relative: advises P over
Robert P's will, 2/181; 3/218; social:
2/146, 147
CLAXTON, [Paulina], wife of Ham-
mond, housekeeper to Roger P:
3/219; 4/159
CLAYPOLE, John ('Lord') (d. 1688):
enquires for lease of P's Axe Yard
house, 1/218 & n. 1; ~ his footman,
ib.
CLAYTON, Sir Thomas, Warden of
Merton College, Oxford 1661–93:
9/352 & n. 2
CLEGGAT, Col. [?Thomas], Greenwich: political news from, 6/286;
social: 6/245, 316
CLEMENT IX, Pope 1667–70: election, 8/336 & n. 1
CLEMENTS [?John], bo'sun: 3/155
CLEOPATRA: alluded to in sermon,
5/97; picture, 9/430
CLERGES: see Clarges
CLERK OF THE ACTS, the [i.e. P's
principal activities as Clerk. References to his attendance at the Board
and to his share in its collective deci-
sions are indexed under Navy Board.
See also Royal Exchange; for his
relations with colleagues and associates, *see* under names.]:
GENERAL: career summarised, vol. i,

303–4 & n.; 5/215–16 & n., 333 & n. 1; 7/2–3 & n.; deals, 4/232 & n. 4, 233; tar, 4/364 & n. 1; 5/136 & n. 3; glazing, 5/44 & n. 4; hammocks, 6/40 & n. 2; plank, 6/99 & n. 6, 185 & n. 2; defends Warren's contracts, 4/326, 421 & n. 3; 7/2–3 & n.; 9/254, 255; criticises Winter's, 4/326; ahd Murford for alleged breach of, 4/353 & n. 1; makes calculation about Wood's masts, 5/51 & n. 4, 52

DOCKYARDS [for his work at individual yards *see* Blackwall; Chatham; Deptford; Portsmouth; Woolwich]: drafts letter 'of reprehension and direction', 3/164 & n. 5; introduces new call-book, 3/234 & n. 2, 289 & n. 2; 4/14–15; to visit Deptford and Woolwich at least once a week, 4/425; defends his administration, 4/256; proposes employment of workmen in fire-fighting, 7/274

FINANCIAL [*see also* Exchequer; Navy Board; Treasury; Warwick, Sir P.]: *general*: prepares statement on debts for parliament, 1/211, 214 & n. 4, 226 & n. 4, 227, 228, 246 & n. 3, 247, 288 & n. 1; drafts scheme for paying off seamen, 1/309 & n. 5; makes estimates for boats, 3/52; drafts statement of navy estimates, 3/179 & n. 4; prepares answer to Lord Treasurer, 3/250, 258, 261, 280 & n. 1; and account of expenses (1660–2), 4/49 & n. 2; calculates debts, 4/304; introduces new method of accountancy, 5/7; proposes separation of posts of deputy-treasurer and muster-master, 5/8 & n. 1; drafts letter to Lord Treasurer on cost of war, 5/325, 326, 329; inflates estimate, 5/330 & n. 2; to be fully informed by Treasury, 6/46; works on accounts, 6/256 & n. 3, 257 & n. 4; 7/76(2); comments on proposal to pay bills in course, 6/304 & n. 3; and on value of Additional Aid (1665), 6/327, 334; 7/4, 87; presents statements of need for money: to Lord Treasurer, 7/48 & n. 2, 294 & n. 1, 295; to Duke of York, 7/122(2) & n. 1, 205–6 & n., 373 & n. 2, 374(2), 381; 8/138 & n. 2, 274 & n. 3; 9/49, 94; to Cabinet/

Council, 7/311–12 & n.; 8/111(2), 111–12 & n., 114 & n. 3; enquires about loans at Guildhall, 7/72 & n. 2, 76, 88 & n. 2; prepares statement on cost of war for Commons, 7/233, 285–8 passim & nn., 291–4 passim & n., 300, 301–2 & n., 308 & nn., 310, 314; 8/90; compares costs of First and Second Dutch Wars, 7/307 & n. 5, 308; calculates extraordinary charges, 7/310; his imprests authorised by Board, 7/328, 330; prepares accounts for parliament, 7/417; examines petty warrant accounts, 8/50; attempts to get creditors paid, 8/203(2); 9/140, 146, 149; works on report to Treasury Commission on accounts (1660–7), 8/250, 349, 372 & n. 1, 373 & n. 2; consults Treasury about commanders' pay, 8/398; works on Navy Treasurer's accounts, 8/448 & n. 4, 458 & n. 2; drafts Council order about Exchequer certificates, 9/152–3; applies to city for cash, 9/169; ordered by Council to calculate charge of summer fleet, 9/216; reforms storekeepers' accounts, 9/300, 374 & n. 1, 474; defends Board against criticisms from new Treasurers, 9/447; examines old accounts, 9/479; prepares estimates, 9/493–4 & n., 501, 530; also, 4/305, 306; 6/75; 7/77; 8/89, 273, 274, 277, 524; 9/40, 109, 110, 119, 271

pays [*see also* Navy Treasury; and under names of dockyards]: signs tickets, 6/158; 7/366; 8/280; discusses order of pay, 7/308, 327; and methods of expediting, 8/433 & n. 1, 558 & n. 3; inspects Ticket Office, 7/76, 418; to draw up rules for issue of tickets, 9/15 & n. 4

pursers: plans reform of, 6/325, 341; memorandum on, 7/1(3) & n. 1, 2(3), 5, 9, 10 & n. 1, 13; plan adopted, 7/27, 28, 105, 106 & n. 2; offers to help Mennes with pursers' accounts, 7/421 & n. 2; new proposals, 9/459, 460 & n. 2

JUDICIAL/DISCIPLINARY BUSINESS [*see also* Carkesse, [J.]; Field, [E.]]: memorandum on bill empowering Principal Officers as city magistrates,

CLIFFORD, family of: in Fuller's *Worthies*, 5/118 & n. 1

CLIFFORD, Martin, Buckingham's secretary: to mediate between Buckingham and Clarendon, 9/361 & n. 2

[CLIFFORD, Rosamund], (d. ?1176) 'fair Rosamund', mistress of Henry II: alluded to in sermon, 5/97 & n. 2

CLIFFORD, Sir Thomas, M.P. Totnes, Devon, Comptroller and Treasurer of the Household, Treasury Commissioner, cr. Baron Clifford of Chudleigh 1672:
PUBLIC CAREER: origin and estate, 8/185 & nn.; 9/205; at Fishery Committee, 5/294; naval service, 7/288 & n. 3; to be Comptroller of Household, 7/390 & n. 2; attacks Pett in Commons, 8/526; appointed to Treasury Commission, 8/229–30; dealings with Navy Board: about Exchequer certificates, 9/122; victualling contract, 9/303, 316–17; debts, 9/444–5; reform of office, 9/525; and other business, 8/249, 278; 9/501
RELATIONS WITH P: P's opinion, 5/294; 7/288; his regard/support for P, 9/487, 493, 501, 503, 512
RELATIONS WITH OTHERS: ally of Sandwich, 7/54; protégé and ally of Arlington, 8/185, 289; unpopular with colleagues, 9/205; disliked by Coventry, 9/472
SOCIAL: 8/79; 9/118, 352

CLIFFORD, Mrs ('Madam') ——: social: 2/151, 169, 193, 201

CLINKE, ——, a Dutchman: fights with waterman, 1/215

CLOCKS: see Watches and Clocks

CLODIUS (Clod), [Frederick], physician: 1/92, 196; ~ his wife (Mary Hartlib), 1/90 & n. 2

CLOTHIER, [John], rope-merchant, Woolwich: 5/190–1, 253 & n. 1

CLOTHWORKERS' COMPANY: see London: livery companies

CLOTHWORKERS' HALL: P visits, 1/187; destroyed in Fire, 7/278–9; alluded to: 9/245, 518

'CLUB', P's: meets weekly in Cromwell's time, 1/208 & n. 4; 2/127; 4/10; 5/30; 6/147–8; 7/375

CLUN, [Walter], actor: replaced by Lacey, 4/128 & n. 4; murdered, 5/232 & n. 5, 233; his talent, 9/411, 438, 523 & n. 1

CLUTTERBUCK, [Richard], merchant: 5/37

CLUTTERBUCK, [Thomas], consul at Leghorn: 9/346 & n. 2

COAL [see also Newcastle-upon-Tyne: Woodmongers, Company of]: P's domestic supplies, 1/11; 2/179; 3/25–6; 8/187, 435; distributed to poor, 4/410 & n. 2; price, 7/401 & n. 5; 8/98 & n. 5, 187, 285, 295–6 & n., 435; scarcity in war, 8/102, 285, 295–6, 576; mined in Nova Scotia, 8/426 & n. 1; exported to Tangier, 9/249 & n. 2

COBHAM, Kent: 8/184; 9/497

COBHAM, Surrey: 9/273

COCKE, [Anna Maria], b. Solomons, wife of George: her good looks etc., 2/218; 3/143, 152; feared consumptive, 4/235; her valuable linen, 4/283

COCKE, Col. Charles George: his reduced condition, 9/113 & n. 2; ~ his daughter, 4/94–5

COCKE, George (Capt. Cocke), hemp merchant, Commissioner for the Sick and Wounded and Prisoners of War 1664–7:
CHARACTER: P's critical comments, 4/283; 5/51; 6/192, 199, 238–41 passim, 282, 290; well thought of, 5/300; good company, 6/227, 342
NAVY BOARD BUSINESS: contracts for hemp, 3/114 & n. 1, 116, 129–30; 6/327 & n. 1; 7/358–9 & n., 385 & n. 2; proposes to provide anonymously, 7/132 & n. 3, 150, 184, 206, 220–1, 228, 359, 361; hemp criticised, 3/155; 4/194 & n. 3; and timber, 4/241–2 & n.; his tar, 4/364 & n. 1; canvas, 7/68; accounts, 4/49, 57, 58, 72, 141; payments to, 6/312, 313, 327, 328, 329; 7/115; 9/140, 146; rumoured appointment as Surveyor, 4/287 & n. 2; discusses exemptions from press, 6/24–5; unspecified business, 3/152–6 passim; 4/235; 6/216, 279, 307; 7/133; 8/447
CHATHAM CHEST: attends meeting, 3/257

COMMISSIONER OF THE SICK AND
WOUNDED AND PRISONERS OF WAR:
appointed Treasurer, 5/329 & n. 1;
business, 8/112; also, 6/217
HIS SHARE IN SANDWICH'S PRIZE-GOODS:
bargains and agreements with P and
others, 6/230, 238 & n. 4, 241, 243,
245, 297; acquires certificate from
Sandwich, 6/247; goods threatened
with seizure, 6/243, 252, 256, 259,
260–5 passim, 269–70; profit, 6/313–
14, 327, 328, 329, 334, 340, 341;
7/65; affair investigated by Brooke
House Committee, 9/48–50 passim
& nn., 57, 61, 63, 66, 72; also, 6/228,
234, 239, 246, 247, 248, 271–2, 272,
312, 318; 7/6
POLITICAL VIEWS ETC.: on Dutch war,
5/35, 105; 6/282; 7/286–7; fears parliament will withold supply, 2/196–7;
8/68–70; pessimism about government and state of nation, 6/210–11,
218, 245; 7/14, 375; 8/125, 409; 9/96;
believes active King the only solution,
8/37; on danger of civil war, 8/70;
help to Coventry, 9/303; news from,
7/220, 287, 309, 311, 317, 402; 8/18, 24,
37, 68–70, 80, 105, 153, 176, 275–6,
409, 447, 535, 568, 572; 9/278
COMMERCIAL NEWS: about Guinea
trade, 4/363; loss of rents in Fire,
7/286 & n. 2; bankers' wartime credit,
8/285
HOUSES: at Greenwich: P visits, 3/142,
143; 6/233, 291, 297; stable, 6/233;
garden, 6/291, 297; door by the
water, 6/297; in London: 8/441, 497
RELATIONS WITH P: gifts of fish etc.,
2/225; 3/81; silver plate, 7/90, 91, 121,
132, 405, 409, 416–17, 420; money,
7/132; lends coach, 7/269; warns
against Brouncker, 8/203; asks for
loan, 8/598; praises parliamentary
speech, 9/105, 113; advises about proposed reform of Board, 9/290; also,
7/305; 8/572; 9/285
SOCIAL: drunk, 2/?232, 238; 3/4;
6/290; atheistical talk, 5/335–6; on
river trip, 3/30–1; talks of Poland,
3/154; of Roman history, 4/362; of
Cromwell's betrayal of Charles I,
5/335 & n. 2; plays billiards, 6/190;
enjoys Mrs Penington's company,

6/273, 297, 299, 308, 310; at Twelfth
Night party, 7/6; dance, 7/18; taverns, 2/208, 218, 219, 233; 6/325;
7/68, 74, 89; 8/95; houses/lodgings of
associates in London and Greenwich,
2/211, 218–19; 3/10, 88; 5/277;
6/186, 187, 204, 209, 217, 236, 237,
275, 285, 303, 307–8, 311, 313, 317;
7/14, 67, 376; 8/65, 66; 9/410; at his
Greenwich house, 3/142, 143; 6/191,
192, 212, 220, 222, 227, 228, 275, 291,
296, 316, 324, 335–6, 339; London
house, 7/34, 38, 404, 408; 8/394–5,
441, 497; 9/15; also, 2/220, 223–4;
?4/212; 6/226, 248, 303
ALLUDED TO: 9/286, 501
~ his son: 2/218; at school, 6/223; his
black footboy (?Jack) dies of suspected
plague, 6/232, 233, 236, 244, 283, 285;
his servant Jacob, 6/259; his maid,
7/63
COCKE, [Robert], navy victualler at
Lisbon: gift to P, 4/290 & n. 2;
accounts, 4/325
COCKE, ——, ?a prostitute, Fleet
Alley: P entertained by, 5/225–6
COCKER, [Edward], calligrapher
and engraver: P's regard, 5/237–8 &
n.; engraves P's slide-rule, ib.; sells
him reading glass, 5/290, 291–2
COCKPIT, the: see Whitehall Palace
COCKPIT, the new, King's Gate,
Holborn: P at, 9/136, 141, 154
[COENDERS, Rudolf], Dutch naval
commander: killed in action, 7/229 &
n. 3, 231 & n. 4
COFFEE-HOUSES:
GENERAL: political talk/debate in [see
also below, Miles's]: 5/30, 228, 321;
8/304; Presbyterians' bold talk, 4/15;
literary/scientific talk, 5/14, 27–8, 37,
108, 123; music, 5/12; in Plague, 7/45;
chocolate drunk, 5/329
P VISITS [business talk/transactions not
noted]: [Miles's, the 'Turk's Head',
New Palace Yard, Rota Club at], 1/13,
14, 17, 20–1, 61, 63, 288; Grant's,
4/64–5; coffee-house(s) near Navy
Office [all or most in Cornhill],
1/318; 2/11, 108, 111, 151; 3/2, 35;
4/340, 353, 371, 378, 380, 434, 438;
5/1, 12, 34, 293, 295; in Covent
Garden, 5/37 & n. 2 (the 'great' coffee

political/court news from, 7/353–4; 8/11, 86, 368–9, 544, 597; alluded to: 2/97; 9/139; ~ his brother, 1/206

COLLADON (Collidon), Sir John, physician: patent for smoky chimneys, 4/315 & n. 1

COLLAR: *see* Collier

COLLETON (Collidon), Sir John, merchant: report on Fishery lottery, 5/299–300 & n.

COLLIER, [?John] ('Blacke Coller'): Hawley's case against, 1/199–200 & n.

COLLINS, [Jerome], surgeon: to sail with Rupert, 5/275 & n. 1

COLLINS, ——: employed by Brooke House Committee, 9/43

COLNBROOK, Mdx: 9/243

COLVILL(E), John, goldsmith banker, Lombard St:

BUSINESS WITH P: Tangier: cashes tallies, 6/108, 115, 163, 164; 7/214, 242; and bills of exchange, 6/169; 7/66; his accounts settled, 6/204–5, 325; also, 9/265; private: sells salts, 6/131; arranges loan on Treasury warrants, 7/85, 89–90 & n., 230, 243, 244, 251; advances money for Paulina P's portion, 9/97; unspecified: 6/184, 297; 9/214

HIS NEWS/OPINIONS: critical of ministers, 7/244; news of Dutch fleet, 6/184; of court and parliament, 7/323; low view of government credit, 6/268; 7/171; praises P's parliamentary speech, 9/109; also, 6/318

MISC.: credit survives Fire, 7/323; moves to Lime St after Fire, 7/323; new house in Lombard St, 9/112 ~ his beautiful wife: 6/131–2

COLWALL, [Daniel], Treasurer of the Royal Society: supports Carkesse in dispute with Navy Board, 8/555; at Royal Society, 9/147, 334

COMBERFORD, [Nicholas], chartmaker, Ratcliffe: P admires his methods, 4/240

COMETS and meteors: *see* Science and Mathematics: astronomy

COMINGES, Gaston Jean-Baptiste, Comte de, French ambassador 1663–5: at review of troops, 4/217; takes offence at Lord Mayor's banquet,

4/355; house [Exeter House, Strand], 5/103 & n. 4

COMMANDER, [Henry], scrivener, Warwick Lane: draws up deed for Sandwich, 4/343; and P's will, 5/20, 25, 26, 29, 31, 192; negotiates P's purchase of land etc. for coachhouse and stable, 8/209, 224, 225, 246, 250

COMMON GARDEN: *see* Covent Garden

COMMONWEALTH, the:

GENERAL: P reproached for service to, 6/329–30; return predicted, 8/337–8, 390, 556; 9/373; political/military efficiency, 3/90; 6/45–6; 8/250, 377–8, 390–1

POLITICAL HISTORY: successive régimes in 1659, 5/8 & n. 2; Committee of Safety (1659), 1/39, 51; 2/92; Council of State (1660): clerks dismissed, 1/23; members chosen, 1/65 & n. 4; appoints Sandwich general-at-sea, 1/71; orders Cavaliers and disbanded soldiers to leave London, 1/91 & n. 2; prepares agreement with King, 1/103 & n. 2, 111; also, 1/48

ARMY: high repute abroad, 4/215 & n. 3; and at home, 4/217, 373–4 & n.; disbandment, 1/242 & n. 1, 249, 257, 295 & n. 3, 304; political activity: officers submit to Rump, 1/1, 13, 14; soldiers mutinous, 1/36 & n. 4, 36–7 & n., 38 & n. 1, 40 & n. 3, 59 & n. 4; officers' attempted remonstrance to parliament, 1/81–2 & n., 88 & n. 1; soldiers said to be anti-royalist, 1/86; Dunkirk garrison royalist, 1/101; army's engagement to support parliament, 1/108 & n. 3; envoy sent to King, 1/128 & n. 2; also, 1/121

FINANCIAL ADMINISTRATION: coinage, 4/148 & n. 2; efficient collection of excise, 4/374–5 & n.; revenue, 5/68 & n. 3

NAVAL ADMINISTRATION: alleged corruption, 1/308; praised, 6/45; compared with Navy Board, 7/307 & n. 5, 308; 9/444, 484 & n. 3; methods, 9/485; creditors to be paid (1663), 4/158–9 & n.; promotion by sanctity, 4/375; Cromwell's expenditure, 5/59 & n. 4

COMPTON, James, 3rd Earl of

establishing Brooke House Committee, 9/8

AS CHANCELLOR OF THE EXCHEQUER: navy business, 4/158–9; 5/321; Tangier business, 6/91(2) [see also below]; alluded to: 8/180

AS TREASURER OF THE COMMISSION FOR PRIZES: orders payment to navy, 6/319; resists Navy Board's request for ships, 7/80; accounts, · 7/309; 8/446; quarrels with Board over sale of goods, 8/16, 20, 144; sits as Commissioner of Appeal, 8/231; alluded to: 8/252

AS TREASURY COMMISSIONER: appointment, 8/223, 229–30; low view of colleagues, 8/244; and unpopularity with them, 9/205; proposes method of paying off fleet, 8/456; opposes Navy Board's application for money, 9/152, 171, 174, 444–5; unspecified business, 9/525; alluded to: 8/249

AS MEMBER OF TANGIER COMMITTEE: examines Povey's accounts, 6/13, 14, 15–16, 33, 77–8, 79; 9/371, 449; Rutherford's, 6/95; Yeabsley's, 7/121, 156; bribed by Yeabsley, 7/128, 129, 137; supports his claims, 7/156, 167; 8/445, 446, 461; cool with Peterborough, 7/156, 163; examines Belasyse's accounts, 9/199; approves P's fees, 9/340; attends meetings, 5/174; 6/58; 8/347; unspecified business, 6/71 8/197; 9/152

~ his wife [Margaret], 8/446; for his clerk, see Blany, R.

COOPER, [Henry], officer of the King's Works: 1/314; provides seat for P at coronation, 2/83

COOPER, [Richard], sailing master: P's opinion, 4/84; 'one-eyed', 4/133; mate of Royal James, 3/128; master of Reserve, 3/159, 160; quarrels with Holmes, 4/67, 78, 81; dismissed, 4/84; teaches P mathematics, 3/128, 131–4 passim, 136, 140, 148, 149; ships' rigging etc., 3/138, 149, 152, 158, 160, 161, 163; and cartography, 4/133–4; 5/303

COOPER, Samuel, miniaturist (d. 1672): painting of EP, 9/138 & n. 3, 253, 256, 258, 259, 261, 263, 264, 267, 268, 276–7; its cost, 9/277; other

paintings by, 9/139–40; his house, 9/139 & n. 1; musical and other talents, 9/259–60; good company, 9/256; social: 9/265; alluded to; 3/2; ~ his cousin Jack [Hoskins], 9/265

COOPER, [William], timber purveyor to the Navy Board: report by, 3/169; his dullness, 4/231

COOPER, Maj. ——: 7/68, 404

COPENHAGEN: 1/140; 4/69 & n. 2

COPPIN, Capt. [John], naval officer: transferred from Langport to Newbury, 1/109; killed in action, 7/154

CORBET, Miles, regicide: arrested in Delft, 3/45 & n. 1, 47–8 & n.; in Tower, 3/47; executed, 3/66

CORBET, Mrs ——: social: 7/362; 8/384, 502; 9/12, 128, 133, 186

[CORBETTA], Francesco, court musician: 8/374 & n. 3

CORDERY, Mr ——: 6/108

CORDERY, Mrs ——: 2/153, 157

COREY, [Katherine], ('Doll Common'), actress: performance in The scornful lady, 7/422 & n. 6; quarrels with Lady Hervey, 9/415 & n. 1

CORNBURY, Viscount: see Hyde, L.

CORNHILL [see also Coffee-houses; Taverns etc.: Globe; Pope's Head; Three Golden Lions; White Bear]: coronation arch, 3/138 & n. 2; Fire, 8/151–2 & n.; Backwell's building development, 9/517 & n. 1; stocks, 1/314; carrefour at conduit, 3/268

CORNWALL, rebellion in (1549): 9/167 & n. 5

CORNWALLIS, Charles, 2nd Baron Cornwallis, Gentleman of the Privy Chamber 1660–d. 73: pimps for King, 9/264

CORNWALLIS, Frederick, 1st Baron Cornwallis, Treasurer of the Household 1660–d. 62: distributes medals at coronation banquet, 2/84; death and funeral, 3/10 & n. 4; character, ib.

CORNWALLIS, [Henrietta Maria, of the Queen-Mother's Household]: 9/23

CORONEL(L), [Sir Augustine], financial agent of the Portuguese government: in dispute over customs dues, 5/43 & n. 2

CORRESPONDENCE (P) [omitting

cookmaid: (wages) 6/29; E. Knepp: (signing herself 'Barbary Allen') 7/4; Lambert: (a simple letter) 1/183; Lanyon: (news) 6/8 & n. 2; R. Matthews: (pay) 1/33; Moore: (news) 1/113, 170; (lawsuit) 3/83; J. Pearse: (invitation) 4/10; Mrs J. Pearse: (social) 8/25;

EP: (health) 1/128; (family news) 1/166; (her loneliness) 3/257–8; 4/9; (country life) 4/199; (quarrels with father-in-law) 4/210; (quarrels with Ashwell) 4/262; (journeys) 7/93; 8/272; (stay at Roger P's) 9/310; (unspecified) 1/106, 137; 4/221; John P, sen.: (Brampton business) 2/180, 194, 195; 3/212, 240; 4/15; 7/80; (storm) 3/35; (family news) 3/106; 4/271; 5/154; 6/314; 9/308–9; (employment for relative) 3/119; (Ferrer's fight) 3/196; (Tom's match) 4/12; (Tom's children) 5/154, 158; (household arrangements) 4/180; (Pall's match) 7/78; (illness) 8/119; (J. Trice's difficulties) 8/158; (EP's return) 8/286; (unspecified) 9/18; John P, jun.: (request for books) 1/243; (asks favour) 2/26; (his ordination; in Latin) 7/50; (mother's illness) 8/122, 129; (and death) 8/134; (unspecified; in Latin) 1/137; Paulina P: (mother's illness), 3/103; Robert P: (asks favour) 2/96; (land purchase) 2/117; (unspecified) 1/218; Roger P: (Pall's match) 9/18–19; Tom P: (family news) 3/107; Tom P the turner: (Robert P's will) 3/48;

Sandwich: (shipping), 1/302; (alterations at Hinchingbrooke) 1/313–14; (Lisbon news) 2/209; (Tangier news) 2/221; 3/33 & n. 2; (requests visit) 3/240; (comet) 5/352; (return) 6/41; (Lady Jem's marriage) 6/163, 202; (return) 6/237; (prize-goods) 6/269, 309; (rebuke) 9/217; J. Scott: (Tom P's estate) 5/124, 149–50; (unspecified) 1/22 (in cipher); 1/44 (in cipher); 2/163; 5/225

CORTENAER, Egbert Meüssen, Dutch naval commander: sails from Holland, 6/108 & n. 3

COSIN (Cosens), John, Bishop of Durham 1660–d.72: votes for

Clarendon's impeachment, 8/542 & n. 1

COTTENHAM, Cambs.: Pepys family in, 8/261 & n. 4, 274 & n. 2 ~ 'Cottenhamshire', 8/517

COTTERELL, Sir Charles, courtier, (d. 1702): story of Russian diplomatists, 8/428 & n. 3; at Danckert's, 9/504; ~ his son [Clement], ib. & n. 3

COTTINGTON, Francis, 1st Baron Cottington (d. 1652), diplomatist: advises Charles I to seize Spanish bullion, 7/253 & n. 1; stories of disinheriting nephew, 8/566–7 & n.; and of mission to Spain, 9/256 & nn.

COTTLE (Cuttle), [Mark], registrar of the Prerogative Court of Canterbury: house at Greenwich, 6/339 & n. 2; at Twelfth Night party, 7/5; alluded to: 6/334; 7/68; ~ his wife, 7/5

COTTON, Cambs.: 2/148

COUNCIL OF TRADE: *see* Privy Council

COUNTER, the, the city prison (in the Poultry): prisoners sent to, 2/73 & n. 3; 3/44; 5/114; and conventiclers, 4/129; also, 4/421

COUNTRY, Capt. [Richard], naval officer: sails with P to Baltic (1659), 2/185 & n. 5; gift of fruit, 2/185–6

COUNTRYSIDE, P's appreciation of [his visits to the country are indexed under place names]: expresses enjoyment of pastoral scene near Brampton, 3/221 & n. 2; nightingales near Woolwich, 4/151; 5/130; walks/rides: near Rotherhithe, 4/112; Woolwich, 4/149; Epsom, 4/245–9; 8/335–40; Brampton, 4/312; Islington, 5/132–3; 8/175; Kingsland, 8/211–12; and Hatfield, 8/381; river outing, 8/236; journey in West Country, 9/229, 231, 232, 234; and Medway valley, 9/495; would rather take trips to country than own country retreat, 8/339–40 & n.

COURLAND, Duke of [? Jacob, Duke 1642–82]: method of hunting, 4/413–14

[COURTIN, Pierre], French ambassador-extraordinary 1665: arrives incognito, 6/76 & n. 1

other news of 1666 campaign, 7/181, 224, 228, 288, 304; Dutch raid on Medway: disapproves of reduction of fleet, 8/140; orders fireships, 8/256 & n. 2, 259, 260 & n. 1; discharges ships at Chatham, 8/271 & n. 1; blamed for disaster, 8/298; criticises Deane and Spragge, 8/358, 379; defence against parliamentary criticism, 8/490 & n. 2, 492 & n. 2, 497–8, 524, 536; examined on use of tickets, 8/497; incriminating letter suppressed, 8/507 & n. 1; also, 5/321; 6/112

ACCUSATIONS OF CORRUPTION: criticised for selling offices, 3/104 & n. 3; for selling offices and charging excessive fees, 4/156 & n. 4, 166, 169 & n. 3; defence, 3/243, 4/330–2 & nn., 383; 7/306–7; takes salary in lieu of fees, 4/331 & n. 4; 9/92; cases cited, 4/71; 5/231 & n. 4, 235, 248–9 & nn.; to be attacked in Commons, 8/18, 69–70; examined by Committee on Miscarriages, 8/504, 505, 507; to be attacked in Commons, 9/87, 92, 98 & n. 2, 108 & n. 2, 128–9, 169; Sir F. Holles's part in attack, 9/92, 129, 173; and Tatnell's, 9/108; petition against him, 9/87 & n. 2, 129, 173; fears Brooke House Committee, 9/258, 277; accused of treason. 7/242 & n. 1

OTHER APPOINTMENTS:

AS TREASURY COMMISSIONER: appointed, 8/223, 229–30; asks for P's help, 8/230–1; dominates colleagues, 8/398; depressed by lack of money, 8/290, 591; 9/101, 248; reorganises Wardrobe, 9/7; concentrates on Treasury work, 9/316, 447; praises Southampton, 9/448; dismissed, 9/478–9 & n.; also, 9/465

AS TANGIER COMMISSIONER: appointed, 3/171, 238 & n. 3; critical of Povey, 3/177; supports P in disputes, 5/279; 9/418; encourages him to accept treasurership, 6/60, 106; other business: Povey's accounts, 5/48, 52, 123, 124, 127, 132, 135, 139; shipping, 5/177; victualling, 5/210; new commission, 5/229; reduction of garrison, 5/310; and of costs, 8/347; P's report on lack of money, 7/383; reform of

government, 8/160, 201; Belasyse's profits, 9/205; construction of mole, 9/364; puts low value on overseas possessions, 8/347–8; misc. and unspecified business, 3/272, 287; 4/335, 341; 5/168, 204; 6/154; 7/156, 166, 167; 8/210

AS M.P.: opposes motion to farm administration of navy, 7/304; defends Carteret, 7/322; libel against, 7/342; assures House King will disband army, 8/353; speaks in defence of clergy, 9/121 & n. 2

AS PRIVY COUNCILLOR: business: Lord Treasurer's accounts, 7/295; state of navy, 7/312; report on Navy Board, 7/374; on Tangier, 7/383; Navy Treasurer's accounts, 8/449; naval bounties, 8/460–1; manning fleet, 9/121; size of fleet, 9/216–17; unspecified, 7/354; 8/317

ON FISHERY COUNCIL: attends meeting, 3/269–70; anxious for its success, 4/366

RELATIONS WITH P: regard for/kindness to, 2/24; 3/134, 151, 171, 183, 185, 202, 210, 216, 272, 282, 302; 4/39, 232, 289; 6/63, 64(2), 172; 7/26–7, 28, 67–8; 8/420; 9/502–3; with P/Pett dominates office, 3/284, 290; P fears his reforming zeal, 3/83; welcomes it, 3/105; supports P's reform of victualling, 6/279–80; of pursers, 7/1 & n. 1, 5, 9 & n. 3, 10, 13, 28, 106; of office in general, 9/205, 253, 293–4, 312, 523 & n. 2; shows him MSS, 5/177 & n. 2; 9/523 & n. 2; supports claim to purveyorship, 2/54; gives silver pen, 4/263–4 & n., 268; suggests he write war history, 5/177–8; proposes increased pay for his clerk, 5/228 & n. 1; advises on dealing with parliamentary critics, 8/303–4, 524, 560; 9/79, 178; and with Brooke House Committee, 9/42, 79, 117; provides office papers for his defence, 9/255; urges him to lend to government, 8/392, 393; helps obtain *Maybolt*, 8/477; congratulates on parliamentary speech, 9/104–5; urges him to enter parliament, 9/454; when in Tower and afterwards advises on office matters, 9/481, 488, 503–4, 523, 563; P values

at meetings, 4/13, 27, 31–2, 102; 5/97, 105, 124, 139, 154, 210, 339; 6/13, 22, 61, 134, 151; 7/95, 121, 228, 254, 265; 8/61, 210; 9/355, 562; also, 3/238 SOCIAL [on some of these occasions, e.g. visits to dockyards, Creed may have transacted Tangier business]: at Trinity House dinners, 1/177; 3/246; 6/35; coronation banquet, 2/86; walks round Tower, 2/213–14; at funerals, 3/269; 6/114, 127; 8/101; christening, 4/82; visits Epsom, 4/245–9 passim; at Bartholomew Fair, 4/298; 5/265; Lord Mayor's banquet, 4/354–6; visits Greenwich, 5/178; Rochester and Chatham, 8/306, 307, 311–14 passim; sees freaks at Charing Cross, 8/326; prize fight, 8/429, 430; and cockfight, 9/154; calls on P with his bride, 9/408; at Twelfth Night party, 9/409; inhospitable to P and EP, 9/520; at taverns/coffee-houses etc., 1/75, 174, 207, 217, 221, 263, 267, 284, 303; 2/36, 63, 79, 88, 95, 101, 103, 116, 117; 3/94, 152, 248, 298; 4/12, 23–4, 58, 130, 179, 196, 349, 353, 361, 371, 427, 435; 6/115, 251; 9/163, 164, 169; at P's house, 1/173; 2/113; 3/91, 116, 132; 4/32, 40, 55, 133, 141, 157, 164, 188, 214, 266, 389; 5/128, 155, 175, 185, 242, 256, 259, 282, 304, 321, 323, 344; 6/41, 61, 109, 118; 7/131, 168; 8/130, 209, 232, 255, 362, 451, 511, 578; 9/51, 57, 61, 116, 197; at theatre, 1/224, 264; 2/34, 35, 54, 56, 66, 80, 89; 3/260; 4/4, 6, 16, 55–6, 162, 163; 5/240; 6/73, 83; 7/421–3; 8/399, 486; 9/162, 186, 248; at houses of other colleagues and associates, 1/268; 5/257; 6/63, 68–9, 87, 172–3; 7/29–30, 191; 9/130, 165, 176; at Sandwich's lodgings, 2/100; 3/288, 299; 4/5, 21–2, 101, 160; 9/334; at his own, 3/226–7, 281, 282; 4/22; 9/345; walks with P in St James's Park, Whitehall, to Deptford, Woolwich etc., 4/30–1, 37, 87, 113, 131, 151, 286, 297, 348; 5/47, 127, 133, 155, 186, 198, 215, 269; 6/118; 7/144, 148–9, 155, 221, 242, 265, 375, 376; 8/94, 368, 412, 464, 544, 545, 590; 9/141–2, 206–7, 215; on pleasure trips to Hackney/ Islington/Vauxhall etc., 5/176, 180–1,

190; 6/74, 136; 7/136, 223; 8/240–1, 249–50; also, 4/124, 125, 142, 163
MISC.: admires France, 2/33; at Backwell's, 3/94; belittles Lawson's achievements, 4/73; proposed as joint-secretary to Fishery corporation, 5/251; at Fire, 7/269, 271; at riot, 9/129–30
ALLUDED TO: 1/190; 9/272, 487
~ his footboy, 4/12; 5/45, 180
CREED, Richard, brother of John: his Puritan views, 1/91 & n. 2; alluded to: 1/86
CREEVEY, Thomas, diarist (d. 1838): opinion of P's diary, vol i, p. lxxxiii
CREIGHTON (Creeton), Robert, Dean of Wells 1660–70, Bishop 1670– d. 72: P admires his preaching, 5/96; comical sermon, 3/42–3 & n.; preaches against nonconformity, 4/92–3; 5/96– 7; and (in King's presence) against adultery, 8/362–3, 366; social: 8/417
[CRÉQUI, Charles Duc de], French ambassador to the Papacy 1662, 1664–5: 4/24 & n. 1
CRESSET, ——, 8/425 & n. 3
CREW, Jemima, Lady Crew (b. Waldegrave), wife of John Crew, 1st Baron: her 'saintly questions', 7/17; also, 1/41; 3/2; 5/209; ~ her page, 8/333
CREW, John, cr. Baron Crew of Stene 1661:
PUBLIC AFFAIRS: his part in return of secluded M.P.s, 1/18, 57, 60, 62; elected Councillor of State, 1/65, 82; and M.P., 1/116; created baron, 2/80; views: on constitution of House of Lords, 1/118, 125–6; contribution of Presbyterian clergy to restoration, 3/290–1; Dutch War, 5/244; 6/6; 7/125, 387; poll tax, 7/387–8; Brooke House Committee, 8/193–5; management of royal finances, 8/195; dissolution, 8/558; Dutch alliance, 9/1, 30; toleration, 9/31; the court, 9/190; also, 8/99, 251
PRIVATE AFFAIRS: new house in Lincoln's Inn Fields, 2/153 & n. 2, 213; ill, 9/265, 268, 550
RELATIONS WITH P: their mutual regard, 2/124–5; 3/55, 265; 7/355–6; 9/1; his advice about fees etc., 1/122 & n. 1; offers bargain of land, 5/196; also, 3/11

RELATIONS WITH SANDWICH: consulted about his lodgings, 1/22; his finances 3/11; 8/405-6, 461-2, 463, 480; his involvement in Tangier, 3/204; his naval command, 5/207; and the prize-goods scandal, 7/17, 219; 9/165, 176, 177; discreet about his liaison, 4/305, 316; to help arrange Hinching-brooke's match, 8/190; advises him how to obtain Lord Treasurership, 8/195; regrets his abandonment of Presbyterian interest, 9/164; also, 3/203

POLITICAL/COURT NEWS FROM: 1/44-5, 65; 3/253, 290-1; 4/126; 8/480, 558; 9/190, 222

SOCIAL: reminiscences of Elizabethan nobility, 2/114; at Lady Catherine Mountagu's christening, 2/171; at Lady Jemima Mountagu's wedding, 6/159-60, 176, 179, 180; P visits/dines with: 1/227; 3/2, 22, 33, 68, 78, 112, 203; 4/44, 239; 6/115; 7/423; 8/333; 9/130, 162(3)

ALLUDED TO: 1/73; house in Lincoln's Inn Fields alluded to [P's visits to servants and others]: 1/4, 5, 14, 15, 20, 25, 32, 43, 56, 64, 71, 73, 77, 79, 83, 89, 90, 91, 94, 173, 174, 176, 177, 178, 180-4 passim, 189, 222, 238, 247, 254, 255, 261, 278, 295, 310, 322, 325; 4/26, 123, 135, 237

~ Jane, servant, 1/20; John, coachman: buried, 1/73

CREW, John, son of the 1st Baron: at Dover with Sandwich, 1/158; social: 2/232; 7/356, 388(2); 8/558; 9/1

CREW, John, son of Sir Thomas: 4/239; 7/357

CREW, Nathaniel, brother of the 1st Baron: inherits estate, 7/423

CREW, Dr Nathaniel, son of the 1st Baron, Fellow of Lincoln College, Oxford; later Bishop of Durham and 3rd Baron: appointed proctor, 4/199; views city ruins after Fire, 7/357; preaches at Whitehall, 8/144-5; social: 3/84; 7/356-8 passim

CREW, Samuel, son of the 1st Baron: death, 2/131 & n. 4

CREW, Sir Thomas, son of the 1st Baron, kted 1660; succ. as 2nd Baron 1679:

PRIVATE AFFAIRS: portraits, 1/28-9 & n.; 4/139; copy of Van Dyck's self-portrait, ib.; prints, 7/211; ill, 3/55, 68; 4/136, 239; also, 1/223; 4/316

PUBLIC AFFAIRS: presents address to Rump, 1/73; on *Naseby*, 1/135, 151, 154, 161; views on taxation, 7/356; criticises Navy Board's accounts, ib.; views on Louis XIV, 8/335-6; defends Sandwich in Commons, 9/64, 177; regrets Sandwich's abandonment of Presbyterian interest, 9/164

NEWS FROM: political/court: 2/213; 3/78; 4/127; 5/244; 7/376; 8/333, 530, 538; theatrical: 8/334; also, 4/139

SOCIAL: 1/95, 187, 309; 4/305; 5/185; 7/388; 9/115

~ his children, 3/76; two daughters, 8/145; servant Pedro, 2/30

[CREW], Waldegrave; son of the 1st Baron: 1/15, 56, 57

CREW, ——, [?Nathaniel, ?Salathiel], brother of the 1st Baron: 3/253 & n. 2

CRIPPLEGATE [*see also* Taverns etc.: Cross Keys]: Brampton carrier in, 5/122-3; 6/90, 95

[CRISP, Agnes], daughter of Commissioner Pett: 4/168 & n. 1; 6/262

CRISP, Diana: no better than she should be, 1/237, 239, 246; fails to keep assignation, 1/251, 252; social: 1/91, 94, 226; ~ her old suitor, Meade, 1/219

CRISP, Capt. [Edward]: chosen Elder Brother, Trinity House, 6/84; and Master, 6/298

CRISP (Crips), Laud, brother of Diana: to go to sea, 1/91, 92, 237; his singing, 3/147; 8/65; place in Wardrobe, 8/65; social: 1/90; 7/44; alluded to: 1/93

CRISP, Sir Nicholas, merchant: project for dock at Deptford, 3/18 & n. 1, 29, 30, 32-3; social: 3/188; alluded to: 1/52; ~ his son [Ellis] dies of eating cucumbers, 4/285

CRISP, Mrs ——, mother of Diana and Laud: P lodges with, 1/90-4 passim; plays harpsichord, 1/90; advises on furnishing house, 1/210; also, 1/94; 2/166; social: 1/190, 237

CRISPIN, [Arthur], waterman: gives evidence against H. Brouncker, 8/501

CRITZ (Cretz), Emanuel de, Serjeant-Painter to the King (d. 1665):
shows P royal collection of sculpture,
1/188–9 & n.; copies Lely's portrait
of Sandwich, 1/272, 273, 290, 292,
301–2; other copies, 3/80 & n. 1;
social: 5/84

CROCKFORD, ——, ?porter: 1/92 &
n. 2; 2/87

CROFTON, Zachary, Presbyterian
minister (d. 1672): imprisoned, 2/58–9
& n.

CROFT(S), Herbert, Bishop of Hereford 1661–d. 91: his preaching, 1/265;
8/116 & nn.; convert from Catholicism, 8/116 & n. 4; votes for Clarendon's impeachment, 8/532 & n. 3

CROFTS, [?Thomas], clerk in the
Signet Office: 1/208, 211

CROFTS, William, 1st Baron Crofts:
3/149 & n. 5; 9/336, n. 4

CROFTS, Mr: see Scott, James, Duke
of Monmouth

CROFTS, Mrs ——, shopkeeper, of
Westminster: her shop, 9/129, 142;
social: 6/115, 163: 7/392

CROMLEHOLME (Crumlum),
Samuel, High Master of St Paul's
School: a conceited pedagogue, 6/53;
advises on John P's exhibition, 1/27;
given book for school by P, 2/239 &
n. 3; 4/33, 132–3; 5/38; his drinking a
warning to P, 3/199–200; losses in
Fire, 7/297; also, 1/44; 3/142; social:
2/238; ~ his wife, 4/133

CROMWELL, Elizabeth, widow of
Oliver: 1/248 & n. 1

CROMWELL, Frances, daughter of
Oliver: her impending marriage,
1/248 & n. 1; proposed marriage to
Charles II, 5/296–7 & n.

CROMWELL, Mary: see Belasyse

CROMWELL, Oliver:

CHRON. SERIES: at meetings of Eastern
Association, 3/224 & n. 3; attitude to
Charles I (1648), 5/335 & n. 2; to
Charles II, 5/296–7; story of his
tampering with royal tombs, 5/297 &
n. 2; storm at his death, 3/32 & n. 2;
body exhumed, 1/309 & n. 4; 2/24 &
n. 3, 26–7, 31; effigy hanged, 4/418 &
n. 2, 420; portrait by Simon, 4/70

REPUTATION: praised for: strong government, 4/376; promotion of trade,
5/52; 8/426; encouragement of navy,
5/59 & n. 4; Irish settlement, 5/346;
financial credit, 6/78; prestige abroad,
8/249, 332; sobriety of court, 8/355;
and intelligence service, 9/70–1; a
'coquin', 5/264; a 'rogue', 8/355;
biography, 8/382 & n. 2

ALLUDED TO: 1/12; 3/46

~ his family, 5/297

CROMWELL, Richard: downfall,
1/21 & nn. 3, 4; rumours of restoration, 1/74, 76, 79; Sandwich's advice
to in 1659, 1/180; life in exile, 5/296 &
n. 2; 7/94 & n. 6

CROONE, [William], physician: describes blood transfusion experiment,
7/370–1 & nn.

CROPP, ——, waterman: appointed
government waterman, 1/37 & n. 2;
also, 7/319

CROUCHED FRIARS: see Crutched
Friars

CROW, Capt. [?George], naval officer:
8/266–7

CROW, ——, footman to John
Claypole: 1/218

CROWE, Ald. [William], upholsterer
in St Bartholomew's: denied title of
alderman, 4/404 & n. 1; P/EP inspect(s)
tapestries, 9/329, 330; and beds, 9/333,
334, 356; also, 1/269; 9/362

CROWLAND, Abbot of: P's family
connection with, 8/261 & n. 4

[CROWTHER, Joseph]: unnamed
clergyman who married Duke and
Duchess of York, 2/40–1 & n.

CROXTON, [?Jane], of Salisbury
Court: P consults on flags, 3/205 & n.
1; also, 5/86

CRUMLUM: see Cromleholme

CRUTCHED (Crouched) FRIARS
[see also Taverns etc.: Three Tuns]:
7/152; 9/188, 519

CUCKOLD'S POINT, nr Deptford:
4/50

CULAN, Henry Fleury de, Heer van
Buat: executed, 7/315 & n. 1

CUMBERFORD: see Comberford

CUMBERLAND, [Henry], tailor, of
Salisbury Court: burial, 4/32 & n. 2

CUMBERLAND, Richard, P's contemporary at St Paul's and Magdalene,

Bishop of Peterborough 1691–
d.1718: in London, 1/43 & n. 1; P
visits, 1/54; P's regard, 8/118; 9/17,
56 ~ his brother, 8/118
CURLE, Capt. [Edmund], naval officer: gifts to P and EP for captain's
commission, 1/180
CURSITORS' ALLEY, Chancery
Lane: 9/140
CURTIS, Capt. [Edmund], naval
officer: to go to Mediterranean, 1/119
& n. 3; social: 2/33
CUSTIS (Custos), [Edmund], merchant: dispute about freightage, 4/404;
5/23, 36
CUSTOM HOUSE: P visits, 3/163;
new site, 7/280; alluded to: 4/163;
8/566
CUSTOM HOUSE (STAIRS): 3/119,
180; 4/144
CUSTOMS DUES: navy expenses
charged on, 4/206; merchants' cheats
(unspecified), 7/31; farmers of: listed,
3/188 & n. 3; dine with Lord Mayor,
4/341; farm criticised by Treasury,
8/373 & n. 4; officers attempt to
seize prize-goods, 6/256, 258, 259
CUTLER, Sir John, merchant: story
of beer and thunder, 4/365; on commission for repair of St Paul's, 4/430;
social: 4/22, 65, 100, 256
CUTLER, [William], merchant: P's
opinion of, 4/188, 322; 5/136; 6/166,
331; his regard for P, 4/296–7; his
rise, 5/52; contracts for hemp, 3/114,
116; 6/77; for tar, 5/136; discusses
navy victualling, 4/181, 398; breaks
with Cocke, 5/51; opposed by P,
5/352; provides cash, 6/191; bargain
for freight to Tangier, 7/65; unspecified business, 4/296; 5/332, 354;
foreign news from, 4/322; 5/51, 141,
343; house in city, 4/398; in Hackney,
6/331; housing property in city,
5/282–3; social: 4/216; 5/19, 23, 62,
159, 186, 255, 336, 341; 6/25, 83, 166;
~ his wife and mother [?]-in-law,
4/398; 6/331
CUTLER, P's: 8/136, 232
CUTTANCE, Capt. Henry, naval
officer: receives commission for *Cheriton*, 1/121; on *Royal Charles*, 1/160;
also, 1/221

CUTTANCE, Capt. Roger, kted
1665, naval commander:
CHRON. SERIES: supports Mountagu
(Sandwich) as parliamentary candidate, 1/103 & n. 4; loyalty to Mountagu questioned, 1/107; transactions
concerning ships' pay, 1/162, 167;
3/128; part in prize-goods affair,
6/230, 240, 241, 247, 313; 9/91, 402 &
n. 3; at council of war, 6/230; news
from, 6/306–7; 8/549–50 & n.; influence with Sandwich, 7/19; out of
favour with Coventry, 7/34; criticised
by Sir J. Chicheley, 8/549; gifts to
Sandwich and P, 1/57, 130, 232; also,
2/15–16, 16–17
TANGIER: appointed to committee,
3/238; attends meetings, 3/272; 4/319,
335; his design for jetty, 3/238; to
visit, 4/132
SOCIAL: 1/56, 265, 267, 321; 2/22, 23,
45, 49, 72, 74; 3/269; on *Swiftsure*,
1/97, 98; on *Naseby*, 1/113, 114, 119,
123, 141, 159, 160, 164
ALLUDED TO: 1/101, 104, 158, 161, 166,
179
CUTTLE, Capt. [John], naval officer:
killed in action, 6/219, 225; also, 2/33,
50
CUTTLE, lawyer: *see* Cottle
CUTTS, Sir John, of Childerley,
Cambs.: proposed match with Lady
Jemima Mountagu, 4/174 & n. 2

DAGENHAMS (Dagnams), Essex: P
visits for wedding, 6/175–7; his other
visits, 6/158–61, 167, 180–1; 7/17–18;
gallery, 6/159, 160; gardens, 6/160;
buttery, 6/180; also, 6/163, 173, 188,
193, 225
DAKING (Deking), Capt. [George],
naval officer: discharged, 1/109 &
n. 2, 110; (?the same), 3/50
DALMAHOY (Dormehoy), [Tho-
mas]: on *Naseby*, 1/134 & n. 6
DALTON, [Richard], Serjeant of the
Wine-cellar to the King: buys lease of
P's house in Axe Yard, 1/235, 244–8
passim; social: 4/4
[DALZIEL, Lt-Gen. Thomas]: defeats
Scots rebels, 7/390 & n. 6
DAMFORD, ——: anecdote about,
1/262

DAMPORT: *see* Davenport

DANCING: P dances for first time, 2/61, 71; 7/18; dislikes/disapproves of, 2/212; 4/176; 6/79; admires at court, 3/300–1; 6/29; takes lessons/ practises, 4/111, 122, 124, 126, 129, 132, 133, 134, 141, 149, 150, 153, 161, 265; finds useful for a gentleman, 4/122; Sandwich's dancing-master, 2/117; dancing at court, 3/300–1; 5/56; 6/29; 7/341, 371–3; 9/507; King's French dancing-master, 9/507; dancing schools: in Broad St, 1/253; Fleet St, 2/212; in city, 4/107; Bow, 7/238; at private parties: 6/262, 279, 284; 7/73, 230, 263, 360, 362, 363, 422; 8/28–9, 104, 493, 511; 9/8, 12–13, 42, 128, 134, 172, 227, 458, 464, 511; at schools: 8/392, 396; theatres: 3/32; 8/27, 101, 171, 375, 388, 440, 451, 487; 9/24, 48, 107, 144, 183–4, 219, 420, 459; particular dances: branle, 3/300; 7/372; coranto (courant), 3/300; 4/122, 124, 126; 6/88 & n. 1; 7/372; Cuckolds all a'row, 3/300–1; country, 3/300–1; 4/126, 149, 150, 161; 8/232; 9/464; French, 7/372; jig, 6/79; 7/246; 8/101; 9/120, 219, 464; La Duchesse, 4/141, 265; military, 8/451; 9/459; morris, 4/120; Spanish, 9/440

DANCKERTS (Dancre), [Hendrick], painter (d.? 1680): paintings for P's dining room, 9/421, 423 & n. 1, 434, 487; of Greenwich Palace, 9/438, 445, 465, 485; Rome substituted for Hampton Court, 9/504; painting of Windsor, 9/539; of Tangier, 9/541 & n. 2

DANIEL, [Richard], of the Victualling Office: 1/249; death, 5/286

DANIEL, [Samuel], naval officer: wife solicits commission for, 6/335; 7/417; 8/367; on *Royal Charles*, 7/141; brings news of Four Days Fight, 7/145–7; social: 8/76; alluded to: 6/336

DANIEL, Mrs ——, of Greenwich, wife of Samuel: fondled by Lord Rutherford, 6/274; with child, 6/274, 336; dogged by P, 6/332(2); asks favour for husband, 6/335; 7/417; 8/233, 244, 367; P kisses, 6/336;

7/202; ?brings news of plague, 7/236; fondled by P, 7/417; 8/233, 244, 282; 9/132, 248; tries to borrow money from, 9/306; also, 7/7; social: at Greenwich, 6/315, 333, 338; 7/141; at P's house/office, 7/211, 341; 8/45, 76; 9/265; ~ her son, 7/128; ?her mother-in-law, 7/341

DANVERS, Col. [Henry], Fifth-Monarchist: arrest and escape, 6/184 & n. 3

DARCY, [Marmaduke], Cavalier: on *Naseby*, 1/154, 157; alluded to: 2/29

DARCY, Sir William: Fishery business, 3/269–70 & n.

[DARLING, Edward and Thomas] *see* Taverns etc.: Three Tuns, Charing Cross

DARNELL, [?Richard, jun.], musician: P buys music from, 8/24–5

DARTFORD, Kent: P visits, 2/15, 16, 17, 57, 72; 6/242; 9/495, 499; post-house, 2/17; alluded to: 2/32

DARTMOUTH, Devon: Straits fleet at, 8/345

DASHWOOD, Ald. [Francis]: 6/182

DA SILVA, Don Duarte, merchant: 3/114 & n. 2

DAVENANT, Sir William, playwright and producer [*see also* Musical Compositions; Plays]: reinstates Harris, 4/239 & n. 3, 347; opera *The siege of Rhodes*, 6/284 & n. 1; 8/25, 59; allegedly taught by Capt. H. Cooke, 8/59; criticised by Dr Clerke, ib.; death and burial, 9/156 & n. 1, 158 & n. 3; ~ his sons, 9/158 & n. 4

DAVENPORT, [Frances], actress: leaves stage, 9/156 & n. 2

[DAVENPORT, Hester] ('Roxalana'), actress: leaves stage to live with Earl of Oxford, 3/32 & n. 6, 58 & n. 3, 86; alluded to: 3/273, 295

DAVENPORT (Damport), [?John], of Brampton, Hunts.: social: 2/24, 137, 208, 210, 213

DAVIES, [John], Storekeeper, Deptford: character, 1/286; 4/151; P stays with, 2/12; complains of treatment under Commonwealth, 1/308; his stores, 3/111, 173; bookkeeping, 3/129, 234; in disputes over contracts, 4/73 & n. 2, 151 & n. 1; also, 2/13;

alluded to: 4/318; ~ his wife, 2/12; his kinswoman, 3/129

DAVIES, [Thomas], bookseller and P's schoolfellow: heir to T. Audley, 3/264 & n. 2; knighted as sheriff, 8/497

DAVIS (Davy), [John], clerk to Lord Berkeley of Stratton: P's dislike, 2/26; 3/259; attempted burglary at house, 1/305; news from, 2/10; to go to Ireland, 2/55; alluded to: 1/289, 291, 315; 2/9; 4/408

DAVIS, Jack, son of the foregoing, Navy Office clerk: lends Tower Hill lodgings to P, 3/182, 188–209 passim; alleged fraud by, 4/152; Batten wants dismissed, 5/32; social: ?1/289; ?2/8, 26; ~ his Tower Hill landlord, 3/200

DAVIS, [Jane], ('Lady Davis'), wife of John, clerk to Berkeley: P's dislike, 2/55; 3/259; annoys P by closing door to leads, 1/277; resents EP's neglect, 2/10; to go to Ireland, 2/55; social: 2/25–6; alluded to: 2/114

DAVIS, Mary (Mall), actress: (untrue) rumour of death, 7/102 & n. 1; role in *Richard III*, 8/101 & n. 4; in *Love-tricks*, 8/375 & n. 2; her dancing, 8/101, 375; 9/24, 219; leaves stage to become King's mistress, 9/19 & n. 3, 24 & n. 2, 219, 388, 422, 450; alleged parentage, 9/24 & n. 2

DAVIS, [Thomas], messenger, Admiralty office: 1/103

DAVIS, Mr ——: employs Wayneman Birch, 4/382

DAVY: *see* Davis, [John]

DAWES, [Henry], merchant: shipping business, 1/267 & n. 4; a slave in Algiers, 2/34

DAWES, Sir [John], merchant: clandestine marriage, 4/121–2 & n., 269, 355; baronetcy, 4/269

DAWS, Mr —— [?identical with Henry Dawes]: 1/147

[DAWSON, William], naval officer: 9/488 & n. 2

DAY, [John], of Leverington, Cambs., P's great-uncle by marriage: P's claim on estate, 4/231 & n. 1, 300 & n. 2, 310–12

DAY, [John], 'old Day', fishmonger: 5/53

DAY, ——, carpenter: 1/78

DEAL, Kent: fleet off, 1/105–34 passim; forts near, 1/105 & n. 3; provisions from, 1/107, 134, 136; P visits, 1/119 & n. 4; Fuller's tavern, 1/119; Poole's, ib.; royalist demonstrations, 1/121(2), 129, 163; naval guns heard, 6/65; plague, 7/241 & n. 3; alluded to: 1/134; 5/212; 6/29

DEAN, Forest of: storm damage, 3/35 & n. 5; (1362), 3/165; ironworks, ib. & n. 1; 'forbid' trees, ib. & n. 2; timber, 4/20; alluded to: 3/114

DEANE, Anthony, kted 1675, shipwright:

CHARACTER: able but conceited, 3/170 & n. 1; 4/124, 176, 236, 381; 5/130; 9/152; a fanatic, 5/203

RELATIONS WITH P: instructs P in timber measurement, 3/151, 163, 169; 4/189–90; demonstrates slide-rule, 4/124; gives P ship model, 3/163 & n. 1, 208; instructs about ships/ship-building, 4/157, 172, 236, 262, 396; 5/29–30, 144, 146, 159, 189, 309; 8/489; 9/250; 'Doctrine of Naval Architecture' written at P's request, 9/531 & n. 1; tells of abuses in yards, 4/19, 79, 219; 8/489; 9/249; gift to P, 6/338; offers money, 9/528; P's gift to, 9/531

NAVY BOARD BUSINESS: rivalry with Petts, 3/170; complains of timber, 4/326; of timber contract, 4/381; and of colleagues, 4/384, 433; to fell Clarendon's timber, 5/203, 205, 210, 214, 238; discusses shipbuilding with Brouncker, 6/281; his *Rupert* praised by King and Duke of York, 7/119, 127; his drawing of, 8/142 & n. 2; and of *Resolution*, 9/262 & n. 4; his calculations of ship's draught, 7/127–8 & n.; his fireship design, 8/358 & n. 1; and gun design, 9/528 & n. 1; also, 5/155, 308–9; 8/39; unspecified business, 4/176, 425; 5/137; 9/175

SOCIAL: 4/141, 318; 5/185; 6/282

DEBUSSY (Debusty), [Lawrence], merchant: his tallies, 6/224 & n. 2; letter of credit, 7/174; poor English, 7/404; ~ his house and fine tapestry, 7/174

DEKING: *see* Daking

DEKINS: *see* Dickons, [J.]

DELABARR, [Vincent], merchant: social: 1/212; 2/65 & n. 2

DELAUNE, [George], merchant, Lothbury, and wife [Dorothea]: death, with family, in fire, 3/296 & n. 4

DELFT: P visits, 1/145–7; description, 1/145–6 & nn.; regicides arrested, 3/45, 47

DELKES 'old', waterman: appeals to P against son-in-law's impressment, 6/187, 202

DELL, [William], formerly Rector of Yelden, Beds.: his puritanism, 3/123 & n. 1

DENHAM, Sir John, poet and Surveyor-General of the King's Works: alterations at Hinchingbrooke, 1/313, 314 & n. 1; attends coronation, 2/83; as friend of Mennes, 4/436–7; pox cured by Mennes, 5/242; builds Burlington House, Piccadilly, 6/39 & n. 2; 9/321; death, 9/491 & n. 1

DENHAM, [Margaret], Lady Denham, wife of Sir John: liaison with Duke of York, 7/158–9 & n., 297, 315, 320, 323, 404–5; cabals with Coventry and Brouncker, 7/323; with Bristol, 7/404–5 & n.; rumoured poisoning by Duchess of York, 7/365 & n. 2, 366, 405; 8/6 & n. 2; postmortem, 8/8; house in Scotland Yard, 7/158

DENMARK [see also Copenhagen; Frederick III; Zeeland]: peace with, 8/399 & n. 1, 426 & n. 2; also, 1/41, 43, 83; 6/229

DEPTFORD, Kent [see also Baddiley, W.; Carteret, Sir G.; Cowley, T.; Davis, John; Pett, Christopher; Trinity House; Uthwayt, J.]:

TOWN: storm, 4/317–18; Plague, 6/253, 294, 331–2; 7/236 & n. 3, 239, 241, 285; pretty woman at, 8/141, 170 & n. 6; Balty St Michel lives at, 9/195, 261, 349; P to live with him, 9/349, 369; church [St Nicholas], 2/12 & n. 1; Globe, 1/254; 2/12, 77; 3/274; 6/96, 201; 7/285; ferry, 6/167; King's Head, 6/295; upper town, 6/331; Halfway tree, 8/188

DOCKYARD:

GENERAL: guard, 2/11, 12–13, 15; royal yachts at, 2/14, 120; ships built,

2/14 & n. 4; 5/24–5 & n.; launched, 7/160 & n. 3; project for new dock, 3/18 & n. 1, 29, 30 & n. 1, 32–3; timber frames for Navy Office houses built at, 3/111, 179, 188, 203; abuses, 3/128, 135–6, 274; 4/289 & n. 1, 293; 7/176(2); fire, 5/257; Navy Board meets at during Plague, 6/173, 184; plague in ships, 6/189, 204; workmen sent to fight Fire, 7/274, 276; P stores goods at during Fire, 7/273, 276, 278, 285, 290; Elizabethan wreck discovered, 8/188; measures taken against Dutch raiders, 8/256–7 & n., 259, 270, 282, 313; *Maybolt* at, 8/503–4; 9/29

VISITS BY P (sometimes with colleagues) on official business: pays: 1/253–4, 283, 286 & n. 2; 3/53 & n. 1, 58, 124, 179–80 & n., 185 & n. 1, 192, 193 & n. 2, 195, 198, 200–1 & n.; 4/7, 386 & n. 1, 425; 7/339; sales: 2/45 & n. 3; 3/185–6 & n.; criticises method, 4/319 & n. 2; shipping: ships fitted out/provisioned/despatched: 2/104, 112, 127; 3/31, 51, 63; 4/103–4; 5/165, 176; 7/157, 158, 162, 176(2), 177, 181; 8/176; measured, 5/217; 7/69; built, 8/124; launched, 9/101 & n. 2; inspects stores, 3/129, 173, 188; 4/79(2), 219; flags, 3/149; 4/151; 5/182; masts, 3/273–4; plank, 4/266; ironwork, 5/16; 7/119; canvas, 5/106, 155; poop lantern, 5/116–17; cordage, 5/287; timber, 5/312; and wet dock, 8/188; at musters, 3/160 & n. 1; 4/15, 50, 80, 222; consults officers about callbooks, 3/234; 4/7, 15, 80; investigates fire risks, 4/7; leases ground for mastdock, 5/231 & n. 1; also, 1/287; 2/12–13, 36, 45, 75–7, 104, 112, 127, 204; 3/19, 31, 111, 129, 135–6, 137, 140, 149, 160, 173, 179, 188, 192, 203, 211, 214, 227, 234, 273–4; 4/20, 67, 87, 103, 253, 277, 283, 288–9, 322, 425; 5/29, 39, 54, 72, 75, 80, 95, 138, 146, 156, 192, 213, 263, 303, 347, 351, 357; 6/74, 93, 118, 125, 128, 162, 201, 278; 7/19, 20, 21, 31, 115, 125, 126(2), 129, 134, 137, 138, 149, 166, 168, 175, 186, 191, 198, 249, 255, 319, 352, 358; 8/23, 39, 84, 95, 99, 124, 141, 162

VISITS BY P ON PRIVATE BUSINESS [*see also* Bagwell, Mrs]: 4/205; 6/155; 9/261; stores goods at in Fire, 7/273, 276, 278, 285, 290

VISITS BY P'S COLLEAGUES ON OFFICIAL BUSINESS: pays: 1/262 & n. 1, 290; 2/94, 171; 3/128; 4/126, 175; 6/319; sales: 3/180; surveys: 5/35, 39; also, 2/95; 4/204, 317–18

DERING, Sir Edward, 2nd Bt: contract for timber, 6/77 & n. 3

DERING, Edward, kted 1680, merchant, half-brother of the foregoing: appointed King's merchant, 4/415 & n. 4; 5/6; P critical of, 5/331; 6/245; gives/offers presents to P, 4/415, 422, 426, 436; 5/1, 5, 8, 330–1; 6/185, 242, 245; contracts for deals, 4/415 & n. 4; hemp, 6/77; plank, 6/99 & n. 6, 245 & n. 3; provisions at Hamburg, 9/542; unspecified business, 6/304

[DERWENTDALE PLOT, the]: 4/377 & n. 1

DESBOROUGH, Maj.-Gen. John, Cromwellian general: disloyalty to Richard Cromwell, 1/21 & n. 4; released from Tower, 8/169 & n. 4

DESCARTES, René: works studied at Cambridge, 4/263 & n. 2

DEVEREUX, Robert, 3rd Earl of Essex, parliamentary general: bust at Swakeleys, 6/215 & n. 1; lying in state, 9/425 & n. 3

DE VIC, [Anne Charlotte], daughter of Sir Henry: at court ball, 3/301 & n. 2

DEVONSHIRE HOUSE, Bishopsgate St: burial, 8/101

DIAMOND, Capt. [Thomas], naval officer: acquitted of murder, 3/124; bawdy remarks about King's marriage, ib.

DIARIES: Sir W. Rider's, 5/98; Sir W. Coventry's, 9/475

DIARY (P):

GENERAL: tells Lieut. Lambert of it, 1/107; and Coventry, 9/475

THE MANUSCRIPT: described, vol. i, pp. xli–xlviii; its history, vol. i, pp. lxviii–lxxi; sent away during Fire, 7/272, 282; during Medway raid, 8/264; volumes covering two years, 4/205; 6/143; 'bye-book', 5/25

THE SHORTHAND: described, vol. i, pp.

xlviii–liv; changes symbol for full stop, 8/104

EDITIONS: by Lord Braybrooke, first (1825), vol. i, pp. lxxv–lxxxiii; second (1828), vol. i, p. lxxxiii; third (1848–9), vol. i, pp. lxxxiii–iv; fourth (1851), vol. i, p. lxxxv; fifth (1854), vol. i, pp. lxxxv–vi; by Mynors Bright (1875–9): vol. i, pp. lxxxvii–xci; by H. B. Wheatley (1893–9): vol. i, pp. xc–xcvi

CRITICISM ETC.: value as historical evidence, vol. i, pp. cxiv–cxxxvii; sources, vol. i, pp. cxviii–ix, cxxi, cxxv–vi, cxxix; literary style, vol. i, pp. civ–vi, cx–xiii; P's motives in keeping, vol. i, pp. xxvi–vii, cvi–cx, cxiv

METHOD OF COMPOSITION: vol. i, pp. xcvii–ciii; enters up journeys, 2/73, 96, 140; 3/77, 226; 4/316; 8/316; his 'old way' of entering it daily, 6/270; enters account of Fire from loose leaves, 7/318, 402; 8/18; rough notes bound in, 9/160–8, 224–43; vows to keep, 5/25; 7/15, 25, 35, 40; enters it [normally at home or in his office but exceptionally]: on board ship, 1/152; at Admiralty, 1/204; on yacht, 6/240; in lodgings, 6/307, 337; writes it for stated periods, in days: one day, 3/141, 177, 215; 4/54, 128, 193, 273, 352, 378, 429, 438; 5/357; 7/421; 8/341; 9/424; two days, 1/143, 164; 7/74; 8/30, 162; two-three, 3/96; 4/2; 8/557; three, 2/88; 4/6, 252; 7/61, 262; 8/57, 391; 9/89, 386; three-four, 1/243; 7/299; four, 1/152, 204; 2/52; 5/236; 6/171; 7/112; four-five, 9/397; five, 1/251; 2/19; 6/327; 7/282, 309; 9/16, 319; five-six, 2/81; 9/409; six, 2/185; 4/231; six-seven, 9/363–4; seven, 6/240; 9/295, 433, 451, 492; seven-eight, 7/35, 40; eight, 6/270; eight-nine, 6/337; twelve, 6/307; 9/533; thirteen (from memory), 6/295; fourteen, 9/516; enters/writes it for unstated periods: 1/18; 2/241; 3/137, 162, 243, 251; 4/41, 67, 350, 356, 364, 423; 6/201; 7/25, 49, 63, 109, 167, 168, 170, 182, 205, 249, 258, 283, 291, 315, 323, 375, 385, 397; 8/3, 7, 17, 82, 114, 189, 271, 465, 478, 535,

579; 9/28, 331, 372, 455, 460, 473, 482, 500, 545

P'S COMMENTS WHILE WRITING: hears bellman's cry, 1/19; notes mistakes in entries, 1/92–3, 94, 207; 9/349, 353, 357, 363, 515; notes striking of clock, 2/14; receives funeral invitation, 2/73; makes entry for future reference, 3/3–4; writes 'slubberingly' in poor light, 3/236 & n.*c*; writes shakily because shocked, 8/208 & n.*a*; consults it, 4/296; makes entries for his justification, 7/331, 331–2; 8/548–9; values it, 8/264; confesses to tiredness, 6/16; 7/74

INCIDENTS AND PHRASES [i.e. some memorable passages which are difficult or impossible to retrieve by the use of the rest of the Index]:

CHILDHOOD: 'But Lord, how in every point I find myself to overvalue things when a child', 5/132

CHURCH: 'And when the parson begins, he begins "Right Worshipfull and dearly beloved" to us', 2/147

DEATH: 'all die alike, no more matter being made of the death of one then another', 4/339; 'but Lord, to see how the world makes nothing of the memory of a man an hour after he is dead', 5/91; 'This day Sir W. Batten, who hath been sick four or five days, is now very bad, so as that people begin to fear his death – and I at a loss whether it will be better for me to have him die, because he is a bad man, or live, for fear a worse should come', 6/32; 'Sir Wm. Petty came, among other things, to tell me that Mr. Barlow is dead; for which, God knows my heart, I could be as sorry as is possible for one to be for a stranger by whose death he gets 100*l* per annum', 6/33; '[Sir W. Batten] is so ill, that it is believed he cannot live till tomorrow; which troubles me and my wife mightily, partly out of kindness, he being a good neighbour, and partly because of the money he owes me upon our bargain of the late prize', 8/462; 'And here do see what creatures widows are in weeping for their husbands, and then presently leaving off; but I cannot wonder at it, the cares of the world taking place of all other passions', 8/483

FOOD: 'And strange it is, to see how a good dinner and feasting reconciles everybody', 6/295

LONDON LIFE AND MANNERS: 'I sat up till the bell-man came by with his bell, just under my window as I was writing of this very line, and cried, "Past one of the clock, and a cold, frosty, windy morning." I then went to bed and left my wife and the maid a-washing still', 1/19; 'And here, I sitting behind me in a dark place, a lady spat backward upon me by a mistake, not seeing me. But after seeing her to be a very pretty lady, I was not troubled at it at all', 2/25; 'But Lord, to see the absurd nature of Englishmen, that cannot forbear laughing and jeering at everything that looks strange', 3/268; 'But it is very pleasant to hear how [Will Stankes of Brampton] rails at the rumbling and ado that is in London over it is in the country, that he cannot endure it', 4/118; 'it being very pleasant to see how everybody [on Epsom Downs] turns up his tail, here one and there another, in a bush, and the women in their Quarters the like', 4/246; 'I went out, and running up (her friend however before me) I perceive by my dear Lady's blushing that in my dining-room she was doing something upon the pott; which I also was ashamed of and so fell to some discourse, but without pleasure, through very pity to my Lady', 5/129; 'I lacked a pot but there was none, and bitter cold, so was forced to rise and piss in the chimny, and to bed again', 5/357

LOVE AFFAIRS: 'When weary, I did give over, and somebody having seen some of our dalliance, called aloud in the street, "Sir, why do you kiss the gentlewoman so?" and flung a stone at the window – which vexed me', 4/203; 'a strange slavery that I stand in to beauty, that I value nothing near it', 5/264; 'Up, and to the office (having a mighty pain in my forefinger of my left hand, from a strain that it received last night in struggling avec la femme que je mentioned yesterday)', 6/40; 'I am not, as I ought to be, able to command myself in the pleasures of my eye', 7/110; 'into St Dunstan's church. . . . And stood by a pretty, modest maid, whom I did labour to take by the hand and the body; but she would not, but got further and further from me, and at last I could perceive her to take pins out of her pocket to prick me if I should touch her again; which seeing, I did forbear, and was glad I did espy her design', 8/389

MARRIAGE: 'myself somewhat vexed at my wife's neglect in leaving of her scarfe, waistcoat, and night-dressings in the coach today that brought us from Westminster, though I confess she did give them to me to look after – yet it was her fault not to see that I did take them out of the coach', 4/6; 'Coming home tonight, I did go to examine my wife's house-accounts; and finding things that seemed somewhat doubtful, I was angry, though she did make it pretty plain; but confessed that when she doth misse a sum, she doth add something to other things to make it', 5/283; 'To church in the morning, and there saw a wedding in the church, which I have not seen many a day, and the young people so merry one with another; and strange, to see what delight we married people have to see these poor fools decoyed into our condition, every man and wife gazing and smiling at them', 6/338–9; 'high words between us. But I fell to read a book (Boyle's *Hydrostatickes*) aloud in my chamber and let her talk till she was tired, and vexed that I would not hear her; and so become friends and to bed together', 8/250–1

MONEY: 'talking long in bed with my wife about our frugall life for the time to come, proposing to her what I could and would do if I were worth 2000*l*; that is, be a Knight and keep my coach – which pleased her',

3/39–40; 'it is high time to betake myself to my . . . vows, . . . so I may for a great while do my duty, as I have well begun, and encrease my good name and esteem in the world and get money, which sweetens all things and whereof I have much need', 4/6–7; 'And I bless God, I do find that I am worth more than ever I yet was, which is 6200*l* – for which the holy name of God be praised', 7/348–9; 'but it is pretty to see what money will do', 8/123

MUSIC: 'However, music and women I cannot but give way to, whatever my business is', 7/69–70; 'music is the thing of the world that I love most, and all the pleasure almost that I can now take', 7/228; 'but that which did please me beyond anything in the whole world was the wind-musique when the Angell comes down, which is so sweet that it ravished me; and indeed, in a word, did wrap up my soul so that it made me really sick, just as I have formerly been when in love with my wife; that neither then, nor all the evening going home and at home, I was able to think of anything, but remained all night transported, so as I could not believe that ever any music hath that real command over the soul of a man as this did upon me', 9/94

PLEASURE: 'I do think it best to enjoy some degree of pleasure, now that we have health, money and opportunities, rather then to leave pleasures to old age or poverty, when we cannot have them so properly' 3/86; 'I . . . do look upon myself at this time in the happiest occasion a man can be; and whereas we take pains in expectation of future comfort and ease, I have taught myself to reflect upon myself at present as happy and enjoy myself in that consideration, and not only please myself with thoughts of future wealth, and forget the pleasures we at present enjoy', 7/57; 'We eat with great pleasure, and I enjoyed myself in it with reflections upon the pleasures which I at best can expect, yet not to exceed this – eating in silver plates, and all things mighty rich and handsome about me', 7/388; 'they being gone, I paid the fiddler 3*l* among the four, and so away to bed, weary and mightily pleased; and have the happiness to reflect upon it as I do sometimes on other things, as going to a play or the like, to be the greatest real comforts that I am to expect in the world, and that it is that that we do really labour in the hopes of; and so I do really enjoy myself, and understand that if I do not do it now, I shall not hereafter, it may be, be able to pay for it or have health to take pleasure in it, and so fool myself with vain expectation of pleasure and go without it', 9/13; 'I did, as I love to do, enjoy myself in my pleasure, as being the heighth of what we take pains for and can hope for in this world – and therefore to be enjoyed while we are young and capable of these joys', 9/134

PUBLIC AFFAIRS: 'But methought it lessened my esteem of a king, that he should not be able to command the rain', 3/140; 'I see it is impossible for the King to have things done as cheap as other men', 3/143; 'He showed me a very excellent argument to prove that our Importing lesse then we export doth not impoverish the kingdom, according to the received opinion – which though it be a paradox and that I do not remember the argument, yet methought there was a great deal in what he said', 5/70; 'While we were talking, came by several poor creatures, carried by by constables for being at a conventicle. They go like lambs, without any resistance. I would to God they would either conform, or be more wise and not be ketched', 5/235; '[He] did . . . inform me mightily in several things; among others, that the heightening or lowering of money is only a cheat, and doth good to some perticular men; which, if I can but remember how, I am now by him fully convinced of', 7/304; 'by bringing over

one discontented man you raise up three in his room', 7/311; 'Most things moved were referred to committees – and so we broke up', 7/321; 'Englishmen on board the Dutch ships . . . did cry and say, "We did heretofore fight for tickets; now we fight for Dollers!"', 8/267; 'some rude people have been . . . at my Lord Chancellor's, . . . and a Gibbet either set up before or painted upon his gate, and these words writ – "Three sights to be seen; Dunkirke, Tanger, and a barren Queen"', 8/269; 'But it was pretty, news came the other day so fast, of the Duch fleets being in so many places, that Sir W. Batten at table cried, "By God!" says he, "I think the Devil shits Dutchmen"', 8/345; '[Coling] told us his horse was a Bribe, and his boots a bribe; . . . and that he makes every sort of tradesman to bribe him; and invited me home to his house to taste of his bribe wine', 8/369

SERVANTS: 'To the office, where . . . I sent my boy home for some papers; where, he staying longer then I would have him and being vexed at the business and to be kept from my fellows in the office longer then was fit, I became angry and boxed my boy when he came, that I do hurt my Thumb so much, that I was not able to stir all the day after and in great pain', 7/19; 'coming homeward again, saw my door and hatch open, left so by Luce our cookmaid; which so vexed me, that I did give her a kick in our entry and offered a blow at her, and was seen doing so by Sir W. Penn's footboy, which did vex me to the heart because I know he will be telling their family of it, though I did put on presently a very pleasant face to the boy and spoke kindly to him as one without passion, so as it may be he might not think I was angry; but yet I was troubled at it', 8/164

SOCIAL OCCASIONS: 'Went to hear Mrs. Turner's daughter . . . play on the Harpsicon; but Lord! it was enough to make any man sick to hear her; yet was I forced to commend her highly', 4/120; 'They have a kins-woman they call daughter in the house, a short, ugly, red-haired slut that plays upon the virginalls and sings, but after such a country manner, I was weary of it, but yet could not but commend it', 4/242; 'We were as merry as I could be with people that I do wish well to but know not what discourse either to give them or find from them', 4/427; 'A very good dinner among the old Sokers', 6/36

SUCCESS: 'There was also [a letter] for me from Mr. Blackburne, who with his own hand superscribes it to *S.P. Esqr.*, of which, God knows, I was not a little proud', 1/96–7; 'Lay very long in bed, discoursing with Mr Hill of most things of a man's life, and how little merit doth prevail in the world, but only favour – and that for myself, chance without merit brought me in, and that diligence only keeps me so', 6/285; 'We had much talk of all our old acquaintance of the College, concerning their various fortunes; wherein, to my joy, I met not with any that have sped better then myself', 8/51; 'my Lord Chan-cellor did say . . . that no man in Eng-land was of more method nor made himself better understood then my-self', 8/60

THEATRE: 'Burt acted the Moore; by the same token, a very pretty lady that sot by me cried to see Desdimona smothered', 1/264; 'I sitting behind in a dark place, a lady spat backward upon me by a mistake, not seeing me. But after seeing her to be a very pretty lady, I was not troubled at it at all', 2/25; 'And it was observable how a gentleman of good habit, sitting just before us eating of some fruit, in the midst of the play did drop down as dead; but with much ado, Orange Mall did thrust her finger down his throat and brought him to life again', 8/516–17; 'It pleased us mightily to see the natural affection of a poor woman, the mother of one of the children brought on the stage – the child crying, she by

force got upon the stage, and took up her child and carried it away off of the stage from Hart', 8/594; 'I was prettily served this day at the playhouse-door; where giving six shillings into the fellow's hand for us three, the fellow by legerdemain did convey one away, and with so much grace face me down that I did give him but five, that though I knew the contrary, yet I was overpowered by his so grave and serious demanding the other shilling that I could not deny him, but was forced by myself to give it him', 9/90

WORK: 'having so many [letters] to write . . . that I have no heart to go about them', 1/215; 'here I had a most eminent experience of the evil of being behind-hand in business; I was the most backward to begin anything, and would fain have framed to myself an occasion of going abroad . . . but some business coming in . . . kept me there, and I fell to the ridding away of a great deal of business . . . and . . . I could have continued there with delight all night long', 7/249

WORKMEN: 'At home all the after-noon looking after my workmen in my house, whose lazinesse doth much trouble me', 1/243; 'All the after-noon at home among my workmen; work till 10 or 11 at night; and did give them drink and were very merry with them – it being my luck to meet with a sort of Drolling work-men upon all occasions', 1/255; 'a poor fellow, a working goldsmith, that goes without gloves to his hands', 8/437

MISC.: 'Lay long; that is, till 6 and past before I rose', 3/190; 'so home to dinner, where I find my wife hath been with Ashwell at La Roches to have her tooth drawn, which it seems akes much. But my wife could not get her to be contented to have it drawn after the first twitch, but would let it alone; and so they came home with it undone, which made my wife and me good sport', 4/97; 'By and by news is brought us that one of our horses is stole out of the Stable; which proves my uncles, at which I was inwardly glad; I mean, that it was not mine', 4/310; 'the fellow coming out again of a shop, I did give him a good cuff or two on the chops; and seeing him not oppose me, I did give him another; at last, found him drunk, of which I was glad and so left him and home', 4/342; 'it is not greatest wits but the steady man that is a good merchant', 5/300; 'where a Trade hath once been and doth decay, it never recovers again', ib.; 'one Mr Tripp, who dances well', 7/362; 'He told me also a story of my Lord Cottington: who wanting a son, entended to make his Nephew his heir, a country boy, but did alter his mind upon the boy's being persuaded by another young heir (in roguery) to Crow like a cock at my Lord's table, much company being there and the boy having a great trick at doing that perfectly – my Lord bade them take away that fool from the table, and so gave over the thoughts of making him his heir from this piece of folly', 8/566–7

DICK (Dike) SHORE: see Duke Shore

DICKENSON, Esther ('Widow'): see Pepys, Esther

DICKONS (Dekins), [John], hemp merchant: dies of grief, 3/213, 233; social: 3/19

DICKONS, [Elizabeth], ('my Morena'): at St Olave's, 2/192; illness and death, 3/213, 233; alluded to: 3/19

DIGBY, Lady Anne, daughter of the 2nd Earl of Bristol: jilted, 4/208–9 & n.

DIGBY, Capt. [Francis], naval officer, son of the 2nd Earl of Bristol: opinion of 'tarpaulins', 7/333

DIGBY, George, 2nd Earl of Bristol, succ. 1653 [occasionally referred to by his original title of Lord Digby], politician: a Papist, 4/224; 9/17; said to have turned Protestant, 5/58; 9/120; a public danger, 9/120; responsible for failure of Treaty of Uxbridge (1645), 4/212 & n. 1; sells

Irish peerage (1646), 8/126; in France and Flanders during Interregnum, 4/212–13 & nn.; enmity to Clarendon: 2/142; opposes over bill of uniformity, 3/49 & n. 1; brings articles of impeachment against (1663) 4/115, 219–20, 223–5 & nn., 229, 231 & n. 2, 367; 8/445 & n. 4; renews attack (1664), 5/34, 60 & n. 4, 73, 85, 89, 137, 208; influence over King, 4/137; part in scheme for parliamentary management, 4/200, 207, 207–8 & nn., 211 & nn., 213; supports marriage alliance with Parma, 4/224 & n. 1; flees to escape arrest, 4/271 & n. 1, 272, 298 & n. 4; 5/85, 89 & n. 3; Lady Denman supports him, 7/405; his faction, 7/261; appears in Lords, 8/362; recovers King's favour, 8/530, 532, 533, 597; ~ his chaplain, 5/58–9 & n.

DIKE: see Dyke

[DILLINGHAM, Theophilus], Master of Clare Hall and Vice-Chancellor, Cambridge: 3/218 & n. 4

DILLON, Col. Cary, succ. as 5th Earl of Roscommon 1685: courtship of Frances Butler, 1/209 & n. 3, 217; 2/152; 3/299 & n. 1; 9/311; duel, 3/171 & n. 1; alluded to: 1/214

DILLON, [William]: hanged, 4/60 & n. 1

DIPLOMATS [for individuals, see under personal names]: disputes about precedence among in London, 2/187–9 & nn.; in Paris, 4/419–20 & n.; (rumour of) in Madrid, 8/36 & n. 2

DIVES: see Dyve

DIXON, Mr ——: matchmaker for Tom P, 4/19, 21

DIXWELL, Col. [Basil], cr. bt 1660, of Broome, Barham, Kent (d. 1668): 1/172, 176, 182

DOBBINS, Capt. [Joseph]: feast as Elder Brother, Trinity House, 6/155

DOCTORS' COMMONS, St Benet's Hill: P visits, 1/229; 2/216; 4/368; 5/351

DOLBEN, Catherine, wife of John: story of, 9/89 & n. 5; ~ her two children, 9/89

DOLBEN, John, Dean of Westminster 1662–83, Bishop of Rochester 1666–83,

Archbishop of York 1683–d.86: sermon before King, 7/245 & n. 4; rumoured suspension, 8/587 & n. 2; slanders against, 8/596 & n. 2; dismissed from court office, 9/53 & n. 2, 89

DOLING, Thomas, messenger, Council of State: news from, 1/14 & n. 4; P's letters to, 1/116, 126 & n. 2; to go to Ireland, 1/311; visits Overton in prison, 1/319; social: 1/37, 38, 80, 92, 95, 174–5, 208, 230, 282

DOLL, milliner at the New Exchange: see Stacey

DOMESDAY BOOK: P to consult, 2/236 & n. 3

DONCASTER, ——, waterman: 3/156

DONNE: see Dunn

DONNE, John, poet (1573–1631): takes holy orders, 9/215 & n. 2

DORCHESTER, Lord: see Pierrepont

DORMEHOY: see Dalmahoy

DORMER, Charles, 2nd Earl of Caernarvon (1632–1709): on value of timber, 8/201 & n. 3

DORRINGTON, [?Francis, ?John], merchant: compensation for loss of ship, 9/69 & n. 1; bid for victualling contract, 9/288 & n. 2

DORSET, Earl of: see Sackville, R.

DORSET HOUSE, Salisbury Court: Clarendon at, 1/173, 184

DOUCE: see Doves

DOUGLAS, James, 2nd Marquess of Douglas (d. 1700): at court ball, 7/372; commands troops, 8/306, 308, 309, 311

DOUGLAS, William, 9th Earl of Morton (d. 1681): 9/534 & n. 2

DOVER, Kent: parliamentary elections, 1/96–7, 111(2), 167, 179 & n. 1, 183; clerk of castle, 1/97; jurats visit Naseby, 1/130; mayor welcomes King, 1/158; Dutch ships brought into, 5/326; Rupert's fleet at, 7/143–5 passim; Governor prepares against invasion, 7/187 & n. 1; squadron to be stationed at, 8/149 & n. 1; Dutch attack feared, 8/327 & n. 1, 328; Duke of York as Lord Warden, 9/280 & n. 4; also, 1/134, 279; 7/300

DOVES (?Douce, ?Dowes), Capt.——: 2/207

DOWGATE [see also Taverns etc.: Swan]: Fire, 7/270

DOWNE(S), [Elkanah], Vicar of Ashtead, Surrey, 1662–d.83: dull sermon, 4/247 & n. 1

[DOWNES, John], actor and writer: in Davenant's Siege of Rhodes, 2/131 & n. 3

DOWNES, [John], regicide: reprieved 3/16 & n. 1

DOWNING, [Frances], b. Howard, wife of Sir George: praises Holland, 1/249; alluded to: 1/153

DOWNING, George, kted 1660, cr. bt 1663; Teller of the Receipt in the Exchequer 1656–60; reappointed 1660; envoy to United Provinces, 1657–60, 1660–7, 1671–2; Secretary to the Treasury Commissioners, 1667–71; M.P. Morpeth, 1660, 1661–79, 1679, 1679–81, 1681

CHARACTER: parsimonious, 1/186 & n. 2; 8/85; rogue, 3/45; vain, 8/425; efficient, 8/238, 240

AS ENVOY TO UNITED PROVINCES: offers P clerkship, 1/18, 31; P writes ciphers for, 1/28, 30, 31; leaves for Holland, 1/23, 25, 29, 31, 33; returns, 1/136 & n. 1, 249; knighted, 1/153; has regicides extradited, 3/44–5 & n., 48; news from, 5/121 & nn.; 6/103 & n. 2; protests against Dutch detaining English cargo, 5/321; assists in relief of English prisoners of war, 7/201 & n. 1, 380 & n. 3; 8/407–8 & n., 425; complains of peace terms, 8/425–7 & nn.; intelligence service, 9/401–2 & nn.

IN EXCHEQUER: as P's master, 1/2 & n. 1, 83, 107–8, 238; offers P council clerkship, 1/22 & n. 5, 35; lawsuit against Squibb, 1/31 & n. 1, 33–6 passim, 40, 45, 48, 49; encourages loans on Additional Aid (1665), 6/322, 327, 330, 334; 7/9, 23, 87, 124 & n. 2; 8/131–2, 397–8, 407

AS M.P.: part in drafting Additional Aid bill (1665), 6/292 & n. 3; 7/122; 8/30; project for leather trade, 8/425 & n. 4; introduces bill for Treasury orders, 8/520 & n. 2; parliamentary news from, 7/380; 8/520

AT TREASURY: appointed secretary, 8/238, 240; Tangier accounts, 8/249

fashion (vest, coat, belt, sword), 7/353; changes in September from silk to cloth suit, 8/455

SWORDS: Prynne's basket-hilt, 1/62; (P): rapier stick, 1/95, 138; sword 'refreshed', 2/24; smallsword with gilt handle, 4/80, 105; silver-hilted, 7/353; gilded for May Day, 9/537; wears to escort Sandwich, 1/93; starts wearing 'as manner among gentlemen is', 2/29 & n. 2; 3/241 & n. 2; equips footboy with, 3/77 & n. 2; 9/537

TOPS: *see* cannons

TRAVELLING-CLOTHES: 8/233

TUNICS: (P): velvet, 8/489; laced, 9/201 & n. 2; coloured camlet, 9/540

TURBANS: 7/378; worn by giant, 5/243

VEILS: at synagogue, 4/335 & n. 2

VESTS: new fashion, 7/315; first worn by Duke of York, 7/320; description, 7/324, 328; Louis XIV puts footmen into, 7/379 & n. 4; also, 8/154; (P): first wears, 7/346, 353(2), 362, 366; made from old suit, 8/295, 314, 341, 404; his new laced vest, 9/201; and flowered tabby, 9/533, 540

WAISTCOATS (P) (outer garments): green watered moiré, 1/298; false tabby with gold lace, 2/195; black baize faced with silk, 4/360; thin silk, 7/172; (under garments): leaves off/puts on according to season, 2/116, 195, 198; 3/138; 5/198; 6/67; 7/182; 8/235; 9/175, 180, 400, 549

WALKING STICKS (canes) (P): knotted, 1/104; rattan, painted and gilded, 1/244; buys at cane shop, 5/117; varnished for walking, 7/211; silver-headed Japan, 8/84

COMPLETE OUTFITS (P): 4/105, 400; 6/175; 9/201, 533

FASHION: changes at Easter, 8/63; King's new, 7/315, 320–1; description, 7/324 & n. 3, 328; worn by M.P.s, 7/324; hat 'cocked behind', 8/249; French ambassador's unfashionable dress, 9/284 & n. 3; (P): buys/wears to keep up with: buckled shoes, 1/26 & n. 2; short cloak, 1/260; coat and sword, 2/29; longer hair, 2/97; new coat, 2/203; suit with linings showing under breeches, 4/130; low-crowned beaver, 4/280; suits in new fashion, 7/353(2); 8/295; suit with shoulder belt for sword, 9/201

COURT/CEREMONIAL/PROFESSIONAL [*see also* clerical, above]: coronation robes, 2/80, 82, 84; regalia, 2/84; costumes at court ball, 7/372 & n. 3; Russian envoys' costumes, 4/360; 8/428; Persian envoy's, 9/17; Garter robes, 8/184–5; academic, 9/544

MOURNING: purple worn by King, 1/246; (P): hat band, 1/247; short black stockings, 1/251(2); rings, 2/74 & n. 2; 3/269; 4/21; belt, 2/203; shoes blacked, 5/90; white gloves, 5/90 & n. 2; servants', 8/134

BEARDS: Spanish fashion, 8/453 & n. 1; (P): shaves off beard/moustache, 3/97; 5/22–3 & n.

HAIRDRESSING: wigs worn at court, 4/136; King and Duke of York start wearing, 4/360; 5/49, 126; and W. Howe, 4/390; Rupert's, 8/146; (P): hair cut by: barber, 2/97; 4/237; 5/352; EP, 5/72; 8/35; 9/424; maids, 8/280; 9/201; and sister-in-law, 9/175; close-cropped, 7/112, 302; because lousy, 9/424; foul with powder, 3/96; combed by maids, 3/96; 6/21, 185; 8/531; 9/20, 37, 48, 73, 109, 277, 328, 337; head inspected, 9/239; finds difficulty in keeping hair clean, 3/96, 196; 4/130; to wear periwig, 4/130, 290, 343, 350, 357, 358, 378; first appearances in, 4/362, 363, 365, 369; periwig cleaned, 5/212; repaired, 6/74; fears to wear one made during Plague, 6/210; refuses to buy infested periwig, 8/133, 146; buys from French wigmaker, 8/136, 137, 138, 146, 177; 9/334; barber to keep in repair, 9/217; catches fire in candle, 9/322; periwig case, 4/363; also, 6/89, 97

SHAVING (P): trimmed by barber, 1/90, 113, 136, 142, 148, 152, 162, 200, 208, 214, 219, 224, 252, 298, 308; 2/32, 76, 97, 112, 135, 180, 241; 3/24, 41, 64, 71, 81, 187, 201, 215, 220, 233, 289, 299; 4/16, 20, 23, 43, 96, 130, 154, 186, 190, 258, 261, 312; 5/246; 6/257, 266, 288, 303, 306, 322, 331, 334; 7/6, 278,

293; 9/234, 496; employs barber on giving up pumice-stone, 3/196; for first time for a year, 6/233; pays barber, 9/225; shaves with pumice, 3/91, 97; shaves off beard/moustache, 3/97; begins using razor, 5/6; shaves off beard/moustache, 5/22–3 & n.; cuts himself, 5/29; shaves after week's growth during Fire, 7/288; shaves himself, 5/52, 55, 87; 6/159, 228, 311; 8/247

WASHING (P): washes regularly, 5/320; washes on hottest day of year, 3/75; and at EP's request, 6/44; washes feet/legs, 3/47; 4/165; 7/172, 206; catches cold, 7/207; ears washed, 6/21; lousy, 9/424

DRESS AND PERSONAL APPEARANCE (WOMEN AND GIRLS):

GARMENTS AND ACCESSORIES:

APRONS: Queen Catherine, 9/557

BANDS: lace, 6/172

BODICE: Nell Gwyn, 8/193; (EP): pair, 4/357

CAPS: Duchess of Newcastle's velvet, 8/186, 196

COATS (EP): velvet, 4/316

CUFFS (EP): laced, 8/392–3, 396

DRAWERS: 9/194; (EP): 4/140 & n. 1, 172

DRESS: lying-in, 6/55; 7/329; 'paysan', 8/375; riding, 6/162; 7/162; travelling, 7/142

DRESSING-BOX: 8/46, 53; (EP): 9/91

FANS (EP): 4/172

FARTHINGALES: Portuguese ladies-in-waiting, 3/92 & n. 2

GALLOSHES: 6/299

GARTERS: valentine gift, 9/449; (EP): valentine gift, 2/40

GLOVES: embroidered, 2/38; white, 2/38; 4/68; 7/344; Jessamy, 7/344; 9/449; (EP): valentine gift, 2/40; painted leather, 4/100; with yellow ribbons, 5/264; perfumed French, 9/427

GORGET: 4/279

GOWNS: velvet, 3/299; 4/2, 400; silver-laced, 5/188; flowered tabby, 9/521; (EP): black silk, laced with black gimp, 2/117; moiré to replace taffeta, 3/298; 4/10, 13; trimmed with point, 4/337; Indian, 4/391; 5/8;

Japanese, 4/415; laced, 5/100, 110, 118; 9/455–6; morning, 5/103; 8/465, 468; light coloured silk, 6/76; similar to Lady Castlemaine's, 7/298; coloured flowered tabby, 7/302; 9/540; cloth, 8/242

HANDKERCHIEVES ('han(d)kirchers'): ('lace', worn as collar), 7/341; 8/576; (EP): 2/211, 212, 214; 7/243, 379; 9/6

HATS: plumed, 4/230; straw, 8/382; (EP): straw, 8/382

HOODS: black, 1/42; (EP): yellow bird's-eye, 6/102 & n. 2; white, 8/124; French, 9/453

JEWELRY: posy ring, 1/39; diamonds and pearls at court ball, 7/371–2; (EP): pearl necklace, 1/240; 6/200–1; 7/108, 111, 112, 113, 412; pendants, 4/100; 5/196; diamond ring, 6/190–1; 9/67–8, 78, 88–9

JUSTE-AU-CORPS: black, 8/187; gold laced, 9/213

LACE: see Textiles etc.; when worn as collar, see above, handkerchieves

MANTLE: frieze, 1/60–1; white flannel, 8/79; (EP): 1/320

MASK [see also below, vizard]: at theatre, 8/71–2; at Vauxhall, 9/220; travelling 2/91 & n. 1; (EP): 5/28

MUFF (EP): 1/320; 3/271; 4/7; 7/39

NECKCLOTH: 8/224

NIGHTGOWN: Lady Castlemaine's, 8/404; (EP): 7/18; 8/210, 424, 458

PATCHES: worn by Dutch ladies, 1/138; shop girl, 3/239 & n. 2; Duchess of Newcastle, 8/186; Peg Lowther, 6/9; 8/196, 197; Lady Castlemaine, 9/186; Lady Sandwich and daughter, 1/269; (EP): first wears, 1/234, 283, 299

PATTENS (EP): 1/27

PETTICOATS: satin, 3/83; linen, trimmed with lace (Lady Castlemaine), 3/87; short crimson (Queen Catherine), 4/229; (EP): paragon, 1/82; trimmed with silver lace, 1/225; 5/239; 8/242; and gold lace, 5/44; sarcenet, trimmed with black lace, 3/65; yellow, 3/85; 5/264; green flowered satin trimmed with gimp lace, 3/125; silk striped, 4/199; silk, 5/114; 7/296; blue, 8/124; laced, 9/400

PINNER: (Lady Castlemaine), 5/126;

moderation, 3/130, 151, 163, 197; 4/235; mixes wine with beer, 4/343, 410; 5/236; relaxes vow during Plague, 6/226; 7/49; alleged to be a drinker, 6/243; drinks sack despite oath, 7/23; and burnt wine, 8/130; first morning visit to tavern for seven years, 9/220

HEALTHS: puritan objections, 2/105 & n. 5; 5/172 & n. 4; French method, 4/189; loyal toast accompanied by gun salute, 1/152; drunk kneeling, 1/121, 122; 2/87; ladies toasted, 2/220; 7/246; 8/130–1

VARIETIES:

  BRANDY: 9/103, 498; burned, 8/20

  BRISTOL MILK: *see* wine

  BUTTERMILK: 5/152

  CHOCOLATE: 1/178; 3/226–7; 4/5; 5/64, 139; at coffee house, 5/329

  CIDER: 3/300; 4/28, 121; 7/115; 8/315; French, 4/254

  COFFEE: 5/76, 77, 105

  ELDER SPIRITS: 4/221

  GRUEL: 4/40

  HIPPOCRAS: *see* wine

  JULEP: 1/181

  LAMB'S WOOL: *see* ale

  MEAD: 8/460

  METHEGLIN: 1/72; 7/218

  MILK: 4/29; 7/207; 9/224; from milkmaid on Epsom Downs, 8/339; from Keeper's Lodge, Hyde Park, 9/142 & n. 1, ? 154, 175, 184, 222, 260, 533–4

  MUM: *see* ale

  MUSCADINE: *see* wine

  ORANGE JUICE: 9/477 & n. 3

  POSSET: 3/274; 4/40, 202, 319; 5/77; sack posset: 1/9, 10, 11; 4/14, 38; 9/13; in Davenant play, 9/134

  PURLE: *see* beer

  SACK: *see* wine

  STRONG WATERS: EP for fainting fit, 4/307; also, 2/24; 4/284; 6/40, 198; 7/157; 8/412, 504, 544; 9/99

  TEA: 'cupp of tee', 1/253 & n. 5; also, 6/328 & n. 1; 8/302

  WATER: [for spa water, *see* Health]: public supply, 3/92 & n. 3; 4/295 & n. 3; 8/370 & n. 2; also, 4/265; 6/23

  WHEY: 3/116; 4/164 & n. 2, 175,

179–80, 286; 5/152; 6/120; 7/170 & n. 4; 8/215; 9/215

  WINE: Bristol milk: 9/236 & n. 1; burnt: 7/295, 425; 8/47, 120, 130, 589; canary: 2/211; 6/151; claret: 1/277; 2/25; 4/65, 171; 6/151; 7/175, 375; 8/393; burnt, 5/90; 7/386; 8/124; English: from Walthamstow, 1/317; 8/341–2; Florence wine: 1/324; 2/8; Haut Brion ('Ho Bryan'): 4/100 & n. 4; hippocras ('hypocras'): 4/354; 5/118; Malaga (*see also* sack): 3/14; 6/151; muscadine: 1/296; Navarre: 9/443 & n. 1; Rhenish: 2/125; 8/156; with sugar, 2/38; 3/24; Bleakard, 4/189 & n. 3; sack: with wormwood, 2/9; raspberry sack, 2/212; Malaga, 4/235; 6/151; mulled, 6/266; 7/424; 9/103; anecdote of its killing toad, 7/290; also, 1/57, 230, 292, 308; 2/25, 217, 219, 224; 5/32, 37; 6/224; 7/23, 166; 8/5; 9/227; sherry: 3/14, 180; tent: 4/405; 5/11, 222; 6/151; wormwood: 1/301; 4/25, 58; misc.: wine and sugar, 1/167; 4/179; mulled white, 1/292; wine traders' tricks, 7/256

WINE CELLARS: P orders jointly with colleagues, 3/14 & n. 3; crested bottles, 4/346 & n. 1; pride in stock, 6/151; cellars at Audley End, 1/70 & n. 1; 8/467–8; Whitehall palace, 1/193, 246, 247; 2/175; and at Povey's, 4/18 & n. 2, 298; 5/161

DRUMBLEBY (Drumbelly), ——, flageolet maker, Strand: the best in town, 8/53; supplies flageolets, 8/53, 87; 9/30, 51, 160; recorder, 9/157; moulds for eye tubes, 9/278; ~ his boy, 9/364

DRURY LANE [*see also* Coffee-houses; Taverns etc.: Bear; Theatres]: plague in, 7/72–3; milkmaids in, 8/193

DRYDEN (Draydon), John (1631–1700) [*see also* Plays]: known to P at Cambridge, 5/37 & n. 2; share in authorship of *Sir Martin Mar-all*, 8/387 & n. 1, 468, n. 2; alluded to: 8/363

DUBLIN: Castle Plot, 4/168 & n. 2, 170; packet boat, 4/256; alluded to: 3/162

DUTTON, ——, servant to T. Povey: his wife, 6/267

'DYAN', Ursula: *see* Ursler, Barbara

DYKE (Dike), [Elizabeth]: mourns brother Edward P, 4/424; social: 1/268; 5/19, 29; 7/391; 9/407, 409, 416, 422, 425, 463–4

DYMOKE, [Sir Edward], the King's Champion (d. 1664): at coronation banquet, 2/85

DYVE (Dives), Sir Lewis: story of prison escape, 8/566 & n. 3; a gamester, 9/3 & n. 2

EAGLE COURT, Strand: 9/254, 364

EARLE, [John], King's chaplain, Dean of Westminster 1660–2; Bishop of Worcester 1662–3; of Salisbury 1663–d. 65: on *Royal Charles*, 1/157; at coronation, 2/84

EAST, ——, porter at Sandwich's Whitehall lodgings: 1/4, 25, 57, 244; social: 3/3, 12; alluded to: 2/103; ~ his wife, 1/36

EAST INDIA COMPANY: chron. series: disputes with Navy Board, 2/228 & n. 1; 4/368 & n. 3, 399; 5/26, 76, 232 & n. 2; 9/37 & n. 3, 66 & n. 1, 410 & n. 1, 494; with Dutch, 5/52, 108–9, 175; with customs, 5/66 & n. 1; with T. Skinner, 9/182–3 & n., 184–91 passim; to sell prize goods, 6/273–4, 280, 291, 319 & n. 4; loan to navy, 6/298, 325; its credit, 8/456; ships: 2/46, 62, 65; 4/204, 210, 299; taken by French, 8/162; attacked by Algerines, 9/492 & n. 5; also, 3/298 & nn.

EAST INDIA HOUSE, Leadenhall St: P visits, 4/384; 6/319, 329; 7/12; also, 2/77; 5/132

EAST INDIES [i.e. India]: trade with, 3/91; Dutch power in, 5/41, 49–50 & n.

EASTCHEAP: 4/20

EASTLAND: *see* Baltic

EAST PRUSSIA: fishing and hunting in, 4/413–14; late marriages in, 4/414

EASTWOOD, [Roger], assistant-shipwright, Deptford and Woolwich: 9/160 & n. 1

EASTWOOD, Mrs ——, of Portsmouth: 3/73, 74; ~ her maid, 3/74

EASTWOOD, Mrs ——, widow, of Westminster: 7/232

[ECCLES, Solomon], Quaker: calls for repentance in Westminster Hall, 8/360 & n. 1

EDEN, [Robert], cr. bt 1672 (d. 1720): marriage, 9/512 & n. 2

EDGAR, King of England (d. 975): charter to Worcester, 6/81 & n. 1

EDGAR, Duke of Cambridge (1667–71): *see* Stuart

EDINBURGH: alluded to, 7/397 & n. 1

EDISBURY (Edgeborough), [Kenrick], Surveyor of Navy 1632–8: his ghost, 2/68 & n. 3; 4/227

EDLIN (Eglin), [?Samuel]: subject of bawdy story, 1/59 & n. 2; social: 1/74, 78, 196, 200; 3/58; alluded to: 2/139

EDWARDS, Jane (b. Birch), wife of Tom and P's servant:

CHRON. SERIES: 'our old little Jane', 7/42, 84; P's first servant at Axe Yard, 1/1 & n. 2; injures leg, 1/187, 188, 191; P beats with broom, 1/307; troubled at her leaving, 2/162, 167; she returns, 3/51 & n. 3, 53; upset at P's beating Wayneman, 3/66; 4/7–8; with P in EP's absence, 3/141, 148, 151, 182; P attracted by, 3/152, 157; cuts off carpenter's moustache, 3/198; mimics Lady Batten, 3/249–50; P/EP displeased with, 3/295, 301; 4/8; dismissed, 4/30, 31, 32; begs P to take back Wayneman, 4/252; returns to P's service, 7/42, 84–5; witnesses start of Fire, 7/267, 268; at Brampton with EP, 9/98, 145, 210; P caresses, 9/307; EP's jealousy, 9/439, 440–1; marriage, 9/63–4 & n., 283, 483, 484, 493, 494, 499, 500, 513; leaves Seething Lane, 9/502; wedding gift, 9/526 & n. 2; also, 1/26, 178; 7/275, 284; 8/134, 340

AS SERVANT: a good servant, 7/85; promoted chambermaid, 3/273 & n. 2, 275, 278, 279; returns as cookmaid, 7/85; washes/cleans house etc., 1/19, 85, 243, 296, 316; her cooking/baking, 3/54, 81; 4/30; 8/589; 9/13; refuses to kill turkey, 1/41; combs P's hair, 1/222; mends his breeches,

1/317; helps him rearrange books etc.
after Fire, 7/292, 336, 367; gathers
May-dew with EP, 8/240; also, 1/59,
251; 3/113, 156; 4/9; 5/13; 8/552;
9/116
SOCIAL: at Twelfth Night supper, 1/10;
sees pre-coronation procession, 2/83;
at Vauxhall, 3/95; on river trips,
7/235; 8/325; visits previous mistress,
8/315; also, 1/76; 3/115; 8/167, 376,
443; 9/516
~ her mother, 2/162
EDWARDS, Tom, P's servant:
CHRON. SERIES: P given allowance for,
5/228 & n. 2; engaged from Chapel
Royal, 5/234 & n. 1, 255; given suit
from Wardrobe, 5/234, 245, 246, 251;
his schoolboy ways, 5/256, 260, 266;
neglects music, 6/7, 77, 86; spoilt by
EP, 6/26, 28, 29; P boxes his ears,
7/19, 150; beats, 8/176; scolds, 8/202;
courtship of Jane Birch, 9/63-4, 283;
to leave P's service, 9/441, 483;
marriage, 9/483, 484, 493, 499, 500;
leaves Seething Lane, 9/502; gifts to,
9/526 & n. 2, 537; also, 5/329; 8/134,
420
AS SERVANT: accompanies P on visits to
dockyards/ships etc., 5/305, 317;
6/103, 119, 128, 228, 286-7, 299;
7/112, 202; 8/165; to Westminster/
Whitehall, 6/35; 9/422, 444, 449;
church, 5/256, 267, 285; 6/5; Brampton, 9/207, 209-10, 212-13; reads to
P, 7/283; 9/202, 215, 271, 300, 311,
313, 315, 317, 318, 320, 337, 354, 381,
382, 400, 433, 482, 501, 502, 542;
helps in office, 6/226; 9/524, 526, 548;
helps to stow prize goods, 6/259;
arrange books/papers, 7/290; 8/432;
9/354; to secure P's money after Fire,
7/284, 336, 367; escorts P after Deb
Willet affair, 9/397; also, 6/143, 205,
217; 7/95, 100, 266, 425; 8/444, 540,
551; 9/331
MUSICAL: talented, 5/258; 266; lute/
theorbo lessons, 5/344; 6/86; 7/182,
226-7, 375; 8/558; teaches Barker
song, 8/113; writes down P's compositions, 9/412; sings/plays lute/
theorbo, 5/261, 266, 305, 310, 320,
321, 332, 339; 6/138; 7/68, 338; 8/113,
394, 413, 504; 9/179, 213, 300, 401

SOCIAL: looks for comet with P, 5/355;
at Bartholomew Fair, 5/260; Vauxhall, 7/198; Islington, 8/376; at
taverns with P/EP, 6/27; 9/445, 516,
538; also, 6/263; 8/590
ALLUDED TO: 9/464
~ his father's death from plague,
6/225, 235
EGERTON, John, 2nd Earl of Bridgewater (d. 1686): appointed to Brooke
House Committee, 8/194; at Privy
Council committee, 8/278; rumoured
appointment to Treasury Commission, 8/367-8 & n.; rumoured dismissal from Privy Council, 8/596 &
n. 1, 600
EGLIN: see Edlin
EGLIN(G)TON, 6th Earl of: see
Montgomerie
EGYPT: 5/274
ELBOROUGH, [Robert], Curate of
St Laurence Poultney, and P's schoolfellow: foolish, 1/178 & n. 3; 4/5, 34;
preaches well, 7/235; alluded to: 7/269
ELBE (Elve) river: naval squadron in,
7/71
ELIEZER: see [Jenkins]
ELIZABETH I, Queen of England
1558-1603: Armada fleet, 3/187 &
n. 2; embassy to Russia, 3/188-9 &
n.; coinage, 4/148; letter from
Cranmer (recte Grindal), 4/329-30 &
n.; letters from, 6/308 & n. 2; Roman
Catholic disloyalty, 7/394; avoids
summoning parliament (1588), 8/293
ELIZABETH, Dowager Queen of
Bohemia (d. 1662): at The Hague,
1/138 & n. 1, 144; 'debonaire but
plain', 1/144; on Naseby, 1/154; at
theatre, 2/131, 156; death, 3/28, 81;
alluded to: 1/140
[ELKINS, RICHARD], Clerk of the
Cheque, Gravesend: news from,
8/349 & n. 1, 350
ELLINGTON, Hunts.: 9/211, 553
[ELLIOTT, James], servant to Lord
Middleton: killed in affray, 5/32 &
n. 3
ELLIOTT, Capt. [Thomas], naval
officer: naval news from, 7/142, 143
ELLIS, [William], Solicitor-General
1654: 1/40
ELVETHAM, Hants.: 4/102

Tower Hill: market established after Fire, 7/281

FAITHORNE, [William sen.], engraver and printseller: P buys from, 1/174 & n. 2; 3/2; 7/173, 359, 393; 8/10; engraving of Lady Castlemaine, 7/359 & n. 3, 393; instrument for drawing perspectives, 9/513

FALCONBRIDGE: see Belasyse, Thomas, Lord Fauconberg and Fauconberg, Edward

FALCONER, [Edward] (ed. error): see Fauconberg, [Edward]

FALCONER, [Elizabeth], widow of John: formerly his maid, 4/67; claims compensation on his death, 5/231, 248 & n. 2, 249, 253; ill, 5/213; social: 5/155, 192

FALCONER, [John], Clerk of the Ropeyard, Woolwich: marriage, 4/67; gift to EP, 5/45, 47; P inspects ropeyard with, 5/54; illness and death, 5/109, 125, 130, 137, 155, 213, 217, 248 & n. 2; stories of gifts to Penn and Coventry, 5/231 & n. 4, 248, 249, 253; 8/228; social: 2/121, 155, 227; 3/19, 102, 142, 159, 179; 4/103; 5/156, 182, 192; ~ his friend, 5/155

FALMOUTH, Viscount: see Berkeley, Sir C.

FALMOUTH, Cornwall: 7/397

FANATICS [P uses both 'fanatics' and 'sectaries' to describe the extreme Puritans. See also Anabaptists; Fifth-Monarchists; Nonconformists; Plots and risings, minor]: strength in London, 1/109, 111; 4/373 & n. 3; blame King for persecution, 3/127; rising feared, 3/186, 236, 303; prophesy end of world next Tuesday, 3/266–7; want court and church purified, 3/275; alleged loyalty, 4/373; 5/264 & n. 1; rebel in Yorkshire, 4/391 & n. 1; riot in churches, 9/96 & n. 1

FANCHURCH ST: see Fenchurch St

FANSHAWE, Anne, Lady Fanshawe, wife of Sir Richard: 3/126; 7/379–80

FANSHAWE, [Henry], brother of Thomas Fanshawe, 2nd Viscount Fanshawe: seeks place in navy, 9/86 & n. 3

FANSHAWE, [Lyonel], 2/163 & n. 3; 3/57

FANSHAWE, Sir Richard, diplomatist: drafts preambles to patents of nobility, 1/188 & n. 1, 189; ambassador to Portugal, 2/163 & n. 3; 3/2 & n. 3, 57; death, 7/214 & n. 1, 380

[FARRINER, Thomas], King's Baker, Pudding Lane: Fire alleged to have started at his bakery, 7/268 & n. 1; 8/81, 82

FAUCONBERG (Falconbridge etc.), [Edward], Deputy-Chamberlain of the Receipt at the Exchequer: agrees to P's resigning, 1/80; consulted by P, 2/236; alluded to: 7/303, 304, 314, 319; 8/212; social: 1/24; 2/239–40, 241; 6/162, 235; 7/398; ~ his kinsman, R. Knightley; his kinswoman, Barker, EP's companion (qq.v.)

FAUNTLEROY (FONTLEROY), [?Thomas]: 1/294

FAVERSHAM, Kent: 8/358

FAZEBY, Capt. [William], naval officer: 7/141–2

FÉCAMP (Feckam): King lands at (1651), 1/156

FEE LANE: see Fleet Lane

FELTON, Sir Henry, Bt, M.P. Suffolk (d. 1690): 6/118

FELTON, [John], assassin of Buckingham: 2/93 & n. 2

FENCHURCH ST [see also Taverns, etc.: Mitre]: Plague, 6/124, 128, 225; Fire, 7/276; P shops in, 8/173; 9/322; St Gabriel's church, 6/76 & n. 2

FENN, John, Paymaster to the Navy Treasurer: financial business: with P, 4/422; 6/192(2); 8/259; Penn, 7/65; and B. St Michel, 8/153, 162, 163; also, 7/169, 312; 8/121–2, 177, 281, 285; 9/169, 362, 428; malpractices: 6/40, 117; enquired into by Brooke House Committee, 9/82; rudeness, 7/89; a tool of Backwell, 7/214; P warns Carteret against, 6/190; usefulness to Carteret, 8/48 & n. 1, 180, 327; dismissed, 9/357 & n. 2; news from, 8/299, 354, 416; social: 3/14; 6/187, 198; 7/48, 74, 89, 404; 9/337; ~ his pretty wife, 9/337; his son, 6/24

FENNER, family of: dine at P's father's, 1/266; at funeral, 2/179

Bailey, ib.; Post-house, ib.; Fleet St, 7/275, 279; Cheapside, 7/275, 277; All Hallows Barking, 7/275, 276; St Paul's, 7/275, 279, 367–8; 9/22–3; Fenchurch St, 7/276; Gracechurch St, ib.; Lombard St, ib.; Royal Exchange, ib.; Newgate market, 7/277; Mercers' chapel, ib.; Bishopsgate, ib.; Clothworkers' Hall, 7/278–9; St Paul's School, 7/279; St Faith's-under-Paul's, 7/279, 309; Ludgate, 7/279; St Bride, Fleet St, ib.; Seething Lane, 7/282; Holborn, ib.; St Paul's Churchyard, 7/309; Tower Hill, 7/357

COUNTER-MEASURES: lack of, 7/269, 270; Lord Mayor blamed, 7/280; use of soldiers, 7/269, 273; dockyard workmen, 7/274, 276, 278; water, 7/278; houses pulled down, 7/269, 271, 274; blown up, 7/275, 276; King's part in, 7/269, 271; Duke of York's, 7/271, 273; Albemarle's, 7/279; courtiers', 7/298; P's, 7/269, 274; Penn's, 7/276

INCIDENTS: panic on river, 7/268, 271, 273; pigeons killed, 7/268; cat survives, 7/277; goods stored in churches, 7/270; virginals in boats, 7/271; looting, 7/278, 282; ungenerous rewards to firefighters, 7/282; Bishop Braybrooke's corpse exposed, 7/367–8 & n.; paper fragments blown to Windsor Park, 8/42–3

LOSS AND DAMAGE: P/EP view(s) ruins, 7/291, 357, 419; 8/5–6, 46, 60; loss of life, 9/23; destruction of book stocks, 7/297 & nn., 309; of Sir E. Walker's MSS, 7/410 & n. 3; effect on merchants' credit, 7/287; 8/450; number of churches destroyed, 9/46; loss in rents, 7/286; establishment of Fire Court, 7/357 & n. 2; 9/23 & n. 1; case in, 8/562–3 & n.

EFFECTS: on relations between King and Parliament, 7/286; King's power, 7/307; movement of shopkeepers to Westminster, 7/426; 9/250; theatre audiences, 8/55; rents, 7/280; on prices: of bread, 7/277; eels, 7/281; guineas, 7/346; books, 8/121 & n. 2, 156 & n. 2; land, 8/563

RECOVERY AND REBUILDING: Exchange

moved to Gresham College, 7/280 & n. 2; new markets, 7/280–1 & n.; theatres reopen, 7/341 & n. 3; temporary shops, 7/404; government and city to cooperate, 7/281, 384–5 & n.; the Rebuilding Acts, 8/35, 72 & n. 2, 81, 87 & n. 4; P's timber project, 7/298 & n. 3, 300; Birch's proposal, 8/81; new streets, 8/108, 136 & n. 2, 155, 201 & n. 1, 562 & n. 3; 9/245, 258, 285; new churches, 8/151–2 & n.; new St Paul's, 9/288 & n. 1, 305, 307–8 & n.; Mincing Lane, 9/245; Surgeons' Hall, 9/292 & n. 5; also, 9/223, 289, 392

FIREWORKS: 7/152, 246

FIRTH OF FORTH (the Frith): Dutch fleet in, 8/200, 202

FISH, Mrs ——: 5/214

FISH [see also Fishery, Royal; Food]: in E. Europe, 4/412; ?paradise fish, 6/111 & n. 1; sturgeon in Thames, 8/232–3; Huntingdon sturgeon, ib. & n.

FISHER, Anne (Nan), P's cousin: P sends pamphlets to, 1/56 & n. 4; alluded to: 1/196; 3/107 & n. 3, 110

FISHER, Payne (Pagan), author (d. 1693): dedicates book to P, 1/200 & n. 2; panegyric on Charles II, 1/209 & n. 1; borrows money, ib.

FISHER, [?Robert], husband of Anne P of Worcs.: 3/107, 110

FISHER, Capt. [?Robert]: ship hired for Tangier, 5/281

FISHER, Capt. [Thomas], customs officer: seizes Cocke's prize-goods, 6/258, 259, 261, 269, 340; and Pierce's, 6/317; bribed by Cocke, 6/260, 264, 265

FISHER, ——: in Carkesse's case, 8/200; his wife, ib.

FISHERY, the Royal:

COUNCIL OF (1661): its herring fleet, 2/198 & n. 4; 3/268–9 & n., 269–70 & n., 274; proposed farthing monopoly, 4/365–6 & n.; P hopes for profit, 4/365

CORPORATION OF (1664): established, 5/79 & n. 3, 198; P appointed member of Council, 5/76, 79, 83; hopes for profit, 5/79; Council debates oath, 5/199 & n. 3; appointment of secretary,

5/251, 262; P appointed to committee for raising funds, 5/262; lottery proposed, 5/269 & n. 2, 276, 279, 294, 299–300, 323; 6/53; farthing monopoly, 5/269, 336; voluntary collections, 5/293–4 & n., 304, 304–5, 312; P prepares proposals, 5/314, 315; fears he may neglect Navy Office for, 5/280; unspecified business, 5/202, 214, 260, 269, 276, 281, 315, 341, 348

FISHMONGERS' HALL: 5/269, 276

FISH ST (Old Fish St) [*see also* Taverns etc.: Feathers; Swan]: 7/237

FISH ST (New Fish St, Fish Street Hill) [*see also* Taverns etc.: King's Head; Sun]: P buys lobsters, 1/212; 7/103; gradient, 2/214; 7/103–4; Fire, 7/268(2), 270, 272; rebuilt, 9/285 & n. 1

FISH YARD, the, Westminster: 3/67

FISSANT, Mrs ——: 6/173; ~ her daughter, ib.

FIST, [Anthony], clerk to Sir W. Batten: 8/213–15 passim, 277, 278; 9/259, 394

FITCH, Col. [Thomas]: handles mutiny, 1/36–7; dismissed from command of Tower, 1/39 & n. 2

FITTON, Alexander, cr. Baron Fytton of Gosworth, co. Limerick 1689: suit against Lord Gerard, 9/83–4 & n.

FITZGERALD, Lt-Col. [John], Deputy-Governor of Tangier 1662–6: criticised, 5/302 & n. 1, 344–5 & n.; good company, 9/274; commands Irish regiment, 3/204; favourite of Duke of York, 4/116; of Falmouth, 5/345; financial business, 7/173; 8/76; 9/272; ill at Woolwich, 8/403; returns from Tangier, 9/272; arrested to prevent duel, 9/273; alluded to: 8/61; 9/275

FITZHARDING: *see* Berkeley, Sir C.

FITZROY, Lady Charlotte: daughter of Lady Castlemaine, 6/41 & n. 2

FLANDERS: *see* Spanish Netherlands

FLEET ALLEY: prostitutes, 4/164, 301; 5/219–20, 224, 225–6

FLEET BRIDGE: rebuilt after Fire, 9/223 & n. 1, 258

FLEET (Fee) LANE: 5/101, 220–21

FLEET PRISON: 2/118

FLEET ST [*see also* Taverns etc.: Devil; Globe; Greyhound; Hercules Pillars; Mitre; Penell's; Standing's]: storm damage, 3/32; Fire, 7/275, 279, 288–9; conduit, 1/3; 5/269

FLEETWOOD, Lt-Gen. Charles, parliamentarian (d. 1692): letter to Rump, 1/34–5 & nn.; reprieved, 3/16 & n. 1; alluded to: 1/21, 76

FLETCHER, Capt. [John], naval officer: 3/150

FLOWER, old Mr ——: 1/307

FLOYD: *see* Lloyd

FLUSHING: peace commissioners at, 8/216; alluded to: 1/131, 132; 7/229, 234

FLY, the: *see* Vlie

FOGARTY (Fogourdy, Fougourdy), ——, Catholic priest: P fears influence on EP, 5/39, 103; news from, 5/40

FOLEY, [Robert], ironmonger to the Navy: provides chest for P, 5/323; and tools, 7/245; provides locks for Brouncker, 8/226; social: entertains Navy Board, 3/266; 5/308; also, 9/157; ~ his man, 4/409; 7/245

FOLEY, [Thomas], ironmaster: endows almshouse, 9/227 & n. 3

FONTLEROY: *see* Fauntleroy

FOOD [*see also* Health: diet]:
MEALS ON SPECIAL OCCASIONS [asterisks denote entries at which dishes are listed]: colly feast, 1/24; Shrove Tuesday club dinner, 1/78*; Lenten dinners, 1/80; 2/50, 73; 4/70, 71; 5/44; P's New Year breakfast, 2/2*; P's Lenten dinners, 2/52*; 4/104*; 5/117*; P's stone feasts, 2/60; 3/53*; 4/95*; 5/98; 6/124*; coronation banquet, 2/85; Lord Mayor's banquets, 2/201, 203; 4/354–6 & nn.; P's dinner for Exchequer colleagues, 2/241; Penn's wedding anniversary dinner, 3/4*; P's Christmas dinner, 3/293*; P's dinner for Mountagu children, 5/180*; club dinners, 6/39, 132; bad dinner given by Sir W. Hicks, 6/222*; P's six-course dinner, 7/388; P's seven-course dinner, 8/4; Downing's dinner for poor neighbours, 8/85*; French tavern dinner, 8/211*; bad dinner given by Penn, 8/371*; breakfast after dancing party, 9/289; also, 1/6*, 29*; 2/228*; 4/14*, 247*,

fee etc., 1/293; gift from Sandwich, 1/292, 293, 298; also, 8/430

AS PAYMASTER-GENERAL: management of funds, 8/16; discusses allocation of excise money, 6/136; 7/92, 133; 8/123-4, 198, 586 & n. 3; 9/197, 199; obtains funds from Excise Office/ Treasury for army, 7/133; 8/112, 193, 198, 199, 572, 586 & n. 3; 9/14, 280, 306 & n. 2

NEWS ETC. FROM: suggests P enter parliament, 7/322; stories of Spain, 8/111; pessimistic about public affairs, 8/149; also, 7/322-3; 8/80, 294

SOCIAL: 1/157, 299-300; 2/21, 22, 29; 3/190, 202; 4/63; 6/114; 9/320

FOX(E), Dr [Thomas], physician: daughter's marriage, 1/141

FRAISER, Dr Alexander, physician, kted ?1667: blamed for death of Princess Mary, 1/323 & n. 1; influence at court, 5/275 & n. 1; attends Rupert, 8/41 & n. 4; Duke of Cambridge, 8/192; Mennes, 8/324; and Duke of York, 8/524; arrested for debt, 9/561 & n. 2

FRAMPTON, Robert, chaplain to Levant Company 1655-70; Bishop of Gloucester, 1680-91 (d. 1708): P admires his preaching, 7/316 & n. 4; 8/21 & n. 1, 32, 34 & n. 1

FRANCE:

NATIONAL CHARACTERISTICS, MANNERS, CUSTOMS etc. [for English imitation of French manners, *see* Food; Humfrey, P.; Mountagu, E., 1st Earl of Sandwich; Penn, W., jun.]: volatility, 1/10; 2/189; 3/160; 'humours', 6/213; English prefer Spaniards, 2/188 & n. 4; mottoes in taverns, 3/204; and bargaining for meals in, 4/131; hiring of servants, ib.

GOVERNMENT: marshals, 4/213 & n. 1; nobility, 4/416 & n. 1; princes of blood, 4/419-20 & n.; taxation, 5/68; 8/300; praised by Evelyn, 8/181-2; by others, 8/335; 9/352; King's arbitrary powers, 8/300 & n. 5; his achievements, ib.

FOREIGN RELATIONS:

GENERAL: ambassador claims precedence in England, 2/187-91 & nn.; and in Spain (untrue rumour), 8/36 &

n. 2, 37, 42; ambassador affronted at Lord Mayor's banquet, 4/355 & n. 2

WITH THE EMPIRE: 4/340, 439; 8/107

WITH ENGLAND: relations deteriorate, 5/343; 6/165, 270, 307; claims wine from Dutch prize, 5/354; attack on English merchantman, 6/278 & n. 3; attempts mediation, 6/76 & n. 1; war declared, 7/24, 40 & n. 2; quarrel over Charles II's new fashion, 7/324 & n.3, 379-80 & n.; embargo on trade, 7/403 & n. 5; fleet movements (1666), 7/139 & n. 3, 216, 300, 327-8; threatens invasion of England, 7/185(2) & n. 1, 186, 286, 287, 395; and of Ireland, 8/1; suspected involvement in Pentland Rising, 7/384 & n. 2; French victories in St Kitt's, 7/171 & n. 3, 390 & n. 3; fleet sent to W. Indies, 8/2 & n. 1; takes Antigua, 8/38 & n. 1; defeated off Martinique, 8/430 & n. 1; peace negotiations, 7/420; 8/11 & n. 3, 69 & n. 2, 72, 74, 96, 106-7 & n., 113, 128, 151, 170 & n. 5, 212, 244, 289, 294 & n. 4; fleet movements (1667), 8/38, 170, 248, 250, 266; threatens invasion, 8/265, 277, 432, 602; peace proclaimed, 8/399 & n. 1; published, 8/453 & n. 3; renewed threat of invasion, 9/7, 18, 30, 181; fleet movements (1668), 9/26, 141 & n. 3, 250-1 & nn., 251; rumoured demand for salute from English ships, 9/397 & n. 3; anxious for alliance, 9/7 & n. 1; alienated by Anglo-Dutch alliance, 9/35 & n. 4; French intentions uncertain, 9/417; English alliance almost achieved, 9/536 & n. 2

WITH THE PAPACY: quarrel with Alexander VII, 3/253 & n. 3; 4/24 & n. 1, 26, 63 & n. 3; 5/40 & n. 1, 42, 60; 6/156 & n. 1; rumour of establishment of patriarchate, 3/253; influence in election of Clement IX, 8/335-6 & n.

WITH PORTUGAL: peace with, 8/191 & n. 6

WITH SPAIN: designs against, 4/340 & n. 5, 439; said to have hired ships against, 4/407, 420; designs on Flanders, 8/74, 92 & n. 3, 175; on Poland, 8/92, 95; diplomatic prepara-

tions, 8/96, 107 & n. 2; Louis XIV's claim to Flanders, 8/186 & n. 2, 253–4 & n.; military preparations, 8/285, 300; 9/7, 38 & n. 1; recruits English seamen, 8/601; peace negotiations, 9/18, 153, 161 & n. 5, 176 & n. 3, 181; (untrue) rumour of renewal of war, 9/264 & n. 3
WITH THE UNITED PROVINCES: alliance, 3/7 & n. 5; 5/354; 6/248; 7/216
VISITS BY P/EP: proposed visit in royal yacht, 4/399 & n. 4; EP in (c. 1652–3), 5/39 & n. 4; proposed holiday, 3/393, 462 & n. 3, 555–6
MISC.: famine, 3/62 & n. 2, 200; breadmaking, 6/48 & n. 3; partridge-shooting, 7/79; gardens inferior to English, 7/213 & n. 2; kid leather from, 8/425; blood transfusion in, 8/554 & n. 4; book on overseas trade, 9/431–2 & n.
'FRANK': see Udall, Frances
FRANK, [?Ald. Francis], of Worcester: 1/80 & n. 3
FRANKE, [Edward], landlord of John P's house: 9/399
FRANKLIN, Mrs ——: at coronation, 2/86–8 passim
FRAZIER: see Fraiser
FREDERICK III, King of Denmark and Norway 1648–70: his part in Bergen action, 6/198, 229; 7/335; allies with England (untrue rumour), 6/286; cancels debt to English merchants, 8/426 & n. 2
FREDERICK, Ald. Sir John, Lord Mayor 1661–2: revives ceremonial visit to St Paul's, 2/203 & n. 4; at Spital sermon, 3/57–8; and parish dinner, 9/179; also, 8/218
FREEMAN, Sir Ralph, Master of the Mint: 1/135
FREEMANTLE, [?John]: 4/139
FRENCH CHURCH, the, in the Savoy, Strand: P at, 3/207 & n. 1; alluded to: 8/137 & n. 3
FRENCH CHURCH, the, Thread-needle St: exchange of congregations with Dutch Church, 3/276–7 & n.; sermons, 3/270, 296; 5/17, 342; baptisms, 3/296; catechising of children, 5/18
FREWEN (Fruen), Accepted, Bishop

of Coventry and Lichfield (d. 1664): translated to York, 1/259 & n. 2
FRIDAY ST: 3/178
FRIESENDORFF (Frezendorfe), Johan Fredrik von, Swedish envoy 1657–61: 1/182
FROST, [Gualter, jun.], Treasurer for Contingencies (Council of State) 1660: 1/28, 29, 31, 33
FROWDE, Col. Sir Philip, kted 1665, secretary to the Duchess of York: court news from, 8/384; also, 5/123; 7/150
FRUITS: see Food; Plants etc.
FRYER, Mr ——: news from, 8/266
FUDGE, Capt. ——, captain of merchantman: to sail to Tangier, 5/176, 177
FULHAM, Mdx: 9/555
FULLER, [Richard], merchant: 6/202
FULLER, Thomas, author: [see also Books]: at The Hague, 1/144 & n. 3, 145; views on tragedy, 1/239; his remarkable memory, 2/21 & n. 2; his preaching, 2/29, 98 & n. 3; death, 2/155 & n. 4; also, 2/6 & n. 3
FULLER, Thomas, Fellow of Christ's College, Cambridge 1649–61; Rector of Navenby, Lincs. 1659–1701: his account of college factions, 1/63–4; university prævaricator, 5/278 & n. 1; requests discharge for impressed waterman, 5/278, 292; preaches, 5/292; tells ghost stories, 5/349; social: 5/303
FULLER, William, Dean of St Patrick's, Dublin 1660; Bishop of Limerick 1663; Bishop of Lincoln 1667 (d. 1675): P's regard, 3/86; 7/209–10; 9/35, 36; his school at Twickenham, 1/20 & n. 2, 65 & n. 3, 165; adversities under Commonwealth, 1/65 & n. 3; appointed Dean of St Patrick's, 1/181 & n.3; Bishop of Limerick, 7/209–10; translated to Lincoln, 8/449 & n. 2, 521; account of Irish church affairs, 2/67 & n. 2, 117–18 & n.; political news from, 8/113; 9/35–6; episcopal seat at Buckden, 9/35 & n. 3; also, 1/85; 3/162; 7/302; social: dines with Lady Sandwich, 2/126, 149; also, 1/21, 217–18; 3/8; alluded to: 9/127

FULWOOD, Gervase, Rector of Coton, Cambs.: his preaching, 9/211 & n. 2

FUNERALS:
GENERAL: invitation by ticket, 2/73; held at night, 1/249 & n. 2; 2/204; 5/230; 7/414; at parish charge, 7/414
PARTICULAR: Robert P, 2/133; K. Fenner, 2/159; Sir R. Stayner, 3/268–9; Edward P, 4/432; Tom P, 5/90–1; T. Fenner, 5/158; Sir T. Vyner, 6/114; Earl of Marlborough, 6/127; Sir J. Lawson, 6/145; Sir C. Myngs, 7/165; A. Joyce, 9/36; Sir W. Davenant, 9/158; Sir T. Teddeman, 9/200; Mrs Middleton, 9/452
CUSTOMS [for mourning clothes and rings, see Dress etc.]: procession, 3/269; 4/432; 6/114 & n. 1; 8/475; 9/158; pew draped in black, 3/153; biscuit and wine, 4/21; 5/90 & n. 2

FURBISHER, Mr ——: 2/208, 210
FURNITURE, furnishings: see Household etc.
FURZER, [Daniel], shipbuilder, Bristol: 9/235
FYGE: see Fage

GALE: 3/58
GALEN, Christopher Bernard von, Prince-Bishop of Münster 1650–78: letter to States-General, 6/274–5 & n.; allies with Dutch, 7/93 & n. 5, 107 & n. 1
GALLIPOLI: 8/374 & n. 6
GALLOP, [?John], parson: 1/178
GALLOPER SAND, Thames estuary: ships aground, 7/153 & n. 1, 195; 8/359
GAMBIA (Gambo): stories of, 3/10–11 & n.
GAME, [John]: see Taverns etc: Coach and Horses
GAMES, SPORTS AND PASTIMES [Asterisks denote the occasions on which P takes part. See also Entertainments; Gaming]:
ARCHERY: 8/211* & n. 3
BACKGAMMON: see tables
BILLIARDS: 6/160*, 179*, 190*, 220*
BOB-CHERRY: 6/132
BOWLS: 3/146; 5/233*; 8/377; 9/447
CARDS [SELECT]: beast, 2/3*; cribbage,

1/5*, 142*; gleek, 3/9*, 14*, 31*; ombre, 6/218
CHESS: in Russia, 5/272
DRAUGHTS: 1/70*
FISHING: through ice, 4/412; with gut for line, 8/119; also, 1/169; 6/225
FLINGING AT COCKS: 2/44 & n. 1
FOOTBALL: 6/3
FOOTRACES: in Hyde Park, 1/218 & n. 1; on Banstead Down, 4/160, 255; at Newmarket, 9/473; between P's maids, 8/167
HAWKING: in Russia, 5/272
HORSE RACES: at Epsom/Banstead, 4/160 & n. 5, 243 & n. 4, 249; Newmarket, 4/324 & n. 2; 9/209, 473; Putney, 8/203–4
HUNTING [select]: King's prowess, 2/152 & n. 2; Duke of York's, 4/371; language of, 4/394; 8/475; P dislikes, 6/295; at Bartholomew Fair, 4/288; in Courland, 4/413–14; in St James's Park, 5/239; in Siam (elephant), 7/251
NINEPINS: on board ship, 1/118*, 119*, 121*, 129*, 131*, 132*, 142*, 160*, 162*, 166*, 169*; 4/99; elsewhere, 4/144*, 160*, 197*
PARTY GAMES: blindman's buff, 5/357; crambo, 1/149; cross-purposes, 7/422 & n. 3; flinging cushions, 7/56; handicap, 1/248; 'I love my love', 9/469 & n. 2; mock-marriage, 1/175; questions and commands, 2/30 & n. 2
PIGEON FLYING: in Russia, 5/272
PELL MELL: 2/64 & n. 2; 4/135; 5/4; 9/542
SHOOTING: at Bartholomew Fair, 4/288; battue in France, 7/79
SHUFFLEBOARD: 3/150*; 5/175*; 6/74*
SHUTTLECOCK (SHITTLECOCK): 1/15*
SKATING: 3/272 & n. 2, 277, 282
TABLES (BACKGAMMON ETC.): 6/221, 227, 236*
TENNIS: 4/435; 5/4, 11, 19; 8/418, 419
TRAP-BALL: 9/191
WRESTLING: in Moorfields, (between North and West countrymen), 2/127; 3/93; at Bartholomew Fair, 4/288
YACHT-RACES: 3/188; 4/256 & n. 3
GAMING [omitting casual wagers and bets]: P plays at 'selling of a horse for a dish of eggs and herrings', 1/38 &

Turks into, 4/315–16 & n., 349 & n. 2, 358
GERMIN: *see* Jermyn
GERVAS: *see* Jervas
[GERY, ——]: 1/126 & n. 3
GHOSTS: *see* Popular Beliefs etc.
GIBBONS, [Charles]: his tennis-court, 1/297 & n. 2
GIBBONS, Dr Christopher, organist (d. 1676): performs at Sandwich's house, 2/103; 3/108, 287; 4/160; to set parts for P, 7/418; inspects organ with, 9/89; promises music for flageolets, 9/271
[GIBBS, Ann], actress ('the little girl'): in *The slighted maid*, 4/56 & n. 2; *Heraclius*, 5/78–9 & n.
GIBBS, Mr ——, clerk: his calligraphy, 8/545–6; 9/21, 330
GIBRALTAR, BAY OF: 6/19
GIBSON, Richard, clerk in the Navy Office:
P'S REGARD: 9/16 & n. 1
AS CLERK: compares costs of Dutch Wars, 8/297 & n. 1; stories of commanders, 9/26; carries gold to Brampton, 8/263–4, 268, 272, 273, 473, 474, 487; works for P, 7/284, 294, 305; 8/212, 373–4, 539, 540; 9/22, 42, 101, 283, 286, 308, 315, 316, 340(2), 342, 344, 358, 360, 394, 478, 500, 511, 521, 524, 547, 548, 556
AS SURVEYOR OF VICTUALLING AT YARMOUTH: appointment, 6/315 & n. 3; instructs P on pursers, 6/316, 321; 7/1; also, 7/139
SOCIAL: story of meteor, 9/207–8; accompanies P to Maidstone, 9/495, 497; to Hyde Park, 9/564; also, 9/100, 208, 297, 310, 562
MISC.: house, 8/590; Warren's offer of employment to, 9/16; also, 8/253–4 & n.
GIFFORD, [George], Rector of St Dunstan-in-the-East: his preaching, 4/268 & n. 4; 9/482
GIFFORD, [?Henry]: political news, 1/75–6
GIFFORD, [?Thomas], merchant: Tangier business, 6/27, 28; social: 6/21, 44
GIGERY: *see* Jijelli
GILES (Gyles), Sarah (b. Kite), P's cousin and wife of Thomas: borrows

money, 4/154–5; P deposits diary etc. with in Medway crisis, 8/264; social: 5/266; 7/174; 8/448; alluded to: 8/262; ~ her children die of plague, 6/342; also, 2/173; her pretty boy, 8/442
GILES, Thomas, of St Giles's parish, Cripplegate: 5/266; 8/264
GILLINGHAM, Kent: P at, 6/248; Dutch raid, 8/309
GILSTHROPP [?Gilsthorpe], ——, clerk to Sir W. Batten: alleged to have paid for place, 5/141; illness and death, 8/337, 560; accusations against Navy Board, 8/560 & n. 1, 564–5; also, 6/244
GIPSIES: *see* Popular Beliefs etc.
GLANVILL(E), [William], of Greenwich: friend of Cocke, 6/243 & n. 5; stores prize-goods, 6/243, 259, 270; P lodges with, 6/243–4, 245, 288, 290, 293, 294; alluded to: 6/273, 297, 299
GLASCOCK, Charles, relative of P: political views, 1/54 & n. 4; house, 2/83; visits dying brother, 2/144; social: 1/81, 85
GLASCOCK, John, Rector of Little Canfield, Essex, brother of Charles: death, 2/144 & n. 1
GLEMHAM, Henry, Bishop of St Asaph 1667 – d. 70: scandalous life, 8/364–5 & n.
GLYNNE, Sir John, lawyer (d. 1666): unpopularity, 2/87–8 & n.
GOA, India: 2/62
GODALMING (Godlyman), Surrey: P visits, 2/91
GODDARD, Dr [Jonathan], physician: attends Royal Society Club, 6/36; defends doctors leaving London in Plague, 7/21
GODFREY, Sir Edmund Berry, magistrate: arrests royal physician, 9/561 & nn.
GODFREY, [Henry]: dispute with P over debt, 3/34 & n. 1, 80
GODFREY, [Richard]: 4/384–5 & n.
GODMANCHESTER, Hunts.: P visits, 4/307
GODOLPHIN, William, diplomat, kted 1668: arrives from Spain, 9/46 & n. 2; Sandwich's regard, 9/52 & n. 3;

and P's, 9/59; praises Sandwich as ambassador, 9/59–60; and P's parliamentary speech, 9/105; stories of Spain, 9/118; news of Sandwich, 9/164, 320; also, 9/65; social: 9/116, 162, 176, 321–2, 423–4

GOFFE (Gough), Stephen, divine: anecdote of, 7/290 & n. 2

[GOGH, Michiel van], Dutch ambassador 1664–5: arrives, 5/175 & n. 3; conciliatory, 5/181 & n. 3; audience with Duke of York, 5/264; and King, 5/301; imprisoned (rumour), 6/273 & n. 1; also, 5/283

GOLD (Gould), [Elizabeth], Lady Gold, widow of Sir Nicholas: wealth, 5/1; marriage to T. Neale, 5/1, 184 & n. 2; 6/126; ~ her brother, 5/184

GOLD (Gould), [John], hemp merchant: his knavery, 5/117

GOLD (Gould), [?John, ?Edward], merchant: 9/421

GOLD (Gould), Sir Nicholas, merchant: attends Rota Club, 1/14 & n. 3; death, 5/1

GOLDEN EAGLE, New St (?shop): 1/205

GOLDING, Capt. [John], naval officer: killed in action, 6/82

GOLDING, ——, barber, Greenwich: plays fiddle, 3/164; 6/227 & n. 3, 263, 279

GOLDSBOROUGH, Mrs ——: debt to Robert P, 2/195–6 & n., 197, 198; 3/44; estate, 3/232; 4/203, 362; alluded to: 9/451; ~ her son, 3/232; 4/203, 362

GOLDSMITH, Capt. [Ralph], naval officer: 9/160 & n. 5

GOLDSMITHS: see Banks and Bankers

GOLDSMITHS' HALL, Foster Lane: funeral, 6/114

[GOLOVIN, Mikhail], Russian envoy: 8/428 & n. 2

GOMBOUST, [Jacques]: map of Paris, 7/379 & n. 2

GOMME (Gum), Sir Bernard de, military engineer: advises King on Medway defences, 8/126 & n. 4

[GONSON, Benjamin], Treasurer of the Navy 1549–1577: ledger, 6/307–8 & n.

GOODENOUGH, [Edward], plasterer: sends P gift, 2/32 & n. 2; consulted about rooms at Navy Office, 3/197

[GOODFELLOW, Christopher], Reader, Inner Temple (d. 1690): 9/465–6 & n.

GOODGROOME, [John], musician: gives P/EP singing lessons, 2/126 & n. 2, 130, 144, 145, 190; 7/397; 8/411, 424; teaches P to trill, 8/424; P critical of, 8/109, 378; given copy of *Beauty Retire*, 7/397; sings with P and EP, 8/171; social: 3/108, 298; 7/412; 8/209; 9/414

GOOD HOPE, CAPE OF: stories of natives, 3/298 & n. 3

GOODMAN, ——: 1/236

GOODS, John, servant to Lord Sandwich: on *Naseby*, 1/105, 108, 110, 116, 134, 151, 160; also, 2/16, 26; 4/210; social: 2/3, 90

GOODSON, [William], naval commander: P's regard, 5/30

GOODWIN [SANDS], the (off the E. Kent coast): 6/29; 7/145

GOODYEAR, [Aaron]: 8/171 & n. 5; 9/13; ~ his sister [Hester], 8/171 & n. 5

GORDON, Eleanor, Lady Byron: King's gift to, 8/182 & n. 1

GORHAM (Gorrum), Goody [Margaret], alehouse keeper, Brampton: P visits alehouse, 2/138 & n. 1, 148; 4/309; 9/212; lease, 3/222; 8/471 & n. 4

GORING, George, 1st Baron Goring and Earl of Norwich (d. 1663): returns from France, 1/106 & n. 2; stories of, 2/29 & n. 3; 7/290

GORING HOUSE, St James's Park: wedding at, 1/196; P admires, 7/203 & n. 1

GOSNELL, [?Winifred], companion to EP; later an actress: to enter EP's service, 3/256 & n. 2, 258, 260, 261, 263, 267, 269, 270, 271; arrives, 3/276; leaves, 3/277, 278; sings well, 3/256, 260, 276; dances, 3/263; at theatre, 3/294; becomes actress, 4/162 & n. 5; 7/422; 9/219; in *The slighted maid*, 4/163; 9/268; *The Rivals*, 5/267 & n. 2; *The Tempest*, 9/422; ~ her

sister, 3/256, 260, 294; her mother, 3/260, 261, 269, 278
GOSPORT, Hants.: P visits, 3/70
GÖTEBORG (Gothenburg, Gottenburg), Sweden: masts from, 5/215; Dutch ships wrecked at, 5/279; shipping to/from, 7/287, 390, 408, 420, 424 & n. 3; convoy for, 7/216 & n. 1; insurance for shipping, 7/25
GOTIER: see Gaultier
GOUGE, [Thomas], Presbyterian divine (d. 1681): refuses to use Prayer Book, 3/161 & n. 4
GRABU (Grebus), [Luis], court musician: appointment, 8/73 & n. 3; performances criticised, 8/458, 530; at rehearsal, 9/163
GRACE, Mrs, servant to Lady Sandwich: 2/16
GRACECHURCH (Gracious) ST: conduit in carrefour, 3/268; St Benet's church, 6/225 & n. 2; Fire, 7/276; road reconstructed, 9/285
GRAFHAM, Hunts.: 4/312
[GRAHAM, James, 2nd Marquess of Montrose]: poem by, 1/33 & n. 1
GRAMONT, Antoine, Duc de (d. 1678): Bristol's ingratitude, 4/212–3 & n.
[GRAMONT, Armand de], Comte de Guiche (d. 1673): praises English in Four Days Fight, 7/222 & n. 4
GRANDISON, Viscount: see Villiers, G.
GRANGER, [Abraham Gowrie]: forgeries, 5/12 & n. 5; 9/83–4 & n.
GRANT, ——, coffee-house keeper: 4/64–5
GRAUNT, Capt. John, statistician [see also Books]: collects Barlow's annuity, 2/103; 4/22; 7/40; his prints, 4/106; reports to Royal Society on Petty's ship, 4/263; social: on growth of population, 4/22; and music, 5/12; stories of suicides, 9/175; at Royal Society music meeting, 5/290; also, 4/100, 256, 334, 437; alluded to: 3/2
GRAVELEY, Cambs.: dispute over Robert P's land, 2/136, 148, 156, 174, 178, 180, 182, 205; Cotton closes, 2/148; courthouse, 2/182
GRAVES, ——: a drowsy preacher, 3/264

GRAVESEND, Kent: P/EP visit(s), 1/172–3; 2/67; 3/153, 156; 4/258, 260, 261; 5/190; 6/119, 181, 182, 183, 240; plague, 6/195, 249; naval action off, 8/349, 350, 351; ships, 8/379; defences, 8/257–8, 276, 313 & n. 1, 351; White's, 6/240; Swan Inn, 3/153 & n. 1, 156; Ship Inn, 8/258, 351; 9/300
GRAY: see Grey, [T.]
GRAY'S INN: P visits, 7/184; 9/311, 480; students' rebellion, 8/223 & n. 3; garden, 3/275
GRAY'S INN FIELDS: 7/72, 169; 8/453; 9/311
GRAY'S INN WALKS: 1/176; 2/98, 125, 128, 152; 3/60, 64, 77; 4/101; 9/311
GRAYS (Grayes-market), Essex: 1/104; 6/240; 8/257
GREAT LEVER HALL, Lancs.: 3/254 & n. 3
GREATOREX, [Ralph], mathematical-instrument maker, Strand: his armillary sphere, 1/14; waterpump in St James's Park, 1/263–4 & n.; lampglasses, 1/273; varnish, 4/153 & n. 2; schemes for fen drainage, 4/356 & n. 2; diving experiments, 5/268–9 & n.; to visit Tenerife, 2/21 & n. 4; sells P drawing pen, 1/273; and weather glass, 3/203; 8/84; teaches him mathematics etc., 2/112; mends his ruler, 3/266; engraves almanac on, 4/270, 277; social: 1/174; 2/110; 3/105; alluded to: 2/55; 4/152; ~ his apprentice, 9/437 & n. 3
GREBUS: see Grabu
GREEN(E), Major [John], fishmonger: 5/312
GREEN, [John], merchant: in customs dispute, 5/43 & n. 2
GREENE, [John], of Brampton: 2/138; 3/223
GREENE, [Levi], naval officer: dismissed for drunkenness, 9/5–6 & n.; made captain against Duke of York's wishes, 9/39
GREENE, [William], tar merchant: 3/137 & n. 3
GREENLAND: whale fishing, 4/125
GREENLEAF (Greenlife), Mrs ——: 1/190
GREENWICH, Kent   [omitting

passing visits. For P's stay in the Plague, see Clerke, Mrs]:
P VISITS TOWN: 3/63, 142–3, 152, 159, 164; 4/20, 79, 131, 149, 151, 219; 5/24, 129–30, 146, 193; 6/180, 188, 209; P/EP visit(s) on river outings, 4/283; 5/138; 6/106, 111; 7/134
PALACE: P visits, 3/63, 111; Queen's House, 3/63 & n. 5; building works, 5/75 & n. 3, 178; 6/169, 200; 9/485; King and Duke of York visit, 7/38, 141; Danckerts's painting of, 9/423 & n. 1, 438, 445, 465, 485; H. May's lodgings, 6/200; Navy Office moved to in Plague, 6/195 & n. 1, 200 & n. 3, 201, 203, 206, 208, 210, 213, 217, 221, 223, 253, 255, 293, 294; 7/19; garden, 6/212; park: replanted etc., 3/63 & n. 4; 4/99; gate, 6/335; P visits, 3/63, 111, 126, 152; 5/180; 6/169, 212; 9/485
PLACES: the Bear, 6/336; 7/181; castle, 3/63; 'common garden', 4/197, 273; Coombe Farm, 6/200, 201, 212 & n. 3; church (St Alphege), 2/12 & n. 3; 6/210, 227, 272, 316, 320, 338–9; 9/502; ferry, 6/158, 168; Globe inn, 2/115; 3/63; King's Head, 6/242, 250, 251, 254, 264, 294, 334; 7/141; 'music-house', 4/283; Ship inn, 3/164
MISC.: royal yachts at, 3/164, 173; 6/193; 7/141; plague, 6/200, 206 & n. 1, 210, 211, 212; 7/236, 239; 'riding', 8/257
ALLUDED TO: 4/149; 5/24
GREETING, [Thomas], musician: teaches P/EP flageolet, 8/87 & n. 2, 89, 110, 146, 205–6, 220–1, 223, 237, 286, 325, 329, 344, 369, 396, 400; 9/279; plays violin to P's viol, 8/325; and for P's dance at Navy Office, 9/464; P buys pipes from, 8/344; and music, 9/164 & n. 4; alluded to: 9/13
GREGORY, [Edward], sen., Clerk of the Cheque, Chatham 1661: house, 3/155, 156; social: 3/153
GREGORY, [Edward], jun., Clerk of the Cheque, Chatham 1665: Chest business, 5/196
GREGORY, [?Henry, ?William], musician: to teach EP viol, 7/377
GREGORY, [John], of the Exchequer, later of the Secretary of State's office:

court news from, 8/532–4; on Brooke House Committee, 9/254; social: 1/61; 2/127, 232; 7/116
GRENVILLE, Sir John, 1st Earl of Bath (d. 1701): brings Declaration of Breda to parliament, 1/122; awarded £500 by Commons, 1/128; on Naseby, 1/133; title-patent, 1/187–8 & n.; alluded to: 1/143; ~ his wife [Jane, b. Wyche], 7/394
GRESHAM, Sir Thomas (d. 1579): statue at Royal Exchange, 7/276 & n. 3
GRESHAM COLLEGE [see also Royal Society]: Exchange moves to after Fire, 7/280 & n. 2; aldermen meet at, 7/281–2 & n.; also, 6/7; 9/544, 562
GREVILLE, [Robert], 4th Baron Brooke (d. 1677): house and gardens at Hackney, 7/181–2 & n.
GREY (Gray), [Thomas], member of Fishery Corporation and M.P. Ludgershall, Wilts. 1669–72: opposes Creed as Secretary to Corporation, 5/251; views on trade, 5/300; approves P's report for committee, 5/315; political news from, 5/348; 7/360 & n. 4, 361; 8/422; alluded to: 5/262
GREY [?Henry, 6th] Earl of Kent (d. 1615): anecdote of, 2/114–15 & n.
GRIFFIN: see Griffith(s)
GRIFFIN, Col. ——: reports on Fishery lottery, 5/300
[GRIFFITH, George, Bishop of St Asaph 1660–d. 66]: consecrated, 1/276 & n. 2
GRIFFITH (Griffen), Sir John, soldier: to defend Gravesend, 8/258 & n. 3
GRIFFITH, [Matthew], Rector of St Mary Magdalen, Old Fish St (d. 1665): preaches at Temple, 2/75 & n. 2
[GRIFFITH], Will, alehouse keeper in Westminster [see also Taverns etc: Will's]: dies from plague, 6/186 & n. 1
GRIFFITH (Griffin), William, doorkeeper at Navy Office: reprimanded by P, 3/50; as messenger, 3/51; 4/220, 306, 421, 422; 7/388; 8/296; annoys P by sitting in Navy Office pew, 3/177; arranges lodgings for, 3/182; finds

maid for, 4/284; in search for Barkstead's treasure, 3/242; advises P on
coachhouse, 9/39, 46; also, 1/278,
298, 314; 3/199, 264; 4/54, 113, 154,
363; 6/27, 224, 258; 7/202, 305;
8/217; 9/43; ~ his wife [Alice],
8/226; son [William] dies, 4/416 &
n. 2; son [Thomas] christened, 5/176
& n. 1; maidservant: 5/249; 7/124; P
attracted by, 3/126; 8/120
GRIFFITH, ——, courtier: at court
ball, 7/372
GRIFFITHS [Griffin], [William], ward
of Sir W. Batten: 4/296; 8/433
GRIMSBY, Lincs.: M.P.s for, 8/454–5
GRIMSTON, Sir Harbottle, M.P.
Colchester, Essex: chosen Speaker,
1/115–16 & n.
[GRINDAL, Edmund; 'Cranmer' in
error], Archbishop of Canterbury
1576–d. 83: letter to Queen Elizabeth,
4/329–30 & n.
GROCERS' COMPANY: see London: livery companies
GROCERS' HALL: 1/71
GROOME, ——, clerk in the Signet
Office: 1/212
GROVE, Capt. [Edward], river agent
for the Navy Board: character, 4/73
& n. 1; defends P against Exchequer
Court bailiffs, 4/52; appointed shipping agent for Tangier, 4/85, 93; gifts
to P, 4/93, 120; wife's death, 5/38, 42;
match projected with Paulina P,
5/42–3; cowardice in Battle of
Lowestoft, 6/130 & n. 2; social:
4/157, 231, 365, 406; 5/95
GUERNSEY, Channel Is.: garrison,
6/142–3
GUILDFORD, Surrey: P/EP visit(s),
2/93–4; 3/69, 75; 9/273–5 passim;
King visits, 3/86; places: Red Lion
inn, 2/93–4 & n.; 3/69; 9/274–5;
Abbot's Hospital and grammar school,
2/93–4 & n.; 9/273 & n. 3; Holy
Trinity church, 2/94 & n. 2; 9/274 &
n. 1; St Catherine's Hill, 9/275
GUILDHALL (Yildhall): seamen paid
off, 2/45, 50, 53, 55; trials, 3/120;
4/402, 403; 9/382; Lord Mayor's
banquet, 4/354–6; P consults officials,
7/72; 9/33; rebuilt after Fire, 8/583 &
n. 1; 9/545–6 & n.

GUINEA: ships to, 1/313, 316; Anglo-
Dutch rivalry, 5/115, 160; Dutch
intentions, 5/121 & n. 2; conflicting
news from, 5/127 & n. 2; Holmes's
attack on Dutch, 5/160 & n. 4, 283 &
n. 1, 285, 341; de Ruyter's counter-
attack, 5/352–3 & n., 355 & n. 1; 6/42
& nn., 43, 46; English losses, 9/401;
fleets sail to: Dutch: 5/225, 231, 242,
273 & n. 1, 283, 295 & n. 2; English:
5/242, 246, 248, 250, 258, 264, 265,
295; also, 2/160; 4/363
GUINEA COMPANY: see Royal
African Company
GUINEA HOUSE: see Africa(n)
House
GUMBLETON, Mr ——: 9/289, 458
GUNFLEET, the, shoal off Essex
coast: fleet in, 6/99; 7/139, 140;
alluded to: 7/178, 300
GUNNING, Peter, Master of Clare
College, Cambridge 1660; Master of
St John's and Regius Professor 1661;
Bishop of Chichester 1669–75, of Ely
1675–d. 84: his London congregation,
1/42; weekly fast, 1/58; sermons, 1/3
& n. 1, 11, 32, 60, 76; 2/239; admini-
sters communion to Commons,
2/107; active against puritans, 2/147 &
n. 2
GUNPOWDER PLOT DAY:
observation of, 1/283; 2/208; 5/314;
7/358
GUNS, pistols [see also Ships: guns]:
P's pistol, 2/9; his French gun, 8/137
& n. 1; repeater guns, 3/310 & n. 4;
5/75 & n. 1
GUY, Capt. [Thomas], army officer:
1/101; social: 1/116, 182
GUY, Capt. [Thomas], naval officer:
7/344–5 & n.
GUYAT (Gayet), Susan: P takes to
Islington, 9/197; theatre, 9/198–9,
203; and Vauxhall, 9/216; sings with,
9/202, 217
'GUYLAND' ('Gayland', 'Guild-
land') [recte 'Abd Allāh al-Ghailān],
Moroccan warlord: relations with,
3/172 & n. 2; 4/283 & n. 1, 337 &
n. 1; 7/167 & n. 3; overthrown, 7/214
& n. 2; 8/347–8 & n.
GWYN, Nell, actress:
CHRON. SERIES: P's admiration, 6/73 &

n. 2; 8/193, 463; 9/189, 410; lodges in Drury Lane, 8/193 & n. 3; he meets at theatre, 8/27–8, 463 & n. 5; kisses, 8/27–8; she leaves stage for Lord Buckhurst, 8/334 & n. 2, 337, 371, 503; returns, 8/395, 402; poverty, 8/402; brought up in brothel, 8/503; King's affection, 9/19
HER PERFORMANCES: P admires in *The English monsieur*, 7/401 & n. 2; *The humourous lieutenant*, 8/27 & n. 3; *Secret Love*, 8/91 & n. 2, 101, 129, 235; *The mad couple*, 8/594 & n. 1; *The Duke of Lerma*, 9/81 & n. 3; criticises in *The Indian Emperor*, 8/395 & n. 2, 525; in *The Surprizall*, 8/590 & n. 3
ALLUDED TO: 8/196
GYLES: *see* Giles
GYSBY, Betty: 6/197

HAARLEM GAZETTE: *see* Newspapers
HABERDASHERS' HALL: funeral, 6/114; Committee for Compounding, 8/219
HACKER, Col. Francis, regicide: executed, 1/268, 269 & nn.
HACKET (Hacker), John, Bishop of Lichfield 1661–d.70: preaches at Whitehall, 3/84 & nn.; quarrels with Dean Wood, 9/45 & n. 2
HACKNEY: P boarded as child, 5/132; P/EP drive(s) to for pleasure [select]: 5/132, 175, 201; 6/74; 7/121, 133, 170, 181, 182, 202, 207; 8/150, 174, 296; 9/184, 197, 251, 272, 276, 546, 559; places: Drake's house and garden, 7/181 & n. 3; Brooke House and garden, 7/182 & n. 1; tavern by church, ib. & n. 3; church (St Augustine's) with organ, 8/150, 174; girls' schools, 8/174 & n. 4; 9/512; marshes, 9/546
HADLEY, [James], parish clerk of St Olave's, Hart St: falsifies plague returns, 6/206–7 & n.
HAES, Adriaen de, Dutch naval commander: 7/229 & n. 5
HAGUE, The: P visits, 1/138–50; description of town and people, 1/138–9 & nn.; [Binnenhof], 1/140 & n. 1; [Huis ten Bosch], 1/144 &

n. 4, 147; Voorhout, 1/145 & n. 1; bellman, 1/150; Sandwich to visit, 1/239; proposed venue for peace negotiations, 8/61 & n. 3, 69, 80 & n. 4, 92 & n. 2, 106; alluded to: 1/137; 2/103
HAILES (Hales), [?Thomas], of the Exchequer: death, 3/174 & n. 1; social: 1/24, 320
HAIRDRESSING: *see* Dress and Personal Appearance
HALE, Sir Matthew, Chief Baron of the Exchequer: 3/262 & n. 1
HALE(S), child of: *see* Middleton, John
HALES: *see* Hayls
HALFORD, Sir Thomas, of Wistow, Leics.: arrested for manslaughter, 9/111 & n. 1
HALIFAX, Lord: *see* Savile, Sir G.
HALL, Betty, actress: 8/27, 138; 9/395
HALL, George, Bishop of Chester 1662–d. 68: 9/10 & n. 1
HALL, Jacob, acrobat: 9/293, 313
HALL, Capt. [Robert], naval officer: acquitted of cowardice, 3/124
HALL, ——, husband of Anne (Nan) P of Worcs.: meets P, 1/196; death, 3/107
HALLWORTHY: *see* Hollworthy
HALSALL (Halsey), Maj. [James], Scoutmaster-General: sights Prince Rupert's fleet, 7/145 & n. 6; brings news of Four Days Fight, 7/177–8; Albemarle's protégé, 7/177, 203; navy business, 8/369–70 & n.; praises P, 8/370; social: 9/477–8
HALY, Lord: *see* Hawley
HAMBLETON: *see* Hamilton
HAMBURG: plague, 4/340; quarantine on ships from, 4/399 & n. 2; river frozen, 6/305, 308; Dutch capture/threaten ships bound for, 6/111, 112 & n. 5, 202, 248; shipping to/ from, 6/296, 300, 322; 7/9, 76, 408; possible refuge for English nonconformists, 8/275 & n. 1; provisions at, 9/542
HAM CREEK, nr Woolwich: 2/15; 3/178–9; 4/425
HAMILTON, Lady Anne: *see* Carnegie

HAMILTON, James, Bishop of Gallo-
way 1661–d. 74: besieged in house,
4/130–1 & n., 138
HAMILTON (Hambleton), [James,
George and Anthony], courtiers:
5/21 & n. 1; alleged liaisons with
Lady Castlemaine, 5/21; 'Hamilton'
[?Anthony], a favourite of King's,
5/56; 'Mr Hamilton' at court ball,
7/372
HAMMERSMITH: 9/531, 557
HAMMON(D), [Mary]: 6/212; 7/255
& n. 2; death, 9/161
HAMPSTEAD, Mdx: P visits, 6/155;
Belsize House, 9/281 & n. 4
HAMPTON COURT: Queen-
Mother at, 2/4; court at: on Queen's
arrival from Portugal, 3/89, 95, 97, 99,
100, 127, 146, 150, 157, 175; during
Plague, 6/142 & n. 1, 166–7; 7/24, 26;
Sandwich and family visit, 2/25; 3/94,
96, 103, 104, 120; P visits, 3/81–2 &
n.; 6/153, 154, 156, 166, 171; 7/24–7
passim; Charles I's escape from
(1647), 6/316–17 & n.; painting by
Danckerts, 9/423 & n. 1, 504; rooms
etc.: furniture and pictures, 3/82 &
n. 2; chapel, 6/166; council chamber,
ib.; garden, ib.; alluded to: 8/430
HAMPTON WICK, Mdx: P's lodgings, 7/26, 28, 29
HANBURY, [?Lucy], of Brampton:
3/220
HANES, Joseph: see Haynes
HANES, Lettice: see Howlett
HANNAM, Capt. [Willoughby],
naval officer: in St James's Day
Fight, 7/222 & n. 2; Coventry's
regard for, 7/409–10 & n.
HANSON (Henson), [Edward]: bullet
clock, 1/209
HARBING, ——, a poor fiddler: to
marry Jane Welsh, 6/16, 19, 22,
74–5; 7/103
HARBORD (Herbert), Sir Charles,
sen.: 3/57
HARBORD (Herbert), Sir Charles,
jun.: brings letters from Sandwich to
King, 3/57 & n. 1; knighted, 6/275 &
n. 3; serves in Tangier, 9/374 & n. 2,
418–19 & n., 422; his painting of
Tangier, 9/541 & n. 2; social: at P's
dinner for Sandwich, 9/423–4; and

for Hinchingbrooke, 9/552, 553;
also, 7/54; 9/345
HARBY (Harvy), Sir Job, Bt, customs
farmer, d. 1663: 3/188
HARDING, [John], court musician:
sings at party, 1/10–11 & n.
HARDWICKE, old: 5/272
HARDY, Nathaniel, Dean of Roch-
ester 1660–d. 70: at The Hague, 1/144;
sermon on death of Duke of Glouc-
ester, 1/245; poor sermon on Fire,
7/283
HARE, Mrs [Alice]: see Taverns etc:
Trumpet
HARGRAVE, [Richard], cornchand-
ler, St Martin's Lane: 1/182–3
HARGRAVE, Mrs: see Taverns etc:
Dog, New Palace Yard
HARLEY (Harlow), Sir Edward, ex-
Governor of Dunkirk: to be Governor of Tangier, 9/492 & n. 2
HARLEY, Maj. [Robert], brother of
Sir Edward: at The Hague, 1/147 &
n. 2
HARLINGTON, Mdx: P at, 6/216;
Arlington's title taken from, ib. &
n. 1
HARMAN, Capt. John, kted 1665,
naval commander: made rear-admiral, 6/129; serves under Allin,
6/147; convoys ships from Baltic,
6/328; conduct in Four Days Fight,
7/143, 154; voyage to W. Indies,
8/132, 147, 156; (untrue) story of
capture of Dutch E. Indiaman, 8/374,
375; victory over French, 8/430 &
n. 1; award of bounty to, 8/460–1 &
n.; conduct at Battle of Lowestoft,
8/491, 492; 9/80 & n. 3, 142, 158–9;
committed by Commons, 9/166–7 &
n. 167; released, 9/170; portrait by
Lely, 7/102; also, 7/97, 110; 8/130,
149; 9/142
HARMAN, Mary (b. Bromfield),
wife of Philip: marriage. 4/345 &
n. 2; P admires, 4/265; 5/223, 228,
229, 347; 6/164; 7/15; dies in childbed, 6/125, 152, 164; social: 5/266,
280; ~ her father [Thomas], 6/152
HARMAN, [Philip], upholsterer,
Cornhill: P's regard, 7/15, 73;
marriage, 4/345 & n. 2; son christened, 6/152; proposed match with

Paulina P, 6/164 & n. 1; 7/15, 23, 73, 78, 81(2); offers marriage to Kate Joyce, 9/127; P orders chairs etc. from, 5/251; 7/256, 286, 289; 9/332(2); social: 5/223, 228, 266, 280; 6/86, 126; 7/398; 9/111

[HARMOND, John], shoemaker: marriage, 7/355 & n. 2

HARPER, James, son of Mary: 1/83; 5/17

HARPER, [Mary], widow, tavern keeper, King St, Westminster [see also Taverns etc.: Harper's]: foolish talk, 1/83; 5/71; recommends maids for EP, 4/274, 276, 290, 297, 305; speaks ill of Pepyses, 5/185; alluded to: 4/341

HARPER, Tom: political news from, 1/48

HARPER, [Thomas], Storekeeper, Deptford: gossips about Brouncker, 8/226; helps P with accounts, 8/350; dies, 9/325, 330

HARPER, Mr ——: see Taverns etc.: Harper's

HARRINGTON, Sir James, of Swakeleys, Mdx; M.P. Rutland 1646–53: 6/215

HARRINGTON, James, republican author (d. 1677) [see also Books]: at Rota Club, 1/14 & n. 3, 61; political theories, 1/17 & n. 2, 20

HARRINGTON, William, merchant, of St Olave's parish: stories of fishing in Baltic, 4/412 & n. 3, 413, 414; attends Apposition Court of Mercers' Company, 5/37; death rumoured, 6/296 & n. 1, 305; at parish dinner, 9/179

HARRIS, [Henry], actor:

CHRON. SERIES: conversation, 8/29; 9/12, 138; leaves Duke's Company, 4/239 & n. 3; returns, 4/347, 411; ill, 8/73, 86; criticises Burt's acting, 8/575 & n. 3; and Orrery's Guzman, 9/522; portrait painted for P, 9/138, 140, 175, 206, 299

HIS PERFORMANCES: praised in Henry VIII, 8/73 & n. 2; P admires in Worse and worse, 5/215 & n. 1; Orrery's Henry V, 5/240 & n. 3; The Rivals, 5/267 & n. 2, 335; The man is the master, 9/133–4 & n.; The

royal shepherdess, 9/458–9; criticised in Mustapha, 8/421 & n. 6; and She would if she could, 9/53–4; his singing, 5/267; 9/53–4, 133–4 & n., 195; dancing, 9/458–9

SOCIAL: sings/dances at parties etc., 8/28, 29, 242; 9/13, 128, 134, 175, 289; to learn It is decreed, 9/131, 136; P visits at theatre, 9/178; with P and actors at Vauxhall, 9/218–19; also, 5/37; 9/139, 220, 256, 265, 292–3

ALLUDED TO: 9/108, 546

HARRIS, [John], sailmaker to the navy: gives dinner to Navy Board, 2/61; instructs P on sails, 4/7; gift to P, 6/57 & n. 2

HARRISON, Capt. [Brian], Deputy-Master, Trinity House: defeated in Trinity House election, 5/172 & n. 3

HARRISON, [James], doorkeeper at Whitehall Palace: 1/300

HARRISON, [?the foregoing]: social: 1/19, 21–2

HARRISON, Sir John, Customs Commissioner: 3/188 & n. 3

HARRISON, Maj.-Gen. Thomas, regicide: tried, 1/263 & n. 1; executed, 1/265 & nn.; head displayed, 1/269–70

HART, [Charles], actor: liaison with Nell Gwyn, 8/402 & n. 5; with Lady Castlemaine, 9/156 & n. 4; quarrels with Mohun, 8/569 & n. 3; P admires in The mad couple, 8/594 & nn.; alluded to: 8/196; 9/438

HART, Capt. [John], sen., naval officer: navy business, 8/283

HART, Maj. [Theo]: criticises Commons' committee, 1/249; administers oaths to P, 1/257; pays P as secretary to Sandwich's troop, 1/304; social: 1/232, 242

HARTLIB, Anne: see Rothe

HARTLIB, Mary: see Clodius

HARTLIB, Samuel, sen., author (d. 1662): 5/30

HARTLIB, Samuel, jun.: business with Lord Holland, 1/216; story of Duke of York's marriage, 2/40; accosts EP, 8/423; social: 1/206; 2/127; also, 1/219(2)

HARVEY, Sir Daniel, merchant: security for loan, 3/157 & n. 3; (erroneous) account of Four Days

Fight, 7/152 & n. 3; Lady Castlemaine lodges with, 8/366 & n. 1,
376, 377
HARVEY, [Elizabeth], Lady Harvey,
wife of Sir Daniel: 2/193; 3/12;
offended by Doll Common's mimicry, 9/415 & n. 1, 417
HARVEY, Sir Thomas: *see* Hervey
HARVEY'S: *see* Taverns etc.
HARVY, Sir Job: *see* Harby
HARWICH, Essex: lighthouse, 5/314;
6/3 & n. 4; English/Dutch ships at/off,
6/76, 86, 90, 104, 126, 296; 7/146, 148;
8/254(2), 281, 345, 357; hailstorm,
7/208; Duke of York inspects fortifications, 8/115 & n. 2, 125, 126;
militia raised, 8/255; Dutch attack,
8/317 & nn., 322 & n. 2; Duke of
York visits, 8/328; dockyard [*see also*
Deane, Anthony; Taylor, Capt.
John; Taylor, Capt. Silas]: visits by
Batten, 6/83, 115, 119; Brouncker,
7/408; pay at, 6/90; also, 6/330
HASLERIG: *see* Heselrige
HASLERIGGE, Mrs ——: her child
attributed to King or Duke of York,
3/227, 255
HASTINGS, Sussex: parliamentary
election, 1/102 & n. 2
HATCHAM, Surrey: 4/235
HATFIELD, Herts.: P/EP visit(s),
2/138–9, 149; 4/314; 5/298–9; 8/381–
2; places: Hatfield House: gardens
and vineyard, 2/139 & n. 2; 8/381;
chapel (St Etheldreda), 2/139 & n. 3;
5/298–9 & n.; 8/381 & n. 1; Salisbury
Arms: 2/138, 139; 8/381, 382
HATTON, Christopher, 1st Baron
Hatton (d. 1670): 2/221
HATTON, Sir Thomas, of Long
Stanton, Cambs., royalist agent: joins
King at Breda, 1/117 & n. 1
HATTON GARDEN: P visits, 8/110,
167, 597; Wardrobe moves to after
Fire, 8/597 & n. 1
HAVANT, Hants.: 3/69
[HAWKINS, Christian]: marriage,
4/121–3 & n., 260, 355
HAWKINS, Mr ——, shopkeeper, of
Rochester: P kisses wife, 8/312
HAWKYNS, [William], Canon of
Winchester: preaches at St Paul's,
5/66–7 & n.

HAWLES (Hollis), [Anthony], chaplain to the King: 1/157
HAWLEY [Haly], Francis, 1st Baron
Hawley (d. 1684): 6/110 & n. 2
HAWLEY, [John], Exchequer clerk:
PERSONAL: witnesses P's will, 1/90;
moves from Bowyers', 1/244; lives in
Westminster, 5/185; proposed by P
as match for Betty Lane, 4/431; 5/9,
41, 42, 71, 113, 242; also, 1/94
CAREER: P's substitute during absence,
1/18, 83, 238; 2/9; hopes for promotion, 1/35; accounts, 1/41–2, 61;
offered bribe, 1/77–8; said to have
resigned, 1/186; legal action against
Collier, 1/199–200 & n.; unspecified
Exchequer business, 1/13–14, 30, 33,
43, 49, 65; to serve Bishop of London,
2/9; refuses post as Sandwich's
steward, 5/185; becomes parish under-
clerk, 7/211
SOCIAL: visits/dines with P, 1/6, 10, 31,
57, 58, 189; 3/255; 4/51, 66; 5/25, 287,
304; gives P cane, 1/244; also, 1/8, 25,
88; 2/40, 227
HAYES, [James], secretary to Prince
Rupert: victualling business, 7/265,
266; fees, 7/323–4 & n.; news from,
7/339, 340; also, 7/84; 8/34, 52
[HAYES, Walter], mathematical-
instrument maker, Moorfields: com-
passes from, 5/271 & n. 3
HAYES, ——: to marry Jane Welsh,
6/16–17
HAYLS (Hales), [John], portrait painter:
GENERAL: to paint P and EP, 7/42–3 &
n.; looks at pictures in Whitehall,
7/97–8; and at S. Cooper's portraits,
9/139–40; P compares with Lely,
8/129; dines with P, 9/265; his house,
7/70 & n. 1, 396; 9/175
HIS PORTRAITS:
HENRY HARRIS: 9/138 & n. 2, 140, 175,
206; P criticises, 9/299
THOMAS HILL: P admires, 7/42–3 &
n.; displeased with finished version,
7/52, 53; buys copy, 7/125
ELIZABETH PEARSE: 7/93 & n. 1, 97,
108; a poor likeness, 7/111, 117, 120,
131; her son James, 8/439; 9/188; and
daughter Betty, 9/188
P's FATHER: sittings, 7/151 & n. 2,

8/149; 9/476; for fever/cold, 2/163; 4/17, 55; 5/197 & n. 3, 198; in pregnancy, 8/164; for smallpox, 8/524; for eye-strain, 9/261; amounts recorded, 3/76–7 & n.; 9/261

MAGIC: hare's foot, for colic, 5/359 & n. 1; 6/17, 18, 67; charms for staunching blood, etc., 5/361–2 & nn.

OPHTHALMIC: P tries globe light, 5/290, 291–2; green spectacles, 7/406, 419, 420, 424–5; new spectacles from Turlington, 8/486 & n. 3, 519; paper tubes, 9/270 & n. 3, 277, 278, 279, 286, 337, 384, 451, 482–3, 516; plaster vizard with tube, 9/463, 533, 547

SWEATING: for inflammation/itching, 4/39, 57, 89, 300; 5/260, 261; for pox, 8/217; in Russia, 5/272

MISC.: suitable clothing, 2/129; 5/240, 359; 6/66–7, 101; removal of earwax, 3/124; fluxing, for pox, 6/12; head shaved in smallpox, 4/339; gargling, 4/339; ten rules for curing infertility, 5/222

HEART, ——, landlord of Abingdon inn: 9/228

HEATH, [John], Attorney-General of the Duchy of Lancaster: to examine Chatham Chest accounts, 3/257 & n. 2

HEBDON, Sir John, merchant, agent for the Tsar of Muscovy: supplies hemp, 4/175 & n. 5; views on English court, 4/176; admires Lord Ashley's efficiency, ib.; and Dutch efficiency, ib. & n. 1

HEEMSKERCK, Laurens van, naval officer: in Holmes's Bonfire, 7/247; his ship design, 9/171 & n. 2, 198, 206, 488; dispute with lieutenant, 9/488

HELLEVOETSLUIS (Helversluce): 1/127

HELY, Mrs ——: gave P his 'first sentiments of love and pleasure', 4/247

HEMPSON, [William], Clerk of the Survey, Chatham: house, 2/70; cunning, 4/226; criticises Comm. Pett, 5/28; dismissed, 5/36, 140–1; stories of Batten's corruption, 5/141; also, 3/153; social: 2/68, 125, 126; ~ his wife, 2/68, 69, 125, 127; 5/141

HENCHMAN, Humphrey, Bishop of Salisbury 1660–3, London 1663–d.75: consecrated, 1/276 & n. 2; preaches at Whitehall, 7/99 & n. 1; at Maundy ceremony, 8/150 & n. 1; his patronage of city churches, 8/151–2 & n.; severity as landlord, 9/23 & n. 1; also, 1/259; 2/9; 5/67 & n. 2; 6/87

HENLEY, Sir Andrew: assaulted in court of Common Pleas, 7/391 & n. 1

HENRIETTA, Princess, Duchess of Orleans, sister of Charles II (d. 1670): marriage to Duc d'Anjou, 1/240 & n. 3; 2/56 & n. 1; dines in public, 1/299; appearance, ib. & nn.; sails to France, 2/1, 23; has measles, 2/11, 14; also, 4/26, 430 & n. 1

HENRIETTA-MARIA, Queen Mother (d.1669):

PERSONAL: appearance, 1/299; in debt, 5/59; portrait by Van Dyck, 6/222 & n. 2; 8/181 & n. 3; by Huysmans, 5/254; piety, 7/384; marriage negotiations (1624–5), 3/253–4 & n.; rumoured marriage to St Albans, 3/263 & n. 3, 303; 5/57–8 & n.; 8/564 & n. 1

CHRON. SERIES: returns to England, 1/260, 278, 279, 281, 282 & n. 2; to France, 1/302, 303, 322; 2/1, 3, 23, 93; to England, 3/128, 139, 143, 148; at public functions etc., 3/297; 4/216; 5/193, 196; relations with Frances Stuart, 4/366; 8/184; ill and goes to France, 6/142 & n. 3; 9/508 & n. 3; promotes peace/alliance with France, 7/420 & n. 2; 9/536 & n. 2; enmity to Secretary Nicholas, 8/534 & n. 1

HER COURT: dines in public, 1/299; at Somerset House, 3/191; keeps great state, 3/299, 303; 4/48–9; new buildings, 4/127 & n. 3; 5/63 & nn., 300; paintings, 6/17 & n. 3; also, 5/56

SOCIAL: at court lottery, 5/214, 215; dines with Lord Mayor, 4/193; seldom at public theatre, 8/55–6 & n.; dancing, 9/507; also, 1/297; 4/229

MISC.: sells reversion to Brampton manor, 3/176 & n. 3; her liking for pears, 8/417; also, 2/33; 4/20

ALLUDED TO: 3/82; 7/253; 8/161

~ her servants, 5/58 & n. 3; confessor, 4/111 & n. 3; Capuchins, 7/329

HENRY, Duke of Gloucester, son of Charles I: on *Naseby*, 1/152, 153; sails to England, 1/154, 157, 158; at theatre, 1/171; entertained by Speaker, 1/174 & n. 1; ill with smallpox, 1/240, 243; dies, 1/244, 245, 248; buried in Westminster Abbey, 1/249 & n. 2

HENRY VIII: portrait: at Audley End House, 1/70; 8/467 & n. 4; at Barber-Surgeons' Hall, 4/59 & n. 3; tomb, 7/58 & n. 6; 'King Harry's chair', 1/280 & n. 1; alluded to: 5/69

HENSHAW, Joseph, Bishop of Peterborough 1663–d.79: preaches at Whitehall, 9/563 & n. 2

HENSON: *see* Hanson

HERALDRY: P's arms, 3/50 & n. 3; 8/128 & n. 1; armorial glass at Great Lever, Lancs., 3/254; arms etc. of Duke of Monmouth, 4/107 & n. 2; 5/318 & n. 4; of Royal African Co., 4/152–3 & n.; hatchments etc. at funeral, 4/424–5, 427, 432; arms and title of Sandwich, 5/319; loss of Heralds' rolls in Fire, 7/410 & n. 3; book on, 8/422 & n. 4; also, 4/175

[HÉRAULT, Louis], minister of the French Church, Threadneedle St: sermons by, 3/296 & n. 2; 5/342

HERBERT, Sir C. sen. and jun.: *see* Harbord

HERBERT, Capt. [Charles], naval officer: 6/237, 238

[HERBERT], John, servant to Tom P: 4/183 & n. 2; servant to P. Honywood, 5/88, 244, 252; character, 5/241

HERBERT, Philip, 5th Earl of Pembroke (d. 1669): rumoured expulsion from Lords, 1/127 & n. 1; a founder of Royal African Company, 1/258 & n. 2; inefficient in financing Royal Fishery, 5/294 & n. 1; plays tennis, 9/150; views on Genesis, 9/150–1 & n.; alluded to: 9/230

HERBERT, William, styled Lord Herbert, 6th Earl of Pembroke 1669 (d. 1674): suitor to Elizabeth Malet, 7/385

HERBERT, [William], landlord of the Swan, New Palace Yard [*see also* Taverns etc.]: unwell, 8/124; finds P

tumbling Frances Udall, 8/224

HERBERT, Mrs ——, of Newington Green: 5/132

HERCULES PILLARS ALLEY: 9/42

HERMITAGE, the: 3/163

HERRING, John, Vicar of St Bride, Fleet St: preaches, 1/26 & n. 1; extruded, 3/162 & n. 1, 167; farewell sermon, 3/168; social: 1/229

HERRING, [Michael], merchant: lends money to Sandwich, 1/56 & n. 5, 72, 75, 80

HERRINGMAN, [Henry], bookseller at the New Exchange: P visits shop, 8/380 & n. 3, 383, 597–8; 9/248, 367

HERTFORDSHIRE: parliamentary election, 9/150 & n. 2

HERVEY (Harvey), Sir Thomas, Navy Commissioner 1665–8:

CHARACTER: 6/119; 7/359–60; 8/531–2

AS COMMISSIONER: appointed, 6/37 & n. 2; absent during Plague, 7/39; expects dismissal, 8/293–4 & n.; at pay, 7/359–60; in Carkesse affair, 8/76, 215; examines Gauden's accounts, 8/322; at Ticket Office, 8/531–2; in enquiries of Committee on Miscarriages, 8/494–5, 538; 9/80, 83, 84, 103; at launch, 9/100–1; unspecified business, 8/77, 178, 180, 314–15, 328, 479, 581

HOUSE: to occupy Turner's lodgings, 6/37 & n. 2; 7/105, 296, 359

NEWS FROM: 7/152; 8/328

SOCIAL: 6/77; 7/364; 8/65, 77, 220, 563–4; 9/82, 104, 115

HESELRIGE (Haslerig), Sir Arthur, Bt, republican politician (d. 1661): his quarrel with City of London, 1/16 & n. 1, 53 & n. 2, 60; and parliament, 1/50, 74 & n. 4, 81 & n. 1; raises support against army leaders, (Dec. 1659), 2/92 & n. 3

HETLEY, [William], of Brampton, Hunts.: on *Royal Charles*, 1/162, 168; gifts to P and Howe, 1/182; death, 2/18; property at Brampton, 2/28 & n. 2; social: 1/163, 177, 324; alluded to: 1/172

HEWER, [Ann], wife of Thomas: P meets, 1/268; moves to Islington after Fire, 7/275; 'well-favoured',

8/24; social: 8/48, 101, 158, 193, 197, 254; 9/417; alluded to: 1/215

HEWER, [Thomas], printer and stationer: P meets, 1/268; dies of plague, 6/225, 235; alluded to: 2/96; 4/106, 114

HEWER, Will, P's clerk in the Navy Office [P spells the name variously: Eure, Ewere, Ewre, Hewers]:

P'S OPINION: favourable, 1/202–3; 5/255; 8/207; 9/75, 368–9; unfavourable, 2/199, 201; 3/105; 5/301; 9/53

PERSONAL: ailments, 1/215, 216; 2/96; 4/28, 106, 114, 194, 291; 6/174, 175; 9/242; money etc. stolen, 1/233; 2/140; banking account, 8/263; hears common prayer for first time, 1/245; in mourning for father, 6/235; suggests Mercer as EP's companion, 5/229, 257, 258, 265; tries to negotiate her return, 7/300, 301, 303; admires EP, 9/398; gives her diamonds, 9/7; criticises P to EP, 8/171; P jealous of, 5/13, 19, 29, 44, 301; refuses proposal to marry Paulina P, 8/17; brideman to Jane Birch, 9/500; intermediary in Deb Willet affair, 9/367–71 passim, 373, 379, 411, 413, 518; also, 9/19

HIS WORK IN HOUSEHOLD:

GENERAL: arrives, 1/204; sent to church, 4/43; misdeeds, 1/219, 254–5; 2/34, 63, 79, 97; 3/35; 4/97, 171, 356, 358, 365; 5/13; P thinks of dismissing, 3/4–5; 4/318, 323; ears boxed, 3/105, 180; 4/166; to lodge elsewhere, 4/358, 363, 367, 371–2, 381, 382

ERRANDS/MESSAGES: 1/226, 232, 237; 2/10, 191, 212, 221; 3/80; 7/176; 9/405, 420

ESCORTS/ACCOMPANIES P/EP ON HOUSEHOLD/NAVAL BUSINESS IN LONDON: 1/212, 213, 218, 289, 324; 2/8; 4/435; 9/32, 256, 259, 382–4 passim, 401, 406, 408, 417, 421, 422, 430, 451, 465, 474, 484, 493, 519, 520; on journeys: Brampton etc., 3/206, 217–23 passim; 5/200–1; 7/92–3, 137; 8/381, 465, 468, 471–2, 474–5, 479; 9/145, 306, 310; Woolwich, 8/240; West Country, 9/223, 224, 226, 228–30 passim, 233, 234; Deptford, 9/335

MISC.: helps with accounts, 1/209;

9/564; puts P to bed, 3/182; reads Latin testament, 4/189, 190, 193, 204, 236; examined in Latin, 4/271; reads to P, 9/372, 387, 506; copies words of song, 9/242; helps to store cash, 7/367; 8/473–4; gives first aid to P's father, 8/237; in mourning for P's mother, 8/134; witnesses P's will, 8/266; also, 3/152; 4/166; 6/141; 9/209

HIS MOVEMENTS: his new chamber, 4/320, 323; lodges at Mercers', 5/256 & n. 1; his rooms, 7/152; returns to P's house in Plague, 6/154, 156, 174, 175; lodges at Greenwich, 6/233, 251; moves to Woolwich after Fire, 7/275, 280; returns to P's house, 7/287; in lodgings again, 9/458 & n. 2

NEWS FROM: 8/269–70, 297, 538; 9/99–100, 104, 397

HIS WORK IN NAVY OFFICE: allowance, 1/305 & n. 5; 4/353, 358; accused of leaking information, 3/5; fraud, 4/152; receiving gift, 9/283; and conspiring to get contract, 9/288 & n. 2, 389–91 passim, 393, 394; at Deptford, 2/95; 3/111, 180; Portsmouth, 3/69–75 passim; 7/75; Harwich, 6/90; accounts/estimates, 1/226–7; 6/205, 256, 271; 7/305; 8/48, 372; 9/260, 376; other financial business, 2/54–5; 4/20, 337; 7/25; 8/259; 9/376, 377, 486, 513; at launch, 5/305; in Carkesse affair, 8/94, 204, 212; inspects sunken ship, 8/293; organisation of office, 9/151; parliamentary business, 9/99, 102–3; clerical business (general): writes shorthand notes, 7/374; 9/480, 483; also, 3/119; 5/257; 6/108, 109; 7/100; 8/503, 557; 9/344, 478, 479; unspecified business, 6/32, 201, 202; 9/281, 282, 325, 364, 392, 547; ~ Tangier business, 5/267; 7/255; 9/267, 414

SOCIAL: sees pre-coronation procession, 2/83; on river trips, 3/95; 6/119; to see E. Indiaman, 4/210; entertains P/EP and others at lodgings, 6/130; 7/152; 9/458, 459; and Barnet, 8/382; at riotous party, 7/246; on trips to Islington, 7/317; and Epsom, 8/337–9 passim; at theatre, 7/423; 8/158, 435, 481, 521; 9/249, 296, 326, 521–2; in

Hyde Park, 8/193, 197; at Bartholomew Fair, 8/421; 9/299; at taverns,
1/263; 2/18; 9/443, 456, 494; at P's
house, 5/357; 6/263; 7/198, 249, 405,
421; 8/67, 82, 128, 146, 154, 187, 254,
276, 400, 442, 594, 599; 9/21, 30, 37,
107, 118–19, 194, 202, 219, 410, 454,
455; also, 4/267; 6/272; 7/351; 8/590;
9/477
ALLUDED TO: 1/267; 2/241; 3/113, 151,
301; 4/88
HEWET, [?Howet], Tom, clerk to
Sir W. Penn: accompanies Penn to
Portsmouth, 3/69, 75; offends P,
3/177
HEWITT, Capt. [Simon], merchant:
Tangier business, 6/163, 164
HEWLETT, [William], Irish rebel:
arrested, 4/80 & n. 4
HEWSON, Col. John, regicide: hanged in effigy, 1/28 & n. 4
[HEYDON, John], astrologer: im-
prisoned, 8/93, 94 & n. 1
HICKES, Baptist, 3rd Viscount Camp-
den (d. 1682): 1/210 & n. 2
HICKES, [Edward], Rector of St
Margaret Pattens 1662–d.82: dull
preacher, 9/311, 431; remarries, 9/311
& n. 1
HICKES, Sir William, Keeper of
Waltham Forest: entertains Navy
Board, 6/220–1, 222; house, 6/222 &
n. 1
HICKES, Capt. William, of Deptford:
reports on Deptford officers, 4/289 &
n. 1, 293; gives shells to EP, 4/293,
295, 298–9
HICKES'S HALL, Clerkenwell: quar-
ter sessions at, 1/311 & n. 3
HICKMAN, [Henry], ejected Fellow
of Magdalen College, Oxford (d.
1692): objects to reinstatement of
dons, 1/227 & n. 1
HICKMAN, Sir William, M.P. East
Retford, Notts.: 5/111
HIDE: see Hyde [?J.]
HIGHGATE, Mdx: rebels at, 2/10; P
visits, 5/64, 233; 6/155; 7/224;
Lauderdale's house, 7/224 & n. 2
HILL, [George], musical-instrument
maker: 1/58, 76
HILL, [?John], of Axe Yard: on board
Swiftsure, 1/100; also, 1/215

HILL, [John], merchant: victualling
business, 9/297–8, 312
HILL, [John], tar merchant: his high
prices, 4/184; forms ring, 4/187
HILL, Joseph, Fellow of Magdalene
College, Cambridge: P visits, 1/67 &
n. 5; his hopes of Savoy Conference,
2/141 & n. 2; and for religious
toleration, 4/243 & nn.
HILL, [Roger], court musician: ?1/276;
?2/209
HILL, [?Thomas], courtier: ?1/276
HILL, Thomas, merchant and P's
friend:
PERSONAL: P's affection for, 5/12, 83,
124 & n. 1; 6/18, 324; 7/41; portrait
by Hayls, 7/42–3 & n., 52, 53; P's
copy, 7/125; also, 6/98
CHRON. SERIES: assistant to secretary of
Prize Office, 6/21; in country during
Plague, 6/323, 327, 336; 7/36; goes to
Portugal for Houblons, 7/39, 64–5;
business with P, 7/53; draft letter from
P, 9/236–7
MUSICAL: 5/12, 124; 6/210, 282–3; sings,
5/120, 136, 194, 199, 209, 217, 226,
227, 261, 290, 321, 332, 337, 349; 6/24,
27, 32, 34, 50, 55, 73, 88, 125, 284, 323,
324, 326; sets three-part song, 6/219;
alluded to, 9/327
SOCIAL: talks of Rome and Italy, 5/332;
6/44; and 'of most things of a man's
life', 6/285; EP's valentine, 7/42;
visits Clarendon House, 7/42–3; at
P's house, 6/283, 323; 7/51; also, 5/83;
6/59, 63–4, 336–7
~ his brother [?Abraham]: 6/336–7
HILL, Capt. [William], naval officer:
brings gifts to Lady Sandwich, 3/25;
his ship founders, 5/321 & n. 3;
captured by French at Barbados, 8/511
& n. 2
HILL, ——, [?servant to Sandwich]:
1/84, 177, 181, 182
HILL, Mr ——, of Worcestershire:
1/55–6, 57
HILL, Mrs ——: blithe and young,
7/206
HILTON'S: 1/46
HINCHINGBROOKE, Hunts. [see
also Mountagu, Edward, 1st Earl of
Sandwich; Mountagu, Edward, 2nd
Earl of Sandwich]: P visits, 2/183;

3/219, 220, 223; 4/307, 308(2), 313; 5/298; 8/469–72 passim; 9/211; King to visit, 4/324; alterations, 1/313–14 & n., 324; 2/8, 27, 35, 48–9 & n., 79, 135, 183; 3/110, 220 & n. 5; 4/308; 5/298; 8/470; cloister, 2/183; courtyard, 4/313; garden (crooked wall, the Mount), ib.; 8/472; waterworks, 5/298; summer house, 8/472; park, 8/472; grove, ib.; drawbridge, ib.; Nuns' Bridge, ib.; chapel, 9/211; alluded to: 9/495

HIND COURT, off Fleet St: 1/199

HINDHEAD, Surrey: P and EP at, 9/274

HINGSTON (Hinxton), [John], organist: sets bass to *It is decreed*, 7/414 & n. 1, 420; court news from, 7/414; P consults, 8/574

HINTON, [Edmund], goldsmith: 6/332

HINTON, [John], physician in ordinary to the King: 6/332 & n. 2

HISTORY: P comments on uncertainty of historical knowledge, 8/99

HOARE, [James], sen., joint-Comptroller of the Mint: shows Mint to P and Mennes, 4/143–8 & nn.; social: 7/22; alluded to: 9/410–11 & n.

HOARE (Whore), [James], jun., Joint-Comptroller of the Mint: 9/410–11 & n.

HOARE (Whore), [Richard], clerk in the Prerogative Court of Canterbury: his calligraphy, 1/132–3 & n.; 6/339 & n. 3; also, 2/145

HOARE (Whore), [William], physician: social/musical, 1/10–11 & n.; 4/18; 5/174; 6/61; ~ his wife [Hester], 6/61

[HOBART, Sir Richard], Groom Porter: rebuked in sermon, 3/292–3 & n.

HOBELL, Mrs ——, of Banbury: proposed wife for Tom P, 3/176 & n. 1, 183, 192, 195, 201, 207, 210, 226; match broken off, 3/231 & n. 1, 232–3; 4/12, 253

HODDESDON, Herts.: P at, 9/213

HODGES, [?Edmund], of Lincoln's Inn Fields: 2/125

HODGES, [Thomas], Dean of Hereford (d. 1672): Lady Sandwich stays

with at Kensington, 5/178 & n. 5

[HODGKIN, Roger], Fifth-monarchist: executed, 2/18 & n. 2

HOGG, Capt. [Edward], commander of privateer *Flying Greyhound*: captures prizes, 7/418, 424; 8/7, 115–16, 341, 344; his knavery, 8/159 & n. 1, 352, 385; ordered to sea, 8/180; alluded to: 8/392

HOGSDEN: *see* Hoxton

HOLBEIN: portraits of Henry VIII at Audley End, 1/70; 8/467 & n. 4; and in Barber-Surgeons' Hall, 9/293 & n. 1; work at Nonsuch House attributed to, 6/235 & n. 3

HOLBORN [*see also* Taverns etc.: Black Swan; Chequer; George]: subsidence in, 5/82–3 & n.; Fire, 7/282; bearded lady, 9/398; Conduit, 3/148; 9/265, 375, 438; terminus for Brampton coach, 5/200; and York coach, 5/234; Cockpit at King's Gate, 9/154; alluded to: 4/44

HOLBORN CONDUIT HILL: 8/448; 9/520

HOLCROFT, John, P's cousin: 2/109, 111, 114

HOLDEN (Holding), [Joseph], haberdasher, Bride Lane: P buys hats from, 2/25, 104, 127; 4/274, 280, 300, 411; alluded to: 7/394

HOLDEN, [Priscilla], wife of Joseph: to recommend maid for EP, 4/279; finds nurse for Tom P, 5/82; at his death and funeral, 5/86, 87, 91; godmother, 7/394 & n. 2

HOLDER, [Thomas], Auditor-General to the Duke of York and Treasurer of the Royal African Company: 6/170; 8/27; 9/313 & n. 4

HOLDER [?Holden], ——: 7/394 & n. 2

HOLE HAVEN, Essex: quarantine harbour, 4/399 & n. 2; Dutch ship aground, 8/306

HOLINSHED, ——, tobacconist: marries widowed Kate Joyce, 9/127, 195

HOLLAND, Gilbert: gift to P, 1/95; social: 1/94

[HOLLAND, John], Rector of Holy Trinity, Guildford: 2/94 & n. 2

HOLLAND, Capt. Philip, naval

officer: advises P on perquisites, 1/82; commission renewed, 1/167 & n. 2, 168; political news from, ib.; P pays debt to, 2/116; attempts suicide and turns Quaker, 4/109; social: 1/15, 17, 56, 59, 196, 205; alluded to: 1/313, 316 & n. 2; 3/163; ~ his mother, 2/116; sons, 9/184

HOLLAND, ——, wife of Capt. Philip: a plain dowdy, 2/116; her mother a Quaker, 4/109; social: 1/17, 205

HOLLAND, Earls of: see Rich

HOLLAR, Wenceslaus, engraver (d. 1677): appointed royal scenographer, 7/378–9 & n.; engraving of city after Fire, ib.

HOLLES, Denzil, cr. Baron Holles 1661, ambassador to France 1663–6: Privy Councillor, 1/171; (untrue) rumour of dismissal, 8/596, 600; and of affronts to, 4/419–20 & n., 5/59–60 & n.; plenipotentiary in peace negotiations, 8/61, 63, 138 & n. 4, 175, 189 & n. 2, 216, 218, 249, 352; bewails state of country, 7/370; said to be wise, 8/70

HOLLES, Sir Frescheville, naval officer, M.P. Grimsby, Lincs.: conceited, 8/275, 292, 304; 9/516; service with fireships, 8/256 & n. 4, 272, 275, 379; at odds with Coventry, 8/304; 9/76, 92, 108–9, 129, 173; defends Brouncker in Commons, 9/62; attacks Sandwich, 9/68; his family in parliament, 8/454–5 & n.; Sir J. Smith's enmity to, 9/118; parliamentary news from, 9/135

HOLLES, [Gervase], father of Sir Frescheville: as M.P. for Grimsby, 8/454–5 & n.

HOLLIER (Holliard, Holyard), [Thomas], P's surgeon:

AS SURGEON: treats P for stone, 2/17; 4/327, 345–6; 5/162, 165, 241; colic, 4/280, 328, 329, 332, 345, 385–6; and deafness, 4/319, 320; bleeds P, 3/66, 76/7; his laxative pills, 4/153, 386; and draught, 4/332; consulted about sore, 4/252; general advice, 2/17, 201; 3/10; on diet, 4/280, 345–6, 385–6; treats EP for earache, 3/124; and abscess, 4/379, 382, 383–4, 385; 5/145;

8/584; his bill, 4/435; examines Tom Edwards for stone, 3/329; treats P's father for rupture, 8/110, 213–14, 237; denies efficacy of touching for King's Evil, 1/281; supports claims of naval surgeons, 5/261 & n. 1; also, 9/558

GENERAL: praises Luther and Calvin, 4/386; anti-Catholic, 5/256; 8/586, 587; 9/16; losses in Fire, 8/87 & n. 4; house in Hatton Garden, 8/110

SOCIAL: fuddled, 4/386; 5/309; 9/142; talks Latin, 4/386; 9/142, 279; also, 4/434; 6/9; 7/127; 8/64; 9/72–3, 356, 561

HOLLINS, [John], Fellow of Magdalene College, Cambridge, physician: P visits, 1/67; also: 9/212

HOLLIS: see Hawles

HOLLOND, [John], Surveyor of the Navy 1649–52: scheme for paying off seamen, 1/306 & n. 1, 308; MS. discourse(s) on naval administration, 3/145 & n. 1, 280, 285; 9/489 & n. 2

HOLLOWAY: P at, 2/184

HOLLWORTHY, [Mary], widow of Richard: spurns advances of Spragge, 8/141; reputation for gossip, 8/544; conceited, 9/13; social: 9/220, 245; alluded to: 8/172 & n. 3; 9/433

HOLLWORTHY, [Richard], merchant, of St Olave's parish: dies in fall from horse, 6/296

HOLMES, Gabriel: tried for arson, 8/319–21 passim & nn.

HOLMES, Capt. John, kted 1672, naval officer: P's low opinion, 9/157; wounded, 7/155; under Harman's command, 7/409–10 & n.; marriage, 9/157 & n. 2

HOLMES, Margaret (b. Lowther), wife of John: pretty, 8/241; marriage, 9/157 & n. 2; at Lady Penn's, 7/96

HOLMES, [Nathaniel], Rector of St Mary Staining 1643–62, and preacher to the Council of State (d. 1678): preaches at Whitehall, 1/53; n. 1

HOLMES, Capt. Robert, kted 1666, naval commander:

CHARACTER AND REPUTATION: 2/169; 4/196; 6/129; 7/180, 344, 409–10

CHRON. SERIES: friend of Sandwich, 2/169; fails to enforce salute from Swedish ambassador, 2/212 & n. 3,

222, 229; 3/14; returns from Mediterranean, 4/67; quarrels with sailing master, 4/67, 78, 81, 83, 84, 91–2; violent words against Mennes, 4/92; returns from Tangier, 4/299; voyage to Guinea, 5/160 & n. 4, 341; 6/42 & n. 2; sent to Tower, 6/6 & n. 2, 56; in Battle of Lowestoft, 6/122; resigns commission, 6/129 & n. 2; in Four Days Fight, 7/143; quarrel (?duel) with Sir J. Smith, 7/339–40 & n., 348; 9/107 & n. 3, 118, 123; influence in fleet, 7/158, 178, 332, 333; alliance with Rupert, 7/332; and with Buckingham, 9/382, 467; criticised, 7/204; attack on Dutch ships in Vlie ('Holmes's Bonfire'), 7/247 & n. 1, 257; in St James's Day Fight, 7/344–5; appointed 'land admiral', 8/149; his part in Buckingham – Shrewsbury duel, 9/26–7; also, 7/409–10; 9/148, 352

SOCIAL: 1/317; 2/175, 240; 3/14, 22

MISC.: brings ape from Guinea, 2/160; his advances to EP, 2/237; 3/4; offered king's wife in Guinea, 3/11; objects to brother's marriage, 9/157

ALLUDED TO: 1/176, 182

HOLT, Mr ——, of Portsmouth: 3/70

HOLYARD: *see* Hollier

HOLYHEAD, Anglesey: 4/256

HOMEWOOD, [?Edward], Navy Office clerk: victualling business, 7/139; social: 3/5

HOMOSEXUALITY: increase of, 4/210; P's innocence of, ib.

HONYWOOD, Col. Henry: good natured, 3/9 & n. 2; killed by fall from horse, 4/25 & n. 2; alluded to: 3/7

HONYWOOD, Michael, Dean of Lincoln: good natured, 3/9; 4/167 & n. 1; 5/192, 233; P's gift to, 4/171–2, 173; alluded to: 3/7

HONYWOOD, Peter: lodges with P's parents, 2/5 & n. 3; demonstrates 'Prince Rupert's drops', 3/9 & n. 3; lame, 5/20; pays allowance to John P, 5/142 & n. 3; 6/49; social: at P's stone feast, 5/98; 6/124; also, 4/167; 5/91; 7/173; alluded to: 3/7

HONYWOOD, Col. Philip, kted ?1662: 1/130; 9/74

HONYWOOD, Sir Robert, M.P.

New Romney, Kent: 1/199 & n. 3; ~ his wife, ib.

HONYWOOD, Sir Thomas: 1/181 & n. 1, 220; ~ his daughter, 1/220

[HOOGSTRATEN, Samuel van] painter (d. c.1678): perspective painting, 4/18 & n. 1, 26; 5/277

HOOKE, [Robert], curator of experiments to the Royal Society [*see also* Books]: P's admiration, 6/36–7, 95; at Royal Society, 6/36–7 & n.; lectures on comet, 6/48 & n. 1; and felt-making, 7/51 & n. 3; experiments in coach design, 6/94–5; 7/12, 20 & n. 2; borrows book of naval terms, 7/148; explains nature of sound, 7/239 & n. 1; 9/147; and blood transfusion, 7/373; social: 8/64; 9/544

HOOKE, [Theophilus], clergyman, P's contemporary at Cambridge: 2/44

HOOKER, Ald. Sir William, merchant, kted 1666, Sheriff 1665–6: drafts plague regulations, 6/211 & n. 5; story of child saved from plague, 6/212; dirty house, 6/328 & n. 3; supplies tallow, 7/41; criticises Penn, 9/170; alluded to: 8/152

HOOKER (of the Privy Seal): *see* Hooper

HOOPER, [William], minor canon of Westminster: 2/240 & n. 2

HOOPER (Hooker), ——, of the Privy Seal: 1/208, 212

HOPE, the, reach of the Thames: P at, 5/197(2), 317; 6/287; Coventry at, 7/70; fleet/ships in, 1/98; 2/95; 5/190, 193, 196; 6/65, 103; 8/251, 257, 263, 266, 298, 349; Rupert sails from, 5/291; pontoon bridge, 8/254 & n. 4

HORACE: ode recited, 8/472

HORE (Whore), Philip: dispute about Irish estate, 5/324 & n. 1

[?HORNECK, Anthony], German minister: his preaching, 8/580 & n. 1

HORSE DEALERS: tricks, 4/120; 9/384, 391

HORSE GUARD HOUSE: fire, 7/362–3 & n.

HORSE SAND, off Portsmouth: 2/11

HORSLEY, Mrs —— [also Horsfall, Horsfield]: P admires ('my new Morena'), 5/349 & n. 3; 7/135–6 &

politician, M.P. Stockbridge, Hants. (d. 1698) [*see also* Plays]: his proviso to poll bill, 7/399–400 & nn.; speech against royal prerogative, 8/9 & n. 1; adherent of Buckingham, 8/342; unpopular in Commons, 9/71 & n. 2; his phrase 'rowling out', 9/76; favours Penn's impeachment, 9/165; moves to have Sandwich recalled, 9/176; caricatured as Sir Positive At-All, 9/186 & n. 3, 190; caricatures Coventry in *The country gentleman*, 9/467, 471 & n. 2

HOWARD, Thomas, 2nd Earl of Arundel (d. 1646): 8/6–7 & n. 11

HOWARD, Thomas, 2nd Earl of Berkshire, Gentleman of the Bedchamber to the King (d. 1669): in 'dirty pickle', 7/218 & n. 2; Moll Davis his daughter, 9/24 & n. 2

HOWARD, Thomas: in duel, 3/171; flatters Albemarle, 8/147, 148

HOWE, Jack, brother of Will; deputy-clerk in Patent Office: 9/?202, 480

HOWE, Will, servant to Sandwich and Muster-Master:

CHARACTER: P's opinion: favourable, 3/90; 6/333–4; unfavourable, 4/390; 5/41; 6/50, 79, 231, 301; 7/22; disliked by Sandwich, 5/108; 6/54, 301

PERSONAL: ill, 1/178, 212; wears periwig, 4/390; his chamber and books in Gray's Inn, 9/480

AS SANDWICH'S SERVANT: accompanies to Holland, 1/85, 95, 143, 147–8, 173; and to Mediterranean, 2/120–1; 3/90; 5/302; as messenger, 1/93; 5/36; dislikes Creed, 1/101; 5/65, 107; his chamber in Whitehall, 1/222; at coronation banquet, 2/86; in Becke affair, 4/270, 281, 313, 379, 390, 395, 402, 419, 429; 5/36, 65, 70, 74; claims credit for P's appointment as Sandwich's secretary, 5/174; unspecified business, 4/173; 5/187; 7/52; 9/402; also, 1/191, 197, 267; 4/38

MUSTER-MASTER ETC. TO FLEET: appointed, 6/54–5 & n.; accounts, 6/62; 7/7, 31, 42; in prize-goods scandal, 6/230, 231, 299–300, 301, 303; arrested, 6/306, 309, 329; examined by Navy Board, 6/333–4; and by

Brooke House Committee, 9/91, 92, 363–4; scandal alluded to, 7/20, 22; also, 7/19

OTHER APPOINTMENTS: in Patent Office, 9/372 & n. 2, 480; asks for loan, 9/492 & n. 4; shows P Patent Office records, 9/479–80

MUSICAL: sings, 1/111, 113, 118, 144, 162, 164, 185–6, 194, 215, 285; 2/118, 121; 3/281; 4/63, 84, 149; 8/413, 429; 9/202; plays viol/violin, 1/104, 107, 114, 129, 285; 3/184, 187, 216, 281

SOCIAL: at taverns, 1/75, 259; 2/102; 3/248, 298; on *Swiftsure*, 1/96, 98, 100(2); and *Naseby*, 1/103, 105, 110, 115, 116, 120, 131, 166; visits Deal, 1/119; and The Hague, 1/149; at Wardrobe dinner, 2/104; dines with/ visits P, 1/195; 5/162, 196; 8/5, 223, 365, 464, 570; 9/138, 255, 260, 279, 286, 464, 482, 533; at Sandwich's lodgings, 2/37, 41; 3/266, 282; 4/21–2, 117; 5/40; in Hyde Park, 4/119–20; at Vauxhall, 9/219; at theatre, 9/304, 322; also, 1/71, 74, 208, 209; 2/102–3

HOWELL, [Richard], turner to the navy: supplies files, 2/171; tells P of malpractices, 6/117 & n. 1; also, 2/231, 232; 3/298; 6/309 & n. 1; 7/274; ~ his widow, 9/311 & n. 1

HOWELL (Houle), [William], historian, Fellow of Magdalene College, Cambridge, 1652–?60 (d. 1683): news from, 4/274–5 & n.; at coffee-house with Dryden, 5/37; social: 1/45

HOWET: see Hewet

HOWLETT, Betty: see Mitchell

HOWLETT, Lettice (Lissett), P's aunt: to live with P's father at Brampton, 2/183; visits P, 8/442 & n. 1, 448; 9/195 & n. 1; at theatre, 8/450; ~ her son, 2/183

HOWLETT, Mr ——, shopkeeper, Westminster Hall: as tax-collector, 8/121; social: 5/41; 7/123, 197; 8/34, 72, 236; 9/99; alluded to: 4/234, 368; 5/71; 7/284, 337, 338, 378, 418

HOWLETT, Mrs ——, shopkeeper, wife of the foregoing: ill, 8/120, 121, 151; complains of son-in-law, 8/479; social: at her shop, 4/242; 5/41; 7/61, 378; 8/47; at christenings, 7/394; 8/202; also, 7/123; 8/34, 72;

9/99, 594; alluded to: 4/234; 8/400; 9/103

[HOWORTH, John], Master of Magdalene College, Cambridge 1664–8 and Vice-Chancellor 1667–d.68: 8/469 & n. 1

HOXTON, Mdx: P visits, 5/272; 9/197, 513; Baumes House, 5/272 & n. 2; 9/197

HUBBARD (Hubbert, Hulbert), Capt. [John jun.], naval officer: reputation, 7/333–4; 8/485–6 & n.; refuses to strike flag to French, 9/560 & n. 2

[HUBERT, Robert]: hanged for starting Fire, 7/357 & n. 2; 8/81 & n. 4

HUDSON, [James], wine cooper: 6/151; 8/265–6

HUDSON, [?John], of Westminster: 1/10, 17

HUDSON, [Michael], chaplain to Chatham Dockyard: his preaching, 4/258 & n. 2

HUDSON, [Nathaniel], scrivener, the Old Bailey: 5/114, 168

[HUGHES], Peg, actress: 9/189 & n. 3

HUGHES, [William], ropemaker, Woolwich: reports on yard, 3/101 & n. 3; dismissed, 3/197; to swear against Coventry, 4/170; a rogue, ib.; also, 5/256–7

HUGHES, ——, housekeeper to Parliament: 7/305

HULBERT: see Hubbard

HULL, Yorks.: garrison prepared against invasion, 7/185 & n. 1; prize ships at, 8/341, 344, 349, 352, 369, 385

HUMFREY, Pelham, composer (d. 1674) [see also Musical Compositions]: returns from France, 8/515 & n. 5; disparages King's music, 8/529–30; conducts at court, 8/532, 534

HUNGARY: Turkish advance into, 4/316 & n. 1, 321, 372 & n. 2

HUNGERFORD, Margaret, Lady Hungerford, widow of Sir Edward: 9/534–5 & n.

HUNGERFORD, Wilts.: P visits, 9/228

HUNT, [Elizabeth], of Axe Yard, wife of John:
CHRON. SERIES: P's regard, 4/3; 6/142; 7/92, 219; ill, 2/15; birth of son, 2/234,

235, 236; fat, 7/52; related to Cromwells, 7/94; returns from Cambridge, 7/219 & n. 2; also, 1/94, 254, 257; 2/10, 35, 53; 3/180; 4/361; 5/174
SOCIAL: at P's house, 1/6, 37, 202–3; 3/36, 75; 4/4, 114, 293, 365; 5/146, 340; 6/37; P/EP visit(s) etc., 1/217; 2/55, 87, 207, 240; 3/7, 51; 4/182, 274, 276; 5/51, 79; in Hyde Park, 4/73; 5/126; at P's stone feast, 5/98
~ her cousin, 5/146

HUNT, [?George], musical-instrument maker, Paul's Churchyard: alters theorbo, 2/201, 203; brings bass viol, 4/104–5; makes viol, 4/282, 284; lends lute, 5/258; alluded to: 2/209

HUNT, [John], of Axe Yard, friend and neighbour of P; sub-commissioner of the Excise:
CHRON. SERIES: P's regard, 4/3; 7/219; political news from, 1/58, 77; troubled at return of secluded members, 1/63 & n. 5; dismissed (temporarily) from Excise, 1/254 & n. 4, 257 & n. 2; 2/53 & n. 2; returns from duties in Cambridge, 7/44, 219 & n. 2; 8/84–5 & n.; prospers, 7/92; informs P of Betty Becke, 4/392; stands bail for Hayter, 6/116
SOCIAL: at P's house, 1/6, 37, 49, 53; 2/216; 3/25, 36, 75, 86, 105; 4/83, 118, 293; 5/72, 174, 340; 7/132; in Hyde Park, 5/126; also, 1/8, 27; 2/67, 87; 3/76, 191; 4/231; 9/165
ALLUDED TO: 4/42; 5/167
~ his kinswoman, 5/174

HUNT, John, son of John: birth and christening, 2/234, 235, 236; EP's gift as godmother, 3/7; also, 4/276, 293; 5/146

HUNT, Mrs ——, of Jewen St, Deb Willet's aunt: her conversation, 8/569; 9/332; also, 9/346, 520

HUNTINGDON, Maj. Robert: intermediary between Charles I and Cromwell, 5/335 & n. 2

HUNTINGDON, Hunts.: P visits, 2/137, 148; 3/220; 4/312, 313; 9/212, 224; at school, 1/87 & n. 4; town waits, 8/474; parliamentary elections, 1/86–7 & n., 99 & n. 1; assizes, 2/145, 148; Sandwich appointed Recorder, 4/30 & n. 1, 62; anecdote about

Mayor, 8/232–3 & n.; Mountagus at school at, 8/472 & n. 1; places: Crown Inn, 2/137; 3/220; 4/312; church, 4/313; bridge, 8/220; Chequers Inn, 9/212

HUNTINGDONSHIRE: list of J.P.s, 1/184 & n. 1

HUNTSMOOR, Bucks.: Bowyers' house, 1/85, 88, 131, 170, 177; alluded to: 3/65

HURLESTONE, [Nicholas]: elected Master of Trinity House, 6/107 & n. 1; dies, 6/298

HUSON: *see* Hewson

HUTCHINSON, [Richard], Treasurer of the Navy 1651–60: helps check accounts, 1/312; his accounts scrutinised, 2/100 & n. 1; paymaster to Navy Treasurer, 9/357 & n. 1; at Chatham dockyard, 9/495, 499; his religious bent, 9/495; also, 1/82, 188

HUYSMANS, Jacob, painter (d. 1696): reputation, 5/254, 276 & n. 3; P views his work, 5/254 & n. 4; to paint EP, 5/276 & n. 3; 6/113

HYDE, Anne: *see* Anne, Duchess of York

HYDE, Edward, cr. Earl of Clarendon 1661, Lord Chancellor 1658–67 (d. 1674):

PERSONAL: created earl, 2/80; patent of nobility, 2/75 & n. 3; illnesses, 1/144; 3/290; 5/205, 328, 329; 6/11; 8/181; King's grants, 2/157 & n. 3; poor, 8/402 & n. 2; rich, 8/592; ungenerous, 8/418; eloquent, 7/321; as father-in-law to Duke of York, 8/214, 438; also, 6/252 & n. 1

POLITICAL CAREER [for relations with colleagues, *see* under names; for formal speeches to parliament, *see* Parliament]: at Worcester House Conference, 1/271; daughter's marriage to Duke of York resented, 1/284; 2/40–1 & n.; 4/223 & n. 5; 5/60 & n. 4; 8/287, 367; accused of cupidity, 2/213; 4/223 & nn.; 6/39, 218; 7/55; 8/185–6, 265, 269, 270, 402, 592; of selling places, 4/166; and of raising army, 3/15 & n. 2; proposes proviso in bill of uniformity, 3/49 & n. 1; fluctuating influence with King, 3/290, 303; 4/115, 123, 137, 195, 196,

213; 5/73, 345; 9/387; unpopular in Parliament, 3/290–1; and court, 5/73, 345; Bristol's abortive impeachment of, 4/219, 223–5 & nn., 229, 231 & n. 2, 367; 8/445; attempts to obtain loan from city, 7/174; hostile to war, 7/411; 8/145, 287–8; despairs of its conduct, 8/330; alleged responsibility for disasters, 9/40; said to favour standing army, 8/366–7 & n.; appointed Treasury Commissioner, 8/223; opposes parliamentary appropriation of revenue, 8/140 & n. 4; and Downing's plan for Treasury bills, 8/520 & n. 2; house attacked by mob, 8/269, 270; opposes recall of Parliament in Medway crisis, 8/293 & n. 1, 506; dismissed, 8/304, 401–2 & nn., 406, 409–10; 9/476; asks for common law trial, 8/401–2, 403, 544–5; his hopes from parliament, 8/432, 434; parliament thanks King for dismissal, 8/476 & n. 2, 479, 480, 482 & n. 2, 525; impeached for high treason, 8/427, 478, 502, 506, 507, 509, 518, 521, 522, 523 & n. 3, 526–9 passim, 534, 541–5 passim, 555–6, 557–8 & n.; factions in parliament, 8/532–3, 542, 544, 571, 596; flight and petition, 8/561 & n. 4, 563, 566, 568, 577; banished, 8/565–6 & n., 578, 583; satirised, 9/256; rumours of dismissal of supporters, 8/596, 597, 600; 9/2, 9–10, 17; rumours of return, 9/153–4, 341, 347, 417, 536; said to favour French alliance, 9/536 & n. 2

NAVY BOARD BUSINESS: high opinion of P, 3/171, 172; 5/321; 6/91, 292; 8/60; criticises him, 7/334; receives P's papers on navy debts, 1/225, 226; advises P on treatment of parliament, 1/226; and Board in Field case, 4/52; his timber, 5/203–6 passim, 210, 212–14 passim, 216, 218, 219, 238, 318; hears navy business in Council/ Cabinet, 6/10–12; 7/260, 312, 377; approves Carteret's replacement, 8/301; unspecified business, 7/242; 8/30

TANGIER BUSINESS: P applies to for money, 6/154; 7/336; 8/74, 75; criticises P, 6/277; and committee, 8/61; also, 7/321; 8/60

AT COUNCIL/CABINET MEETINGS (business unspecified): asleep, 7/260, 377; also, 5/317; 6/76, 78, 91, 105, 154; 7/107, 260, 312, 336; 9/425
JUDICIAL WORK: in trials, 1/225; 5/204, 205; also, 1/226, 272
HOUSES [see also Berkshire House; Clarendon Park, Wilts.; Dorset House; Worcester House]: Clarendon House, Piccadilly: building, 6/39 & n. 1; P visits/admires, 6/39; 7/32, 42, 49, 87, 93, 220; 8/175; attacked by mob, 8/269, 270; pictures, 8/175 & n., 346–7; furnishings, 8/207
SOCIAL: 4/173; at Lord Mayor's banquet, 4/355
MISC.: with King at The Hague, 1/144; attends coronation, 2/84; in town during Plague, 6/142; his bookbinder, 9/480
ALLUDED TO: 2/118; 4/61
HYDE, Edward, son of the Lord Chancellor: 4/341
HYDE, Frances, Countess of Clarendon, wife of the Lord Chancellor: plain, 2/80; at court, 8/33; death, 8/570 & n. 2
HYDE, Lady Henrietta, wife of Laurence: marriage, 8/190 & n. 3; social: 9/468
HYDE, Henry, styled Viscount Cornbury, eldest son of the Lord Chancellor; M.P. Wiltshire; succ. as 2nd Earl of Clarendon 1674 (d. 1709): attitude to Clarendon's impeachment, 8/427, 544–5 & n.; expelled from court, 9/53 & n. 2; social: 4/341
HYDE, Laurence, son of the Lord Chancellor, M.P. Oxford University, cr. Earl of Rochester 1681 (d. 1711): marriage, 8/190 & n. 3; speech on Clarendon's impeachment, 8/539 & n. 3; expelled from court, 9/53 & n. 2; social: 4/341
HYDE, Sir Robert, Chief Justice of the King's Bench 1663–5: tries marine insurance case, 4/403–4; ignorant of sea terms, 4/403; death, 6/96 & n. 3; alluded to: 5/73
HYDE (Hide), [?John], of St Olave's parish: 8/224; ~ his brother, 8/225
HYDE PARK [see also Gardens; Mulberry Garden]: May Day parade,

1/121 & n. 1; 2/91; 4/119–20; 5/139; 8/196–7; 9/182, 537, 540–1; 'the Tour': 4/95 & n. 3; first day of, 6/60; also, 6/89; 9/141–2, 143, 555; P complains of dust, 5/130, 139; 6/77; 8/196; 9/136; footrace, 1/218 & n. 1; King/Duke of York review(s) troops, 4/216–17 & n.; 9/308, 557; other visits by King, 5/126; 7/106; 8/288; the (Keeper's) Lodge: P visits for first time in year, 9/533–4; also, 9/142 & n. 1, ?154, 156, 175, 184, 222, 260, 541; other visits by P/EP to Park: for first time in year, 7/106; 9/122, 533–4; for first time in own coach, 9/487; find gates locked, 9/549; also, 3/78, 288; 4/73, 95, 120; 5/100, 130, 138; 7/144, 178; 8/207; 9/154, 168, 170, 269, 270, 282, 504, 515, 530–1, 541–2, 549, 556, 563

'IANTHE': see Betterton, M.
IBBOT, [Edmund], naval chaplain: P's opinion, 1/107; sermons etc. on voyage to Holland, 1/97, 101, 137; believes in extemporary prayer, 1/105; at Delft, 1/145; social: 1/100, 147, 149, 162; also, 1/95, 129
ILFORD, Essex: P at, 3/169; 6/126
IMPERIALE, Cardinal (Lorenzo), Cardinal-Governor of Rome: 4/24 & n. 2
IMPINGTON, Cambs.: P/EP visit(s), 2/136, 147–8, 180; 3/218; 9/253, 301, 306, 309; church and parson, 2/147 & n. 3; Roger P's house, 4/159; alluded to: 9/348
INCHIQUIN, Lord: see O'Brien, M.
INDIA: see East Indies
INDUSTRIES [for shipbuilding, see principally Ships; and under dockyards]: bricks, 9/314 & n. 3; cloth, in England, 5/300; in Spain, 8/79–80 & n. ; felt, 7/51 & n. 3; glass, 9/457 & n. 2; gloves, 8/425 & n. 4; ironworks in Forest of Dean, 3/165 & n. 1; mining in Nova Scotia, 8/426 & n. 1; mint (royal), 2/38–9; 3/265 & n. 2; 4/70, 143–7 & nn.; ropes, 6/34 & n. 3; sails, 4/7; textiles, at New Bridewell, 6/65–6 & n
INGOLDSBY, Col. [Richard]: captures Lambert, 1/115 & n. 1, 117; given commission, 8/265 & n. 5, 323

INGRAM, Sir Arthur, merchant: 6/108; 7/169

INGRAM, Sir Thomas, Privy Councillor: courteous, 7/20; appointed to Tangier Committee, 6/7; financial business, 6/33, 121, 133; 9/371; victualling business, 6/117, 171; attends meetings/unspecified business, 6/58, 61, 166; at Council committee, 8/278; ~ his clerk, 1/186

INGRAM, Mrs ——: 5/304

INNER TEMPLE: Reader's Feast, 2/155 & n. 2; 9/465–6 & n.; revels, 4/32 & n. 1; gaming in hall, 9/3 & n. 1; riot, 9/465–6 & n., 511–12

INNS: *see* Taverns etc.

INNS OF COURT: *see* under names

INSECTS: spontaneous generation, 2/105 & n. 4; bees: in Baltic, 4/413; apiary, 6/97 & n. 3; fleas: in P's bed, 5/260; also, 3/70; glow-worms: 8/340; gnats (?mosquitoes): at Brampton, 2/135, 138; in Fens, 4/311 & n. 1; lice: P suffers from, 9/231, 424; lice or nits: in P's hair/periwig, 5/212, 8/133, 146; 9/239, 424; moth: courtiers chase, 8/282

INSURANCE (marine): peacetime rates, 4/395 & n. 3, 394–7 passim; wartime, 5/126; story of fraud, 4/401, 403; also, 6/202, 328, 329; 7/25

INVENTIONS and machines [*see also* Entertainments: clockworks; Guns; Royal Society; Scientific and Mathematical Instruments; Ships; Watches and Clocks]: calculating machine, 9/116–17 & n.; chimney design (to prevent smoking), 4/315 & n. 1; claviorganum, 8/25 & n. 4; coins with milled edges, 4/147; diving bell, 5/268–9 & n.; false teeth, 5/293; fire-engines, 8/191, 320; fountain pen, 4/263–4 & n., 278; glass apiary, 6/97 & n. 2; glass coach, 8/396, 446; joke chair, 1/280 & n. 1; lamp glasses, 1/273; 5/237, 291–2; lighthouses, 5/314; 6/3 & n. 4; mechanical organ, 2/115–16 & n.; mine, 3/45–6 & n.; 4/378; sawmill, 3/118; smoke jack, 1/273; theatrical machinery, 2/155 & n. 1; 4/126 & n. 2, 182 & n. 3; 7/76, 77; varnish, 4/153 & n. 2; 7/147–8; waterwheel, 1/263–4; windmill, 9/520

IPSWICH, Suff.: 6/217

IRELAND: appointment of Lord-Lieutenant, 1/227–8 & n.; his establishment reduced, 9/41 & n. 1; declaration against nonconformity, 2/67 & n. 2; troops transported to Portugal, 3/85; land settlement, 4/66 & n. 1, 80, 82, 223 & n. 4, 295; 5/61, 324, 346; 9/119; rumour of dissolution of parliament, 4/80; Castle Plot, 4/94 & n. 2, 100, 285 & n. 3; controversy over cattle trade, 7/313–14 & n., 343; free quartering of soldiers, 8/518–19 & n.; Irish as French recruiting agents, 8/601

IRETON, Henry, regicide (d. 1651): body exhumed and hanged, 1/309 & n. 4; 2/24, 27; head displayed, 2/31 & n. 4

IRETON, [?Jerman, of Gray's Inn]: 9/464

IRETON, John, republican (d. 1689): imprisoned after Yarranton plot, 2/225 & n. 1

IRONGATE [Stairs], Little Tower Hill: 7/273

IRONMONGERS' HALL, Fenchurch St: funeral, 3/268

ISACKSON, ——, linendraper at the Key in Cheapside: 1/277

ISHAM, Capt. [Henry]: accompanies Sandwich to Holland, 1/95, 96, 102, 115, 126, 136, 137 & n. 2; to go to Portugal, 2/161, 163; brings letters from Lisbon, 3/51; social: 1/92, 97; 2/142

ISLE OF DOGS, the: P and party spend night on, 6/168; stranded on, 6/175; also, 6/331

ISLE OF MAN, the: 4/240

ISLE OF WIGHT [*see also* St Helen's Point; Newport]: 7/334; Charles I's escape to (1647), 6/316

[ISLEWORTH, Mdx]: P at, 6/199 & n. 1

ISLINGTON: P/EP visit (their 'grand tour'): 5/132; 6/86; 7/108, 122, 126, 129, 167, 170, 202, 223, 265, 267, 317; 8/211; 9/251, 271–2, 521, 558; plague in, 6/175–6; the fields/ponds: P visits, 3/57, 59; 9/32; boyhood memories, 5/101 & n. 1; Katherine Wheel, 7/167, 261; King's Head ('the old house', 'the great house'): boyhood memories, 5/101; P/EP visit(s), 2/98, 125; 5/133; 6/112; 7/149, 220; 8/174–5, 219, 234, 296, 344, 390; 9/47, 133, 184, 197, 513; J. Birch's wedding at, 9/500; White Lion, 9/32

ITALY: homosexuality, 4/210; gardens, 7/213

IVAN IV, Tsar of Russia 1547–84: anecdotes of, 3/188–9 & n.

IVY LANE: 9/494

JACKSON, John, sen., of Ellington, Hunts.: P's opinion, 9/56, 57; marries Paulina P, 8/585 & n. 6; 9/17, 18–19, 100 & n. 2; marriage settlement, 9/55, 64–5; P's father to live with, 9/212; also, 9/61, 210, 215

JACKSON, John, jun., P's nephew and heir: vol. i, pp. xxxix, lxxi–lxxii

JACKSON, Paulina (b. Pepys), P's sister and wife of John Jackson sen.:
P's OPINION ETC.: ill-natured, 1/290; 3/223; 4/3; 5/54; 8/475; 'good bodied' but 'full of freckles', 7/138; old and ugly, 8/471; fatter and comelier, 9/210

CHRON. SERIES: birth date recorded, 5/361 & n. 1; servant in P's household, 1/288, 290–1, 324; 2/1, 4; proud and idle, 2/139; dismissed and moves to Brampton, 2/153, 161/2, 167; 5/234; P's small money gifts to, 2/172; 3/223; 5/268; 8/474; unworthy of becoming EP's gentlewoman, 4/3, 15, 49; father defends, 4/108; and seeks dowry for, 4/366; 5/44; growing old, 4/439 & n. 1; P's hopes of marrying her off, 5/42–3, 152, 183; plans match with Harman, 6/163–4 & n., 170; 7/15, 23, 72, 73, 81–2; match proposed with Ensum, 7/78 & n. 2, 81–2, 86, 91, 104, 170, 405; and with B. Gauden, 7/88–9; P's legacy to, 7/134; stays with P in London, 7/40, 137, 138, 140, 175; match proposed with Hewer, 8/17; with Cumberland, 8/118 & n. 3; 9/17; and with Barnes, 8/261 & n. 2; her match with Jackson, 8/539 & n. 1, 585; 9/16–17, 18–19, 47, 55, 56, 58, 61, 64–5; P provides dowry, 9/16–17, 19, 56, 61, 97; marriage, 9/79, 100, 108; to live at Ellington, 9/211, 212, 293; pregnant,

9/553 & n. 4; also, 1/27, 81; 2/64; 3/103, 106; 4/134, 210; 7/40; 8/280, 314, 470

SOCIAL: at Twelfth Night party, 1/10; christening, 2/125; Woolwich, 7/142; Islington, 7/149, 167; and Hinchingbrooke, 8/471–2; also, 2/40, 54, 160; 3/219; 4/313; 7/169, 172, 174

JACKSON, [?Stephen], merchant: 6/164

JACKSON, ——; 2/148

JACOB, Sir John, Customs farmer: 3/188 & n. 3

JACOB'S: see Taverns etc.

JACOMBE, [Thomas], Rector of St Martin-infra-Ludgate: sermons, 2/74–5 & n.; 3/30 & n. 3; friendship with Jane Turner, 3/30

JAGGARD, [Abraham], merchant: victualling business, 5/53; country house, ib. & n. 3; at Gauden's, 7/29; builds house in Thames St, 9/124 & n. 1; ~ his wife [Sarah], 5/53(2), 54

JAMAICA: ships to, 2/6 & n. 3; new Governor sails to, 3/52, 62–3 & nn.; returns, 4/41 & n. 4; its capture (1655), 3/115; 4/376 & n. 2; privateers at, 8/75 & n. 1; also, 2/56; 3/52

JAMAICA HOUSE, Bermondsey: see Gardens; Taverns etc.

JAMES I, of Great Britain: monopolies 3/159 & n. 2; coinage, 4/148; Mennes's memories of, 6/127; privy purse expenditure, 8/324, 331 & n. 2

JAMES, Duke of Cambridge: see Stuart

JAMES, Duke of York, Lord High Admiral:
CHARACTER: independence, 4/116; industry, 4/367; 5/21 & n. 2, 167, 185–6; 'like to be a noble prince', 5/21; courage and modesty, 5/170–1; good judgement, 7/93–4; unpopularity, 4/24; neglects business for pleasure, 7/320, 323, 350

PERSONAL APPEARANCE ETC.: 'very plain' in nightshirt, 2/79; adopts periwig, 4/360; 5/49; 'better' after voyage, 5/339; adopts King's new fashion, 7/320–1; health: ague, 5/249; smallpox, 8/522(2), 524, 526, 527, 551, 565, 575; venereal disease (rumour), 6/60; also, 9/155

CHRON. SERIES: quarrels with King (1656), 8/431 & n. 1; returns from exile, 1/131, 152(2), 154, 157, 158, 162, 166; meets Princess Henrietta from France, 1/242, 243, 252; birthday, 2/195; 9/328, 329; visits Portsmouth, 3/80 & n. 4, 122; 4/24; meets Queen Mother in Downs, 3/139, 140; visits Bath, 4/287, 288, 321; leaves London in Plague, 6/172; 7/24, 34; visits Greenwich Palace, 7/38; and Audley End, 7/68, 71; 9/325

NAVAL ADMINISTRATION:

GENERAL: appointed Admiral of Kingdom, 1/143 & n. 1; profits, 4/195; Instructions to Navy Board and dockyards, 3/23–4 & n., 100; 6/336 & n. 2; 9/282, 525; abstract of, 3/148 & n. 1; orders revival of meetings with Board, 3/184; arrangements during absence at sea, 5/315 & n. 1; 6/58 & n. 2; fears parliamentary criticism, 8/510; 9/83, 280, 370; encourages reform of Board and yards, 9/253, 258–9, 267, 280–3 passim, 286, 287, 289–93 passim & n., 295, 304, 306, 308, 309, 312, 314, 321, 338, 349, 360, 370, 374, 377, 444, 445, 519, 521, 523–6 passim; jealous of his authority, 9/256, 350 & n. 2; answers criticisms of Board, 9/290, 291–2 & n.; rumour of replacement by commission, 9/278 & n. 5, 279, 347 & n. 2

RELATIONS WITH P [see also Clerk of the Acts]: regard for, 3/47, 302; 4/194, 196; 5/65, 75; 6/61(2), 61–2, 64, 65; 7/26, 31, 39; 9/375, 407, 415, 418–19, 445, 447; commends to Sandwich, 3/215–16; praises memorandum on pursers, 7/27, 28, 106; and on victualling, 7/216–17 & n.; lends navy MS., 7/50 & n. 3; 9/501 & n. 2; praises parliamentary speech, 9/105; P petitions for grant of *Maybolt*, 8/115–16, 455, 464–5 & n., 477–8; and for long leave, 9/222, 275–6, 556(2) & n. 1, 558, 560; also, 4/369; 5/125; 9/506, 529, 541; ~ admires EP, 9/515

APPOINTMENT OF OFFICIALS: views on officials' profits, 4/331–2; on merchants in public service, 5/300; on trading by Principal Officers, 8/231;

9/355, 358, 399; on appointments of merchants to Board, 9/507; advised about appointments by Coventry and P, 9/506; 'bears with' Anabaptist as Navy Office clerk, 4/135 & n. 2, 140; approves of 'fanatic' as Commissioner, 5/350; of P as Surveyor-General of Victualling, 6/280; 7/28; and of new posts of assistant to Mennes, 7/413, 421; and physician-general, 7/79 & n. 1; rewards B. St Michel, 8/15, 18–19; loyalty to 'old servants', 9/317; his nominee rejected by King, 9/349–50; suspends Anglesey, 9/310, 340–1 & n., 345; critical of Anglesey's successors, 9/410, 445, 447, 512; approves of Middleton, 9/543, 545; also, 8/301; 9/128

CHATHAM CHEST: orders enquiry, 3/174 & n. 5, 179

CONTRACTS AND TENDERS: 5/300–1, 303; 8/114

FINANCIAL BUSINESS [mostly with Navy Board]: receives report on navy's debts, 2/154; asks for statement on, 2/240 & n. 1; discusses use of Dunkirk money, 3/265; enquires about bills, 6/336 & n. 2; discusses supply, 7/43, 313; 8/112; 9/101, 530; receives complaints of shortages, 7/123, 307, 311–13, 331, 339, 349, 377; 8/62–3, 67, 392; 9/115; and detailed statements, 8/138 & n. 2, 140, 141; 9/125 & n. 1; asks for statement 9/216, 220 & n. 2; Exchequer certificates, 9/149, 150, 152, 153; flag-officers' pensions, 9/257 & n. 2, invites Board to lend to government, 8/399 & n. 5; authorises Brouncker's issue of tickets, 9/69; also, 1/225; 4/215–16; 8/73

JUDICIAL/DISCIPLINARY BUSINESS: Field's case, 3/64; adjudicates, 7/93–4, 380; Carkesse's case, 8/101, 103; punishes Jennens, 9/430; court-martials, 9/498, 511

ROYAL FISHERY: nominated Governor, 5/79; attends meetings, 5/198, 262, 315, 341

SHIPPING: inspects wreck, 1/313, 315; 8/67; 9/494; setting out/calling in ships, 2/127, 128; 3/119 & n. 3; 5/155, 156, 168, 262, 287 & n. 2; 7/102, 154;

9/418, 422; unspecified, 3/272, 282, 300; 4/4; 5/177, 223; 6/58, 134; 7/82, 166, 321; 8/60–1, 347, 459, 521, 591, 600; 9/135, 316, 449

MILITARY CAREER: in Flanders (1658): 5/170–1 & n.; 6/302; 8/75; reminiscences, of, 9/396; rumoured appointment to new army, 3/15 & n. 2; 6/277 & n. 2, 302; 7/395; and as general of land and sea forces, 6/321 & n. 1; commands troops during Fire, 7/269, 271, 273; favours standing army, 8/355, 361, 366–7; reviews troops, 4/216–17 & n.; 9/308, 557 & n. 1; Governor of Portsmouth, 2/199 & n. 2; Lord Warden of Cinque Ports, 9/280 & n. 4

OTHER PUBLIC WORK: patron of R. African Company, 1/258; 4/335; 5/11; 9/350; and of E. India Company, 2/228; profits from wine licences, 9/132 & n. 1, 319 & n. 1; low opinion of new Council of Trade, 9/549 & n. 2

POLITICS [see also below, Court]:

GENERAL: favours papists, 2/38; prefers Irish to English subordinates, 5/345; fears/resents Monmouth's claims, 3/238, 290, 303 & n. 1; 4/123, 138; 5/21, 58; 7/411; 8/434; advises tax by prerogative, 8/292–3; favours government by army on French model, 8/332; political news from, 5/13; 8/186, 384; 9/173–4, 310

RELATIONS WITH KING AND MINISTERS: attitude to Clarendon's dismissal, 8/406, 409, 410 & n. 1, 412, 414, 416, 419, 420, 424, 476, 506; power reduced by, 8/434, 597; relations with King deteriorate, 8/431, 480, 482, 530, 532, 535, 558, 596, 602; improve, 8/568; 9/153; fears Clarendon's impeachment, 8/518; rumours of his own impeachment, 8/532, 533–4; reconciled with Coventry, 9/79, 336; power weakened by Buckingham's rise, 9/340, 341, 361, 373, 472, 550–1, 558; relations improve, 9/319, 490–1

AS PRIVY COUNCILLOR: discusses state of navy, 7/311–13; money for navy, 7/377; 8/112; 9/216, 220; flag-officers' pensions, 9/257 & n. 2; attends cabinet meetings, 8/117, 138,

600; other council meetings, 7/26, 353; 8/111; 9/87, 122

PARLIAMENT: candidate defeated, 7/337 & n. 2; attends Lords, 7/406; 8/46; 9/176; opposes recall, 8/292–3 & n.; members attend on, 8/477; instructions to friends, 8/482

FOREIGN AFFAIRS: relations with Algiers, 3/121–2 & n.; 9/473, 516; favours Dutch war, 5/107, 111, 212, 242, 355; warns Dutch ambassador, 5/264 & n. 4; favours French alliance, 9/536; also, 8/452

COURT: reconciled to Queen-Mother, 2/2–3 & n.; association with Fitzharding and Muskerry, 4/116; 5/345; dislike of E. Mountagu of Boughton, 5/207; laughs at Sir R. Howard, 9/190–1; chides Bab May, 9/336–7; fears King may marry F. Stuart, 8/438; allies with Lady Castlemaine, 9/417; resents disgrace of H. Savile, 9/466, 469, 493; dines in public, 4/407; 8/161; attends Garter ceremony, 8/177; 9/246; and court balls, 3/300–01; 7/372; drunk at Cranbourne, 8/446–7; also, 3/191

MARRIAGE [for his mistresses, see Carnegie, Lady; Chesterfield, Lady; Churchill, Arabella; Denman, Lady; Hamilton, Lady Anne; Stuart, Frances]: rumours of, 1/260–1 & n., 273, 275, 284 & n. 1, 315, 319; publicly acknowledged, 1/320; 2/1; the ceremony, 2/40–1 & n.; dalliance with wife, 4/4; her jealousy, 4/138; his mistresses, 8/6, 286; henpecked (nicknamed 'Tom Otter'), 8/368 & n. 2; 9/342; marriage said to have 'undone the nation', 8/367; alluded to: 7/261; 8/287

FAMILY [see also Stuart]: children, 4/238, n. 1; untroubled by death of son Charles, 2/95 & n. 1; plays with daughter, Princess Mary, 5/268; also, 1/247–8; 2/213

RELIGION: friend of Catholics, 2/38; 'silly devotions', 9/163–4; attends Whitehall chapel, 3/42; 4/31, 401

SPORTS [for his yacht, see Ships: Anne]: plays pell-mell, 2/64; 9/542; hunts, 3/76, 198, 247, 260; 4/167, 192; 7/136–7, 228, 388; 8/382, 446–7;

9/442, 443, 455; 'a desperate hunts-
man', 4/371; injured hunting, 7/239;
hunts thrice weekly, 7/320; skates,
3/282; watches footrace, 4/255; races
horses at Putney, 8/204; visits Newmarket, 9/209, 340–1, 473
HOUSES AND HOUSEHOLD [seasonal
moves from Whitehall to St James's
are not indexed]:
WHITEHALL: Lely's portraits of flag
officers to hang in chamber, 7/102 &
n. 3; dressing chamber, 8/115; 9/491;
closet burgled, 9/489 & n. 3; little
chapel, 9/163–4
ST JAMES'S: hangings, 4/217; dressing
room, 8/374; pictures, 9/284; P
admires chamber, 8/198; moves to for
Duchess's lying-in, 6/19; and own
illness, 8/524
HOUSEHOLD: clerk of kitchen dismissed, 3/214 & n. 1; H. Killigrew
jun. banished, 7/336–7 & n.; H.
Brouncker dismissed, 8/416, 447;
corruption/extravagance, 5/120; 7/
191–2; 8/286, 287, 434; commissioners of, 8/287; 8/592 & n. 1; 9/290;
appoints Milles chaplain, 8/241, 248;
tenants include brothel keepers, 9/132
& n. 1; P admires 'little pretty
squinting girl', 9/295
SOCIAL: entertained by Speaker, 1/174;
Sir H. Finch, 2/155 & n. 2; Berkeley,
3/184; and Carteret, 6/169–70; at
Hinchingbrooke's wedding, 9/51;
plays 'I love my love', 9/468–9; at
theatre, 1/171; 2/80, 164, 174; 4/431;
5/33; 7/347; 8/91, 167, 388, 487;
9/183, 398; walks etc. in parks, 3/47,
60, 288; 8/68; 9/118, 414
MISC.: his horse Pen, 5/71; elected
Fellow of Royal Society, 6/6 & n. 1;
views ruins of St Paul's after Fire,
7/367; rules for forecasting weather,
9/150; recommends sauce, 9/443;
love of Navarre wine, ib.; in coach
accident, 9/474
ALLUDED TO: 9/425
JAMES, porter: news from, 1/36, 38
JAMES, Mrs —— (Aunt James): piety,
4/164–5; 5/266; P ashamed of neglecting, 4/163–4 & n.; 5/263; at Brampton, 5/263, 266, 282; breast amputated, 6/97 & n. 5; death, 7/36; social:

5/288, 289; 6/125, 133
JANE (Seymour), third Queen of
Henry VIII (d. 1537): tomb, 7/58 &
n. 6
JAPANNING: *see* Crafts
JEFFERIES, [Thomas], apothecary,
Westminster; P's kinsman: 8/517 &
n. 2
JEFFERY, Francis, Lord Jeffery, editor
of the *Edinburgh Review* (d. 1850):
opinion of Diary, vol. i, p. lxxxii
JEFFERYS, Capt. [?John]: on *Naseby*,
1/166
JEFFERYS, ——: a 'fumbler', 3/50 &
n. 1
JEFFREYS, ——: 6/65
JEGON (Jiggins), [Robert], Westminster magistrate: 3/278
JENIFER, Capt. [James], naval
officer: political gossip from, 8/118–19
& n.; account of St James's Day
Fight, 8/357–60 & nn.
[JENKINS], Eliezer (Ely), P's footboy: hired, 1/87; on Dutch voyage,
1/95, 96, 100, 101, 134, 135, 138, 139,
140, 143, 147; sad to leave P's service,
1/232; P meets again, 9/117; also,
1/89, 233; ~ his father, 1/87, 233
JENKINS, Leoline, kted 1670; judge
of the Court of Admiralty; Secretary
of State 1680–4 (d. 1685): character,
8/131, 133; his appointment, 8/133 &
nn.; hears prize case, 8/130–4 passim
JENKINS, [Capt. William], soldier:
killed in duel, 9/26–7 & n.
JENNENS (Jennings), Sir William,
naval commander: P's low opinion,
9/430; courage in Four Days Fight,
7/148; ill-government of fleet, 7/332;
quarrel with Le Neve, 7/380 & n. 2;
conduct at Gravesend criticised, 8/351,
379; also, 9/430 & n. 1
JENNINGS, ——, of the Privy Seal:
social: 1/206, 217; ?5/330
JENNINGS, ——, clerk to quarter-
master of Sandwich's troop: business,
1/14; social: 1/13; ?5/330
JENNINGS, Frances: her prank, 6/41
& n. 1
JENNINGS, Capt. W.: *see* Jennens
JERMYN (Germin), Henry, 1st Earl of
St Albans, courtier and diplomat:
PERSONAL: character, 1/307; rumoured

marriage to Queen Mother, 3/263 & n. 3, 303; 5/57–8 & n.; 8/564 & n. 1; new buildings in St James's Fields, 4/295–6; 7/87–8 & n.; dress, 7/328; reckless gamester, 8/190 & n. 2; fine coach, 8/196; also, 6/316 & n. 4

PUBLIC CAREER: ambassador to France, 1/300, 307; rumoured appointment as Lord Treasurer, 3/227; negotiations with France, 8/107 & n. 1; 9/530 & n. 2, 536; also, 2/33; 8/294

SOCIAL: 2/32; 4/229

JERMYN, Henry, Master of the Horse to the Duke of York; cr. Baron Dover 1685: rumoured marriage to Princess Dowager, 1/320; duel, 3/170–1; attempt at abduction, 5/58 & n. 2; at sea with Rupert, 5/311; affair with Lady Castlemaine, 8/366, 368; wealth, 8/196, 563–4; also, 9/473; ~ his brother [Thomas], 8/563–4

JERSEY, Channel Is.: Carteret's government during Civil War, 3/243 & n. 2; 4/195, 306; Sir T. Allin's flight to (1650), 8/161 & n. 4

JERVAS (Gervas), [Richard], barber, New Palace Yard: trims P, 1/90; 4/130, 290; his man hired for Dutch voyage, 1/90; P inspects periwigs, 4/130, 290, 350; 5/224; 6/74; other visits, 5/246, 257, 260, 267–8, 275, 287, 316, 332, 340; 6/1, 6, 9, 16; 8/177; supplies infested periwig, 8/133, 146; sees diving experiment, 5/268–9; ~ his wife [Grace], 4/261–2; 5/268–9; 6/6, 16; child [Ann] buried, 5/221; mother-in-law, —— Palmer, ventriloquist, 4/261–2

JESSOP, [William], Clerk of the House of Commons 1660: 'an old-fashion man of Cromwell's', 9/44; parliamentary business, 1/29; 2/32 & n. 3; secretary to Brooke House Committee, 9/30 & n. 1, 44, 298

JESUITS, the: Leopold I's reliance on, 4/350 & n. 2

JEWEN ST: Deb Willet lodges in, 9/543; also, 9/332, 520(2)

[JEWKES, Roland], lawyer: tomb, 8/545 & n. 2

JEWS: P attends synagogue, 4/335 & nn.; story of new Messiah, 7/47 & n. 4

JIGGINS: see Jegon

JIJELLI (Gigery), Algeria; captured by French, 5/295 & n. 1

JOHN GEORGE II, Elector of Saxony 1656–80: made Knight of Garter, 9/246 & n. 2

JOHNSON, [Henry], shipbuilder, Blackwall: story of petrified trees, 6/236 & n. 4; repairs ships, 8/135; social: 1/280

JOHNSON, Mrs ——, servant to Sandwich: 1/38

JOHNSON, Mrs ——, sister of Lady Mordaunt: 9/476 & n. 5

JOLLIFFE (Jolly), [George], physician: 4/60 & n. 3

JOLLIFFE, [John], merchant: 5/300

JONES, Anne, of St Olave's parish: social: 7/136; 8/29, 104, 150; 9/197

[JONES, John]: elected M.P. for London, 2/57 & n. 1

JONES, Col. John, republican: impeached, 1/34 & n. 2

JONES; Col. [Philip], parliamentarian: influence over R. Cromwell, 1/180 & n. 4; ~ his son, 2/34 & n. 2, 56

JONES, Sir Theophilus, Scoutmaster-General of Ireland 1661–d.85: 2/173

JONES, ——, a young merchant: 8/76

JORDAN, Joseph, kted 1665, naval commander: in Battle of Lowestoft, 6/122; serves under Penn, 6/147; at council of war, 6/230; poor tactics in St James's Day Fight, 8/354 & n. 3, 357–60; portrait by Lely, 7/102 & n. 3

JORDAN, Mrs —— [?Mary, wife of Joseph]: as godmother, 2/109

JOURNAL: see Diary

JOWLES, Lieut. [Henry], naval officer: P's low opinion, 4/229; 5/1; marriage to Rebecca Allen, 4/229 & n. 1; challenges his captain to duel, 8/140–1; ~ his mother, 4/227

JOWLES, Rebecca (b. Allen), wife of Henry: P admires, 2/68, 71, 72; 5/1; dallies with, 9/495, 497; married, 4/229 & n. 1; churched, 4/227; pleads for husband, 5/1; 8/140–1; social: 2/69, 125, 126, 127; 3/153; ~ her pretty cousin, 9/497

JOWLES, Capt. [Valentine], naval officer: commissioned, 1/100; gift to P, ib.

KEMBE, Harry, Navy Office messenger: damages awarded against, 3/280; dies, 7/412

KEMPTHORNE, [John], naval commander; kted 1670: in Downs, 8/43; presides over court martial, 9/488, 497 & n. 1, 505 & n. 1

KENASTON: see Kinaston

KENDAL, Duke of: see Anne, Duchess of York

KENERSLY: see Kinnersley

KENNARD: see Kinward

KENSINGTON: P visits: Holland House, 1/216 & n. 2; tavern with garden and grotto, 9/166, 170, 203; other visits, 5/178, 180–1; 7/54, 95, 100; Sandwich/Lady Sandwich at, 1/210, 215; 5/174, 178; Queen at, 5/163; duel, 1/20

KENT, [John]: see Taverns etc.: Three Tuns, Crutched Friars

KENT, Earl of: see Grey, [?Henry]

KENT ST: Plague, 6/279, 297

KENTISH KNOCK, the (shoal off the mouth of the Thames): 1/254

KENTISH TOWN: 5/233

[KERKHOVEN, D.], Dutch naval commander: 6/108 & n. 3

KERNEGUY: see Carnegie

KEVET: see Kievet

KIEVET, Johan, Burgomaster of Rotterdam ('Amsterdam'):⁹ in peace negotiations, 8/68–9 & n.

KILLIGREW, Henry, chaplain to the King: preaches at Whitehall, 4/393 & n. 2

KILLIGREW, Henry, Groom of the Bedchamber to the Duke of York: at puppet play, 7/267 & n. 1; banished from court, 7/336–7; in affray with Buckingham, 8/348 & n. 1; bawdy talk, 9/218; attacked by Lady Shrewsbury's footmen, 9/557 & n. 2, 558; also, 3/229–30, 265

KILLIGREW, Sir Peter: on Naseby, 1/132 & n. 2

KILLIGREW, Thomas, dramatist, manager of the Theatre Royal and Groom of the Bedchamber [see also Plays]:

AS MANAGER OF THEATRE ROYAL: his plans for opera, 5/230; 8/56; and for training actors, 5/230 & n. 3;

love of Italian music, 8/54–7 passim; brings Italian consort to court, 8/56, 65–6; on improvement in theatre, 8/55–6; praises Knepp's acting, 8/55, 430; employs whore for actors, 9/425; warned against putting on satirical play, 9/471

AS GROOM OF THE BEDCHAMBER: frank advice to Charles II, 7/400; repartee with, 8/368 & n. 2; appointed King's jester, 9/66–7 & n.; struck by Rochester in King's presence, 9/451–2 & n.; also, 8/497; 9/558

SOCIAL: 5/27; 8/429–30; 9/200

MISC.: his (joke) letter to Queen of Bohemia, 1/157; early passion for theatre, 3/243–4 & n.; early poverty, 9/256 & n. 4

KILLIGREW, Sir William, dramatist and courtier: at Greenwich and Deptford with King, 6/169

KINASTON (Kenaston), [Edward], merchant: P's high opinion, 8/295; Tangier business, 7/19; 8/251 & n. 1, 292, 295, 369–70, 372

KING, Col. [Edward]: 2/53

KING, Henry, Bishop of Chichester 1642–d.69: sermons, 1/195; 4/69; 6/54 & n. 3

KING, [Thomas], M.P. Harwich, Essex: lends P copy of impeachment against Clarendon, 8/523; social: 9/474

[KING, William], landlord of the Crown, Hercules Pillars Lane: wealth, 9/42 & n. 3

KING, [William], Vicar of Ashtead, Surrey ?1648–62: dull preacher, 4/247 & n. 1

KING, [?William], late of the Treasurers at War: dismissed, 1/82

KING, Dr ——, physician, of Huntingdon: 4/313

KING ST, the city: constructed after Fire, 8/562–3 & n.

KING ST, Westminster [see also Taverns etc.: Angel; Axe; Bell; Crown; Fox; Harper's; Leg; Red Lion; Rhenish winehouse; Rose; ?Ship; Sun; Swan; Trumpet; White Horse]: flood, 1/93 & n. 1; traffic block, 1/303 & n. 1; alluded to: 3/201

KINGDON, Capt. [Richard], Comptroller of the Excise Office: service under Commonwealth, 6/319–20 & n.; business with, 6/319, 332; 8/16

KING'S CHANNEL, the (off the Essex Coast): Dutch fleet in, 8/256

[KINGSDOWN], Deal, Kent: wager on height of cliff, 1/163

KING'S GATE, Holborn: 9/154, 474

KINGSLAND, Mdx: P's boyhood memories, 5/132 & n. 4; 8/211 & n. 3; P/EP at, 2/180; 5/133, 201; 7/121, 132, 220; 8/174, 211–12, 390; 9/197, 513

KINGSMILL, family of: 5/118 & n. 1

KINGSTON, Catherine, Lady Kingston, wife of John, 1st Baron: alluded to, 2/54 & n. 3

KING'S LYNN, Norf.: as port, 1/179; 2/27, 156

KINGSTON, Surrey: P visits, 3/75; 6/154, 166, 167; 7/28; Quakers to be tried, 4/271; alluded to: 2/202

KINNERSLEY, ——, of the Wardrobe: 2/121

KINWARD (Kennard), [Thomas], Master-Joiner of the King's Works, Whitehall: his work at Hinchingbrooke, 1/314, 324; 2/35; and on Penn's lodgings, 3/28, 31, 41; ~ his servant, 1/314

KIPPS, [Thomas], Seal-bearer to the Lord Chancellor: at Whitehall chapel, 1/195; Chancery business, 1/197, 204; in P's 'old clubb', 2/221; also, 1/44, 184; 2/127

KIRBY, Capt. [Robert], naval officer: killed in action, 6/122

KIRTON, [Joshua], bookseller, Paul's Churchyard [until the Fire often 'my bookseller']: P: buys books/pays bills, 3/105, 290; 4/234; 5/38, 358, 359; 6/70, 151; 7/41, 47, 64; orders books, 1/281–2; 2/239; 5/342, 343–4, 355; 6/109; collects books, 6/28; has books bound, 5/355; 6/2, 14, 28; visits shop, 2/22, 165, 238; 4/342; 5/190; 7/46, 116; lends P money, 7/101; ruined by Fire, 7/297, 309; death, 8/526 & n. 2; ~ his apprentice, 1/53–4, 307; his kinsman, 4/80; 7/309

KITE, Ellen, P's aunt: 4/131; 5/132

KITE, Margaret (Peg), P's cousin: orphaned, 2/172; left legacy, 2/173;

troublesome to P as executor, 2/179, 190, 192; marries weaver, 2/209, 231; husband demands marriage portion, 3/161

KITE, Sarah: see Giles

KITE, Mrs —— (Aunt Kite; 'my aunt the Butcher'): see Clarke, Julian

KIUPRILLI, Ahmed, Turkish Grand Vizier 1661–d.76: death reported, 5/236, 237, n. 1

KNAPP, [John]: solicits for places in navy, 4/407 & n. 1; claims to be royal physician, ib.

KNEPP, [Christopher], horse dealer, husband of Elizabeth: 9/391; jealous of P, 6/323; 7/2; social: 7/16, 369

KNEPP (Knipp), [Elizabeth], actress:
CHRON. SERIES: P meets at Greenwich, 6/320 & n. 5; admires, 6/321; 7/1; she signs letter 'Bab Allen', 7/4; P replies as 'Dapper Dicky', 7/5; gives her money, 7/61; 9/309; and gloves, 7/70; his valentine, 8/86, 100; her unhappy marriage, 7/5, 7; pregnant, 7/133, 173; birth and death of son Samuel, 7/196, 198, 236; P fondles, 7/2; 8/29; 9/170, 172, 188, 189–90, 218; EP's jealousy of, 7/120, 236–8 passim; 8/25, 211, 371–2, 399, 599; 9/1, 108, 436, 469; P vows to see no more, 9/339, 368, 391; avoids in theatre, 9/381, 405

HER PERFORMANCES: T. Killigrew's opinion, 8/55, 430; P admires in *The scornful lady*, 7/422; *The custom of the country*, 8/3; *The Indian emperor*, 8/14 & n. 2; *The humourous lieutenant*, 8/27; *The Chances*, 8/46; *The troubles of Queen Elizabeth*, 8/388–9; *The northern lass*, 8/437; *The Duke of Lerma*, 9/81; *The Storm*, 9/133 & n. 1; *The sea voyage*, 9/201 & n. 1; *The silent woman*, 9/310 & n. 2; also acts in *The Goblins*, 8/28–9, 232; *Flora's Vagaries*, 8/463 & n. 5; *The Surprizal*, 9/166 & n. 2; *The Heiress*, 9/435–6; P admires her singing, 8/3, 27, 46; 9/436; and dancing, 8/388–9; alluded to, 8/196; 9/200, 282, 320

HER SINGING (at parties etc.): P enraptured by, 6/321; sings *Barbara Allen*, 7/1; Italian song, 8/57; English songs, 8/599; with P, 7/44, 69, 92–3, 95, 237, 362; he teaches her *Beauty Retire*, 7/53,

54; and *It is decreed*, 7/369; teaches P *The Lark*, 9/299; also, 6/323–4; 7/341, 343–4; 8/65, 86; 9/128, 131, 189
SOCIAL: dances, 7/73; 9/12–13, 134, 289; introduces P to Nell Gwyn, 8/27; at theatre, 7/347; 8/137–8, 156, 383, 395, 463; 9/12; theatre gossip from, 8/168–9; 9/19–20, 155–6; at Vauxhall, 9/219; also, 7/18, 84, 103–4, 257; 8/598; 9/276
ALLUDED TO: 6/342; 7/3, 15–16; 8/242
~ her daughter, 8/57; her pretty maid Betty: 9/156; P kisses, 9/201, 320–1
KNIGHT, [John], Surgeon to the King: 3/299; ~ his wife, ib.
KNIGHT, [Mary], singer: P admires her voice, 8/453 & n. 4; 9/299
KNIGHT, Sir John, navy agent, Bristol: 9/235 & n. 2
KNIGHTLEY, [Richard], Rector of Charwelton, Northants., 1663–95: proposed as husband for Lady Jemima Mountagu, 3/84 & n. 1
KNIGHTLY, [Robert], merchant, of Seething Lane: wants churchyard limed during Plague, 7/31; social: 2/239–40; 7/31–2, 278, 280; alluded to: 6/142; ~ Mary, ?his daughter, 9/221 & n. 1
KNIGHTSBRIDGE [*see also* Taverns etc.: World's End]: P visits, 5/181; 6/89
KNIPP: *see* Knepp
KÖNIGSBERG (Quinsborough), East Prussia: stories of, 4/412
KRAG (Kragh), Otte, Danish ambassador-extraordinary to the United Provinces 1659–60: 1/153–4
KUFFELER, Johannes Siberius, inventor: his explosive mine, 3/45–6 & n.
KYNASTON, [Edward], actor: in *The loyal subject*, 1/224 & n. 3; *The silent woman*, 2/7 & n. 4; *The island princess*, 9/441 & n. 4; assaulted for mimicking Sedley in *The Heiress*, 9/435 & n. 3, 435–6

LACEY, [John], actor and dramatist [*see also* Plays]: imprisoned for part in *The change of crowns*, 8/168 & n. 1, 172–3; said to be dying, 8/334 & n. 3; imitated in puppet play, 9/445 & n. 2; P admires in *The French dancing*

master, 3/87–8 & nn.; *Love in a maze*, 3/88 & nn.; 4/179 & n. 3; 8/195–6; 9/177–8; *The Committee*, 4/181 & n. 1; 8/384 & n. 3; *The faithful shepherdess*, 4/182; *The change of crowns*, 8/167–8 & n.; also acts in *The humourous lieutenant*, 4/128 & n. 4; in own adaptation of *The taming of the shrew*, 8/158 & n. 2; dances in *The jovial crew*, 9/411–12 & n.; and in *Horace*, 9/420 & n. 2; alluded to: 7/77
[LAFRERI, Antonio, d. 1577]: print by, 7/102–3 & n.
LAM, Mother: *see* Taverns etc.
LAMB, [James], Canon of Westminster: sermon, 1/261
LAMBART (Lambert), [Rose], Viscountess Lambart (d. 1649), first wife of Richard Lambart, succ. 1660 as 2nd Earl of Cavan: 9/215 & n. 3
LAMBERT, [David], naval officer: lieutenant on *Naseby*, 1/105; P tells of diary, 1/107; his gittern, 1/169; instructs P on naval matters, 1/259; 2/13, 115; married, 2/23; house, 2/116, 123; transferred to 4th-rate, 2/90; captain of *Norwich*, 2/115, 203–4; stories of Lisbon, 2/196–7; sails for Mediterranean, 2/214, 219; and Tangier, 3/67; 4/100–1; social: 1/75, 102, 106, 107, 120, 162, 164, 166, 258–9; 2/23, 25, 49, 101, 196–7, 207; alluded to: 1/27; ~ his wife, 2/123; father-in-law, 2/197
LAMBERT, [James], naval officer: captain of *Anne* yacht, 3/63; killed in action, 6/225
LAMBERT, Maj.-Gen. John, republican (d. 1683): opposes Rump, 1/1 & n. 4; rumoured advance on London, 1/4 & n. 5; support in army, 1/7; indemnity offered to, 1/6, 7; submits to Rump, 1/8; defies Rump, 1/51 & n. 2; to appear before Council of State, 1/74 & n. 3; imprisoned in Tower, 1/81; escapes, 1/108 & n. 1; captured, 1/114–15, 117; sent to Guernsey, 2/204 & n. 1; old lodgings in Whitehall, 5/164; alluded to: 2/92
LAMBERT, ——, servant to Coventry: 4/258
LAMBETH, Surrey [For Lambeth ale, *see* Drink. *See also* Taverns etc.:

Three Mariners]: P visits, 2/25, 120; 4/213–14, 317; 7/103; 8/346; yacht building, 3/164; Plague, 6/289; bonfire, 9/172; gipsies, 9/278 & n. 2

LAMBETH MARSH etc.: 4/317; 5/219

LAMBETH PALACE: P admires, 9/554; new hall, 6/164 & n. 2; other visits, 4/217; also, 9/550

LAMBTON, [Margaret] (d. 1730): marriage, 9/512 & n. 2

LANDGUARD FORT, Harwich: Dutch attack, 8/317

LANE, Betty: see Martin

LANE, Doll: see Powell

LANE, Sir George, cr. Viscount Lanesborough 1676; secretary to Ormond (d. 1683): profits and corruption, 4/331–2 & n.; 5/73 & n. 6; lawsuit concerning Irish land, 5/324 & n. 1; also, 2/140; 3/52

LANEY, Benjamin, Bishop of Peterborough 1660–3, Lincoln 1663–7, Ely 1667–d. 75: 4/98–9 & n.

LANGFORD, [William], tailor: P's good opinion 5/106; leases Tom P's house, 5/106; 9/399; recommends cook-maid, 5/158; complains about P's father, 5/244, 251–2; in country during Plague, 7/13; as P's tailor, 5/142, 144, 240, 308; 6/62, 104, 124, 125; ~ his wife, 5/244, 252

LANGLEY, ——, government (?Exchequer) clerk: 2/31, 40; 5/30

LANGUAGES [No attempt is made to index the occasional foreign phrases, mottoes and inscriptions in the text. Asterisks denote books read.]:

GENERAL: sign language, 2/160; 7/363; 'universal characters', 5/12 & n. 4; Wilkins's book, 7/12 & n. 6; 8/554 & n. 2; dialect, 9/232; hunting jargon, 8/475; de Cordemoy's book, 9/385–6 & n.

FRENCH [see also Pepys, Elizabeth; her reading]: spoken in The Hague, 1/139; proverb quoted by Tom P, 5/86–7; Coventry requires of clerks, 8/207; (P): speaks, 1/99, 260–1; comments on spoken French, 1/139; 4/58; 9/197; hears sermons/services in, 3/207, 270, 296; 5/17, 18, 342; writes, 1/153–4; argues about word, 6/223;

reads/buys books/songs in; anon., 2/35; 4/411–12 & n.; 5/58; 9/428, 431–2★ & n.; Psalms, 1/140 & n. 3; by [Besongne], 9/428 & n. 2; [de Bussy], 7/114 & n. 3; Fournier, 9/17 & n. 5; [Furetière], 6/302★ & n. 2; [Gomberville], 1/35 & n. 2; [La Calprenède], 9/365 & n. 1, 545★ & n. 1, Marnix, 9/428 & n. 3; Mersenne, 9/148 & n. 3, 216★; [Millot et l'Ange], 9/21–2★ & n., 57–8★, 59★; [Parival], 4/410–11★ & n.; Sorbière, 5/297 & n. 2; 9/206★; also, 1/90; 2/35★

GREEK: schoolboys examined in, 4/33; neglected in Colet's time, 5/38 & n. 2; (P): corrects brother's speech, 1/18; quotes Epictetus, 3/194, 231; 4/16; objects to false Greek, 4/259; examines brother, 4/269; uses in polyglot, 6/202; examines Mountagu twins, 8/472; buys lexicon, 5/198 & n. 3

HEBREW: schoolboys examined in, 4/33 & n. 4; (P): buys grammar, 1/28 & n. 5; hears in synagogue, 4/335

ITALIAN: (P): sings, 1/63; 2/126; listens to songs, 8/56; fails to understand, 8/54, 55, 599; misquotes, 3/7–8 & n.; quotes proverb, 4/137; reads translations, 7/206★ & n. 4; 9/535★ & n. 3, 542★; alludes to La puttana errante, 9/22 & n. 1

LATIN: spoken in The Hague, 1/139; by woman, 2/68; extemporary, 2/21; schoolboys examined, 4/33; restored in legal proceedings, 7/114 & n. 2; English pronunciation, 9/544 & n. 5; Seneca alluded to, 8/507; (P): speaks, 1/99, 142; 4/386; sings, 1/63 & n. 3; 9/194; receives letters, 1/137; 7/50; teaches young Edward Mountagu, 1/165; and Mountagu twins, 8/472; examines Sandwich's page, 1/312; objects to 'false Latin', 4/190; shocked at Carteret's ignorance, 4/217; takes sermon notes in, 4/268, 278; hears speech at Royal Society, 8/554; reads/acquires books: Alsted, 1/275 & n. 4; Bacon, Faber Fortunae, 2/102★ & n. 1, 5/39★; 7/72★, 129★, 242★, 346; Bacon, Organum, 1/140 & n. 4; Barclay, 1/231 & n. 1; 4/369★; Bartholinus, 1/243 & n. 2; [Bate], 1/67 & n. 3; 4/42 & n. 1; Bible, 4/189, 190, 193, 204, 236, 269;

theatre, 8/172–3 & n.; affray at prize-
fight, 8/239; assault in King's presence,
9/451–2 & n.; by hired bullies,
9/435–6 & n., 441, 471, 557 & n. 2,
558; P fears for EP's safety, 9/549;
also, 1/215, 303; 2/30, 228–9; 3/34
& n. 2, 35–6 & n., 196, 212; 5/32 &
n. 3; 6/306–7; 7/369 & n. 3, 380;
8/90 & n. 3, 206, 208–9, 319, 321 &
n. 3, 348–9 & n.; 9/111 & n. 1, 166,
412 & n. 2, 470 & n. 1
DUELS:
    GENERAL: P disapproves, 3/171;
proclamations against, ib. & n. 2; bill
against, 9/53 & n. 1; serving officers
arrested to prevent, 8/140–1; 9/273
    PARTICULAR: Chesterfield and
Wolley, 1/20 & n. 1; Sandwich and
Buckingham (challenge), 2/32–3;
Cholmley and Ned Mountagu, 3/157
& n. 2; 4/47; Jermyn and Rawlins,
3/170–1 & nn.; P fears challenge from
Holmes, 4/83–4; Seymour and Commissioner Pett (challenge), 7/212 &
n. 1; Spragge and Commissioner Pett
(challenge), ib.; Ossory and Buckingham (challenge), 7/343 & n. 3, 350;
Holmes and Smith, 7/348; Porter and
Belasyse, 8/363–4 & n., 377, 384;
Buckingham and Shrewsbury, 9/26–7
& nn.; Halifax or Coventry and
Buckingham (rumoured challenge),
9/462; Leijonbergh and P (challenge,
1670), 8/22, n. 1; also, 3/53; 4/47;
7/376; 8/173
HIGHWAY ROBBERY: 3/34 & n. 2
RIOTS AND DISORDERS [for seamen's
mutinies, see Navy: seamen]: by
apprentices, 1/39 & n. 1, 54; 5/99–100
& n.; in churches, 3/178 & n. 2;
9/96 & n. 1; by seamen, 4/292 & n. 2,
294; 6/255, 288 & n. 5, 303; 7/330 &
n. 3, 415–16; 8/60 & n. 1, 62–3, 272;
fanatics, 6/184 & n. 3; in inns of
court, 8/223 & n. 3; 9/465–6 & n.; by
mob: for recall of parliament, 8/268;
against Clarendon, 8/269 & n. 2; for
'Reformation and Reducement', 9/
129–34 passim & nn., 152; ~ in
Paris, 8/299–300 & nn.
LAWES, Henry, composer (d. 1662)
[see also Musical Compositions]: ill,
1/324

LAWES, William, composer, brother
of Henry (d. 1645): see Musical
Compositions
LAWRENCE, Goody, P's nurse:
house at Kingsland, 5/132
LAWRENCE, [Henry], merchant: to
go to Algiers, 1/321 & n. 2
LAWRENCE, Sir John, Lord Mayor
1664–5: gives dinner, 6/126; ~ his
father [Abraham], ib.
LAWRENCE, [Samuel]: 4/265; ~ his
wife, ib.
LAWSON, [Abigail], daughter of Sir
John: her funeral, 2/131–2 & n.
LAWSON, [Isabella], wife of Sir
John: at Penn's, 4/23; 5/6, 7; also,
7/264
LAWSON, [Isabella], daughter of Sir
John: see Norton
LAWSON, Sir John, kted 1660, naval
commander (in 1660 'the Vice-
Admiral') and member of the Tangier Committee:
CHARACTER: 1/106, 159; 4/12, 24, 376;
6/138; 7/195; ~ cartoon, 1/45
NAVAL CAREER: under Commonwealth,
1/1, 62, 79 & n. 1; 4/375; 8/125;
relations with Sandwich, 1/95, 98,
107; 3/121–2 & n.; agrees to serve
King, 1/100, 130; commissioned,
1/110; knighted, 1/254; voyages to
N. Africa, 3/79 & n. 2, 89, 121, 263 &
n. 4, 271; 4/3–4 & n., 6, 73, 369 & n. 2,
415 & n. 1; 5/141 & n. 4, 295, 299;
accounts etc., 4/12, 104, 325, 414–15;
his ship blown up, 6/52 & n. 1;
wounded in action, 6/122, 129; death,
6/131, 132, 138; funeral, 6/145;
family impoverished, 6/150–1; alleged
plundering, 6/276; also, 1/249; 4/73;
5/15, 17; 6/10, 11; 7/227 & n. 2
TANGIER BUSINESS: proposals for construction of mole, 4/13, 26–7, 31, 35–
6; contract signed, 4/88 & n. 3; new
proposals opposed, 5/303, 343; profits, 6/71, 101, 103; 8/593; attends
meetings, 4/23; 5/11; 6/61; also, 6/39
SOCIAL: 1/114, 115, 167, 317; 2/66;
4/23, 53; 5/6
ALLUDED TO: 1/134, 153, 159
~ his daughters, 6/150
LAWSON, [?Samuel, son of Sir
John]: 6/100–1 & n., 185

[LAWSON, Miss ——]: 5/58 & n. 2
LAXTON, —— [?error for Layton],
Sandwich's apothecary: 1/73; 5/178;
~ his wife and daughters, 5/178
LAYTON: *see* Leighton
LEA (Leigh), [Matthias and Thomas],
under-clerks of Council of State: 1/23
LEA BAILEY, Forest of Dean: 3/114 &
n. 5
LEAD, Mr ——: makes vizard for P,
9/533(2), 547
LEADENHALL MARKET: *see* Fairs
and Markets
LEADENHALL ST [*see also* Taverns
etc.: Sun; Swan]: mum-house, 3/94;
5/191; morris-dancing, 4/120; execu-
tion, 5/23; conventicle, 9/385
LEATHERHEAD, Surrey: P at, 2/91
LE BLANC, Mlle ——, governess in
Sandwich's household: at Bartholo-
mew Fair, 2/166; at theatre, 2/214;
5/138-9; social: 2/198; 3/68; alluded
to: 2/232; 4/29
LE BRUN, [?Christian, of St Olave's
parish]: 7/246
LECHMERE (Leechmore), [Nicholas],
lawyer, kted 1689, Judge of Exchequer
Bench 1689-1700 (d. 1701): in Field's
case, 3/231
LECTURER, our: *see* St Olave's
Church, Hart St
LEE, Sir Thomas, M.P. Aylesbury,
Bucks.: critic of Navy Board, 9/103-4
LEE, ——, lawyer: to prosecute Vane,
3/88
LEE, Essex: *see* Leigh
LEESON, [Robert], barber-surgeon:
extracts EP's tooth, 9/557
LEGGE, George, son of Col. William;
cr. Baron Dartmouth 1682: his early
promotion, 9/40 & n. 1
LEGGE, Col. William, Lieutenant-
General and Treasurer of the Ordnance: to supply Tangier garrison,
5/279 & n. 3; allowance reduced,
8/178 & n. 3; at gun trial, 9/528; lends
money to Carteret, 8/180; reputedly
Catholic, 8/265 & n. 1; Duke of York's
affection, 9/39; his part in Charles I's
escape from Hampton Court (1648),
6/316-17 & n.
LEGHORN: quarantine, 4/417-18 &
n.; also, 4/201

LE HAVRE: Sandwich at, 2/32
LEICESTER HOUSE: 9/333
LEIGH: *see* Lea
LEIGH (Lee), [Robert]: in search for
Barkstead's treasure, 3/240-1 & n.,
246, 250-1, 284, 285, 286; stories
of Spain (alluded to), 3/251
LEIGH (Lee) ROAD, off Leigh-on-
Sea: ships in, 1/103; 6/54
LEIGH-ON-SEA (Lee), Essex: 8/136,
343, 344, 354
LEIGHTON, Sir Ellis, secretary of the
Prize Commission: his wit, 5/300 &
n. 5; counsel to Navy Board, 8/27,
131, 133; news from, 7/160; social:
5/11
LEIJONBERGH, Baron: *see* Barck-
mann
LEITH: 7/224; 8/425
LELY, Sir Peter: proud, 8/129; successful, 3/230; 7/209; compared with
J. M. Wright, 3/113; Huysmans,
5/254; and Hayls, 8/129; portraits:
Sandwich, 1/262 & n. 2, 271 & n. 1;
Duchess of York, 3/112-13 & n.; 7/82
& n. 1; Charles II, 3/113 & n. 2;
Lady Castlemaine, 3/113 & n. 3;
7/359 & n. 3; Lady Carteret, 5/104 &
n. 4; flag-officers, 7/102 & n. 3, 209;
maids of honour, 9/284 & n. 4; his
table book, 7/209; social: 6/166
LEMING (Lemon), Mary (b. Batten):
?1/317; ?2/19, 22, 23; 2/57, 59,
61, 78, 82; 4/218; ~ her old nurse,
3/205
LEMING, ——, of Colchester, husband of the foregoing: fatally ill,
3/169-70
LE NEVE, [Richard], naval officer:
drunken quarrel, 7/380
LEN(N)OX, Duke of: *see* Stuart,
Charles, Duke of Richmond and
Duke of Lennox
LENTHALL, [Sir] John, brother of
William: arrests Quakers, 4/271 &
n. 2
LENTHALL, (Sir) John, son of William; M.P. Abingdon, Berks.: cen-
sured by Commons, 1/151 & n. 3
LENTHALL, William, Speaker of the
House of Commons: resumes chair,
1/25 & n. 5; refuses to sign warrants
for elections, 1/61 & n. 2

LENTHROPP: *see* Leventhorpe
LEONARD, [John], under-clerk to the Council of State: 1/49
LEOPOLD I, Holy Roman Emperor 1658–1705: under Jesuit influence, 4/350 & n. 2; persecution of Protestants, 4/372 & n. 2; Louis XIV's friendly offers, 4/349 & n. 3; 8/107 & n. 2; victory over Turks, 5/236–7 & n., 247
LE SQUIRE, Scipio, Vice-Chamberlain of the Receipt in the Exchequer: P hopes for his place, 1/80 & n. 2
L'ESTRANGE, Roger, kted 1685, journalist: *Intelligencer*, 4/297 & n. 2; fine manners, 5/348; P to provide news, ib. & n. 1; account of Battle of Lowestoft, 6/128, 135 & nn.
LETHIEULLIER, [Anne], wife of John: P admires, 6/316, 328, 338, 339; 7/35, 41, 322
LETHIEULLIER, [John], merchant, kted 1674: 6/328; 7/41
LEVANT (Turkey) Company: convoy, 6/10–12; export of cloth, 6/11–12 & n.; to transport troops to Tangier, 6/20; also, 3/259–60
LEVENTHORPE, Sir Thomas Bt (d. 1679): on *Naseby*, 1/130 & n. 3
LEVER, family of: at Great Lever Hall, Lancs., 3/254
LEVER, [William], Purser-General: gift to EP, 5/316–17; P's 'disservice', 5/317
LEVITT, [William], cook: 9/116
LEWIN (Luein), [?John], of the King's Lifeguard: at P's stone feast, 3/53; also, 3/78
LEWIS (Lewes), Sir John, merchant: 3/50
[LEWIS, John], pilot: negligence, 3/213 & n. 1
LEWIS, [?John], cook: 9/116
LEWIS, [Thomas], clerk, Victualling Office: Chatham Chest (memorandum), 3/130; navy victualling, 3/135; 4/322; 6/325; 7/259, 262, 265; Tangier victualling, 5/210; 6/207; Batten's accounts, 8/561; prize business, 8/582, 584; instructs P in pursers' accounts, 3/181, 195; 4/28; unspecified business, 8/483; news from, 8/267, 475; social: 2/60; 8/180; ~ his daughter, 6/225

LEWIS, Ald. [Thomas], merchant: 3/50
LEWIS, [William], prebendary of Winchester (d. 1667): inaudible sermon, 4/63 & n. 1
LEY, James, 3rd Earl of Marlborough, Governor of Bombay and naval officer: P's regard, 5/30; surrender of Bombay, 4/139; stories of India, 5/30; in government's dispute with E. India Company, 5/76, 230; killed in action, 6/122; funeral, 6/127 & n. 3
LEYCESTER, 'Peter' [Ralph], antiquary (d. 1777): letter about P's diary (1728), vol. i, pp. lxxiii, lxxiv
LEYDEN: 1/148
LIDCOTT, Capt. [Robert], republican army officer: 1/45 & n. 3
LIDDELL, Sir Thomas: 7/142
LIGHTHOUSES: at mouth of Humber, 2/41 & n. 2, 44; at Harwich, 5/314; 6/3 & n. 4
LIGNE, Claude Lamoral, Prince de, Spanish ambassador-extraordinary 1660: arrival, 1/237 & n. 1, 247; departure, 1/260; ~ his sister, 2/38 & n.1
LILLY, [William], astrologer (d. 1681) [*see also* Books]: his astrology criticised by Booker, 1/274 & n. 3; laughed at by P, 8/270 & n. 2; his club, 1/274; social: 1/198–9
LILLY, ——, varnisher: death, 9/534; ~ his wife and brother, 9/534, 538
LILLY: *see* Lely
LIMEHOUSE: P visits, 2/198; 4/287; 5/265; 6/34; floods, 1/95 & n. 2; project for dock, 2/198; herring-boats built, 3/274; ropeyards, 5/265; 6/34
LIME ST: robbery, 5/8–9 & n.; execution, 5/23 & n. 2
LINCOLN, Will, of Cow Lane: hires coach and horses to P, 8/460, 464
LINCOLNSHIRE: magistrate imprisoned, 8/252 & n. 2
LINCOLN'S INN: Christmas revels, 3/2; new garden, 4/201 & n. 3; chapel, ib.
LINCOLN'S INN FIELDS/WALKS [*see also* Taverns etc.: Blue Balls]: P/EP walk(s) in, 1/173; 2/177; 3/112; 4/34, 297; 7/423; 8/422; improved, 4/297; coachhouses, 8/224, 225; riot, 9/129

LINCOLN'S INN FIELDS
THEATRE [*see also* Theatres]: Dav-
enant buried from, 9/158 & n. 2
LION QUAY: 4/273
LIPHOOK, Hants.: 9/274
LISBON: dirt and poverty, 2/197 &
n. 1; Sandwich's prints, 4/286 & n. 1;
Sandwich at, 2/186, 209; 3/51;
Spanish fleet off, 3/110; Stayner's
death, 3/249 & n. 1; also, 8/374-5 &
n.
[LISLE, Thomas], Master of the
Barber-Surgeons' Company: at ana-
tomy lecture, 4/59 & n. 1
LISOLA, Franz Paul de, Imperial
Resident 1666-7, 1667-8 [*see also*
Books]: at theatre, 8/383-4 & n.; ~
his wife and pretty daughter [Elean-
ora], ib.
LISSON GREEN, Mdx: P visits,
1/210; 7/204-5, 240
LITTLECOTE HOUSE, Wilts.: P
admires, 9/241-2 & n.
LITTLE SAXHAM, Suff.: King at,
9/336 & n. 4
LITTLETON, [James], merchant: victualling contract, 9/287 & n. 1;
appointed cashier to Navy Treasurer,
9/357 & n. 2
LITTLETON, Sir Thomas, M.P.
Much Wenlock, Salop 1661-79;
Joint-Treasurer of the Navy 1668-
71: his conversation, 7/210 & n. 1; on
commission of accounts, 8/194, 252;
opposes standing army, 8/353; to
undertake parliamentary management, 9/71 & n. 2; criticises Navy
Board, 9/103-4; appointed Joint-
Treasurer, 9/341, 346, 351; claims
precedence at office table, 9/365;
overbearing, 9/412; critical of Board's
constitution, 9/550; Duke of York
distrusts, 9/408, 410, 507; at dockyard
pay, 9/412, 419; navy estimates and
debts, 9/444-5, 447, 493-4, 525;
supports Child as Penn's successor,
9/549-50; attends meetings, 9/357,
369, 383, 393
LITTLE TOWER HILL: 4/55
LITTLE TURNSTILE (off Holborn):
9/435
LLEWELLYN, [Peter], clerk to E.
Dering, timber merchant: dismissed

from underclerkship to Council, 1/23;
on *Naseby*, 1/111, 114; returns from
Ireland, 4/295 & n. 2; Irish news
from, ib.; Dering's business, 4/422,
436; 5/1, 2, 5; 6/185, 242, 245; dies in
Plague, 6/304; social: in mock
marriage, 1/175; drunk and amorous,
1/244; bawdy story, 2/43, 50; at
Bartholomew Fair, 2/166; in Hyde
Park, 3/78; at taverns/cookshops etc.,
1/25, 27, 31, 37, 38, 87, 92, 174, 195,
208, 212, 232, 233, 248, 257, 311;
2/193; 5/330; visits/dines with P,
2/39, 201; 3/48; 4/326, 415, 421; 5/7,
26, 78, 106, 270, 281, 294, 308, 351;
6/38, 65, 98; also, 1/26, 59, 86; 2/42,
125, 208; alluded to: 1/116; ~ his
brother to go to Constantinople,
1/250
LLOYD, Sir Godfrey, military engineer: on fortifications, 8/126 &
n. 2
LLOYD, [Philip], clerk to Sir W.
Coventry, kted 1674: dances, 7/362;
?9/128; dismissed for idleness, 8/206
LLOYD (Floyd), Sir Richard, M.P.
Radnorshire: 4/77
LLOYD, [Thomas], secretary to the
Prize Commissioners: 8/58
LLOYD (Floyd), [William], chaplain
to the King 1666, Bishop of St Asaph
1680; Lichfield and Coventry 1692;
Worcester 1700 (d. 1717) [*see also*
Books]: sermons, 7/382-3; 8/587
& n. 3; also, 8/541 & n. 1
LLOYD (Floyd), ——, captain of
merchantman: 5/30
LOCK(E), Matthew, composer (d.
1677) [*see also* Music; Musical Com-
positions]: sings with P, 1/63
LOCK, [Matthew], secretary to Albe-
marle: political news from, 1/50-1;
exorbitant fees, 6/260; 7/323-4 & n.
[LOCKETT, Adam]: *see* Taverns etc.
[LOCKHART, Sir William], Governor of Dunkirk 1658-60 (d. 1676):
5/62 & n. 2
LODUM, Mrs ——: B. St Michel's
landlady, 3/286; niece to be EP's
companion, 4/19, 21; social: 4/45
LOGGIN(G)S, [John], chorister
Chapel Royal: 8/393-4 & n.
LOMBARD (Lumber) ST [*see also*

Taverns etc.: Royal Oak; Pope's Head; White Horse]: fire, 3/94; destroyed in Fire, 7/270, 276; rebuilt, 9/112, 517 & n. 1; new house collapses, 9/392
LONDON [for streets, buildings etc., *see* under names. *See also* Fire, the Great; Justice, administration of; Plague, the]
GENERAL: the diary as document of London history, vol. i, pp. xvii–xviii; its evidence on public opinion, vol. i, pp. cxxiv–cxxviii, cxxxiii–cxxxvii; unpopularity of bishops in, 2/57; 3/255, 271; favours Presbyterians, 2/141; and ejected ministers, 3/169, 255; resents rise of Arlington's faction, 3/229; political importance of, 4/131
BISHOPS: *see* Henchman, H.; Sheldon, G.
COMPANIES: *see* livery companies
CITY, CORPORATION OF:
  GENERAL: rights of freemen, 2/81 & n. 1; water supplies, 4/295 & n. 3; 8/370 & n. 2; granaries, 5/187–8 & n.
  CHRON. SERIES: supports free parliament, 1/1 & n. 5, 9 & n. 3, 16 & n. 3; sets up posts for defence, 1/3 & n. 2; sends delegation to Monck, 1/24 & n. 6, 25 & n. 3; friendly to army, 1/38; discourages payment of taxes to Rump, 1/47 & n. 1; Monck's actions against, 1/47, 48 & nn., 51; Monck allies with, 1/52 & nn., 55 & n. 2; imprisoned councilmen freed, 1/63; declares for Restoration, 1/122 & n. 3; to lend money to King, 1/128; sends deputation to The Hague, 1/138 & n. 4; entertains King at Guildhall, 1/193 & n. 1; elects puritan M.P.s, 2/57 & nn.; pays for *Loyal London*, 6/53 & n. 4; 8/105 & n. 3, 152; dispute over water baillage, 9/420–1 & n.; and with the Temple, 9/465–6 & n., 511–12 & n.
  FINANCES: loans to King, 1/128, 299 & n. 1; 5/307 & n. 2; 6/211; shortage of money, 3/100–1; 7/88 & n. 2, 159, 160, 171, 172, 174 & n. 5; 8/283–4, 370, 432, 456
  MILITIA: under arms, 1/70, 74; routed in Venner's rising, 2/9–11 *passim*;

mustered, 2/95; patrols streets, 3/92, 183, 229; at envoy's entry, 3/267–8; P assessed for, 3/283; quells riots, 5/99, 100, 9/132, 134, 466; under arms during Fire, 7/279; and Medway raid, 8/260, 264, 268; lieutenancy commission meets, 3/275 & n. 1
ORDERS/PRECEPTS OF LORD MAYOR AND ALDERMEN: about coachmen, 4/77–8 & n.; bonfires, 6/213 & n. 5
OFFICERS: Lord Mayor [*see also* Bateman, Sir A.; Bludworth, Sir T.; Bolton, Sir W.; Browne, Sir R.; Frederick, Sir J.; Laurence, Sir J.; Robinson, Sir J.; Turner, Sir W.]: annual show, 1/276–7 & n.; 4/356 & n. 1; 5/309; banquet, 2/201, 203; 3/240; 4/354–6 & nn.; ceremonial swords, 4/295 & n. 1; installation at St Paul's revived, 2/203 & n. 4; sworn in, 7/346 & n. 2; dinners, 4/294; 7/149; 8/321, 370; at St Mary Cree, 8/389; at Spital sermon, 3/57–8 & n.; 9/517–8; others: Aldermen: present gifts to Queen, 3/100; Chamberlain [*see* Player, Sir T.]; Clerk to the Market: opens Bartholomew Fair, 4/287; Common Crier: makes arrests, 4/292; profits, 5/248 & n. 1; Recorder [*see* Wilde, Sir W.]; Remembrancer: 1/183 & n. 1; 7/187 & n. 4; Sheriffs [*see also* Chaplin, [F.]; Ford, Sir R.; Gauden, Sir D.; Hooker, Sir W.; Waterman, G.]: nominated under Corporation Act, 3/162 & n. 4; Swordbearer: *see* Man, [W.]; Town Clerk: 9/33; Water-bailiff: 6/43 & n. 1
LIVERY COMPANIES: general: gifts to King, 1/128; granaries, 5/187–8 & n.; Barber-Surgeons': lecture, 4/59–60 & nn.; privileges, 5/261, n. 1, 271; Clothworkers': dinner, 1/186–7; P as Master (1677–8), vol. i, p.xxxix; Grocers': entertains Monck, 1/71; Mercers': Apposition court, 1/42, 43–4; Apposition Day feast, 5/37–8 & n.; as trustee of St Paul's school, 1/42 & n. 4; 8/218 & n. 3; entertains Monck, 1/79; as trustee of Royal Exchange, 1/113 & n. 5; Merchant Strangers': contests city tax, 9/420–1 & n.; Painter-Stainers': dispute over patent,

9/531–2 & n.; Parish Clerks': P dines with, 1/19; Skinners': entertains Monck, 1/106; liverymen, 4/21; Watermen's: 3/196 & n. 4; Wood-mongers': surrenders charter, 8/520 & n. 4

LONDON BRIDGE: piles for, 5/188; P falls into hole, 5/307; pavers at work, 6/312; pales blown off, 7/22; difficulty of passage through: anec-dote of Frenchman's fear, 3/160; tides, 3/52; 6/143, 327; 8/202; also, 1/323; 2/59, 101; 3/68, 198, 260; P shoots at night, 6/143, 156

LONDON GAZETTE, the: see Newspapers

LONDON WALL: Plague, 6/150; P drives by to avoid ruins after Fire, 7/358, 364, 395; 8/448, 451, 458, 459; 9/55, 134, 172; ruins in, 8/6

LONG, [?Israel], attorney: in Field's case, 4/201

LONG, Sir Robert, Auditor of the Receipt at the Exchequer: financial business, 4/81; 6/95, 96; 7/76, 79, 137; 8/102, 205, 576; 9/302, 387; defends Additional Aid, 6/311, 312; submits poll tax accounts, 9/82; story of battue, 7/79; house at Westminster, 4/272; and in Surrey, 6/312 & n. 2; ~ his niece, 4/272; kinswomen, 6/312

LONG ACRE: brothels, 5/50

LONG LANE: Plague, 6/150

LONGRACK, [John], purveyor of timber to the navy: wedding recep-tion, 7/262–3

LONG REACH (in the Thames): 1/95; 7/149

LOOKER, Mr ——, gardener to the Earl of Salisbury: bawdy story, 1/59; shows P Hatfield House and garden, 2/139

LOOSDUINEN, Holland: described, 1/149; monument to 365 children, 1/148–9 & n.

LOOTEN, Jan, landscape-painter (d. ?1681): 9/514 & n. 2

LORIMERS' HALL: funeral, 9/200 & n. 2

LOTTERIES: at court, 5/214–15 & n.; management by Fishery Corpora-tion, 5/269 & n., 276, 279, 294, 299–300 & n., 323; 6/53; Virginia lottery

alluded to, 5/323; P wins books, 7/48 & n. 1

LOUD, ——, page to Sandwich: examined by P in Latin, 1/312; also, 1/300; 2/15, 17; ~ his mother, 1/312

LOUIS XIV, King of France 1643–1715 [for his public policy, *see* France]: admiration for Mazarin, 4/26 & n. 2; love of work, ib.; illness, 4/156–7 & n., 159, 162, 163, 166, 169, 189; reviews guards, 4/189; rumoured assassination, 6/257, 259; shoots partridges, 7/79; his attitude to mistresses, 8/183 & n. 2; gift to Frances Stuart, 8/184 & n. 1; association with Elizabeth Berkeley, 8/338 & n. 1; prints of, 9/427 & n. 1, 451 & n. 1

LOVE, Ald. William: elected M.P. for London, 2/57 & n. 1

LOVELACE, Col. [Francis], of Can-non Row: P consults on tax assess-ment, 3/285 & n. 1

LOVELL (Loven), [?Charles], lawyer: P consults, 4/22, 33

LOVETT, ——, varnisher: pleasant, 7/124; lazy rogue, 7/258; 8/124, 206; new varnish, 6/97; varnishes paper for P, 6/97; 7/119–20, 124, 130, 184, 198–9, 211, 232, 353; P dissatisfied, 7/151, 258; imitation tortoise-shell, 7/184–5; varnishes prints, 7/185, 409; 8/23, 171, 204, 206; of crucifixion, 7/211, 218, 353; and of St Clara, 7/409; P god-father at son's (Catholic) christening, 7/329; to go to Spain, 8/23; social: 7/134

LOVETT, ——, wife of the varnisher: P admires, 6/97; 7/120, 134, 329; works with husband, 7/130, 198; 8/124; plays lute, 7/134, 199

LOWDER: *see* Lowther

[LOWE, Timothy], of Greenwich: 4/283; 6/242 & n. 1

LOWER (Lowre), [Richard], physi-cian: at dissection of eyes, 9/254–5

LOWESTOFT (Lastoffe): 6/130

LOWESTOFT, BATTLE OF: *see* War, the Second Dutch: naval movements and actions (1665)

[LOWMAN, John], keeper of the White Lion prison: 8/81 & n. 5

LOWTHER (Lowder), Anthony:

Marquess of Antrim, Irish royalist
(d. 1682): dispute over his estates,
5/57–8 & nn.

MACE: see Maes

MACHINES: see Inventions and Machines

MACKWORTH, Mr ——: 1/297;
2/119

MACNACHAN, Col. [Alexander]:
9/534 & n. 2

MADDEN, [John], Surveyor of the
Woods south of Trent: 7/263; 8/191;
~ his wife, 7/263

MADDOX, Robert, clerk, Navy
Office: 4/226

MADEIRA (Maderas): ships to, 3/47,
51; convoy, 7/316

MADEMOISELLE, governess to
Sandwich's daughters: see Le Blanc

MADGE, [Humphrey], court musician: sings, 1/10; 3/287; 4/428; recommends singing teacher to P, 2/126 &
n. 2; defends English music, 2/150;
social: 1/85, 223

MAES (Mace, Mawes), [Iudoco],
merchant: in customs dispute, 5/38,
43 & n. 3, 50, 147; Carteret consulted,
5/54–5, 76; escapes arrest, 5/72 & n. 1;
case discussed by Privy Council
committee, 5/251 & n. 3; social:
5/47, 53, 75, 191

MAGIC: see Popular Beliefs etc.

MAGNA CARTA: invoked by Sir H.
Vane, jun., 3/109; disregarded by
Chief Justice Kelyng, 8/577

MAIDENHEAD, Berks.: P at, 9/234

MAIDSTONE, Kent: assizes, 3/137; P
visits, 9/495–6 & nn.; Bell inn, 9/496
& n. 2

MAITLAND, John, 2nd Earl of
Lauderdale, cr. Duke 1672; Secretary
for Scottish affairs: on Naseby, 1/133;
hostile to Clarendon, 5/34, 57; influence with King, 5/56, 57 & n. 1, 73;
cunning, 5/73; Navy Office business,
7/224; house at Highgate, 7/224–5 &
n.; on music, 7/225; belittles Pentland
Rising, 7/384; at theatre, 8/196; at
Council committee, 8/278; also,
7/220; social: 1/325; 3/241; ~ his
wife [Anne], 7/224

MALAGA (Malago), Spain: fleet at,
7/45; alluded to: 6/14

MALET, [Elizabeth]: abducted by
Rochester, 6/110 & n. 2; Hinchingbrooke's proposed match, 6/110 &
n. 4, 119, 193 & n. 2; 7/56, 260;
suitors, 7/385; 8/45; marries Rochester, 8/44 & n. 4

MALLARD, (Maylard, Maylord),
[Thomas], musician: plays viol, 1/8 &
n. 3, 11; 3/287; 5/25, 64; sets tune for
P, 5/18; accompanies Sandwich to
Portugal, 3/112 & n. 1; also, 4/428;
social: 1/19, 24, 272; alluded to:
4/261; 5/349

[MALYN, Thomas], city Waterbailiff: 6/43 & n. 1

MAN, [William], City Swordbearer:
emissary to Monck, 1/1; offers £1000
for Clerkship of Acts, 1/210, 216, 219

MANCHESTER, Lord: see Mountagu,
Edward, 2nd Earl of Manchester

MANDEVILLE, Lord: see Mountagu,
Robert

MANLEY, Maj. [John]: 9/497; ~ his
wife and daughter-in-law, ib.

[MANNING, Edward], City Remembrancer 1665–6: 7/187 & n. 4

MANSELL [Francis]: pension, 8/74 &
also, 1/111 & n. 3, 256

MANUEL, Mrs ——: formerly actress, 8/384; P admires her singing,
8/384, 599; 9/128; social: 9/134, 172,
219; alluded to: 9/156; ~ her husband, 9/134, 172

MAPLESDEN, [Gervase], timber merchant: gifts to P, 4/361 & n. 1

MAPS [see also Books]: P examines at
Cade's, 3/1; at Dutch shops, 4/350;
his maps of Paris, 4/320; 9/286 & n. 1;
and of Brest, 9/437; buys books of
maps of cities, 5/55; his collection,
7/111, 124, 258, 290; his sea-charts,
7/290, 292; at Navy Office: Northern
Seas, 4/390; Tangier, by J. Moore,
5/98 & n. 2; Deptford, 6/111 & n. 5,
144; elsewhere: Portsmouth by Sandwich, 6/38, 46, 49, 50(2); city of London by Hollar, 7/378–9 & n.; Paris by
Gomboust, 7/379 & n.; England and
Wales by Hollar, 8/255 & n. 2

MARDYCK, Flanders: demolition of
fort, 1/250 & n. 2; siege (1657–8), 9/6
& n. 2

MARESCOE, (Morisco), [Charles],

merchant: 6/166 & n. 3

MARGATE (Margetts), Kent [*see also* Drink: ale]: Princess Mary at, 1/252; Dutch fleet off, 6/8, 268

MARGETTS, [George], rope merchant, Limehouse: 5/265 & n. 1

MARGETTS, ——, merchant, of Fenchurch St: 9/518

MARGUERITE de Valois, Queen of Navarre (d. 1549): 9/31 & n. 2

[MARIA–ANNA], Queen Regent of Portugal 1665–75: Duke of York's letter to, 8/452 & n. 1

[MARIA-TERESA], Queen of France, wife of Louis XIV (d. 1683): 4/189; 8/254

MARIUS, Gaius (186–57 B.C.): alluded to in sermon, 5/97

MARKHAM, [?George, ?William], kinsman of Sir W. Penn: marriage, 7/235

MARKHAM, Nan (b. Wright), maid to Lady Penn: marriage, 7/235; P kisses, 7/418; 9/177; allegedly Penn's mistress, 8/322; in Navy Board pew, 8/322, 437; pregnant, 8/371; social: 7/246, 249, 280, 353, 422; 8/29, 274, 284; 9/312, 314

MARK LANE: Fire, 7/268, 276; effigy hanged, 8/89

MARLBOROUGH, Wilts.: P visits, 9/241 & nn.

MARLOW, [Thomas], Navy Office messenger: 6/226, 244; 8/538

MARR(E), Mr ——: at Dagenhams, Essex, 6/180; 7/17

MARRIAGE:

GENERAL: 'fools decoyed into', 6/339; special licence, 9/493; divorce, 2/6 & n. 2

MARRIAGE SETTLEMENTS [asterisks denote entries at which amounts of portions etc. are given]: 2/159*, 242*; 3/3*, 176* & n. 1, 226, 228*, 231* & n. 1, 232*; 4/19*, 159*, 345*; 6/138* & n. 1, 150*, 180* & n. 3, 191* & n. 4, 252*; 7/15*, 73*, 78*, 81*, 88–9*, 104*, 170* & n. 1, 241*, 264*; 8/63*, 118*, 190*, 217*, 300* & n. 2, 365*, 539*; 9/16–17, 51* & n. 4, 55, 56* & n. 5, 61* & n. 1, 97*, 157, 170*

WEDDING CEREMONIES: posy ring, 1/39–40; bridemen, 4/345; 9/500; dinner, 7/262–3; untying ribbons etc., 2/23; 3/22; flinging stockings, 4/38; sackposset, ib.; putting to bed, 6/176; 9/51; music on morning after, 8/66; favours/gifts to guests, 4/218; 8/73, 77, 79; 9/28, 335; mock weddings, 1/27; 4/37–8

WEDDING (P) [*see also* Pepys, Samuel: marriage etc.]: anniversary, 2/194; 6/262; forgets it, 5/294; unsure of number of years of marriage, 7/318

MARRIOT(T), [Benjamin], attorney: the great eater, 1/40–1 & n.

MARRIOTT, [James], housekeeper, Hampton Court: 6/166

MARRIOTT, [Richard], housekeeper, Hampton Court: 3/82 & n. 1

MARROWBONE: *see* Marylebone

MARSEILLES: 8/421

MARSH, [Alphonso], court musician: 2/158 & n. 3; ~ his wife, ib.

MARSH, [George], son of Capt. Richard: 3/72

MARSH, Capt. [Richard], Storekeeper, Ordnance Office, the Tower: house at Limehouse, 2/198; also, 3/72; 91; 4/28; 5/215

MARSH, Thomas, Clerk Assistant, the House of Commons: 4/281

MARSH, [James], cook, Whitehall: P visits, 1/23, 25, 27, 61, 64–5, 87, 92

MARSHALL, Anne (Nan), actress: P admires in *The Indian queen*, 5/33–4 & n.; and criticises, 9/250; alleged parentage, 8/502–3 & n.

MARSHALL, Rebecca, actress: her good looks, 8/433; 9/189; alleged parentage, 8/502–3 & n.; P admires in *The maid's tragedy*, 7/399 & n. 2; *The maiden queen*, 8/235 & n. 2; *The virgin martyr*, 9/93–4 & n.; *Hyde Park*, 9/260; also, 9/156

MARSHALL, Stephen, Presbyterian divine (d. 1655): sermons, 4/111 & n. 4; also, 8/502–3 & n.

MARSHALL, ——, timber merchant: 3/169

MARTIN, Betty (b. Lane), wife of Samuel; linendraper in Westminster Hall and P's mistress:

P'S LOW OPINION: 5/216–17; 8/167, 375–6; 9/552

CHRON. SERIES: sells goods to P, 1/214,

231; 4/234; 8/440, 456; her sweet-
hearts, 1/282; 2/9; match with
Hawley favoured by P, 4/431; 5/41,
42, 71, 112–13; consults palmist,
4/234–5; marries Martin, 5/215; a
bad marriage, 5/219, 262, 331;
pregnant, 5/242, 331, 338; asks P to be
godfather, 5/338; and for place for
husband, 5/242, 285, 286, 338; 6/55;
7/218, 262; 9/165; birth of son
Charles, 6/52, 53, 65; out of town,
6/141; 7/49; borrows money, 7/50,
62; new lodgings, 7/218; pregnant,
7/218, 319; accompanies husband to
Portsmouth, 9/527, 551, 552
AMOROUS ENCOUNTERS WITH P: at P's
house, 1/220; at taverns, 4/203, 234,
263, 317; 5/9, 17, 127–8, 219, 242;
7/104; P catches cold in consequence,
4/318; at lodgings, 5/216, 338; Bow
St lodgings, 6/1–2, 68; last lodgings,
7/49; new lodgings, 7/61, 75, 128,
142, 284, 319, 345; 8/64, 120, 139,
177, 224, 236, 255–6, 393, 456, 461,
478, 601; 9/99, 118, 126, 136, 165,
208, 220, 249, 514; fails to keep
assignations, 4/232, 261, 297, 316;
7/101; 8/166, 167; 9/168; P sends
wine, 5/11; 7/375; relieved she is not
pregnant, 5/33; 8/318, 323;? also,
6/114, 115
SOCIAL: at funeral, 1/24; at her lodgings, 7/134, 173, 230, 231, 232, 337,
409; 8/110–11, 128, 479; at tavern,
8/58; at P's house, 9/297
~ her cousins, 5/217; starling, 9/99,
208, 209
MARTIN, [Catherine], daughter of
Betty: birth, 7/382, 386; P godfather,
7/394; possibly father, 7/413; his gifts,
8/456, 498; her death, 9/187
MARTIN, [John], bookseller, Temple
Bar: describes burning of St Paul's,
9/22–3; P buys from/has books bound
by, 9/17–18 & n., 22–3, 57–8, 89, 97,
101–2 & n., 120, 121, 144, 166, 200,
216, 365; P visits, 9/21, 158, 183, 439
MARTIN, [Samuel], husband of
Betty: P's low opinion, 5/216–17,
286, 302; 8/601; 9/552; servant of
Capt. Marsh, 5/215; marriage, 5/215,
219, 331; 6/71; asks P for place, 5/242,
262, 285, 286, 302, 338; 6/55; pay-

master to marines, 5/331; in France,
6/68, 141; appointed purser, 7/75, 218,
360; 8/97, 318; later career, 8/461;
9/165, 514, 527, 552; also, 8/102–3;
9/43; social: 7/134, 142–3, 409;
8/110–11; 9/274; alluded to: 9/168,
209, 514
MARTIN, [Capt. William], naval
officer: killed in action, 7/231
MARTIN ABBEY: see Merton Priory
MARY I, Queen of England 1553–8:
7/394
MARY, Queen of Scots (d. 1587):
letters, 6/308 & n. 2; crucifix, 8/26 &
n. 3
MARY, Princess, daughter of the Duke
of York, later Mary II Queen of
England (d. 1694): born, 3/75 & n. 1;
her dancing, 9/507; also, 5/268
MARY, Princess Royal of England,
Princess Dowager of Holland (d.
1660): at The Hague, 1/144 & n. 1,
147; her portrait, 1/144 & n. 5; on
Naseby, 1/154; sails to England, 1/234
& n. 4, 236, 242, 247, 252, 254; dines
in public at Whitehall, 1/299; rumoured marriage to H. Jermyn, 1/320 &
n. 3; death from smallpox, 1/320,
322; 2/1; doctors blamed for, 1/323 &
n. 1; also, 1/157, 297
MARY, Princess of Orange (d. 1688):
marries Count Palatine of Simmern,
7/250 & n. 1
MARYLEBONE (Marrowbone, Mar-
bone): Lord Mayor and aldermen
dine at, 8/370 & n. 2; also, 1/95, 210
MARYLEBONE GARDENS: 9/189
MARYS, ——, a tanner of Greenwich:
9/543
MASHAM (Massam), Orlando: 4/26
MASHAM, Massom: see Mossom
MASON, [John], timber merchant,
Maidstone: (alleged) gift to P, 9/90;
gift to Hewer, 9/283; ~ his wife, 9/90
MASQUES: at school, 4/45, 58–9, 112
& n. 2; at court, 6/29 & n. 6
MASSEY, Maj. Gen. Sir Edward:
2/219 & n. 3
MATHEMATICS / MATHEMATI-
CAL INSTRUMENTS: see Science
etc.; Scientific etc. Instruments
MATTHEWS, [John], of the Privy
Seal Office: 1/207, 211, 212, 235

erhithe, 4/296; increase after Plague, 7/3; at Bishop's Stortford and Cambridge, 8/469; P gives to, 9/227–8

MENNES (Mince, Minnes), Sir John, Comptroller of the Navy 1661–71, and naval commander:

CHARACTER: fine gentleman and good scholar, 2/210; good company, 3/112; 4/67, 196, 346; 5/227; 8/95; honest, 7/255; P criticises, 5/118, 120, 121; foolish/inefficient/senile, 4/67, 97, 98, 104, 151, 152, 233, 324–5; 5/67–8, 80, 182, 318, 322, 326; 6/226, 228, 309; 7/76, 235, 300, 305–6; 8/12, 550; 9/384, 393, 408, 501; criticised by Sandwich, 3/122–3; 4/196; Coventry, 4/97, 196, 341; 5/218, 313–14; 7/235, 302, 308, 310, 409, 413; 8/570, 571; Commissioner Pett, 4/98; and Brouncker, 6/237

AS COMPTROLLER:

APPOINTMENT ETC.: appointed, 2/206 & n. 4; loses right to draft contracts, 3/99–100 & n.; assistants proposed for, 3/236–7 & n.; 4/61 & n. 1, 66, 67, 71, 75, 397–8; 5/15; 7/421; Brouncker and Penn to assist, 8/20 & n. 2, 24, 25, 30, 38; desires place in Prize Office, 5/328; objects to arrangements for tickets, 9/383; rumoured dismissal/resignation, 7/321, 324, 328, 361, 380; 8/586; 9/100, 337, 386, 555; dismissal recommended, 9/131, 151, 205–6, 400

FINANCIAL BUSINESS: estimates etc.: 5/325, 326; 6/72; 7/48, 311–12; 8/140; 9/80, 174, 220, 444–5; at pays, 3/193, 215, 225, 234, 289, 290; 4/175, 219, 222, 225, 253, 291–2; 7/133, 253, 327, 339; 8/114, 257; works on accounts: Creed's, 3/278–9; 4/215–16; Navy Treasurer's, 3/240; 5/104, 105; 7/305–6; 9/222; R. Cocke's, 4/290 & n. 3, 325 & n. 2; Warren's, 8/550; his carelessness, 4/11; 6/119: 9/394; on commanders' pay, 4/7; investigates Exchequer methods, 5/7(2); and new method of paying bills, 6/336 & n. 2; makes proposals about storekeepers' accounts, 9/444

DOCKYARD BUSINESS (other than pays): visits, 3/205, 280; 4/12, 67, 203–4, 284, 317–18, 389; 5/39; 6/83, 171; 8/95;

launch, 4/102; sale of provisions, 4/319; survey, 5/35; mast-dock, 5/202, 353; 6/96

THE PRIZE-GOODS AFFAIR: responsibility for captured E. Indiamen, 6/234, 236, 242, 262, 273, 280, 286; complains of pillage, 6/249; examines Howe, 6/333–4; allowance, 8/446

OTHER BUSINESS: Field's case, 4/51, 52, 54, 71; slops, 4/74; victualling, 4/84; shipping, 4/204, 227; 6/193–4, 226, 228; 9/251; seamen's riot, 4/294, 295; contracts, 4/326, 380–1, 421; 5/318; 6/38; 7/2; 9/542; burning of figurehead, 4/318, 420; Clarendon's timber, 5/205, 218; gun-wadding, 5/316; wreck, 6/54; Board's Greenwich offices, 6/200, 201; Plague at Greenwich, 6/211; Carkesse case, 8/76, 83, 204(2), 213, 215, 386; Dutch raid on Medway, 8/259, 268, 272, 394; defence of office against parliamentary charges, 8/504; 9/80, 103; Duke of York's proposed reforms, 9/305, 525; also, 6/126–7; 9/327; unspecified: 3/106, 201, 203, 229, 236–7, 252, 265, 272; 4/4, 12, 21, 31, 43, 50, 69, 81, 91, 97, 106, 110, 152, 154, 177, 178, 213, 226, 234, 241, 243, 278, 296, 332, 338, 435; 5/98, 138, 156–7, 157, 228, 241–2, 286, 303, 318, 333, 349; 6/39, 140, 145(2), 203, 222, 233, 334, 339; 7/13, 18, 26, 50, 419; 8/62, 178, 198, 346, 403, 413, 565; 9/5, 156, 251, 267, 315, 316, 428, 508

RELATIONS WITH COLLEAGUES AND OTHERS: failure to collaborate, 5/235; enmity to Commissioner Pett, 3/227; 4/91, 228; 6/104; and to P, 4/161; criticises him for neglect of business, 6/92; supports, 5/238; subservient to Batten, 4/194, 205, 436; 5/108; quarrels with, 5/293; complains of Hayter, 4/97, 100; unjust to Steventon, 4/151; accuses Hewer of fraud, 4/152

AS NAVAL COMMANDER: appointed Vice-Admiral, 2/70 & n. 5; salary, 4/325; on flag honour, 2/229; 3/4, 14; at Council of War, 3/124; reminiscences, 3/252; 4/124 & n. 1; 6/127 & n. 1; enmity to Sandwich, 2/169, 216–17, 229; 3/123

OTHER APPOINTMENTS: Master of

Trinity House, 3/93; 4/185; dines at, 3/190; 4/209; 7/381–2; on Chatham Chest Commission, 3/257; 6/68; Tangier Committee, 3/272; 4/319; 6/139; 9/316; and Royal Fishery, 5/199

HEALTH: lame, 4/314; 8/4; seriously ill, 7/253, 255(2), 261, 289; 8/296, 298, 314, 315, 324; also, 4/110; 5/268; 6/21, 23; 7/405; 9/276

HOUSE/HOUSEHOLD: official lodgings at Seething Lane: upper room used by P, 3/38; to exchange lodgings with Turner, 3/111; affected by P's alterations, 3/193, 194, 195, 197, 199, 205, 216, 231, 244, 252, 255, 261; 5/356; P admires, 3/262; new entry, 3/247, 249, 250; complains of accommodation, 5/278 & n. 3; lodgings at Greenwich: 6/190; leaves Turner's lodgings, 7/296; also, 3/259; 4/51, 278; 6/210; 8/552, 555; ~ his servant George, 6/200; coachman, 9/527

INTELLECTUAL INTERESTS ETC.: visits Mint, 4/143–8; quotes Chaucer, 4/184; his pictures, 4/187, 191, 319; views royal collection, 8/403; recites verse, 4/200 & n. 4; interest in chemistry, 4/218; and anatomy, 4/334; prescribes medicines for P, 4/39, 40, 329; medical attendant at court in exile, 5/242 & n. 2; claims to have translated from Dutch, 5/235

POLITICS: opposes test bill, 4/125; friend of Clarendon, 4/196

SOCIAL: his mirth and mimicry, 6/220; 7/1–2; stories: of sanitation in Portugal, 3/205; longevity, 6/237 & n. 3; ancestor's murder, 8/141; and Sir L. Dyve and others, 8/566–7 & nn.; tells bawdy story, 3/243; his stories entered in P's book of anecdotes, 4/346; 8/95; at christenings, 4/165; 8/540; gives dinner for Clarendon, 4/173; at dinners given by Lord Mayor, 4/341; Carteret, 5/15; Coventry, 5/102, 166; Lieutenant of Tower, 6/56; Sir G. Smith, 6/187; Brouncker, 6/204; 7/1–2; Cocke, 6/220; Hickes, 6/222; Sandwich, 6/273; Penn, 8/3, 77; 9/283, 505; and Gauden, 9/214; gives dinners for colleagues and associates, 5/227, 357;

6/191, 237, 333; lends coach to EP, 6/45; his tiff with Battens, 6/233, 234; dines with P, 7/353; at parish dinners, 8/218; 9/179, 559; theatre, 9/269–70; Bartholomew Fair, 9/301; and taverns, 3/279; 5/308; 6/119; 8/220; 9/115, 222, 359; visits/dines with etc. Batten, 3/189; 4/171, 230, 237; 5/216; 6/220–1; 7/226, 8/376; P visits/dines with etc., 4/28; 5/335; 6/206, 210, 212; also, 4/155, 212, 225; 5/176, 217; 6/141; 7/76; 8/389

MISC.: almost drowned near Portsmouth, 3/283–4; praises beauty of Suffolk women, 4/186; on homosexuality, 4/210; on Spanish stamp tax, 7/332; inspects new Exchange Alley, 4/214; King's bawdy joke against, 5/12; Denham's verses on, 8/380 & n. 2; news from Holland, 7/228; 8/88; assessed for poll-tax, 8/120; foundling on doorstep, 9/304

ALLUDED TO: 3/198

~ his sister, 4/74; 6/233; 8/4; niece, 4/74; 8/4; 9/505

MERCER, Anne, Mary's sister: at dances at P's house, 7/230; 8/28, 493, 511; 9/42; runs for wagers, 8/167; also, 7/200, 246; 8/11, 19; 9/12, 96, 111, 197

MERCER, Mary, companion to EP:

CHRON. SERIES: pretty, 5/360; 8/375; growing fat, 8/508; proposed as companion, 5/229 & n. 2, 256 & n. 1; engaged, 5/257, 265, 267; with EP to Woolwich in Plague, 6/143, 183, 340; returns, 7/7; dress, 6/238; helps rule Navy Office books, 7/63, 100; washes P's ears, combs/cuts his hair, 6/21; 7/95; 8/280; quarrels with EP, 6/205, 206; 7/60, 175, 176; EP's jealousy of, 5/274; 7/228, 238; P fondles, 7/104, 172; dismissed by EP, 7/273; P misses her, 7/294; unwilling to return, 7/298–303 passim; visits EP, 7/360; P fondles/kisses again, 7/364; 8/37, 150; 9/55; EP displeased with, 8/79, 118; P's valentine, 9/67; visits Cambridge with EP and others, 9/306; also, 6/25, 66, 85; 7/138; 9/19, 98

MUSICAL: plays harpsichord/viol, 5/266, 282; sings with P/EP/others, 5/266; 6/138; 7/44, 53, 110, 111, 117, 172,

183, 195, 199, 205, 212, 216, 227, 228, 230, 267; 8/37, 165, 174, 223, 283, 289, 328, 375; 9/14, 85, 120, 179, 196, 197, 199, 201, 202, 204, 216, 217, 221, 249; her talent, 7/228; 8/29; P teaches *It is decreed*, 8/35; 9/14, 16; *Canite Jehovae*, 9/194; and the Lark's song, 9/304; her style of singing, 8/165–6
SOCIAL: at theatre, 5/267, 289, 335; 6/73; 7/412; 8/27, 157, 439–40, 508; 9/14, 19, 54, 85, 100, 189, 195, 198–9, 249, 269, 278, 280–1, 296, 304, 326; visits/shopping etc., 5/301; 6/40, 48–9, 87, 89, 102, 104, 121, 128, 223, 250, 251, 270, 282, 320–1; 7/18, 72, 78, 81, 84, 128, 131, 137, 152, 169, 172, 220; 8/431–2; river trips to Gravesend, Woolwich, etc., 5/305; 6/106, 111, 119; 7/142, 233, 235; 8/346; jaunts to Islington, Bow, Hackney, etc., 6/74, 112; 7/54–5, 108, 113, 126, 129, 133, 167, 170, 181–2, 240, 267; 8/150, 174–5, 296; 9/197, 208, 221, 271–2; at Vauxhall, 7/198; 9/195–6, 198–9, 203–4, 216; and Bartholomew Fair, 9/293, 296, 299; dances, 6/262, 279; 7/43–4, 246, 362; 8/29, 493, 511; 9/12, 42, 289; toasted at Bear garden, 7/245–6; visits P's house after leaving household, 7/200, 374, 403, 419, 421; 8/11, 13, 19, 157, 166, 282, 289, 594; 9/111, 213, 244, 250; also, 7/257, 267; 8/165, 167; 9/278
ALLUDED TO: 7/15; 9/454, 519
~ her sisters, 7/230
MERCER, [Nicola], Mary's mother: ends quarrel between EP and Mary, 7/176; annoyed at Mary's dismissal, 7/273, 300, 301; social: gives parties for naval victories, 7/152, 246; also, 5/257; 6/340; 7/43, 101, 200; 9/110, 111, 197, 276; alluded to: 7/175
MERCER, William, Mary's brother: ?provides fireworks for party, 7/152; makes valentine for EP, 8/62
MERCER, [William], Mary's father: 5/265
MERCER, P's: *see* Finch
MERCERS' CHAPEL, Cheapside: P visits, 2/20; in Fire, 7/277
MERCERS' COMPANY: *see* London: livery companies
MERCERS' HALL, Cheapside: P as

schoolboy at, 2/20; Council of Trade meets, ib.
MERCHANT STRANGERS' COMPANY: *see* London: livery companies
MERCHANT TAYLORS' HALL, Threadneedle St: 7/235
MERES, Sir Thomas, M.P. Lincoln: eloquent, 8/2; supports Buckingham, 8/342
MERITON, [John], Rector of St Michael, Cornhill: his high reputation, 7/365 & n. 3; also, 6/152
MERITON, [Thomas], Rector of St Nicholas Cole Abbey: an 'old dunce', 7/365 & n. 3; preaches well, 7/365; 8/222
MERRETT, Christopher, physician: on anatomy, 3/228 & n. 2; at Dr Wilkins's, 7/12; drunk at Royal Society club, 7/21
MERSTON, Messum: *see* Mossom
MERTON PRIORY, Surrey: bought by Thomas P of Hatcham, 9/207 & n. 2
MERVIN, [John], merchant: 6/164
MESSIAH, the false: *see* Sabbatai Zevi
METEORS: *see* Science and Mathematics: astronomy
MEXICO: coinage, 4/146
MEYNELL (Maynall), Ald. Francis, goldsmith-banker; Sheriff 1661–2: entertains P and colleagues, 3/200; income, 4/17; refuses to lend to Navy, 6/121; advances money to victualler, 6/254; death, 7/315; also, 5/33
MICHELANGELO: paintings copied, 3/80 & n. 1
MICO, [Edward], merchant: Dutch compensation to, 5/52 & n. 1
MIDDLEBURG, Holland: 1/137
MIDDLEBURGH, ——, merchant: 4/396
MIDDLEGROUND, the (shoal at mouth of Thames estuary): Dutch fleet in, 8/359
MIDDLESEX, Lord: *see* Sackville, Charles, 1st Earl of Middlesex
MIDDLESEX, Lady: *see* Cranfield
MIDDLE TEMPLE: Readers' Feast, 6/28 & n. 2, 49 & n. 2; gaming in Hall, 9/3 & n. 1; riot, 9/465–6 & n., 511–12
MIDDLETON, Elizabeth/Jane: *see* Myddelton

MIDDLETON, John, 1st Earl of Middleton, soldier and Governor of Tangier 1668–d.74: character, 8/167 & n. 1, 201 & n. 2, 306, 600–1; 9/326, 328, 551; Lauderdale's hostility, 5/57 & n. 1; conduct in Medway raid, 8/306–7, 311; 9/11; Governor of Tangier, 8/167 & n. 1; payment to, 9/294, 325, 328 & n. 3; to go to Tangier, 9/492, 504; favoured by Duke of York, 9/543, 545; asks for loan, 9/534; ~ his servant, 9/326

[MIDDLETON, John], 'the child of Hales', wrestler (d. 1623): 9/226 & n. 3

MIDDLETON, Col. Thomas, Navy Commissioner at Portsmouth 1664, Surveyor of the Navy 1667:

p's OPINION: 8/462, 582; 9/500

OFFICIAL CAREER: appointed to Portsmouth, 5/314 & n. 2; at pay, 7/75; reports to Board, 7/333; 8/142; appointed Surveyor, 8/462 & n. 3, 575 & n. 1, 582; at launch, 9/100–01; defends master-attendants, 9/267; replies to Duke of York's great letter, 9/314 & n. 1; allegations against Hewer, 9/388 & n. 2, 390–5 passim; criticised about pay, 9/412; on refitting fleet, 9/425–6; proposals about pursers etc., 9/459, 460 & n. 2; assessor at court martial, 9/488–9, 498, 505, 508, 510–11; at Chatham, 9/494, 495, 499; attends meetings/unspecified business, 7/75, 313, 418; 8/594; 9/335, 410, 430; also, 9/525

SOCIAL: his stories of Barbados etc., 8/275; 9/499–500 & n.; at parish dinner, 9/559; also, 5/1; 9/253, 359

MISC.: coach, 9/206; ill, 9/533

~ his wife, [Elizabeth], death of, 9/444, 452

MILDMAY, Sir Henry, regicide (d.? 1664): his sentence, 3/19 & n. 1; house forfeited, 6/102 & n. 4

MILE END/MILE END GREEN [see also Taverns etc.: Gun; Rose and Crown]: P/EP and others at, 5/201; 6/80; 8/389, 393, 398, 399, 419, 424, 443, 485, 500; 9/88, 177, 180, 202, 221, 254, 255; market established at after Fire, 7/280

MILFORD STAIRS: 2/110

MILITIA, the [see also London]: in Yorkshire, 8/154; in Medway raid, 8/308; favoured by country party in parliament, 8/352–3 & n.

MILK HOUSE, the, Hyde Park: P visits, 9/142, ?154, 156, 175, 184, 222, 260, 533–4, 541

MILK ST: 5/122

MILLER, Lt-Col. [John]: holds Tower for Committee of Safety, 1/39 & n. 2

MILLES, [Anna]: christened, 2/192 & n. 3

MILLES, Daniel, Rector of St Olave's, Hart St 1657–89:

CHARACTER: 1/225; 3/134–5; 8/247–8, 564

CHRON. SERIES: adopts Prayer Book service, 1/282, 289; and surplice, 3/213, 235, 247; to begin catechising, 5/49; leaves parish in Plague, 7/35; chaplain to Duke of York and Rector of Wanstead, 8/241 & n. 1, 247–8; also 2/24; 3/81, 104; 5/125; 8/540; 9/325

SERMONS [an asterisk denotes comment by P. See also Sermons (in main series)]: 1/225, 241, 251★, 270★, 308★, 322★; 2/24★, 26★, 42★, 52★, 59★, 67, 112, 161, 210, 225, 238★; 3/12–13★, 20, 104★, 110★, 132★, 178, 247★, 264, 270★; 4/29★, 30★, 177, 268, 369★, 426★, 433★; 5/49, 356★; 6/131★, 132; 7/35★ & n. 3, 112★, 283★, 420★, 425★; 8/51★, 91★, 154★, 437, 535★, 557★, 589★; 9/325, 385, 452, 514★, 548★

SOCIAL: first dinner at P's house in five years, 8/437; P's first visit to, 9/220; his story of suicide, 3/239; at parish dinner, 8/218; 9/179; christening, 8/540; and P's house, 9/24, 184, 219, 260, 406; also, 2/28, 131; 3/22; 9/245

MILLES, [Daniel], son of Daniel and Mary: EP godmother, 8/540 & n. 5; P's gift, 8/544

MILLES, [Elizabeth], daughter of Daniel and Mary: christened, 5/265 & n. 3

MILLES, [Mary], wife of Daniel: family connection with Brampton, 2/28; 8/437 & n. 3; at P's house, 2/28; 9/24, 184, 219, 260, 406; alluded to: 9/245; ~ her (unnamed) daughter, 9/219

MILLET, Capt. [Henry]: book of ships' rates, 6/217 & n. 2; evidence against Commissioner Pett, 8/502

MILLICENT, Sir John, of Barham, Cambs: anecdote of, 3/159 & nn.

MINCING (Minchen) Lane: fire, 9/245

MINNES, Mince: *see* Mennes, Sir John; Myngs, Christopher

MINORIES, the: 4/84, 434; 7/423; 8/224; 9/204

MINORS, Capt. [Richard], naval officer: E. India Company business, 4/299 & n. 2, 396; 9/37

MITCHELL, Mrs [Ann], bookseller in Westminster Hall:
GENERAL: her illegitimate daughter, 5/9; leaves town in Plague, 6/162; kinswoman as maid to EP, 7/108, 109; asks P to help son, 8/341; also, 7/394; 8/72, 202, 479, 583; 9/99
AS BOOKSELLER: P pays, 1/26, 87; buys newspapers from, 6/162; and book, 8/10; reads pamphlets at, 7/393–4; P/EP visit(s), 1/30, 31, 66, 204, 222, 279; 2/31, 139; 3/296; 4/242, 251; 7/61, 123, 186, 295; 8/47, 68, 177, 440; 9/81, 486
~ her daughter, 9/265

MITCHELL, Betty, (b. Howlett), wife of Michael:
CHRON. SERIES: betrothed to Michael's brother, 5/9; 7/75; marries Michael, 7/75, 81; moves to Thames St, 7/98, 108, 114; to Shadwell after Fire, 7/351; unhappily married, 7/284; 8/479; keeps shop for mother, 8/121
P'S FONDNESS FOR: calls her 'wife', 4/234, 242; 7/75, 89; admires, 5/9, 41; 6/330–1; 7/61, 157, 175, 235, 365; 8/20, 21, 47, 51, 91, 121, 138, 159, 224, 236, 273; 9/548–9; mistakes another woman for, 7/303; 8/400; gifts to, 8/46, 53; kisses/fondles, 7/123, 197, 207, 230, 234, 338–9, 395, 419; 8/32, 46, 53, 110, 511; 9/564; she avoids/is cold to, 7/245, 418–19; 8/34, 68, 70, 440; 9/173
SOCIAL: with husband dines at/visits P's house, 7/206–7, 243, 311, 344, 418; 8/5–6, 166, 289, 412–13, 524; 9/255, 276; P visits, 7/255; 8/37, 58, 146, 151; 9/114, 198, 297, 328; at christen-

ing, 7/394; wedding anniversary, 8/72; also, 7/142, 161, 186, 337; 8/45, 66, 255
ALLUDED TO: 8/52, 504, 514; 9/124, 168
~ her first daughter (Betty) born, 8/53, 177, 186, 199–200, 202, 224; baptised, 8/202; dies, 8/273, 277, 289; her second daughter (Betty) born, 9/260, 264; her maid, 8/54

MITCHELL, [John], flagmaker: supplies, 4/73 & n. 2; gift to P, 4/220

MITCHELL, [Michael], keeper of strong-water house:
CHRON. SERIES: marries Betty Howlett, 7/75, 81; succeeds to brother's trade and house, 7/81, 114; P calls there, 7/157, 234–5; 8/20, 32, 34, 37, 58, 66, 94, 102, 120, 151, 175, 186, 199, 224, 504; 9/198, 249, 297; cashes pay tickets, 7/174–5 & n., 319, 338; employed on cork business, 7/206; house burnt in Fire, 7/268; moves to Shadwell, 7/284, 338; new shop, 7/339; house rebuilt, 8/20; 9/75, 114, 124; relations with wife, 7/284; 8/479, 511; prevents P from seeing her, 8/316; 9/173; out of town, 9/564
SOCIAL: on river, 7/161; 8/34, 66, 68; to Hackney, 7/207; at christenings, 7/394; 8/202; wedding anniversary party, 8/72; at P's house, 7/206, 243, 311, 344, 365–6, 418; 8/5–6, 21, 51, 91, 138, 166, 236, 289, 413, 524; 9/255; also, 7/123; 8/493
ALLUDED TO: 9/99, 161

MITCHELL, [Miles], bookseller in Westminster Hall: at coronation banquet, 2/86; leaves town in Plague, 6/162; garden, 7/123; social: 1/204, 222; 8/68, 72, 202; alluded to: 7/308;
~ his (unnamed) son: betrothed to Betty Howlett, 5/9; 7/75; dies of plague, 7/75; ?alluded to, 6/186; another (unnamed) son: 8/341

[MODERS, Mary], 'the German princess'; imposter [*see also* Plays: *The German princess*]: in prison, 4/163 & n. 4; tried and acquitted, 4/177 & n. 2

MOFFETT (Muffett), [Thomas], physician and author (d. 1604): story of Dr Caius, 8/543 & n. 2

MOHUN (Moone), [Michael], actor: high reputation, 1/297; his part in

Lacy's quarrel with King, 8/168 & n. 6; quarrels with Hart, 8/569; P admires in *The beggar's bush*, 1/297 & n. 3; in *The Traitor*, 1/300 & n. 1; criticises in *The Moor of Venice*, 9/438
MOHUN (Moone), Capt. [Robert], naval officer: ship wrecked off Cadiz, 6/19 & n. 3; reputation for ill-luck, ib. & n. 4, 6/20
[MOLINA, Antonio Francesca Mesia, de Tobar y Paz, Conde de], Spanish ambassador 1665–9: 8/107; 9/544 & n.4
MOLINS (Mullins), Edward, surgeon: leg amputated, 4/340 & n.1; death, 4/345
MOLINS, [James], surgeon: operates on Rupert, 8/41 & n.2
MONCK, Anne, Duchess of Albemarle:
LOOKS AND CHARACTER (critical comments): 2/51; 6/324; 7/10, 56 & n. 2, 57, 354; 8/147
CHRON. SERIES: trades in appointments, 1/181 & n. 4, 184; 3/43 & n. 3; 8/219–20; book fulsomely dedicated to, 1/275 & n. 2; speaks well of P, 4/231; 8/490; slanders Sandwich, 6/324; 7/10; and Penn, 9/138–9; dislikes Coventry, 7/196; comments on du Teil's incompetent gunnery, 8/147 & n. 3; and on division of fleet (1666), 8/148; also, 1/53
SOCIAL: 2/51; 3/79; 6/268
ALLUDED TO: 8/228
MONCK, Christopher, styled Earl of Torrington, succ. as 2nd Duke of Albemarle 1670 (d. 1688): said to be illegitimate, 8/536 & n. 2; also, 7/240
MONCK, George, cr. Duke of Albemarle 1660, ('the General'); Captain-General of the Kingdom:
CHARACTER: P's low opinion, 1/87; 4/435; 6/68, 298; 7/11, 12, 204, 354; 8/499, 536, 586–7, 591; Sandwich's, 1/125; Blackborne's, 4/372–3; Coventry's, 7/203, 204; satire on, 8/21 & n. 3; popularity, 7/203, 281; 9/205; trusted by bankers, 7/178; ballad in praise of, 8/99 & n. 2; bravery, 8/499
CHRON. SERIES: in Scotland, 1/1; ordered to London, 1/8 & n. 5, 13; political intentions, 1/16 & n. 3, 22 & n. 4, 30 &

n. 1, 33, 58, 75 & n. 5, 79, 102, 111; 5/297; arrives, 1/39, 40 & n. 2; attends on Rump, 1/43 & n. 2; his power, 1/45, 74(2); action against city, 1/46–51 passim & nn.; requires Rump to fill vacancies, 1/50 & n. 1, 51 & n. 1, 54 & n. 2; in city, 1/52, 53, 71; allies with city, 1/54–5 & n.; addresses to, 1/55 & n.4, 73 & n. 1; allies with secluded M.P.s, 1/60, 62 & nn.; made general, 1/62; entertained by livery companies, 1/71 & n. 2, 79, 106; made joint general-at-sea, 1/71 & n. 4, 75; actions against republicans, 1/81, 84, 109; elected M.P., 1/109 & n. 1; relations with Presbyterians, 1/117, 118–19; granted money, 1/118; welcomes King at Dover, 1/158; invested with Garter, 1/161; appointed Treasury Commissioner, 1/170 & n. 3; patent of nobility, 1/188 & n. 1; appointed Lord Lieutenant of Ireland, 1/227–8 & n., 228–9; in trial of regicides, 1/263; Overton's plot against, 1/318–19 & n.; attends coronation, 2/82, 85, 86; exempted from place bill, 4/136 & n. 1; at Oxford in Plague, 6/310, 320; appointed to Treasury Commission, 8/223, 229–30; rumoured appointment as Lord High Constable, 8/269 & n. 3, 270; sharp practice in Moyer case, 8/325; godfather to Duke of Cambridge, 8/438; misunderstanding with King about Buckingham, 9/27
AS CAPTAIN-GENERAL OF THE KINGDOM: severity against plotters, 3/237, 252; quells brawl, 4/136; sends soldiers to guard pressed men, 6/99; victuals Guernsey garrison, 6/142–3; discusses apportionment of money for army, 6/154, 155; 8/591; resents proposal to make Duke of York general, 6/277 & n. 2, 321 & n. 1; sent for in Fire, 7/279–80, 281; dismisses Catholic officers, 7/354; quells seamen's riot, 7/416; sends soldiers to man ships, 8/83, 147; confident of peace, 8/128; his measures to defend Medway, 8/257–8, 260–1 & n.; blames Lord Brouncker for disaster, 8/271, 315; is himself blamed by Coventry, 8/490, 492 & n. 2, 497, 505, 515, 524, 536;

orders removal of *Royal Charles*, 8/495, 502

AS ADMIRAL OF THE KINGDOM, 1665: to act in Duke of York's absence, 6/58 & n. 2; high opinion of P, 4/231; 6/68, 88–9, 197, 239, 258, 298, 305, 310, 310–11, 324; 7/17, 37, 69, 107; 8/370; offers him victualling post, 6/266, 279; gives P/Navy Board news of naval campaign, 6/81–2, 99, 103, 121, 135, 195–6, 214, 223, 243, 255–6; financial business with Board, 6/74, 75, 78, 322; victualling business, 6/91, 103, 109, 239, 269; ordnance business, 6/131; examines captains charged with cowardice, 6/104; receives report on dockyard strike, 6/144; orders fleet to be made ready, 6/192, 195–6, 196, 233, 257; in Dutch prize-goods affair, 6/258, 260, 262, 263, 273–3, 280, 291, 298; arranges convoy, 6/296; ships' insurance, 6/328; requires Board to meet over Christmas, 6/337; receives P's memorandum on pursers, 7/5, 10, 14; favours recall of tickets, 7/11; also, 6/169, 264; unspecified business: 6/68, 73, 94, 98, 107, 111, 125, 145, 162, 163, 165, 168–9, 186, 199, 233, 243, 305, 334, 341; 7/2, 12, 18, 23, 24, 32, 37, 79, 97

AS NAVAL COMMANDER: appointed joint general-at-sea, 1/71 & n. 4, 75, 109; discusses paying off ships, 2/19; to command battle fleet (rumour), 5/183; 6/258, 259, 310, 323, 324, 342; goes to sea, 7/107, 108, 109, 139, 140; in Four Days Fight, 7/143, 146–50 passim & nn.; wounded, 7/147 & n. 1; blames officers, 7/154 & n. 2, 163, 177, 222; 8/147–8; 9/5; tactics criticised, 7/158 (2), 160, 168, 179; 8/125, 359; 9/70; his defence, 7/177–8; 8/147–8; loses reputation at court, 7/196, 213–14, 248, 317–18, 334, 350, 354; quarrels with Duke of York over appointments, 7/163, 314–15; 8/147; 9/39, 76; sails again, 7/210; poor discipline, 7/212; in St James's Day Fight, 7/225, 227–30 & nn.; blames Board for lack of victuals, 7/259, 260, 263, 264, 265; 8/512, 513; quarrels with Rupert, 7/315, 323, 333, 340; his landlubber's language, 8/148

& n. 2; hopes for peace, 8/347; thanked by Commons, 8/499 & n. 2; his 'Narrative', 8/511–12 & n., 514–15, 518, 519, 571; also, 9/25–6, 138

PERSONAL: lodgings in Whitehall, 1/8 & n. 5; in Broad St, 1/53, 58; at Cockpit, Whitehall, 1/179, pictures, 3/198; his nasty food and household, 7/84; 9/294; land grants confirmed 4/156; granted Clarendon Park, 5/61 & n. 1, 203, 218; bank account, 8/276; ill, 2/155, 157; 8/181; portrait by Lely, 7/102 & n. 3; miniature by Cooper, 9/139 & n. 2; plaster cast, 9/487–8

AS PRIVY COUNCILLOR ETC.: his power, 3/291; 4/138; 7/55; 8/585; careless, 7/10; sleeps in meeting, 8/317; relations with Sandwich, 6/313; 7/31; 8/117; with Coventry, 7/172, 174, 231; 9/478; tries to reconcile King and Clarendon, 8/401, 402; naval business, 7/48, 312; 8/278; also, 6/104–5, 209; 7/28

TANGIER: appointed to committee, 3/238; offends Teviot, 4/102; advises on garrison, 5/310 & n. 1; financial business, 5/337; 6/214; 7/20; 8/521; victualling business, 6/252–3, 254(2); also, 5/174; unspecified business, 3/272; 5/11, 51, 114–15, 204, 321; 6/22, 58, 61, 153, 166; 7/321; 8/60, 347

SOCIAL: entertains Sandwich, 1/179; 4/187; royal family, 1/297; P, 6/272–3, 279; P and Carteret, 6/310–11; entertained by Trinity House, 2/4; Archbishop Sheldon, 6/164; and Sir J. Robinson, 6/268–9

MISC.: patronage of T. Turner, 7/31; 9/328

~ his chaplain, 6/289

MONMOUTH, Duke and Duchess of: *see* Scott, Anne; Scott, James

[MONSON, Sir William], naval commander: naval tracts, 9/447, 524 & n. 2

[MONSON, William, 1st Viscount Monson, regicide (d.?1672)]: his sentence, 3/19 & n. 1

MONTACUTE, family of ['Mountagus,' in error]: tombs, 9/230 & n. 3

MONTAGU(E): *see* Mountagu

MONTGOMERIE, Alexander, 6th Earl of Eglintoun: 9/554 & n. 5

calculating machine, 9/116–17 & n.; also, 1/190; 5/342; 8/420; ~ his man Herbert, 5/88

MORLAND, [Suzanne], Lady Morland, wife of Sir Samuel: visits France, 4/274 & n. 2; reproaches King for failure to reward husband, 4/275; her appearance, 5/342; 8/440

MORLEY, George, Bishop of Worcester 1660–2, Winchester 1662–d.84: consecrated, 1/276 & n. 2; preaches at Whitehall against Christmas revels, 3/292–3; alleged lack of charity, 3/293 & n. 2; rumoured suspension, 8/587 & n. 2; dismissed from court office, 9/53 & n. 2

MORLEY, Col. [Herbert], republican (d. 1667): 1/16 & n. 1

MORRICE, Mr ——: at P's stone feast, 2/60; also, 4/272; ~ his wife, 1/3, 10; 4/65, 272, 273; his sister-in-law, 4/272;? his niece, ib.

MORRICE, ——: 1/19

MORRIS (Morrice), [John], landlord of Ship Tavern, Billiter Lane: 9/284, 485–6; ~ his pretty wife, 9/284, 486

MORRIS (Morrice), Capt. [Robert], court upholsterer: supplies furniture for Sandwich, 1/181; in militia against Venner, 2/11; shows P King's Privy Kitchen, 2/175

MORRIS (Morrice), [Roger], wine cooper, of St Olave's, Hart St: business with Navy Board, 3/14; 8/135, 159

MORTALITY, BILLS OF [see also Plague, the]: 3/292 & n. 1; cited, 6/180, 191, 207–8, 208, 214, 234, 243, 284, 305, 314, 340; 7/2, 21, 32, 52, 63, 71, 91, 95

MORTLAKE (Moreclack(e)), Surrey: P at, 3/81; 6/154, 156; 7/235

MORTON, Sir John, Bt, M.P. Poole, Dorset (d. 1699): quarrel with H. Brouncker, 9/470 & n. 1

MORTON, Sir William, Judge, King's Bench 1665–d.72: 9/470 & n. 1

MORTON, bookseller: see Morden

MORTON, Lord: see Douglas

MOSCOW: described, 5/272 & nn.

[MOSELEY HALL, Staffs.]: Charles II hides at (1651), 1/156 & n. 5

MOSSOM (Masham, Massam, Merston, Messum, Mossum), [Robert], Dean of Christ Church, Dublin 1661–6, Bishop of Derry 1666–d.79: his congregation at Cary House, Strand, 1/11 & n. 3, 76, 173, 183; sermons, 1/25, 60, 91, 176; reputation, 1/25; also, 8/553 & n. 3

MOTHAM (Mootham), Capt. [Peter], naval officer: reminiscences as slave in Algiers, 2/33–4 & n.; killed in action, 7/154

MOUNT, [Jeremiah], Gentleman-Usher to the Duchess of Albemarle: 2/51; social: 1/26, 95, 232, 233, 244, 311; 4/101, 421, 436; 5/7, 136

MOUNTAGU, family of: stories of longevity, 6/237–8 & n.

MOUNTAGU, Anne, Lady Mountagu, widow of Sir Sidney; stepmother of Sandwich: at christening, 2/171; alluded to: 2/98

MOUNTAGU, Lady Anne, daughter of Sandwich [see also Mountagu, Edward, 1st Earl of Sandwich: his children]: 3/68; 8/470

MOUNTAGU, Anne, (b. Boyle), Viscountess Hinchingbrooke(d. 1671): marriage, 8/190–1 & nn., 208, 216, 252, 469; 9/28, 51; P admires, 8/498; 9/115, 117; dines with P, 9/109, 116–17; also, 9/211, 321, 322

MOUNTAGU, Lady Catherine, daughter of Sandwich (d. 1757): birth, 2/159 & n. 1; christening, 2/171; ailments, 5/189–90; 9/218 & n. 2; alluded to: 2/195

MOUNTAGU, Sir Edward, Lord Chief Justice (d. 1557): descendants, 6/238 & nn.

MOUNTAGU, Sir Edward (d. 1602): 6/238 & n. 1

MOUNTAGU, Edward, 2nd Earl of Manchester, Lord Chamberlain: PUBLIC AFFAIRS: Presbyterian peers meet at his house, 1/111 & n. 1; chosen Speaker of Lords, 1/115; at Portsmouth, 3/70, 71; unpopular at court, 3/291; closes New Exchange after attack on King's coachman, 4/431 & n. 5; intervenes to prevent duels, 7/414; 9/467; orders M.P.s out of theatres etc. to vote, 7/399–400;

rumoured appointment to Treasury commission, 8/367–8 & n.; imprisons Doll Common, 9/415 & n. 1; also, 1/106, 266; 2/96, 97; 4/229; 8/176, 278

PRIVATE AFFAIRS: quarrels with Ned Mountagu, 4/47; dines with Sandwich, 1/75, 220

ALLUDED TO: 8/544; 9/139, 471

MOUNTAGU, Edward, (often referred to as 'my Lord'), cr. Earl of Sandwich July 1660, politician and naval commander; ambassador to Spain 1665–8; P's patron:

CHARACTER: 'a perfect Courtier', 1/269; secretive, 1/285; brave, 3/149; noble, 4/115; grown 'very high and stately', 5/42; neglectful of business, 4/28; 5/155; 9/374; Teddeman's high opinion, 7/345

PHYSICAL APPEARANCE AND PORTRAITS: moustache, 7/26; Spanish beard, 8/452–3; portrait by Lely, 1/262, 271 & n. 1, 296; copies of, 1/270–3 passim, 284, 286, 290, 292, 296, 301–2; miniature by Salusbury, 2/23; second portrait by Lely, 7/102 & n. 3

AS NAVAL COMMANDER:

UNDER COMMONWEALTH: voyage to Mediterranean (1656), 1/238; to Baltic (1659), 1/23 & n. 2, 80; his Swedish medal, 1/238 & n. 1

VOYAGE TO HOLLAND, March–Apr. 1660, to bring over King: joint general-at-sea, 1/71 & n. 4, 75; prepares to sail, 1/78, 82, 83, 84, 90; embarks, 1/95; civil to Cavaliers, 1/99, 112, 117; opposed by Lawson's captains, 1/100; shifts flag from *Swiftsure* to *Naseby*, 1/101; dismisses Anabaptist, 1/101, 109 & n. 2; Declaration of Breda etc. read to fleet, 1/123 & n. 2, 124 & n. 1, 125, 126–7, 129 & n. 2; Commonwealth flags etc. replaced, 1/130, 133–4, 136–7; sets sail from Downs, 1/133–5 passim; surrenders command to Duke of York, 1/152; accompanies King ashore at Dover, 1/158; invested with Garter, 1/160–1 & nn.; distributes royal bounty, 1/162, 164; returns to London, 1/171; pay, 1/174, 192; 2/49, 55; voted thanks by Commons,

1/176, 177 & nn.; also, 1/96, 98, 115, 167

VOYAGE TO HOLLAND, Sept. 1660, to bring over Dowager Princess Mary: his orders, 1/234 & n. 4, 239; preparations, 1/236, 241; sets sail, 1/238, 241; returns, 1/254, 258; alluded to: 1/247, 251

VOYAGE TO THE MEDITERRANEAN AND PORTUGAL, 1661–2, to bring over Queen Catherine: preparations, 2/45–7 passim, 62 & n. 3, 77, 79, 95, 99, 103, 104/(2), 108, 112(2), 114, 118, 120, 121, 127; his instructions, 2/118 & n. 3; gift of cloth to Algerines, 2/120, 122, 123, 126; expenses granted, 2/150–1 & n., 163; illness at Alicante, 2/152–4 passim, 163; action at Algiers, 2/184 & n. 2, 185, 189; in Lisbon, 2/185–6; provisions sent, 2/186; sees bull-fight, 2/209 & n. 2; action at Tangier, 2/221 & n. 3; asks for astronomical information, 3/7; ambassador-extraordinary to Portugal, 3/12 & n. 3; puts troops into Tangier, 3/18, 33; news from, 3/21 & n. 2; gifts to wife, 3/25; sends map of Tangier to Duke of York, 3/37 & n. 2; returns, 3/84, 89, 97, 120; report on Queen etc., 3/89, 90–1 & n.; gift from Queen, 3/90; his part in treaty with Algiers, 3/121–2 & nn.; determines fleet's rate of pay, 3/128 & n. 1, 129; his cash/pay/allowances/accounts, 3/93, 99 & n. 2, 115, 121; 4/101, 104, 113, 114, 116–17 & n., 135, 136, 156, 204; also, 2/167, 242; 3/18, 105

VOYAGE TO FRANCE, July 1662, to bring over Queen Mother: 3/128; in storm, 3/143, 144 & n. 1, 145, 146; bravery, 3/149; returns, 3/148, 149

1664 COMMAND: rumours of, 5/160–3 passim & n., 183; visits fleet, 5/187, 196, 197; made admiral, 5/206, 207 & n. 4; departs, 5/208–9, 211–12; at sea, 5/225, 256 & n. 3; in river, 5/265; returns, 5/299; at sea again, 5/360; also, 5/303–4

1665 CAMPAIGN: at sea, 6/13, 29 & n.1, 35, 39, 41, 50; repute, 6/50; at Nore, 6/64–5; death rumoured, 6/120; in Battle of Lowestoft, 6/121 & nn., 123 & n. 2, 127, 129, 137; his account of,

6/134–5 & n.; newspaper account,
6/128 & n. 3; unfair official account,
6/135 & nn., 149, 276; failure to
pursue enemy, 8/494, 550; conduct
defended by King, 8/573; returns,
6/134; at sea, 6/141; given sole command, 6/147 & n. 4; proposed joint
command with Rupert, 6/148 & n. 2;
jealousy of Penn, 6/148–9, 151, 230;
fails to intercept Dutch E. Indiamen,
6/165, 178, 184 & n. 2; action in
Bergen harbour, 6/193, 195–6 & n.,
198; his defence of, 6/229; criticised
for failure to capture E. Indiamen,
6/218 & n. 2, 231, 277; 8/494, 515,
538, 550; 9/68 & n. 1; puts out again,
6/205, 208; captures *Phoenix* and
Slothany etc., 6/219 & n. 1, 223 [*see
also* below, The prize-goods affair];
captures warships, 6/223–4 & n.; at
Nore, 6/226, 228; lack of provisions,
6/228–9, 229, 230, 239; ability as
commander, 6/230; at sea again,
6/275, 278, 287; leaves fleet to go to
court, 6/307; 9/70 & n. 1, 87; criticised
for failure to engage Dutch in
October, 6/291 & n. 1; parliamentary
motion against, ib.; criticism dies
down, 7/148–9, 168, 376, 406; 8/2;
also, 6/247, 300–1

THE PRIZE-GOODS AFFAIR: breaks bulk
in *Phoenix* and *Slothany*, 6/219, 223,
226, 230–1 & n., 238–9; his profit,
6/238–9, 240, 241, 297–8, 334, 342;
navy's allocation, 6/239; 7/27, 45, 54;
distribution of goods authorised by
King and Duke of York, 6/247 & n. 3,
264, 269 & n. 2, 318; 9/50; goods
declared prize, 6/263–4; his action
criticised by Myngs, 6/261, 266; in
Commons, 6/262, ?291; in Lords,
7/309, 325; at court, 6/262, 263, 268,
276, 287, 301, 302, 311, 323; 7/6, 8; by
Colvill, 6/268; Albemarle, 6/273, 313;
7/31; Coventry, 6/276, 301; 9/165;
Penn, 9/165; and Duke of York,
6/287, 291, 302; Cuttance's influence,
8/549; 9/402; bill against breaking
bulk, 6/274 & n. 4, 277; recovers
King's favour, 6/276, 291, 301, 311,
318, 321; 7/8, 52, 54, 55; 9/67;
Rupert's, 6/276; and Duke of York's,
6/311; 7/55–6; pardoned by King,

7/13, 17, 27, 55, 260, 262; exculpated
by Prize Commissioners, 7/10, 52;
attacked in *Second advice*, 7/407–8;
affair investigated by Committee on
Miscarriages, 8/485, 486, 494, 499,
521, 527, 572, 576; 9/51, 64 & n. 3,
70; and by Brooke House Committee, 9/87, 91, 92, 96, 111, 135,
165, 204, 363–4; discussed by Commons, 9/?174 & n. 5, 176 & n. 2, 177;
alluded to: 7/203, 219, 260–1; 8/517,
530; 9/180

AS VICE-ADMIRAL OF THE KINGDOM:
appointed, 1/221 & n. 1, 222, 225, 229,
236; subordinate appointments, 1/188;
5/162–3 & n.; with King on yacht,
1/222; provides ships, 1/249, 300; new
barge, 2/110; quarrels with Mennes
over flags, 3/122–3; fee, 8/405–6 & n.;
attends Navy Board, 1/197, 211;
3/265, 272, 282; 4/12, 31, 418

AS ARMY OFFICER: pay, 1/7 & n. 1;
regimental dinner, 1/185; regiment
disbanded, 1/242, 295; also, 1/13, 14

AS CLERK TO PRIVY SEAL [*see also* Privy
Seal]: takes office, 1/128 & n. 1, 176;
sworn in, 1/206, 207; fees, 1/237, 238;
appoints P his deputy, 1/205 & n. 3;
and Moore, 3/168; also, 1/212

AS MASTER OF THE WARDROBE: appointed, 1/170, 175; visits building,
1/180; attendance, 1/303; P his deputy, 2/113 & n. 2, 116; profits, 3/287;
4/251; poundage, 8/418; is owed
£7000, 5/206; accounts, 4/257, 390;
5/208; 8/253; 9/52; advised to
surrender place, 8/195; also, 1/258;
5/32

TANGIER: appointed to committee,
3/238; nominates P as member, 3/170,
171, 172; rumoured appointment as
Governor, 5/313; 9/387; receives
money from contractors, 8/592–3 &
n.; visits and reports on, 9/135 & n. 3,
355–6 & n.; other business: victualling, 4/30; mole, 4/35; 5/343; mercantile court, 4/102; Peterborough's
accounts, 5/74–5, 140; local paymaster, 9/418, 419, 422; also, 9/326;
unspecified, 3/232, 272; 4/97, 123,
269, 408; 5/173; 6/58, 61, 134; 9/340,
364

AS AMBASSADOR TO SPAIN: appointed,

6/320–3 passim & n.; departure, 6/342; 7/6, 52, 57; untrue rumour of recall, 7/354, 406; 8/52; and of quarrel with French ambassador, 8/36 & n. 2, 37, 42; negotiates treaty, 8/45, 107; anecdotes of his embassy, 8/451–2; overspends, 8/461–2; accounts, 8/462; 9/387, 440; return expected, 8/189, 190, 207–8, 476; recalled, 8/511; mediates in Spanish-Portuguese peace negotiations, 8/578 & n. 3; 9/59–60, 80, 222; high repute in Spain, 8/578–9; returns, 9/320

OTHER APPOINTMENTS: Deputy-Lieutenant for Huntingdonshire, 1/310 & n. 5; Master of Trinity House, 2/119; 3/29; 4/185; 5/172; work for Royal Fishery, 3/268–70 passim; 4/365–6

FINANCES [for fees etc. *see* under offices]: state of summarised, 5/206 & n. 1; makes will, 1/94, 95; King's grant to [*see also* Fox, Sir S.], 1/271–2, 285 & n. 4, 288, 290–4 passim, 297; 2/3, 47; 3/121; 4/87–8 & n., 156; 8/530 & n. 3; acquires Brampton manor, 3/102, 176 & nn.; debts, 3/55, 118; 5/186, 187(2), 192, 238–9; 7/56, 370; extravagance/insolvency, 4/37; 7/45; 8/187–8 & n., 444, 463, 470, 480, 516, 517; 9/331; lends money to Calthorpe, 1/4, 6 & n. 3, 24, 36; to Sir R. Parkhurst, 1/310 & n. 2, 311; 2/48; 4/94; Worcester money, 1/56 & n. 5, 57, 80, 91–2; borrows £1000 from T. Pepys, 2/43, 61, 62–3 & n.; 3/17 & n. 1; 5/186, 187; 6/331, 333; 7/13, 14–15, 31–2; from P, 2/61 & n. 5; 4/199–200, 286, 288, 290, 438; 5/42, 131, 211; 6/33–4; again from P, 8/579, 580, 582; P refuses to lend, 7/260; 8/187, 199; his borrowings amount to £7000, 3/92; over £9000, 5/132; £10, 000, 5/206; needs loan of £1000, 4/43, 45–6, 57; and of £2000, 9/321–2

RELATIONS WITH COVENTRY [*see* Coventry, Sir W.]

RELATIONS WITH P:

HIS REGARD FOR: 1/141, 206, 303, 323; 2/49, 113; 3/102, 133–4, 139, 187, 232, 248, 304; 5/74; 6/237, 239(2), 248, 287, 302

AS P'S PATRON: 1/129, 167; P as secretary to regiment, 1/7, 14, 25, 257, 304; and to fleet, 1/77(2); 5/65; deputy in Privy Seal, 1/169–70, 205 & n. 3; and in Wardrobe, 2/113 & n. 2, 116; promises P Clerkship of Acts, 1/184, 185, 222–3; thanked by Duke of York for introducing him, 3/215–16; advises him about Clarendon's timber, 5/202, 203, 206, 207, 208; secures his appointment to Tangier committee, 3/170, 171, 172; and to Royal Fishery, 4/366; 5/76, 79; also, 1/202; 2/121, 192; 4/196

AS P'S EMPLOYER [In the diary period P was primarily Sandwich's man of business; his domestic duties were light after his appointment as Clerk of the Acts, and varied with circumstances.]:

P as domestic steward/man of business [*see also* Andrews, J.; Creed, J.; Moore, H.; Shipley, E.; and above: The prize-goods affair; Finances]: appointment: vol. i, pp. xxii–iii; hopes for profits, 3/133; 4/422; his 'little chamber'/'turret' in Whitehall lodgings, 1/59, 186, 222; 4/22; 8/82; moves from, 2/126; overnight at, 3/187, 199, 301; 5/142; domestic duties: in charge of Whitehall lodgings, 1/24, 64; 3/146; and of servants, 3/288, 293; financial business: accounts, 1/24, 32, 104, 297, 305, 306, 307; 2/37, 56, 57, 67, 97, 106; 3/92–3, 99, 116, 120–3 passim, 124, 126, 133, 136, 138, 139, 266; 4/281, 285, 286, 416; 7/7, 41, 42; supervises Wardrobe finances during Sandwich's absence, 2/112; 3/132, 133–4, 147; 4/58; 8/253, 418; advises him on land purchase, 3/176 & n. 2; negotiates Lady Jemima's marriage settlement, 6/29, 135–6, 137; business with bankers, 6/334; misc.: sends deals to Hinchingbrooke, 1/313–14, 324; 2/8, 27, 35, 48–9, 79; advises him on garden design, 4/313; also, 1/29, 40, 78, 310–11, 312; 2/49; 4/343; unspecified business, 2/3; 3/94, 212, 215, 260, 281, 288; 4/23; 9/211

the Becke affair: P disapproves of Sandwich's liaison, 4/238, 270–1, 278, 281, 282, 286, 292, 301, 303, 313, 379; writes 'great letter of reproof', 4/382,

385–8 passim, its effects on Sandwich and on relations between them, 4/390–3 passim, 395, 396, 397, 402, 407, 408, 421, 422, 427, 428, 429, 437; 5/4, 9, 10, 18, 21–2, 26, 42, 43, 65, 70, 80, 83, 108, 110, 120, 185, 189, 192, 200; relations re-established, 5/76, 161, 203, 211, 225

misc.: gives New Year present, 1/4; advises about Robert P's estate, 1/170; 3/220, 226; 4/42; designs alterations to Brampton house, 3/206, 210; urges P to provide for Pall, 4/366; advises about W. Joyce's arrest, 5/110; and about sale of land, 5/211; concerned for during Plague, 6/231; confides in about his political standing, 7/54–6; P fails to write to in Spain, 9/321; and to pay visit of condolence, 9/474; P distrusts his associates, 9/372, 374 & n. 2; P dines/talks with, 2/54, 56, 79, 115; 3/126, 134; 4/82; 6/54–5, 60; P gives dinner for, 9/420, 423–4; also, 4/313

RELATIONS WITH EP: his regard for, 1/293, 294; 3/206, 210; admires her beauty, 4/186; makes advances to, 9/356

POLITICS [*see also* below, Court]:

HIS VIEWS: on restoration of monarchy, 1/77, 79, 107, 110, 285 & n. 2; Presbyterian discontent, 3/176; state of court and kingdom, 6/248, 277; likely effects of war, 7/55; a 'politique', 3/122

HIS POLITICAL CAREER: under Commonwealth, vol. i, pp. xxii, xxiii–vi; corresponds with King (1659), 1/125 & n. 1, 285; 4/69 & n. 2; takes out pardon, 3/121 & n. 1; returns to London, 1/44, 60, 62; elected to Council of State, 1/65; resumes seat in parliament, 1/72; dines with Presbyterian leaders, 1/75; and Lord Mayor, 1/92; elected M.P. for Weymouth, 1/108(3) & n. 2; and Dover, 1/110–11; resigns on becoming peer, 1/179; electoral influence at Harwich, 1/98 & n. 3; Cinque Ports, 1/93 & n. 2, 94, 96, 97; Weymouth, 1/103 & n. 4, 179; Dover, 1/167, 179 & n. 1; Huntingdon, 1/86–7 & n., 99 & n. 2; supports candidate at Huntingdon (1661), 2/3 & n. 5; opposes Sir R. Bernard's

influence there, 3/281–2 & n.; sworn Privy Councillor, 1/179; raised to peerage, 1/184–5 & n., 187–8 & n., 196 & n. 5; attends Lords, 1/208; 2/107; gifts of plate to Secretary and King, 1/185, 192, 193; 2/5; as judge at regicides' trial, 1/263, 266; exempted from place bill, 4/136 & n. 1; member of King's 'private council', 5/207; fears may be blamed for sale of Dunkirk, 7/55 & n. 4; rumoured appointment to Treasury, 8/195, 217; alliance with Clarendon, 1/173; 2/209–10, 221; 3/33, 122; 4/115, 366; 5/207, 208; 6/148, 291, 311; 7/5, 55; 8/418; relations cool, 6/276–7; with Duke of York and his party, 4/115; relations cool, 5/133; with Arlington, 4/115; 5/208; 6/276 & n. 5; with Albemarle, 6/313; and with Carteret, 6/148; also, 1/66, 68; 2/75; 7/28

POLITICAL NEWS FROM: 1/271; 3/237; 4/24, 57, 115–17, 366–7

COURT: attends coronation, 2/82, 86; advised to avoid court, 3/291; standing at court, 3/304; 5/207; 6/273, 276, 287, 291, 301, 302, 311, 318, 323; 7/5, 26–7, 132; 8/149, 207–8; 9/331, 339, 342; absence from court remarked on, 4/370, 379, 387–8; allies with Lady Castlemaine, 4/13, 115; also, 3/94, 157; 4/115, 239, 255; 5/161

RESIDENCES:

AT MRS BECKE'S, Chelsea: 4/97, 101, 112, 114, 117, 123–4, 160, 278, 281, 286, 402, 419; 5/173

AT LORD CREW'S, Lincoln's Inn Fields: 1/77, 87, 89, 94

HINCHINGBROOKE, Hunts. [for the house, *see* under name]: to entertain King, 4/324; visits, 1/221–3 passim, 234, 310, 312, 320; 2/47, 48, 49, 52; 3/116, ?160, 187, 287, 288, 304; 4/12, 251, 292, 313, 348; 5/32, 36, 64, 185; 7/34; 9/541; also, 1/66; 2/108

AT DEAN HODGES'S, Kensington: 5/184, 192

LINCOLN'S INN FIELDS: takes lease, 5/19–20, 43; P visits, 5/65, 74, 75, 79, 132, 202; admires house and garden, 5/74; christening in dining-room, 7/49; let to Carteret, 8/450

LODGINGS AT THE WARDROBE [P's

numerous visits – mostly social – are not indexed. His first mention of them is at 1/277; his last at 5/316.]: roomy but ugly, 1/291; 'pretty pleasant', 2/97; kitchen, 2/106; dining-room, 3/89; parlour, ib.; Capt. Ferrers's chamber, 3/81

LODGINGS IN WHITEHALL [He had lodgings in the palace from c. 1654 onwards and throughout the diary period – whether the same set is not known. P's numerous visits are not indexed. His first mention of them is at 1/17; his last at 9/553.]: next door to Lady Castlemaine's, 3/215; claimed by A. A. Cooper, 1/17, 22, 23; re-paired and decorated, 3/49, 146; King's tennis court in garden, 3/147; damaged by collapse of tennis court, 4/197; Hinchingbrooke's chamber, 8/516; Sandwich's study, 1/22, ?251; stair door, 1/71; ? garden, 1/77, 220; nursery, 1/186, 203; house of office, 1/250; buttery, 2/90; drawing-room, 2/102; little new room, 2/103; great dining-room, 1/287; 3/266; also, 2/121

HOUSEHOLD [see also Lady Sandwich: household; Burfett, ——; Carleton, ——; Creed, J.; Crisp, L.; Ferrers, R.; Loud, ——; [Luffe, E.]; Turner, John]: to have French cook and master of horse, 1/269, 311; angry at servants' improvidence, 2/64; new liveries for coronation, 2/79; footboy (Tom), 1/14, 58; black footman, (Jasper), 1/82, 92, 166; other footmen, 3/196, 212; 4/348; porter, 5/202; Spanish dancer, 9/440; great coach, 1/181; 5/200

PERSONAL:

INTEREST IN ARTS AND SCIENCES: on engravings, 6/50; paints miniature of Charles II, 2/59; plans alterations to P's Brampton house, 3/206, 210; his drawings of Lisbon, 4/286 & n. 1; and of Portsmouth harbour, 6/38, 46, 50; admires Danckerts's view of Tangier, 9/541 & n. 2; musical tastes, 1/298; 4/160; composes three-part anthem, 4/418–19, 428; borrows lute, 1/218; plays and commends guitar, 6/301; plays viol, 1/114 (bass), 285; 2/39, 57;

organ, 1/287, 292, 297; his virginals, 2/121–2; sings, 1/114, 115, 118, 129, 133, 169, 285; 2/57; musical parties, 2/66, 103; 3/255, 287; takes dancing-master on voyage, 2/117; sceptical about ghost, 4/185–6; given load-stone, 4/397; astronomical observa-tions, 5/346 & n. 3, 352; also, 3/7; 4/283

RELIGIOUS VIEWS: a 'sceptic' and favours uniformity, 1/141, 201; 'in-different', 1/261; prefers homilies to sermons, 1/271 & n. 2

HEALTH: heavy cold, 1/202; bruised foot, 1/254; unwell, 1/262; ill (? mal-aria) at Alicante, 2/152–3, 154, 163; ill (? recurrent malaria), 4/17, 21, 22, 24, 25, 28, 30, 55, 58, 62, 63, 66, 68, 69, 89; 5/207; takes physic, 1/164, 166; 2/42; 3/92; 9/338

DRESS ETC.: rich new clothes, 1/141; garter dress and insignia, 1/160; 2/49; comb-case, 1/239; toilet cap, ib.; French coronation suit, 2/83; gold-buttoned suit, 4/187; watch, 1/120

LIAISONS: affair with Betty Becke, 4/97, 101, 112, 174, 238 & n. 3, 270–1, 281, 286, 292, 301, 303, 305; neglects attendance at court, 4/370, 379; P's letter of reproof, 4/383, 387–8 (see also Relations with P, above); leaves Chelsea, 4/399–400, 402, 419; still visits her, 5/173–4; affair alluded to, 9/455; liaison with Lady Castlemaine, 5/21; his portrait of, 5/200

CHILDREN [The following references are to children/daughters whose names are not given in the text. See also Mountagu, Anne, Catherine; Edward (Hinchingbrooke); James; John; Oliver; Paulina and Sidney.]: in London for coronation, 2/75; P/EP take to theatre, 2/151–2, 173–4; Tower, 3/76; Hampton Court, 3/81–2; Greenwich, 3/111; to see ship, 6/56, 57; also, 2/165, 170, 206; 3/47, 79, 94, 223

CHILDREN'S MARRIAGES: agrees terms for Lady Jemima's marriage, 6/138, 145, 148, 173; his pleasure at, 6/202; refers Hinchingbrooke's marriage negotiations to advisers, 8/190–1 & n.

SOCIAL: plays ninepins on board ship,

1/131, 142, 162, 164, 169; goes fishing with Vice-Admiral, 1/169; dines with Lord Campden, 1/210; with King, 1/214, 297–8; Manchester, 1/220; Albemarle, 4/187; Peterborough, 4/270; and Povey, 9/345; entertains Ormond, 2/100; officers of Wardrobe, 2/104; and Coventry, 3/138–9; at theatre, 3/211, 216; at Lady Castlemaine's, 3/214–15; 4/238; plays at dice, 4/28; loses £100 at cards, 4/134; at Boughton, 4/307; at Whitehall chapel, 4/401; visits Lady Pulteney, 5/163; and Archbishop Sheldon, 6/239
MISC.: challenges Buckingham to duel, 2/32–3; in search for treasure in Tower, 3/240–4 passim
MOUNTAGU, Edward, styled Viscount Hinchingbrooke, eldest son of Lord Sandwich [often referred to as 'Mr Edward' before July 1660]:
CHARACTER: 'a noble and hopeful gentleman', 6/13; 'a most sweet youth', 6/188; his sobriety, 7/235–6, 358; 8/516
CHRON. SERIES: at school at Twickenham, 1/18 & n. 3, 19, 20; on *Naseby*, 1/133; has audience with King, 1/143–4; visits The Hague, Delft and Scheveningen, 1/143–4, 145, 147–50 passim; at Deal, 1/163; Latin lesson from P, 1/165; returns to London, 1/173; continues education, 2/114 & n. 1, 142, 163; 4/25, 121, 187; suspected smallpox, 2/152, 153, 154(2), 157; false report of death, 3/11 & n. 2; kills page in shooting accident, 4/138; visits Rome, 6/13; returns to England, 6/169 & n. 3, 178, 183; has smallpox, 6/191, 193; P's impression of, 7/47 & n. 2; proposed match with Elizabeth Malet, 6/110 & n. 4, 119, 193 & n. 2; 7/56, 260, 385; marriage with Lady Anne Boyle, 8/190–1 and nn., 208, 216, 252, 377, 418, 469, 498, 598; 9/28, 51; short of money, 8/276, 333; assistance in father's financial difficulties, 8/199, 463, 516, 573 & n. 2, 579, 580; dishonourable advances to EP, 9/356; also, 2/107; 3/291; 6/190; 7/46, 54, 94, 234, 356, 368; 9/318, 321
SOCIAL: plays shuttlecock, 1/15; at theatre, 2/8; sees Lord Mayor's Show,

1/276 & n. 3, 277; at christening, 7/49; visits city ruins after Fire, 7/357–8; dines with P, 7/387, 388–9; 9/109, 115, 116–17, 423–4, 553; also, 9/211, 345
ALLUDED TO: 1/151
MOUNTAGU, Edward, 1st Baron Mountagu of Boughton (d. 1644): ?6/238 & n. 2
MOUNTAGU, Edward, 2nd Lord Mountagu of Boughton (d. 1684): dines with Sandwich, 4/136; ill, 5/154; quarrels with son Edward, 5/244; alluded to: 6/155
MOUNTAGU, Edward (Ned), son of the 2nd Baron Mountagu of Boughton; Master of the Horse to the Queen Mother:
CHRON. SERIES: parliamentary candidate, 1/102 & n. 2, 167; carries letters between Sandwich and King, 1/110 & n. 2, 112, 113; on Dutch voyage, 1/135, 171, 173; manages Sandwich's business during absence abroad (1661–2), 2/118, 121, 163, 185, 186, 195, 197, 206, 229; distrusted by Lady Sandwich and P, 2/163; visits Tangier, 2/186; 3/12 & n. 1., 78; low repute at court, 3/15, 43, 289; 4/47 & n. 1; 5/207, 208; mismanagement of Sandwich's business, 3/29, 55–6; duel with Cholmley, 3/157 & n. 2; 4/47; borrows money from Sandwich, 3/157; dispute with Chesterfield, 3/289–90 & n.; 4/25; quarrel with Sandwich, 4/46–7 & nn., 114–15, 366; 5/207, 208; with father and uncle, 4/47, 187–8; 5/244; to procure Frances Stuart for King, 4/366; tries to make mischief between Sandwich and Clarendon, 4/366–7; rusticated for affront to Queen, 5/153 & n. 2, 155, 244; owes Sandwich £2000, 5/206; killed in action, 6/196
SOCIAL: 1/187; 3/139
ALLUDED TO: 2/142, 191, 193
MOUNTAGU, George, son of the 1st Earl of Manchester (d. 1681): with Sandwich on Baltic voyage, 1/44 & n. 3; custos rotulorum for Westminster, 1/79–80 & n.; M.P. for Dover, 1/167, 179 & n. 2, 183, 228; parliamentary candidate for Huntingdon, 2/3 & n. 6, 4; political news

108; 5/119, 120, 185, 200, 238, 244–5, 333, 339, 347, 358; 6/5, 13, 17, 115; also, 1/309; 3/83

ALLUDED TO: 1/46; 2/101; 4/176; 7/154

MOUNTAGU, Lady Jemima, ('Mrs'/ 'Lady Jem'): *see* Carteret, Jemima

MOUNTAGU, John and Oliver, twin sons of Lord Sandwich: stay with P and EP to avoid smallpox, 2/153, 155, 157, 158; P examines in Greek and Latin, 8/472 & n. 1; alluded to: 9/335

MOUNTAGU, [Mary], (b. Aubrey) wife of (Sir) William (d. 1700): 3/1; 5/19; 8/598

MOUNTAGU, [Mary], ('Lady Mountagu'): 8/319

MOUNTAGU, Oliver: *see* Mountagu, John

MOUNTAGU, Lady Paulina, daughter of Lord Sandwich:

CHRON. SERIES: given page by Sandwich, 3/95; and parrot, 3/105; sent to Brampton to avoid smallpox, 4/439; 5/74 & n. 1, 95; returns to London, 5/32, 53; resents father's liaison, 5/173–4; frightened at shooting London Bridge, 5/180; 'a proper lady', 8/470; fatally ill, 9/455; death, 9/462 & n. 1; piety, 9/520

SOCIAL: on river trip, 2/142–3; at Bartholomew Fair, 2/166; at theatre, 3/57; also, 3/59, 89; 5/64, 65, 132, 184, 358; 9/211

ALLUDED TO: 5/153; 9/474

MOUNTAGU (Montagu), Ralph, son of the 2nd Lord Mountagu of Boughton, succ. as 3rd baron 1683, cr. Duke of Montagu 1705; Gentleman of the Horse to the Duchess of York (d. 1709): anecdote of, 3/43; alluded to: 3/12, 139

MOUNTAGU, Robert, styled Lord Mandeville, succ. as 3rd Earl of Manchester 1671 (d. 1683): on *Naseby*, 1/157; a gallant, 3/15; visits Louis XIV as ambassador extraordinary, 4/156 & n. 2; at Hampton Court, 7/27; valentine gift to Frances Stuart, 8/184; at Harwich in Medway crisis, 8/255; alluded to: 1/86

MOUNTAGU, Sir Sidney, father of Lord Sandwich (d. 1644): coarse

anecdote about, 1/261; his rise, 1/285 & n. 2; alluded to: 6/238 & n. 1

MOUNTAGU, Sidney, second son of Lord Sandwich (d. 1727):

CHRON. SERIES: stays with P and EP to avoid smallpox, 2/153, 155, 157, 158; education in Paris, 2/114 & n. 1, 142, 163 & n. 4; 4/25, 187; returns, 5/185 & n. 1; ill, 6/225; at Cranbourne, 7/54; returns from Spain, 9/321–2 & n.; welcomed at court, 9/323; to visit Flanders and Italy, 9/552; also, 3/291; 5/200

SOCIAL: sees Lord Mayor's Show, 1/276 & n. 3, 277; at theatre, 2/8; 9/419; dines with P, 9/423–4, 553; also, 9/345, 420, 541

MOUNTAGU, Abbot Walter (d. 1677): prevents duel between Sandwich and Buckingham, 2/33 & n. 1; to take charge of Sandwich's sons in Paris, 2/114 & n. 1; alluded to: 4/211 & n. 2

MOUNTAGU, Sir William, lawyer: given charge of Sandwich's will, 1/94 & n. 2, 95; his legal adviser, 1/271, 294, 310; 2/3; 4/45; loyalty to, 7/54; helps arrange Hinchingbrooke's marriage, 8/190 & n. 4; social: 3/1; 4/136; 8/598; alluded to: 8/22; 9/28

MOUNTAGU, ——, grandson of 1st Earl of Manchester: tried for arson and robbery, 8/316 & n. 2, 319; ~ his mother [Mary], 8/319

MOUNTNEY, [Richard], of the Customs House: 7/12

MOUNT'S BAY, Cornwall: 3/79; 9/320, 321

MOXON, [Joseph], type-founder and instrument maker, Cornhill: his shop, 4/302; P buys globes, 4/302 & n. 3; 5/83, 136; also, 4/350

MOYER, [Laurence], merchant, brother of Samuel (d. 1685): secures brother's release, 8/219–20 & n.

MOYER, Samuel, republican (d. 1683): imprisoned, 2/225 & n. 1; dispute over release, 8/219–20 & n., 325

MOYSE(S), Capt. [Richard], army officer: 1/57 & n. 3

MUDDIMAN, [Henry], journalist: his newsbooks, 1/12 & n. 3; 4/297, n. 2; 6/305, n. 3; at Rota Club, 1/13

MUFFETT: *see* Moffett

MULBERRY Garden: *see* Gardens: Hyde Park

MULGRAVE, Lord: *see* Sheffield, John, 3rd Earl of

MULLINER, Goody, of Cambridge: her stewed prunes, 9/212

MULLINER, ——, butler's man at Magdalene College: college news from, 9/212

MULLINS: *see* Molins

MUMFORD, Mrs ——, shopkeeper in Westminster Hall: 1/66; 6/186

MÜNSTER: *see* Galen, Christopher Bernard von, Prince Bishop of

MURFORD, [Will], Navy Office messenger: accompanies P to Brampton, 8/465, 474–5; and to West Country, 9/229; nickname, 8/467

MURFORD, Capt. [William], timber merchant: solicits naval commission for friend, 1/175, 177, 178, 180; offers gift, 1/273; projected light-house, 2/41 & n. 2, 44; breach of contract, 4/353 & n. 1; also, 1/80; 2/31, 32; 3/284; ~ his widow, [Bridget], 8/231

MURFORD, Mrs ——, shopkeeper in Westminster Hall [?identical with Mrs Mumford]: 1/204, 222

MURREY: *see* Moray

MUSIC [*see also* Books]:

GENERAL:

P'S LOVE OF: 4/48; 6/320–1; 7/69, 228; 9/94; fears its distractions, 4/104–5; his music room, 5/230; also, 5/12, 235; 8/432

P'S TASTES: vol. i, p. xxi; finds professionals spoil 'ingenuity' of domestic music, 5/226; prefers vocal to instrumental, 5/238, 290; dislikes 'old-fashion' singing, 1/19 & n. 2; critical of Ravenscroft's psalms, 5/342; prefers English to French songs, 7/171; and to Italian, 8/384, 599; critical of Carissimi, 5/217; admires composition of Italian songs, 8/54–5, 65; reflects on relation of words and music, 8/54–5, 64–5, 154; critical of elaborately contrapuntal songs/anthems, 8/438, 458, 515; 9/59, 251; dislikes trumpets and kettledrums, 2/29; 4/355–6; guitar, 2/142; Scottish tunes, 7/224–5; and bagpipes, 9/131

MUSIC THEORY: P attempts to invent simpler method of composition, 8/574–5; 9/125, 127 (2), 138, 151(2), 152, 155, 412; studies 'scale'/'gamut', 6/227, 236; 9/151, 159, 161; inquires about physical nature of sound, 9/147; his 'music papers', 8/177

P'S COMPOSITIONS [sometimes voice-line only]: takes lessons from Birchensha, 3/8–9 & n., 9, 10, 16, 19, 35, 36; studies Birchensha's rules, 3/35, 36–7; 5/174–5 & n.; 6/282–3; practises 'music' (composition), 3/14, 15, 19, 20, 21, 24, 26, 27, 32, 33; 4/212, 213, 219, 220, 221, 266; orders music-card, 7/219; dislikes 'unnecessary' octaves, 7/414 & n. 3; attempts to compose a song, 2/207; composes airs, 3/26; 7/227; composes/sings/teaches/listens to: 'Gaze not on swans', 3/27 & n. 4, 34–5, 46; 'Nulla Nulla', 3/35 & n. 1; 'This cursed jealousy', 3/36 & n. 2; 'Beauty Retire', 6/320 & n. 4, 324; 7/2 53, 54, 257, 362, 397; 'It is decreed', 7/91 & n. 4, 104, 223, 257, 366(2), 369, 403, 414, 420; 8/35, 36, 50, 54, 142; 9/14, 16, 131, 136; 'I wonder what the grave', 8/555 & n. 3; a duo, 6/266; a bass to 'the lark's song', 9/299 & n. 3, 303; also, 7/418; 8/167

INSTRUMENTAL CONSORTS: King's twenty-four violins, 2/86; 8/73, 404, 458; music meeting, 5/238; Buckingham's band, 9/12–13; bands for dancing, 8/29; 9/128, 458, 464; band of fiddles (alluded to), 8/65

PARTICULAR INSTRUMENTS:

angelica: 1/183

bagpipes: 2/101; 9/131

bandore: 3/224

claviorganum: 8/25 & n. 4

'cymbals' (barber's music), 1/169

dulcimer: P hears for first time, 3/90; also, 3/118

flageolet: P buys, 8/53, 87, 344; 9/30, 162; has lessons from Greeting, 8/205–6, 223, 237, 286, 325, 329; 9/279; plays (alone), at 'echo', 1/58, 70, 147; also, 1/19, 33, 38, 45, 121, 138; 2/65, 115; 3/53, 80; 4/189; 5/215; 8/224, 253, 272, 273, 277, 326, 327, 344, 376, 384, 385(2), 443; 9/163, 184; (with others), 1/71; 8/224, 235(2),

250, 253(2), 305, 369, 370, 380, 384,
396, 430, 433–7 passim; 9/279, 280;
asks Gibbons for duets, 9/271; listens
to, 1/180; 4/377; 8/367; 9/138, 476
   gittern: (barber's music), 1/169; also,
2/17
   guitar: P listens to, 7/56, 378; 9/153;
dislikes, 2/142; 8/374; Sandwich plays
and commends, 6/301; King's guitar
alluded to, 1/172 & n. 2
   harp: at taverns, 1/15; 2/89; on
board ship, 1/119, 153; at Vauxhall,
8/240
   harpsichord (harpsichon): P listens
to, 1/90; 2/71, 90, 104, 123; 4/75, 120;
5/88, 266; 7/364; 8/55, 57, 65; 9/261;
price of, 2/44; plans to buy, 9/127, 149
   Jew's harp (trump): 8/240
   lute: P listens to, 5/119, 258, 305,
344; 6/283; 7/68, 134, 182, 199, 375;
8/118, 325, 333, 558; 9/401; his instrument altered, 1/58; lent, 1/91, 218;
strung, 1/270; 4/282; plays, 1/29, 33,
40, 41, 56, 57, 58, 61, 288, 298, 322,
324; 2/9, 23, 115, 209; 3/2, 46, 63, 93,
113, 148, 195; 4/194, 204, 211, 235;
French lute: P listens to, 8/530; also,
8/558; 9/259
   lyra viol: P plays, 1/295 & n. 4;
4/155, 245; 7/377; also, 5/18; 7/327
   organ [i.e. chamber-organ: see also
below, Church Music]: Sandwich's
organ 'in the form of Bridewell',
1/287 & n. 2; P hears it played, 1/292,
297; hears organ at 'music-house',
Greenwich, 4/283; admires one in
music room at Whitehall, 8/532; in-
tends to buy one, ib.; hears one at
Carteret's, 9/11; inspects one at
Deanery, Westminster, 9/89
   recorder: P's love of, 9/94 & nn.,
157; buys one, 9/157; begins to learn,
9/164
   singing glasses: 9/457
   spinet/triangle: P listens to, 4/87, 93,
99, 103, 120, 122, 242; 5/194; Sandwich's instrument brought to P's
house, 2/121–2; tuned, 4/79, 90; its
stand, 5/194; P tries out chords on,
4/190, 201; buys one, 9/149, 259, 261,
262; its tuning key, 9/265
   theorbo: P listens to, 7/227, 338;
8/530; 9/138; used in consort for

dancing, 9/12, 128, 464; P's instrument strung, 1/76; altered, 2/193, 201,
203; its cost, 2/203; its excellence,
2/228; 4/284; Child writes tablatures
for, 1/302, 324; 3/33
   triangle: see spinet
   trump marine: 8/500
   viol: P listens to, 2/71; 5/52, 53, 54,
64; 6/183, 279; 7/422; 8/104, 193;
9/42; and to bass-viol, 1/116; 2/71;
3/131, 286; 4/48; 8/40; P's instrument
altered, 1/58; his new instrument,
4/174, 232, 242, 252, 255, 266, 277,
280, 282; 5/25; its cost, 4/284; thinks
of buying bass viol, 4/104; P plays
viol: 1/8, 10, 59, 78, 114 & n. 1; 4/48,
110, 212, 214, 220, 232, 293, 296–8
passim, 300–2 passim, 304, 361, 363;
5/50, 282; 6/5, 201; 7/396; 8/325, 530;
9/125, 198; 'thrums on' to voice,
9/517; P 'fiddles' [it is unclear
whether he is playing viol or violin]:
1/308; 2/61; 3/187; 5/266; P 'plays'
[viol or violin is implied, but which is
uncertain]: 2/39; 3/216, 281
   violin: P listens to, 1/78, 85, 297;
2/116; 3/164; 4/237; 6/227; 7/171,
224–5; 8/325; 9/128; also, 8/468; bass
violin, 9/12; his instrument, 4/284; P
plays, 1/104, 106, 107, 298; 4/109,
186, 187, 188; 8/40
   virginals: 1/313; great number in
London, 7/271
   whistling: P considers having lessons,
2/101
VOCAL:
   GENERAL: Italian manner, 8/430;
Spanish serenades, 8/452
   P SINGS [apparently alone, but this
not always certain. See also Musical
Compositions]: sight-reads, 1/19;
sings to echo, 1/144; 6/18; practises
trillo, 2/128 & n. 4; has lessons, 2/126,
144, 145; to be taught trillo,
8/424; also, 1/32–3, 59, 64, 76, 115,
129, 162, 164, 169; 2/71, 77, 121, 126;
3/46, 68, 82, 147; 4/110, 149, 235;
5/120, 179, 180, 194; 6/217, 303;
7/113; 8/89, 90, 109, 157, 166, 176,
322(2), 325, 346, 458; 9/517
   P SINGS WITH OTHERS: Italian and
Spanish part songs, 1/63; canons and
catches, 1/63, 205; psalms, 1/111, 215,

285; 5/120, 194, 261, 321; 6/138; 7/95, 100; 8/444; 9/202, 219; improvised duets, 1/194; with choir, 1/313; 2/240; 'holy things', 3/67–8; French psalms, 3/99; new tunes, 4/63; sings with EP/Mercer, 7/111; 8/29, 171, 198, 203, 206, 209, 223, 238, 244, 250, 253(2), 289, 327, 328, 340, 344, 351, 380, 390, 429, 437–8, 465, 467–8, 504, 557; 9/13, 14, 35, 55, 58–9, 81, 85, 119, 128, 134, 152, 166, 172, 175, 179, 196, 197(2), 199, 201, 203, 204, 213, 216, 217, 221(2), 227, 249, 250, 261, 269, 273, 300, 320, 513, 552, 555, 563

also, 1/113, 118, 268, 272, 274; 2/57, 101, 118; 3/86; 5/136, 199, 209, 229, 266, 282, 325, 337, 339, 342, 349; 6/24, 32, 34, 39, 44, 50, 73, 77, 79, 86, 88, 98, 125, 156, 219, 283, 294, 321, 323–6, passim; 7/44, 53–4, 69, 73, 92–3, 95, 110, 113, 117, 172–4 passim, 183, 191, 195, 197, 200, 205, 206, 212, 216, 227, 228, 230, 236, 237, 240, 348, 362

P LISTENS TO OTHERS [see also Musical Compositions]: impromptu part songs, 4/249; part songs in tavern, 4/377; Italian songs, 4/428; 5/217; 8/29, 54, 56, 57, 59, 154; a Dutchman, 5/19; sailors, 6/287; French song, 7/199; Irish songs, 8/29; recitativo, 8/55, 57; 'a boat full of spaniards', 8/325; also, 2/104; 5/53, 126, 242; 6/28, 34, 64, 137, 215, 235, 267; 7/12, 30, 341, 343–4; 8/97, 108, 119, 204, 283, 325, 384, 394, 599; 9/11, 20, 111

CHURCH MUSIC: Bath Abbey: organ, 9/238; Chesterton, Cambs.: bells, 9/212; Hackney church (St Augustine's): organ, 8/150, 174; King's College, Cambridge: organ, 2/135–6 & n.; Norton St Philip, Som.: bells, 9/232; Roman Catholic (general): 8/26; St George's Chapel, Windsor: anthem, 7/58; St James's Palace, Queen's chapel at: choir: P dislikes, 3/202; his opinion changes, 7/87, 99; 8/588; 9/319, 515; eunuchs, 8/154; harsh voices, 8/427–8; also, 9/126; St Olave's, Hart St: long psalm, 2/6 & n. 5; 9/21; new psalm, 4/269; clerk out of tune, 5/320; P hopes for organ for, 8/150 & n. 2; St Paul's Cathedral: poor choir, 5/67; Salisbury Cathedral:

organ, 9/229; Westminster Abbey: organ, 1/283 & n. 1, 324; anthem, 6/18; Whitehall Chapel [see also Cooke, Capt. Henry]: anthems: dull, 1/237; badly sung, 1/265; 7/99; rehearsal, 2/41; with symphonies, 3/190, 197, 293; discontinued in Lent, 4/69; in five parts, 4/393; by Sandwich, 4/418–19, 428; on Ps. 150, 6/5; with wind music, 6/5; 9/163; by Humfrey, 8/515; by Silas Taylor, 9/251; also, 1/195, 220; 3/84, 85; 4/63; 7/99, 245, 383, 409; 8/32, 41, 425, 478; 9/294, 563; organ, 1/176, 195; 8/145; wind music, 9/163; unspecified music, 6/109

COURT MUSIC: French musicians, 1/297–8 & n.; 8/73 & n. 3; musicians unpaid, 7/414; disparaged, 8/529–30; Italian musicians, 8/56–7; 9/322; concerts on occasion of peace, 8/458; on Duke of York's birthday, 9/328; also, 8/456, 532, 534; rehearsal of twenty-four violins, 9/163; violins play during dinner, 8/404; undefined music, 8/456, 458

MILITARY MUSIC: reveilles by drums and trumpets, 7/422; 9/403; drums summon militia, 5/99, 101; 7/362; Scottish march, 8/311; Louis XIV's drums and trumpets, 4/189; Italian trumpet music, 7/352; also, 2/29; 8/496; 9/129

OPERA: T. Killigrew's plans for, 5/230; 8/56

THEATRE MUSIC [see also Dancing]: T. Killigrew on improvement in, 8/55 & n. 3; P's comments on acoustics, 4/128; 9/459; in If you know not me, you know nobody (song to Queen Elizabeth), 8/388; The faithful shepherdess, 9/327, 329; The Heiress, 9/436; Macbeth, 8/171; The man is the maister, 9/134; She would if she could, 9/54; The siege of Rhodes, 1/187; 6/284 & nn.; 8/25 & n. 1, 59 & n. 1; The Surprizall, 9/166; The Tempest (echo song), 8/522 & n. 1; 9/189; (seamen's dance), 9/48; The virgin-martyr (wind music), 9/94, 100, 188; also, 8/396; 9/89

TOWN WAITS: Cambridge, 3/224; 8/469; Huntingdon, 8/474; Bath,

MEETINGS: to meet Duke of York weekly, 3/192 & n. 1; rules about morning/afternoon sessions, 2/143, 217; 3/31, 181; 4/49, 253; 5/88, 330; 7/95; time of the clock noted, 8/213; 9/47, 395; meets on Sunday, 5/349; at Christmas, 6/337; on Thursdays only during Plague, 6/188; interrupted by Fire, 7/281, 301, 316; by Dutch raid on Medway, 8/314; extraordinary meetings, 5/167; 7/13, 31, 82, 129, 419; 8/104, 385, 522; 9/125; meeting places (other than at Navy Office): Admiralty, 1/229, 241; Deptford and Greenwich in Plague, 6/173, 195 & n. 1, 200, 203; 7/7; Ruckholts, Essex, 6/222; Coventry's chamber, St James's Palace, 7/281; Brouncker's house, 7/284; Penn's parlour, 8/481; also, 4/322

RECORDS ETC.: books of precedents, 4/88; 'seabooks', 4/97; muster books, 7/100, 326; J. Humphrey's collection, 7/50 & n. 3; warrant book of First Dutch War, 9/300; office seal, 7/82–3; P buys books for, 4/395 & nn.; and globes, 5/117, 136; office furniture, 4/409, 436; 7/388

CHRON. SERIES [select]: given control of fleet in Duke of York's absence, 2/200; prepares for war, 5/111, 131, 262, 267, 273, 285, 293; preparations held up for lack of money, 7/210, 221, 233, 234–5, 239–40, 241, 248, 249, 255–6, 281, 284, 289, 307, 315, 339, 341, 349, 353, 383, 413; accused of negligence in supplying victuals, 7/172, 259 & n. 1, 260, 263, 264, 265; 8/513, 514, 517–18; 9/98; discusses fortification of Medway, 8/126 & n. 2; 9/56–7; provides fireships for Medway, 8/256(2) & n. 2, 259, 260 & n. 2; unpopularity in Medway crisis, 8/297–8, 302, 315, 337, 579; rumours of purge, 8/575; 9/100, 285, 290–1, 337, 380, 385, 504, 506–7, 509; attends Council enquiry into Medway raid, 8/460, 460–1; attends Commons to answer charges of Committee on Miscarriages, 8/494–6, 501, 502, 509–10, 512; its defence against charge concerning tickets, 9/97, 101, 103–4; answers enquiries

of Brooke House Committee, 9/34 & n. 4, 39, 42 & n. 1, 335, 394

BUSINESS

CONTRACTS [see also below, Business: victualling]: canvas, 5/136 & n. 3, 157 & n. 3, 238; deals, 4/232 & n. 4; fireships, 7/233; flags, 3/164; 5/178 & n. 4, 313; hemp, 3/114 & n. 1, 116, 129–30; 6/327 & n. 1; 7/150, 183–4, 358–9 & n., 385 & n. 2; lanterns, 5/117 & n. 1; masts, 3/268; 4/303–4 & n.; 5/6 & n. 4, 52, 108, 123, 215–16 & n., 239 & n. 1, 333; 7/2–3 & n.; Norway goods, 5/333 & n. 1; 6/330 & n. 2; provisions, 3/193; 5/73; tallow, 6/327 & n. 1; tar, 5/136 & n. 3, 352; timber, 4/326, 421; 5/299 & n. 3, 300–1, 303, 304; 6/77 & n. 3; timber and iron, 3/112 & n. 2, 114; yarn, 3/130; with E. India Company, 2/227–8 & n.; Board fails to scrutinise, 4/303

DOCKYARDS [indexed principally under Chatham; Deptford; Harwich; Portsmouth; Woolwich]: guard for, 2/11 & n. 1; accounts, 2/29 & n. 1; Admiral's Instructions to, 3/129 & n. 1; letter of 'reprehension and direction' to, 3/164 & n. 5; new mast-docks, 5/202, 231 & n. 1, 353; 6/95–6 & n.; strike, 6/216; difficulty of paying, 9/130, 419; reform of storekeepers' accounts, 9/444

SALES: (ships), 1/284, 305; 3/185–6; 8/484 & n. 3, 485; (stores), 2/45 & n. 3, 50 & n. 2, 68–9, 93 & n. 1; 4/319; Board criticised for, 9/562

FINANCIAL [general]: draws up estimates of debts, 1/231 & n. 4, 312; 2/240 & n. 1; of salaries, 2/50 & n. 1; and of ordinary charge, 4/152; is asked for estimates, 3/179 & n. 4; writes to/ consults Duke of York about insolvency, 2/119, 120, 154 & n. 1, 213 & n. 2; 3/47; 7/35(2), 36–7, 43, 123, 205–6 & n.; 8/41, 58, 62–3, 69, 70, 73, 78, 138, 140, 141, 142, 241, 274, 346, 392; 9/49, 94, 101, 115, 125, 126; applies to Lord Treasurer, Cabinet etc. for supply, 4/121 & n. 2; 6/77, 78; 7/48, 311 & n. 3; 9/122 & n. 1, 147–8, 152, 154, 171, 174, 444–5, 525, 530; presents accounts to Treasury, 3/6 &

n. 2, 280 & n. 1; 4/302 & n. 1; 5/325, 326, 330 & n. 2; 6/72; 7/294 & n. 1 (totals given); 8/57–8, 372 & n. 1, 373; and to Parliament, 7/64, 78, 93, 294, 295, 298, 305, 306, 308, 314, 356; 8/71 & n. 1, 303, 351, 448, 449; orders pursers' accounts etc. 2/29 & n. 1; examines/passes Navy Treasurer's accounts, 3/14, 240; 4/96–7, 99; 5/104 & n. 2, 105, 318, 329; 6/119(2), 203; 7/289; 8/141, 169–70, 448, 449, 458, 460; 9/222, 250; examines Comptroller's accounts, 7/76; 8/50; discusses paying off fleet, 3/252–3, 265; 6/149; hopes for money from sale of Dunkirk, 3/265, 271; assigned £200,000 p.a. by Exchequer, 3/297 & n. 1, 302; 4/81; discusses exchange rate of pieces-of-eight, 4/132, 133; draws up instructions for paying bills, 6/336 & n. 2; 'libel' against Board's failure to pay bills, 7/388; allotted £35,000 from poll tax, 8/57–8 & n., 89, 90; and £500,000 from Eleven Months Tax, 8/111–12, 205 & n. 1; bills sold at 35–40% discount, 8/201; receives £10,000 from Treasury, 8/252; discusses allocation from Treasury, 8/334; discusses pay tickets, 9/80, 263, 266; and cost of new fleet, 9/220 & n. 2; discusses expenses with Treasury, 9/444–5, 525–6, 530; credit good, 4/405 & n. 1; insolvency alluded to: 2/168; 3/210; 6/208, 211, 266, 273, 291–2, 293, 307, 322, 323, 324, 341; 7/256, 312, 313, 327, 331, 383; 8/66–7, 72, 96–7, 122 & n. 1, 206, 277 & n. 2, 315, 430–1; 9/18, 155, 180; also, 7/64, 78, 93, 383; 9/303

JUDICIAL AND DISCIPLINARY [see also Field, [E.]; Carkesse, [J.]]: Officers appointed J.P.s, 1/240, 252–3 & n.; 3/231; 4/78, 81–2 & n.; 8/31; commits alleged forger, 3/43–4 & n.; charges alleged thief, 3/137 & n. 2; adjudicates in dispute between captain and purser, 3/284 & n. 1; commits naval officers to trial for cowardice, 6/104 & n. 4; adjudicates between captain and master, 4/84; between captain and lieutenant, 7/380; between commander and Waith of Treasury, 7/93–4 & n.; investigates

loss of ships, 8/12 & n. 1, 28; investigates charges against dockyard officers 9/258–9 & n., 267 & n. 2

SEAMEN AND OFFICERS: chooses ship's masters etc., 2/103; 4/72; discusses establishments, 4/290; 6/339 & n. 1; (peacetime), 8/448 & n. 2; the press, 5/168 & n. 2; 6/45; 7/188; 8/394; discharges men etc., 7/327; discusses riot, 8/62–3

SHIPS AND SHIPBUILDING: hires ships, 1/242; 5/349, 350; (fireships), 7/161; (for Portugal), 3/63, 72, 85, 196; pays off ships, 1/245 & n. 1, 246, 247, 249, 283, 288, 308–9; 2/18, 19, 28, 30, 33; 8/396–7; appoints winter guard, 1/257, 266: 8/485–6; sets out ships, 2/127; 3/30–1, 125 & n. 2; 5/287 & n. 2; 6/233; 9/101, 121–2, 123, 125, 126, 130, 155, 180, 216–17, 220 & n. 2, 223(2); (for Guinea), 5/246 & n. 3, 248, 265; (fireships), 8/256(2) & n. 2, 259, 260 & n. 2; (merchantmen), 8/314–15, 316; (for Mediterranean), 9/424, 425–6, 510, 513 ~ to build ten ships, 7/193 & n. 5, 201; discusses design of masts, 9/5 & n. 1; and Heemskerck's project, 9/198 & n. 1, 206; values ships, 9/96 & n. 1; also, 5/111, 131

SICK AND WOUNDED: orders money for, 6/239 & n. 1, 243 & n. 2; approves proposal for infirmary, 7/49 & n. 2; discusses relief of prisoners, 7/201

VICTUALLING: examines/passes accounts, 3/41–2 & n., 52, 55, 62, 103, 106; 4/337; 7/74(2), 373, 403, 405; 8/47, 49, 50, 77, 208, 322; 9/250; inspects victualling office, 3/135 & n. 3; 4/84; obtains cash by sale of prize-goods, 6/239 & n. 1; discusses P's report, 7/219–20 & n.; examined by Council about complaints of Rupert and Albemarle, 7/259 & n. 1, 260; concludes new contract with Gauden, 9/252, 253, 261, 263, 287(2) & n. 1, 288 & n. 2, 301, 303(2) & n. 1, 428 & n. 4, 429; decides against direct management, 9/315–18 passim & nn.; prepares supplies for Mediterranean fleet, 9/508 & n. 2; also, 1/212–13; 4/36, 282; 7/13, 129, 135; 8/245; 9/24–5, 142

NEW BRIDEWELL, Clerkenwell: P visits, 5/250 & n. 4, 289; 6/65–6, & n. 3
NEWBURY, Berks.: P at, 9/242
NEWCASTLE, Duke and Duchess of: *see* Cavendish
NEWCASTLE UPON TYNE, Northumberland: parliamentary election, 2/76 & n. 1; dispute between city and Gerard, 9/359 & nn.; shipping from/ to, 4/395, 397; 8/263, 285, 602; coals from, 8/426, 435, 576
NEW CHAPEL, Orchard St, Westminster: plague burials, 6/162
NEWELL, ——, clergyman: 3/199
NEW ENGLAND: masts/mastships from, 5/123, 127, 239, 321; 7/395, 397; alluded to: 4/71
NEW EXCHANGE, Strand (the Exchange): shut by King's order, 4/431 & n. 5; P spreads news at, 7/151; makes assignation, 7/385; drafts memorandum, 9/84(2); P/EP shop(s) at: for pendants, 4/100; mercers' and drapers' goods, 4/100; 7/70, 344; 8/104, 322, 424; 9/84, 188, 206–7, 400; dressing-boxes, 8/53; 9/91(2); books, 7/103, 104, 117; 8/380, 383, 387, 439, 508; 9/29, 216, 411, 449; baubles, 7/386; knives, 8/433; also visit(s) (to pay bills, or for unspecified purposes): 1/85, 251; 3/52, 65, 215; 4/58, 100, 124, 164, 286, 290, 324, 332, 336, 341, 357, 363; 5/9, 48, 55, 118, 134, 144, 155, 186, 238, 269; 6/17, 52, 100; 7/124, 131, 208, 256, 367, 369, 425; 8/27, 30, 46, 86, 99, 100, 110, 121, 151, 213, 334, 341, 353, 393, 403, 431, 460, 463; 9/6, 28, 39, 46, 89, 113, 120, 124, 158, 178, 179, 182, 215, 218, 247, 264, 269, 295, 304, 313, 333, 393, 397, 412, 419, 422, 437, 465, 449, 474, 511, 532
NEW EXCHANGE STAIRS: 7/233, 284; 8/517; 9/128
NEWGATE: 9/258
NEWGATE MARKET: P shops in: for grate, 4/409; poultry, 5/264; also, 3/294; 9/268; shambles, 3/283; Fire, 7/277
NEWGATE PRISON: prisoners escape, 8/371; malpractices of keeper, 8/562 & n. 2; alluded to: 4/5; 9/111
NEW HALL, Essex: timber at, 4/435 & n. 3

NEWINGTON, Surrey: P's father married, 5/360; alluded to: 2/91
NEWINGTON GREEN, Mdx: 5/132, ?360
NEWMAN, Col. [George]: 4/260
NEWMAN, Samuel, Puritan divine [*see also* Books]: foretells his death, 9/31 & n. 3
NEWMAN, ——, barber: 1/15
NEWMARKET, Suff.: King/Duke of York visit(s) races at, 4/324 & n. 2; 9/209 & n. 2, 264, 341, 343, 473 & n. 5, 535 & n. 2
NEW NETHERLAND (N. America): surrender of, 5/283 & n. 2
NEW PALACE YARD, [New York] Westminster [*see also* Taverns etc.: Crown; Leg; Swan]: soldiers in, 1/40, 43; Quaker meeting, 1/44 & n. 2; also, 3/177; 4/234
NEWPORT, Andrew, Comptroller of the Great Wardrobe: appointed, 9/41 & n. 3; at Exchequer, 9/477; social: 9/112
NEWPORT [Richard]: at Vauxhall, 9/218 & n. 4, 220
NEWPORT, Essex: 8/467
NEWPORT (I. of Wight), TREATY OF (1648): 4/473 & n. 2
NEWPORT PAGNELL, Bucks.: P visits, 9/224, 225 & nn.
NEWPORT ST, Westminster: 9/431
NEWSPAPERS: Muddiman's parliamentary newsbooks, 1/12 & n. 3; P's letters quoted in, 1/126, n. 2; Buckhurst's defence in, 3/35–6 & n.; Scottish news, 4/138 & n. 3; 7/387 & n. 2; Portuguese news, 4/203 & n. 1; P reads first number of *The Intelligencer*, 4/297 & n. 2; asked to contribute news to, 5/348 & n. 1; Moore's account of Battle of Lowestoft in, 6/128 & n. 3; P pays for newsbooks, 6/162; *Oxford Gazette*: P reads first number, 6/305 & n. 3; Chatham Chest business in 7/116 & n. 2; Great Fire foretold, 7/405 & n. 3, 406; report on Carkesse case, 8/216 & n. 1; French news, 9/38 & n. 1; P reads newsbooks at Brouncker's, 9/161; Lisbon gazette, 4/215 & n. 1; Dutch gazette, 8/126–7 & n. 1; also, 7/242

during Plague, 6/188 & n. 1; and after
Fire, 7/278 & n. 1; P visits, 6/234, 235,
244, 303, 304, 311, 312, 313; alluded
to: 7/299
NORBURY, [George], P's uncle:
social: 2/215, 220; 4/427; 5/47, 49,
151, 340; 7/115, 134
NORBURY, [Katherine], daughter of
George: ? 4/312; 5/61
NORBURY, Mary, daughter of
George: ?4/312; 5/61
NORBURY, [Sarah], wife of George:
offers to sell Brampton property to
P, 2/124 & n. 5; 3/13; social: 2/200,
215, 220; 4/312; 5/140, 340; ~ ?her
sister, 4/312
NORE, the: English fleet at, 6/275;
7/123, 223, 304, 326, 332, 355, 360;
Dutch fleet at, 8/256, 258, 354, 359;
P visits *Royal Sovereign*, 6/188, 194;
pay at, 8/144
NORMAN, [James], clerk to Sir W.
Batten; Clerk of the Survey, Chat-
ham 1664: new design for storekeeper's books, 5/104 & n. 1; alluded
to: 3/164; 5/36, 141
NORRIS, ——, frame-maker: 9/538
NORTH, Catherine, Lady North,
wife of Sir Charles: 8/600 & n. 3
NORTH, Sir Charles, kted before
1667, succ. as 5th Baron North 1677;
relative of Sandwich: P's opinion,
8/600; on Dutch voyage with
Sandwich, 1/138, 142, 153, 159;
marriage, 8/600 & n. 3; musical:
1/123 & n. 1, 129; social: 1/135
NORTH, Sir Dudley, succ. as 4th
Baron North 1666: defeated in elec-
tions for Cambridgeshire, 1/112 & n.
2; social: 1/75
NORTH, [Francis; Lord Keeper
(as Baron Guilford) 1682–5]: 9/140
NORTHAMPTON, Earl of: *see*
Compton
NORTHAMPTON: floods, 4/139 &
n. 1
NORTHAMPTONSHIRE: declara-
tion for free parliament, 1/28 & n. 6
NORTHUMBERLAND, Lord: *see*
Percy, Sir Henry, 9th Earl; Percy,
Algernon, 10th Earl
NORTON, [Daniel], of Southwick,
Hants.: marriage, 6/150 & n. 3; death

and will, 7/264; also, 6/60; ~ his son,
7/264
[NORTON, George], innkeeper at
Abbotsleigh, nr Bristol: 1/155 & n. 3
NORTON, [Isabella], (b. Lawson),
wife of Daniel: her beauty, 4/23; 5/7;
marriage, 6/150–1 & n. 3; widowed,
7/264; also, 6/60
NORTON, Joyce, relative of P: P
shows her Parliament chamber, 1/39;
buys mourning for Duke of Gloucester, 1/251; gives silver cup to P and
EP, 5/47; at Tom P's funeral, 5/90;
grown old, 9/425; social: at P's
father's, 1/65, 81, 85, 88, 176; 2/40; at
P's stone feast, 2/60; 3/53; 4/94–5;
5/98; 6/124; also, 1/10, 72; 2/43, 53;
3/207; 5/87, 166; 5/391; 9/530–1;
alluded to: 4/272
NORTON, [Mary], actress: P admires
in *Le Cid*, 3/273 & n. 1; in *The siege of
Rhodes*, 3/295; P meets, 7/190–1
NORTON, Col. [Richard]: given
commission, 8/265 & n. 5; alluded to:
6/150
NORTON, [Roger], King's printer:
Chancery dispute, 7/261 & n. 5
NORTON ST PHILIP, Som.: church
and tombs, 9/232 & nn.
NORWAY: timber, 3/118 & n. 3;
4/103; sawmills, 3/118; transport of
timber, ib.; naval supplies from,
5/333; 6/330
NORWICH, Earl of: *see* Goring
NORWICH: flags from, 5/182 &
n. 1
NORWOOD, Henry, Maj./Col.,
Deputy Governor of Dunkirk 1662,
and Tangier 1665–8: carries letters
between Sandwich and King, 1/112,
125; at surrender of Dunkirk, 3/272;
quarrels with Fitzgerald, 5/344–5 &
n.; Tangier business, 6/144; 7/18–20
passim; 8/372; invites P to join in
trading venture, 7/23, 24; quarrels
with Houblons, 7/38, 45; P's low
opinion, 7/99; dispute with Bland,
9/392 & n. 1, 430–1; enemy of
Cholmley, 9/455; social: 1/264; 7/38,
44, 61
NOSTRADAMUS   (Notredame,
Michel de), astrologer (d. 1566):
anecdote of, 8/42 & nn.

NOTT, [William], bookbinder: 9/480 & n. 2

NOVA SCOTIA: ceded to France, 8/212–13 & n., 426 & n. 1; mineral deposits, 8/426 & n. 1

NUN, [?Elizabeth], servant in Queen's household: 9/560, 563

NYE, Philip, Independent divine (d. 1672): sermons mimicked, 1/280 & n. 3

OAKESHOTT, Capt. [Benjamin], soldier: 1/14

OATES, Capt. [Thomas], rebel: in Derwentdale Plot, 4/377 & n. 1; 5/13 & n. 2

OBDAM (Updam), Jacob, Heer van Wassenaer, naval commander: sends envoy to Sandwich, 1/142; plague on his ship, 5/231 & n. 3; commands Dutch fleet, 6/108; killed in action, 6/122; social: 1/152

O'BRIEN, Capt. [Charles], naval officer: given ship by King, 8/489 & n. 4; at court, 9/23–4; at Teddeman's funeral, 9/200

O'BRIEN, Murrough, 1st Earl of Inchiquin: 1/321 & n. 2

OFFICES, SALE OF [see also Barlow, T.; Coventry, Sir W.; Titles, sale of. Asterisks denote the references at which a price is given.]:
GENERAL: prevalence, 1/223, n. 1*; bill (1663) to prevent fraud, 4/156 & n. 4, 169 & n. 2; Duchess of Albemarle's trade in, 1/181 & n. 4, 184; 3/43 & n. 3; 8/219–20; Clarendon's, 4/166; and Lady Castlemaine's, 8/427; secretary to Admiral's income from, 4/170, 330, 331; M. Wren's attitude, 8/447; forbidden in Ordnance Office, 8/178
PARTICULAR: court and administration: coachmaker to King, 1/181*; Groom of Privy Chamber, 4/255*; Master of Wardrobe, 8/195; Patent Office, clerk in, 9/372 & n. 2, 480, 492*; Secretary of State, 1/223, n. 1*; 3/226* & n. 2; 9/302* & n. 4; Surveyor of King's Works, 9/491* & n. 3; Treasurer to Duke of York, 9/38* & n. 2; naval administration: Navy Treasurer, 7/334; 8/222, 277, 295 & n. 3; Clerk of the Acts, 1/185*, 189*,

191*, 202*, & n. 1, 210*, 216*, 219; 2/55* & n. 2; Clerk of Ropeyard, 4/429; 5/231*, 248*, 253; 8/228*; Navy Commissioner, 4/71*; 8/294* & n. 1; Navy Office clerk, 1/194*; 4/71*; 5/141; purser, 1/77–8*; 9/382 & n. 4; Purveyor of Petty Provisions, 8/228*; unspecified, 5/235; other offices: commission in Lifeguards, 4/371; 8/436*; 9/308 & n. 2*; Governor of Tangier, 8/117 & n. 1, 127; Treasurer of Tangier Committee, 6/68* & n. 2

OFFLEY, [Robert], lawyer: attorney for navy creditors, 9/140; counsel for Newcastle upon Tyne, 9/359

OFFORD, Hunts.: P visits, 2/136, 182; his land at, 2/182 & n. 2; alluded to: 8/158

OGILBY, John, author and publisher [see also Books]: lottery, 7/48 & n. 1; to publish fables, 7/184 & n. 3

OGLE, [Anne], Maid of Honour to the Duchess of York: 9/468

OKEY, [John], regicide: arrested in Delft, 3/45 & n. 1; imprisoned and executed, 3/47, 66

OLD BAILEY [see also Sessions House; Taverns etc.: Fountain; Short's]: Fire in, 7/275

OLDENBURG, Henry, secretary to the Royal Society 1663–77: imprisoned for treasonable correspondence, 8/292 & n. 2; shows P drawing instrument, 9/537–8; also, 5/290 & n. 1

OLD FISH ST [see also Taverns etc.: Swan]: 7/237

OLD FORD, Mdx: P/EP at, 5/175; 9/221, 546

OLD PALACE YARD, Westminster [see also Coffee-houses: Miles; Taverns etc.: Heaven]: 2/222; 7/160

OLD SARUM, Wilts.: P at, 9/228

OLD ST: 9/184

OLD SWAN, the [usually the jetty of that name; occasionally the district; see also Taverns etc.: Old Swan]: 1/249, 294, 313; 2/59; 3/52, 177; 4/92, 262; 6/154, 313, 331; 7/93, 157, 161, 221, 230, 234, 245, 255, 339; 8/13, 20, 32, 34, 39, 91, 102, 120, 151, 175, 224, 241, 247, 293; 9/114, 288, 320

O'NEILL (Oneale), [Daniel],

6/41; quarrels with Dowager Duchess of Richmond, 3/68 & n. 4; and Lady Hervey, 9/415 & n. 1; encourages Duke of York's affair with Lady Denham, 7/159; at balls, 3/215, 300; 4/68; 7/373; Garter service, 4/112; lottery, 5/214; masque, 6/29; and court play, 9/24; hunts moth, 8/282; gaming for high stakes, 9/71

CHILDREN: by ?her husband, 3/175; by the King: 8/355, n. 1; birth and christening of Charles (later Duke of Southampton), 3/81 & n. 1, 87, 146; birth of Henry (later Duke of Grafton), 4/315 & n. 2; 5/56; George (later Duke of Northumberland), 7/8 & n. 2; Charlotte, 6/41 & n. 2; also, 8/376

HOUSES ETC.: in King St, Westminster, 1/199 & n. 4; 3/147; Pall Mall, 7/159; Whitehall, 5/164; fire at lodgings, 5/27; aviary, 8/404; Berkshire House, 9/190 & n. 3

PORTRAITS: by Lely, 3/113 & n. 3; version acquired by Sandwich, 5/200 & n. 3; P buys prints, 7/359 & n. 3, 393, 417; 8/23, 124, 171, 206; also, 3/230

SOCIAL: at dinner party, 9/468, 469; mock-wedding to Frances Stuart, 4/37-8, 48; at theatre, 2/139, 164, 174; 3/87, 260; 4/56; 5/33, 77; 6/73; 7/347; 8/46, 225; 9/186, 398; puppet play, 8/409; in Hyde Park, 4/95; 5/126; 6/60; 8/196; 9/282

ALLUDED TO: 8/45

~ her servants: her black boy, 8/33; —— Willson, her woman, 8/288, 325; 9/186; her nurse, 8/288

PALMER, Benjamin: 1/246

PALMER, ——, lawyer [?identical with the foregoing]: 4/277; ~ his wife, ib.

PALMER, Sir Geoffrey, Attorney-General 1660-d.70: advises Sandwich on patent of nobility, 1/187-8 & n.; and P on Clerkship of Acts, 1/194; issues warrant for P's appointment, 1/196 & n. 1; and for Tangier commission, 5/229; P consults, 5/325-6; 6/101; 9/281, 291; rumoured appointment as Chief Justice, 8/412 & n. 2; draws up Tangier charter, 9/149;

house at Hampstead, 9/281 & n. 2; alluded to: 8/67; 9/122

PALMER, [James], Vicar of St Bride, Fleet St, 1616-45: death, 1/11 & n. 4

PALMER, [Roger], 1st Earl of Castlemaine [see also Books]: patent of nobility, 2/229 & n. 1; deserted by wife, 3/139, 146-7 & n.; their mutual indifference, 3/175, 248; said to have entered French monastery, 3/147 & n. 1; returns from France, 6/41, 55-6; their amicable separation, 7/404 & n. 2; alluded to: 1/199 & n. 4

PALMER, Mrs ——: entertains P with bawdy songs and ventriloquy, 4/261-2

PANNIER ALLEY: 7/98, 101(2)

PAPILLON, [Thomas], merchant: victualling contract, 9/287 & n. 1; dispute with excise farmers, 9/532 & n. 2

PARGITER, [Francis], of the Muscovy Company: stories of Russia, 5/272 & n. 1; alluded to: 2/142

PARGITER, [John, sen.], goldsmith: loses by purchase of Crown lands, 2/199 & n. 3

PARHAM, [Richard], of the Fishmongers' Company: Fishery business, 3/269-70 & n.; 5/309; gives P oysters, 5/312

PARIS: famine (1661), 3/200 & n. 2; cleanliness and order, 8/299-300 & nn.; peace celebrations, 9/257 & n. 3; also, 8/74

PARISH CLERKS' Company: see London: livery companies

PARKE: see Packer

PARKER, Capt. [John], naval officer: 1/121

PARKER, [?John], merchant, of Mark Lane: ship retaken from Algerines, 2/221 & n. 3

PARKER, Mrs ——: 8/511

PARKHURST, [John and Catherine]: 9/176-7 & n.

PARKHURST, Sir Robert, of Pyrford, Surrey: borrows £2000 from Sandwich, 1/310 & n. 2, 311, 312; 2/48; 4/94; his prescription for colic, 4/441; social: 5/149

PARLIAMENT: (general):

P's EVIDENCE, vol. i, pp. cxxxi-iii; his

views on, 7/416; 8/292–3, 305, 353, 485

P'S ASSOCIATION WITH (omitting official business): visits: hears law cases in Lords, 1/225; 5/139–40 & n.; 8/22 & n. 3; 9/85 & n. 2; observes proceedings from lobby, 4/207; gains entrance to Commons committee, 7/386 & n. 1; and to conferences between Houses, 8/2 & n. 5, 34 & n. 2; observes proceedings from Speaker's chamber, 9/169; also, 3/33, 60–1; 6/8, 20, 25, 39; 7/295, 304, 414; 8/521; as candidate: decides not to stand, 2/42; urged to, 7/322 & n. 2; decides to, 9/376–7 & n., 385, 454; parliamentary career, vol. i, p. xxxvii

BUILDING, PLACES IN: lobby, 1/17, 82; 2/107; 4/207, 222; 8/491, 501, 511; 9/65, 83, 85, 103; Painted Chamber, 1/83; 4/251; 5/110, 112, 147; 8/2, 360, 521; parliament door, 3/19, 60; 8/520; Prince's Chamber, 9/190, 191; Speaker's Chamber, 4/395; 9/169

HOUSE OF LORDS: status of judges, 8/445 & n. 4; powers, 8/542, 561; order of precedence among barons, 9/106–7 & n.; Black Rod, 5/110, 111; 9/184

HOUSE OF COMMONS: number of naval officers and merchants, 5/95 & n. 1; nature of members' privileges, 7/50–1 & n.; payment of members' wages, 9/15, 140–1 & n.; representation of boroughs, 9/15 & n. 3, 140; officers: clerk-assistant, 4/281; doorkeeper, 7/305; housekeeper, ib.

PARLIAMENT (the Long): proceedings cited, 8/547 & n. 3; 9/74

PARLIAMENT (the Rump), 27 Dec. 1659–16 March 1660:

GENERAL: reassembles, 1/1 & nn.; members meet Monck, 1/40; Monck attends on, 1/43 & n. 2; unpopularity, 1/45; 3/95; 'the Burning of the Rump', 1/52 & n. 4; ordered by Monck to fill vacancies, 1/50 & n. 1, 51 & n. 1, 54 & n. 2, 57; issues writs for elections, 1/57; secluded members admitted, 1/57, 58, 60–3 passim & nn.; dissolves itself, 1/73, 74, 76, 86, 88, 89; Lords intend to sit, 1/78 & n. 2; supports King, 1/86

BILLS AND ACTS: reconstituting Council

of State, 1/4–5 & n.; on indemnity for army, 1/4–5 & n., 6; on members' qualifications, 1/56 & n. 2

VOTES, ORDERS AND RESOLUTIONS: for fast, 1/7–8; to fill vacancies, 1/6, 8, 41 & n. 3, 56; of censure on Clerk, 1/12 & n. 4; for 'law and gospel', 1/26, 27 & n. 4; summoning Committee of Safety, 1/27–8 & n.; for demolition of city's defences, 1/48; for elections to common council of city, 1/49 & n. 3; rusticating Sir H. Vane, 1/56; appointing Monck general of all forces, 1/62; for re-erection of city gates, 1/63, 65; electing Councillors of State, 1/65 & n. 4; re-issuing Covenant, 1/77 & n. 1; on Lords, 1/86 & n. 3

PARLIAMENT (the Convention), 16 March–29 Dec. 1660:

ELECTIONS: Huntingdon, 1/86–7 & n., 99 & n. 2; Cinque Ports, 1/93 & n. 2, 94, 96, 97; Hastings, 1/102 & n. 2; Weymouth, 1/103, 108 & n. 2; Dover, 1/110–11, 167, 179 & n. 1; Cambridgeshire, 1/112 & n. 2; Cavaliers' majority, 1/116 & n. 4

GENERAL: assembles, 1/115; Houses agree to fast, 1/116; passes indemnity act, poll tax act and act confirming judicial proceedings, 1/234 & n. 1; adjourns, 1/243; reassembles, 1/284; dissolved, 2/1

HOUSE OF LORDS: Presbyterian peers resolve to sit, 1/111 & n. 1, 113; assembles and chooses Speaker, 1/115; 'young' Lords sit, 1/118; chooses commissioners to wait on King, 1/128, 132, 335, 141, 156; sits as court, 1/225 & n. 3; quarrels with Commons over indemnity bill, 1/229 & n. 1

HOUSE OF COMMONS: chooses Speaker, 1/115–16; inaugural sermon, 1/116; receives Declaration of Breda, 1/118, 122, 128; votes for government by King, Lords and Commons, 1/121–2 & n.; votes supply for King, 1/122; chooses commissioners to wait on King, 1/128 & n. 2, 131; orders arrest and trial of regicides, 1/151; establishes annual thanksgiving service on King's birthday, 1/166 & n. 2; entertains royal dukes, 1/174 & n. 1; debates indemnity bill, 1/177, 229,

232, 234 & n. 1; abortive motion to reward Sandwich, 1/178 & n. 2; allocates excise to King, 1/303 & n. 4; orders exhumation of regicides' corpses, 1/309 & n. 4; Committee for disbandment of armed forces: appointment and proceedings, 1/245 & n. 1, 246 & n. 3, 247, 249, 283, 288 & n. 1, 308–9; 2/18 & n. 3, 19 & n. 2, 28 & n. 3, 30, 33 & n. 3, 45 & n. 1, 50; parties: Presbyterians to impose terms on King, 1/117, 118; Cavaliers and Presbyterians, 1/118 & n. 4; Episcopalians and Presbyterians, 1/229; 'factions', 2/1

PARLIAMENT (the Cavalier):
ELECTIONS: Cambridge borough, 2/56 & n. 2; London, 2/57 & n. 1; Newcastle-upon-Tyne, 2/76 & n. 1; bye-elections: court candidates defeated, 7/337 & n. 2; Quakers' candidate, 9/150 & n. 2; expenses, 8/454–5 & n.

FIRST SESSION, 8 May 1661–19 May 1662:
HOUSE OF LORDS: examines Hutchinson's accounts, 2/100; dispute with Commons over licensing bill, 2/144 & n. 3; bishops resume seats, 2/216 & n. 4; debates Clarendon's proviso to bill of uniformity, 3/49 & n. 1; prayers, 3/61

HOUSE OF COMMONS: receives communion, 2/107 & n. 1; orders Commonwealth legislation to be burnt, 2/108 & n. 4; bill restoring bishops to Lords, 2/111 & n. 2; benevolences, ib. & n. 4; grants supply, 2/217–18 & n.; lack of government control, 2/141 & n. 3; examines regicides, 2/224 & n. 1; orders fast, 3/10 & n. 2; militia bill, 3/15 & n. 2; hearth tax bill, 3/41 & n. 2, 43, 78; uniformity bill, 3/49; hastens business, 3/85

SECOND SESSION, 18 Feb.–27 July 1663:
GENERAL: reassembles, 4/49; King's speech, 4/50 & n. 2; King calls on to hasten business, 4/159 & n. 3; prorogation, 4/239, 240, 249–51 & nn.; forms of royal assent to bills, 4/249–50 & nn.

HOUSE OF LORDS: Bristol's attempted impeachment of Clarendon, 4/222–5 passim & nn., 229 & n. 3, 231 & n. 2;

defeats conventicle bill, 4/249; debates bill on popery, ib.; 'mislays' bill for sabbath observance, ib. & n. 2

HOUSE OF COMMONS: opposes King's declaration of indulgence, 4/44 & n. 2, 57 & n. 4, 58 & n. 1, 62, 63, 82; to disqualify members refusing to abjure Covenant, 4/53 & n. 1; bill encouraging wearing of English cloth, ib. & n. 2; bill and address against popery, 4/67–8, 90 & n. 1, 92, 95 & n. 2, 249; resumption of crown lands, 4/87–8; to enquire into navy expenses, 4/103; and Queen's, 4/127 & n. 1; bill to disqualify ex-rebels from office, 3/291; 4/125 & n. 1, 126, 136 & n. 1; bill to suppress abuses in sale of offices, 4/156 & n. 4, 166, 169 & n. 2, 190; enquiries into revenue, 4/166, 193 & n. 2; bill to suppress conventicles, 4/159–60, 161, 243 & n. 3, 249; votes supply, 4/183, 187, 191, 205–6 & n., 249–50; votes £200,000 p.a. to navy from customs, 4/206 & n. 3; votes on Temple's attempt to manage House, 4/191–2 & n., 200, 207, 208, 211; Bristol's speech on, 4/207–8 & nn.; fast day for weather, 4/237 & n. 3; bill to enforce sabbath observance, 4/249 & n. 2; parties: court party, 4/57, 58

THIRD SESSION, 16 March–17 May 1664:
GENERAL: reassembles, 5/88; adjourned and reassembles, 5/93; King's speech on triennial bill, 5/112 & n. 4; act about writs of error, 5/112; joint address against Dutch, 5/131, 135, 137; King's reply, 5/137; conference on conventicle bill, 5/147–8 & nn.; (untrue) rumour of prorogation, 5/151; prorogued, 5/247 & n. 4

HOUSE OF LORDS: Lady Petre's case, 5/109–12 passim & nn., 126, 128–9; joint address with Commons against Dutch, 5/131

HOUSE OF COMMONS: triennial bill, 5/93–4, 99 & nn., 102–3; Navy Board enabling bill, 5/99 & n. 1, 104, 105; merchants' petitions against Dutch, 5/107–9 passim, 113, 127, 129 & n. 2; grants £2½m. for war, 5/331 & n. 1; parties: Bristol's faction, 5/89; Presbyterian faction, 5/103, 327–8; King's party, 5/331

Commons over Carr, 8/583, 587; 9/57, 85; bill establishing Brooke House Committee, 9/8, 9; Penn's impeachment, 9/173-4 & n., 175-6, 178; dispute with Commons over Skinner v. E. India Company, 9/182-96 passim & nn.; parties: Duke of York's friends, 8/482

HOUSE OF COMMONS: *supply business:* backward in granting, 8/324, 331, 395, 534, 568, 591; 9/82-3, 140, 141, 163, 171-2, 173, 180, 184; demands accounts of expenditure, 9/82-3 & n.; votes £300,000 from wine and poll tax, 9/92-3 & n., 120, 123, 141, 192; clergy excused from poll, 9/120-1 & n.; also, 9/114, 115, 167; *Clarendon's impeachment:* thanks King for dismissal, 8/476, 479, 480; impeachment process, 8/478, 499 & n. 1, 502 & nn., 509, 522, 523 & n. 2, 526, 532-3, 533 & n. 1, 539 & n. 3; replies to Lords' objections, 8/534, 557-8 & n., 559, 561; condemns Clarendon's petition, 8/563; bill of banishment, 8/578 & n. 1; also, 8/532, 555-6; *Committee on Miscarriages:* appointed, 8/484-5 & n.; revived, 9/135 & n. 2, 138; terms of reference, 8/485, 494; enquires into division of fleet (1666), 8/489 & n. 1, 502; voted a miscarriage, 9/70, 74, 75; enquires into prize-goods scandal (1665), 8/486, 494, 499, 549, 576; 9/64, 80, 96; into failure to pursue Dutch fleet (1665), 8/489-90 & n., 491-2; 9/142, 166-7 & n.; voted a miscarriage, 9/80 & n. 3; into issue of tickets and failure to defend Medway (1667), 8/493-8 passim & nn., 501, 502, 504, 508-11 passim, 526-7, 538 & n. 1, 540, 545-6; 9/11, 62, 69, 70, 76, 77, 79, 84, 85; Board defended by P before committee, 8/494-6 & nn.; voted a miscarriage, 9/76, 86-7, 95, 97, 98; enquires into sale of places by Coventry, 8/504, 505; into Bergen affair, 8/538; orders to Navy Board, 8/489, 493, 501, 537-8 & n.; examines P, 8/493; and Navy Board, 8/494-6 passim & nn., 501-2, 510; criticises victualling, 9/98, 107, 142; Board defended by P before House, 9/102-6 & nn.; Committee attends Privy

Council, 9/122; *Brooke House Committee (the Commissioners of Accounts):* appointed, 8/559-60 & n.; 9/8-9, 63; membership, 8/559-60 & n., 569-70, 571-2, 576-7, 586; 9/30, 44; powers, 8/601; 9/50 & n. 1, 179-80 & n.; efficiency, 8/586; 9/43-4 & n., 292; enquiries into pay tickets, 9/43-4, 56, 97; prize-goods scandal (1665), 9/49-50, 63, 64, 66, 68, 92, 162, 363-4; Warren's gifts, 9/73 & n. 2, 92, 220, 254 & n. 1, 277; Navy Treasury, 9/82, 179, 214 & n. 5; allegations against Coventry, 9/258; Hewer, 9/283; Waith, 9/358 & n. 1; and P, 9/562 & n. 1; into contracts, 9/394; interim report, 9/117; also, 8/599, 602; 9/34, 162(2), 335, 394; *other business:* opposes standing army, 8/324 & n. 3, 332 & n. 1, 352-3, 355, 361; resents adjournment, 8/352 & n. 1, 361, & n. 1; condemns Kelyng, 8/483-4 & n., 577, 578, 579; receives petitions against Mordaunt, 8/501-2 & n.; thanks Rupert and Albemarle, 8/515; condemns Woodmongers' charter, 8/520 & n. 4; proceedings against Commissioner Pett, 8/526-7; resolution on freedom of speech, 8/547 & n. 3; proceedings against Gerard of Brandon, 8/573-4 & n., 581, 583, 587; 9/57; hostile to bill for comprehension and toleration, 9/31 & n. 4, 35, 45-6 & n., 51-2, 60 & n. 2, 104, 111, 112; vehement against nonconformists, 9/96 & n. 1, 181; debates conventicle bill, 9/177 & n. 3, 192; bill prohibiting duelling, 9/53 & n. 1; libel distributed, 9/65 & n. 2; debates King's speech, 9/70; secretary of state's intelligence service, 9/70-1 & n., 74 & nn.; Temple's 'undertakers', 9/71 & n. 2; King's evil counsellors, 9/74; Temple's triennial bill, 9/77 & n. 2; petition against Ormond, 9/119, 169; impeachment of Penn, 9/162, 163, 165, 170; expulsion and impeachment of H. Brouncker, 9/170; dispute with Lords over Skinner v. E. India Company, 9/182-3 & n., 184, 191, 192, 196; second bill for rebuilding London, 9/187-8 & n.; *parties:* power of 'discontented party', 8/324, 352; Duke

17; at her house in Covent Garden, 7/18, 73, 362–3; 9/128; at P's house, 8/25, 28, 29, 104; 9/12; and tavern, 9/134; at theatre, 5/246; 7/347; 8/27, 64, 101, 383, 511; 9/12, 133, 186; P's valentine, 7/44, 49, 70; visits Kensington, 7/95, 100; and Islington, 7/121–2; at court ball, 7/341, 371–3; court news from, 7/99–100; 8/169; 9/23–4, 311, 320; hears Italian singer, 8/599; 9/172, 219; sees crown jewels, 9/172; at review in Hyde Park, 9/308; at P's house, 1/29, 259; 2/23; 4/14, 89; 5/291; 7/92, 118, 343–4, 399–400, 401; 8/151, 157, 502, 598; P/EP visit(s), 1/215; 2/169; 3/8, 301; 4/73, 124; 5/318; 8/103, 105, 242; 9/218; also, 1/32, 86–7, 96, 214, 312–13; 5/245; 6/49, 294; 7/53, 84, 93, 100, 103–4, 136; 8/58
ALLUDED TO: 6/316; 7/53
~ her servant Mary, 6/317; 7/93, 103, 238, 257
PEARSE (Pierce), James, surgeon; surgeon to the Duke of York 1662; Groom of the Privy Chamber to the Queen 1664; Surgeon-General to the fleet 1665:
CHRON. SERIES: visits regiment, 1/64–6 passim, 68; on Dutch voyage, 1/102, 119, 145, 148, 151, 154; on sea service, 1/186; shows P Somerset House, 3/191; and Whitehall, 5/188; promised place as Queen's surgeon, 3/234–5; dissects cadavers, 4/132; injects opium into dog, 5/151; attends dissection, 9/254; buys place as Groom of Queen's Privy Chamber, 4/255; attends Sandwich, 4/17; Sandwich's favour to, 5/22; his part in prize-goods affair, 6/230, 240, 247, 294, 317, 328, 333; away from London in Plague, 6/321; 7/16; account of Four Days Fight, 7/158; applies for place in hospital, 8/91–2; continued in pay as Surgeon-General, 8/198 & n. 1; banking account, 8/270; in privateer business, 8/342; and prize-goods scandal, 9/91; consults P on pay, 8/436; P godfather to son, 8/454 & n. 3; evidence about Battle of Lowestoft, 8/491; treats Arabella Churchill for ?pox, 9/413; also, 1/80, 251; 4/91; 5/131–2,

197; 8/20
COURT/POLITICAL NEWS FROM: 3/157, 227, 234, 248, 289; 4/132, 174, 187, 222, 272, 348, 370, 392, 399–400; 5/4, 20, 33, 40, 50, 245, 275; 6/321; 7/8, 99–100, 314–15, 323–4, 399, 400; 8/47, 192, 235, 253, 270, 297, 334, 376, 403–4, 436, 475, 476, 550–1; 9/204–5, 335–6, 501–2
HIS HOUSE: in St Margaret's churchyard, 1/186, 212, 215; new house [?nr Covent Garden], 5/151; 7/136, 296, 341; 8/169; lets rooms after fire, 7/296
SOCIAL: at P's stone feast, 2/60; his 'foul discourse', 4/436; at music/dancing parties, 6/320–1, 323; 7/16; visits Bear Garden, 7/246; attends court ball, 7/371–3; at Teddeman's funeral, 9/200; Vauxhall, 9/219; and Mulberry Gardens, 9/286; to see execution, 9/335; at taverns, 1/26; 2/49, 89, 108, 117; 9/134, 172; P visits etc., 1/27, 47, 208, 283; 2/3, 48; 4/14; 7/92, 100; 8/28, 65; 9/4, 188, 311; at P's house, 1/29–30, 53, 259; 2/23; 3/138; 5/7, 291; 7/236, 352; 8/20, 64, 104, 157, 502; 9/12, 128, 145, 376; on *Naseby*, 1/103, 105, 107; at theatre, 1/214; 2/60; 7/347; 9/522; also, 1/173, 214, 313; 4/21–2; 8/58, 238; 9/126–7, 289
ALLUDED TO: 1/32, 86, 93, 145, 173, 203, 251, 252; 2/114; 9/293
~ his man, 1/68; brother, 2/149; sister, 5/197; kinswoman, ib.; brother-in-law, 8/104
PEARSE, James, son of James and Elizabeth: P delights in his company, 6/317–18; 7/70, 100; 8/188; portrait by Hayls, 9/188; at school, 9/413; social: with mother at P's house, 7/343; 8/104, 157; 9/12, 128; also, 7/93, 95; 8/599; 9/286, 289; his master, 8/188
PEARSON, John, Master of Trinity College, Cambridge 1662–73, Bishop of Chester 1672–d. 86: 8/337 & n. 2
PEARSON, Richard, Vicar of St Bride, Fleet St 1660–6, Canon of Exeter 1643–4, 1660–d. 68: conducts Tom P's funeral service, 5/91
PEDLEY, [Nicholas], lawyer, kted 1672: elected M.P. for Huntingdon,

3/249; garden-door, 4/11; new dining-room, 4/121; new chimney-piece, 5/7; goods removed in Fire, 7/272, 274; land attached, 8/209; house at Walthamstow, 3/64; 6/102; 8/197, 235, 389, 408; plan to buy Wanstead House, 8/172, 197 & n. 2; Irish estate, 2/200 & n. 1, 201; visits to, 3/79, 123, 126, 132, 134, 151, 181–2; also, 5/183; 9/170
HOUSEHOLD: dishes 'deadly foul', 5/18; mean dinners, 7/287; 8/3, 122, 129, 234, 408; 9/505; bad food, 8/284, 371, 375; 9/202, 283; borrows silver etc. for daughter's wedding, 8/63, 77; housekeeping showy but mean/slatternly, 8/73, 122, 142, 197, 217, 408, 423; 9/84; servants [see also Markham, Nan]: footboys, 2/36; 3/77; 4/177; 7/282, 304, 305; 8/164; Harry (boy), 7/292; Jack (black servant), 2/61; John (ex-coachman), 8/173; Tom (coachman), 8/436; Betty (maid), 3/152; Sarah (once at P's), 3/302; chaplain in Ireland, 5/190
SOCIAL: sings bawdy songs, 1/262; visits Batten at Walthamstow, 1/279, 280–1; 2/78; 8/423; fuddled, 1/321; 2/208; at funerals of R. Blake, 2/74; and Batten, 8/476–7; at christenings, 2/109, 146; 4/165; 8/405; watches pre-coronation procession, 2/82; chariot race with Batten, 2/110; sings with P on roof, 2/115; sees wrestling at Moorfields, 2/127; tankard stolen as joke, 2/164, 169, 170, 175–6, 178; makes Cocke drunk, 2/238; gives dinners on wedding anniversaries, 3/4; 5/3, 6–7; and to Navy Board, 3/217; 5/358; 7/11; dines with Lieutenant of Tower, 4/70; dines with Coventry, 5/102; visits Lawson on deathbed, 6/132; takes P, for his health, on coach ride, 7/208; outings to Islington, 7/261; 9/184; and Mile End, 8/485; 9/88, 202; P stays with in Fire, 7/280, 282, 283, 284; at P's New Year party, 8/4–5; gives favours for daughter's wedding, 8/73, 77; in Hyde Park, 8/196–7; 9/122; at parish dinner, 8/218; Bartholomew Fair, 9/301; taverns, 1/292; 2/30, 54, 61, 78, 173, 185, 192, 200, 219, 227, 233, 239; 3/42,

91; 5/149, 308; 7/63; 8/49, 108, 130, 133, 220; 9/82, 115; at theatre, 2/154, 155, 186, 194, 202, 206, 212, 220, 223, 227, 241; 3/24, 31, 56, 86, 88; 5/232; 6/9, 10; 7/267; 8/129, 138, 195, 235, 384, 386, 388, 402, 421, 443, 521–2, 590; 9/57, 78, 104, 193, 310, 329; in garden at Seething Lane, 1/248; 2/24; 5/81; 7/208; 8/315; visits/dines etc. with P, 1/242, 324; 2/22–3, 29, 126, 143, 192, 218–19; 3/8, 34; 4/315; 7/209–10, 259; 8/106, 260, 284, 433; 9/312; and with Batten, 1/293, 295, 309; 2/90, 125; 8/105, 376; P/EP dine(s) with/visit(s) etc., 2/21, 66, 123, 215, 240; 3/3, 18, 60, 77, 90, 125, 183, 209, 286, 293; 4/12, 23, 28, 45, 171, 278, 338; 5/122, 125; 6/38; 7/190–1, 233; 8/146, 508; 9/149, 174, 177, 179, 187, 191; also, 3/5; 5/128, 240
ALLUDED TO: 8/248, 396
PENN, William, founder of Pennsylvania, son of Sir William [see also Books]:
CHRON. SERIES: sent down from Oxford, 2/206 & n. 3; proposed removal to Cambridge, 3/17 & n. 4, 21; nonconformist opinions, 3/73 & n. 1; returns from France, 5/255 & n. 1; 6/213, 222; French affectations, 5/257; with father in fleet, 6/89; returns from Ireland, 8/565 & n. 1; becomes a Quaker, 8/595 & n. 3; also, 3/47; 6/223; 8/228
SOCIAL: sees pre-coronation procession, 2/82; at theatre, 2/241; 3/1; also, 2/239; 3/5, 132; 5/270
PENNY, [Nicholas], tailor, Fleet St ('my tailor', 7/13 onwards): recommended to P, 7/13; work for/visits by P, 7/15, 16, 172, 346; 8/34, 134, 136, 138, 146, 281, 295, 460, 461, 463, 525, 529, 599; 9/197, 198, 201, 203, 215, 333, 455, 456, 534, 537, 540, 551; makes cloak and cassock for John P, 7/299; alluded to: 9/366, 456; ~ his boy, 8/315
PENROSE, Capt. [Thomas], naval officer: 1/172
PEPPER, [Robert], Fellow of Christ's College, Cambridge: John P's tutor, 2/44; Proctor, 3/217–18; social: 1/68
PEPYS, family of: history, vol. i,

pp. xix–xx; 3/26–7 & n.; 8/261 &
nn., 274 & n. 2; decay of, 5/134; P's
immediate family listed with birth-
dates, 5/360–1 & nn.; lack of handsome women, 8/365
PEPYS, [Anne], wife of Robert, of
Brampton, Hunts., P's aunt: ill of the
stone, 1/320–1 & n.; 2/5, 17, 27, 52,
133, 134; sends for P's father in husband's last illness, 2/126, 127; troublesome, 2/134 & n. 1, 137; provisions of
husband's will, 2/134 & n. 1, 138, 148;
dispute over bond, 2/164; 4/384;
5/353
PEPYS, Anne (Nan), of Worcs.: see
Fisher, ——; Hall, ——
PEPYS, Bab and Betty, Roger's
daughters, P's cousins: visit London
with father, 9/446, 450; comely,
9/453; stay at P's house, 9/453–4, 455,
460; at theatre, 9/453, 454, 456, 458,
459, 476; visit Bedlam, 9/454;
Westminster Abbey, 9/456–7; and
glasshouse, 9/457; at P's dance,
9/463–5 passim; return to Impington,
9/477; also, 9/475; ~ their maid
Martha, 9/454
PEPYS, Charles ('the joiner'), son of
Thomas Pepys of London: at reading
of Robert P's will, 2/153; his legacy,
4/20, 42–3, 102, 345, 346; 5/157;
social: 2/172
PEPYS, Edith, P's aunt: see Bell
PEPYS, Edward, of Broomsthorpe,
Norf., P's cousin: dies, 4/421 & n. 2,
425; funeral scutcheons and hatchments, 4/424–5 & n., 427; buried,
4/426; 5/10; funeral procession, 4/432;
social: 1/54, 60; alluded to: 1/72;
5/76; 8/365
PEPYS, Elizabeth, (b. St Michel), wife
of the diarist [see also entries under
Dress etc.; Health: Household Goods
etc.; Servants. For her relations with
the Pepyses, Mountagus, St Michels
and others, see under names.]:
PERSONAL: her beauty admired at
wedding, 1/196; at theatre, 9/398; by
Sandwich, 4/186; by Duke of York,
9/515; pretty wearing black patch,
1/283; in black laced gown, 2/117; in
flowered tabby, 9/134; better looking
than Princess Henrietta Maria, 1/299;

the only pretty woman in theatre,
9/450; her 'comely person', 6/31;
washes before going to court, 1/298 &
n. 3; visits bath house, 6/40 & n. 1, 41,
45; spends day getting clean, 9/372;
snores, 1/266–7; rides well, 2/180; her
watch, 8/51, 146
PORTRAITS: by Savill: 2/218 & n. 4, 227,
233, 234, 235; her dog added, 2/241;
altered because unlike, 3/17, 19, 21;
hung in dining room, 3/25, 34, 106;
P wishes Huysmans to paint, 5/276 &
& n. 3; 6/113; by Hayls: 7/43, 44 & n.
2, 48, 52, 53–4, 61, 65, 69, 72; a good
likeness, 7/73, 74, 78, 82; improved,
9/292, 297, 299; alluded to, 7/98, 108,
117, 120; 9/138; by Cooper: 9/138 &
n. 3, 139, 140, 253, 256, 258–61
passim, 263, 264, 267, 268, 276–7; not
such a good likeness, 9/264, 267
CHRON. SERIES:
MAIN BIOGRAPHICAL EVENTS: marriage, vol. i, p. xxii & n. 13; early
differences and separation, 2/153 & n.
3; 4/277 & n. 1; 5/196 & n. 2; believes
herself pregnant, 1/1; 4/365; Uncle
Wight's unusual attentions to, 5/14,
16, 24, 55, 65; her child to be his heir,
5/61; he proposes they have child,
5/145–6, 151; death, vol. i, p. xxxv
MOVEMENTS/VISITS TO BRAMPTON ETC:
with Bowyers during P's Dutch
voyage, 1/84, 85, 88, 89–90; returns to
London, 1/131, 166, 177, 178; re-
united with P, 1/173; moves from
Axe Yard to Seething Lane, 1/199–
203 passim; stays with P's father
during alterations to house, 2/64–7
passim, 88, 90, 94, 96; with P visits
Portsmouth, 2/90–4; rides to Brampton and back, 2/180–4; at Brampton
while house altered, 3/134, 140, 141,
144, 145, 148, 151, 182; returns,
3/199, 200, 206, 208, 209; with Tom P
while house cleaned, 3/251; with P at
Sandwich's lodgings, 3/299, 301;
4/1–6 passim; visits Brampton with
Ashwell, 4/174, 176, 178, 179, 180,
183, 184, 199, 210, 212, 262; returns
following quarrels, 4/271, 273, 276;
visits Brampton with P, 4/306–14;
without him, 5/200, 201, 224, 233–4;
to stay at home till after Easter, 5/358;

to stay at Woolwich in Plague, 6/128 & n. 2, 134, 140, 143, 147; settles in with two maids, 6/149; P's visits to, 6/151-2, 153, 162, 170, 174, 183, 185, 190, 200, 205-6; joined by P, 6/207-10 passim, 212, 214, 216, 219, 221, 223, 226, 228; he visits from Greenwich lodgings, 6/242, 246, 249-50, 262, 263, 273, 303; she visits him, 6/250-3 passim, 270, 279, 280, 282, 284, 286, 295, 296; P rents rooms for at Greenwich, 6/261 & n. 3, 271; she moves to, 6/309, 313, 314; returns to London, 6/313-16 passim, 318, 341; visits P at Greenwich, 6/320, 321, 324, 326, 327, 338; 7/2, 3, 5, 6; P visits in London, 6/329(2), 332, 340; they return to house in Seething Lane, 7/7; with P visits Cranbourne and Windsor, 7/54, 56-9 passim; visits Brampton to advise on Pall's marriage, 7/86, 91(2), 92, 93, 104; with P camps in Navy Office during Fire, 7/273, 274, 275; sent to Woolwich with his gold, 7/275, 280, 283, 284, 285, 286, 289; takes gold to Brampton in Medway crisis, 8/262, 263, 264, 273; returns to London with account of burying it, 8/279, 280, 281; visits Brampton with P and Deb Willet, 8/453, 465-75 passim; at Audley End, 8/467-8; Cambridge, 8/468-9; at Brampton with Deb and others, 9/98, 125, 143, 144, 180; P visits her there, 9/210-12; and calls for at start of West Country tour, 9/224; visits Oxford, 9/226; Salisbury, 9/229; Stonehenge, 9/229-30; Chitterne, 9/231; Bath, 9/232-4, 236, 238-9; Bristol, 8/234-5; Avebury, 9/240; Marlborough, 9/241; visits Petersfield with P and Deb Willet, 9/273-4; with Deb and Hewer visits Roger P to see Sturbridge Fair, 9/301, 306, 310, 315

PUBLIC EVENTS/LONDON SIGHTS: sees burning of the Rump, 1/53; Queen-Mother and princesses dine in public, 1/297, 299; Queen in presence chamber, 3/299; hanging of regicides' corpses, 2/26-7; pre-coronation procession, 2/83; coronation banquet, 2/85; drinks King's health at bonfire, 2/87; sees alterations in St James's

Park, 2/171; rides in Hyde Park coach parades on May Day etc., 3/78; 5/126, 130, 163; 6/89; 8/193, 197; 9/142-3, 260, 269, 270, 487, 515-16, 530, 533-4, 540-1, 541-2, 549, 556, 563, 564; sees wrestling at Moorfields, 3/93; visits Bartholomew Fair, 4/298; 5/259-60; 8/405, 421, 423; 9/290, 293, 296, 299; synagogue, 4/335; at Col. Turner's execution, 5/23; service in Whitehall chapel, 6/86, 87; visits Clarendon House, 7/220; sees Fire of London, 7/272; and city ruins, 7/291; watches bull baiting 7/245-6; puppet plays, 3/254-5; 7/257, 265, 267; 8/121, 157, 421; 9/296; at court ball, 7/371, 372, 373; meets Nell Gwyn, 8/27; sees block ships in river, 8/293; giant children, 8/326, 500; prize fights, 8/429, 430; 9/516; bearded woman, 9/398; giantess, 9/440; royal tombs in Westminster Abbey, 9/456-7

MISC.: receives gifts from P's business associates, 1/222; 2/225; 4/293, 295, 298-9, 391, 415; 5/45, 47, 316; interprets French for Lady Sandwich, 1/293; attends women friends in labour, 2/150, 151; 8/177(2); 9/260; on bad terms with Lady Batten, 2/161; 3/146, 249-50, 302; 4/71, 426; 5/356; ends estrangement from, 6/46, 95; helps wounded acquaintance after fight, 2/229; importuned by drunk, 4/342; fortune told by gipsies, 9/278; first rides in P's new coach, 9/379; and with his new horses, 9/399-400

RELATIONS WITH P [for the Deb affair, see Willet]:

HER LOVE: troubled at his going to sea, 1/84; rejoices at his becoming Clerk of the Acts, 1/199; frightened at his injured thumb, 7/37; devotion in early hardships, 8/82; comforts him before parliamentary speech, 9/102; rejoices in its success, 9/104; rejects advances from Sandwich and Hinchingbrooke, 9/356, 404 & n. 2; and from others, 9/369; also, 1/131; 2/75; 7/398

HIS LOVE: concerned at leaving her for Dutch voyage, 1/89, 92, 102, 106; happy in wife and estate, 1/166; 3/234; troubled at her absence, 1/317;

2/14-15; pleased to be her valentine, 2/36; 'her care, thrift and innocence', 3/247; distress at her fainting, 4/307; pleasure in her company, 4/291, 403, 406, 435; 7/104, 351; 9/401; lies close to in grief for Tom P, 5/87; joy at her return from Brampton, 5/233-4; thanks God for love and health on wedding anniversary, 5/294; kisses at New Year, 5/359; grieved at her removal to Woolwich, 6/149, 157; and at lodging without her at Greenwich, 6/226; keeps cheerful for her sake in Plague, 6/225; finds 'all things melancholy' in her absence, 7/92; will keep together and 'let the world go hang', 8/97; also, 2/96; 3/206; 4/183, 186; 5/50, 55, 296; 6/262

HIS BEQUESTS/GIFTS/ALLOWANCES TO: wills in her favour, 1/88; 4/433; 7/134; 8/266; gives her pearl necklace, 1/240; lace handkerchief, 2/210, 211, 212, 214; money for Easter clothes, 3/26; 6/48; silk petticoat, 5/114, 118; cabinet, 5/152; diamond ring (£10), 6/190-1; pearl necklace (£80), 6/200-01; 7/108, 111, 112, 113; his gifts to equal those to other women, 8/100; gives her Guillim's *Heraldry*, 8/422 & n. 4; lace handkerchief as New Year gift, 9/6; diamond ring for valentine gift, 9/78, 88-9; *Cassandra* and other French books, 9/365; walnut cabinet as New Year gift, 9/405, 406; clothing allowance (£30 p.a.), 9/406, 408, 412; also, 1/106, 107, 139; 5/155; 7/344; 9/98, 501

THEIR SHARED TASTES/PLEASURES [for his teaching her music etc., *see below*: her accomplishments]: distaste for mock wedding, 1/27; amused by absurd book, 1/275; plan French holiday, 2/35; 4/399 & n. 4; 9/462 & n. 3, 546; dislike of Lady Batten, 3/55; and Penn, 3/117; plan improvements at Seething Lane, 4/300; 7/7; enjoy riding through Brampton fields, 4/312; joy at returning home after absence, 4/314; 7/7; play cards together, 6/3, 221; 7/392

HE CONSULTS/CONFIDES IN: on intentions to live frugally and become a knight, 3/39-40; finances, 5/42-3,

131; quarrel with Creed, 5/48; troubles over prize-goods, 6/242; standing at court, 7/31; plan to live at Brampton, 7/202, 235, 340, 344; fears in Medway crisis, 8/260, 262; giving up victualling post, 8/367

HER HELP/ADVICE: on his health, 4/409, 414; his demeanour to Sandwich, 5/65; helps him to catalogue books, 7/419; 9/49, 72; cuts his hair, 5/72; 8/35; 9/424; searches him for lice, 9/424; rules pursers' books, 7/63; helps him to pack up goods in Fire, 7/272-3; to dig up gold at Brampton, 8/472; and carry it to London, 8/475; tells Hewer of P's dissatisfaction with, 9/52-3; reads to when ill, 4/40; and to save his eyes, 8/413, 438, 440, 444, 455, 535, 537, 538, 547, 548, 564, 568, 572, 582, 589; 9/11, 61, 241, 242, 247, 255, 277, 281, 305, 325, 328, 331-5 passim, 337, 344, 372, 374-9 passim, 385, 396, 401, 402-3, 416, 426, 429(2), 431(2), 432, 433, 444, 446, 460, 472, 475, 481, 482, 483, 493, 508, 535(2), 541, 542, 545, 547

HIS JEALOUSY: annoyed at stranger kissing her, 2/10; jealous of T. Somerset, 2/165 & n. 2, 170, 172-3; J. Hunt, 2/216; Capt. Holmes, 2/237 & n. 1; 3/4; Pembleton (dancing master), 4/140, 141, 144, 148-9, 150, 153-4, 157-8, 161, 165, 166, 172, 173, 179, 183, 205, 229, 277-8, 285, 291, 300, 318, 337-8, 347, 369; 5/17, 125; Hewer, 5/13, 19, 29, 44, 301; W. Penn, jun., 5/263, 270; Llewellin, 6/38; Browne (drawing master), 6/246; W. Batelier, 7/238; Coleman (fellow traveller in coach), 8/286, 305, 588; H. Sheeres, 9/504, 522, 532, 533, 540, 541; she shows him P. Sydney's letter on jealousy, 6/2; troubled at her staying out late, 9/529, 531; also, 5/18, 64, 111; 6/214, 216

HER JEALOUSY: jealous of E. Pearse, 2/201; E. Pearse/E. Knepp, 7/120, 122; her uncivil behaviour to both, 7/236-7, 238, 322, 341; continuing jealousy of, 8/25, 210-11, 371-2, 399, 599, 600; 9/1, 108, 339, 368, 376, 391, 405, 413, 436, 469-70; jealous of Ashwell, 4/122, 165, 180; Mercer, 5/274; 7/228;

9/304; teases P over handsome maids, 6/40; 9/479; comments on his high colour after clandestine dalliance, 8/233; P prevents her meeting Martin and Burroughs, 8/375–6; mistrusts his roving eye in theatre, 9/375, 390, 395–6, 405, 421, 436; and at church, 9/482; jealous of E. Turner and daughter, 9/380; makes jealous scene over J. Birch, 9/439, 440–1; distrusts his being out late, 9/494; also, 1/16–17
HIS GUILTY FEELINGS TOWARDS: at going to theatre without, 2/177; 3/294; 6/9; 8/3, 123; at deceiving her with Betty Lane, 4/317; self-reproach for his jealousy, 4/140; for criticising her painting, 6/303; and her singing, 7/348; 8/89; dines twice to prevent her dining alone, 4/318; keeps theatre visits secret from, 8/169, 384, 395; 9/78
THEIR QUARRELS / P'S ANNOYANCE WITH:
over servants/household management: her dog's fouling house, 1/54, 284–5; badly served/cooked meals, 1/308; 2/237, 238; 4/13, 29; maid's dismissal, 3/258, 263, 264, 273; her negligence, 4/121, 287; call each other 'beggar' and 'prick louse', 4/121 & n. 1; her neglecting household business for dancing, 4/183; and for painting, 7/115–16; her complaints of: maid's lying, 4/361, 417; badly kept household accounts, 5/283; 6/46–7; 7/125, 243, 397; exchange blows over badly served food, 5/291; he gives her black eye, 5/349, 350, 356; further quarrels over dismissal of servants, 6/4(2), 26–31 passim, 295, 296; she brings him 'only trouble and discontent', 6/31; P throws trenchers about, 7/398; her failure to prepare for party, 8/104; dirty table linen, 9/402; also, 1/311; 3/7; 4/177–8, 337; 6/340; 9/411
over her extravagance: expenditure on dress, 1/247; 5/84, 100, 310; 8/392–3, 413; 9/427, 450–1; earrings, 5/196; dancing lessons, 4/133(2); 'snappish' at his refusing her money, 7/256
over her dress/appearance: ill-matched ribbons, 2/235; P calls her 'whore', ib.; unsuitable dress in church, 3/110; false

hair, 6/55; 7/346–7; 8/210–11; low décolletage, 7/379; unsuitable mourning, 8/242, 250–1; also, 2/11; 8/124, 202
over her complaints of dull life/love of pleasure etc.: her 'letter of discontent', 3/257–8; P burns it with her love letters, 4/9–10; fears losing command over, 4/150; accuses him of keeping house dirty to occupy her, 4/289; his wish 'to keep her head down', 4/262, 276; refuses to let her attend christening, 5/176; his 'gadding abroad to look after beauties', 5/286; her bad temper from too much liberty, 7/284; 9/243; he pulls her nose in quarrel over his dining out, 8/333; her want of money and liberty, 9/20–1, 245–6; his going to plays in her absence, 9/244; also, 3/85; 4/347; 8/189
misc. quarrels: P kicks her china basket, 1/265; annoyed with for leaving parcel in coach, 4/6; for being robbed of waistcoat, 4/28; for bad spelling, 4/29; pulls her nose, 5/113; for failing to keep count of singing lessons, 7/397; his silence prevents quarrels, 9/136, 304; also, 1/225; 2/94, 189; 4/133; 6/83; 8/488
SEXUAL RELATIONS: 1/217, 279; ?2/75; 3/234; 4/274, 291, 336, 347; 5/94, 200; 8/588; 9/184, 439; have not lain together for six months, 8/372–3; make love after three-month interval, 8/382; after her being unwell, 8/594; 9/90; after Deb affair, 9/363
MISC.: he dictates her letter to Lady Sandwich, 4/176; troubled at her quarrels at Brampton, 4/210, 212, 271, 273, 274, 276, 293; and at her visiting her father in poor area, 5/50; will not permit her to accept diamond locket from Hewer, 9/7
AS HOUSEWIFE:
COOKING ETC.: makes Christmas pies etc., 1/29, 291; 2/170; 3/293, 295; 4/433; kills turkey, 1/41; and pigeons, 1/189; makes marmalade, 4/361, 363; also, 1/3, 321; 4/62; 7/420; 8/82
LAUNDERING: helps with/supervises, 1/19, 301; 4/65; 5/62; calls maids early for, 1/296; 5/11, 55; promises them a holiday after, 4/348; takes washing to

be bleached, 8/383–6 passim, 401; 9/283

RELATIONS WITH UNNAMED SERVANTS [for relations with named servants, see Servants in main series]: annoyed with for complaining of Suffolk cheese, 2/191; forgets to buy food for, 2/198; servants spoiled by her familiarity, 4/9; with P hears them read Bible, 4/383; scolds for failing to search beds for fleas, 5/260; buys presents for, ib.; permits to attend Lord Mayor's Show, 5/309; joins in Christmas games, 5/357, 358; 6/4–5; dances, 6/252; cards, 7/358

MISC.: makes caps for P, 1/85; worsted cushions, 4/180; tears up flags for bed linen, 5/48; makes shirts and smocks, 8/187; settles household accounts with P, 3/132, 289; 5/283; 6/46–7; 7/125, 243, 397; 8/444; sets up closet, 4/317, 318, 322, 324, 328, 329; works 'like a horse', 7/14; and a drudge, 7/24; helps clean house, 9/365; to learn to fold napkins, 9/423

HER ACCOMPLISHMENTS:

MUSIC: singing: to learn from Goodgroome, 2/190; P teaches song to, 7/111; neglects to teach, 7/228; will learn in return for dancing lessons, 7/300; lessons with Goodgroome, 7/348 & n. 1, 397; sings out of tune, 7/348; 8/89; P teaches her 'It is decreed', 7/420; learning to trill, 8/49, 108, 109; P pleased with progress, 8/119, 171, 203, 204, 209; Goodgroome's neglect, 8/109, 378, 411; sings with P/Mercer/ others, 8/90, 166, 198, 206, 209, 238, 244, 250, 253, 325, 327, 344, 351, 380, 390, 458; in garden, 5/266; 7/117, 172, 183, 195, 212, 228, 230; 8/37, 165, 322, 328; on roof, 3/86; 7/110, 174; in coach, 7/267; 9/513; on river, 8/325, 346; 9/552, 555, 563; in cellars at Audley End, 8/468; flageolet: lessons from Greeting, 8/87 & n. 2, 89, 110, 400; fails to practise, 8/146, 205–6, 221(2); P pleased with her progress, 8/96, 232, 291, 295, 396, 430, 433, 434, 435; has lessons to encourage her, 8/205–6; she 'pipes' with him, 8/224, 235(2), 250, 253, 305, 327, 367, 369, 370, 380, 384, 436, 437, 443; resumes

lessons, 9/25, 94, 279; plays to P, 9/280; misc.: is taught 'some skill in' by P, 1/232, 233, 239; repeats words of French song 'D'un air tout interdit', 6/223; to learn viol, 7/377

DANCING: wishes to learn, 3/213–14; 4/106, 109; 7/300; lessons from Pembleton, 4/111, 113, 114, 122, 126, 129, 132, 133, 134, 140, 148, 149, 150, 155, 156, 161; at dances/dancing parties, 6/279, 315, 323–4; 7/18, 43–4, 73, 362–4, 422; 8/29, 104, 493, 511; 9/1, 4, 42, 128, 134

DRAWING AND PAINTING: lessons from Browne, 6/98(2) and n.; P's pride in her progress, 6/143, 162, 170, 174, 183, 200, 242; 7/232; 9/25; her talent superior to Peg Penn's, 6/185, 210; her picture of Christ, 6/242; and the Virgin, 7/241, 242, 251, 262; resumes lessons, 7/115; also, 6/303; 7/359; 9/424, 534

OTHER INTERESTS: reading: reads Polixandre, 1/35; Le grand Cyrus, 1/312; 7/122; Imposture, 3/247; with P reads Ovid (trans.), 3/289; Iter Boreale, 4/285; Fuller's Worthies, 5/118; he reads to her Life of Henrietta Maria, 1/275; The siege of Rhodes, 5/278; and Chaucer, 7/378; her books separated from P's, 1/268; misc.: P teaches her astronomy, 4/43; use of globes/geography, 4/302, 343, 344, 433–4; 5/6, 8, 16, 25–6, 49; arithmetic, 4/357, 360, 363, 364, 378, 402, 404, 406; with P experiments with microscope, 5/241

HER RELIGIOUS OPINIONS: enjoys reading missal, 1/282 & n. 1; P fears her becoming catholic, 5/39 & n. 4, 92, 103, 250; 9/378; she claims to be one, 5/92 & n. 2; 9/338, 385; attributes juggler's tricks to the Devil, 8/234; fasts on Good Friday, 6/66

SOCIAL:

ON RIVER TRIPS: sees wreck of Assurance, 1/315, 316–17; dines on Rosebush, 2/36; sees royal yachts, 2/179; fleet in the Hope, 5/197; at launch of Royal Catherine, 5/305, 307; and Greenwich, 7/153; visits the Prince, 6/56, 57, 59; on river trips to Hampton Court, 3/81–2; Gravesend,

190, 191, 193; portrait by Hayls, 7/151 & n. 2, 161, 164, 166, 170–1, 173, 184, 199; takes P's gold to Brampton, 8/262, 263, 264, 280–1, 472–3, 474, 539; visits P in London, 3/85, 93–4, 97, 99, 103, 104, 106; 4/89, 90, 92, 93, 95, 98–101 passim, 103–6 passim, 108–12 passim, 114, 118, 274, 276, 280; 7/137–40 passim, 142, 149, 151, 152, 161, 164, 166, 167, 169–76 passim, 306, 308, 309, 311, 313, 316, 317, 318, 329; 8/214, 216, 231, 232, 233, 235; death, vol. i, pp. xxxv–vi; also, 1/72, 220; 2/132, 140; 3/6; 5/104, 118

AS TAILOR: work for P/EP, 1/171, 224, 245, 251, 260, 268, 320; 2/104; advises about hangings, 1/256, 261; supplies cloth to Sandwich for gift to Algerines, 2/122, 126; hopes for place at Wardrobe, 1/201, 203; 2/42 & n. 1, 113; 5/168 & n. 3, 172 & n. 1, 185; 8/508

MARRIAGE: date, 5/360; quarrels with wife, 2/64, 81, 89–90, 111, 160, 183; 'unquiet life' with, 3/207; 4/90, 96; 5/234; grief at her dying, 8/129

RELATIONS WITH P: P's affection, 5/120, 298; 7/137, 164, 175, 306; 8/90, 166, 232, 233, 237; P takes leave of before Dutch voyage, 1/93; gives financial support to, 1/222, 274, 317; 4/127; 5/360; 7/169–70, 173, 318; 8/90, 91; other gifts, 3/33; 4/6; 5/52, 261, 344, 346; 6/149; 8/565; plans alterations with at Brampton, 2/182–3; 8/237, 469, 471; helps/scolds him over accounts, 2/162, 183; 4/87, 106, 108, 119, 121, 141 & n. 3; fears his maintenance becoming a burden, 3/276, 302; 4/106; urges him to live on £50 p.a., 4/119, 280, 308; defends his reputation for paying debts, 5/244, 251–2, 253; hopes to maintain at Brampton, 8/508; vol. i, pp. xxxv–xxxvi; bequeaths money to, 7/134; 8/266; also, 3/119, 219

RELATIONS WITH OTHER CHILDREN:

WITH JOHN: enters at Christ's College, Cambridge, 1/26, 27, 66–9 passim; troubled by P's quarrel with, 5/93, 135, 137; John to stay with at Brampton, 8/14, 48, 49, 471; also, 1/46

WITH PAULINA: troubled at her pilfering, 1/27; agrees to her becoming P's servant, 1/288, 290, 291; and to her leaving, 2/161–2; defends against P, 4/108; attempts match-making for, 7/78, 86, 170; lives with after her marriage, 9/212 & n. 1; also, 4/90; 9/293

WITH TOM: angry with for sleeping out, 1/256; Tom disrespectful to, 2/103; matchmakes for, 2/158, 159, 163, 165; tailoring business handed over to, 2/144; 5/250 & n. 2, 351; also, 3/131; 4/410

HEALTH: sight and hearing deteriorate, 2/103; 7/137; deaf, 8/473; hernia, 4/117–18; 7/104; 8/13, 14, 88, 90, 110, 119, 122, 123, 129, 162; acute attacks of, 4/117–18; 8/237; treatment from Hollier, 8/110, 166, 214, 220; truss, 8/232, 237, 252; unwell, 3/48; 4/100, 310, 312, 313, 321, 348, 358; 5/92, 123

HOUSE in Salisbury Court [see also Langford, [W.]; for his house at Brampton, q.v.]: little room, 1/27, 291; cutting house, 1/84; three storeys, 1/181; burnt in Fire, 7/279

HOUSEHOLD: man Ned, 2/163; John Noble, 5/113; boy, 4/313; 9/210; man, 9/210

SOCIAL: at Twelfth Night parties, 1/10; 2/7; first visits P in Seething Lane, 1/210; wedding anniversary dinner, 1/266; at P's stone feasts, 2/60; 5/98; at K. Fenner's funeral, 2/159; dines with Penn, 8/252–3; at Hinchingbrooke, 8/471–2; visits Greenwich, 4/99; Woolwich, 7/142, 153; Islington, 7/149, 167, 170, 317; at taverns, 1/221, 229, 303; 2/17, 25, 45, 114, 124; at theatre, 8/253; Joyces visit at Brampton, 5/263, 266, 268, 273, 282; with P at Axe Yard, 1/43; and Seething Lane, 1/274, 294, 302; 2/9, 28, 44, 52, 113, 125, 155–6, 157; 3/96, 99; with other London relatives, 1/28, 252; 2/2, 162, 164; 3/94; 4/100, 101, 108; 5/119; 7/140, 169, 172, 174; P/EP visit(s) etc. in Salisbury Court, 1/3, 9, 11, 25–6, 32, 42, 54, 64, 65, 85, 88, 179, 195, 205, 230, 289, 319, 324; 2/40, 47, 65, 66, 67, 75, 89, 152

PEPYS, John, P's older brother (d.

1631): his birthdate and death, 5/361
& n. 1
PEPYS, John, P's brother (d. 1677):
EDUCATION: gives speeches at St Paul's
School, 1/11–12 & n., 18, 44; gains
exhibition, 1/42 & n. 4, 46; enters
Christ's College, Cambridge, 1/26,
60, 61, 64–9 passim; transfers from
Magdalene, 1/68 & n. 2; P gives him
books/money/advice, 1/61, 69, 90,
222, 243; 2/95; 3/33; a good scholar,
2/25; elected a scholar of Christ's,
2/44; P dissuades from becoming
moderator, 3/160–1 & n.; takes his
B.A., 4/27 & n. 1; has studied
Descartes, 4/263; and Aristotle's
physics, 4/267; P complains of his
idleness, 4/291, 292, 316–17, 439; is
ordained and takes his M.A., 7/50 &
n. 2, 112, 170
CHRON. SERIES: his birthdate recorded,
5/361 & n. 1; at Brampton, 3/219,
220, 223; with P in London, 4/261–3
passim, 266, 269, 273, 282, 300, 317;
complains of EP's unkindness, 4/293;
comes to London on Tom P's death,
5/91, 122; P angry with over his
'roguish' letters to Tom P, 5/91, 92,
93, 135, 137, 298; 6/134; his allowance, 5/142 & n. 3; 6/49; P makes up
quarrel, 7/111–12, 170; stays with P,
7/281–3 passim, 293, 306, 316, 318,
344, 349, 362, 420, 426; 8/14, 31;
wears clerical dress, 7/299, 310, 313;
his lack of scholarship, 7/327, 346;
helps P store his money and plate,
7/367; and to catalogue his books,
7/419, 421; 8/8, 40(2); 9/559–60; has
fainting fit, 8/48–9; returns to
Brampton, 8/49; 'melancholy and
harmless', ib.; his prospects, 8/471 &
n. 2; stays with P, 8/474, 477, 478;
9/553, 555, 563; also, 4/27; 5/157, 261;
8/122, 134, 207, 469; 9/144, 210, 212
SOCIAL: at Twelfth Night party, 1/10;
P visits at Cambridge, 2/135, 181;
visits Westminster Abbey, 7/322, 323,
345; plays lyra viol, 7/327; and bass
viol, 8/40; at theatre, 7/398; 8/481;
9/556; dines at Hinchingbrooke,
8/471–2; also, 1/9; 7/317, 351, 366
ALLUDED TO: 1/81; 8/473
PEPYS, John, P's cousin, of Ashtead,

Surrey, lawyer (d. 1652): house,
3/152 & n. 1; 4/247; 8/338; servants,
4/247; 8/338; marshal to Chief
Justice Coke, 9/42 & n. 4; alluded to:
9/383
PEPYS, Dr John, lawyer, Fellow of
Trinity Hall, Cambridge, P's cousin
(d. 1692): P's opinion, 4/211, 389;
advises on Robert P's will, 2/136;
arbitrator in dispute, 3/265; recovers
from illness, 4/211; also, 2/146, 147;
3/218; 4/389
PEPYS, [Margaret], (b. Kite), P's
mother:
CHRON. SERIES: washmaid, 2/31 & n. 2;
marriage date, 5/360; children's birth-
dates, 5/361 & n. 1; argues about
religion, 1/76 & n. 3; unwell, 1/230,
233, 244, 245; suffers from stone,
1/283, 302, 310, 314; at Brampton,
2/5, 26, 27; quarrels with husband,
2/64, 81, 89–90, 111, 160, 183; has
become simple, 2/111, 153, 160,
171; extravagance, 2/144; moves to
Brampton, 2/151, 162, 165, 171, 172;
ill, 3/103, 106; quarrels with EP,
3/206; 4/274; unquiet life with husband, 3/207; 4/90, 96; 5/234; quarrels
with servants, 5/154; P's gifts to, 4/7;
5/268; begs him to forgive brother,
5/298; 6/134; stays with P, 6/90, 95,
99, 132, 133–4; 'impatient and
troublesome', 7/104; P's bequest,
7/134; ill, 8/88, 119, 122, 123, 129,
131; dies, 8/134, 135; P's grief, 8/134;
also, 1/54, 75, 93, 203; 5/85
SOCIAL: at Twelfth Night party, 1/10;
P's stone feast, 2/60; christening,
6/102; visits Woolwich, 6/111; Islington, 6/112; Gravesend, 6/119; P
visits at Salisbury Court, 1/9, 28, 71,
72, 205, 215, 324; 2/65, 67, 139, 141,
169; at Brampton, 3/219, 223; visits/
dines with P, 1/29; 2/28, 165; also,
1/252; 2/164; 5/266; 6/107–8, 121,
128, 130
ALLUDED TO: 1/60, 81; 3/167; 9/134
PEPYS, Mary, P's aunt: birthdate,
5/360 & n. 1
PEPYS, Mary, P's sister: birthdate and
death, 5/361 & n. 1
PEPYS, Mary, P's cousin; daughter of
Thomas P of London: see Santhune, de

PEPYS, Paulina, P's older sister: birthdate and death, 5/361 & n. 1
PEPYS, Paulina, P's younger sister: see Jackson, J.
PEPYS, Richard, of Ashen, Essex, P's cousin: 1/252 & n. 3
PEPYS, Richard, draper, of Great St Bartholomew's, P's relative: to supply flags for navy, 5/181–2 & n.
PEPYS, Robert, P's brother: birthdate and death, 5/361 & n. 1
PEPYS, Robert, of Brampton, Hunts., P's uncle:
CHRON. SERIES: lease of Hetley's land, 2/28; business with Sir P. Neile, 2/47; surety for loan to Sandwich, 2/62–3; proposes P buy land at Brampton, 2/117; illness and death, 1/81, 321; 2/5, 27, 126, 129, 130, 132, 133 & n. 2; mourning for, 3/7; also, 1/46, 72, 218; 2/3, 96
HIS WILL: P's expectations, 1/73, 77, 81, 170, 264; its terms, 2/133 & n. 1, 134 & n. 2, 135 & n. 1; estate, 2/134–5, 144; 3/275 & n. 3; P exaggerates its value, 2/140; will discussed, 2/153; proved, 2/160 & n. 1, 162; copied, 3/269; legacies: to P and his father, 2/133 & n. 1; 5/143; Pall, 7/15; the Wights, 4/86; the Perkinses, 8/90, 91; debt to Thomas P 'the Executor', 3/17; 6/100; P's papers concerning estate, 2/140; 3/48, 274, 275 & n. 2; 4/121, 122; land sold to meet debts etc., 4/119 & n. 2; 5/211 & n. 2: 6/100; accounts as tax-receiver (1647), 5/31, 39, 135; 6/65
DISPUTES OVER WILL [see also Brampton; Godfrey, [R.]; Goldsborough, Mrs ——; Graveley; Moore, H.; Offord; Pepys, Anne; Pepys, Charles; Pepys, Dr John; Pepys, Roger; Pepys, Talbot; Pepys, Thomas of London; Pepys, Thomas, the turner; Prior, [W.]; Trice, J.; Trice, T.; Stirtloe; Turner, Dr John; Williams, Dr John]: copyhold lands at Brampton etc., 2/135; 4/42–3 & nn.; annuities to Thomas P of London and sons, 3/275 & n. 3; 4/42–3 & nn.; debt to Trices, 2/134 & n. 2; 3/265, 274; 4/384; 5/353; also, 2/134–5, 177, 194–5; 3/7, 27, 34, 48, 80, 83, 96, 100, 219–23 passim,

232, 240, 244, 253, 256, 265, 269, 271, 274, 275, 281, 302; 4/15, 20, 28, 34, 63, 119, 126, 132, 153, 203, 344–5 & n., 351–2, 379; 5/36, 157, 225
PEPYS, Roger, son of Talbot, and P's cousin; lawyer; M.P. and Recorder, Cambridge borough:
CHARACTER: simple and well-meaning, 4/389, 402; 5/351; honest, 9/377
CHRON. SERIES: at Cambridge assizes, 2/146; bound over by Kelyng at assizes, 8/484 & n. 2, 578; advises on dispute over Robert P's will, 2/145, 147; 3/113, 218, 253, 263; 4/28, 34, 35, 41; arbitrator between P and Uncle Thomas, 3/256, 261, 265, 267; 4/42; advises on Robert P's Exchequer business, 5/135; Tom P's debts, 5/149, 250, 351; and land purchase, 8/517; 9/95; advises P's father on Robert P's estate, 5/44, 45; intercedes for Pall, 5/44; and for John, 5/135; offers match for Pall, 8/261 & n. 2; arranges her marriage settlement, 9/18–19, 55, 56, 61 & n. 1, 64–5; P's gifts to, 4/232; 8/393; on committee of Canary Company, 7/314; stories of family history, 8/261 & n. 4, 274; reports slander about Archbishop Sheldon, 8/364 & n. 1; also, 1/195; 8/522; 9/83–4
AS M.P.: election, 2/56 & n. 2; critical of Cavalier M.P.s, 2/147–8; and court, 4/193, 197; 8/33, 274; finds politics distasteful, 4/159–60; his independence, 8/33, 85–6 & n., 512; 9/114–15; helps P in defence before Committee on Miscarriages, 8/493, 496; 9/162; congratulates him on parliamentary speech, 9/113; attends debates on ecclesiastical bills, 4/95; 4/159; journeys to and from London for sessions, 4/66, 242, 402; 8/47, 261, 365, 575; 9/113, 477; also, 9/65
NEWS FROM (mostly parliamentary): 4/65, 90, 159, 200, 229; 8/32–3, 274, 361, 510, 512, 527, 558–9, 579; 9/70, 95, 121, 171, 174, 186–7, 463
PERSONAL: marries third wife, 1/39 & n. 3, 45, 46; enquires for rich widow, 4/159; 7/387; woos E. Wyld, 8/365; marries E. Dickenson, 9/431 & n. 2, 441; health, 5/36–7; 9/450; income,

4/159; borrows £1000 from P, 9/357–8, 369, 375, 377; house at Impington, 3/219; London lodgings, 9/348, 353, 473
SOCIAL: at Trinity House, 4/185; funeral, 5/347; visits court, 8/33, 70; EP's valentine, 9/67; at theatre, 9/429; entertains P/EP, 2/147; 3/219; 9/222, 301, 306, 310, 315, 379, 450, 474; attends P's stone-feast, 6/124; dines with/visits P, 4/94–5; 5/337; 7/391–2; 8/362, 577, 578; 9/57, 116, 167–8, 253, 343, 430, 455, 463–4, 553, 559; at tavern, 9/163; also, 1/54; 2/130; 4/235; 9/68, 461, 475, 552
~ his maid Martha, 9/454; his man Arthur, 9/460
PEPYS, Samuel, of Ireland, clergyman; P's cousin: godfather to J. Scott's child, 2/216 & n. 2; also,3/123 & n. 2
PEPYS, Samuel, the diarist, recollections of early life of [i.e. his life before the start of the diary. The dating implied in the organisation of this section is in some cases tentative. The principal entries in the Index dealing with his life during the diary period are listed above, p. xiii.]:
CHILDHOOD AND YOUTH: put out to nurse in Kingsland, 5/132; carried to see Christmas revels in Temple, 9/3; taken to church, 3/167; plays bows and arrows in Islington fields, 5/101; plays games, 4/433; beats parish bounds, 2/106; carries clothes to father's customers, 9/113
SCHOOLDAYS AND ADOLESCENCE: witnesses execution of King, 1/280; eats oysters at Bardsey, 1/104; his 'first sentiments of love', 4/247; writes anagram on Elizabeth Whittle's name, 1/290; at Ashtead, 3/152 & n. 1; at Durdans, 4/246; cast in female part in play, 9/218; his 'boyish' papers, 5/31, 360; examined for leaving exhibition at St Paul's, 2/20; 5/221–2
UNIVERSITY: at Magdalene College, vol. i, p. xxi; 1/67; 2/220; 3/54 & & n. 1; 5/31, 203, 361; 9/212
MARRIAGE AND EARLY MANHOOD: love letters exchanged with EP, 4/9–10; 5/360; wedding ring, 1/238; marriage

ceremonies (1655), 2/194, n. 3; wedding dinner, 7/237; their temporary separation, ?2/153 & n. 3; 4/277 & n. 1; and early privations, 8/82–3; efficiency as Mountagu's servant, 5/192; member of 'club' of government clerks, 1/208 & n. 4; 2/127; 4/10; 5/30; 6/147–8; 7/375; attends Scott's divorce proceedings, 4/254 & n. 2; operated on for stone (1658), 1/1 & n. 1, 97 & n. 3; 3/153; speaks 'privately' of King during Rump, 1/204; visits Baltic fleet as messenger, 1/140, 285; 2/185 & n. 5; pawns lute, 1/91; makes notes on family history and writes out medical charms, 5/360–2
PEPYS, Sarah, P's sister: birthdate and death, 5/361 & n. 1
PEPYS, Talbot, of Impington, Cambs.; lawyer; P's great-uncle: advises on disputes over Robert P's will, 2/136 & n. 1, 181; 3/218; P overnight with, 2/147–8; Clarendon acquainted with, 2/209; 7/71 & n. 1; debts, 9/357; alluded to: 8/85
PEPYS, Talbot, Roger's son and P's cousin: law student at Middle Temple, 8/273–4 & n.; brideman to Jane Birch, 9/500; social: visits/dines with P, 9/167, 343, 519, 559; at theatre, 9/398, 414, 453, 456; Mulberry Garden, 9/510; and Hyde Park, 9/530; also, 9/511, 512
PEPYS, Thomas, of St Alphage's parish, P's uncle:
CHARACTER: P's low opinion, 2/178; 4/305
DISPUTE WITH P OVER BRAMPTON ESTATE: claims copyhold land, 2/135, 137; 139, 151, 153; denied possession by manorial court, 2/182; 3/222–3; disputes over rents, 3/219, 221; 4/15, 20, 28; arbitration attempted, 3/42, 256, 261, 265, 270, 302; enters complaint in Court of Arches, 4/33; out-of-court settlement, 4/34, 35, 36, 42–3 & nn., 72, 86, 119, 206; 6/100; surrenders mortgaged lands, 4/133, 308–9; enquires into J. Day's estate, 4/300, 310, 312; P objects to bargain with daughter, 4/344–5 & n., 346, 351; 5/303; reversionary right, 5/225 &

business, 5/82, 97; also, 1/205, 267; 2/126; 3/290; 4/417

DEBTS AND CHILDREN: P learns of debts, 5/82, 84–5, 97; examines papers, 5/87, 91, 92; makes inventory of goods, 5/88 & n. 2; arranges administration of his estate, 5/101, 102, 122 & n. 3, 142, 149–50, 157; debt to Dr Thomas P, 5/225, 249–50, 351; and to others, 6/252, 253, 258, 259; 7/80; his two illegitimate daughters, 5/113–14; demands made on P, 5/115, 142, 154, 158, 252, 253; also, 5/164, 360; 8/264

HOUSE/HOUSEHOLD: rebuilt, 4/236, 274, 291, 292, 341; cutting house, 5/81; alluded to (usually as rendezvous): 2/205, 207, 210, 235, 238; 3/61, 77, 85, 93, 96, 99, 105, 108, 206, 212, 214, 215, 230, 285; 4/18, 32, 58, 100, 111, 114, 130; Honywoods lodge at, 3/7 & n. 4; 4/167; 5/91; apprentices, 3/184; 194; 4/421; maid (Margaret), ?4/80; 5/113–14

SOCIAL: visits Cambridge, 3/224, 225; gives dinner, 4/167; brideman, 4/345; P visits/dines with, 1/15–16 & n., 32; 3/161, 275; 4/6, 25, 164; EP stays with while P's house altered, 3/230, 251, 252, 254, 255; visits/dines with P, 1/29, 75, 225, 243, 322; 2/2, 28, 146, 174, 194, 196, 208, 231, 237, 240; 3/10, 110, 132, 138, 140, 259, 296; 4/106, 202, 338, 427; 5/10, 54; at theatre, 2/7; at taverns, 2/114; 3/224; also, 1/10; 2/196; 3/7, 148

MISC.: P gives him old suit, 2/60; and bass viol, 3/131; speech impediment, 4/21; sends P maid, 4/279, 283; silver tankard, 5/90

ALLUDED TO: 1/81, 289; 2/180; 4/237, 308; 9/477

PEPYS, [Ursula], (b. Stapelton), wife of Thomas Pepys 'the Executor': 2/2, 43

PEPYS, Mrs —— (unidentified): 2/193–4 & n.

PERCY, Sir Algernon, 10th Earl of Northumberland, Lord High Admiral 1638–42 (d. 1668): gift of classical busts to Charles I, 1/188 & n. 3; instructions to Navy Board (1640), 2/23 & n. 1; at coronation banquet, 2/85; alluded to: 9/447, 524; ~ his

wife [Elizabeth], 8/138

PERCY, Sir Henry, 9th Earl of Northumberland (d. 1632): his Walk in Tower of London, 9/479 & n. 2

PERCY (Piercy), Lady Joscelin: P admires, 8/139 & n. 1

PEREPOINT, Pierpoint: see Pierrepont

PERKIN, Frank, P's cousin: a miller, 2/96; P's meeting with, 4/310; ~ his wife and children, ib.

PERKIN, Jane, sen. (b. Pepys), of Parson Drove, Cambs. P's aunt: annuity from Robert P's estate, 4/119 & n. 2; evidence about John Day's estate, 4/300, 310; P visits, 4/310; death, 8/90; ~ her children's legacy, 8/90, 91

PERKIN, Jane, jun., of Parson Drove, Cambs., P's cousin: 2/137; 4/310

PERKIN, [John], of Parson Drove, Cambs., P's uncle: P visits, 4/310; ~ his daughters, ib.

PERKINS, [?George]: witness in Carkesse case, 8/109, 200

PERRIMAN, Capt. [John], river agent to the Navy Board: complains of abuses, 8/124; news from, 8/251, 601; 9/147; advice about *Maybolt*, 8/601; navy business, 9/29; social: 8/188–9

PERSIA, envoy from: see [?Cisii, Pietro]

PETER(S), Hugh, Independent divine (d. 1660): arrested and tried, 1/240 & n. 4, 263; style of preaching, 3/42; 4/93 & n. 3; abused, 4/93; also, 4/418

PETERSEN, ——: spreads rumours of Dutch atrocities, 6/42 & n. 1, 43–4

PETERSFIELD, Hants.: P at, 2/92, 93; 3/69, 75; 9/274; King at, 2/92; plague, 8/148; Red Lion, 2/93

PETIT, Kate ('Catau'), (b. Sterpin): marriage, 1/217 & n. 2; bequests from Lady Pye, 1/272 & n. 4; lodgings, ib.; social: 1/16 & n. 6, 54, 78, 94; 2/11

PETIT, Monsieur [Henri]: marriage, 1/217, 272; educational projects, 1/272; visits P, 2/11

PETITION OF RIGHT (1628): 9/196 & n. 2

PETRE (Peters), [Elizabeth], Lady Petre (b. Savage), wife of the 4th Baron (d. 1665): 'a drunken jade',

5/133; W. Joyce attempts to have
arrested for debt, 5/109–12 passim,
125–6, 128–9 & n.; portrait by Hayls,
7/44, 53, 61
PETRE, William, 4th Baron Petre
(d. 1684): quarrels with wife, 5/111;
~ his steward, ib.
PETT, [Agnes]: *see* Crisp
PETT, [Ann], wife of Christopher:
once handsome, 2/13; gift to P, 8/84;
applies to Duke of York for widow's
relief, 9/158 & n. 1, 171, 173
PETT, Christopher, Master-Shipwright, Deptford and Woolwich
yards 1660–8: builds *Anne* yacht, 2/14,
104; *Henrietta* yacht, 4/149; 5/24;
Royal Catherine, 5/136, 305 & n. 2,
306; 6/80; *Greenwich*, 7/153; gifts to
P, 4/29 & n. 4; 8/84 & n 3; and
Coventry, 4/437; inspects deals, 3/135,
136; to instruct P in ship-building,
4/433; discusses ironwork, 5/75; and
despatch of ships, 5/155; complains of
Warren's timber, 4/326; hostile to
Deane, 4/384; criticises Batten, 5/109;
King's opinion of, 7/106; death,
9/128 & n. 1; social: 2/13; 3/179;
7/253; ~ his pretty daughter, 7/263;
9/158
PETT, [Mary] (b. Smith), wife of
Commissioner Pett: at church, 2/12;
3/153; also, 2/13; 5/307
PETT, Peter, Navy Commissioner at
Chatham 1648–67, Master-Shipwright, Chatham 1664–7
CHARACTER: P's low opinion, 5/28 &
n. 1, 122, 210; 8/275
EARLY CAREER: alleged anti-royalism,
4/53–4 & n., 91, 253; 8/526
AS COMMISSIONER:
    ADMINISTRATION OF YARD: appoint-
ment, 1/241, 322; proposed as assistant to Surveyor, 3/327 & n.; 4/75;
criticised by P and Coventry, 4/227–8,
258, 259, 260, 275, 282, 328, 365;
neglect of duty, 6/104; inefficiency in
getting fleet out, 7/186; to be transferred, 7/186; trades with navy under
alias, 8/206 & n. 3, 230–1; blamed for
Medway disaster, 8/259, 263, 272–3,
298, 309; reports to Navy Board,
8/259 & n. 1, 271; arrested and examined by Council, 8/276–7, 278–9, 282,

394, 460, 461; examined by Committee on Miscarriages, 8/495–6 & n.,
498, 501, 502; re-arrested, 8/511–12 &
n.; to be impeached, 8/526–7, 538;
defence by Brouncker, 8/311; by Sir
P. Howard, 9/11
RELATIONS WITH COLLEAGUES: 'of a
knot' with P and Coventry, 3/284;
friendly to P, 4/196; on bad terms
with P, 4/282; 8/103, 200; Rupert,
Albemarle and Coventry, 7/186;
Penn, 7/212–13; Batten, 8/100, 101;
and Brouncker, 8/101, 166; criticises
Batten and Mennes, 4/98
BUSINESS [sometimes in combination
with colleague(s)]: fits out *Naseby*,
1/142; entertains King, 1/240; inspects timber contract, 3/112, 113;
attends launch, 4/225; on *Charles*,
5/317; and *Catherine*, 6/194; inspects
Navy Office houses, 1/192; Deptford
yard, 3/129; 4/50; Woolwich yard,
4/64, 65; Chatham, 6/248–9; musters
guard ships, 3/155; proposes new yard
at Sheerness, 6/194–5; inspects masts,
3/227, 273–4; reports on Sherwood
forest, 4/158, n. 1; project for dock at
St Mary's creek, 4/225–6 & n.;
inspects site for mast-dock at Deptford, 6/96 & n. 5; conducts survey at
Chatham, 1/204; at pays, 3/129, 193;
also, 1/147, 197, 212; 3/106; 6/131,
206; unspecified, 2/221; 3/146, 154;
4/20, 258, 259, 328, 380; 5/146; 6/183;
alluded to: 3/25
AS SHIPBUILDER: builds *Catherine*,
1/286–7 & n.; 2/12, 14, 36, 76, 104;
4/91; his part in building *Jemmy*, 3/164
& n. 4, 188; 4/64; visits yachts, 4/227;
explains ship-drawings, 4/227; 6/7;
jealous of Petty's design, 5/28; also,
4/420, 421
CHATHAM CHEST: profits, 3/274; 5/122
HIS HOUSE AT CHATHAM: P visits/
admires, 2/69; 8/307; 9/499; closet,
3/154; parlour, 4/260; garden, 4/219,
260; upper arbour, 4/258; banqueting
house, 6/182
SOCIAL: with P on Dutch voyage,
1/118, 145, 147, 150; at Navy Board
dinner, 2/210; visits portrait painters,
3/21, 230; attends anatomy lecture,
4/59–60; entertains colleagues at

Deptford, 2/77; Chatham, 3/153, 154; 6/182, 232; and Woolwich, 3/289; dines with/visits P, 2/209; 3/120; 4/21, 45; 5/307; 6/205–6; at taverns, 3/165; 5/329; 6/77; 7/223; also, 2/218
MISC.: ill, 4/168; barber, 6/227
~ daughter [?Agnes Crisp], 4/168 & n. 1; 6/262; daughters, 2/12; step-daughter, 2/12; kinsman, 6/262
PETT [Peter], lawyer, son of Peter: 3/113
PETT, [Phineas], Master-Shipwright, Chatham 1605–29: 8/84 & n. 3
PETT, Phineas, (Capt. Pett), Assistant-Shipwright, Chatham 1660, Master-Shipwright, 1661–80; kted 1680: to be suspended, 1/229 & n. 4, 239, 240; house, 2/69; consulted on masts, 4/287; to join in P's timber deal, 7/298 & n. 3, 300, 301; accused of selling boats, 9/499 & n. 2; dismissed but reinstated, 9/267 & n. 2; social: 2/71
PETT, Phineas, shipwright, son of John: 5/109 & n. 1
PETTUS, Sir John, of Chediston, Suff. (d. 1685): on *Naseby*, 1/103 & n. 3
PETTY, William, kted 1661, scientist and economist [*see also* Books]: P's regard, 5/12, 27; 6/38; at Rota Club, 1/14; as T. Barlow's agent, 1/191, 305; 6/33; double-keeled ships: [*Invention* II], 4/256 & n. 3, 263 & n. 1, 334, 437; 5/24–5 & n., 28, 30, 32, 47; [*Experiment*], 5/353 & n. 3; 6/35, 38, 63 & n. 1; views on public taste, 5/27–8; and dreams, 5/108; proposed bequests for scientific research, 6/63 & n. 2
PHELPS, Mr —— [?John, Auditor of the revenue at the Exchequer]: 1/47; 2/163; 9/465–6 & n.
PHILIP IV, King of Spain 1621–65: prepares for Portuguese war, 4/349 & n. 5; death, 6/257 & n. 5; mourning for, 7/39; also, 7/55
PHILIPPE, Duc d' Anjou, later Duc d'Orleans (d. 1701): marriage, 1/240 & n. 3; 2/56; anecdote, 2/29
PHILIPS, [?John], cook: 9/116
PHILIPS, —— [?Robert, Groom of the Bedchamber to the King]: 5/279

& n. 1
PHILLIPS, [Henry], Council messenger: 1/123, 126
PHILLIPS, Lewis, lawyer, of Brampton and Huntingdon: character, 9/211; consulted in disputes about Robert P's estate, 2/135, 138, 148, 183, 223, 227; 3/27, 31, 33, 221; 4/34, 45, 221; 5/40; as arbiter, 3/261, 265; consulted about land purchase, 8/282–3; political news from, 4/155; leaves Brampton, 8/220; estate, 8/585; social: 2/137, 210, 213; 9/559; ~ his wife [Judith] dies, 9/211
PHILLIPS, [?Philip]: drawing of yacht, 4/301 & n. 2
PHILPOT LANE: 7/262
PHIPPS, [?Thomas], of Rochester: 7/177
PHYSICIANS, ROYAL COLLEGE OF: 4/156
PICKERING, Dorothy, (b. Weld, Wilde), wife of Edward: social: 5/34; 9/431, 487, 504
PICKERING, Edward (Ned):
CHARACTER: a fool but well informed, 2/170; a coxcomb, 1/101; 4/239, 255; 7/295
CHRON. SERIES: on *Naseby*, 1/101, 105, 133; carries letters for Sandwich, 1/105, 137, 142, 156; in Holland, 1/144, 145, 150; disappointed of place in Queen's Household, 4/239 & n. 2; dismissed from place at court, 4/255–6 & n.; involvement in Sandwich's love affair, 4/270, 301, 303, 371 & n. 4, 392; 5/22, 184; advises P on coach horses, 9/384, 391(2), 431; house in Lincoln's Inn Fields, 7/423; also, 1/251; 3/72, 212; 6/13; 7/295
COURT/POLITICAL NEWS FROM: 1/101–2; 2/152, 156, 170, 216–17; 3/64; 4/48–9; 5/34
SOCIAL: dines/plays cards etc. with Sandwich, 2/64, 115; 3/7; 4/28, 46; at Bartholomew Fair, 2/166; 4/301; theatre, 5/34; also, 8/181; 9/431, 487
PICKERING, Elizabeth, Lady Pickering (b. Mountagu), wife of Sir Gilbert: solicits Sandwich's help for husband, 1/174, 178 & n. 4; poor lodging in Blackfriars, 1/277; visits P, 9/261–2 & n.; also, 1/179

PICKERING, Sir Gilbert, Lord Chamberlain to Oliver Cromwell: pardoned by Parliament, 1/178 & n. 4; death, 9/334 & n. 1

PICKERING, Gilbert, son of Sir Gilbert: marries heiress, 7/358 & n. 2; rogue, 8/181 & n. 4

PICKERING, John, son of Sir Gilbert: fool, 1/116, 161, 295; on *Naseby*, 1/112, 153, 161; annoys Sandwich, 1/142 & n. 5; proposed match, 1/220–1, 295; also, 2/35

PICKERING, Oliver, son of Sir Gilbert: dies of smallpox, 9/487 & n. 2

PICKERING, Sidney, son of Sir Gilbert: 9/335

PICTURES:

COLLECTIONS [*see* under owners or houses: i.e. Charles II; Clarendon; Crew, Sir T.; Evelyn, J.; Graunt, J.; James, Duke of York; Mary, Princess Dowager of Holland, Povey, T.; Audley End House]

PORTRAITS [*see* under subjects: Albemarle, by Cooper; Allin, Sir T., by Lely; Anne Duchess of York, by Lely; Arlington, by Cooper; Ascue, Sir G., by Lely; Ashley, by Cooper; Berkeley, Sir W., by Lely; Lady Castlemaine, by Lely; Catherine of Braganza, by Huysmans; Charles I, by Van Dyke; by Marshall; Charles II, by Luttichuys; by Lely; Archbishop Chichele, by S. Strong; Cleopatra, artist unknown; Colbert, engr. by Nanteuil: Lord Coventry, ?by S. Stone; Crew, Sir T., ?by Lely; Harman, by Lely; Henrietta-Maria, by Huysmans; by Van Dyck; Henry VIII, by Holbein; anon.; Hill, T., by Hayls: Jordan, Sir J., by Lely; Louis XIV, engr. by Nanteuil; Mary, Princess Dowager, by van Honthorst; Myngs, Sir C., by Lely; Ormond, ?by Loggan; Pearse, Mrs J., by Hayls; Pearse, James jun., by Hayls; Penn, Sir W., by Lely; Sarah Robartes, artist unknown; Prince Rupert, by Lely; Sandwich, by Lely; by Salisbury; Smith, Sir J., by Lely; Stuart, Frances, by Cooper; by Huysmans; Swynfen, ——, by Cooper; Teddeman, Sir T., by Lely;

Van Dyck, self-portrait]; ~ the fashion for portraits *en déshabillé*, 6/335 & n. 1

OTHER PICTURES: cartoons, 1/45; 4/400 & n. 2; *The Four Evangelists* (artist unknown), 1/70 & n. 2; *trompe-l'œuil*, 1/148, 257–8 & n.; 4/18 & n. 1, 26 (by Hoogstraten); 9/119, 352; *The Embarkation of Henry VIII* (artist unknown), 3/292 & n. 4; *Henry VIII and the Barber-Surgeons' Company* (by Holbein), 4/59 & n. 3; 9/293; Dutch drawing, 4/109; etchings of Lisbon and the Tagus (by Sandwich), 4/286 & n. 1; Venetian scene (by Fialetti), 7/60 & n. 2; landscape and still life (artist unknown), 7/81; landscape (by Looten), 9/514 & n. 2; flower-piece (by Verelst), 9/515, 516

MEDIA: on cloth, 1/148; 'paper pictures', 4/320; Evelyn explains mezzotints, 6/289 & n. 3; pastels, 7/359; chalk, ib. & n. 3; ink, 8/181; tempera, 9/434–5 & n., 465

PICTURES (P) [including those acquired for the office. It is not always possible to distinguish prints from other pictures. *See also* Prices.]:

HIS COLLECTION:

GENERAL: hangs/rehangs pictures, 3/3; 5/235–6; 7/122, 258, 409, 417; 9/271, 331(2); also, 8/455; buys pictures at The Hague, 1/148; in London, 1/298; 9/373; buys prints, 1/296; 3/2; 4/434; 5/41; 7/173, 208–9, 409; shown to guests, 9/424; also, 3/1; 7/102

ITEMS: portraits in oil [*see* under artists: P by Savill; by Hayls; EP by Hayls; by Cooper; John P, sen., by Hayls; T. Hill by Bosse after Hayls; H. Harris by Hayls]; other pictures: Dutch landscape, 7/208–9; marine scenes, 7/290, 292; Santa Clara, 7/409; royal palaces by Danckerts, 9/423 & n. 1; Rome by Danckerts, 9/504; drawings: *Resolution* by A. Deane, 9/262 & n. 4; also, 8/142 & n. 2; prints etc.: by Ragot after Rubens, 1/194; *Royal Sovereign*, 4/29 & n. 4, 43; by Lafreri, 7/102–3 & n.; the Thames, 7/290; Lady Castlemaine by Faithorne after Lely, 7/359 & n. 3,

393; crucifixion, 7/211 & n. 2, 218, 232, 353; Ormond ?by Loggan, 8/10 & n. 3; cities, 8/383 & n. 4; Thames dockyards, 9/266, 268; Louis XIV, Colbert and others by Nanteuil, 9/427 & n. 1, 451; frames etc.: vellum covers, 3/10; mock-tortoise-shell frame, 7/184–5; gilt frames, 7/290, 292; album, 9/266; 'paper pictures' (? water-colours), 4/320

HIS TASTE: admires *trompe l'œuil*, 1/148, 257–8; 4/18; 9/119, 352; and still life, 7/81; love of verisimilitude, 9/515, 516; comments on likenesses in portraits, 7/171; prefers oil to tempera, 9/434–5, 465; admires pictures in royal collection, 1/257; 3/82; compares them with Hayls's, 7/97; admires Duke of York's collection, 7/102; and Clarendon's, 8/175; criticises Povey's, 9/521; admires portraits by Huysmans, 5/254, 276; 6/43; Van Dyck, 6/222; ?S. Stone, 7/183; Cooper, 9/139

PIERCE: *see* Pearse

PIERCE, [Thomas], President of Magdalen College, Oxford 1661–72; Dean of Salisbury 1675–d.91: sermons before King on temptation, and against papists, 4/98 & n. 1

[PIERCE, (Peirs) William], Bishop of Bath and Wells 1632–d.70; 1/259 & n. 3

PIERCE, Serjeant ——: news from, 3/29, 43; 4/187; ? also, 2/149

PIERCE, Mr ——, formerly a soldier [? identical with the foregoing]: 1/311; ? 2/149

PIERREPONT, [Henry], 1st Marquess of Dorchester (d. 1680): quarrels with Buckingham, 7/414–15 & n.; alluded to: 7/366

PIERREPONT (Perepoint, Pierpoint), [William], politician, brother of the foregoing (d. 1678): elected to Council of State, 1/65; rumoured appointment to Privy Council, 8/265 & n. 3; appointed to commission of accounts, 8/577 & n. 3

PIERSON: *see* Pearson

PIGGOT, [Francis], musician: 8/437 & n. 4, 557

PIGOTT, [Richard], of Brampton,

Hunts.: dispute over mortgage, 2/137 & n. 4, 138, 182; 3/219–20, 222, 223 & n. 1, 261; to sell land in order to pay, 4/133, 179, 237 & n. 4, 309; 5/149, 281, 282; dispute alluded to, 4/308, 352; debt, 4/309; ∼ his wife's interest, 4/309

PIGOTT, Sir Richard, Clerk of the Patents: 9/372, n. 2, 492 & n. 4

PILLAU (the Pillow), E. Prussia: 6/305

PINCHBECK (Pinchbacke), [John]: swallows toad with drink, 7/290 & n. 2

PINKNEY, [Charles]: 1/132; ? also, 1/19

PINKNEY, [George], King's embroiderer: anecdote of loyalty, 1/77; petitions for place, 1/132–3 & n.; in Holland, 1/148, 149; also, 1/184; social: entertains P at Parish Clerks' Hall, 1/16, 19; also, 1/21, 76–7, 229, 304; 2/99; alluded to: 2/57; ∼ his sons, 1/148

PINKNEY, [? Henry], goldsmith, Fleet St: 1/307

[PIOSSASCO, Filiberto, Conte di], Savoyard envoy, June–July 1666: 7/202 & n. 2

PITT(S), [John], Secretary and Deputy-Treasurer to Lawson's fleet: irregular accounts, 4/104, 132; alluded to: 1/133

PITTS, ——, landlord of the King's Head, Islington: 5/101, 133; 7/149; death, 7/317

PLAGUE, the:

IN HOLLAND: 4/340 & n. 2, 399; 5/142, 186, 220; Dutch fleet, 5/231, 279; quarantine on ships from Holland etc., 4/340, 399 & n. 2

IN ENGLAND: 6/93, n. 2

P'S REACTION [for the movements of his household and office during the outbreak, *see* Pepys, Elizabeth; Navy Office]: fear, 6/120, 121, 136, 164, 173–4, 187, 192, 199, 200, 208, 217, 232, 265, 288; 7/50, 166; fears infection from periwig, 6/210; from hackney coaches, 6/311; from graveyard, 7/30, 31, 35; calmness in face of, 6/145, 192, 225, 240, 246; makes will etc., 6/125, 188(2), 189(3), 190, 192; hardened to sight of corpses, 6/256;

lives 'merrily' at Greenwich, 6/342
ITS SPREAD AND INCIDENCE IN
LONDON AND ENVIRONS: first signs,
6/93; houses marked in Drury Lane,
6/120 & n. 1; reported in city, 6/124,
125, 128, 142, 168, 205–7 passim, 225;
Bell Alley, Westminster, 6/132; near
St Clement's, 6/140; Palace Yard,
6/141; King St, Westminster, 6/141,
163; increases in Westminster, 6/144,
154, 210, 268, 289; reported in
Basinghall St, 6/144; Pall Mall,
6/147–8; Long Lane, 6/150; Covent
Garden, ib.; London Wall, ib.;
Rotherhithe, 6/163, 201; Axe Yard,
6/163; St Olave's parish, 6/171 & n. 2,
175, 329, 335; Islington, 6/175–6;
Dagenhams, 6/181; Deptford, 6/189,
204, 206, 253, 294, 332; 7/236 & n. 3,
239, 241, 285; Woolwich, 6/189, 206,
309; Gravesend, 6/195, 249; Hounslow, 6/199; Greenwich, 6/200, 201,
206, 210, 212, 256; 7/236, 239; St
Sepulchre's, Newgate St, 6/225; near
Tower, 6/251(2); Steelyard, 6/270;
Kent St, 6/279, 297; St Martin's-in-
the-Fields, 6/289; Lambeth, ib.; St
Martin's Lane, 6/304; Chatham, 7/42
& n. 1, 253; Drury Lane, 7/73; the
Swan, Chelsea, 7/95; the Mitre,
Fenchurch St, 7/236, 241, 242; fear of,
6/154, 161, 174, 192; (unspecified)
increase of, 6/143, 164, 171, 206–7,
226, 328; 7/41, 108, 123
ITS SPREAD AND INCIDENCE ELSE-
WHERE: at Salisbury, 6/189; Colchester, 6/307 & n. 2; 7/193; Cambridge,
7/219 & n. 2; 8/468; Deal, 7/241 & n.
3; Petersfield, 8/148
MORTALITY [mostly P's summaries of
statistical returns in weekly bills of
mortality]: P notes worst increase,
6/234; other increases, 6/128, 132–3 &
n., 142, 173, 178, 187, 191 & n. 2,
207–8, 208, 214, 295, 335; 7/9, 14, 17,
52, 71, 80, 91–2, 94, 95, 193; decreases,
6/157 & n. 1, 224–5, 243, 353, 264,
284, 299, 305, 314, 340; 7/2, 21, 32, 63,
110; also, 6/163, 170, 180, 206–7;
bills' unreliability, 6/206–7 & n.
BURIALS: plague-pits, 6/162 & n. 2,
164–5 & n., 207, 213; by day, 6/189,
213, 225; coffin left out all night,

6/201; St Olave's churchyard piled
high, 7/30 & n. 3; attended by infected persons, 7/40–1
ANECDOTES: P's coachman stricken,
6/131; his physician accused of killing
servant, 6/165 & n. 2; P encounters
corpse, 6/192; child rescued from
infected house, 6/212; P meets search-
ers, 6/283 & n. 4; victims beg in street,
6/297; breathe on passers-by, 7/41
FAST FOR: proclaimed, 6/155 & n. 4;
observed, 6/179, 294, 320; 7/37, 68,
91, 150, 151, 193, 231, 306, 359(2)
MEASURES AGAINST: discussed, 6/108,
211, 212; houses shut up, 6/120, 125,
192, 203, 212, 224, 225; fumigated,
6/288; whitewashed, 7/166; pest-
houses, 6/165, 181; pest-coaches,
6/181; bonfires in streets, 6/213 & n.
5; churchyards covered in lime, 7/31;
tobacco, 6/120 & n. 2; plague-water,
6/163 & n. 3; 'good drink', 6/226;
burials by night, 6/189, 199, 282;
(untrue) story of curfew, 6/189
FLIGHT FROM: 6/133, 141–2 & n.; Clarendon, Albemarle and Arlington remain,
6/142; streets empty/shops shut, 6/165,
168, 186, 192, 205, 207, 233, 268, 311;
effect on Royal Exchange, 6/192, 224;
river traffic, 6/233, 293; meetings of
Royal Society, 7/21 & n. 1; physicians
leave, 7/21 & n. 2
CESSATION OF: P notes/hopes for decrease, 6/313, 337, 341; 7/29; decrease
in frosty weather, 6/305, 306; town
fills up, 6/278, 328, 342; 7/3, 18, 38,
52; Brampton carrier resumes, 6/314;
theatres reopen, 7/376–7, 399;
Thanksgiving Day appointed, 7/376 &
n. 2; King's presentations for services
during, 8/196 & n. 3
PLANTS, fruits and trees [For timber
trees used in shipbuilding, see Clerk of
the Acts; Navy Board. See also Food.]:
GENERAL: P admires plantations in
Greenwich Park, 3/63 & n. 4; St
James's Park, 5/127 & n. 1; Wricklemarsh, 6/94; discusses botany with
Evelyn, 6/253, 289
PARTICULAR: cowslips: 4/112; goose-
berries: at Hatfield, 2/139; grapes: in
London, 2/176; Walthamstow, 8/341
–2; lemon-trees: in Hampstead, 9/281;

orange-trees: in St James's Park, 5/127; Hackney, 7/182; Hampstead, 9/281; petrified trees: at Blackwall, 6/236 & n. 4; pinks: 3/95, 116; roses: 3/95; 7/204; rushes: by Thames, 8/320; sage: 3/70–1; 5/222; sensitive plant: P given seeds, 1/80; tobacco: grown in Gloucestershire, 8/442 & n. 2; vineyards: at Hatfield, 2/138–9 & n.; Wricklemarsh, 6/94 & n. 4
PLAYER, Sir Thomas, sen., City Chamberlain 1651–d.72: consulted about navy's credit, 7/72, 76; 9/169
PLAYFORD, [John], bookseller and publisher, Inner Temple [see also Books; Musical Compositions]: P visits shop/buys books, 1/54 & n. 6; 2/106; 4/127; 7/381; 8/440–1; Fire delays publication, 7/381 & n. 4; also, 3/263; ~ his man, 7/381
PLAYS [Asterisks denote entries at which P comments either on the play or the production; daggers indicate that EP attended. Square brackets indicate that the play is not named in the text. If the play was published, the title given here is that of one of the 17th-century editions; P's titles, if substantially different, are added. TR is an abbreviation for Theatre Royal, and LIF for the theatre at Lincoln's Inn Fields. For plays which P read, see Books. See also Theatre.]:
[BEAUMONT, F., ?AND FLETCHER J.], The knight of the burning pestle, at TR, Vere St, 3/78★ & n. 3
[BEAUMONT, F. AND FLETCHER, J.], The Coxcomb, at TR, Drury Lane, 9/486★† & nn.; Cupid's Revenge, at LIF, 9/282★ & n. 2; A king and no king, at TR, Vere St, 2/54★ & n. 2, 185★†; The maid's tragedy, at TR, Vere St, 2/100★ & n. 4; at TR, Drury Lane, 7/399★ & n. 2; 8/71†; 9/164★ & n. 2, 193★; Philaster, at TR, Vere St, 2/216★† & n. 3; at TR, Drury Lane, 9/217–18 & n. 1; The scornful lady, at TR, Vere St, 1/303 & n. 3; 2/6★, 35★ & n. 6; at Cockpit, Whitehall, 3/260★†; at TR, Drury Lane, 7/422★†; 9/222; alluded to: 8/440 & n. 1
[BERKELEY, SIR W.], The lost lady, at TR, Vere St, 2/18★ & n. 5, 25★

[BRISTOL, 2nd EARL OF], Worse and worse, at LIF, 5/215★ & n. 1
[BROME, R], The Antipodes, at TR, Vere St, 2/162★ & n. 3; The jovial crew, or The merry beggars, at TR, Vere St, 2/141★ & n. 1, 164★†, 206; at TR, Drury Lane, 9/411–12★† & n.; The northern lass, at TR, Drury Lane, 8/436–7★† & n.
BUCKINGHAM, GEORGE, DUKE OF, AND HOWARD, SIR R., [The country gentleman], alluded to, at TR, Drury Lane, 9/467, 471 & n. 2
BUCKINGHAM, DUKE OF: see also Dryden, J.
[CARYL, J.], The English princess, or The death of Richard the III, at LIF, 8/101★† & n. 3
[CHAPMAN, G.], Bussy d'Ambois, at TR, Vere St, 2/241† & n. 1
[CHAPOTON, JEAN, completed by], Le mariage d'Orphée et d'Eurydice, at Cockpit, Drury Lane, 2/165† & n. 1
[COOKE, J.]–Davenant, Tu Quoque, or The city gallant, at LIF, 8/435★† & n. 1, 440★†
[CORNEILLE, P.], The valiant Cid, at Cockpit, Whitehall, 3/272–3★ & n.; Heraclius, at LIF, 5/78–9★† & nn.; 8/44★†, 421–2★†; Horace, at TR, Drury Lane, 9/420★† & n. 2; The mistaken beauty, or The Liar, at TR, Drury Lane, 8/551–2★† & n.
[?CORNEILLE, T.], The Labyrinth, 5/138★† & n. 1
[COWLEY, A.], The Guardian (formerly The cutter of Coleman Street), at LIF, 2/234★† & n. 3; 9/272★ & n. 2
DAVENANT, SIR W., Love and honour, at LIF, 2/200★ & n. 2, 201(2)★†; The man's the master, at LIF, 9/133–4★† & nn., 148, 189★; The siege of Rhodes, at LIF, 2/130–1★ & nn., 214★†; 3/86★, 295★† & n. 3; alluded to, 8/225; The unfortunate lovers, at LIF, 5/77★† & n. 2; ?8/433† & n. 2; 9/157★, 383★†; The Wits, at LIF, 2/155★ & n. 1, 156★, 160★†; 8/170–1★† & n. 1, 172★†; 9/419★†
DAVENANT, SIR W.: see also Cooke-Davenant; Fletcher-Davenant; Shakespeare-Davenant
DEKKER, T. and MASSINGER, J., The

you know not me, you know nobody, or The troubles of Queen Elizabeth, at TR, Drury Lane, 8/388*† & n. 2; alluded to : 8/387

[?HOLDEN, J.], *The German princess*, at LIF, 5/124*† & n. 2; *The Ghosts*, at LIF, 6/83*† & n. 1

HOWARD, E., *The change of crownes*, at TR, Drury Lane, 8/167–8* & nn.; alluded to : 8/169; *The Usurper*, at TR, Drury Lane, 5/3*† & n. 2; 9/381*† & n. 4

[HOWARD, J.], *The English monsieur*, at TR, Drury Lane, 7/401* & n.; 9/155* *All mistaken, or The mad couple*, at TR, Drury Lane, 8/443*† & n. 1, 594*† & n. 1; 9/269*†

[HOWARD, SIR R.], *The Committee*, at TR, Drury Lane, 4/181*† & n. 1; 8/384*, 508*†; 9/200; *The great favourite, or The Duke of Lerma*, at TR, Drury Lane, 9/81*† & n. 2; alluded to : 9/20 & n. 1; *The Surprisal*, at TR, Drury Lane, 8/157*† & n. 3, 402*, 590*† & n. 3; 9/166*, 182

[HOWARD, SIR R. AND DRYDEN, J.], *The Indian queen*, at TR, Drury Lane, 5/28–9* & n., 33–4*†; 9/250*† & n. 1

HOWARD, SIR R.: *see also* Buckingham, Duke of

[JONSON, B.], *The Alchemist*, at TR, Vere St, 2/125* & n. 1, 154; at TR, Drury Lane, 9/522–3*† & n.; alluded to : 5/232; 9/85 & n. 4; *Bartholomew Fair*, at TR, Vere St, 2/116–17* & n., 127*, 174*† & n. 1, 212*†; at TR, Drury Lane, 5/230*; 9/299†; *Great Hall*, Whitehall, 9/456†; *Catiline his conspiracy*, at TR, Drury Lane, 8/569, 575*; 9/395*† & n. 1; alluded to : 5/349 & n. 4; 9/20; *Epicoene, or The silent woman*, at Cockpit, Whitehall, [1/297–8]; at TR, Vere St, 2/7*†, 106*; at TR, Drury Lane, 5/165*† & n. 3; 8/168†, 169*; 9/310*; alluded to : 1/171 & n. 2, 309 & n. 2; *Volpone*, at TR, Drury Lane, 6/10*† & n. 2; *Works*, alluded to : 4/410 & n. 4

[KILLIGREW, T., sen.], *Claracilla*, at TR, Vere St, 2/223* & n. 2; at Cockpit, Whitehall, 4/4*† & n. 4; at TR, Drury Lane, 9/476*†; *The parson's wedding* ('*The parson's dreame*') alluded to, at TR, Drury Lane, 5/289 & n. 1, 294; *The Princess, or Love at first sight*, at TR, Vere St, 2/132* & n. 2;

[KYD, T.], *The Spanish tragedy, or Hieronymo is mad again*, at Nursery, Hatton Garden, 9/89–90*† & n. ; *The Labyrinth*, at TR, Drury Lane, 5/139*†; alluded to : 5/138 & n. 1

LACY, J., *The old troop, or Monsieur Raggou*, at TR, Drury Lane, 9/270*† & n. 1, 271*†

LACY, J.: *see also* Shakespeare

Love's Quarrel, at Salisbury Court, 2/66* & n. 3

[MARLOWE, C.], *Dr Faustus*, at Red Bull, Clerkenwell, 3/93*† & n. 4

[MASSINGER, P.], *The Bondman*, at Salisbury Court, 2/47* & n. 2, 56, 60†; at LIF, 2/207*†, 220 & n. 3; 3/58*† & n. 3; 5/224* & nn.

MASSINGER, P.: *see also* Dekker, T.; Fletcher, J.

[MAYNE, J.], *The city match*, at TR, Drury Lane, 9/322* & n. 1

The merry devil of Edmonton, at TR, Vere St, 2/151* & n. 6

[MIDDLETON, T.], *The Widow*, at TR, Vere St, 2/8* & n. 2

[MIDDLETON, T. AND ROWLEY, W.], *The Changeling*, at Salisbury Court, 2/41* & n. 3; *The Spanish gipsie*, at TR, Drury Lane, 9/107*† & n. 4

NEWCASTLE, WILLIAM, DUKE OF, *The country captain*, at TR, Vere St, 2/202*† & n. 2, 220*; at TR, Drury Lane, 8/386*; 9/198–9*; *The Heiress*, at TR, Drury Lane, 9/435–6*† & nn.; *The humorous lovers*, at LIF, 8/137* & n. 4, 163*; *The humours of Monsieur Galliard* (based upon *The Variety*), at TR, Vere St, 3/87–8*† & nn.; *Sir Martin Marall: see* Dryden, J.

ORRERY, ROGER BOYLE, EARL OF, *The Black Prince*, at TR, Drury Lane, 8/487–8*† & n., 498*; 9/144* & n. 1; *The General*, at TR, Drury Lane, 5/281–2* & n., 288–9*† & n.; 9/533*†; *Guzman*, at LIF, 9/521–2*† & n.; *Henry the fifth*, at LIF, 5/240–1*† & nn., 282; 9/256–7† & n.; at Great Hall, Whitehall, 7/424*; 8/487–8*; alluded to : 5/245*; 8/380;

PLOTS and minor risings [for major plots and risings, *see* [Derwentdale Plot]; Dublin; Fire, the Great; Pentland Rising; Venner, T.]: P's scepticism, 2/225; 3/236; Yarranton or Baxter Plot, 2/225 & n. 1; 3/15; fanatics in London, 3/92 & n. 4; Southwark, 3/165 & n. 3; Dorset, 3/236 & n. 1, 237, 239, 240, 245; P dreams of, 3/250; in W. Country, 6/209 & n. 2

PLOUGH, the, Fleet St (shop): 1/71

PLUME, Thomas, Vicar of St Alphege, Greenwich 1658–d.1704: sermons, 6/227 & n. 4, 316; 9/502

PLYMOUTH, Devon: damaged ships return, 7/9; convoy, 7/395; prize-ships, 8/7, 115–16 & n.; squadron, 8/149; victuals for, 8/88, 560; Dutch fleet off, 8/345; French raids, 9/79–80; also, 5/341

POINTER (Poynter), [Thomas], Navy Office clerk: P's clerk for victualling, 6/315, 315–16; 7/266; 9/37; recommended to Mennes, 6/336

POLAND: hangmen, 3/154 & n. 2; French designs on, 8/92 & n. 3; state treasuries, 8/454 & n. 2

POLICE: *see* Burglary etc.

POLITICAL OPINIONS (P) [For his views on the King and the politicians, *see* under names. *See also* War, the Second Dutch.]: approves of Charles I's execution, 1/280; recalls talking 'privately' of King during Rump, 1/204; drinks King's health (Feb. 1660), 1/58, 67, 68, 70; sympathetic to arrested Cavalier (March 1660), 1/99; kisses King's letter to Sandwich (May 1660), 6/237; views on: state of nation, 3/127; parliament, 7/416; 9/326; parliamentary enquiries, 8/292–3, 305, 353, 485; power of King to save nation, 7/197, 350, 371; French military absolutism as model for England, 8/332; new balance of power in government, 8/584; ~ regrets failure to keep abreast of news, 1/219; 2/124

POLLARD, Sir Hugh, Comptroller of the King's Household 1660–d.66: replaced, 7/390 & n. 2

POLLEROON, Poleron: *see* Pulo Run

PONT: *see* Punt

POOLE, Capt. Jonas, naval officer: at Greenwich, 2/121; loses commission, 6/129 & n. 1; social: 2/?112, 186; ~ his wife, 2/186

POOLE, Matthew, biblical commentator (d. 1679): dispute about *Synopsis Criticorum*, 9/259 & n. 2

POOLE, Capt. William, naval officer, kted 1672: ship disabled in action, 6/19; social: 2/121; ~ wife, 3/5; 8/403, 405; boy 3/5; daughter christened, 8/403, 405

POOLEY, Sir Edmund, M.P. for Bury St Edmunds, Suff.: fine gentleman, 5/330; 6/309; discontented Cavalier, 6/303; shows P prize-goods, 6/300; social: 6/285, 303, 324; ~ his wife, 7/240

POOR, the [*see also* Mendicancy]: P's poor box, 3/230; 4/56, 123, 149–50, 431; 5/55, 192, 193, 284; 6/29; 7/205, 401; employs parish girl, 4/282, 283; ragpicker, 2/60; city orphanage, 1/180 & n. 1; at cockfights, 4/428; foundling, 9/304

POORTMANS (Portman), [John], naval official under Commonwealth: supports rise of Penn, 4/375

POPE'S HEAD ALLEY: P shops in, 1/80, 298; 3/17, 115; also, 2/141

POPHAM, Alexander, M.P. Bath, Som. 1661–d.69: house (Littlecote House, Wilts.), 9/241–2 & n.

POPHAM, Sir —— [?Francis: son of the foregoing; M.P. Bath, Som. 1669–d. 74]: 7/385 & n. 3

POPINJAY ALLEY: 4/279

POPISH PLOT, the: effects on P's career, vol. i, p. xxxvii

POPULAR BELIEFS and customs [*see also* Ashmole, E.; Booker, J.; Lilly, W.; Nostradamus]:

ASTROLOGY: horoscopes, 1/274 & nn.; P buys mock almanac, 1/288–9 & n.; laughs at Lilly's prophecies, 8/270 & n. 2; Buckingham accused of having King's horoscope cast, 8/93–4 & n.; and of being influenced by 'conjurors', 9/373 & n. 2; fear of meteor, 9/208

GHOSTS: P meets, 2/68; 4/227; sceptical of Wiltshire drummer, 4/185–6 & n.;

POSTAL SERVICES: management, 7/375 & n. 2; express, 4/306; 6/257, 260, 271(2); 7/2; 8/263-4, 429; 9/74; carrier, 1/15, 36, 46, 57; delayed by floods, 7/328-9; post-boy, 1/32; post-houses: Southwark, 2/15, 231; Charing Cross, 6/197

POST OFFICE, Threadneedle St: P rides post from, 2/133; music-meetings at, 5/238 & n. 2, 290; destroyed in Fire, 7/275; also, 1/53

POTTLE, ——, shopkeeper in New Exchange: 8/53

POULTNY: see Pulteney

POULTRY, the: 1/246; 8/180

POUNDY, [?James], waterman: witness against P in prize-goods affair, 8/531; also, 7/202, 275

POVEY (Puvy), [Thomas], Treasurer for Tangier:

CHARACTER: vain, 4/17-18; 'most excellent in anything but business', 6/215; also, 3/300; 4/297-8; 5/139, 339; 6/13, 24, 63, 87; 7/191

AS TREASURER FOR TANGIER: appointed, 3/177 & n. 1, 238; incompetence, 5/97-8, 102, 106, 123, 124, 127, 135, 139, 154; 6/18, 37, 69-70, 84-5; 7/191, 330; neglects to provide boats, 3/291; loses his papers, 6/65; victualling business, 4/30; 5/212-13, 223; Gauden's gift, 8/37, 44; drafts civil constitution, 4/88-9; freightage business, 5/23, 26, 276, 332, 336-8 passim, 340, 348; accounts criticised, 5/105; 6/13-18 passim, 33, 38, 58-60 passim, 71, 77, 77-8; 8/75; examined, 9/244, 247, 371, 449; part in examining Peter-borough's accounts, 5/123, 124, 135, 154, 187, 199, 201-2; 6/68-9; other financial business, 6/100-1, 144, 157, 185, 214-15; 9/416; cheated by Vernatty, 7/342; 8/52; resigns office to P on terms, 6/58-63 passim, 79, 84, 89, 91, 94, 108, 109, 121, 130, 139; accounts with P, 7/19, 51, 71, 74, 83, 321, 335(2), 338; 8/593; 9/341-2; at committee meetings, 3/300; 4/21, 23, 269, 341; 5/11, 97, 139, 204; 7/228; unspecified business, 3/232; 4/21, 31, 394; 6/76, 103, 131, 136, 137, 151, 163; 7/156, 245, 265; 8/286-7; 9/437, 543; also, 6/22, 65-6

AS TREASURER FOR THE MANAGEMENT OF THE HOUSEHOLD OF THE DUKE OF YORK: Duke's debts, 7/191-2; 8/287; dismissed, 8/592 & n. 1; 9/38

POLITICAL/COURT NEWS FROM: criticises court, 6/266, 267; 7/228-9; pessimism, 8/286-7; also, 6/215-16; 8/295, 297, 366-7, 431-2; 9/341-2, 373, 414, 416

HOUSES, WEALTH ETC.: house in Lincoln's Inn Fields: cellar, bathroom etc., 4/18 & n. 2, 272 & n. 3, 298; 5/161 & n. 2, 199, 277; 6/139; 8/128-9; 9/345; aviary, 4/272; grotto, 4/298; 5/161; pictures, 4/18 & n. 1, 26; 5/161 & n. 3, 161-2, 212, 277 & n. 2; house at Hounslow, 6/153 & n. 3, 198, 266, 267; chariot, 6/153, 266; horses, 6/266; forced to economise, 6/267; also, 9/443

PERSONAL: bold dalliance with Mary Mercer, 6/85; unwell, 6/97; leaves London in Plague, 6/154; 7/4

SOCIAL: at court ball, 3/300; Hinching-brooke, 5/65; at funeral, 6/114; at theatre, 8/435; at his house, 4/17-18, 26, 31, 35, 297; 5/161-2, 276; 6/13, 17, 18, 22, 76, 87, 99; 9/345, 521; elsewhere, 4/242; 5/265, 270, 330, 338; 9/434-5

MISC.: gifts to P, 4/306; 5/269, 274; nominates P to Royal Society, 6/36; attends its meetings, 6/84; 9/379; advises P to enter parliament, 9/376-7; helps choose coach, 9/342, 344, 352; introduces to Danckerts, 9/421; warns against ostentation in dress, 9/551; relations with Creed, 5/338-9 & n.; 6/89-90; 9/244, 247; advises Arlington not to buy Euston, 8/288-9 & n.; also, 5/74

~ his wife [Mary], 4/297 & n. 4; 6/199; his man Dutton's wife, 6/266, 267; his man, 7/229

POWELL, Doll, (b. Lane), of Westminster: P's valentine, 9/121, 126; has baby, 9/486; claims to be Rowland Powell's widow, 9/486, 514; amorous encounters with P: 7/337, 342, 345, 359, 386, 406; 8/3, 39-40, 393, 422; 9/78, 121, 527; misses assignations, 8/111, 113-14; 9/317; fails to find privacy for, 8/193; false modesty,

8/323; social: sings a jig, 7/232; drinks with P, 7/425; 8/435, 478; 9/208, 551; also, 9/118

POWELL, [John], P's schoolfellow and contemporary at Cambridge: preaches at St Olave's, 1/295; social: 2/44

POWELL, [John], steward to diplomatic mission to Sweden 1659: 1/83 & n. 1 ~ his son/?sons, 1/50, 183, 199

POWELL, Rowland, alleged husband of Doll Lane: drowned, 9/514

POWELL, [Rowland], clerk to Brouncker: 8/217

POWELL, [Rowland], clerk to Sir W. Coventry: 8/261; 9/275

POWELL, Dr ——, the Welsh doctor: visits Kate Joyce, 7/72

POWELL, Mr ——, Tom P's doctor (?identical with the foregoing): 5/81, 84, 85, 86

POWLE (Powell), Sir Richard, Master of the Horse to the Duchess of York (d. 1678): 9/468

POYNTER: *see* Pointer

POYNTON [? Boynton], Col. ——: 9/438

POYNTZ, [Francis], Master of the New Bridewell, Clerkenwell: consulted about flags, 5/289; 6/65–6 & n.; ~ his clerk, 5/289

POYNTZ, Capt. [John], Clerk-Comptroller of the office of the Master of the Revels: consulted about lotteries, 5/276 & n. 1

PRAT, Monsieur, —— du: Hinchingbrooke's tutor: 8/276 & n. 2

PRETYMAN, [Theodosia], Lady Pretyman, [wife of Sir John, 1st Bt] (d. c. 1692): 7/362

[PRICE, Gervase], Sergeant-Trumpeter to the King: 7/352 & n. 4

PRICE, [Goditha] (d. 1678): Duke of York's mistress, 7/159 & n. 1

PRICE, Sir Herbert, 1st Bt, Master of the King's Household 1661–5, 1666–d. 78; father of the foregoing: 9/153

PRICE, Jack, underclerk of Council of State: 1/12, 21

[PRICE], ——, receiver of royal aid for Herefordshire: at Treasury, 8/249

& n. 2

PRICE'S; *see* Taverns etc.

PRICES [omitting tips, and including only those references which give sufficient information to establish a specific price. *See also* Offices, sale of; Theatre; Travel.]

GENERAL: rise of after Fire, 7/277, 280, 310; 8/121, 156; in war, 7/401 & n. 5; 8/98, 187, 296

PARTICULAR:

BOOKS: 1/54, 158, n. 2, 275, 281, 281–2; 2/239; 3/290, 292 & n. 1, 294; 4/33, 178, n. 1; 5/55; 6/101; 7/48; 8/121, 156; 9/85, 161(2), 164, 216, 226, 298, 543, 561; bookbinding, 1/281; 4/240; 9/102, n. 1

COAL: 7/401 & n. 5; 8/98 & n. 5, 187, 296, 435

DRESS (m) [including clothes, materials and accessories]: belt, 2/203; 4/80; boots, 3/204; cane, 5/117; cap, 7/346; cloak, 3/84; 7/208; gloves, ?8/425; gown (Indian), 2/130; 4/391; gown, 8/462; hat, 2/25, 127; periwigs, 4/358, 362, 380; 8/136; 9/217; ribbons, ?9/165, 230; shoes, 3/217; silk, ?6/241; stockings, 4/80; 6/334; suits, 2/83; 5/309–10; 6/114; swords, 4/80; 9/537; vizard, 9/547

DRESS (f) [including clothes, materials and accessories]: gloves, 5/264; ?8/425; gown, 8/498; lace, 2/212; 4/332; 9/6; nightgown, 8/424; petticoat, 1/224; ribbons, ?9/165, 230; scallop, 2/228; 3/216; silk, ?6/241

DRINK: ale, 1/287; beer, 7/131 & n. 2; sack, 9/227; tea, 1/253, n. 5

FOOD: meals: P's dinner parties, 2/22; 4/14; 9/472; christening feast, 4/265; parish dinner, 8/218; Royal Society club dinner, 8/555; at taverns, etc., 2/95, 218; 3/238, 248; 4/216, 300–1; 6/39, 132; 8/211, 461; 9/54, 78, 82, 83, 85, 115, 134, 213, 224, 225, 228, 232, 235, 356, 391; asparagus, 8/173; beef, 2/291; cake, 9/13; cheese, 4/64; cherries, 9/221; eels, 7/166, 281; fowl (roasted), 4/14; lemons, 6/322; oranges, 6/322; 9/133, 163, 195; salmon, 1/88; spices, 6/240

FURNITURE AND FURNISHINGS: cabinet (walnut), 9/405; chairs and couch,

n. 2; accounts, 8/448 & n. 4, 449; 9/445; retrenchments, 8/374 & n. 2, 591; pay, 8/396–7; 9/130; compensation for sunk ship, 9/69; flag-officers' pensions, 9/257; instructions to Sandwich, 3/90; seamen's riot, 4/294; committee acts in Duke of York's absence, 5/315 & n. 1, 318–19, 321, 322, 325, 333, 357–8; criticised by P, 5/332, 333, 357–8; 6/58; standing committee appointed, 9/67 & n. 3; impressment of men and ships, 6/45, 91; 8/290; insurance of cargo, 6/104–5; embezzlement of stores, 6/115 & n. 3, 118; victualling, 6/142, 143; 9/315–18 passim & nn., 429; Marescoe's tar, 6/166 & n. 3; pursers, 7/28; Medway disaster, 8/269, 278–9, 287–8, 317, 396–7, 404, 454, 456, 460, 461, 567, 571; committee for seamen's complaints, 8/297; fitting out merchantmen, 8/316; Carkesse's dismissal, 8/379, 385, 386, 388; design of masts, 9/5–6; acts of war by foreign ships, 9/87–8; calling in fleet, 9/251; Anglesey's complaints, 9/253 & n. 2, 256; tickets, 9/263; supernumeraries, 9/350–1 & n.; also, 8/67

JUDICIAL: Lane v. Hore, 5/324 & nn.; desertion of ship, 8/16 & n. 4; private case, 8/316–17; Buckingham examined, 8/330–1; Barker's case, 8/404, 407, 420–1 & n.; 9/119; Bee's case, 9/259 & n. 2; the Temple's claim to immunity, 9/511–12 & n.; excise disputes, 9/529 & n. 2, 532 & n. 1; Painter-Stainers' case, 9/531–2 & n.

MISC.: parliamentary bills, 3/85 & n. 2; indulgence to Presbyterians, 3/186 & n. 2; plotters examined, 3/241 & n. 2; disorders in Scotland, 4/168–9 & n.; Portuguese customs dues, 5/251 & n. 3; King's new fashion, 7/315 & n. 1; Tangier, 7/321, 336; 9/14–15, 272; poll-tax commissioner committed, 8/252 & n. 2; patent of Canary Company, 8/297 & n. 4; peace terms, 8/328, 329–30, 426; retrenchment, 8/391 & nn., 394–5 & n., 405; treaty with Portugal, 9/59 & n. 3, 222 & n. 4; Anglesey's dismissal, 9/342–3, 344–5; also, 5/58; un-

specified: 4/390; 7/26, 137, 158, 159, 177, 178, 186, 252, 353, 354, 385; 8/67, 80, 86; 9/26, 28, 280

ORDERS IN COUNCIL: constituting Navy Board, 1/191, n. 2, 193; boats for Jamaica, 3/52 & n. 3; ships for Portugal, 3/85 & n. 3; inspection of Victualling Office, 3/135 & n. 3; quarantine regulations in Thames, 4/399 & n. 2; house for Navy Treasury, Broad St, 5/278 & n. 2; impressment, 6/96; building ships, 7/193 & n. 5; re-organising work of Comptroller, 8/20 & n. 2, 24, 25, 30; impressment of ships, 8/260 & n. 2, 291–2 & n.; bankers' assignments, 8/285 & n. 3; petitions to Navy Board, 8/393 & n. 1; government loans, 8/400 & n. 1; enforcing oaths, 8/425 & n. 2; payment of seamen, 8/454 & n. 1; payment of Tangier garrison, 9/14–15 & n.; setting out fleet, 9/25(2) & n. 1; 25–6; payment of navy creditors, 9/152, 153–4; storekeepers' accounts, 9/474 & n. 1; also, 8/219 & n. 3

CABINET [meeting usually on Sundays; also 'cabal', 'cabinet council', 'the Committee for Foreign Affairs', 'King's private council']:

COMPOSITION: 4/138; 5/317; 7/312; 8/585

MEETING PLACES [usually 'at Whitehall' but also]: in the Green Room, Whitehall, 7/260, 311–12; at Secretary's chamber, Whitehall, 9/427; at Lord Chancellor's, 8/21; Lord Treasurer's, 8/138; Lord Keeper's, 9/424–6; Secretary Arlington's, 9/473, 525

BUSINESS: victualling, 6/266, 275; 7/259, 260; state of navy, 7/311–13; Tangier, 7/321, 336; 8/82; 9/492; peace terms, 8/138; preparation of fleet, 9/424, 425–6, 427–8 & n. 1, 473; Sandwich's allowances as ambassador, 9/440 & n. 2; constitution of Navy Board, 9/443, 525–6; supply, 7/311–12; 8/111(2), 111–12, 114; 9/525; unspecified, 5/317; 7/260, 374; 8/21

COUNCIL OF TRADE: (of 1660) proposals for convoys, 2/20 & n. 4; secretary, 5/223; (of 1668) angers Duke of York, 9/549 & n. 2

PRIVY SEAL OFFICE:
GENERAL: warrants issued, 1/197; 3/83;
4/62, 65; 5/61 & n. 1, 79; 6/3, 8; P
examines records, 4/188–9 & n.;
9/474, 477, 478; lack of method,
9/478; also, 1/295
P'S SERVICE IN: appointed Sandwich's
deputy, 1/205 & n. 3, 206, 207; begins
work, 1/208, 212; attends by the
month, 1/218–19, 235, 303; 2/226;
busy, 1/213, 218–19, 232; 2/235; 3/61;
idle in King's absence from town,
1/227, 229, 230; alleged error, 1/245 &
n. 2; issues free pardons, 1/310, 312,
316, 317, 320; attends sealing-day,
2/149, 150, 156, 159, 186, 187, 229,
232; misses Navy Board meeting,
2/177; fees: amounts, 1/213 & n. 1,
219, 225, 233, 320; 2/2, 3; divided between Sandwich, P and Moore, 1/237,
238 & n. 4; 2/63, 64; 4/378; decrease,
1/262; 3/80; table of, 2/209, 214; unspecified business, 1/214, 216, 217,
220, 221, 223, 224, 228, 231, 307, 318,
320; 2/64, 66, 79, 149, 150, 153, 157,
171, 175, 177, 199–200, 226, 228, 236;
3/66, 83; official stall in Whitehall
Chapel, 3/67; ?5/96; resigns, 3/168;
also, 1/173; 2/234; 3/66
PRIZE OFFICE, Whitehall: commissioners appointed, 5/322, 327 &
n. 2, 328, 333; T. Hill assistant secretary, 6/21; officers dismissed, 7/78 &
n. 1; sale of goods at, 8/14, 16; new
office in Aldersgate St, 8/16; case
before special commissioners, 8/231 &
n. 2
PRIZES and privateers:
PRIZES:
   GENERAL: act against breaking bulk,
   3/118 & n. 2; revenue from, 7/130,
   317; 8/446 & n. 3; dividends, 8/23–4
   & n.
   PRIZE-GOODS TAKEN BY SANDWICH
   1665 [see also Cocke, G.; Cuttance,
   R.; Howe, W.; Sandwich; Penn]:
   capture of Dutch E. Indiamen, 6/223,
   226; cargoes rifled, 6/230–1 & n. 1;
   goods stored, 6/236; navy's share of
   proceeds, 6/239 & n. 1; sold by E.
   India Company, 6/273 & n. 3, 280–1;
   P joins with Cocke to buy goods,
   6/230, 238–42 passim, 244; P's profit,

6/231 & n. 1, 243, 245; advice from
broker, 6/250, 254; 7/140; clears
customs, 6/247, 256, 258; sells out to
Cocke, 6/314, 327, 328, 341; enquiries
by Brooke House Committee (and P's
defence), 9/48–53 passim, 57, 61, 72,
118, 163; his narrative, 9/64 & n. 2,
68; also, 6/271–2; 7/6, 65, 80, 305;
8/531
   OTHER PRIZES: Dutch ships, 5/341 &
   n. 1; 7/224, 249, 250, 251 & n. 3,
   296–7 & n.; French, 7/350 & n. 1, 352;
   9/160; Ostender, 9/96, 97 & n. 1;
   goods sold contrary to order, 8/14,
   15–16 & nn., 20 & n. 2, 58, 144;
   Rupert's licence for discovery of
   stolen goods, 8/52; ships sold, 8/484 &
   n. 3, 485
   PRIVATEERS [see also Algiers; Ostend;
   Tangier; Tunis]:
   The Flying Greyhound: lent to P,
   Batten and Penn, 7/299, 300–1 & n.;
   to trade with Madeira, 7/316; prizes:
   at Plymouth, 8/115–16 & n.; Hull,
   8/341 & n. 3, 344, 345, 349, 351–2,
   369, 385 & n. 2; Newcastle, 8/435; in
   Holland, 9/117; *St John Baptist,* 9/147;
   other ships: 7/418, 424; 8/1, 7, 8; dispute with Swedish resident, 8/17, 21–
   4 passim & nn., 27, 123 & n. 1, 130 &
   n. 2, 133–6 passim, 169, 180, 181, 231;
   P calculates dividends, 8/232; 9/147;
   sells out to Batten, 8/341, 385; settles
   with Batten's widow, 8/462, 477, 483,
   561, 569, 579, 582, 584; and with
   Duke of York, 9/290, 298; asked to
   lend to government from profits,
   8/392, 393; accused of favouring
   ship's seamen in pays, 9/99; also,
   7/360; 8/135, 159, 579; alluded to:
   9/168
   OTHERS: French caper, 8/162; Scottish, 8/200; Rupert's *Panther* and
   Fanfan, 8/341
PROBY, [Peter], son [-in-law] of Sir
R. Ford: 4/354
PROCTOR, [William], landlord of
the Mitre, Wood St [see also Taverns
etc.]: with son dies of plague, 6/175–6
& n.
PROGER, [Edward], Groom of the
Bedchamber to the King: influence,
5/56; news from, 8/429–30 & n.;

against Rupert (1648), 5/169 & n. 1; 8/306

RICHARDS, ——, tailor: 9/218

RICHARDSON, [Sir Thomas], Chief Justice, King's Bench (d. 1635): anecdote of, 8/428–9 & n.

RICHARDSON, [William], bookbinder: work for P, 7/243, 303–4, 307; 8/237, 551; 9/24, 32, 46, 547–8; also, 8/71; 9/43

RICHMOND, Duke/Dowager Duchess/Duchess of: see Stuart, Charles/Mary/Frances Teresa

RICHMOND, Surrey: P visits, 3/81; 6/154; Lady Castlemaine at, 3/139; 4/238

RIDER, Sir William, hemp merchant, kted 1661:

NAVY BOARD BUSINESS: consulted about provisioning ships, 2/62; hemp contract, 3/114 & n. 1, 116, 129–30; to insure ship, 4/394, 395, 398; quarrels with Cocke, 5/51; contract for tar and canvas, 5/136 & n. 3, 352; hemp business, 6/77; payments to Carteret, 6/191; also, 4/343; 6/256

TANGIER: appointed to committee, 3/238; helps draft civil constitution, 4/89 & n. 1; and examine Peterborough's accounts, 5/48, 105, 123, 132; at meetings, 3/272; 4/83, 320, 335; 5/11, 97, 124, 135, 139; also, 5/212; 7/65

TRINITY HOUSE: Deputy-Master for Sandwich, 3/18, 29; Batten's attempt to make him Master, 6/107; blamed for sinking ships, 8/270–1; dinners, 5/15, 94, 186; also, 2/4, 26

HIS HOUSE AT BETHNAL GREEN: P admires, 4/200 & n. 5; sends valuables in Fire, 7/272, 282, 283

SOCIAL: dines with P, 1/14; 5/62; gives dinner, 4/200; at taverns, 5/341; 6/25, 83, 145; also, 5/255

MISC.: stories of Genoa, 3/7–8 & nn.; 4/201; Chatham Chest, 3/257; 7/110; arbitrates in dispute, 4/426; 5/15, 19, 36; his rise alluded to, 5/52; diary, 5/98; ill, 5/159; fears issue of war, ib.; Fishery business, 5/336; opposes building of New London, 6/170

ALLUDED to: 2/193

~ his wife [Priscilla], 4/200

RIDER, Mr ——, merchant: 4/247

RIGA, Latvia (Sweden): yarn/cordage from, 3/101 & n. 3, 5/182; hemp, 4/49, 259 & n. 4

RIGGS, ——, servant to Albemarle: 7/203

RINGSTEAD'S: see Taverns etc.: Star, Cheapside

RIOTS: see Law and Order, offences against

ROBARTES, Sir John, 2nd Baron Robartes, cr. Earl of Radnor 1679; Lord Privy Seal 1661–73 (d. 1685):

CHARACTER: 2/149, 150; 5/73; 8/450

AS LORD PRIVY SEAL: introduces register of fees, 2/214; refuses P a deputy, 3/61; refuses to seal royal pardon, 9/52 & nn.; affixes seal, 2/150, 158, 187, 232–3, 234, 237; 6/83, 84; at Chelsea house, 2/158, 187, 201, 234, 237; unspecified business, 2/228; out of town, 2/170, 171, 175, 236; also, 2/214; 3/66, 168

OTHER APPOINTMENTS ETC.: Treasury Commissioner, 1/170 & n. 3; Lord Deputy of Ireland, 1/227–8 & n.; to be Lord-Lieutenant, 9/452 & n. 2; in cabal, 8/585; 9/427

HOUSES ETC.: Whitehall chamber, 2/150; in Chelsea: P admires, 2/187–8 & n.; visits on Privy Seal business, 2/158, 187, 199, 201, 234, 237; pictures, 2/187; 6/84

SOCIAL: 8/450

ALLUDED TO: 3/66, 168

~ his wife [Laetitia], 9/176, 177 & n. 1; his daughter [Laetitia Isabella], 9/176 & n. 4

ROBARTES, Robert, son of the foregoing: case in Chancery, 5/140 & n. 1; ~ his wife [Sara]: her inheritance, 5/140 & n. 1; P admires, 6/84; 9/176–7; portrait, 6/84

ROBERT, Prince: see Rupert

[ROBERT, Anthony], dancing master: 9/507

[ROBERTS, William], Bishop of Bangor 1637–d. 65: 1/259 & n. 3

ROBERTS, [William], merchant, of St Olave's parish: ship, 8/293 & n. 2

ROBERTS'S: see Taverns etc.: Harp and Ball

ROBINS, [?Judy]: 6/187, 202

ROBINS, Tony, of Westminster: 1/92
ROBINS, Monsieur ——, periwig-
maker and proprietor of ordinary,
Covent Garden: 8/211
ROBINSON, [Anne], Lady Robinson,
wife of Sir John: admired by P, 5/67;
6/290; 7/415; by Cocke, 6/290;
wanton speech, 6/290; 7/415; social:
6/268
ROBINSON, [Henry], merchant and
author (d. ?1673): claims management of Post Office, 7/375 & n. 2
ROBINSON, Ald. Sir John, Lieutenant of the Tower 1660–79; M.P.
London 1660, Rye, Sussex 1661–79;
Lord Mayor 1662–3:
CHARACTER: P's low opinion, 4/77–8 &
n.; 5/12, 307; 6/299; 8/201; love of
food and wine, 7/38
AS LIEUTENANT OF TOWER: account of
Vane's trial and execution, 3/103–4 &
n., 116; allows search for treasure,
3/241 & n. 1, 242, 286; consulted on
exemptions from militia service, 6/24
& n. 3; and on pressed men, 7/200;
arranges coal supplies for poor, 6/264
& n. 3, 265(2); shirks duties in Dutch
raid, 8/266; also, 4/294; 8/278, 299,
394
AS ALDERMAN AND LORD MAYOR: boasts
of influence, 4/77; 5/307 & n. 2; plans
new street, 4/77; 8/201; precept about
coachmen, 4/77–8 & n.; disapproves
of Principal Officers of Navy as city
magistrates, 4/78; revives ceremonial
at Bartholomew Fair, 4/288 & n. 2
SOCIAL: as Lieutenant of Tower: entertains King, 1/214 & n. 3; Navy Board,
2/51; 5/316; Holmes (on his release),
6/56; Albemarle, 6/268; as Lord
Mayor: at Trinity House, 3/103, 187;
entertains customs farmers, 4/341;
other occasions: P dines with, 4/70,
294–5; 5/67; enjoyment of hunting,
6/295; and singing, 6/311–12; dines
with P, 9/410–11; also, 7/11–12,
38, 226, 299; 9/108, 543
MISC.: house in Mincing Lane, 3/241;
news from, 5/333; 7/268; quarrels
with Capt. J. Taylor, 6/56 & n. 3, 295;
as M.P., 9/92–3, 193
ALLUDED TO: 8/394
~ his son [John], 7/268

ROBINSON, Luke, M.P. Scarbor-
ough, Yorks. 1645–8, 1660: delegate
to Monck, 1/51–2 & n.; royalist
speech, 1/122 & n. 2
ROBINSON, Capt. [Robert], kted
1675, naval officer: action against
Dutch, 7/424 & n. 3
[ROBINSON, Robert, painter]: *see*
Rogerson
ROBINSON, ——, cook: 2/102 & n. 3
ROBSON [Robinson], [Thomas],
clerk to Sir W. Coventry: 7/244;
9/87, 169
ROCHE, DE LA [Peter], dentist: 2/53
& n. 1; 4/97
ROCHESTER, Kent: P visits/passes
through, 1/172; 2/68, 70, 72; 3/156;
6/182, 241–2, 249; 8/311; burning of
figurehead, 4/420; bridge, 1/172 & n.
5; 8/306; 9/11; cathedral, 2/70 & nn.;
8/311; castle, 6/249 & nn.; 8/311;
Salutation tavern, 2/70; Crown inn,
3/153 & n. 1; 6/241–2, 249; 8/307;
White Hart inn, 8/311, 312; cherry
gardens, 8/312; alluded to: 2/15, 55,
57, 67; 6/256; 7/162; 9/50
RODER: *see* Rothe
ROETTIER(S) (Rotyr), [John], engraver to the Mint: bust of King on
coins, 4/70 & n. 3; his dies, 4/147 &
n. 2; engraves Navy Board seal,
7/82–3; Breda medal, 8/83 & n. 1;
P admires his work, 4/147; 8/83
ROGERS, [?Matthew], of St
Margaret's parish, Westminster: 1/47
ROGERS, ——: 9/58–9
ROGERSON [?Robinson, Robert],
painter: 9/420 & n. 1
ROLLS CHAPEL: *see* Chancery
ROLT, Capt. [Edward], Gentleman of
the Bedchamber to Oliver Cromwell:
his former greatness, 2/108 & n. 1;
P's admiration, 8/29; cornet, 8/323 &
n. 1; building works in Whitehall,
9/302 & n. 1; social: sings with Mrs
Knepp, 6/320–1, 323; 9/166; and
Harris, 9/175; at dance at Navy
Office, 8/28, 29; at taverns, 2/119, 120;
9/186, 220; also, 2/121; 7/2, 100;
8/51, 172–3, 575; 9/203, 218–19
ROMAN CATHOLICISM [*see also*
Religion (P)]:
STATUS OF/OFFICIAL POLICY TOWARDS:

Catholics befriended by Duke of York, 2/38; long exclusion from office, 4/196; loyalty in Civil War, 7/394; arrest of priest, 4/44; King's Declaration of Indulgence (Dec. 1662), 4/44 & n. 2, 66; Commons fear admission to office, 4/50 & n. 3, 57; 7/343 & n. 5, 354; 8/6; bill and address against indulgence, 4/67–8 & n., 90 & n. 1, 92 & n. 3, 95 & n. 2, 249; book against, 4/111 & n. 2; accused of causing Fire, 7/343 & n. 4, 356–7 & n.; 8/439 & n. 4; fear of further plots, 7/360, 363, 364–5 & n.; 8/264, 269–70; 9/208; proclamation against, 7/343, n.5; order in council, 8/425 & n. 2, 476 & n. 2; Commons address, 9/104
SERVICES: at ambassadors' chapels, 2/102 & n. 2; 5/103; 9/319; Somerset House, 5/63; 9/319; Queen's Chapel, 3/202; 5/63; 7/87, 99, 107; 8/116, 588–9; 9/319; private baptism, 7/329–30; also, 7/94, 97
RELIGIOUS ORDERS: laymen's dress worn by Capuchins, 7/329; Friary at St James's Palace, 8/26–7 & n.; Jesuit to preach at Queen's chapel, 7/94; Jesuit influence in Holy Roman Empire, 4/350 & n. 2; anecdote of Spanish friar, 8/67
MISC.: prohibited degrees of matrimony, 7/329; converts from, 8/99; sermons against, ?1/32; 4/98 & n. 1; 8/587 & n. 3
ROME: Spanish guide-book, 1/49 & n. 4; Corraro's book on, 4/425 & n. 3; print of triumphal column in, 7/102–3 & n.; building works, 8/26 & n. 1; music, 8/26; painting by Danckerts, 9/504, 539; also, 6/177; alluded to: 6/13; 8/56, 336
ROOTH, Capt. [Richard], naval officer: gift to P, 2/23; child christened, 2/110; ill, 3/91; alluded to: 4/205; ~ ?his wife, 3/19; 4/45
ROS (Roos, Rosse), de: disputed barony, 8/22 & n. 3
ROSSE, Alexander: imprisoned for forgery, 2/73 & n. 3
ROTA CLUB, the: P's entry fee, 1/13 & n. 3; attends meetings, 1/14, 24, 61; debates on government, 1/17, 20–1

ROTHE (Roder), John/Johannes; kted Aug. 1660: marriage, 1/190 & n. 2, 196, 215; 7/203; sails to Holland, 1/216, 219
ROTHERHITHE [see also Taverns etc.: Half-way House]: P visits/passes through, 1/262; 2/12, 45, 112; 3/124, 128, 149, 160, 185, 188, 192, 214; 4/79, 151, 175, 233, 234, 296, 386; 5/47, 95; 6/40, 95, 158, 206; 7/69, 112, 114, 134, 176, 249; 8/39, 165, 325, 351; 9/25, 29, 468, 469; ship at, 4/23; launch, 5/353 & n. 3; plague, 6/163, 201; church (St Mary's) flooded, 7/4 & n. 6; burial, 9/200; Cherry Garden, 5/178, 180; Half-way tree, 3/95
ROTHERHITHE STAIRS: 5/29
ROTYR: see Roettier(s)
ROUEN (Roane): Charles II at, 1/156
ROULLES (Reulé), [Pierre], curé of St Barthélemy, Paris (d. 1666): sermon, 5/103 & n. 4
ROUNDTREE, [Ralph]: 2/118 & n. 1
ROUSE, Mr ——, ?tailor to the Queen: 4/245–6
ROWE, John, Independent divine (d. 1677): farewell sermon, 1/251–2 & n.
[ROWLEY, John], Vicar of Brampton, Hunts. (d. 1688): 8/471 & n. 5; ~ his wife, ib.
'ROXALANA': see Davenport
ROYAL AFRICA (Guinea) COMPANY, the [see also African House]: projected, 1/258 & n. 2; arms and motto, 4/152–3; election of assistants, 5/11; Duke of York criticises members, 5/300 & n. 4; forts overrun, 5/352–3 & n.; government negotiates with Dutch on its behalf, 8/426–7 & n.; petition in parliament against, 8/551 & n. 5; its five-guinea pieces, 9/313 & n. 4; Duke of York's business with, 9/350; meetings, 4/335; 5/48, 199–200; 8/181; P studies contract books, 5/14; dines with members, 5/52, 66, 124; also, 4/432 & n. 2
ROYAL EXCHANGE, the (the Exchange, the Old Exchange):
CHRON. SERIES: cartoon hung, 1/45; statue of Charles I, 1/89 & n. 3, 99, 113; Commonwealth legislation

for Council, 7/96 & n. 2; 8/553; Councillor, vol. i, p. xxxix; 7/96, n. 2; President (1684–6), ib.; subscribes to new building, 9/146; pays dues, 9/165 & n. 4
MEETINGS: visitors at, 8/11; Duchess of Newcastle, 8/243 & nn.; meeting day changed, 8/242–3; vacation, 9/334; club meetings, 6/36; 7/148
SUBJECTS OF MEETINGS/DEMONSTRA-TIONS: P lacks 'philosophy' to under-stand, 6/48; effects of heat on glass, 5/123 & n. 3; viol with keyboard, 5/290 & n. 3; French bread, 6/48 & n. 3; comets, ib. & n. 1; effects of poison on dog, 6/57 & n. 1; of vacuum on kitten, 6/64 & n. 1; of poison on hen, dog and cat, 6/84 & n. 4, 95–6; design of coaches, 6/94 & n. 2; human foetus, 6/96 & n. 1; felt making, 7/51 & n. 3; blood transfusion, 7/370–1 & n., 373, 389; 8/543 & n. 1, 554 & n. 4; gun-powder, 8/11 & n. 1; lodestones, microscopes etc., 8/243 & n. 3; re-fraction of light, 8/555; 9/113 & n. 5; otacousticon, 9/146 & n. 3; circulation of blood, 9/263 & n. 1; elections, 7/96; 8/553; 9/379; unspecified subjects, 6/41, 52, 112; 7/21, 43, 79, 147; 8/17, 528, 540–1; 9/334
OFFICERS: the operator, 9/337
ROYSTON, HERTS.: 3/224; 8/268
RUBENS: engravings after, 1/194 & n. 5; work at Nonsuch House (attrib. to), 6/235 & n. 3
RUDDIARD (Ruddyer), [Thomas], of the Excise Office: 1/33, 192; 2/50
RUMBOLD (Rumball), [Henry, jun.]: ?7/23
RUMBOLD (Rumball), [William], Clerk of the Great Wardrobe: his claret, 1/277; son's christening, 2/230 & n. 2; also, 1/301; 3/2; 4/69; ?7/23; ~ his wife, 3/2; 8/369–70 & n.
RUNDELL(S), [Edward], house car-penter at Deptford and Woolwich yards: sends P blackbird, 4/150; over-charges for wharf, 4/284 & n. 2
RUPERT, Prince ('the Prince', Prince Robert), Privy Councillor and naval commander:
CHARACTER: 1/255; 5/169–70, 304; 6/12, 139; 7/332

CHRON. SERIES: defence of Bristol (1645), 5/169–70 & n.; leads mutiny at Newark (1645), 6/30–1 & n.; at court for first time, 1/255 & n. 2; made Privy Councillor, 3/75; at Council committee for navy, 9/152; at Cabinet, 9/525; rumoured to have pox, 6/12; portrait by Lely, 7/102 & n. 3; ill of head wound, 8/15, 16, 38; operated on, 8/34–5, 40, 41 & n. 4, 45, 46–7, 52, 58, 145–6; granted licence for stolen prize-goods, 8/52, 531; privateers, 8/341, 342, 344, 349, 385
AS NAVAL COMMANDER: jealous of Batten (1648), 5/169 & n. 1; given command, 5/183, 258; in *Henrietta*, 5/262; refuses to command whole fleet, ib.; sails to Downs, 5/264, 291, 295; returns to Portsmouth, 5/301; fears attack by Dutch, 5/304; in Battle of Lowestoft, 6/121, 122, 127, 135, 137, 146; refuses joint command with Sandwich, 6/148; parliamentary grant proposed, 6/291; relations with Sand-wich, 6/276, 291; 8/117; new com-mand, 6/323, 342; 7/108, 109; responsibility for dividing fleet before Four Days Fight, 7/139 & n. 3, 141, 143–4 & n., 149; 8/489; 9/70; conduct in, 7/147, 148, 158, 160; sails again, 7/210, 210–11; reputation declines, 7/212, 213–14, 231, 299, 340, 349–50, 354; conduct in St James's Day Fight, 7/225, 344–5; blames Navy Board for victualling deficiencies, 7/172, 259 & n. 1, 260, 263, 264, 312–13; 8/315, 511–12, 513; 9/107; differences with Albemarle, 7/315, 323; his 'narrative' in self-defence, 8/511–12 & n., 513, 514–15, 518, 571; thanked by Com-mons for services, 8/499 & n. 2; appointments to fleet, 9/5–6, 39, 75–6; favours small fleet, 9/121–2, 216; hopes of command frustrated, 9/126, 140, 148, 216; offended by Penn's appointment, 9/125, 126, 131, 140; supports Heemskerck's ship-design, 9/206; also, 8/496
TANGIER: appointed to committee, 3/238; attends meetings, 3/272; 5/167; 7/321; frivolous behaviour, 5/167
SOCIAL: at court ball, 7/372; at theatre, 8/196

MISC.: perspective machine, 7/51 & n.
4; recalls Mother Shipton's prophecy
of Fire, 7/333 & n. 2; plays tennis,
8/418–19; also, 9/302, 474
RUSHWORTH, [John], public servant under the Commonwealth and
historian (d. 1690) [*see also* Books]:
news from, 4/377
RUSSELL, [Elizabeth], widow of
Robert: gifts to EP, 4/409, 415; 5/62;
also, 4/268
RUSSELL, Francis, 2nd Earl of Bed-
ford: anecdote of, 2/114–15 & n.
RUSSELL, Henry, waterman to the
Navy Board: 4/225, 405; 5/176, 317;
8/400; 9/300, 492; also, 6/223; 8/292
RUSSELL, Col. [John]: at court ball,
7/372
RUSSELL, [Robert], ship's chandler:
funeral, 4/21 & nn.
RUSSELL, Maj. [Robert], of Salisbury
Court: 7/173
RUSSELL, Sir William, Navy Treas-
urer under Charles I (d. 1654): daugh-
ter's marriage, 4/244 & n. 4
RUSSELL, ——: gift to P, 8/19
RUSSIA: stories of, 5/272 & nn.; em-
bassies from, 3/267–8 & n., 274, 297;
4/4 & n. 2, 175; 8/428 & n. 2
RUSSIA HOUSE, Moorfields, a
brothel: 8/319, 320, 321
RUTHERFORD, Andrew, Baron
Rutherford, cr. Earl of Teviot 1663;
Governor of Tangier 1663–d. 64:
CHARACTER: 4/102, 269, 408; 5/170,
180; 8/307
CHRON. SERIES: service in French army,
5/170 & n. 2; and at Dunkirk, 8/348;
appointment to Tangier, 3/282–3 &
n.; 4/85; departure, 4/26, 31, 75, 106;
commission, 4/75, 83, 116 & n.; wants
profits of victualling, 4/27; as contractor for mole, 4/88 & n. 3; quarrels
with committee, 4/102, 115–16; beats
off Moors' attacks, 4/240 & n. 5, 283;
makes truce with, 4/283 & n. 1;
accounts, 4/269–70, 273, 320, 324,
326–7, 408; killed in ambush, 5/165 &
n. 2, 166 & n. 4, 167 & n. 1, 179–80;
administration criticised, 4/116;
5/275–6; 6/18; 8/348; 9/294; also,
4/319
RUTHERFORD, Sir Thomas, 2nd

Baron Rutherford (d. 1668): settles
1st Baron's accounts, 5/339; 6/95,
221 & n. 2, 242(2), 250; 7/65; 8/360;
gift to P, 6/250; ~ his wife [Chris-
tian], 6/250 & n. 4
RUYTER, Michiel Adriaanszoon de,
naval commander (d. 1676): voyage
to Mediterranean and W. Africa,
5/121 & n. 2, 181, 309; successes in
Guinea, 5/352–3 & n., 355 & n. 1;
alleged atrocities, 6/42 & n. 1, 43, 46;
returns, 6/146, 157, 178, 184 & n. 2,
186; in Four Days Fight, 7/147, 180;
and St James's Day Fight, 7/227;
(untrue) rumours of death, 7/228, 291,
300; and disgrace, 7/229 & n. 4, 231,
234; wounded, 7/291; also, 8/359
RYE, Sussex: 2/142, 163
RYLEY, [William], sen., Lancaster
Herald, Keeper of the Records in the
Tower (d. 1667): 5/149 & n. 1
RYLEY, [William], jun., son of the
foregoing; Deputy-Keeper of the
Records in the Tower (d. 1675):
criticises Prynne as Keeper of Records,
5/149 & n. 1

SABBATH OBSERVANCE:
GENERAL: taverns etc. closed during
service hours, 1/270; 6/5; 9/86; Bishop
of London's injunctions, 3/196 &
n. 3; strict observance, 3/252; proclamation enforcing, 4/313 & n. 2
BY P: ashamed to string lute, 1/270; to
read French romances, 2/35; to make
up accounts, 2/67; to compose
'ayres', 3/26; refrains from singing
'ordinary' songs, 8/346; reduces
Hewer's punishment out of respect
for, 4/166; travels by boat for first
time, 1/206 & n. 1; has Sandwich's
permit for land travel, 4/313; reserves
for extra work, 5/131, 183
BY OTHERS: Creed abandons rule
against tavern visits, 2/99; Hayter
objects to work, 7/293; Warwick
reluctant to discuss business, 8/32;
courtiers play cards, 8/33, 70
SACKVILLE, Charles, styled Lord
Buckhurst, succ. as 9th Earl of Dorset
1677: acquitted of manslaughter, 3/34
& n. 4, 35–6; 4/210; indecent frolics,
4/210; 9/335–6, 338–9; his part in

ST JAMES'S PALACE [Apartments occupied by individuals are indexed elsewhere under their names. P's visits on business are omitted.]: friary, 8/26–7 & nn.; gallery, 8/459; matted gallery, 8/181; guard, 1/38; Queen's chapel, services [*see also* Music: church; Sermons]: 3/202 & n. 1; 4/130; 5/63, 188; 7/87, 97, 99, 384; 8/116, 154, 427, 588–9; 9/126, 319, 515; also, 7/94

ST JAMES'S PARK [*see also* Gardens: Physic; Pall Mall]:

GENERAL: Echo, 1/38, 58; keeper 1/206; lake and canal, 1/246 & n. 2, 263–4; 2/51, 156, 171; 3/147; 7/207; gondolas, 2/177 & n. 5; inward park, 1/206; aviary, 2/157; skating, 3/272, 277, 282; riding, 3/288; sliding on lake, 4/37; hunting, 5/239; gates locked, 5/254; 6/147; Gravel Pits, 7/145; naval guns allegedly heard, 7/145, 150

PALL MALL (Pell Mell; the alley for the game): 1/246 & n. 2; keeper, 4/135; Duke of York plays, 2/64; 9/542; others play, 5/4; P/members of court stroll in, 4/229, 251–2; 5/55; 7/39, 61; 8/32–3, 92, 431; 9/319, 465; duel in, 3/171

P WALKS/MEETS FRIENDS IN [omitting occasions on which he merely passes through]: 1/53, 58, 80; 2/51, 62; 3/81, 147, 202, 208; 4/24, 70, 73, 100, 131, 135, 142, 158, 189, 192, 197, 203, 204, 229, 274, 288; 5/50, 55, 63, 102, 104, 133, 163, 174, 181, 186, 188, 198, 212, 215; 6/3, 34, 46, 60, 83, 199, 293; 7/5, 39, 46, 61, 84, 87, 97, 100, 107, 116, 148, 215, 216, 221, 223, 231, 240, 248, 265, 271, 375, 411; 8/21, 26, 32, 41, 43, 117–18, 128, 148, 210, 239, 374, 378, 427, 431, 464, 507; 9/105, 118, 151, 223, 256, 294, 295, 309, 319, 320, 401, 414, 415, 465, 483, 504, 515, 518(2), 560, 562; sleeps on grass, 7/207

KING/DUKE OF YORK AND OTHERS IN: watch waterfowl, 3/47; 8/68; Duke speaks to P, 3/47; 9/415; skates, 3/282; borrows P's cloak, 9/155; King speaks to P, 7/146; 9/105, 415; rides with Knights of the Garter, 8/184–5; Queen Mother in, 4/229; Queen in,

5/188; also, 1/173; 3/60; 4/251–2; 7/217; 8/507; 9/415

ST JOHN, Oliver (Lord St John), lawyer and politician (d. 1673): for free parliament, 1/44–5 & n.; defends Richard Cromwell, 1/74 & n. 6; emissary to King, 1/131, 132; at church, 3/220 & n. 1

[ST JOHN] RIVER, Nova Scotia: mining near, 8/426 & n. 1

ST JOHN (Jones), Clerkenwell, church of: 7/75

[ST JOHN THE BAPTIST'S DAY]: 9/249 & n. 3

ST JOHN'S ISLE [?Patmos]: P dreams about, 4/43

ST JOHN ST, Clerkenwell [*see also* Taverns etc.: Bottle of Hay; Theatre: Red Bull]: Newcastle's house, 8/197

ST KATHARINE, precinct of: 3/111; 4/350; 5/158 & n. 4; 6/278; 9/488

ST KATHARINE'S [STAIRS]: 6/278

ST KITT'S, Leeward Is.: French capture, 7/171 & n. 3; expedition to, 7/390 & n. 3

ST LAWRENCE JEWRY, church of: P admires, 6/34

ST LAWRENCE POULTNEY, church of: destroyed in Fire, 7/269; also, 7/235

ST MAGNUS, church of: destroyed in Fire, 7/268

ST MALO (Mellos), France: guard dogs, 7/133 & n. 1

ST MARGARET (Margetts), Westminster, church of: common prayer at, 1/215; House of Commons receives communion, 2/107; gallery, 8/236; sermons, 1/237; 7/123, 316; also, 7/142, 231; 8/167, 255, 400; 9/98–9, 168, 548; parish bellman, 1/19

ST MARGARET'S (Margetts), nr Chatham, Kent: P visits, 9/495

ST MARGARET'S HILL, Southwark: 4/76

ST MARTIN-IN-THE-FIELDS, parish of: plague in, 6/289, 304

ST MARTIN-INFRA-LUDGATE: 2/74

ST MARTIN-LE-GRAND [usually St Martin's]: 2/132; 6/332

[ST MARTIN OUTWICH] church of: P attends service, 7/235

SALISBURY COURT [*see also* Taverns etc.: Standing's; Theatre]: Fire in, 7/386; also, 3/99; 4/427
SALISBURY, Wilts.: P visits, 9/228–31; Siamese twins, 5/319; court at during Plague, 6/189, 221, 243; assizes, 8/428; George Inn, 9/228 & n. 6, 229, 230; Cathedral and close, 9/229, 230 & n.; Bishop's Palace, 9/229 & n. 3; alluded to: 9/529
SALISBURY PLAIN, Wilts.: 9/229, 231, 497
SALLI, (Sally), N. Africa: English interest in, 4/336 & n. 1
SALMON: *see* Soulemont
SALSBURY, ——, painter: P admires his work, 2/59, 145; miniature of Sandwich, 2/23 & n. 2; shows P portraits, 2/59; also, 1/195, 264; 3/80
SALTONSTALL ('Sanderson'), Lady Saltonstall: killed in storm, 3/32 & n. 4
[SALVIATI, Marchese Giovanni Vincenzo], Tuscan ambassador March –Sept. 1661: state entry, 2/55 & n. 3; first audience, 2/57 & n. 3
SALWEY (Salloway), [Maj. Richard], M.P. Appleby, Westmorland (d. 1685): suspended and imprisoned by Rump, 1/21 & n. 2
SAMFORD, Mr —— [? Samuel Sandford, Commonwealth official]: 1/244, 248
SANDERS: *see* Saunders
SANDERSON, Bridget, Lady Sanderson, (b. Tyrrell), wife of Sir William, Mother of the Maids of Honour to the Queen c. 1662–d. 82: 3/83 & n. 6
[SANDERSON, Robert], Bishop of Lincoln 1660–d.63: consecrated, 1/276 & n. 2
SANDERSON, [Sir William], historian, relative of P: book on Charles I, 1/132 & n. 4; travels to Charles II in Holland, 1/132, 133
'SANDERSON', Lady: *see* Saltonstall
[SANDFORD]: *see* Samford
SAN DOMINGO, Hispaniola: 9/556 & n. 1
SANDWICH, Earl and Countess of: *see* Mountagu, Edward and Jemima
SANDYS (Sands), Col. [Samuel],

M.P. Worcestershire (d. 1685): 8/583
SANDYS (Sands), [William], M.P. Evesham, Worcs. (d. 1669): congratulates P on parliamentary speech, 9/105
SANDYS, [William], 6th Baron Sandys (d. 1669): 8/381 & n. 4; ~ his wife [Mary], (b. Cecil, d. 1667), ib.
SANKEY (Zanchy), [Clement], Fellow of Magdalene College, 1660–?9; Rector of St Clement Eastcheap 1666–1707; drinks King's health, 1/67, 68; marriage, 2/220 & n. 4; appointed to living, 8/17 & n. 5; high repute, 8/151; social: in Cambridge, 1/69; 2/136, 146; at theatre, 2/219, 226; 3/58; also, 2/225; 5/135; 8/167
SANSUM, Rear-Adm. [Robert], naval commander: killed in action, 6/122, 129
SANTHUNE, Mary de (b. Pepys), wife of Samuel: legacy, 4/344–5 & n., 346 & n. 3, 351; marriage portion, 4/344–5, 346; death, 8/590 & n. 4, 601
[SANTHUNE, Samuel de], P's relative: repays debt, 5/342 & n. 4; also, 4/307; 5/303
SANTIAGO (St Jago), Cuba: captured, 4/41 & n. 5, 54, 94
SAUNDERS, Capt. [Francis], naval officer: bravery in Four Days Fight, 7/148
[SAUNDERS, Capt. Joseph], naval officer: killed in action, 7/231, n. 4
SAUNDERS, ——, musician, of Cambridge: dies in Plague, 8/468 & n. 4
SAUNDERS (Sanders), ——, porter: 7/185; 8/264, 272
SAUNDERS. Capt. [? Gabriel], naval officer: on pursers, 5/202
SAUNDERSON, Mary, ('Ianthe'): *see* Betterton
SAVAGE, Sir Edward, Gentleman of the Privy Chamber to the King: 8/220; 9/280 & n. 2
SAVILE, Sir George, Viscount Halifax, cr. Marquess of Halifax 1682, politician (d. 1695): created baron and viscount, 9/2 & n. 5; on Brooke House Committee, 9/254, 255; rumoured duel with Buckingham, 9/462; visits Coventry in Tower, 9/468 & n. 3

SUBJECTS: Gal., iv, 4, 1/3; life of Christ, 1/11; authority of St Peter, 1/32; 1 John, iii. 1, 1/42; widowhood, 1/60; commandments, 1/68; charity, 1/76; Ezra, vi. 10, 1/91; Christian duty, 1/97; stewardship, 1/220; 'The Lord is my Shield', 1/237; 'Teach us the old way', ib.; 1 Cor., ix. 24, 1/251; war, 2/37; drunkenness, 2/42; evil imaginings, 2/48; love, 2/74; patience, 2/98; the Restoration, 2/109; Acts, iii. 21, 2/161; Grace, 2/211; 8/381; church music and behaviour in church, 2/215; 5/172; Jas., i. 17, 2/219; miraculous appearance of the Virgin and St John, 2/239 & n. 4; redemption, 3/12–13; regicide, 3/20; 'Cast thy bread upon the waters', 3/21; Micah, i. 10, 3/42; godliness, 3/60; Gal., v. 13, 3/70; John, iv. 14, 3/84; peace, 3/167; Psalms, i. 1, 3/182; uniformity, 3/190; resurrection, 3/270; frivolity at court, 3/292; David and Saul, 4/29; Josh., xxxiv. 5, 4/36–7; sowing and reaping, 4/69; nonconformity, 4/92–3, 185; temptation, 4/98; popery, 4/98 & n. 1; 8/587; brotherly love, 4/112; John, xv. 14, 4/259; Lot's wife, 4/268; Jas., iii. 17, 5/66–7 & n.; puritans, 5/96–7; duty to parents, 5/342; 1 Sam., xii. 24, 6/87; limits of science, 6/289; purgatory, 7/123; truth of Christianity, 7/206; imitation of Christ and the saints, 7/383; Eccles,. xi. 8, 8/21; the meek shall inherit the earth, 8/116; Luke, xii. 31, 8/144–5; 9/286; adultery, 8/362–3, 366; scribes and pharisees, 9/482

P'S APPRECIATION: nature of his reports, vol. i, pp. cxvii–cxviii; takes notes in Latin, 4/268, 278; samples several, 1/205, 302, 324; 2/230; 3/47, 91–2, 252; 4/163; 5/190, 256, 285; reads during, 1/42; sleeps, 1/97, 322; 2/215; 4/106, 165, 177, 190, 348, 369, 435; 5/125; 8/236; dislikes excessive eloquence, 1/60; disapproves of political, 1/195; dislikes Presbyterian, 2/74–5; 3/58, 81, 99; buys *Evangelium Armatum*, 4/111 & n. 4; reads H. King's sermon on regicide, 6/54 & n. 3; borrows volume of Jeremy Taylor, 6/312 & n. 3; enjoys readings from

sermon against Rome, 8/587 & n. 3; reads A. Wright's *Five sermons in five several styles*, 9/300 & n. 5; prefers puritan style, ib.

SERVANTS (P) [Servants named below are those employed by P and referred to by their Christian names only. Those with surnames are entered in the main series, with cross-references here. Servants of other households are indexed with their employers.]:

GENERAL: numbers employed in P's household, 2/1, 241; 3/301–2; 4/438; 5/257, 359–60; 6/143; 7/426; 8/134; black servants, 2/36, 61, 69; 4/51; 6/215, 244, 283, 285, 288; 8/33, 123; 9/464, 510; man cook hired, 3/53; 4/13; 7/388, 389, 392; 9/115–16; table layer, 9/115, 423; testimonials: 4/78–9 & n., 131, 294; wages: cookmaids, 3/53; 4/86; 5/158–9; lady's companion, 7/311; 9/362

SERVANTS IN P'S HOUSEHOLD:

ALICE, COOKMAID: unpromising, 6/70; accompanies EP to Woolwich in Plague, 6/149, 313; leaves, 7/85; alluded to: 6/143

ASHWELL, MARY: see Ashwell

BARKER: see Barker

BESS, COOKMAID: good temper, 4/399, 438; 5/91, 290; recommended by Creed, 4/320–1 & n.; helps at Tom P's death and funeral, 5/88, 91; promoted to chambermaid, 5/101, 360; scolded, 5/185; at Brampton with EP, 5/224, 234; dismissed, 5/270, 290, 318; 6/49, 51; ingratitude, 6/51; also, 4/354, 362, 399; 5/111, 124, 137, 196, 249, 290, 305

BRIDGET, COOKMAID: cooks well, 9/184; leaves, 9/510; a thief, ib.; also, 9/165, 166

DOLL (DOROTHY, DOROTHÉ), CHAMBERMAID: enters service, 2/151, 174; talkative, 2/204, 221; dismissed, 2/220, 221

DOLL, COOKMAID, a 'blackmoore': good cook, 9/510

ELY, FOOTBOY: see Jenkins, Eliezer

GOSNELL, [Winifred]: see Gosnell

HANNAH, COOKMAID: engaged without references, 4/78–9 & n.; good cook, 4/86, 90, 95; stays up all night cleaning kitchen, 4/253; scolded for leaving house dirty, 4/264; dismissed for stealing, 4/279; also, 4/100, 205, 236

JACK, FOOTBOY: arrives from Impington, 9/348; livery described, 9/372; reads to P, 9/372, 373; accompanies in London, 9/453, 530, 550, 557; also, 9/424, 439–40, 464, 469, 527, 530, 552

JANE, COOKMAID: enters service, 5/158–9 & n. 1, 191, 201; P pleased with, 5/225; dismissed by EP, 6/4(2), 26, 28; EP neglects to pay wages, 6/29, 30, 31

JANE (BIRCH). see Edwards

JANE (GENTLEMAN): see Gentleman

JINNY: parish child, engaged by EP, 4/282; runs away, ib.; dismissed, 4/283–4 & n.

LUCE, COOKMAID: arrives, 7/183; 'ugly and plain', ib.; falls downstairs, 7/188; drinks, 8/126; P kicks for carelessness, 8/164; found drunk and departs, 8/221–2

MARY, COOKMAID: arrives, 2/176; and leaves, 2/196

MARY, CHAMBERMAID: to replace Jane Birch, 4/34; works well, 4/40, 41; tries to corrupt cookmaid, 4/100; dismissed, 4/113

MARY, CHAMBERMAID: engaged by EP, 6/40, 51; at Woolwich during Plague, 6/149; EP quarrels with, 6/214, 246, 250, dismissed, 6/295, 296; engaged by E. Pearse, 6/317; 7/93, 103; also, 6/119, 143

MARY, COOKMAID: arrives, 7/121; and leaves, 7/183

MARY, UNDER-COOKMAID: arrives, 8/225; and leaves, 8/328; her love of gaming, ib.

MATT, CHAMBERMAID: EP tells of her good looks, 9/479, 481, 487; arrives, 9/502, 504; dismissed, 9/559

MERCER, MARY: see Mercer

NELL: arrives, 2/196; unwilling to sleep in room with P and EP, 2/213; 'a simple slut', 2/233; lazy, 3/8; dismissed, 3/57; alluded to: 2/241; ~ her mother, 2/196

NELL, COOKMAID: arrives, 8/419;

cooks well, 9/184; cuts P's hair, 9/201; dismissed, 9/332

NELL (PAYNE): see Payne

SARAH: enters service, 2/218 & n. 3, 222; ague, 3/46, 47, 51, 53, 65; combs P's hair, 3/96; washes his feet, 3/97; P pleased with, 3/113, 135; accompanies EP to Brampton, 3/65, 141, 151, 206; EP quarrels with, 3/135, 184; her proposed dismissal, 3/213, 258, 263, 273; departure, 3/274, 278; warns P against B. St Michel, 3/285; joins Penn's household, 3/295, 302; her gossiping, 4/7; dismissed, 4/92; also, 2/241; 3/95, 108, 110, 116, 208; 4/276; 6/141; ?7/268

SUSAN, COOKMAID: recommended by B. St Michel, 3/279; her cooking, 3/301; 4/34; ill, 4/41, 85, 86; replaced by Hannah, 4/86; twice returns temporarily, 4/150, 279; dismissed for drinking, 4/154, 280, 281

SUSAN, ?COOKMAID: 'an admirable slut', 5/55; the 'little girl', 4/438; 5/307, 318, 320; arrives, 4/284; EP angry with, 4/363; beaten for negligence, 5/13; 6/39; combs P's hair, 6/185; 7/95; at Woolwich with EP during Plague, 6/209, 282, 313; sent away with suspected plague, 7/115(3), 116(2); returns, 7/122; also, 5/165, 225, 257, 323, 360; 6/49, 143; 7/100, 108; ~ her father a sexton, 7/116; her mother, 7/116

WAYNEMAN: see Birch

WILL, FOOTBOY: enters service, 1/189, 193; combs P's hair, 1/222; dismissed for stealing, 1/233, 234, 237, 240; also, 1/203, 206; ~ his father, 1/233, 240

WILLET, DEB: see Willet

ANONYMOUS SERVANTS: coachman, 9/393, 464, 527; maids, 4/297, 304; 7/109, 111; 9/332, 510

SERVINGTON: see Cervington

SESSIONS HOUSE, Old Bailey: trials, 1/263, 266; 3/303; 4/294; funeral, 2/159 & n. 3; also, 8/316, 319

SEVERUS, Emperor A.D. 193–211: severity cited in sermon, 5/96 & n. 4

SEVILLE: high standard of coins minted at, 4/146

SEWERS, Commissioners of: 4/45–6 & n.; 5/353

SEX LIFE, P's [omitting minor amorous encounters. *See also* Pepys, Elizabeth: relations with P; Languages: polyglot; Prostitutes; and (principally) Bagwell, Mrs ——; Burroughs, (E); Crisp, D.; Daniel, Mrs ——; Knepp, [E]; Martin, B.; Mitchell, B.; Powell, D.; Udall, F.; Udall, S.; Welsh, J.; Willet, D.]: his innocence about buggery, 4/210; masturbates, 1/222; 2/44; 4/204, 230, 232; 6/331; 7/365, 419; 8/588; 9/184; dreams, 6/191; reads *L'escholle des filles*, 9/21–2, 57–8, 59
SEYMOUR (Seamour), [Edward], M.P. Hindon, Wilts.; Commissioner for Prizes: conceited, 6/288; seizes prize-goods, 6/261 & n. 4, 262, 263–4; dines with W. Coventry, 5/11 & n. 2
SEYMOUR (Seamour), Capt. [Hugh], naval officer: wears hat in presence of Navy Board, 6/339; challenges Peter Pett to duel, 7/212 & n. 1; killed in action, 7/226 & n. 2, 231
SEYMOUR, Jane: see Jane (Seymour)
SEYMOUR, [John], Comptroller of Customs, London: 9/514 & n. 1
SEYMOUR, [John], servant to Sandwich: 9/331 & n. 1
SEYMOUR, William, 3rd/7th Duke of Somerset (1652–71): attends meeting of Royal Society, 8/243
SHA 'BĀN (Shavan Aga), Pasha of Algiers: 4/370 & nn., 386
SHADWELL, [Thomas], clerk in the Exchequer: 2/241
SHADWELL, [Thomas], dramatist and poet (d. 1692) [*see also* Plays]: at theatre, 9/310 & n. 3; theatre news from, 9/522
SHADWELL, Mdx: 7/284, 338
SHAFTESBURY, 1st Earl of: *see* Cooper
SHAFTO, [Robert], Recorder of Newcastle-upon-Tyne: 9/359
SHAKESPEARE [*see also* Plays]: cited by P, 6/191 & n. 3; quoted by Coventry, 7/265 & n. 1
SHALCROSS (Shelcrosse), [Thomas, draper]: 6/165–6
SHALES, Capt. [John], victualling agent, Portsmouth: business, 4/364, 371; gifts to P, 5/72, 152; recom-

mended by P to Brouncker, 9/331 & n. 2
SHAR, Monsieur ——: *see* Esquier, d'
SHARP(E), [James], Archbishop of St Andrew's 1661–d.79: on *Naseby*, 1/128 & n. 2
SHATTERELL, [Robert], actor: 7/77
SHAVAN AGA: *see* Sha 'bān
SHAVING: *see* Dress and Personal Appearance
SHAW, Sir John, merchant and customs farmer: Clarendon's confidant, 5/219; pluralist, 8/398 & n. 3; complains about hemp, 9/214 & n. 1; also, 3/188; 6/126, 258
SHAW, Robin, clerk in the Exchequer 1660; later clerk to Ald. Backwell: political news from, 1/21; ill, 1/215, 257; death of first wife, 1/215 & n. 1; marries rich widow, 3/255–6 & n.; at Backwell's, 2/120; illness and death, 6/165, 169, 171; 7/215; social: 1/7, 8, 57, 259; 2/31
SHEERES, [Henry], military engineer, kted 1685: returns from Spain, 8/429, 443; stories of travels, 8/444, 451–2; 9/404, 509; engraving of Tangier, 9/419 & n. 2; paid for work at Tangier, 9/419, 429–30; gifts to P, 9/429–30, 536–7; teaches EP perspective, 9/534; EP fond of, 9/541; P jealous, 9/504, 522, 532, 533; his poetry, 9/504 & n. 1; leaves for Tangier, 9/541; also, 9/545 & n. 1; social: at theatre, 9/419, 435, 522; in May Day parade, 9/540; also, 9/420, 436, 437, 488, 509–10, 516–17, 539, 544
SHEERNESS, Kent: project for new yard, 6/194 & n. 2, 194–5; ships sail from, 7/189, 211, 212, 231; ship capsizes, 7/345; fortifications planned, 8/84, 98 & n. 2; King and Duke of York visit, 8/125, 126–7 & n.; capture by Dutch, 8/258, 259, 260; Dutch fleet off, 8/365; investigation into failure of defences, 8/496; 9/75
SHEFFIELD, John, 3rd Earl of Mulgrave, cr. Marquess of Normanby 1694, Duke of Normanby and Buckinghamshire 1703 (d. 1721): house, 9/317
SHELCROSSE: *see* Shalcross

SHELDON, Barbara: *see* Wood
SHELDON, Gilbert, Bishop of London 1660–3; Archbishop of Canterbury 1663–d.77:
CHARACTER: courage, 8/593 & n. 4
CHRON. SERIES: consecrated, 1/276 & n. 2; to be archbishop, 4/173 & n. 2; opposes indulgence to Presbyterians, 3/186 & n. 2; his nominations to benefices, 3/186 & n. 4, 190; injunction on sabbath observance, 3/196 & n. 3; his part in imprisonment of Calamy, 4/6 & n. 1; and in arrest of Catholic priest, 4/44; revokes licence for book on Catholicism, 4/111 & nn.; admires Stillingfleet's preaching, 6/87; appoints L. Jenkins judge, 8/133 & n. 3; slander against, 8/364 & n. 1; listens to mock sermon, 9/554; also, 8/151
POLITICAL: high standing with King, 4/137 & n. 2; inactive in Council, 5/73; attends cabinet, 5/317; good relations with Sandwich, 7/54, 56; dislike of Albemarle, 7/56; dismissed from Council, 8/585, 587, 593 & n. 4, 596, 600; 9/1–2
SOCIAL: at Lord Mayor's banquet, 4/355; his public dinners, 9/550 & n. 2, 554; also, 6/164, 188, 239
MISC.: presents naval papers to Coventry, 5/177 & n. 2
SHELDON, Ald. Sir Joseph, Sheriff 1666–7: fire at house, 8/320 & n. 1
SHELDON, William, Clerk of the Cheque, Woolwich:
CHRON. SERIES: poor bookkeeping, 3/136; instructed by P on call books, 4/80; houses EP in Plague, 6/128 & n. 2, 140, 143, 315; 7/3; P visits her, 6/153, 157, 162, 170, 174, 183, 185, 190, 200, 205, 206–9 passim, 212, 213, 214, 216, 219, 221, 222, 224, 226, 228, 242, 244, 246, 249–50, 262–3, 282, 303, 309, 341; EP stays with in Fire, 7/275, 280; also, 6/225
HIS HOUSE: P admires, 6/143; garden, 5/213
SOCIAL: 3/142; 4/79, 267, 284; 5/213, 307; 7/210
ALLUDED TO: 6/128, 140, 143, 253, 280; 7/5
SHELL HAVEN (Shield haven), Essex:

Dutch fleet in, 8/258, 351
SHELLS, shell-work: *see* Crafts
SHELSTON, [?Robert], grocer, [?of Leadenhall St]: gift to P, 1/95; asks for employment, 1/242; 2/32; social: 1/94; ~ his pretty wife [?Judith], 1/95
SHEPHEARD, ——, of Brampton, Hunts.: 3/223
SHEPPARD (Shepheard), [Robert], naval officer: 7/216
SHEPPEY, Isle of, Kent: 1/104
SHERES: *see* Sheeres
SHERGOLL, [Henry], doorkeeper to the Navy Office: 5/344
SHERWOOD FOREST, Notts.: report on, 4/158
SHERWYN, [Richard], Exchequer official: works on Tangier accounts, 6/14, 15, 17; 9/202; also, 1/31; 6/91–2
SHIPLEY (Shepley), [Edward], Sandwich's steward:
CHARACTER: P's regard, 6/32
AS STEWARD: on Dutch voyage with Sandwich, 1/95, 96, 104, 106, 136, 157, 163, 164, 166, 200, 258; financial business and accounts with P/Sandwich, 1/84, 209, 237, 297, 305; 2/3, 34, 56, 61, 67, 98, 105; 3/100, 116, 117, 121, 124, 126; 7/195, 199; 8/188; 9/211; accounts obscure, 3/131; to be transferred to Hinchingbrooke, 3/101 & n. 2; helps in parliamentary elections, 1/110–11, 112; shows P alterations at Hinchingbrooke, 3/220; unspecified business, 2/62, 108; 5/325; gifts to P/EP, 1/41; 4/22; 5/354; 7/15; P's gifts to, 1/166; 9/411; movements to and from Hinchingbrooke, 1/7, 23; 3/101, 131; 5/171, 191–2, 193, 325, 327; 6/32; 7/132, 193, 195, 371, 376; 8/220, 538, 539, 545; 9/455; dismissed, 9/475; also, 1/4, 21, 71, 73, 77, 78, 87, 93, 222, 266, 323, 324; 2/57, 83, 87; 7/371; 9/193
SOCIAL: at P's house, 1/6, 81, 203; 2/47; 3/99, 128; 6/62; 7/134; 8/223; 9/363; at Sandwich's London lodgings, 1/8, 9, 74, 76, 91, 206, 210, 216, 219, 220, 271; 2/37, 41, 48, 57, 66, 83, 87; 3/96, 120; at taverns, 1/15, 19, 85, 88, 201, 217, 234, 259, 265, 287, 295, 296, 301, 304, 307, 325; 2/33, 79, 89, 99, 109, 116, 119; 4/309, 312; 9/224; on

Deptford 1666; wrecked 1694): her men come up from Portsmouth, 8/272 & n. 1, 275; *Catherine* (King's yacht; 8–10 guns; captured by Dutch 1673): built, 2/12 & n. 2, 14, 36, 76; beats *Mary* in race, 2/104; and *Bezan*, 6/194; victualled, 2/122; weathers storm in Channel, 3/140, 143, 146; drawing of, 4/301; returns from Flanders, 7/141–2, 145; also, 2/121, 179; 3/111 & n. 3, 126, 164; 4/99; 5/197; *Charity* (36–46 guns; prize 1653; captured by Dutch 1665): P on board, 2/121; *Charles* (yacht; 6 guns; built Woolwich 1662; given to Ordnance Office 1668): runs aground, 4/50; court-martial aboard, 9/497–8; *Charles: see Royal Charles; Charlotte* (yacht): P on board, 4/296; *Cheriton: see Speedwell; Chestnut* (8–10 guns; built Portsmouth 1656; wrecked 1665) paid off, 1/310; *Church* (20–6 guns; prize 1653; hulk at Harwich 1659): sold, 1/305 & n. 1; *Concord* (merchantman; 28 guns): arrives from Mediterranean, 5/41–2 & n., 49; *Convertine* (4th-rate; 40–50 guns; Portuguese prize 1650; captured by Dutch 1666): alluded to, 3/31; *Coventry* (5th-rate; 20–6 guns; Spanish ship taken from royalists 1658): captured, 7/390 & n. 3; 8/511; *Crown* (merchantman): P on board, 5/30
Dartmouth (5th-rate; 22–32 guns; built Portsmouth 1655; wrecked 1690): paid off, 3/193 & n. 2; court martial concerning, 9/505; [*Defiance*] (3rd-rate; 66 guns): built, 6/7 & n. 2, 169; measured, 7/69 & n. 1; enquiry into her loss by fire, 9/481 & n. 1, 488, 494, 497–8 & nn.; also, 7/119; *Diamond* (40–50 guns; built Deptford 1651; captured by French 1693): in action, 6/82; overturns during careening, 7/345 & n. 2; *Dover* (40–50 guns; built Shoreham 1654; rebuilt 1695): to sail to Constantinople, 1/224; *Drake* (6th-rate; 12–16 guns; built Deptford 1652; condemned 1690): paid off, 3/58; *Dunbar: see Henry;* [*Dunkirk*] (E. Indiaman): mustered, 4/241 & n. 1; alluded to, 7/150 *Eagle* (merchantman; 44–56 guns):

hired to carry victuals to Tangier, 5/167 & n. 3, 276, 292; *Eagle* (hulk bought 1592; sold 1683): her boat, 3/150; *Edgar* (3rd-rate; rebuilt 1700): built at Bristol, 8/270 & n. 4; 9/231, 235 & n. 1; *Elias* (frigate; 5th-rate; 26–32 guns; Dutch prize c. 1646): brings timber from Forest of Dean, 4/20; and masts from N. America, 5/127 & n. 3; founders, 5/321 & n. 3; *Elizabeth* (ketch): 9/160; *Essex* (48–60 guns; built Deptford 1653): captured by Dutch, 7/154, 157
Fanfan (privateer; 6th-rate; 4 guns; built Harwich 1665 or 1666): made a pitch boat 1693): 8/341; *Fellowship* (hulk; 28 guns; taken from royalists 1643): sold, 3/185 & n. 2; *Flying Greyhound* (privateer; 6th-rate; 24 guns; Dutch prize 1665; rebought by Navy Board 1668; sunk for foundation Sheerness 1673): *see* Prizes and Privateers (P); *Foresight* (4th-rate; 34–48 guns; built Deptford 1650; wrecked 1698): overturns during careening, 7/345 & n. 2; also, 3/153; *Fox* (14 guns; prize 1658; fireship and expended 1666): paid off, 2/93 & n. 3; *Franklin* (fly-boat; given away 1669): sunk as part of river defences, 8/270 & n. 4; *French Ruby* (3rd-rate; 66–75 guns; prize (*Rubis*) 1666; made 2nd-rate 1672; wrecked 1682): captured, 7/350 & n. 1; her guns, 7/352; to be altered, 7/352; 8/121
[*George*]: *see St George; Gift: see Great Gift; Gloucester* (3rd-rate; 50–62 guns; built Blackwall 1654; wrecked 1682): in action, 7/148; *Golden Hand* (fireship; 6 guns; Dutch prize 1665; founders 1673): to sail to Holland, 8/257 & n. 3; *Golden Phoenix* (Dutch E. Indiaman; 3rd-rate; 70 guns; sunk to block Thames 1667): captured by Sandwich, 6/219 & n. 1, 230–1 & n., 234; to be unloaded, 6/236; in river off Erith, 6/242, 249, 273; P on board, 6/300; *Grantham* (22–30 guns; built Southampton 1654; renamed *Guardland* 1660; fireship 1688; reconverted 1689; sold 1698): carries royalists to Flushing, 1/117; *Great Charity* (merchantman): captured by Dutch, 6/118

& n. 1; [*Great*] *Gift* (26–40 guns; French prize 1652; fireship and expended 1666): carries deals to King's Lynn, 2/27; paid off, 3/44; in action off W. Africa, 5/355 & n. 1; [*?Great President*]: paid off, 1/262 & n. 3; *Greenwich* (4th-rate; 54 guns; built Woolwich 1666; rebuilt 1699): launched, 7/153; overturns during careening, 7/345 & n. 2; *Greyhound* (merchantman): 5/41–2 & n., 49; [*Griffin*] (12 guns; taken from royalists 1656; wrecked 1664): paid off, 1/262 & n. 1; 2/237 & n. 2; *Guernsey* (5th-rate; 22–30 guns; built Walberswick 1654 as *Basing*; condemned 1693): paid off, 3/53–4 & n.; accidentally rams *Portland*, 7/142

Half Moon (30–6 guns; prize 1653): sold, 1/284 & n. 3; *Hampshire* (38–48 guns; built Deptford 1653; sunk in action 1697): to sail to India, 2/62; paid off, 2/45 & n. 1; ?3/58–9 & n.; returns from Mediterranean, 7/143; *Happy Return* (44–54 guns; built Yarmouth 1654 as *Winceby*; captured 1691): renamed, 1/154; mutiny in, 8/251 & n. 3; *Harp* (frigate; 8–10 guns; built Dublin 1656; sold 1671): alluded to, 1/90; *Hector* (ex-*Three Kings*; 22 guns; prize 1657): paid off, 1/262 & n. 1; lost in action, 6/219; *Henrietta* (50–62 guns; built Horsleydown 1654 as *Langport*; wrecked 1689): renamed, 1/154; paid off, 1/283, 286 & n. 2; *Henrietta* (yacht; 8–12 guns; sunk in action 1673): designed partly by King, 4/123 & n. 1, 149; carving valued, 5/24 & n. 1; Rupert to go to sea in, 5/262; court-martial in, 9/488 & n. 4; *Henry* (64–82 guns; built Deptford 1656 as *Dunbar*; accidentally burnt 1682): renamed, 1/154; Mennes to fly Vice-Admiral's flag in, 2/70; in Four Days Fight, 7/143, 154, 155; cut loose from moorings in Dutch raid, 8/310; also, 5/317; 7/11; *Hope* (4th-rate; 44 guns; Dutch prize (*Hoop*) 1665): wrecked, 7/390 & n. 3

[*Invention II*] (Petty's double-keeled vessel): wins race, 4/256–7 & n.

Jemmy (yacht; 4 guns; broken up 1722): races against *Bezan*, 3/164 &

n. 4, 188; also, 4/64; 5/317; *Jersey* (4th-rate; 40–50 guns; built Maldon 1654; captured 1691): P made her captain, 9/481 & n. 1; under repair, 9/484; [*Joseph*] (fireship; 4 guns; bought 1666; accidentally burnt 1667): alluded to, 8/39 & n. 3

Kentish ('Kent'; 4th-rate; 46–52 guns; built Deptford 1652; wrecked 1672): P's accident on board, 4/64; *Kingfisher* (merchantman): hired for voyage to Tangier, 7/27 & n. 2, 28, 32; *Kinsale* (8–10 guns; prize 1656; sold 1663): accident to, 1/316; paid off, 3/180 & n. 1; *King Solomon* (Dutch merchantman): sunk, 6/19 & n. 3

Langport ('*Lamport*'): renamed *Henrietta*, 1/154; alluded to, 1/109 & n.*a*; *Lark* (frigate; 8–10 guns; prize 1656; sold 1663): her voyage from Holland, 1/135; *Leopard* (4th-rate; 54–8 guns; built Deptford 1659; sunk for foundation Sheerness 1699): runs aground, 6/8 & n. 3; dispute over freightage charges for, 9/410 & n. 1, 494 & n. 2; also, 4/432 & n. 3; 5/160 & n. 2; [*Leopard*] (E. Indiaman): P musters, 4/241 & n. 1; *Lewes* (merchantman; 32 guns): ? to be released from hire, 8/293 & n. 2; also, 3/50; *Lily* (6th-rate; 6 guns; built Deptford 1657; sold 1667): in action, 8/357; *London* (64–76 guns; built Chatham 1656): P on board, 1/114; 4/228; to carry Queen Mother and Princess Henrietta to France, 2/11; Sandwich's flagship, 5/187 & n. 1; wrecked by explosion, 6/52 & n. 1, 54; alluded to, 6/53; 7/106; *Loyal George* (hired; 42–4 guns; captured 1666): missing after action, 7/154; *Loyal London* (2nd-rate; 90 guns): built to replace *London*, 6/53 & n. 4, 170; surveyed, 6/295 & n. 2; launched, 7/160 & n. 3; to be fitted out, 7/181; guns tried, 7/183 & n. 1; its high repute, 7/215; builder's accounts for, 8/105 & n. 3, 108, 152; burnt by Dutch in Chatham raid, 8/266, 308; alluded to, 7/106

Malaga [*Merchant*] (fireship; 4 guns; bought 1666; sold 1667): in action, 8/47 & n. 4; *Maria*: alluded to,

1/180; *Maria Sancta: see Sancta Maria;*
[*Martha and Mary*] (Margate hoy):
hired, 2/123 & n. 2; *Martin* (6th-rate;
12 guns; built Portsmouth 1652; sold
1667): paid off, 3/180 & n. 1; *Mary*
(*see also Speaker*): renamed, 1/154;
returns from Lisbon, 3/249; in action,
6/122, 129, 135; *Mary* (yacht; 8 guns;
wrecked 1675): presented to King by
Amsterdam, 1/222 & n. 1; admired by
P, 1/286-7 & n.; P on board, 4/272-3;
alluded to, 2/104, 179; 4/76, 157;
[*Mary Rose*] (E. Indiaman): built for
voyage to Bombay, 4/241 & n. 1;
Mathias (4th-rate; 38-52 guns; Dutch
prize 1653; burnt 1692): P hears
sermon on, 4/258; *Maybolt* (hoy;
prize 1666): granted to P, 8/464-5 &
n.; sold, 9/29; [*Merlin*] (yacht; 6-8
guns; built Rotherhithe 1666; sold
1698): court-martial held aboard,
9/505 & n. 1; ?also, 7/417; *Milford*
(5th-rate; 24-8 guns; built Wivenhoe
1654; accidentally burnt 1673): paid
off, 4/386 & n. 1; French demand
salute from in Mediterranean, 9/560
& n. 2; alluded to, 6/20; *Monmouth*
(yacht; 8 guns; sold 1895); built 7/38
& n. 3; guards chain across Medway,
8/310; sunk by order, 8/327-8; ?also,
7/417; [*Morning Star*] (E. Indiaman):
taken by Algerines, 9/492 & n. 5;
Mountagu (52-62 guns; built Portsmouth 1654 as *Lyme*; widened 1675;
rebuilt 1698): P admires, 2/93
   Naseby (80-6 guns; built Woolwich
1655; renamed *Royal Charles* 1660;
captured 1667); Sandwich's affection
for, 1/100 & n. 2; P on board, 1/101-
54 passim; P's cabin, 1/101; his
window altered, 1/112; Sandwich's
bedchamber, 1/100; state-room,
1/114; and wine store, 1/116; her
roundhouse, 1/106; great cabin, 1/108
(2), 109, 111, 114, 118, 130, 133, 142,
153, 164; coach, 1/123, 128, 159,
160(2), 164; cook-room, 1/136;
cuddy, 1/137; scuttle, ib.; new flags
etc., 1/136, 142; renamed *Royal
Charles*, 1/154; story of fire when
King aboard, 1/176; alluded to, 1/78,
85; *Newbury* (52-62 guns; built Limehouse 1654; renamed *Revenge* 1660;

condemned 1678): alluded to, 1/109;
Newcastle (40-56 guns; built Ratcliffe
1653; wrecked 1703): P on board,
2/16; *Nonsuch* (frigate; 5th-rate; 36
guns; made 4th-rate 1669; 5th-rate
1691; captured 1695): built to Heemskerck's design, 9/171 & n. 2, 488 & n. 2;
Nonsuch (ketch; 8 guns; bought 1654;
sold 1667): to be fitted for voyage to
India, 2/62; runs aground, 6/8 & n. 3,
10 & n. 1, 19; alluded to, 1/121, 136;
Northwich [?error for *Norwich*]: allu-
ded to, 1/135; *Norwich* (24-30 guns;
built Chatham 1655; wrecked 1682):
P is shown over, 2/204; returns from
Tangier, 4/101; alluded to, 2/115
   Old Success ('*Success*'; 34-8 guns;
French prize *Jules* 1650): formerly
Bradford, 1/154; paid off, 1/253-4 &
n.; 3/73; sold, 3/185 & n. 2; *Orange*
('*Urania*', Dutch prize *Oranje*; 5th-
rate; lost at sea, 1671): 6/122 & n. 5;
Oxford (5th-rate; 22-6 guns; built
Deptford 1656; blown up 1669): in
action, 6/20
   Panther (privateer): 8/341; *Paradox*
(12-14 guns; taken from royalists
1649; sold 1667): paid off, 3/59;
alluded to, 1/114; *Phoenix* (32-40
guns; built Woolwich 1647): runs
aground, 6/8 & n. 3, 10 & n. 1, 19;
Phoenix of Riga (prize): 8/23-4, 123
& n. 1; *Phoenix* (Dutch E. Indiaman):
see *Golden Phoenix*; *Plymouth* (54-60
guns; built Wapping 1653; rebuilt
1705): to take ambassador to Constantinople, 1/217 & n. 3; also, 1/124,
134, 224; 6/141; *Portland* (4th-rate;
40-50 guns; built Wapping 1653;
burnt to avoid capture, 1692): disabled in action, 7/142; *Prince, Prince
Royal: see Royal Prince; Princess* (4th-
rate; 52-4 guns; built Lydney 1660;
broken up 1680): in Medway raid,
8/271-2; *Prosperous* (?horseboat; built
Chatham 1665; burnt by Dutch
1667): given to King by Penn, 8/441
& n. 3; *Providence* (fireship): plague
aboard, 6/189 & n. 2; lost at Tangier,
9/488-9 & n.; alluded to, 7/176
   Rainbow (40-60 guns; built Deptford
1617; sunk at Sheerness 1680):
damaged in action, 7/149; alluded to,

4/110; *Reserve* (4th-rate; 34–48 guns; built Woodbridge 1650; rebuilt 1701): alluded to, 3/159, 163; *Resolution* (originally *Tredagh* q.v.): burnt in action, 7/221, 222, 226; her guns, 7/227; alluded to, 4/101; *Resolution* (3rd-rate; 70 guns; rebuilt 1698): to be built by Deane, 8/489 & n. 3; 'the best ship . . . in the world', 9/262; Deane's drawing of, 9/262 & n. 4, 313, 330 & n. 3; alluded to, 9/178; *Revenge* (3rd-rate; 52–62 guns; built Limehouse 1654 as *Newbury*; condemned 1678): explosion on board, 7/345; *Richard:* renamed *Royal James*, 1/154; *Richmond: see Wakefield; Richmond* (yacht): to be taken into King's service, 9/301–2 & n.; *Rosebush* (24–34 guns; prize 1653; hulk at Harwich 1664; sold 1668): P dines on board, 2/36; to sail to Jamaica, 3/150 & n. 3; *Royal Catherine* (2nd-rate; 70–82 guns; rebuilt 1702): building, 4/91 & n. 1; 5/75, 110, 136, 232, 253; launched, 6/305, 306 & n. 3; admired by King, 6/306; with fleet, 6/80(2), 306; runs aground in Four Days Fight, 7/153–4; *Royal Catherine* (merchantman): 3/156; *Royal Charles* ('*Charles';* see *Naseby*): formerly *Naseby*, 1/154; P on board, 1/154–72 passim; paid off, 1/167; Sandwich sails in from Portugal, 3/128; Cromwellian figurehead replaced, 4/418 & n. 2, 420; Duke of York's flagship in Battle of Lowestoft, 6/122; runs aground in Four Days Fight, 7/153–4; 8/359; captured and towed away by Dutch in Medway raid, 8/262–3 & nn., 266, 267, 283 & n. 1, 310 & n. 4, 343, 495, 501, 502; alluded to, 1/256; 3/128, 131; 7/141, 146; [*Royal Charles II*] (1st-rate; 96 guns; renamed *St George* 1687; 2nd-rate 1691; rebuilt 1701): launched, 9/101 & n. 2; *Royal James* ('*James';* 70–82 guns; built Woolwich 1658 as *Richard*): renamed, 1/154; Sandwich's model of, 2/121 & n. 5, 192; Sandwich sails to Mediterranean in, 3/128; dispute over rating of, 3/128 & n. 1; in dock at Woolwich, 3/142–3; 4/64; launched after repairs, 4/103; P inspects, 4/131; Sandwich on board,

6/287, 301; dispute about pay, 7/93–4 & n., 97 & n. 1; burnt in Medway by Dutch, 8/266, 308; alluded to, 3/95; *Royal Oak* (2nd-rate; 76 guns; built Portsmouth 1664): in action, 6/122; burnt by Dutch in Medway, 8/266, 308; *Royal Oak* (E. Indiaman): to be launched, 2/14 & n. 3; wrecked in storm, 6/36 & n. 1; *Royal Prince* (1st-rate; 64–85 guns; built Woolwich 1641): P visits in dock, 2/69; launched after repair, 4/225 & n. 4; EP visits, 6/56; her reputation for powerfulness, 6/129 & n. 4; Sandwich's flagship, 6/129, 151, 228; damaged in Battle of Lowestoft, 6/135; runs aground in Four Days Fight, 7/153 & n. 1, 158, 352; 8/12 & n. 1, 359; alluded to, 6/65, 241, 287; 8/109; *Royal Sovereign* (1st-rate; 90–100 guns; built Woolwich 1637; cut down 1660 and 1685; burnt by accident 1696): P visits, 2/15–16 & n., 69; and admires, 2/16; 3/155; 6/194; inspected by P, 3/155; 4/228; and by Navy Board, 6/194; print of, 4/29 & n. 4; with fleet, 6/196, 208, 228; alluded to, 6/188, 189; *Rubis: see French Ruby; Ruby* (4th-rate; 40–8 guns; built Deptford 1651; captured by French 1707): in action, 7/148; *Rupert* (3rd-rate; rebuilt 1703): her repute, 7/119, 127; 8/142; in action, 7/142, 155; drawing of, 8/142 & n. 2; to go to sea, 8/485; alluded to, 7/143; 8/39, 95

St George ('*George';* 2nd-rate; 62–70 guns; built Deptford 1622; made a hulk 1687): paid off, 2/227 & n. 5, ?239 & n. 1; in action, 6/122; *St John Baptist* (prize): captured, 9/147 & n. 3; *St Patrick* (4th-rate; 48 guns; built Bristol 1666): captured by Dutch, 8/47, 67; *Sancta Maria* (4th-rate; 50 guns, Dutch prize 1665; burnt by Dutch 1667): runs aground 8/310 & n. 1; *Satisfaction* (26–32 guns; prize 1646): wreck of, 3/213 & n. 1; 6/19; paid off, 3/225–6 & n.; [*Seaflow*] (merchantman): hired, 1/267 & n. 4; *Seven Oaks* (4th-rate; Dutch prize (*Zevenwolden*) 1665; recaptured 1666): in action, 7/154; *Slothany* (*Slot van Honingen*, Dutch E. Indiaman;

3rd-rate; 60 guns; hulk 1667; sold 1686): captured by Sandwich, 6/219 & n. 1, 230–1 & n., 234; to be unloaded, 6/236; in river off Erith, 6/242, 249, 273; P on board, 6/300; *Sophia* (26–34 guns; prize 1652; sold 1667): paid off, 2/237; *Speaker* (50–62 guns; built Woolwich 1650; wrecked 1703): P admires, 1/115; re-named *Mary*, 1/154; alluded to, 1/86; *Speedwell* (20–8 guns; built Deptford 1656; wrecked 1678): formerly *Cheriton*, 1/154; alluded to, 1/221; *Success: see Old Success; [Surprise]* (merchant-man): carries King to France (1651), 1/156 & n. 2; *Swallow* (ketch; 6 guns; bought 1661; sold 1667): sermon on, 3/72; *Sweepstakes* (5th-rate; 36 guns; built Yarmouth 1666; sold 1698): in action, 7/148, 215 & n. 3; *Swiftsure* (44–6 guns; built Deptford 1621; rebuilt 1653): P and Sandwich on board, 1/95–102 passim; reported missing in action, 7/154–7 passim

Tangier-Merchant (merchantman): hired for Tangier, 4/20 & n. 2; 5/139; *Tholen* (Dutch): burnt in action, 7/229 & n. 5; *Tredagh* (50–66 guns; built Ratcliffe 1654; renamed *Resolution* 1660): carries Dowager Princess Mary and Sandwich from Holland, 1/254

Union (merchantman): hired for Tangier, 5/340; *Unity* (4th-rate; 42 guns; Dutch prize 1665): in Medway raid, 8/501; *Urania: see Orange Vanguard* (40–60 guns; built Wool-wich 1631; sold 1667): in action, 6/129; sunk in Medway raid, 8/310 *Wakefield* (22–6 guns; built Ports-mouth 1656; fireship 1688; recon-verted 1689; sold 1698): renamed *Richmond*, 1/154; *Wexford:* alluded to, 8/81, 100; *Weymouth* (12–16 guns; taken from royalists 1646): sold, 3/185 & n. 2; *White Bear* (1st-rate; built 1563; rebuilt 1600): engraving of, 8/84 & n. 3; *Wild Boar* (flyboat; 6th-rate; prize 1665): sold, 8/484 & n. 1; *William* (merchantman): on convoy duty, 5/340 & n. 2; *William and Mary* (merchantman): hired for Tangier, 4/368 & n. 4; *Winceby: see*

Happy Return; Wolf (6–16 guns; Spanish prize 1656; sold 1663): paid off, 1/290; *Worcester* (48–60 guns; built Woolwich 1651; renamed *Dun-kirk* 1660; rebuilt 1704): alluded to, 1/109

Yarmouth (44–54 guns; built Yar-mouth 1653; broken up 1680): in action, 6/82 & n. 1; also, 1/137; *York* (3rd-rate; 52–60 guns; built Black-wall 1654 as *Marston Moor*; wrecked 1703): in action, 7/176 & n. 3; *Young Lion* (6th-rate; 10 guns; prize 1665; sunk for foundation Sheerness 1673): sold and bought back, 9/160 & n. 2

SHIPTON, MOTHER: prophecy of Great Fire, 7/333 & n. 2

SHISH, Jonas, Assistant-Shipwright, Deptford: his yard, 4/104; ketches, ib.; builds *Charles*, 9/101 & n. 2; business, 5/75, 217; 8/188; 9/29; appointed Master-Shipwright, 9/128 & n. 1

SHOE LANE [*see also* Taverns etc.: Gridiron]: cockpit, 4/427; also, 2/156; 9/297

SHOOTER'S HILL, Kent: gibbet, 2/72–3 & n.

SHORE, Jane, mistress of Edward IV: Lady Castlemaine compared to, 3/68 & n. 4; alluded to in sermon, 5/97

SHOREDITCH: 4/432; 7/121; 8/212

SHORTGRAVE (Shotgrave), [Rich-ard], operator to the Royal Society: 9/337

SHORTHAND: P learns Shelton's system, vol. i, p. xxi; the system, vol. i, pp. xlviii–lix & nn., lxxii, lxxvii, lxxxvii & n. 91, xc; problems of transcribing, vol. i, pp. lvii–lxvii & nn.; P records use of, 5/174; 7/374; 8/448, 553; demonstrates it, 9/269; Coventry reads psalms in, 2/76 & n. 3; prefers clerk with knowledge of, 8/207; used by Hewer, 7/374 & n. 1; 9/483

SHORT'S: *see* Taverns etc

SHOTERELL; *see* Shatterell

SHOTT, ——, woodmonger: P orders firing from, 1/81; also, 1/33

SHREWSBURY, Earl and Countess of: *see* Talbot

SHREWSBURY, [William], book-

seller, Duck Lane: P visits/buys from, 9/161 & n. 1, 173, 260-1, 265, 268, 276, 284(2), 297, 327 & n. 2, 335, 345
SHREWSBURY, ——, wife of William: P kisses, 9/161; admires, 9/170, 173, 260, 265, 276; calls to see, 9/268, 284(2); tries to begin acquaintance with, 9/285; finds weeping, 9/297; pregnant, 9/335
SHROVE TUESDAY: club meets on, 1/78; cockshy, 2/44 & n. 1; fritters, 2/43-4; 6/32; Shrovetide verses by Eton boys, 7/59 & n. 6; also, 4/65; 5/62; 8/72; 9/457
SIAM: anecdotes of, 7/250-1 & n.
SICK AND WOUNDED, COMMISSION FOR THE: 8/407-8 & nn.
SIDLEY: see Sedley
SIDNEY, Algernon, republican (d. 1683): parliamentary commissioner in Baltic war (1659), 4/69 & n. 2; enmity to Sandwich, ib.
SIDNEY, Henry, Groom of the Bedchamber to the Duke of York and Master of the Horse to the Duchess, cr. Viscount 1689, Earl of Romney 1694 (d. 1704): alleged affair with Duchess of York, 6/302 & n. 1; 7/8 & n. 1, 323
SIDNEY, Col. [Robert]: 7/73
SIGNET OFFICE, Whitehall: 1/197
SILBURY HILL, Wilts.: P visits, 9/240 & n. 2
SIMCOTES (Symcottes), [John], physician, Huntingdon: 2/137 & n. 6
SIMON (Symons), [Thomas], engraver to the Mint: his engraving of Cromwell's head, 4/70 & nn.
SIMONS, Mr ——, servant to Lord Hatton: 2/221, 222
SIMPSON (Symson) [John], lawyer, kted 1678: 9/420
SIMPSON, John, minister of All Hallows, Thames St: King's arms set up in his church, 1/113 & n. 4
SIMPSON (Sympson), [Thomas], Master-Joiner of Deptford and Woolwich yards: work at P's house, Seething Lane: on dining room, 3/235 & n. 3; chimney pieces, 4/320; 9/266, 267, 279-80; cupboard, 4/353; bookcases, 7/214 & n. 4, 242, 252; helps arrange books etc., 7/258, 290; work

at Navy Office: alters P's closet, 5/143 & n. 1, 144, 145; other alterations, 8/523, 524; social: dines with P, 3/235; 7/258; 8/525
SINGLETON, John, court musician: King's affront, 1/297-8 & n.
SITTINGBOURNE, Kent: 1/172; 6/65
SIVILL: see Seville
SJAELLAND (Is.), Denmark: turkey from, 1/41 & n. 4
SKEFFINGTON, Sir John, P's contemporary at Magdalene; succ. as 2nd Viscount Massereene 1665 (d. 1695): 5/276-7 & n.
SKELTON, Bernard, P's schoolfellow; Fellow of Peterhouse, Cambridge 1659-64 (d. ?1690): university taxor, 3/218 & n. 2
SKINNER, [Thomas], merchant: dispute with E. India Company, 9/85 & n. 2, 182-4 passim & n., 196 & n. 1
SKINNERS' COMPANY: see London: livery companies
SKINNERS' HALL, Dowgate Hill: King's arms in, 1/106
SLANING (Slany), Anne, Lady Slaning (b. Carteret), wife of Sir Nicholas (d. 1691): marriage, 4/254 & n. 3; shares P's taste for cream and brown bread, 6/157; piety, 6/182; at Cranbourne, 7/54, 57
SLANING (Slany), Sir Nicholas, cr. bt 1663 (d. 1668): marriage, 4/254 & n. 3; admitted to Royal Society, 6/48
SLATER, [John], Navy Office messenger: employed as cook, 2/22; alluded to: 2/24, 28, 227
SLINGSBY, Sir Arthur, of Patrixbourne, nr Canterbury, Kent: pension, 4/274-5; partners King at tennis, 4/435; lottery, 5/214 & n. 2; social: 9/276
SLINGSBY, Henry, Deputy-Master of the Mint 1660, Master 1662: 'very ingenious', 6/22; shows P new coins, 2/38-9; 3/265; 4/70; conducts P and Mennes round Mint, 4/143-8; lease of houses etc. from King, 2/104 & n. 2; on amount of money current, 6/22-3; export of bullion, ib.; and revaluation, 7/304; social: 2/120

SLINGSBY, [Margaret], Lady Slingsby, widow of Sir Guildford Slingsby: 2/26
SLINGSBY, Col. Robert, ('the Comptroller'), cr. bt 1661, Comptroller of the Navy 1660–1:
CHARACTER: P's regard, 2/108, 120, 202
AS COMPTROLLER: appointed, 1/240 & n. 1; visits Deptford, 2/11, 12, 76; Woolwich, 2/11; and Portsmouth, 2/89; memorandum on state of navy, 2/20 & n. 3; disbanding business, 2/39; victualling business, 2/62, 104; acquires official logdings, 2/108, 110–11, 114, 119; plans to expand Navy Office, 2/143 & n. 4, 160–1; unspecified business, 1/290; 2/38, 184–5; also, 1/242, 254
SOCIAL: 1/253, 292; 2/24, 25–6, 30, 51, 76, 111, 131, 175, 179
MISC.: news from, 1/315, 318 & n. 2; 2/39; advises P to enter parliament, 2/42; King's debt to, 1/288 & n. 2; house and bowling-alley, 1/290; 2/15, 115; recites his verses, 1/302; projected order of Knights of the Sea, 1/314 & n. 2; created baronet, 2/61; unsuccessful parliamentary candidate, 2/76 & n. 1; illness and death, 2/200, 201, 202, 204
ALLUDED TO: 2/13, 25
~ his wife [Elizabeth], 2/24, 26, 76, 179; his daughter, 2/24; his sister, 1/290
SMALLWOOD, [Matthew], Canon of St Paul's 1660–71, Dean of Lichfield 1671–d.83: examiner at Apposition Day, St Paul's School, 5/38 & n. 3
SMALLWOOD, [William], barrister, Middle Temple: advises P in dispute with Trice, 2/217 & n. 3, 230; 4/352
[SMEGERGILL, alias Caesar, William], musician: plays lute, 5/344; 7/182; 8/118, 325, 333, 529, 530, 558; treble viol, 7/338; teaches lute/theorbo to Tom Edwards, 5/344; 6/86; 7/182, 226–7, 338, 375; to Lady Crew's page, 8/333; recommends gut string as fishing line, 8/119; stays in Westminster in Plague, 7/40–1
[SMETHWICK] (Smithys), [Francis]:

burning-glass, 9/113 & n. 5
SMITH, Sir George, merchant: to leave London during Plague, 6/205; city news from, 6/251–2; 7/174; social: Lady Robinson's crony, 6/290; entertains P and others, 6/187, 192 & n. 1, 307, 311–12; 7/4; also, 6/186, 257, 299; alluded to: 6/234; ~ his wife [Martha], 6/312
SMITH, Capt. Jeremy, naval commander, kted 1665; Navy Commissioner 1669–75: reputation, 4/196; 6/129; 7/158, 333, 344; 9/123, 137; P's opinion, 6/264; 9/382; leader of Albemarle's faction, 7/158, 333; pay, 4/325; conduct at Battle of Lowestoft, 6/122, 135; with fleet, 6/278; sails for Mediterranean, 7/9 & n. 5, 39–40, 45; at Cadiz, 7/46, 71; portrait by Lely, 7/102 & n. 3; commands *Loyal London*, 7/181, 215; accused by Holmes of failure to pursue enemy, 7/339–40 & n.; their duel, 7/348; charges against, 9/107, 118; to be land admiral at Portsmouth, 8/149; to command fleet, 9/123; appointed Navy Commissioner, 9/350, 551 & n. 2; also, 8/263–4; 9/383, 466; social: 8/479; 9/468, 469
SMITH, [John], herald painter: makes hatchment, 4/424–5 & n.
SMITH, John (d. 1870), first transcriber of the diary: vol. i, pp. lxxvi–lxxix, lxxxiii, lxxxviii, xc, xcii; edition of P's Tangier Journal, vol. i, p. lxxxv
SMITH, [Richard], boatswain, Woolwich yard: tells P of malpractices, 5/117
SMITH, [Robert], Navy Office messenger: to prosecute forger of pay tickets, 2/73 & n. 3; his part in Field case, 3/231 & n. 3, 262, 280; 4/16; helps to prepare King's yacht, 3/140; dines with Navy Board, 3/14; also, 1/253; 3/19; 7/250
SMITH, Sydney, author (d. 1845): opinion of diary, vol. i, p. lxxxiii
SMITH, [?Theophilus], mercer: 7/80 & n. 3
SMITH, [Thomas], formerly secretary to the Lord High Admiral and Navy Commissioner: chamber in Navy

Office, 3/197 & n. 3; profits, 4/170 &
n. 2, 330
SMITH, [Walter], scrivener, of Ludgate
Hill: marriage broker, 3/228, 231, 232
SMITH, [William], actor: kills man
accidentally, 7/369 & n. 3; in *The
Villain*, 8/499–500 & n.; P admires in
Mustapha, 9/62
SMITH, ——, clerk to Auditor Wood:
works on Tangier accounts, 9/389,
393, 429
SMITH, ——: 1/19
SMITH, Mrs ——, shopkeeper at New
Exchange: P admires, 8/215, 334, 335,
443; 9/245; also, 9/?263, 412, ?511, ?534
SMITHFIELD: horsedealers at, 9/384,
391; also, 2/99, 139; 8/464; 9/513, 521
SMYRNA: false Messiah at, 7/47 & n.
4; English merchantmen from, 7/390,
404 & n. 3; alluded to: 3/259
SMYTHES (Smithes), [Simon],
clergyman and Cambridge contemp-
orary of P: 3/58
SMYTHYS, [Francis]: *see* Smethwick
SNOW, [John], of Blackwall, P's
'cousin': offers P share in bottomry,
1/294 & n. 2; asks P for favour, 1/242
& n. 3; 2/32; social: 1/308; 2/30, 40,
81, 194, 196; ~ his wife, 2/81
SOISSONS, Maurice Eugène de
Savoie, Comte ['Duc'] de; ambassador
-extraordinary, 5–22 Nov. 1660:
1/275 & n. 1
SOLEBAY (Soale bay, Sold bay),
Suff.: English shipping at, 2/156;
6/115, 202, 223, 256; 7/251
SOLOMONS (Salomon), Mr ——,
Capt. Cocke's brother[-in-law]: 6/257
& n. 2, 273
SOMERSET, Duke of: *see* Seymour
SOMERSET, Henry, 3rd Marquess of
Worcester, cr. Duke of Beaufort
1682 (d. 1700): godfather to Duke of
Cambridge, 8/438
SOMERSET, [Thomas], son of Lord
John Somerset: troubles P by atten-
tions to EP, 2/165 & n. 2, 170
SOMERSET HOUSE, Strand: soldiers
in mutiny, 1/38 & n. 1, 59; Queen
Mother's court, 3/112, 191, 299;
6/142; Duchess of Richmond at,
8/590; 9/134, 205; places in: Queen
Mother's presence chamber, 3/191;

her rebuilding of chapel etc., 4/127 &
n. 3; 5/63 & n. 2, 300; her closet, 6/17;
garden, 5/63; 6/18; echo in garden,
6/18; also, 9/365–6
SOMERSET STAIRS: 1/249; 5/165;
7/146; 9/219
SOUCHE, General: *see* Ratuit
SOULEMONT (Salmon), [Solomon],
clerk to Sir G. Carteret: practical joke
on, 4/226–7
SOUND, the: *see* Baltic
SOUTH (Zouth), [Robert], chaplain
to the Lord Chancellor (d. 1716):
story of his collapsing in pulpit before
King, 3/67 & n. 2
SOUTHAMPTON: P visits, 3/70–1;
description of town and walls, 3/71 &
nn.
SOUTHAMPTON BUILDINGS:
5/286 & n. 2; 9/371
SOUTHAMPTON MARKET,
Bloomsbury: 7/232 & n. 1; 8/169;
9/389
SOUTHERNE (Southorne), James,
Admiralty clerk: clerk to Blackborne,
1/59; to Coventry, 1/183; petitions
Duke of York for storekeeper's place,
9/327 & n. 4; also, 3/138; 6/280; social:
1/27, 59; 3/5
SOUTH FORELAND, Kent: 1/105
SOUTHWARK [*see also* Fairs etc.]:
post house, 2/15 & n. 1, 231 & n. 2;
fields near, 2/115; 4/214; White Lion
prison, 3/165 & n. 3; court of Admiralty, 4/76; ?Artillery House, 6/99 &
n. 4; ?St Olave's church, 8/255 & n. 3;
also, 2/25; 3/35; 5/307; 7/294, 363
SOUTH WEALD, ESSEX: church
(St Peter's), 6/159–60 & n.
SOUTHWELL, Sir Robert, ambassador to Portugal 1665–9, kted 1665:
his news from Tangier, 5/165 & n. 2;
quarrels with Sandwich over Spanish-
Portuguese treaty, 9/59 & n. 3; con-
veys gift from Royal Society to
Portuguese scholars, 9/113–14 & n.;
also, 9/237; social: in Hyde Park tour
with wife [Elizabeth], 6/60 & n. 4
SPAIN [*see also* Charles II of Spain;
Mountagu, E., 1st Earl of Sandwich;
Vatteville, Baron. For wars, *see*
France; Portugal]:
GENERAL: differences between Spaniard

and Frenchmen, 1/10; English natural affection for, 2/188 & n. 4; bullfights, 3/90; revenues 5/68; shortage of bullion, 6/23; stamp tax, 7/332 & n. 2; court, 7/201; 8/452; army, 7/201; 9/6 & n. 2, 396-7 & nn.; anecdote of friar, 8/67; dress at court, 8/79; effects of Inquisition on cloth industry, 8/79-80 & n.; beards, 8/453; customs, 8/111 & n. 3, 451-2 & nn.; the Pantéon at Escorial, 9/118 & n. 5; food: *oleo*, 9/509-10, 544; sauce, 9/443; also, 3/251

CHRON. SERIES: resents loss of Tangier, 3/33; English merchants fear break with, 3/115; Spanish reaction to raid on Santiago, 4/94 & n. 3; trade treaty with England (May 1668), 8/30, 45, 69 & n. 2, 74 & n. 2, 75, 107 & n. 2, 190 & n. 1, 246, 453 & n. 2

SPANISH NETHERLANDS: French threat to Flanders, 8/74, 75, 92 & n. 3, 107-8, 175; Louis XIV's claim, 8/186 & n. 2, 254 & n. 1; French invasion, 8/186, 432; 9/38 & n. 1; English troops for, 8/246 & n. 3; Flemish ships in Thames, 8/266; wars in (1650s), 9/396 & nn.; also, 3/246; 7/229

SPARGUS (asparagus) Garden, ?Whitehall: 9/172

SPARKE(S), [Edward], clergyman: 1/60

SPARLING, Capt. [Thomas], naval officer: on voyage to Holland, 1/102, 119, 168; gift to P, 1/164; changes Dutch money for, 1/168, 178-9; social: 1/167; ~ his harper, 1/119, 124, 153

SPAS: *see* Banbury; Barnet; Bath; Bourbon l'Archambault; Epsom; Tunbridge Wells

SPELMAN, [Clement], Cursitor Baron of the Exchequer 1663-79 (d. 1680): 6/65 & n. 3

SPELMAN (Spillman), Lady: 5/130

SPENCER, Dr [John], Fellow of Corpus Christi College, Cambridge 1655-67; Master 1667-93; Dean of Ely 1677-d.93 [*see also* Books]: his learning, 7/133 & n. 3

SPENCER, Robert, 2nd Earl of Sunderland, Secretary of State 1679-81, 1683-8 (d. 1702): breaks off

engagement with Lady Anne Digby, 4/208-9 & n.

SPICER, Jack, clerk in the Exchequer: Sandwich's money deposited with, 1/290, 291, 292, 294, 312; at Nonsuch in Plague, 6/235-6; deals with P's Tangier tallies, 7/32-3; counts money for P, 7/251; also, 1/43, 44, 317; 3/296-7; 9/78; social: at P's dinner for old Exchequer colleagues, 2/241; at taverns, 1/7, 8, 33, 57, 201, 229, 270; 2/4, 6, 50, 227; 6/162; 7/398; 8/590; also, 1/41, 257, 259

SPITAL (Spittle), [Square], Spital-fields: Spital sermons at, 3/57-8 & n.; 9/517

SPITALFIELDS: 9/528

SPITTS, the (roadstead off Sheppey): 1/104

SPONG, [John], Chancery clerk and optical-instrument maker:

CHARACTER: P admires, 6/92-3; his 'plainness and ingenuity', 9/417; also, 3/120; 5/235

CHRON. SERIES: engrosses P's Chancery bill, 1/197-8, 198, 204; and his agreement with Barlow, 1/205; arrested as suspected plotter, 3/237-8 & n.; experiments with microscope, 5/235; 7/226; visits glass maker, 7/218-19; demonstrates magic lantern, 7/254 & n. 3; and pantograph, 9/340 & n. 1, 389-90 & nn., 417; supplies P with pantograph, 9/437, 443-4; also, 1/273

MUSICAL/SOCIAL: sings with P, 1/63, 205, 268, 272, 274; 3/99, 120; plays flageolet, 1/71; at music meeting, 5/290; dines with P, 8/105-6; 9/406, 524-5; also, 2/161

~ his mother, 1/272

Sports: *see* Games etc.

SPRAGGE, Capt. Edward, kted 1665; naval commander: at council of war, 6/230; influence in fleet, 7/158, 178, 179; protégé of Rupert, 7/178-9; responsibility for division of fleet, ib.; 8/148; enquiry into, 8/515; challenges Commissioner Pett to duel, 7/212; appointed to command in river, 8/149; squadron in action, 8/354, 359; conduct in Medway raid, 8/308, 351, 379, 501; 9/11; criticises officers of Ordnance, 8/496; enemy of

STEPHENS, ——, lawyer, of the Temple: consulted about Downing's dispute with Squibb, 1/40, 48, 49

STEPNEY: Trinity House, 1/177; 7/381; 9/202; churchyard, 8/248; also, 3/5; 8/437

STERNE, Richard, Archbishop of York 1664–d. 83: preaches at Whitehall, 7/94 & n. 4

STERPIN, Kate: see Petit

STERRY, [Nathaniel], secretary to the plenipotentiaries in Denmark 1659: Swedish news from, 1/83

STEVENAGE, Herts.: P at, 2/183; 5/233, 298; 9/224; [Swan Inn], 8/475 & n. 1

STEVENS (Stephens), [Anthony], cashier to the Navy Treasurer: at pays, 2/93; 6/319; to go to Southampton, 3/70; business with, 6/332; 8/103; on theology, 2/94; also, 1/84, 191

STEVENTON, [?John], purser: abused by Mennes, 4/151; to surrender place, 9/381, 382 & n. 4; also, 8/381; 9/188

STEVENTON (Stephenton), St John, Clerk of the Cheque, Portsmouth dockyard: 3/74 & n. 2, 174

STEWARD, Capt. [Francis], naval officer: criticised, 7/174 & n. 2

STEWARD, Mrs ——: 5/126

STEWARD, STEWART: see Stuart

STILLINGFLEET, Edward, chaplain to the King, Rector of St Andrew, Holborn; Bishop of Worcester 1689–d. 99 [see also Books]: his preaching, 6/87 & nn.; preaches at funeral, 9/40, 49; his school, 8/17 & n. 6; also, 6/80; 9/548

STILLINGWORTH: see Stellingwerf

STILLYARD: see Steelyard

STINT, ——, solicitor: 3/280; 4/333

STIRTLOE (Sturtlow), Hunts.: P inherits land, 2/136, 193, 227; sells, 2/138; 3/27, 103, 226, 228; 4/119; also, 5/44, 91

STOAKES (Stokes), Capt. [John], naval officer: to employ B. St Michel, 1/104; Sandwich dislikes, 1/107; dispute with Winter, 1/175 & n. 1; to buy paper in France for Navy Board, 1/201; ship *Assurance* wrecked, 1/313

& n. 2, 316; and paid off, 2/238; stories of Gambia, 3/10–11 & n.; death, 6/35; social: 1/92, 159, 178; 2/210

STOCKDALE, [Robert]: 6/163, 185

STOCKS MARKET (the Stocks), Cornhill [see also Taverns etc.: Three Cranes]: destroyed in Fire, 9/307 & n. 3; also, 7/14 & n. 1, 164

[STOKE] NEWINGTON, Mdx: affray, 3/34; P's parents married [error], 5/360 & n. 2

STOKES [Capt.]: see Stoakes

STOKES, [Humphrey], goldsmith, Lombard St: business, 7/9–10, 244, 367; 8/582; house destroyed in Fire, 7/270; also, 7/361; ~ his pretty wife, 7/9–10, 362

STONE, Capt. [John], Commonwealth Exchequer official: advises in dispute concerning Downing, 1/40, 44, 45

STONE, [Symon], painter: his copy of ?Johnson's portrait of Lord Coventry, 7/183 & n. 3

STONE, Mrs [?Thomas]: 9/116 & n. 1

STONEHENGE, Wilts.: book on, 9/226 & n. 1; P visits, 9/229; also, 9/240

STORY, Capt. [Thomas], receiver of assessments and farmer of excise, Cambridgeshire: business with, 8/85 & n. 2; news from, 8/85–6 & n.

STOWELL, [?Robert]: 1/239

STRACHAN (Straughan), Capt. [John] navy agent, Leith: gift from King, 1/300–1 & n.; advice about ballast, 1/301; P's opinion, ib.

STRADLING, [George], chaplain to the Bishop of London, Dean of Chichester 1672–d.88: a slicenser of books, 4/111 & n. 2

STRADWICK: see Strudwick

STRAITS, the: see Mediterranean

STRAND, the [see also Taverns etc.: Bell; Bull; Castle; Cock; Fountain; Golden Lion; Half Moon]: mutiny, 1/38, 59; affray, 8/206; Maypole, 1/52, 300; 2/127; 4/167; 7/417; 8/206; conduit, 5/91; turnstiles, 9/366

STRAND BRIDGE: 1/52; 8/138; 9/199

STRAND STAIRS: 9/368

STRANGE, Maj. [Edward], solicitor to the Excise: 6/130
STRANGWAYS, Col. [Giles], M.P Dorset 1661–d.75: 4/77
STRATFORD, Mdx: P at, 8/326; 9/528
STREETER, [Robert], Serjeant-painter to the King 1660–d.79: paintings for Sheldonian Theatre, 9/434 & n. 2
[STRODE, Ellen], servant to the Duchess of York: 2/40–1 & n.
STRODE (Strowd), Col. [John], Governor of Dover Castle: 7/145
STROUD GREEN, Mdx: Green Man at, 9/545
STRUDWICK, [Elizabeth], (b. Pepys), P's cousin, wife of Thomas: death of children, 1/244; social: 2/2, 216
STRUDWICK (Stradwick), [Thomas], confectioner, Snow Hill: P orders confectionery from, 2/8; provides funeral biscuits, 5/87, 88; P's liking for, 9/477; social: gives Twelfth Night party, 1/10; 2/7; also, 2/2, 39; 9/375
STRUTT, [Thomas], purser: dispute with Capt. J. Browne, 3/284 & n. 1; 5/32; also, 4/192
STUART, Charles, Duke of Cambridge, 1st son of the Duke of York: birth, 1/273; death, 2/95 & n. 1
[STUART, Charles, Duke of Kendal] (1666–7), 3rd son of the Duke of York: born, 7/201 & n. 2; illness and death, 8/214 & n. 1, 234
STUART, Charles, 3rd Duke of Richmond and 6th Duke of Lennox (d. 1672); alleged immorality, 6/167; marries Frances Stuart, 8/119 & n. 2, 120, 121, 145, 183, 343; King's anger, 1/145 & n. 4, 169; with wife at Somerset House, 8/590; will not permit her return to court, 8/593; yacht to be taken into royal service, 9/301–2 & n.; gives P warrant for doe, 9/302; alluded to: 4/260; ~ his running footman, 4/255
STUART, Edgar, Duke of Cambridge (1667–71), 4th son of the Duke of York (d. 1671): born, 8/436 & n. 2; baptised, 8/438 & n. 2
STUART (Steward, Stewart), Frances Teresa, wife of the 3rd Duke of Richmond:
HER APPEARANCE: beauty, 4/230; 5/209; 7/384; compared with Lady Castlemaine, 5/139; 7/106, 384; dress at court ball, 7/372; marred by smallpox, 9/294; also, 5/107; 7/252, 306; 8/44; 9/302
CHRON. SERIES: said to be King's mistress, 4/37–8 & n., 48, 142 & n. 1, 174, 206; 7/8, 100, 404; and to be supplanting Lady Castlemaine, 4/230 & n. 1, 238; plot to procure for King, 4/366; King's public attentions, 4/371 & n. 1; 5/20–1, 40; Duke of York in love with, 6/302; marries Duke of Richmond, 8/119 & n. 2, 120, 121, 145; King's anger, 8/145 & n. 4, 169; reputation defended by Evelyn, 8/183–4; Louis XIV's admiration, 8/184 & n. 1; story of King's intending to marry her, 8/342–3, 366; at Somerset House, 8/590; will not return to court, 8/593; 9/24; has smallpox, 9/134–5 & n., 139; King visits, 9/190, 205; made Lady of Queen's Bedchamber, 9/257; also, 6/110; 9/282
PORTRAITS: sits for ?Huysmans, ?Lely, 5/209 & n. 2; painted by Huysmans in soldier's dress, 5/254 & n. 4; represents Britannia on medal, 8/83 & n. 1; miniature by Cooper, 9/139 & n. 2
STUART, James, Duke of Cambridge, 2nd son of the Duke of York: born, 4/229 & n. 4; christened, 4/238 & n. 1; Knight of the Garter, 7/398 & n. 2; illness and death, 8/189, 192, 214, 234, 235, 239, 252, 253, 255, 283, 286
STUART, Ludovic, 10th Seigneur d'Aubigny, Almoner to the Queen Mother (d. 1665): story of cardinalate, 4/211 & n. 2, 224 & n. 2; at court, 4/229; organ, 8/25 & n. 2
STUART, [Mary], widow of the 1st Duke of Richmond, wife of Thomas Howard; Lady of the Queen's Bedchamber (d. 1685): quarrels with Lady Castlemaine, 3/68 & n. 3; 8/330–1 & n. 5
STUART, Sophia, sister of Frances Teresa: P admires, 9/294 & n. 4
STUART, Mrs ——, mother of Frances Teresa: 4/366; 8/184 & n. 1

the 14th Earl (d. 1702): Buckingham's mistress and cause of duel, 9/27 & n. 2; her footmen attack H. Killigrew, 9/557 & n. 2, 558

TALBOT, Capt. [Charles], naval officer: account of St James's Day Fight, 7/221-2 & nn.

TALBOT, Francis, 14th Earl of Shrewsbury (d. 1668): injured in duel with Buckingham, 9/26-7 & n., 29; pardoned by King, 9/52 & nn.

TALBOT, Sir John, Gentleman of the Privy Chamber (d. 1714): injured in duel, 9/26-7 & n.; on prize business, 9/168; supports Ormond, 9/348 & n. 4; also, 8/577 & n. 2

TALBOT, Father Peter, Almoner to the Queen: satire on Clarendon, 9/256 & n. 2

TALBOT, Col. [Richard], cr. Earl of Tyrconnel 1685: brings letters from Portugal, 3/62 & n. 3; hostile to Coventry, 3/122

TALBOT, Mr ——: social: 1/21, 76, 287; 2/99

TALLENTS, [Philip], Sheriff's chaplain; P's contemporary at Magdalene: 9/34 & n. 3

TANGIER [for P's services on the Tangier Committee, *see* below, Tangier (P). *See also* Belasyse, Lord; 'Guyland'; Mordaunt, H., Earl of Peterborough; Povey, T.; Rutherford, A., Earl of Teviot]:
GENERAL: establishment of civil government, 4/83 & n. 4, 88-9 & n.; 7/109 & n. 1; 8/207, 210, 459 & n. 2; 9/149 & n. 1, 551; reform of governorship, 8/61, 160 & n. 1, 207; Reymes's report 5/274 & n. 3; Sandwich's report, 9/355 & n. 1; Beckman's map, 3/37 & n. 2; J. Moore's, 5/98 & n. 2; Sandwich's drawing, 3/174 & n. 3; Sheeres's engraving, 9/419 & n. 2; Danckert's print, 9/541 & n. 2; also, 4/304 & n. 3
CHRON. SERIES: acquisition, 2/145 & n. 2; 3/91 & n. 1; garrison sent, 2/189 & n. 2; Peterborough takes up duties as governor, 2/202; 3/12; Sandwich's action, 2/221 & n. 3; Portuguese defeated by Moors, 3/33 & n. 2; Sandwich takes possession, ib.; poor condition, 3/110 & n. 1; Spain resents English possession, 3/115; hopes of peace, 3/172 & n. 2; corruption, 4/27; Moors attack, 4/240 & n. 5, 283 & n. 1, 301 & n. 1; truce with, 4/283 & n. 1, 299, 304, 336, 336-7 & n.; value, 4/319; relations with Salli, 4/335-6 & n.; Moors attempt to bribe garrison, 4/394; Teviot killed in ambush, 5/165 & n. 2, 166-7 & n., 179-80; quarrels among officers, 5/302 & n. 1, 344-5 & n.; rumour of Sandwich as governor, 5/313; 'Guyland' overthrown, 7/214 & n. 2; value doubted, 8/160, 201, 348; Clarendon blamed for acquisition, 8/269; rumour of cession to France, 8/289; 'Guyland' offers Azila, 8/347 & n. 3; relations with Algiers, 9/272 & n. 1; quarrel between civil corporation and Norwood, 9/392 & n. 1, 431; ruinous condition, 9/543(2); also, 3/18, 30, 81; 9/488
COMMITTEE FOR GOVERNMENT:
GENERAL: appointed, 3/170, 238 & n. 3; reconstructed, 6/6-7 & n., 13; quorum, 6/89; 7/156; meetings cancelled in absence of King and Duke of York, 7/228; alleged inefficiency, 4/35-6, 45; 5/167, 168, 173; committees, 7/321
BUSINESS:
financial: Teviot's accounts, 4/269, 273, 320, 326-7; 6/95; Peterborough's, 5/52, 66, 97, 105, 123, 124, 127, 135, 139, 153, 154, 174; Belasyse's, 9/199, 205, 429, 529; Povey's, 6/13, 14, 15, 17, 58(2), 61, 77, 77-8; 9/371, 449; Yeabsley's, 7/115, 162, 163, 166-7; Cholmley's, 9/388; other accounts, 4/408; 7/321, 336, 383-4; compensation for Portuguese, 4/336 & n. 2; 5/239 & n. 3; supply, 6/134, 139; 7/207; 9/253, 415, 493; currency, 9/316; powers of proposed town treasurer, 9/407 & n. 3
garrison: to be reduced, 3/204, 272; 5/310; 9/36; work on fortifications, 3/287; 4/301; cost of garrison, 4/93; reinforcements, 4/319; 5/166; provisions, 5/279; payment, 7/320, 321; proposed paymaster, 9/415, 417, 418, 422
mole: to be constructed, 3/204; contract agreed, 4/26-7, 31, 35-6, 45, 88

Povey, 7/51, 71, 335(2); Belasyse, 7/190, 191, 330, 338, 423; 8/22-3; 9/202; Vernatti, 7/265, 338; Middleton, 9/325, 328

OTHER FINANCIAL BUSINESS: negotiations with bankers, 6/108, 115, 193, 266, 267, 268; 7/170, 174, 242; 9/78 & n. 1, 315 & n. 1, 325, 328; his accounts with, 6/204-5, 207; enquiries into expenditure by Brooke House Committee, 9/562; also, 6/144, 146; 7/66; 8/100, 103, 123, 203, 244, 329, 341, 348, 372, 383, 390, 407, 518, 520(2); 9/152, 214, 249

SHIPPING BUSINESS: freightage, 4/52 & n. 1, 85; 5/167(2) & n. 3, 175, 186, 199, 201, 255, 276, 292, 332-3, 335, 337 & n. 1, 338, 340 & n. 2, 341; hire, 5/252; 6/27, 28, 32, 70; ships' passes, 7/20 & n. 3, 36, 38, 64, 98, 167

VICTUALLING BUSINESS: Yeabsley's accounts, 7/110, 121; 8/515; payments to Gauden, 6/322, 325; 7/402; Andrews, 6/227, 337; and Lanyon, 8/102, 146, 252; empowered to order bread, 4/21; discusses victualling with Sandwich, 4/30; inspects oats, 5/179, 187; his expenses allowed, 5/200; drafts contract with Alsop and Lanyon, 5/195, 196, 202, 204, 213, 223, 226, 229, 236; with Andrews, 6/37, 98; discusses contract with Gauden, 6/171-2, 253-4; with Andrews, 6/185, 201, 226-7; with Yeabsley, 8/438, 483, 515; also, 7/9

MISC. BUSINESS: appointment of river agent, 4/93; supply of deals, 5/277(2), 279; advised not to press enquiries into mole, 5/343; canvas, 6/65-6 & n.; lighters, 6/146 & n. 2, 172; 7/227

PERQUISITES, PROFITS AND BRIBES: general: hopes for, 4/85; 5/167, 249, 252, 258, 267, 277(2) 332-3, 337, 338, 340; 6/7, 27, 28, 32, 37, 70, 109, 146, 157, 172, 204, 208, 251, 252-3; 8/513; receives c. £250 in one month, 5/276; Tangier 'one of the best flowers in my garden', 5/280; fears discovery, 5/340 & n. 2, 348; willing to admit to, 9/99; justifies gains, 5/195, 214, 279; and retainer, 8/593; insists on paying for candlestick, 9/429-30; money: from

Lanyon and partners (victuallers), £300 p.a., 5/210, 223, 224, 226, 227, 263, 267; £36, 6/57; £222, 6/202; £64, 6/227; £210, 6/337, 340; £200, 7/162, 168; from Gauden (victualler), £500, 6/322, 325; £500, 8/35, 37, 44; from Cholmley (contractor for mole), £200 p.a., 6/306; 8/592, 593; £100, 7/19; from Houblons (ship's pass), £200, 7/64, 66, 98, 167; from other merchants (hire and freightage), £26, 5/175; £50, 5/186, 199, 201-2; £30, 5/255, 276; £117, 5/340, 341; £200, 6/286; 7/24; £100, 7/227; from Fitzgerald, £20, 7/173; also, 4/93; 6/26, 37, 242(2); 7/402; 8/372; other gifts, 7/167

TANNER, Mr ――: plays violin with P, 1/78

TAPESTRY: see Textiles etc.

TASBOROUGH, [John], clerk to Povey: 6/73, 153

TATNELL, Capt. [Valentine], naval officer: enmity to Coventry, 9/108 & n. 2, 129; also, 9/147

TAUNTON, Som.: Blake's defence (1644-5), 5/169 & n. 3

TAVERNS, inns, alehouses and eating-houses [mentioned by name and in London, Westminster and immediate environs, i.e. Bow, Chelsea, Clerkenwell, Holloway, Islington, Knightsbridge, Lambeth, Mile End, Rotherhithe and Stroud Green. Those not in this area are indexed under place-names. Those not named are indexed under streets etc. In this list where P gives sufficient information the street location is added. Asterisks denote the occasions on which he had a meal elsewhere than in an eating-house. For other houses of refreshment, see Cakehouses; Cookshops; Coffee-houses; Gardens: pleasure-gardens; Milk-house; Whey-house. See also Entertainments.]

GENERAL: closed during church services, 1/54 & n. 1, 270; 6/5; brewhouse, 1/119; dining clubs, 1/208; 7/375; bar, 1/301; 8/345; convenience of ordinaries, 4/131; French taverns compared with English, ib.; P rarely visits in mornings, 9/220

Covent Garden: murder at, 1/307 &
n. 2; P visits, 2/193, 220; 7/425;
Fleece tavern, by Guildhall: trick
played on landlady, 2/43; P visits,
2/50; Fleece mum-house, Leadenhall
St: P visits, 3/94; 5/142, 191; Folly,
floating house of entertainment on
Thames: P visits, 9/161 & n. 7;
Fountain tavern, Old Bailey: alluded
to, 5/168; Fountain tavern, Strand: P
visits, 2/195, 221; Fox tavern, King
St, Westminster: P visits, 1/88*;
French ordinary, Westminster: 1/23
Game's: see Coach and Horses,
Aldgate; George inn, Holborn: EP
takes coach, 3/148; 'George's, old',
Lambeth (unident.): P and EP dine at,
2/178; alluded to, 4/217; Glasshouse
inn, Broad St: Monck at, 1/53, n. 5;
P visits, 4/88; 5/64*; Globe tavern,
Eastcheap: P visits, 4/20; Globe
tavern, Fleet St: business meetings,
4/350; 6/65; Goat tavern, Charing
Cross: P visits, 2/64, 75; Mountagu
children stay at, 2/75; (Golden)
Fleece: see Fleece; (Golden) Hoop:
see Hoop; Golden Lion tavern,
Charing Cross: P visits, 1/19; Golden
Lion tavern, Strand: P visits, 7/424;
Grange inn, Portugal Row: P visits,
3/57 & n. 5; Great/Old James: see
Old/Great James; Green Dragon,
Lambeth Hill: P visits, 1/19; Green
Man tavern, Stroud Green: alluded to,
8/465; 9/545; Greyhound tavern,.
Fleet St: P visits, 1/71; 2/17, 212;
Gridiron, alehouse, Shoe Lane:
?2/156; 2/178; Gun, Mile End: P
visits, 9/221

Half Moon tavern, Strand: P visits,
1/15, 59, 181, 194, 223; 4/179;
5/205(2); 7/425; alluded to, 4/429;
5/55; 6/121; Halfway House, nr
Rotherhithe: P visits, 2/45, 112; 3/86,
91, 115; 4/99, 112, 144, 151, 162;
5/80, 95, 111, 124, 138, 156, 176;
6/184, 310, 332; 7/115; 8/325; alluded
to, 4/79, 110; 5/155, 347; Hare's, Mrs:
see Trumpet; Harp and Ball tavern,
nr Charing Cross (Roberts's): P
visits, 1/23, 33, 86; 3/298; 6/87, 103,
115, 142, 144, 145, 155; 7/418; 9/163,
248, 474, 542; ~ Mary at, from

Wales, 6/144; P admires, 6/87, 103;
talks with, 6/142, 145(2) takes on
jaunt, 6/155; also, 6/115, 142, 145(2);
Harper's, King St, Westminster [see
also Harper, James; Harper, Mary;
Harper, Tom]: P buys gloves, 1/183;
other visits, 1/9*, 12, 14, 15, 21, 33, 34,
37, 38, 48, 56, 58, 59, 82, 83, 87, 88,
200, 201, 225–6, 251, 286, 325;
2/80–1, 87; Harv(e)y's, Salisbury
Court: P visits, 1/175; Heaven, eating
house, Old Palace Yard: P dines,
1/31, 234, 290; Hell, eating house,
New Palace Yard: P dines, 1/303;
Herbert's: see Swan, New Palace
Yard; Hercules Pillars ordinary, off
Fleet St: 1/264, 278; 2/6, 145; 4/87*,
356; 8/281; 9/54*, 169*, 171*, 177*,
182*, 183*, 197–8*, 249*, 295*,
299*, 356*, 366*, 373*, 390*, 421*,
442–3*, 445*, 456*, 531, 538*;
Hilton's, Axe Yard: soldiers quartered,
1/46; Hoop (Golden Hoop) tavern,
Thames St/Fish St Hill: P visits,
1/249–50, 287*; 2/9; Horn tavern,
Fleet St: P visits, 4/102; ?5/246 & n. 2;
Horseshoe tavern, nr Navy Office:
Betty Lane's foolish visit, 5/285
Jacob's (?Salutation, Charing
Cross): P visits, 1/58; Jamaica House,
Bermondsey: P visits, 8/167
Keeper's lodge ('the Lodge'), Hyde
Park, milk house: P visits, 9/142 &
n. 1, ?154, 156, 175, 184, 222, 260,
533–4, 541; King's Head, Bow: P
visits, 3/169*; King's Head tavern,
Chancery Lane: P visits, 6/139*; with
fellows of Royal Society, 9/146–7;
King's Head inn, Charing Cross:
renamed, 1/179; P visits, 1/179, 206;
3/238*; 4/23*, 37*, 58*, 130*, 216*,
345*, 349*, 371*, 394*, 408*, 419*,
435*; alluded to, 4/12, 196; King's
Head tavern, Fish St Hill: P visits,
5/309; King's Head, Islington ('the old
House'; Pitt's): P visits, 2/98, 125;
5/133; known to P in youth, 5/101;
King's Head, Lambeth Marsh: P
visits, 4/263; King's Head, nr Royal
Exchange: P visits, 4/384 & n. 3;
King's Head, nr Royal Exchange: P
visits, 4/384 & n. 3; King's Head,
Tower St: P's dirty dinner, 2/89*

Lamb's (Mother Lam's) alehouse, Gardiner's Lane, Westminster: P visits, 1/14; Leg, King St, Westminster (Clerke's): P visits, 1/74*, 173*, 183*, 200*, 207*, 208*, 212*, 217-18*, 224*, 229*, 231*, 257*, 263*, 272*, 310*; 2/18*, 108*, 200*; 8/74; Leg tavern, New Palace Yard: P dines, 1/188*, 296*; 2/35*, 66*; Leg, Westminster (probably King St; possibly New Palace Yard): P visits, 2/4; 3/196; 5/102*, 149*; 6/106, 162*; 9/106; food supplied from, 2/219; [Lockett's] ordinary, Charing Cross: newly established, 9/317 & n. 2; P dines, ?9/206, 317

Mitre, Cheapside: P visits, 2/220; Mitre, Fenchurch St (Rawlinson's) [see also Rawlinson, D.]: P pays bill, 4/353; Sandwich's wine bought, 5/36; in ruins after Fire, 8/427; P visits, 1/174, 195, 200, 216, 220, 239, 256, 302; 2/34, 36, 45, 58, 76, 77, 79, 89, 99*, 103, 107, 109*, 132, 153, 161, 167, 170, 191, 202, 207*, 219, 231, 241*; 3/61*, 124*, 165*, 166*, 173*, 276, 294, 298*; 4/10, 364*; 5/36, 47*, 191; alluded to, 3/178; Mitre, Fleet St (Steadman's): music, 1/25 & n. 4, 59; Mitre tavern, Mitre Court, Fleet St (Paget's): alluded to, 1/25; Mitre, Wood St [see also Proctor, [W.]]: 'a house of greatest note', 1/248; P visits, 1/244, 248*; alluded to, 6/175-6; [Mother Redcap], Holloway: alluded to, 2/184 & n. 1; Mouth tavern, Bishopsgate: alluded to (in error), 5/285 & n. 2

Nag's Head tavern, ?Cheapside: P visits, 5/37; New Exchange tavern, nr Royal Exchange [see also Stanley, B.]: landlord P's old playfellow, 4/384; P visits, ib.

Old/Great James, Bishopsgate St: P visits, 5/15, 19, 23*, 136*, 341*; 6/77*, 83; 7/65*; alluded to: 2/26 'Old house, the', Islington: see King's Head; Old Swan, Thames St: P visits, 8/412; alluded to, 7/75, 114; Oxford Kate's: see Cock, Bow St Paget's: see Mitre tavern, Mitre Court; Penell's, Fleet St: P visits,

2/56; Pope's Head tavern, Chancery Lane: P visits, 1/94; 4/352; Pope's Head tavern, Pope's Head Alley, Lombard St: painted room, 9/420; P visits, 3/41; 5/204; 6/311, 322*, 325(2)*, 328, 329*, 332*, 340*; 7/25*, 83*, 104*, 223*, 370*; 9/420; moved after Fire, 7/329 & n. 1; Price's, Old Palace Yard: P visits, 1/270, 319; Prior's: see Rhenish winehouse, Cannon Row

Quaker's, the, eating-house: P dines, 1/211 & n. 1; 9/162, 163; Queen's Head, Bow: P visits, 8/112*

Rawlinson's: see Mitre, Fenchurch St; Red Lion inn, Aldersgate St: P rides for Brampton from, 5/296; P's father to arrive at by coach, 8/231; (Red) Lion, King St, Westminster: P visits, 1/78; 2/187; Reindeer, Westminster: P visits, 1/259; Rhenish winehouse (Prior's), Cannon Row, Westminster: the further Rhenish winehouse, 4/203; new cellar, 2/170; P visits, 1/39; 2/170; 3/285; 4/203; ?9/220; Rhenish winehouse, King St, Westminster: the 'old' Rhenish winehouse, 1/221; P drinks 'Bleakard', 4/189; first visit for seven years, ?9/220; visits, 1/45, 88, 174, 210, 217, 221, 263, 301; 2/34, 105, 230; ?alluded to, 8/323; Rhenish winehouse, Steelyard: P visits, 2/40, 233; 4/58, 101, 343; 6/95; Ringstead's: see Star tavern, Cheapside; Roberts's: see Harp and Ball; Robins, Monsieur, his ordinary, Covent Garden: P dines, 8/211; Rose tavern, King St, Westminster: P visits with Doll Lane, 7/359; 8/3, 111, 193; Rose tavern, Russell St, Covent Garden: P visits, 8/589; 9/193*, 198, 203*; Rose tavern, Tower St: P sends for wine, 2/211; Rose (and Crown), Mile End: P visits, 8/389; 9/88, 255; [?Rose and Crown alehouse, Tower Stairs]: 2/229; shut during Plague, 6/225 & n. 4; Royal Oak tavern, Lombard St: P drinks Haut Brion, 4/100; entertained to dinner, 6/38

Salutation tavern, Billingsgate: P dines, 1/76-7; ?Salutation tavern, Charing Cross: see Jacob's; Sampson,

Paul's Churchyard: P visits, 2/124*, 161; Saracen's Head, nr Wardrobe: P visits, 2/211; Ship tavern, Billiter Lane, Fenchurch St [see also [Brome], ——; Morris, [John]]: P visits to admire landlord's daughter, 8/156, 345, 443; 9/51, 284, 485–6; pays his debts, 8/443; also, 4/404; Ship tavern, [?King St], Westminster: alluded to, 1/95; Ship tavern, ?Temple Bar: P visits, 2/173; Ship tavern, Threadneedle St: P dines, 3/150; Short's alehouse, Old Bailey: P visits, 3/100; Spring Garden, Vauxhall, house at: P visits, 6/164; Standing's, Fleet St: P visits, 1/250, 290, 303; 2/17, 25, 180; Star tavern, Cheapside (Ringstead's): P visits, 1/14, 52, 307; 2/109, 238; 3/91; 4/424; Star Tavern, ?Tower St: P visits, 4/424; Steadman's: see Mitre tavern, Fleet St; Sugar Loaf, Temple Bar: P visits, 1/48, 49; 9/477*; Sun tavern, Chancery Lane: P visits, 1/24; Sun tavern, Fish St Hill: P visits, 1/84*, 88*, 212*, 321*; 2/208, 210*, 213–14*; 7/91*; Sun tavern, King St, Westminster: P visits, 1/57*, 73, 75, 181*, 192, 194, 207, 209, 211, 217, 229, 231, 235, 265, 292, 296, 304; 3/192; 9/271; P's old drawer George alluded to, 1/229; Sun tavern, Threadneedle St ('behind the Exchange'): aviary, 4/85; Buckingham at, 8/299; P visits, 1/80; 2/196, 219; 4/85*, 172; 5/35, 271; 6/27*, 30*, 39*, 44*, 77*, 86*; 7/36, 38*, 299; 8/49*, 108*, 135, 516*; alluded to, 8/302; Swan tavern, Chelsea: 7/94; Swan tavern, Dowgate: 'a poor house', 1/185; Swan tavern, King St, Westminster: P visits, 2/97; 7/305; Swan tavern (Herbert's), New Palace Yard [see also Udall, Frances; Udall, Sarah]: 'my old house', 6/253; P visits, 1/7, 16, 45, 244, 294, 320; 2/219*, 3/296; 5/128; 6/1, 6, 17*, 65, 75*, 103, 111, 132, 141, 145, 253, 310; 7/32, 62, 81*, 99, 103*, 117, 201, 317, 319*, 355, 392, 396, 413; 8/34, 35*, 68, 120, 124, 133, 158–9, 224, 400, 456, 588; 9/75, 136, 161; new maid, 9/551; alluded to, 9/86; Swan tavern, Old Fish St: P dines, 3/165; juggler,

ib.; Swan tavern, Westminster [probably the Swan in New Palace Yard, in some cases possibly that in King St]: P visits, 1/43, 49, 55, 74, 91, 196; 2/49, 117; 3/43, 299; 7/39; 108, 134, 173*, 231–2*, 278, 279, 398; 8/102, 295, 323, 367, 590; 9/36, 56*, 295, 560*; his assignations with Doll Lane, 7/385–6; 8/193, 422; 9/317(2); Swan-with-two-Necks, Tothill St: W. Joyce in custody of Black Rod, 5/111; Swayne's, eating-house, New Palace Yard: P meets Doll Lane, 7/49–50
Three Cranes tavern, Old Bailey: wedding party, 3/16; Three Cranes tavern, Poultry ('at the Stocks'): farewell party, 2/163; Three Mariners, Lambeth: P visits, 2/120; noted for ale, ib.; Three Tuns tavern, Charing Cross: the old Three Tuns, 1/185; P visits, 1/185, 253; 2/206, 227; 9/359–60*; landlord [—— Darling], 2/206; his sister, ib; daughter, 2/228; Three Tuns tavern, Crutched Friars: newly established, 7/373; affray, 8/208; parish dinners, 8/218; 9/559; P visits, 7/373; 8/218*, 220*; 9/222*, 559*; landlord [John Kent], 8/208; Three Tuns tavern, Guildhall yard: P visits, 1/50; Triumph tavern, Charing Cross: Portuguese ladies at, 3/92; Trumpet, King St, Westminster (Mrs Hare's): P visits, 1/214; 5/9, 242, 340; 6/18 [White Hart], post-house, Charing Cross: 6/197 & n. 2; [?White Hind] inn, Cripplegate: coaches at, 6/95 & n. 4; White Horse, King St, Westminster: horse stabled, 1/85; White Horse tavern, Lombard St [see also Browne, Frances]: P visits, 5/330*, 338*; 7/63*, 68*; alluded to, 8/82 & n. 1; White Lion, Islington: alluded to, 9/32; Will's alehouse, Old Palace Yard [see also Griffin, W.]: P visits, 1/5, 6, 7, 14, 15, 16, 20, 21, 26, 32, 33, 34, 37, 40, 43, 45, 56(2), 57, 61, 64, 71, 78, 87, 173, 174, 257, 290, 294; 2/4(2)*, 6, 31, 40; Wood's, Pall Mall: 'our old house for clubbing', 1/208; P visits, ib.; shut in Plague, 6/147–8; World's End, Knightsbridge: P visits, 9/549, 564
TAXATION [for P's taxes, see Finances (P)]:

house, 3/286; 5/67; Iron Gate, 4/55; the hole, 7/191; magazines, 5/316; main guard[house], 3/286; menagerie, 3/76 & n. 2; 4/118; postern gate, 8/224; storehouses, 5/316; Stone Walk, 9/479, 484, 486, 489; Watergate, 3/241; 4/284

TOWER STAIRS: 2/228; alehouse at, 2/229; 6/225 & n. 4

TOWER ST [see also Taverns etc.: Dolphin; King's Head]: Fire, 7/273–4, 274–5, 393; best route to Whitehall, 8/130

TOWER WHARF: P hires ketches at, 1/242; nearby steps mended, 2/74; also, 1/253; 5/197; 6/94; 7/176, 285; 8/81, 153; 9/128

TOWNSHEND, Thomas, Clerk of the King's Wardrobe:
AS WARDROBE OFFICIAL: reappointed Clerk, and Deputy to Sandwich, 1/179; to help secure place for P's father, 2/42 & n. 1; 5/171 & n., 185; 8/508; to act in Sandwich's absence, 2/113, 116, 118; accounts, 4/257, 390; 8/253, 597; complaints against, 8/11; defence, 8/417–18; Treasury's low opinion, 9/41, 52; also, 1/180, 185, 237; 3/81–2; 5/234, 245, 246
SOCIAL: 1/188, 277, 301; 2/142, 211; 3/2, 172, 203; 5/246
MISC.: puts both legs in one leg of breeches, 2/66; matchmaking for Tom P, 3/192, 194, 228; countryhouse, 4/102 & n. 3; also, 2/180; 3/294 ~ his wife, 3/2; his son, 3/81–2; his daughter proposed for Tom P, 2/225; 3/81–2

TRADE (overseas) [see also under countries and trading companies; Insurance (marine); Privy Council; Council of Trade; War, the Second Dutch]: P reads books on, 3/157–8 & n., 291; 4/160 & n. 1; learns about trading practices, 3/157–8, 255; 4/10; Warwick on balance of trade, 5/70; Slingsby on rates of exchange, 7/304; imports of Swedish iron, 4/412 & n. 2; of Irish cattle, 7/313–14 & n., 343; export of bullion, 6/23; of corn, 9/1

TRAVEL (river):
GENERAL [see also London Bridge]: effect of tides, 1/287; 5/180; 6/149,

156, 181, 183, 232, 327; 7/168, 249; petition of watermen, 1/37 & n. 2; shortage of watermen on Sundays, 1/206 & n. 1; 8/32, 34; and in war, 7/176; boatman loses way, 6/241; ice in river, 6/332–3, 334, 340; storm, 7/22; P's arms painted on boat, 8/128 & n. 1; oar broken, 8/400; also, 4/50
COST: boat-hire, 1/281; 2/226; 3/174; 6/141, 181–2; 7/393; 9/162, 163(4), 165(2), 167, 168
VARIETIES OF BOAT [omitting references to P's everyday use of sculls and pairs of oars]: barges: royal, 1/130, 252; 2/145; 3/140, 175; 4/249; 7/141; 9/322, 469; Navy Office, 1/253, 262; 3/19, 59, 129, 153, ?156; 5/197; ?8/95; Trinity House, 4/185, 186; western, 8/254; 9/555, 563; also, 9/128; ferryboats: from Deptford to Isle of Dogs, 6/163, 168, 173, 175, 180, 181, ?190, ?220; from Greenwich to Isle of Dogs, 6/158, ?181, ?190, ?220; (river) galleys: 2/101; 4/425, 432; 5/54, 136, 178, 262, 265, 357; 8/257, 351; lighters: 6/74; 7/271; wherries: 6/240, 241(2)

TRAVEL (road):
JOURNEYS BY P/EP [entailing absence overnight. See also Brampton; Cambridge; Impington; Maidstone; Portsmouth; Stevenage; Wisbech.]: to the West country, 9/223–43 passim
COST: coach-hire within London, 7/330; 9/161(6), 162(3), 163(2), 164(3), 166; elsewhere, 4/83, 183, 314; 8/49; 9/166, 226, 240; purchase of coach/ riding horses, 6/180 & n. 1; 9/391; of coach, 8/289–90; 9/333 & n. 1, 337, 535; overnight accommodation at inns (for six persons), 9/225, 231, 234, 241, 243
DIFFICULTIES:
COACH ACCIDENTS: 1/239; 5/335; 7/14, 88, 394–5, 400–1; 9/9, 204, 225, 438; royal coach overturned, 9/474
TROUBLE WITH HORSES: 1/209; 7/100 (2); 8/390; 9/404, 461
CONDITION OF ROADS: 1/66; 2/180, 184; 3/217, 224, 283–4; 4/41, 310, 313; 5/64; 6/309; 7/328; 8/9, 443, 475; 9/9, 47, 209–10, 212, 213, 234, 236;

Queen at, 4/251, 272; 7/214 & n. 3; King at, 7/228; Lady Sandwich made ill by waters, 6/152; alluded to: 7/260

TUNIS: peace with, 3/263 & n. 4, 271

TURBERVILLE, [Daubigny], eye specialist: P consults, 9/248 & n. 6; 249, 251, 255; sees eyes dissected, 9/254–5

TURENNE (Turin, Turein), Henri de la Tour d'Auvergne, Vicomte, Marshal of France (d. 1675): anecdote of, 8/127 & n. 2; to command in Flanders campaign, 8/186; Colbert his rival, 9/397 & n. 2

TURKEY/Turks: *see* Algiers; Ottoman Empire, the; Tangier; Tunis

TURKEY COMPANY: *see* Levant Company

TURLINGTON, [John], spectacle maker, Cornhill: P buys spectacles from, 8/486 & n. 2; advice to P, 8/519; ~ daughter's advice to, 8/486

TURNER, Betty, daughter of John: her good looks, 5/337–8; 9/409, 464, 481, 512; P glad to have goodlooking kinswoman, 9/407; to go to school, 9/512, 526; social: at P's Twelfth Night party, 9/409; dances a jig, 9/464; at Mulberry Garden, 9/509–10; at her mother's house, 9/446, 482, 506; at P's house, 9/463, 478, 519; at theatre, 9/476; also, 9/510, 511, 521; alluded to: 9/540

TURNER, Betty, daughter of Thomas of the Navy Office:

CHRON. SERIES: plays badly on harpsichord, 4/120; sings worse than EP, 9/35; grown a fine lady, 8/389; in dancing display, 8/392, 396; helps P title books, 9/49; accompanies EP to Brampton, 9/144, 145, 210; and to West Country, 9/229, 231, 233, 234, 238; also, 9/123; ~ her sparrow, 9/225

SOCIAL: dances at P's house, 8/511; 9/42; and at Twelfth Night party, 9/12; at theatre, 9/133; at P's house, 8/557; 9/28, 29, 38, 126, 244, 250, 265, 301, 325, 380; also, 2/175; 9/54–5, 245, 259, 261

'TURNER, Betty' (error): *see* Mordaunt, [Elizabeth], Lady Mordaunt

TURNER, Charles, son of Jane: 3/88; 9/446

TURNER, [Elizabeth], wife of Thomas of the Navy Office:

P'S OPINION: shares Batten's dislike, 5/293; a gossip, 7/105, 121 & n. 1

CHRON. SERIES: supports P in Field case, 4/53; loses lodgings, 7/105, 296 & n. 2, 359; which Brouncker claims, 8/24, 29, 31 & n. 4; his unkindness, 8/36, 40, 51; new lodgings, 8/51, 63, 398; 9/36, 200 & n. 8; her balsam, 7/37, 40; her strong waters, 4/221; 9/145; tends P's sprained ankle, 8/340; gives EP shells, 7/105; joins her in collecting May-dew, 8/240; and at bleacher's, 8/401; seeks employment for son (Frank), 8/155, 172, 457; 9/38–9; consults P about son (Thomas), 9/279; P's help in promoting husband, 9/334–5; P gives her gloves, 9/120; caresses, 9/312, 314; also, 6/23; 7/274; 8/490, 580; 9/115–16

GOSSIP FROM: about court, 4/177; Brouncker's ménage, 8/51, 75, 225–6; Penn's, 8/63, 141–2, 155, 226–9, 423, 595; Batten's, 8/159; also, 8/315; 9/157

SOCIAL: visits Cambridge, 2/136; Deptford, 3/198; 8/435; Epsom, 8/335–40; Barnet and Hatfield, 8/380–2; Mile End, 9/180, 208; at Greenwich, 6/212, 299; 7/1; at dances in Navy Office, 8/29; 9/13; Battens', 2/24; 4/218, 221, 230; Penns', 8/3, 371; in garden at Seething Lane, 8/391; 9/252, 261; at theatre, 8/433; 9/170, 189; P/EP visit(s)/dine(s) with, 4/278; 7/120; 8/395–6; 9/46, 222–3, 276; at P's house, 7/67; 8/4, 282, 433, 437, 441, 447; 9/28, 123–4, 138, 144, 184, 198, 213, 244, 258, 265, 278, 306, 325, 380; also, 2/38, 175; 5/303; 7/53; 8/378, 389, 581; 9/245

TURNER, Frank, naval officer, son of Thomas of the Navy Office: commission expires, 8/150, 155, 172, 228; joins E. India Company, 8/457; 9/38–9; social: 8/437, 580

TURNER, 'Col'. [James], criminal: arrested with wife for robbery, 5/10–11 & n.; trial and conviction, 5/13, 17,

18–19; confesses, 5/20; execution described, 5/23 & nn.; also, 5/24
[TURNER, Sir James], Governor of Dumfries: imprisoned by rebels, 7/377 & n. 4
TURNER, Jane (Madam Turner; b. Pepys), wife of John, lawyer, and P's cousin:
P'S OPINION: 'a good woman', 2/40; values her friendship, 4/273; shapely legs, 6/28
CHRON. SERIES: P's operation at her house, 1/97 & n. 3; ill, 2/214 & n. 1, 219, 227, 235, 237; 3/8, 13, 30, 44, 62; visited by sons, 3/88; brother's death at her house, 4/424, 425, 426, 432; 5/10; warns P of Tom P's illness, 5/29; attends his death and funeral, 5/81, 84–7 passim, 89, 90, 91; in Yorkshire, 7/391–2, 403 & n. 2; London house destroyed in Fire, 7/386, 391; returns to London, 9/353; borrows P's coach horses, 9/529; to leave town, 9/530; P gives her wine, 4/187; oysters, 5/88; and eagle, 5/352; also, 1/225; 6/28 & n. 2, 49
SOCIAL: with P visits Parliament chamber, 1/39; at Roger P's wedding, 1/39–40; gives Shrove Tuesday dinner, 2/43–4; at P's stone feast, 2/60 & n. 1; 3/53; 4/94–5; 5/98; 6/67, 124; 9/484; visits Chatham and Rochester, 2/67–73; Greenwich, 4/272–3; attends funeral, 5/347; Roger P and family on visit to, 9/407, 446, 475, 477; at P's Twelfth Night party, 9/409; P's valentine, 9/449; P/EP visit/dine with, 1/11, 26, 54, 60, 173, 181–2, 196; 2/52, 59, 63, 90; 3/167, 208, 269; 4/124, 175, 276; 5/71, 124, 130; 9/380, 407, 416, 425, 426, 447, 450, 461, 465, 473, 482, 505, 526; at P's house, 1/10; 2/53; 4/5, 65; 5/19, 337; 7/389; 9/463–4, 481, 519; at theatre, 3/78; 4/32; 9/420, 422, 429, 435, 453, 475, 478, 486; also, 1/42, 72; 4/95; 9/510, 511, 512, 521, 530–1
MISC.: pew at St Bride's, 1/42; 2/89; 3/30, 77, 162; coach, 4/95; 5/87, 130
~ her sister Turner, 9/512; her servant John, 4/68
TURNER, John, chaplain to Sandwich and Rector of Eynesbury, Hunts.:

appointed chaplain, 1/295; sermon, 2/133; learning, 8/517; also, 2/74; ?5/64, 80; social: 8/511, 516
TURNER, John, lawyer, of the Middle Temple, Recorder of York 1662–85: P's admiration, 9/429; consulted on dispute with Trices, 2/210, 214, 226, 230; 3/83; 4/346–7; nominated as arbiter, 3/270, 274, 276; insists on living in Yorkshire, 7/391–2, 403; his Reader's Feast, 6/28 & social: 2/24, 25, 211; 9/380, 450; alluded to: 3/88; 9/461, 530; ~ his man Roger, 2/218
TURNER, Moses, son of Thomas: 9/39
TURNER, Theophila ('The'), daughter of John, lawyer:
CHRON. SERIES: ill-mannered, 1/268; new harpsichord, 2/40, 44, 63; disappointed of place at coronation, 2/59; ill, 3/8; in country, 4/272; grown fat, 5/337; in London to put brothers and sisters to school, 8/210 & n. 1; returns to Yorkshire, 8/259, 262; in London, 9/353; to buy coach, ib.; is bled, 9/476; bridesmaid to Jane Birch, 9/500; also, 1/251
SOCIAL: at P's father's, 1/3 & n. 3, 65; runs races, 1/40; at P's stone feast, 2/60; 3/53; 4/94–5; 5/98; 6/124; P's valentine, 4/65, 68; plays harpsichord, 5/88; in Hyde Park, 5/130; 9/530–1; at P's Twelfth Night party, 9/409; composes mock letter with P, 9/463–4; at Mulberry Garden, 9/510; at her mother's, 9/407, 437, 482, 506; at theatre, 3/78; 4/32; 9/416, 420, 422, 429, 435, 453, 486; at P's house, 1/10, 225; 2/53; 3/44; 5/85; 6/98; 9/478, 481; also, 5/347; 8/221; 9/425, 512, 521
ALLUDED TO: 6/312; 8/260, 261
TURNER, Thomas, of Navy Office; after 1668 Storekeeper at Deptford:
CHARACTER: P's low opinion, 3/137; 6/37; 7/31; 8/38
CHRON. SERIES: hopes for Clerkship of Acts, 1/183–4, 189; salary and allowance, 1/191, 228; 5/228; appointed Purveyor of Petty Provisions, 2/54 & n. 1; 5/320; alleged payment for, 8/228 & n. 2; visits Cambridge, 2/136;

VANLEY: *see* Wanley

VATTEVILLE, Carlos, Baron de, Spanish ambassador 1660–2: quarrels with French ambassador over precedence, 2/187–9 passim & nn.

VAUGHAN, [Edward], son of Sir John (d. 1684): 6/338; ~ his wife Letitia (b. Hooker), 7/41 & n. 2

VAUGHAN, John, M.P. Cardiganshire 1661–8; kted 1668; Chief Justice Common Pleas 1668–d. 74: eloquent, 5/102; 7/210; learned but opinionated, 7/192 & n. 2; speaks against repeal of Triennial Act, 5/102; 7/192; and on privileges of peers, 5/148; opposes grant to navy, 5/331; rumoured appointment to Privy Council, 8/265; praises P's parliamentary speech, 9/106, 153; defends Sandwich, 9/87; made Chief Justice, 9/204; also, 8/362; 9/162

VAUGHAN, John, styled Lord Vaughan, succ. as 3rd Earl of Carbery 1686; M.P. Carmarthen borough 1661–79, Carmarthen county 1679, 1681, 1685–7 (d. 1713): in attack on Clarendon, 8/532–3 & n.; parliamentary 'undertaker', 9/71 & n. 2

VAUXHALL: Old Spring Garden: P and EP visit, 3/95; New Spring Garden: compared with Old, 3/95 & n. 1; and with Mulberry Garden, 9/207; empty in Plague, 6/164; P/EP visit(s), 4/243, 249, 251; 5/268; 6/120, 132, 136; 7/198, 294; 8/249–50; 9/172, 194, 196, 198, 199, 204, 216, 219(2), 220, 249, 257, 264, 268; the 'house' at, 6/164; entertainments: contortionist, 4/251; impressionist, 7/136; music, 8/240–1; alluded to: 4/262

VEEZY, Mr ——, [?of St Margaret's, Westminster]: member of P's 'club', 1/78

VENDÔME, François de, Duc de Beaufort; naval commander (d. 1669): 7/265, 327–8 & n.; 9/141 & n. 3

VENICE: painting of city by Fialetti, 7/60 & n. 2; ambassadors in disputes about precedence, 4/419–20 & n.; 9/320 & n. 2; alluded to: 3/8

VENNER, Thomas, Fifth-Monarchist: rebellion, 2/7–11 passim & nn.; 7/190; execution, 2/18 & n. 2

VENNER, [Tobias], physician, of Bath, Som.: his monument, 9/238, & n. 3

VENNER, [?William], physician, of London: 5/61, 340; 7/345

VERE, Aubrey de, 20th Earl of Oxford, Warden etc. of the Royal Forests south of Trent; Colonel of Horse, Lord Lieutenant of Essex etc. (d. 1703): falsely reported dead, 1/246; Hester Davenport his mistress, 3/86; brawl at house, 4/136; proposed as Governor of Tangier, 5/166; gives consent for timber felling, 6/3 & n. 2, 4(2); sent to Harwich, 8/254 & n. 3; also, 3/146; 7/124; 8/185

VERE, [Mary], Lady Vere (b. Tracy) widow of the 1st Baron Vere of Tilbury: employs P's mother as washmaid, 2/31 & n. 2

VERELST, Simon, painter (d. ?1710): 9/514–15 & n.

VERNATTY, [Philibert], clerk to the Earl of Peterborough, Governor of Tangier: accounts examined by Tangier committee, 5/48 & n. 1, 97, 105, 124, 127, 139, 154; and by P, 5/128, 150, 154; 8/52–3; attempts at cheating, 7/264 & n. 2, 265, 338, 342; flight, 7/342

VERNON, Col. [Edward], Gentleman of the Privy Chamber: 9/477–8 & n.

VERNON, [?John, Quartermaster-General]: 1/25

VERSAILLES: partridge-shooting at, 7/79

VICTUALLING: *see* Gauden, Sir D.; Navy Board; Clerk of the Acts; and under names of Principal Officers; Tangier

VICTUALLING OFFICE, East Smithfield: P visits, 2/104; 3/135; 4/84; 5/179; 6/269; 7/118, 134, 135, 140, 150, 232, 263, 265; Coventry visits, 7/118, 135; bakehouse, 4/84; Gauden's house, 9/34; stabling, 9/354

VILLIERS, Barbara: *see* Palmer

VILLIERS, Col. [Edward], Master of the Robes and Groom of the Bedchamber to the Duke of York: 3/139, n. 2; 9/469

VILLIERS, George, 1st Duke of Buckingham (d. 1628): Knight of the

Harwich, 6/111; in sight of Dutch, 6/115; leaves Sole Bay, 6/115; Battle of Lowestoft, 6/116 & n. 1, 117, 119 & n. 1, 121 & nn., 122–3 & nn., 129 & nn., 134–5 & nn., 135, 137; 7/102; losses and casualties at, 6/117–18 & n., 129; failure to pursue Dutch, 8/489–90 & n., 491–2; 9/80 & n. 3, 142, 166–7 & n.; Banckert's squadron fails to meet E. India fleet, 6/133 & n. 2, 146 & n. 3; English fleet fails to intercept E. India fleet and de Ruyter, 6/151, 178, 184 & n. 2, 186; guns heard to the North, 6/192; Tedde-man's attack on E. Indiamen in Bergen harbour, 6/193, 195–6 & nn., 198 & n. 2, 213, 229; 8/549–50; main Dutch fleet out, 6/193; English fleet to sail from Sole Bay, 6/195; reinforced, 6/196; returns, 6/202; out again, 6/205 & n. 2, 208 & n. 3, 211; Dutch regain harbour with E. India fleet, 6/214, 218 & n. 2; Sandwich captures Dutch ships, 9 Sept., 6/223 & n. 4, 226; and two E. Indiamen (*Phoenix* and *Slothany*), 3 Sept., 6/230–1 & n.; Dutch fleet stays out, 6/243, 248; sails into Sole Bay, 6/255–6; in Downs, 6/258; English unable to put fleet out, 6/257, 260; Dutch said to have sailed home, 6/264–5; appear off Margate, 6/268, 269; dispersed by bad weather, 6/278, 279 & n. 2; Sandwich attempts to engage, 6/275, 291 & n. 1; sixteen new Dutch ships launched, 6/281 & n. 3; also, 6/41, 80, 82

1666: English fleet at the Nore, 7/123(2); in Downs, 7/139; Rupert moves to intercept French, 7/139 & n. 3, 143–4, 145, 147, 160; Dutch put to sea, 7/138 & n. 1; Albemarle sights Dutch, 7/140; Rupert ordered to rejoin Albemarle, 7/141; Four Days Fight, 7/142, 143–4 & n., 146–7, 148, 149, 150, 152–3 & n., 153–8 passim & nn., 169, 172, 176, 177–8 & n., 179 & n. 4, 194–5; 9/5; division of fleet before battle, 7/144 & n. 1, 145, 146–7, 149, 160; 8/502, 514–15; 9/74; tactics, 7/146–7, 161 & n. 3, 177–9 & nn.; Penn's criticisms, 7/194–5; losses, 7/150, 152 & n. 3, 177 & n. 4, 209 & n. 1, 344; English fleet refits, 7/153,

157; Dutch put to sea again, 7/177 & n. 1, 181, 182, 185; off French coast, 7/186; English prepare to set fleet out, 7/182, 183, 185, 205, 210, 210–11 & n., 214; English morale broken, 7/188; Dutch in Gunfleet, 7/193; English strength in ships and men, 7/215–16, 223; Dutch pursued, 7/216; guns heard in London, 7/217; St James's Day Fight, 7/221–3 & nn., 225 & nn., 226–30 passim & nn., 344–5; losses, 7/229, 231 & n. 2, 233; official narrative, 7/229 & n. 1, 230, 234; Thanksgiving for, 7/245 & n. 1; English off Dutch coast, 7/227; rumoured landing, 7/243; 'Holmes's Bonfire', 7/247–8 & n., 249, 250, 257; narrative of, 7/252 & n. 2; English in Sole Bay, 7/251; revictualled, 7/253; movements of Dutch and English fleets, 7/253, 257, 260, 262, 265, 281, 287, 288, 299; fleets parted by storm off Calais, 7/279 & n. 3, 286; English chase French squadron, 7/288 & n. 2, 291 & n. 2, 300; English fleet at Gun-fleet, 7/300; at Nore, 7/304; held up by lack of money, 7/331, 334; English losses, 1666, 7/350; French prize taken, ib. & n. 1; fear of invasion next year, ib.; fleet at Nore, 7/355; Dutch move to intercept Smyrna fleet, 7/390; Dutch threaten colliers, 7/401 & n. 5; attack on Gothenburg fleet repulsed, 7/424 & n. 3; other engagements: French capture St Kitt's, 7/171 & n. 3; 390 & n. 3

1667: English decide on 'flying fleet', 8/1, 38, 66, 68, 80–1, 88, 97–8 & n., 98, 100, 110, 115, 117, 140; defence measures, 8/98 & nn., 115 & n. 2; 'land-admirals' given com-mands, 8/149, 166; Dutch fleet off E. coast, 8/186 & n. 5; off Scottish coast, 8/200, 202 & n. 1; Dutch and French fleets out, 8/248 & n. 4, 250; Dutch off Harwich, 8/254(2); English defence measures, 8/254–60 passim; Dutch arrive in Thames, 8/256 & n. 2, 258 & n. 5; the Medway raid, 8/258–63 passim & nn., 266–9 passim & nn., 277 & n. 1, 306–10 passim & nn., 327–8, 495–6, 501, 502; 9/11; danger of French invasion, 8/265, 285, 602;

Dutch off Harwich, 8/281 & n. 4; threaten colliers, 8/285 & n. 5; in Thames, 8/296, 298, 303; land near Harwich, 8/317 & nn., 322 & n. 2; off s. and e. coasts, 8/327 & n. 1, 345 & n. 1; invade Thames again, 8/349 & n. 1; beaten off, 8/350, 351; defeated in Second Battle of N. Foreland, 8/354 & n. 3, 357–60 & nn.; gunfire heard at Whitehall, 8/367; Dutch plans for next year, 8/568; also, 8/163, 170; other engagements: French expedition to W. Indies, 8/2 & n. 1; take Antigua, 8/38 & n. 1; defeated off Martinique, 8/430 & n. 1; English privateers in Caribbean, 8/75 & n. 1; Harman in W. Indies, 8/132 & n. 3, 147, 153, 156; English squadron in Mediterranean, 8/43; also, 8/47, 162
PUBLIC PESSIMISM: 7/395; 8/306; merchants', 7/371; P's, 6/6, 218; 7/371, 374, 376, 378, 395, 426; 8/68, 88, 113, 146, 249, 274, 289, 305, 306, 363, 366, 377, 532, 602; Lord Crew's, 6/6; 7/387; Coventry's, 6/291–2; Cocke's, 6/218; Houblon's, 7/371; Carteret's, 7/383; Evelyn's, 7/406; 8/248–9, 278, 377; 9/484; Batten's, 7/416; Ford's, ib.; Reymes's, 8/68; and Povey's, 8/289
PEACE NEGOTIATIONS: overtures to Dutch and French, 7/411; Dutch demands, 7/369–70 & n.; venue, 8/17 & n. 3, 61–2 & n., 69, 72–3, 74, 80 & n. 4, 92 & n. 2, 106 & n. 2; Breda agreed on, 8/124, 125–6; King's speech to Parliament, 8/52; appoints plenipotentiaries, 8/61 & n. 3; Arlington's part in, 8/68–9 & n.; French part in, 8/69 & n. 2, 106–7 & n., 113, 170 & n. 5, 297; negotiations with Spain, 8/74 & n. 2; Dutch terms, 8/88, 95–6 & n., 100, 113; Dutch fear French making separate treaty, 8/153; plenipotentiaries assemble, 8/138 & n. 4, 145 & n. 3, 155, 161, 189, 216, 218; rumoured terms, 8/176 & n. 1; Dutch demands high, 8/244, 249; draft treaty, 8/322, 323, 326 & n. 3, 327, 329–30; its severity, 8/335; treaty sealed, 8/352; announced to Parliament, 8/361; further Dutch demands, 8/375; peace ratified, 8/378, 396 & n.

1, 397 & n. 1; proclaimed in London, 8/399; terms concerning prisoners, 8/407–8 & nn., 425–6; and territorial disputes, 8/426; printed copies, 8/453 & n. 3
PUBLIC REACTION TO PEACE: need for recognised by court, 8/62; by P, 8/176, 323, 324, 328–9, 329; by bankers, 8/285; and by Albemarle and Council, 8/347; terms feared/disliked by merchants, 8/157–8, 354–5, 362, 398–9; by court and nation, 8/361–2, 398–9; by P, 8/396; by Downing, 8/425–6; opinion in United Provinces, 8/225, 345
PEACE ALLUDED TO: 8/63, 93, 120, 128, 139, 285, 289, 317, 326, 354, 384, 386, 388, 391
WARCUP, Edmund, magistrate, bailiff of Southwark: in prize-goods affair, 6/269 & n. 3; 7/203–4, 219; disgraced, 7/219 & n. 4; allergy to roses, 7/204; social: 7/23
WARD, [Lieut. James], naval officer: questioned by Brooke House Committee, 9/204 & n. 1
WARD, [Richard], Muster-Master: 8/15 & n. 3, 19
WARD, [Seth], Bishop of Salisbury 1667–d. 89, Fellow of the Royal Society: preaching admired by King, 8/116 & n. 5; praises Abraham Cowley, 8/383 & n. 3; P visits, 9/229 & n. 4
WARD, Mr ——, [?of the Exchequer]: 6/235
WARD, Mr ——: 2/7; ~ his wife, ib.
WARDOUR, [William], Clerk of the Pells in the Exchequer: 6/244
WARDROBE, the KING'S GREAT, Puddle Dock [see also Mountagu, E., 1st Earl of Sandwich; Newport, A.; Reymes, Col. B; Townshend, T.]: officers dine together, 3/172; give Christmas dinner for tradesmen, 3/294; houses belonging to, 4/422; debts and shortages, 8/417–18 & nn.; economies proposed, 9/7; reorganisation, 9/41 & nn.; moves to Hatton Garden after Fire, 8/597 & n. 1; the building: an orphanage during Interregnum, 1/180 & n. 1; Jane Shore's Tower, 2/118 & n. 2; Master's

Portland: killed at Battle of Lowestoft, 6/122

WESTWICKE (Estwicke), ——, fencing-master: in prize-fight, 4/167–8

WEYMOUTH, Dorset: parliamentary election, 1/103, 167

WHALLEY, Maj.-Gen. [Edward], regicide (d. ?1675): house, 1/199 & n. 4

WHEATLEY, Mr ——: daughter's proposed match with Tom P, 2/158; 4/19, 21, 410, 417; ~ his wife, 2/158, 159

WHELER, Sir William, of Westminster: helps in Sandwich's financial affairs, 1/45–6 & n.; 4/43–4, 45, 55, 57; appointed commissioner for sewers, 4/45–6; at Trinity House dinner, 4/185; visits Lady Sandwich, 5/179; also, 4/43, 68, 69; ~ his wife [Elizabeth], 5/179

WHETSTONE, [Capt. Sir Thomas], royalist agent: carries letters between King and Sandwich (1659), 4/69 & n. 2

[WHETSTONE, Mdx]: P dines at Cock, 5/64 & n. 3

WHETSTONE PARK, Holborn: 9/364

WHEY HOUSE, ('Milke house'), the, off the Strand: P visits, 4/164 & n. 2, ?175, 179–80, 286; 5/133–4; 6/120; 7/170 & n. 4; 9/207, 215

WHISTLER, [Daniel], physician and Fellow of the Royal Society: ingenious, 2/31; explains principles of mast-storage, 5/14–15; talks about Egypt, 5/274; about blood transfusion experiment, 7/373; anecdote of Dr Caius, 8/543; praises P's parliamentary speech, 9/113; social: at Royal Society club, 6/36; at Penn's, 7/12 & n. 2, 193; also, 5/290; 7/30; 8/541; ~ his wife, 9/194

WHISTLER, [Henry], flagmaker: attempted fraud, 4/151 & n. 1; P refuses to trade with, 5/291, 310 & n. 2; and refuses gratuity from, 8/46; also, 5/30; 7/276; 9/220

WHITE, [Jeremiah], chaplain to Frances, wife of Oliver Cromwell: suitor to Cromwell's daughter, 1/248 & n. 1; stories of Cromwell family, 5/296–7 & n.

WHITE, [Thomas], navy agent at

Dover: on *Charles*, 1/159

WHITE, ——, waterman: complains of bogus petition, 1/37 & n. 2; resigns as waterman to Manchester, 2/96; also, 5/75 ~ his stairs, 5/219

WHITECHAPEL: P at, 5/132; 9/478

WHITEFRIARS: P at, 4/124, 182

WHITEFRIARS [STAIRS]: 1/185, 192, 204, 224, 266, 310, 320; 2/3, 34, 41, 47

WHITEHALL BRIDGE: see Whitehall Stairs

WHITEHALL PALACE [No attempt is made to index completely references to P's visits, court events, or meetings of government bodies. References to lodgings occupied by ministers and others are entered under their names.]:

GENERAL: P recalls seeing Charles I beheaded at, 1/265; building works, 3/175; 8/417 & n. 2; 9/171, 251 & n. 4, 266, 269 & n. 3, 292 & n. 3, 452; flooded at high tide, 4/406; court leaves in Plague, 6/140, 141–2; 7/32; goods removed during Great Fire, 7/279; outbreaks of fire in, 7/362 & n. 2; 9/333; gates shut during Medway raid, 8/275, 287; Danckerts's painting, 9/423

PLACES IN:

backstairs: 9/507

Banqueting House: King touches for King's Evil, 1/182; 2/74; investiture of peers, 2/79–80; Russian envoys' audience, 3/297; King meets parliament, 4/183; lottery, 5/214; ball, 7/371–2; top-gallery/loft, 3/297; 7/371; Rubens ceiling, 9/434

banqueting house by river (new): 3/175

bowling green/alley: 3/146, 175; 4/142; 7/217; 9/302

chair-room: 5/209

chapel: privy seal pew, 3/67 & n. 3, 84; 4/393; 5/96; rules for seating, 5/267; 8/115; P attends services, 1/53, 195, 220, 237, 251, 276, 313; 3/42, 60, 67, 84, 85, 190, 197, 281, 287, 292; 4/3, 36–7, 63, 69, 92–3, 98, 393; 6/5, 86, 87, 109; 7/94, 245, 382, 409; 8/41, 255, 478, 515; 9/126, 251, 294, 319, 563; other services, 1/176; 2/41; 3/67;

licly in, 4/407; King receives deputation from House of Lords in, 9/106;
also, 7/146; 8/145, 600; 9/17
wine cellar: 1/193, 246, 247
WHITEHALL STAIRS (Bridge):
1/272 & n. 2; 2/3; 3/175; 4/124;
6/330; 7/122; 8/232
WHITE'S, ——, of Gravesend, Kent:
6/240
WHITE SEA, the: map of, 4/390
WHITFIELD, [Nathaniel], clerk in the
Ticket Office: inspects guard ships,
4/228; dismissal prevented, 6/138 &
n. 2; on condition of Ticket Office,
7/418
WHIT MONDAY: shops closed, 3/85
WHITMORE, Sir George, Lord
Mayor 1631–2 (d. 1654): house
(Beaumes House), Hoxton, 5/272
& n. 2; 8/211; 9/197
WHITSUNTIDE: 2/96, 112; 3/85
WHITTINGTON, Capt. [Luke],
royalist agent: at The Hague, 1/143
WHITTLE, Elizabeth: see Fox
WHITTLEWOOD FOREST, North-
ants.: timber from, 8/392
WHITTON, Thomas, clerk in the
Navy Office: death, 2/155; also, 2/26,
60
WHITTY, Capt. [John], naval officer:
killed in action, 7/154
WHORE: see Hoare
WICKHAM, ——: 9/?401, 409
WIDDRINGTON, [Ralph], Fellow of
Christ's College, Cambridge: quar-
rels with colleagues, 1/63–4 & n.;
2/44; admits John P, 1/66, 69; social:
1/68
WIDDRINGTON, [Sir Thomas],
('Lord'), Commissioner of the Great
Seal 1660 (d. 1664): to seal judges'
patents, 1/23–4 & n.; control of
parliamentary writs, 1/93 & n. 2;
alluded to: 1/41
WIELINGS (Wheelings), the, roadstead off Netherlands coast: Dutch
fleet in, 7/225
WIGHT, Anne: see Bentley
WIGHT, [?John], of Braboeuf, Guildford, Surrey: 7/385; 9/275
WIGHT, Margaret: pretty, 3/202;
5/268; 6/29; EP admires, 7/135; looks
described, 7/140; alluded to: 3/236

WIGHT, [Mary], (Aunt Wight), wife
of William, sen.:
PERSONAL: ugly hands, 4/108; 5/2; ugly,
7/71, 366; silly, 7/71
CHRON. SERIES: death of infant daughters, 1/244; miscarriage, 3/46; P teases
by commending mass, 3/202–3; in
mourning for sister, 3/202; leads
husband by the nose, 3/276; Robert
P's legacy, 4/86; quarrels with husband, 5/49, 100, 191, 292; his will,
5/61; favours her relations, 5/125;
fondness for Dr Venner, 5/340; 7/345;
fears Plague, 7/71; in country for
summer, 7/199 & n. 1; estrangement
from P and EP, 8/232; 9/275, 330 &
n. 2; also, 2/124; 3/13; 5/273
SOCIAL: shows P cabinet, 2/202; visits
Lady Sandwich, 2/221; plays gleek,
3/9, 14; at P's stone feast, 4/95; 5/98;
shops with EP for Lent provisions,
5/44, 55; at fish dinner, 5/53; in Hyde
Park, 5/126; on outing to Bow,
7/124–5; at P's house, 2/28, 52, 215;
5/14, 27, 77, 128, 256, 273–4, 340;
7/87, 112, 134; 9/334, 383–4, 403, 406,
430; P/EP visit(s)/dine(s) with, at St
Catherine's Hill, 9/275 & n. 1; at
London house, 1/194–5; 2/9, 19, 139,
160, 165, 200, 211; 3/17, 59, 178, 229;
4/102, 106; 5/23, 24, 124, 246; 7/135,
140; 9/405; at the Mitre, Fenchurch
St, 2/170; 3/173, 183; also, 4/434
~ her sister Con and husband, 1/195
[?WIGHT], Mary: ?4/434; 5/14;
7/?46, 87
[?WIGHT], Robert: 5/14
WIGHT, [William], sen. (Uncle
Wight), half-brother of P's father,
fishmonger:
CHRON. SERIES: P consults about investment, 2/76, 124; about prize-goods,
7/140; interest/attitude in disputes
over Robert P's will, 2/140–1, 151,
153; 4/72, 86, 338, 364, 384–5; losses
at sea, 3/13; P's expectations from,
3/13; 4/278, 434; 5/14, 16, 24, 27, 55,
65, 273, 274; negotiates for Hampshire estate, 3/295; 4/257; to help
Roger P to find new wife, 4/159;
advances to EP, 5/14, 16, 24, 55, 65;
and remarkable proposal to, 5/61,
145–6, 151; consults P about dispute

over customs dues, 5/38, 50, 54, 72, 75, 76, 145; ill, 8/231–2; estrangement from P and EP, 8/232; 9/275, 330 & n. 2; portrait, 2/202; house: in London, 2/202; at St Catherine's Hill, nr Guildford, 2/211; 9/275; also, 2/117, 132; 3/64; 6/83; 7/366
MARRIAGE: ruled by wife, 3/276; complains of her relations, 3/295; and cooking, 5/49; unhappiness/quarrels with, 5/100, 191, 292
SOCIAL: gives fish dinner, 1/28 & n. 3; drunk, 1/220; at funeral, 2/159; P gives chine of beef to, 2/219; shares oysters with, 5/269, 274; at P's stone feast, 4/95; 5/98; at fish dinner, 5/53; views Clarendon House, 7/87; P critical of his entertainment, 7/366; P/EP visit(s)/dine(s) with etc., 1/194; 2/9, 19, 37, 162, 202, 208; 3/30, 178, 202, 228, 236; 4/106, 107–8, 269, 306; 5/1–2, 10, 19, 30, 94, 119, 125, 129, 188, 268, 315; 6/29; 7/345; 9/405, 449; at P's house, 2/28, 52, 215; 3/9, 14, 94; 4/427; 5/27, 77, 128, 162, 211, 256, 340; 6/133; 7/46, 71, 112, 134, 385; 9/334, 383, 403, 430; at the Mitre, Fenchurch St, 1/174, 195, 256; 2/36, 45, 58, 99, 107, 170; 3/61, 124, 166, 173, 183; 5/47, 235; also, 1/80, 194; 2/207; 4/291
ALLUDED TO: 9/375
~ his cousins, 9/406
WIGHT, [William], son of the foregoing: legacy from Robert P, 4/86
WILDAY, ——, [?of Worcester]: 1/92
WILDE, Dorothy: see Pickering
WILDE (Wiles), Elizabeth: see Wyld
WILDE, Sir William, Recorder of London 1659–68 (d. 1679): 1/252
WILDMAN, Maj. [John], republican: association with Buckingham, 8/569–70 & n.; 9/347–8 & n.; nominated to Brooke House Committee, 8/569–70 & n., 571, 577 & n. 1
[WILFORD, Francis], Dean of Ely 1662–d. 67: sermon, 3/190 & n. 2
WILGRESS, Capt. [John], naval officer: commissioned, 1/101
WILKES, [Luke], Yeoman of the King's Wardrobe: 4/26

WILKES, [Luke] [?identical with the foregoing]; servant to Secretary Williamson: 7/289–90
WILKINS, John, Bishop of Chester 1668–d.72; Fellow of the Royal Society [see also Books]: P's regard, 6/95; sermons, 1/302; 6/34; examiner at St Paul's School, 4/33; 5/38; experiments on coaches, 6/94; 7/12, 20 & n. 2; asks P for information on naval terms, 7/148; congratulates P on parliamentary speech, 9/113; appointed bishop, 9/331 & n. 3; lodgings at Lincoln's Inn, ib.; rumoured appointment as Bishop of Winchester and Lord Treasurer, 9/485; Buckingham his patron, ib.; also, 8/541, 543, 555; alluded to: 7/72
WILKINSON, Capt. [Robert], naval officer: surrenders to Dutch, 6/117–18 & n.
WILKINSON, of the Six Clerks' Office in Chancery: 4/242, 345, 346, 351, 352
WILKINSON'S (the Crown), cookshop, King St, Westminster: P dines at 1/21, 91, 284; 2/102, 171, 229; 3/3, 87, 269, 382; 4/189; 9/81; buys/orders food from, 1/26, 39; 8/559; drinks at, 1/201; 6/109, also, 1/85,?190; 9/86; death of the landlord, 9/81
WILL, P's boy: see Servants
WILL'S: see Taverns etc.
WILLET, Deb, companion to EP:
APPEARANCE: good looks, 8/448, 451, 456, 465, 468; grave and genteel, 8/456–7
AS EP'S COMPANION: engaged, 8/448, 451, 456; at Cambridge and Brampton, 8/465–75 passim; combs P's hair, 8/531; 9/20, 37; helps to title books, 9/49, 72; EP angry with, 9/61, 119, 143; visits Brampton, 9/98, 125, 143, 145, 210; on West Country tour, 9/229, 231–6 passim, 238, 266, 273–4; visits Impington, 9/306
P'S AFFAIR WITH: P pleased with, 8/451, 453–4, 458(2), 468; EP jealous, 8/477, 481; P kisses, 8/585; 9/145; caresses, 9/143, 144, 274, 277, 282, 328; discovered by EP, 9/337–8; her rage and P's guilt, 9/338–46 passim; P fears she must leave, 9/346, 348–9; is prevented

from seeing, 9/353, 354, 356; her confession, 9/356; and dismissal, 9/357, 358, 361–3; P searches for, 9/364–7 passim; EP threatens to slit her nose, 9/367, 369; P never to see again, 9/368, 370, 371, 378; forced to accept Hewer as escort, 9/368, 373; sees in street, 9/387; EP makes jealous scenes, 9/384, 395, 422, 433, 480–1, 546; threatens him with hot tongs, 9/413–14; he meets by chance, 9/518–21 passim; she breaks assignation, 9/526; winks at P in street, 9/534; moves to Greenwich, 9/543; affair alluded to, 9/502, 564

SOCIAL: accompanies EP to theatre, 8/459, 463, 481(2), 486, 508, 516, 521(2), 525, 527, 594; 9/12, 14, 18, 19, 37, 54, 62, 81, 85, 89, 91, 93, 100, 107, 133(2), 137, 246, 249, 250, 263, 268–71 passim, 278, 280–1, 296, 304, 326; to tailor/shops etc., 8/460, 519, 520, 528, 558, 563–4, 567, 574, 601; 9/16, 22, 28, 29, 39, 46, 64, 66, 79, 100, 113, 124, 256, 258, 259, 301, 329, 330, 332(2), 334; to Islington, Mile End etc., 9/133, 254, 255, 271–2, 276; to S. Cooper's studio, 9/256, 258, 259, 260, 276; Vauxhall, 9/257, 268; Bartholomew Fair, 9/290, 293, 296, 299; dances, 8/493; 9/128, 289; plays cards, 8/594, 599; 9/17, 35, 107; fortune told, 9/278; also, 9/1, 23, 36, 139, 143, 262

~ her mother, 9/235

WILLIAM I, Prince of Orange (the Silent; d. 1584): tomb at Delft, 1/146 & n. 2

WILLIAM II, Prince of Orange (d. 1650): struggle against republicans, 6/146–7 & nn.

WILLIAM III, Prince of Orange (King of England 1689–1702): 'a pretty boy', 1/139; gives audience, 1/138, 139; on *Naseby*, 1/154; at aunt's wedding, 7/250 & n. 1; opposed by republicans, 6/147; his faction and the peace negotiations, 8/69 & n. 1, 92, n. 2, 106 & n. 1

WILLIAMS, [Abigail], 'Madam Williams', Lord Brouncker's mistress: P'S DISLIKE: Brouncker's doxy, 6/213; 8/5; whore, 6/234; 7/237; spiteful, 6/217; ugly, 6/251; impudent, 6/273,

303; 'a prating, vain, idle woman', 9/200; also, 7/76, 91, 221

CHRON. SERIES: P meets, 6/204 & n. 1; Brouncker's attachment, 6/212, 285; 7/68, 74; 8/314; swoons on hearing of rival, 7/237–8; at Erith, 6/244, 249; information on prize-goods affair, 6/299–300, 302, 303, 309; rebukes P for over-familiarity, 6/337; stories of her accepting bribes, 8/51–2, 75, 226; and of her poverty, 8/226, 302; angry with P over Carkesse affair, 8/203, 260; at St Olave's, 9/452; her closet, 7/76; 8/395; 9/199–200; also, 6/217; 8/97

SOCIAL: visits EP at Woolwich, 6/206; dines on East Indiaman, 6/273; birthday party for Brouncker, 6/285; visits P's house, 7/66–7; godmother to Knepp's son, 7/196; at Brouncker's house/lodgings, 6/236; 7/3; 8/431; 9/546; at hers, 7/14; 8/509; 9/106, 133, 331; at other houses/lodgings, 6/220, 228, 233; 7/18, 34, 38, 69, 364, 408; 8/394; 9/15, 505; at theatre, 8/395; 9/310, 381; also, 6/334; 7/3–4, 173; 9/109

~ her woman, 6/204

WILLIAMS, Col. [Henry], of Ramsey, Hunts.: changes name from Cromwell, 4/82–3 & n.; at Hinchingbrooke, 4/313

WILLIAMS, Dr John, physician: treats EP, 1/215, 276; 2/98, 125; 4/162(2), 350: consulted in dispute over Robert P's estate, 2/156, 160, 164, 176–80 passim, 210, 223; 3/12, 16, 100, 215; 4/126, 132, 350, 351, 364; illness, 2/193, 209; love affair, 6/144; garden and dog, 2/176; out of town, 3/118, 294; alluded to: 2/158; ~ his sister, 2/180; Jane, his maid at Cambridge, 1/216

WILLIAMS, [Vincent], Groom of the Chamber to the King: 7/218

WILLIAMSON, Joseph, Under-Secretary to Arlington and Keeper of State Papers, 1660–74; kted 1672; Secretary of State 1674–8:

CHARACTER: 4/35, 270; 5/323; 7/63, 169; 8/318, 556

CHRON. SERIES: manager of Fishery Corporation's lotteries, 5/323 & n. 2;

news from, 6/156; 7/229; 8/323; edits
Oxford Gazette, 6/305 & n. 3; 7/116;
at launch, 7/169; defeated in bye-
election, 7/337 & n. 2; influence,
8/318; praises P's parliamentary
speech, 9/105; consulted by P on
defence of Navy Board, 9/483; reads
P's memorandum to cabinet, 9/525;
also, 7/205; 9/61, 486
SOCIAL: 6/68; 7/38; 9/352, 410–11, 543
WILLIAMSON, Capt. [Robert], naval
officer: commissioned, 1/90
WILLOUGHBY, Francis, 5th Baron
Willoughby of Parham, Governor of
Barbados etc. 1663–6: drowned,
7/390 & n. 3
WILLOUGHBY, Maj. [Francis],
Navy Commissioner, 1653–1660: on
Naseby, 1/105; lodgings, 1/197
WILLS (P): his first (March 1660), 1/90
& n. 1; tears up EP's copy, 4/9; to
make a second, 4/433; 5/20, 25, 26, 29;
concludes and attaches memorandum
(Jan. 1664), 5/31; alters on Tom's
death, 5/192; draws up a third (Aug.
1665), 6/187, 189, 192; copies, 7/134;
his fourth (June 1667), 8/266
WILLYS, Sir Richard, royalist: dismissed from governorship of Newark
(1645), 6/30–1 & n.; plot betrayed
(1659), 1/141 & n. 1, 221; marriage,
1/141
WILLYS, Sir Thomas, M.P. Cambridge borough 1660: defeated in
county election (1660), 1/112 & n. 2;
on corruption of navy, 4/37
WILMOT, John, 2nd Earl of Rochester: attempts to abduct Elizabeth
Malet, 6/110 & n. 2, 119; 7/385;
marries her, 8/44 & n. 4; his poverty,
ib.; at court ball, 7/372; at theatre,
8/44; assaults T. Killigrew in King's
presence, 9/451–2 & n.; also, 9/382
WILSON, Tom, Navy Office clerk;
Surveyor of Victualling, London,
1665–7; Storekeeper, Chatham 1667–
?76: practical joke, 4/226–7, 230;
appointed Surveyor of Victualling,
6/272, 280 & n. 3; victualling business,
6/294, 305–6, 325; 7/135, 262, 265;
8/587; 9/8(2); Tangier accounts,
7/255; stories of Tom Fuller, 8/337; as
Storekeeper, 8/447; ill, 9/300; P

visits at Chatham, 9/499; also, 8/229,
267; ~ his wife [Jane], 9/499
WILSON, Mrs ——, Lady Castle-
maine's lady-in-waiting: her beauty,
8/324–5; said to be pregnant by King,
9/186
WILTON HOUSE, Wilts.: P's com-
ments on, 9/230; court to visit in
Plague, 6/189 & n. 3
WILTSHIRE, excise farmers of: 9/529
& n. 2
WIMBLEDON, Surrey: Bristol's
house at, 5/89
WIN: see Wynn
WINCHCOMBE, Glos.: tobacco cul-
tivation, 8/442; also, 2/225
WINCHELSEA, Sussex: bye-election,
7/337 & n. 2
WINCHILSEA, Lord: see Finch, H.
WINDHAM: see Wyndham
WINDSOR, Thomas, 7th Baron
Windsor, cr. Earl of Plymouth 1682;
Governor of Jamaica 1661–4 (d. 1687):
consults Navy Board, 3/62–3; attack
on Santiago, Cuba, 4/41 & n. 5, 94 &
n. 3; returns, 4/41 & n. 4, 54
WINDSOR, Berks.: painting by
Danckerts, 9/423 & n. 1, 539; Poor
Knights of, 1/78 & n. 1, 7/58 & n. 4;
installation of Knights of Garter, 2/75
& n. 7; 4/108; St George's Chapel,
7/57–8 & nn.; royal tombs in, 7/58 &
n. 6; castle, 7/58–9 & nn.; Garter Inn,
7/57 & n. 1, 59; also, 6/195, 198; 7/54
WINDSOR FOREST: P lost in, 6/197
WINE, (Wyne), [Arthur], purveyor of
fish to the King's household: 1/287;
4/101
WINGATE, [Edward]. M.P. St Albans
Herts. 1640–8: 9/518 & n. 2
WINTER, Sir John, secretary to the
Queen Mother: P's regard, 3/165;
6/62; 8/114; lease of timber and iron
in Forest of Dean, 3/112 & n. 2, 114;
4/193 & n. 3; stories of Forest, 3/165;
business, 6/62 & n. 2; 8/114, 191 & n. 4
WINTER, [Thomas], timber merchant: 4/326 & n. 2, 381
WINTER, [William], merchant: dis-
pute with Capt. Stoakes, 1/175 & n. 1;
dines with P, 1/212
WINTER, —— (old Winter), the
Algiers pirate: 3/124 & n. 1

WOODMONGERS' COMPANY: *see* London: livery companies

WOODROFFE, [Edmund], clerk in the Exchequer: 2/241; 6/235–6

[WOODSTOCK, ——], former husband of Lady Batten: 4/233 & n. 1

WOOD ST [*see also* Taverns etc.: Mitre]: furniture bought, 2/176; 4/6; joiners, 5/251

WOOLLEY, [John], underkeeper of Privy Council records: stationery expenses, 8/176 & n. 2, 182–3

WOOLLEY, [Robert], broker: advises P on Dutch prize-goods, 6/250, 254; 7/140; social: 5/94; 7/366, 385; 9/334; ~ his pretty wife, 7/345, 366; 9/334

WOOLWICH (Woolwige), Kent [*see also* Acworth, W.; Bodham, W.; Deane, A.; Falconer, J.; Pett, Christopher; Sheldon, W.; Ships: *Royal Catherine*; *Royal James*]:

TOWN [for P/EP's stay in Plague, *see* Sheldon, W.]: P/EP visit(s), 2/121; 4/149, 219; 5/45; Plague, 6/189, 282, 309–10; EP gathers May-dew, 8/240–2 passim; White Hart, 3/150, 214; 4/64, 8/95; story of old woman, 9/221; also, 9/555

DOCKYARD: *general*: guard, 2/11, 13–14; 7/275; thefts, 3/137 & n. 2; 4/236; 6/183–4; King visits, 3/265; corruption etc., 4/19, 79; quarrels between Deane and Christopher Pett, 4/384, ?396; float, 5/130 & n.; purchase of ground, 5/190–1 & n.; men laid off, 5/194 & n. 1; rope-stores, 5/325; projected mast-dock, 6/162 & n. 1, 184; workmen sent to Fire, 7/274, 276; fortifications, 8/266, 270, 284–5, 313 & n. 1, 350 & n. 1; war wounded quartered at, 8/403; also, 3/170; *visits by P (sometimes with colleagues) on official business*: inspects wreck, 1/315, 316; studies or inspects cordage/visits ropeyard, 2/14; 3/101, 136, 142, 145, 150, 156, 159, 179, 214; 4/64, 65, 79; 5/24, 130, 182 & n. 2, 190–1, 231, 253; 7/250; inspects frames for Navy Office houses, 3/102 & n. 1; storehouses, 3/136 & n. 1, 188; masts, 4/50; flags, 4/151; ironwork, 4/64; 5/75; new building, 4/284 & n. 2; hemp ship, 4/405; prize ship,

7/352 & n. 1; ballast wharf, 8/95; and fortifications, 8/284–5; shipping business: 2/104, 112; 3/63, 150; 4/20, 102–3, 131; 5/136–7, 146–7, 155, 156, 165, 265, 305, 306; 7/153; 8/124, 257; criticises survey, 3/150–1; musters yard, 3/179 & n. 2, 214; 4/241 & n. 1; reduces pay, 3/201; introduces new call books, 3/289; also, 2/36; 3/19, 31; 4/67, 235, 254, 302, 425; 5/24, 39, 54, 95, 109, 192–3, 213, 262, 325, 357; 6/74, 93, 96, 111, 128; 7/149, 168; 8/84, 176; *visits by P's colleagues on official business*: sale, 2/50 & n. 2; musters, 3/188; pay, 3/201 & n. 1; also, 1/313, 319; 2/36; 4/204

WOOTON: *see* Wotton, [William]

WORCESTER, Marquess of: *see* Somerset

WORCESTER: Charles II's escape after battle, 1/155–6 & n.; 8/526; King Edgar's charter, 6/81 & n. 1

WORCESTER HOUSE, Strand, Clarendon's residence 1660–6: P visits, 1/198, 199, 225, 226; 2/157; 5/204–5; 7/107; Chancery cases at, 5/203–4, 205; Privy Council at, 5/114; 7/107; Great Hall, 1/226; 5/204; garden, 5/205

[WORCESTER HOUSE], near Ewell, Surrey: P visits, 6/312 & n. 2

WORSHIP, Mrs ——: at musical evenings, 6/320–1, 323; 7/73; widowed, 8/58; dines with P, 8/157; alluded to: 6/215

WORSHIP, Mrs ——, daughter of the foregoing: sings well, 6/137, 215; companion to Lady Vyner, 6/215; at musical evenings, 6/320, 323; 7/73; dines with P, 8/157

WOSTENHAM: *see* Wolstenholme

WOTTON, Charles Henry Kirkhoven, 3rd Baron Wotton, cr. Earl of Bellomont (Ireland) 1680 (d. 1683): house and garden, 9/281 & n. 4

WOTTON, Sir Henry, diplomatist and poet, ambassador to Venice 1604–12, 1616–19, 1621–4 (d. 1639): gives picture of Venice to Eton, 7/60 & n. 2; tomb and inscription, ib. & n. 5

WOTTON, [William], shoemaker, Fleet St: work for P, 1/26, 81, 94; 3/204, 217; 4/28; 7/12; 9/295;

LIST OF ILLUSTRATIONS IN VOLUMES I TO IX

MAPS

BIBLIOGRAPHY

In the footnotes to the text of the diary, references to printed books are usually given in a deliberately brief form. Further details, where necessary, are therefore given here. Books listed under 'Editorial Abbreviations' in volumes i and x are not included. Titles are in some cases abbreviated. The place of publication is London unless otherwise stated.

Abbott, Wilbur C., *Conflicts with oblivion*, Cambridge, Mass. 1935
Adair, John E., *Roundhead General: Sir William Waller*, 1969
Adams, John Q., *Dramatic records of Sir Henry Herbert 1623–73*, New Haven, Conn. 1917
Addison, Sir William, *Audley End*, 1953
   English fairs and markets, 1953
Ailesbury, Earl of, *Memoirs* (ed. Buckley), 2 vols. Roxburghe Club 1890
Albion, Robert G., *Forest and sea power . . . 1652–1862*, Cambridge, Mass. 1926
Anderson, Matthew S., *Britain's discovery of Russia 1553–1815*, 1958
Anderson, Roger C., *Lists of men-of-war 1650–1700*, pt i, *English Ships 1649–1702* (Soc. Naut. Research), Cambridge 1939
Anderson, Roger C. and R., *Sailing Ships*, 1947
André, Louis, *Michel le Tellier et Louvois*, Paris 1943
Andrews, Charles M., *British committees of trade 1622–75*, Baltimore 1908
Andrews, William, *Bygone Punishments*, Hull 1890
Arber, Edward (ed.), *The Term Catalogues 1668–1709*, 3 vols., 1903–6
Arlington, Earl of, *Letters to Sir William Temple* [*1665–70*], (ed. T. Bebington), 1701
Ashley, Maurice P., *Financial and commercial policy under the Protectorate*, Oxford 1934
   John Wildman, 1947
Ashton, John, *History of English lotteries*, 1893
   History of gambling in England, 1898
   Hyde Park, 1896
Atkinson, Thomas D. (intro. by J. W. Clark), *Cambridge described and illustrated*, 1897
Auerbach, Bertrand, *La France et le Saint-Empire Romain*, Paris 1912
Aylmer, Gerald E., *The King's servants: the civil service of Charles I*, 1961
Aylward, James de V., *The smallsword in England*, 1945
Bagwell, Richard, *Ireland under the Stuarts*, 3 vols, 1906–16
Baillie, Granville H., *Watches, their history, decoration and mechanism*, 1929
Bankoft, George, *The story of surgery*, 1947

Barber, Richard W., *Samuel Pepys Esquire*, 1970

Barbour, Violet, *Henry Bennet, Earl of Arlington*, Washington, D.C. 1914
Capitalism in Amsterdam in the 17th century, Baltimore 1950

Barlow, Edward, *Journal* (ed. Lubbock), 2 vols, 1934

Barrett, Charles R. B., *The Trinity House of Deptford Strond*, 1893

Barrow, Albert S. ('Sabretache'), *Monarchy and the chase*, 1948

Barton, Margaret, *Tunbridge Wells*, 1937

Bastide, Charles, *The Anglo-French entente in the 17th century*, 1914

Baxter, Stephen B., *The development of the Treasury 1660–1702*, 1957

Beck, William and Ball, T. F., *London Friends' Meetings*, 1869

Beckett, Ronald B., *Lely*, 1951

Beloff, Max, *Public order and popular disturbances 1660–1714*, Oxford 1938

Bent, James T., *Genoa*, 1881

Bentley, Gerald E., *The Jacobean and Caroline stage*, 7 vols, Oxford 1941–68

Beresford, John J., *The Godfather of Downing St: Sir George Downing*, 1925

Beresford, William, *Lichfield*, 1883

Bernbaum, Ernest, *The Mary Carleton narratives 1663–73*, Cambridge, Mass, 1914

Bertin, Ernest, *Les mariages dans l'ancienne société française*, Paris 1879

Beveridge, Sir William (et al.), *Prices and wages in England*, vol. i, 1939

Bewes, Wyndham A., *Church Briefs*, 1896

Birch, Walter de G. (ed.), *Cartularium Saxonicum*, 3 vols, 1883–93
(ed.), *Historical charters of London*, 1884

Black, William G., *Folk-Medicine*, 1883

Bloch, Marc, *Les rois thaumaturges*, Strasbourg 1924

Blundell, William, *Crosby Records: A Cavalier's notebook* (ed. Gibson), 1880

Boseley, Ira, *Ministers of the Abbey Independent Church 1650–60*, 1911

Bosher, Robert S., *The making of the Restoration settlement . . . 1649–62*, 1951

Boswell, Eleanore, *The Restoration court stage*, Cambridge, Mass. 1932

Bourel de la Roncière, Charles G., *Histoire de la marine française*, Paris 1899–

Brady, W. M., *The episcopal succession in England . . . 1400–1875*, 3 vols, Rome 1876–7

Braithwaite, William C., *The beginnings of Quakerism*, 1912
The second period of Quakerism, 1919

Brand, John, *Popular Antiquities* (ed. Hazlitt), 2 vols, 1905

Brereton, Sir W., *Travels in England* etc. (ed. Hawkins), Chetham Soc., 1844

Brett-James, Norman G., *The growth of Stuart London*, 1935

Bridge, Sir Frederick, *Samuel Pepys, lover of musique*, 1903

Brittain, Frederick, *Latin in church: the history of its pronunciation*, Alcuin Club, 1955

Broodbank, Sir Joseph G., *History of the port of London*, 2 vols, 1921

Brooke, George C., *English coins from the 7th century to the present day*, 1950

Brown, Louise F., *Political activities of Baptists etc. during the Interregnum* Washington, D.C. 1912

The first Earl of Shaftesbury, N.Y. 1933

Brown, R. Allen: *see* Colvin

Browne, Sir Thomas, *Works* (ed. Keynes), 4 vols, 1964

Browning, Andrew, *Thomas Osborne, Earl of Danby 1632–1712*, 3 vols, Glasgow 1944–51

Bulstrode Papers [newsletters from the collection of Alfred Morrison], 1897

Bund, John W. Willis (ed.), *Diary of Henry Townshend*, 2 vols, Worc. Hist. Soc., 1920

Burton, Robert, *Anatomy of melancholy* (ed. Shilleto), 3 vols, 1893

Byrom, John, *Private Journal . . .* (ed. Parkinson), 4 vols, Chetham Soc., 1854–7

Callender, Sir Geoffrey, *Portrait of Peter Pett and the Sovereign of the Seas*, Newport (I. of W.) 1930

Carl, Philipp, *Repertorium der Cometen – Astronomie*, Munich 1864

Carlton, William J., *Shorthand Books* (*Descriptive catalogue of the library of S. Pepys*, pt iv), 1940

Carr, Cecil T. (ed.), *Select charters of trading companies 1500–1707*, Selden Soc., 1913

Carte, Thomas, *Ormond*, 3 vols, 1735–6

Cavendish, Margaret, *Life of the Duke of Newcastle* (ed. Firth), 1886

Chappell, William, *Popular music of olden time*, 2 vols, 1853–9

Chapuis, Alfred and Droz, E. (trans.), *Automata*, Neuchatel 1958

Charrington, John, *Catalogue of engraved portraits in the library of S. Pepys*, Cambridge 1936

Chatterton, E. Keble, *Ship-models*, 1923

Chavagnac, Gaspard de (i.e. G. Courtilz de Sandras), *Mémoires*, Paris 1900

Chester, Joseph L., *Marriage etc. registers of . . . the . . . abbey of St Peter, Westminster*, Harl. Soc., 1876

Chéruel, Adolphe, *Histoire de la France sous Mazarin*, 3 vols, Paris 1882

Chettle, George H., *The Queen's House, Greenwich*, 1937

Christie, William D., *Shaftesbury*, 2 vols, 1871

Clark, Alexander F. B., *Boileau and the French classical critics in England 1660–1830*, Paris 1925

Clark, Alice, *The working life of women in the 17th century*, 1919

Clark, Sir George N. (and A. M. Cooke), *History of the Royal College of Physicians*, 3 vols, Oxford 1964–72

War and society in the 17th century, Cambridge 1958

Clark, John W. and Gray, A., *Old plans . . . of Cambridge 1574–1798*, Cambridge 1921

Clarke, Martin L., *Classical education in Britain 1500–1900*, Cambridge 1959

Clarke Papers (ed. Firth), 4 vols, Camden Soc., 1891–1901

Clement, Pierre, *Lettres etc. de Colbert*, 8 vols, Paris 1861–82

Cleveland, John, *Poems* (ed. Morris and Withington), Oxford 1967

Cobbett, Richard S., *Memorials of Twickenham*, 1872

Cole, Charles W., *Colbert and a century of French mercantilism*, 2 vols, N.Y. 1939

Cole, Francis J., *Early theories of sexual generation*, Oxford 1930

Coleman, Donald C., *Sir John Banks*, Oxford 1963

Collinson, John, *History of Somerset*, 3 vols, Bath 1791

Colvin, Howard M., *Biographical dictionary of English architects 1660–1840*, 1954

(ed.), *The King's Works* (vol. ii, ed. R. Allen Brown et al.)

Cooper, Charles H., *Annals of Cambridge*, 5 vols, Cambridge 1842–53
Memorials of Cambridge, 3 vols, Cambridge 1860–6

Corbett, Sir Julian S., *Drake and the Tudor navy*, 2 vols, 1899
England in the Mediterranean 1603–1713, 2 vols, 1904
(ed.) *Fighting Instructions 1530–1816*, Navy Rec. Soc., 1905

Costello, William T., *The scholastic curriculum at early 17th-century Cambridge*, Cambridge, Mass. 1958

Cowper, Francis H., *A prospect of Gray's Inn*, 1951

Craig, Sir John, *The Mint*, Cambridge 1953

Crawfurd, Sir Raymond, *The King's Evil*, Oxford 1911

Creighton, Charles, *History of epidemics in Britain*, 2 vols, 1965

Croft-Murray, Edward F., *Decorative painting in England 1537–1837*, 2 vols, 1962–70

Cunnington, Cecil W. and P., *History of underclothes*, 1951

Curtis, Mark H., *Oxford and Cambridge in transition 1558–1642*, Oxford 1959

Cussans, John E., *History of Hertfordshire* 3 vols, 1870–81

Dale, Hylton B., *The fellowship of woodmongers*, [n.d.]

Danby, Henry C., *The draining of the fens*, Cambridge 1940

Davies, Godfrey, *The restoration of Charles II 1658–60*, San Marino, Calif. 1955

Davies, John S., *History of Southampton*, 1883

Davies, Kenneth G., *The Royal African Company*, 1957

Davies, Randall R. H., *Chelsea Old Church*, 1904

Dawson, Oliver S., *The story of Wanstead Park*, [n.d.]

Defoe, Daniel, *Tour* (ed. Cole), 2 vols, 1927

Desdevises du Dézert, Georges N., *L'Espagne de l'ancien régime*, 3 vols, Paris 1897–1904

Dews, Nathan, *History of Deptford*, 1884

Dietz, Frederick C., *English public finance 1558–1641*, 1932

Dingley, Thomas, *History from marble* (ed. Nichols), Camden Soc., 1867

Dutuit, Eugène, *Manuel de l'amateur d'estampes*, vols 1, 4, 6 only pub., Paris 1881–5

East, Robert, *Extracts from the records of Portsmouth*, Portsmouth 1891

Elder, John R., *Royal fishery companies of the 17th century*, Glasgow 1912

Esdaile, Arundell J. K., *List of English tales etc. published before 1740*, 1912
Esdaile, Katharine A., *English church monuments 1510–1840*, 1946
  English monumental sculpture since the Renaissance, 1927
  Temple Church monuments, 1933
Evans, Florence M. G., *The Principal Secretary of State 1558–1680*, Manchester 1932
Evans, Willa McC., *Henry Lawes*, N.Y. 1941
Evelyn, *Diary and Correspondence* (ed. Wheatley), 4 vols, 1879
  Miscellaneous Writings (ed. Upcott), 1825
Fagan, Louis, *Descriptive catalogue of the engraved works of William Faithorne*, 1888
Fanshawe, Herbert C., *History of the Fanshawe family*, Newcastle upon Tyne 1927
Feavearyear, Sir Albert E., *The pound sterling*, Oxford 1931
Feiling, Sir Keith, *History of the Tory Party 1640–1714*, Oxford 1924
Fellowes, Edmund H., *Charles I, his death, his funeral, his relics*, Windsor 1950
Fiennes, Celia, *Journeys* (ed. C. Morris), 1947
Firth, Sir Charles H. and Lomas, S. C., *Notes on the diplomatic relations of England and France 1603–88*, Oxford 1906
Fisher, Frederick J. (ed.), *Essays in honour of R. H. Tawney*, Cambridge 1961
Fisher, Sir Godfrey, *Barbary Legend 1415–1830*, N.Y. 1957
Foord, Alfred S., *Springs, streams and spas of London*, 1910
Forbes-Leith, William, *The Scots men-at-arms in France*, 2 vols, Edinburgh 1882
Foss, Edward, *Judges of England* [*1066–1864*], 9 vols, 1848–64
Foster, Joseph, *Grantees of arms* (ed. Rylands), Harl. Soc. Pub. vol. 66, 1915
Foster, Sir Michael, *Lectures on the history of physiology*, Cambridge 1901
Foster, Sir William, *English factories in India* [1618–69], 13 vols, Oxford 1906–27
  John Company, 1926
Fox, George, *Journal* (ed. Penney, rev. Nickalls), Cambridge 1952
  Short Journal (ed. Penney), Cambridge 1925
Fox, Levi (ed.), *English historical scholarship in the 16th and 17th centuries*, Dugdale Soc., 1956
Foxcroft, Helen C., *Life and letters of the 1st Marquis of Halifax*, 2 vols, 1898
Foxon, David F., *Libertine literature in England 1660–1745*, 1964
Franklin, Kenneth J., *A short history of physiology*, 1933
Fraser, Peter, *The intelligence of Secretaries of State 1660–88*, Cambridge 1956
Fraser, Sir William, *Memorials of the Montgomeries*, Edinburgh 1859
Freeman, Andrew J., *Father Smith*, 1926
Frost, Maurice, *English and Scottish psalm and hymn tunes c. 1543–1677*, Oxford 1953
Fulton, Thomas W., *The sovereignty of the sea*, 1911
Funke, Otto, *Zum Weltsprachenproblem in England im 17. Jahrhundert*, Heidelberg 1929

Gardiner, Dorothy, *The story of Lambeth Palace*, 1930

Gardiner, Samuel R., *History of the Great Civil War 1642–9*, 4 vols, 1893

Gasztowtt, Anne-Marie, *Une mission diplomatique en Pologne 1665–8*, Paris 1916

Gatty, Charles T., *Mary Davies and the manor of Ebury*, 1921

Gelder, Hendrik E. van, *'s Gravenhage in zeven eeuwen*, Amsterdam 1937

George, John N., *English pistols and revolvers*, Onslow Co., N.C. 1938

George, Mary D., *English political caricatures to 1792*, Oxford 1959

Gérin, Charles, *Louis XIV et le Saint-Siège*, 2 vols, Paris 1894

Goddard, Edward H., *Wiltshire Bibliography*, [?Trowbridge] 1929

Gras, Norman S. B., *The evolution of the English corn market*, Cambridge, Mass. 1915

Gray's Inn: Pension Book 1569–1800 (ed. Fletcher), 2 vols, 1901–10

Green, Henry and Wigram, R., *Chronicles of Blackwall Yard*, 1881

Greville, Charles C. F., *Memoirs 1814–60* (ed. Strachey and Fulford), 8 vols, 1938

Gunning, Henry, *Reminiscences of Cambridge*, 2 vols, 1854

Gunther, Robert W. T., *Oxford Gardens*, Oxford 1912

Haley, Kenneth H. D., *The first Earl of Shaftesbury*, Oxford 1968

Hall, A. Rupert and Marie (eds), *Correspondence of Henry Oldenburg*, Madison 1965–

Handover, Phyllis M., *History of the London Gazette 1665–1965*, 1965

Hardacre, Paul H., *The Royalists during the Puritan Revolution*, The Hague 1956

Haring, Clarence H., *Buccaneers in the W. Indies in the 17th century*, 1910

Hart, Cyril E., *Commoners of the Dean Forest*, Gloucester 1951

   Free Miners of Dean, Gloucester 1953

Hartmann, Cyril H., *Clifford of the Cabal*, 1937

   The King my brother, 1954

   The King's friend, 1951

   La Belle Stuart, 1924

Hasted, Edward, *History and topographical survey of Kent*, pt i (ed. Drake), 1886

Hastings, James (ed.), *Encyclopaedia of religion and ethics*, Edinburgh 1908–26

Havran, Martin J., *Caroline Courtier: the life of Lord Cottington*, 1973

Hawkins, Edward et al., *Medallic illustrations of the history of Great Britain to the death of George II*, 2 vols, 1885

Hayes, Richard F., *Old Irish links with France*, Dublin 1940

Hazlitt, William C., *Old cookery books*, 1902

Herbert, Arthur S., *Historical catalogue of printed editions of the English Bible 1525–1961*, 1968

Hervey, George F. and Hems, J., *The Goldfish*, 1948

[Hill, Frank], *Sackville College*, East Grinstead 1913

Hill, George, *An historical account of the Macdonnells of Antrim*, Belfast 1873

Hind, Arthur M., *Wenceslaus Hollar and his view of London and Westminster*, 1922

Hinton, Raymond W. K., *Eastland trade and the commonweal in the 17th century*, Cambridge 1959

Hodges, Harold W. and Hughes, E. A. (eds), *Select naval documents*, Cambridge 1936

Holdsworth, Sir William, *History of English law*, 13 vols, 1922–52

Hole, Christina, *English home-life 1500–1800*, 1949

Holles, Gervase, *Memorials of the Holles family* (ed. Wood), Camden Soc., 1937

Hollond, John, *Two discourses of the Navy* (ed. Tanner), Navy Rec. Soc., 1896

Hooke, Robert, *Diary 1672–80* (ed. Robinson and Adams), 1935

Horden, John R. R., *Francis Quarles, a bibliography*, Oxford Bibliog. Soc., Oxford 1953

Hore, John P., *History of Newmarket and annals of the turf*, 3 vols, 1886

Horsefield, John K., *British monetary experiments 1650–1710*, 1960

Hoskins, Samuel E., *Charles II in the Channel Islands*, 2 vols, 1854

Houblon, Lady A. Archer, *The Houblon family*, 2 vols, 1907

Howell, James, *Epistolae Ho-Elianae or Familiar Letters* (ed. Jacobs), 2 vols, 1892

Howell, Roger, *Newcastle upon Tyne and the Puritan revolution*, Oxford 1967

Howell, Thomas B. and Howell, T. J. (eds), *A complete collection of state trials*, 34 vols, 1816–28

Hubaud, L-J., *Dissertation littéraire . . . sur deux petits poèmes*, Marseilles 1854

Hughes, George M., *History of Windsor Forest*, 1890

Hulton, Paul H. (ed.), *Drawings of England in the 17th century*, 2 vols, Walpole Soc., 1959

Humpherus, Henry, *History of the Watermen's Company*, 3 vols, [n.d.]

Hutchinson, J. R., *The press-gang afloat and ashore*, 1913

Huygens, Christiaan, *Oeuvres Complètes*, 22 vols, The Hague 1888–1950

Ingram, Bruce S. (ed.), *Three sea journals of Stuart times*, 1936

James, Percival R., *The baths of Bath in the 16th and 17th centuries*, Bristol 1938

Jewitt, Llewellyn, *Corporation plate and insignia of the cities and towns of England and Wales* (ed. Hope), 2 vols, 1895

Johnson, Basil H., *Berkeley Square to Bond Street*, 1952

Jones, E. Alfred, *Plate of St George's Chapel, Windsor Castle*, 1939

Jones, Philip E. (ed.), *The Fire Court*, 1966–

Jonge, Johan C. de, *Geschiedenis van het nederlandsche zeewesen*, 2 vols, Haarlem 1858–9

Josselin, Ralph, *Diary 1616–83* (ed. Hockliffe), Camden Soc., 1908

Josten, Conrad H. (ed.), *Elias Ashmole, his autobiographical notes etc.*, 5 vols, Oxford 1966

Judson, J. Richard, *Gerrit van Honthorst*, The Hague 1959

Jusserand, Jean A. J., *A French Ambassador*, 1892

Kaufman, Helen A., *Conscientious Cavalier: Bullen Reymes 1613–72*, 1962

Keevil, John J. et al., *Medicine and the navy, 1200–1900*, 4 vols, Edinburgh 1957–63

Kennedy, James, *The manor and parish of Hampstead*, 1906

Keynes, Sir Geoffrey (ed.), *Blood Transfusion*, Bristol 1949

Kingsford, Charles L., *The early history of Piccadilly*, Cambridge 1925

Kingston, Alfred, *East Anglia and the Great Civil War*, 1897

Kirby, Ethyn W., *William Prynne*, Cambridge, Mass. 1931

Kitchin, George, *Sir Roger L'Estrange*, 1913
    Survey of burlesque and parody in English, Edinburgh 1931

Lafontaine, Henry C. de (ed.), *The King's Musick: records relating to music and musicians 1460–1700*, [1909]

Lambley, Kathleen, *The teaching of the French language in England in Tudor and Stuart times*, Manchester 1920

Lamont, William M., *Marginal Prynne, 1600–69*, 1963

Lane Poole, Rachel, *Catalogue of portraits in Oxford*, 3 vols, Oxford 1912–25

Lane Poole, Stanley, *The life of . . . Stratford Canning*, 2 vols, 1888

Lang, Jane, *The rebuilding of St Paul's after the Great Fire*, 1956

Latimer, John, *Annals of Bristol in the 17th century*, Bristol 1900

Laughton, Sir John K. (ed.), *State papers relating to the defeat of the Spanish Armada*, 2 vols, Navy Rec. Soc., 1894

Legrelle, Antoine, *La diplomatie française et la succession d'Espagne*, 4 vols, Paris 1888–92

Lemaire, Louis, *Le rachat de Dunkerque: documents inédits*, Dunkirk 1924

Lennard, Reginald V. (ed.), *Englishmen at rest and play 1558–1714*, Oxford 1931

Leuridant, Félicien, *Une ambassade du Prince de Ligne en Angleterre 1660*, Brussels 1923

Lewis, Michael A., *England's Sea-officers: the story of the naval profession*, 1939
    The Spanish Armada, 1960

Lewis, Lady Theresa (ed.), *Lives of friends of Clarendon*, 3 vols, 1852

Liber Albus: the White Book of the City of London (ed. Henry T. Riley), 1861

Loisel, Gustave, *Histoire des ménageries*, Paris 1912

Lowe, Robert W., *Betterton*, 1891

Lower, Sir William, *A relation of the voyage etc. [of Charles II]*, The Hague 1660

Lubimenko, Inna, *Relations commerciales de l'Angleterre avec la Russie avant Pierre le Grand*, Paris 1934

Lufkin, Arthur W., *A history of dentistry*, 1948

Lyons, Sir Henry, *The Royal Society 1660–1940*, Cambridge 1944

McCloy, Shelby T., *French inventions of the 18th century*, Lexington, Ky 1952

McCulloch, John R. (ed.), *Select collection of early English tracts on commerce*, 1856

Macdonald, Hugh and Hargreaves, M., *Thomas Hobbes: a bibliography*, Bibliog. Soc., 1952

McDonnell, Sir Michael, *The registers of St Paul's School 1504–1748*, 1957
  The History of St Paul's School, 1909
McKisack, May, *The parliamentary representation of English boroughs during the Middle Ages*, 1932
McLachlan, Jean O., *Trade and peace with Old Spain 1667–1750*, Cambridge 1940
Maclure, Millar, *Paul's Cross sermons 1534–1642*, Toronto 1958
Madan, Francis F., *A new bibliography of the Eikon Basilike*, Oxford Bibliog. Soc., 1950
Madge, Sidney J. *The Domesday of Crown lands*, 1938
Magne, Emile, *Images de Paris sous Louis XIV*, Paris 1939
Marburg, Clara, *Mr Pepys and Mr Evelyn*, 1935
Markham, Christopher A. and Cox, J. C., *Records of Northampton*, 2 vols, 1898
Marples, Morris, *A history of football*, 1954
Martin, John B., '*The Grasshopper' in Lombard Street*, 1892
Matthews, Arnold G., *Calamy Revised*, Oxford 1934
Maxwell-Lyte, Sir Henry C., *Historical Notes on the Great Seal*, 1926
Mercier, Ernest, *Histoire de l'Afrique septentrionale*, 2 vols, Paris 1888
Millar, Sir Oliver, *Tudor, Stuart and early Georgian pictures in the collection of H.M. the Queen*, 1963
Mitchell, W. Fraser, *English pulpit oratory from Andrewes to Tillotson*, 1932
Monson, Sir William, *Naval Tracts* (ed. Oppenheim), Navy Rec. Soc., 5 vols, 1902–14
Mordaunt, John, Viscount Mordaunt, *Letter Book 1658–60* (ed. Coate), Camden Soc., 1945
Morison, Samuel E., *Harvard College in the 17th century*, 2 pts, Cambridge, Mass. 1936
Morley, Henry, *Memoirs of Bartholomew Fair*, 1859
Muddiman, Joseph G., *A history of English journalism [to 1666]*, 1908
  (ed.) *The trial of Charles I*, 1928
Mullinger, James B., *Cambridge characteristics in the 17th century*, Cambridge 1867
Neale, Sir John, *The Elizabethan House of Commons*, 1950
Needham, Raymond and Webster, A., *Somerset House*, 1905
Nef, John U., *The rise of the British coal industry 1550–1700*, 2 vols, 1932
Nethercot, Arthur H., *Abraham Cowley*, 1931
Nettel, Reginald, *Seven centuries of popular song*, 1956
Newton, Lady Evelyn C. Legh, *Lyme Letters 1660–1760*, 1925
Newton, Samuel, *Diary* (ed. Foster), Camb. Antiq. Soc., Cambridge 1890
Nicholls, Henry G., *The Forest of Dean*, 1858
Nicolson, Marjorie H. (ed.), *The Conway Letters 1642–84*, New Haven, Conn. 1930
  Pepys' diary and the new science, Charlottesville, Va. 1965

Notestein, Wallace (ed.), *The journal of Sir S. D'Ewes*, New Haven, Conn. 1923

Nuttall, Geoffrey F. and Chadwick, O., *From uniformity to unity 1662–1962*, 1962

O'Donoghue, Edward G., *Bridewell Hospital*, 1923

O'Donoghue, Freeman and Hake, H. M., *Catalogue of engraved portraits in the British Museum*, 6 vols, Oxford 1908–25

Ogg, David, *England in the reign of Charles II*, 2 vols, Oxford 1955

Oliver, Harold J., *Sir Robert Howard*, Durham, N.C. 1963

Ollard, Richard L., *The escape of Charles II after the battle of Worcester*, 1966
    Man of War: Sir Robert Holmes and the Restoration navy, 1969

Oman, Sir Charles, *The coinage of England*, 1931

Ornsby, George (ed.), *Correspondence of John Cosin*, 2 vols, Surtees Soc., Durham 1869–72

Osborne, Mary T., *Advice-to-a-painter poems 1633–1856*, Austin, Texas 1949

Overall, William H. and H. C. (eds), *Analytical index to the Remembrancia of the City of London 1579–1664*, 1878

Overton, John H., *Life in the English Church [1660–1714]*, 1885

Page, Frances M., *The estates of Crowland Abbey*, Cambridge 1934

Parkes, Joan, *Travel in England in the 17th century*, Oxford 1925

Parsons, Frederick G., *History of St Thomas's Hospital*, 3 vols, 1932–6

Pastor, Ludwig (trans.), *History of the Popes*, 1891–

Pearce, Ernest H., *Annals of Christ's Hospital*, 1901

Pearsall Smith, Logan, *The life of Sir Henry Wotton*, 2 vols, Oxford 1907

Pearson, Karl and Morant, G. M., *The portraiture of Oliver Cromwell*, 1935

Penn, William, jun., *My Irish journal 1669–70* (ed. Grubb), 1952

Penney, Norman (ed.), *Extracts from state papers relating to Friends 1654–72*, 1913

Percy, Thomas, *Reliques* (ed. Wheatley), 3 vols, 1876

Perrin, William G., *British Flags*, Cambridge 1922

Petitjean, Charles and Wickert, C., *Catalogue de l'œuvre gravé de R. Nanteuil*, Paris 1925

Petty, Sir William, *Economic Writings* (ed. Hull), 2 vols, Cambridge 1899

Petty-Southwell Correspondence 1676–87 (ed. Marquess of Lansdowne), 1928

Pevsner, Sir Nikolaus, *Buildings of England: Hertfordshire*, 1953
    (with Nairn, rev. Cherry), ib.: *Surrey*, 1971

Phillips, Frank T., *History of the Company of Cooks*, London, 1932

Picciotto, James, *Sketches of Anglo-Jewish history*, 1875

Pinks, William J., *The history of Clerkenwell*, 1881

Pinto, Vivian de Sola, *Sir Charles Sedley*, 1927

Playfair, Sir Robert, *The scourge of Christendom*, 1884

Plomer, Henry R. (with A. Esdaile), *Dictionary of printers and booksellers in England*, 2 vols, Bibliog. Soc., Oxford 1907–22

Plumb, J. H. (ed.), *Studies in social history: a tribute to G. M. Trevelyan*, 1955

Pontalis, Antonin L., *John de Witt* (trans.), 1885

Pool, Bernard, *Navy Board contracts 1660–1832*, 1966

Pooley, Charles, *Notes on the old crosses of Gloucestershire*, 1868

Porritt, Anne G. and E., *The unreformed House of Commons*, 2 vols, Cambridge 1903–9

Povah, Alfred, *Annals of St Olave, Hart St*, 1894

Powell, John R., *The navy in the English Civil War*, Hamden, Conn. 1962

Prestage, Edgar, *Diplomatic relations of Portugal 1640–68*, Watford 1925

Preston, Arthur E., *Christ's Hospital, Abingdon, almshouses, hall and portraits*, Oxford 1929

Purnell, Edward K., *Magdalene College*, Camb. Coll. Histories, 1904

Raven, Charles E., *English naturalists from Neckam to Ray*, Cambridge 1947
  John Ray, Cambridge 1942

Records of Lincoln's Inn: Black Books (ed. Baildon), 4 vols, 1897–1902

Reddaway, Thomas F., *The rebuilding of London after the Great Fire*, 1951

Redgrove, Herbert S. and I. M. L., *Joseph Glanvill and psychical research in the 17th century*, 1921

Reresby, Sir John, *Memoirs* (ed. Browning), Glasgow 1936

Rex, Mildred B., *University representation in England 1604–90*, 1954

Riemer, Jacob de, *Beschryving van 's Gravenhage*, 2 vols, Delft and The Hague 1730–9

Roberts, Clayton, *The growth of responsible government in Stuart England*, Cambridge 1966

Rogers, James E. T., *History of agriculture and prices in England 1259–1793*, 7 vols, Oxford 1866–1902

Rogers, Philip G., *The Dutch in the Medway*, 1970

Rohde, Eleanour S. (ed.), *The garden book of Sir T. Hanmer*, 1933

Rollins, Hyder E. (ed.), *A Pepysian garland*, Cambridge 1922

Roncière: *see* Bourel de la Roncière

Rose-Troup, Frances, *The Western rebellion of 1549*, 1913

Roseveare, Henry, *The Treasury*, 1969

Rouse Ball, Walter W., *Notes on the history of Trinity College, Cambridge*, 1899

Roxburghe Ballads (ed. William Chappell and J. W. Ebsworth), 9 vols, Hertford 1871–99

Russell, J. M., *History of Maidstone*, Maidstone 1881

Savile Correspondence (ed. William D. Cooper), Camden Soc., 1858

Sayle, Robert T. D., *The barges of the Merchant Taylors' Company*, 1933
  Lord Mayors' pageants of the Merchant Taylors' Company, Reading 1931

Scholes, Percy A., *The puritans and music in England and New England*, 1934

Scott, James R., *Memorials of the family of Scott of Scot's Hall*, 1876

Scott, Sir William R., *Joint-stock companies to 1720*, 3 vols, Cambridge 1910–12

Selden, John, *Table Talk* (ed. Pollock), 1927

Sergison Papers (ed. Merriman), Navy Rec. Soc., 1950

Shaw, William A., *The Knights of England*, 2 vols, 1906

Shrewsbury, John F. D., *The history of bubonic plague in the British Isles*, Cambridge 1970

Simon, André L., *Bottlescrew days: wine-drinking in England during the 18th century*, 1926

 History of the wine trade in England, 3 vols, 1907–9

Simpson, Claude M., *The British broadside ballad and its music*, New Brunswick, N.J. 1966

Singer, Charles J, et al. (eds), *History of Technology*, 5 vols, Oxford 1954–8

Slothouwer, D. F., *De paleizen van Frederik Hendrik*, Leiden [1946]

Smith, Adam, *The wealth of nations* (ed. Cannan), 2 vols, 1904

Smith, Frederick F., *History of Rochester*, Rochester 1928

Smith, H. Maynard (ed.), *The early life of John Evelyn*, Oxford 1920

Smyth, Charles H. E., *Church and parish: studies in the history of St Margaret's Westminster*, 1955

Smyth, John, *The Berkeley manuscripts: the lives of the Berkeleys* (ed. Maclean), 3 vols, Gloucester 1883–5

[*Somers Tracts*], ed. Walter Scott, 13 vols, 1809–15

Speaight, George G., *The history of the English puppet theatre*, 1955

Speed, John, *History of Southampton* (ed. Aubrey), Southampton Rec. Soc., 1909

Spencer, Hazelton, *Shakespeare Improved: the Restoration versions in quarto and on the stage*, Cambridge, Mass. 1927

Steinman, George S., *A memoir of Barbara, Duchess of Cleveland* (with Addenda), Oxford 1871–8

Stern, Walter M., *The porters of London*, 1960

Straker, Ernest, *Wealden Iron*, 1931

Straus, Ralph, *Carriages and coaches*, 1912

Strode, William, *Poetical Works* (ed. Dobell), 1907

Strong, Sir Roy, *Holbein and Henry VIII*, 1967

Stuart, Dorothy M., *The English Abigail*, 1946

Summers, Montague, *The Playhouse of Pepys*, 1935

 The Restoration Theatre, 1934

Summerson, Sir John, *Architecture in Britain 1530–1830*, 1953

Symonds, Richard, *Diary of the marches of the royal army* [*1644–5*] (ed. Long), Camden Soc., 1859

Swart, Koenraed W., *Sale of offices in the 17th century*, The Hague 1949

Sykes, Norman, *From Sheldon to Secker*, Cambridge 1969

Tanner, James R., *Samuel Pepys and the Royal Navy*, Cambridge 1920

Tate, William E., *The parish chest*, Cambridge 1951

Thompson, Edward M., *Correspondence of the family of Hatton 1601–1704*, 2 vols, Camden Soc., 1878

Thomson, Gladys S., *Life in a noble household 1641–1700*, 1937
Thomson, Mark A., *Constitutional history of England 1642–1801*, 1938
Thorn-Drury, George (ed.), *A little ark of 17th century verse*, 1921
Thorndike, Lynn, *History of magic*, 8 vols, London, 1923–58
Thornton, Archibald P., *West India policy under the Restoration*, Oxford 1956
Thurloe, John, *Collection of state papers* (ed. T. Birch), 7 vols, 1742
Tibbutt, Harry G., *Life and letters of Sir Lewis Dyve 1599–1669*, Beds. Hist. Soc., Streatley 1948
Tighe, Robert R. and Davis, J. E., *Annals of Windsor*, 1858
Townshend, Henry, *Diary* (ed. J. W. Willis Bund), Worc. Hist. Soc., 1920
Turnbull, George H., *Hartlib, Dury, and Comenius*, Liverpool 1947
Turner, Edward R., *The Privy Council 1603–1784*, 2 vols, Baltimore 1927–8
Turner, Francis C., *James II*, 1948
Turner, G. Lyon, *Original records of early nonconformity*, 3 vols, 1911–14
Uffenbach, Z. C. von, *London in 1710* (ed. Quarrell and Mare), 1934
Underwood, Edgar A. (ed.), *Science, medicine and history*, 2 vols, 1953
Varley, Frederick J., *Oliver Cromwell's latter end*, 1939
Vertue, George, *Notebooks*, 7 vols, Walpole Soc., Oxford 1930–55
Villari, Luigi, *The Republic of Ragusa*, 1904
Vincent, William A. L., *The state and school education, 1640–60, in England and Wales*, 1950
Wagner, Sir Anthony R., *Historical heraldry of Britain*, 1939
   Records and collections of the College of Arms, 1952
Walford, Edward, *Greater London, its history etc.* 2 vols, [n.d.]
Walpole, Horace, *Anecdotes of painting* (ed. Wornum), 3 vols, 1849
   Correspondence (ed. Lewis et al.), New Haven, Conn. 1937–
Wardale, John R. (ed.), *Clare College letters and documents*, Cambridge 1903
Warner, Sir George F. (ed.), *The Nicholas Papers*, 4 vols, Camden Soc., 1886–1920
Warnsinck, Johan C. M., *De retourvloot van Pieter de Bitter*, The Hague 1929
Watson, Foster, *English grammar schools to 1660*, Cambridge 1908
Weiss, D. G., *Samuel Pepys, curioso*
Westergaard, W. (ed.), *The First Triple Alliance 1668–72*, New Haven, Conn. 1947
Westrup, Sir Jack A., *Henry Purcell*, 1960
Wheatley, Henry B., *Samuel Pepys and the world he lived in*, 1880
Whitaker, Wilfred B., *Sunday in Tudor and Stuart times*, 1933
White, Eric W., *The rise of English opera*, 1951
Whitelocke, Bulstrode, *Memorials of the English affairs* [*1625–60*], 4 vols, Oxford 1853
Whiting, Charles E., *Studies in English puritanism 1660–88*, 1931
Wickham Legg, John and Hope, W. H. St J. (eds), *Inventories of Christchurch Canterbury*, 1902

Wickham Legg, Leopold G., *English coronation records*, 1901

Wilks, George, *The Barons of the Cinque Ports*, Folkestone 1892

Willcox, William B., *Gloucestershire 1590–1640*, New Haven, Conn. 1940

Williams, J. B. (J. G. Muddiman), *History of English journalism to* [*1666*], 1908

Williams, Neville J., *Powder and paint*, 1957

Williamson, J. Bruce, *History of the Temple*, 1924

Willis, Robert and Clark, J. W., *Architectural history of Cambridge*, 4 vols, Cambridge 1886

Wilson, John H., *Nell Gwyn*, New York 1952

    A rake and his times: George Villiers, 2nd Duke of Buckingham, New York 1954

Winstanley, Denys A., *Unreformed Cambridge*, Cambridge 1935

Withington, Robert, *English Pageantry*, Cambridge, Mass. 1918

Wolf, Abraham, *History of science etc, in the 16th and 17th centuries*, 1950

Wood, Alfred C., *Nottinghamshire in the Civil War*, Oxford 1937

Woodfill, Walter L., *Musicians in English society from Elizabeth to Charles I*, Princeton, N.J. 1953

Woodruff, Charles E. and Danks, W., *Memorials of Canterbury*, 1912

Woodward, John, *Tudor and Stuart drawings*, 1951

Wright, Arthur R. (ed. Lones), *British calendar customs: England*, 3 vols, Folk Lore Soc., 1936–40

Wright, Lawrence, *Clean and decent*, 1962

    Warm and snug, 1960

Yonge, James, *Journal* (ed. Poynter), 1963

Young, Sidney, *Annals of the Barber-Surgeons of London*, 1890

Zook, George F., *The Company of the Royal Adventurers trading into Africa*, Lancaster, Pa. 1919

CORRECTIONS, VOLUMES I TO IX

[Some of these corrections have been made in the reprints issued since 1971. Oblique lines are used to separate the corrigenda from the corrections. A minus sign before a line number indicates its position above the bottom line.]

VOLUME I

Preface and Introduction
p. xiii, l. −7: X/XI
p. xxi, ll. 6–7: Boughton, North-amptonshire/Kimbolton, Hunting-donshire
p. xxxvi, l. 9: depts/debts
p. l, l. 13: September/October
p. lxii, l. 21: 16 March/8 March
p. lxix, l. −2 & n. 11, l. 4: January/December
p. lxxiv, l. −7: 'Cuppe'/'Cupp'
    l. −6: 'tee'/'Tee'
p. lxxxix, l. 11: 15 May/18 May
p. xc, l. −6: than/that
p. cx, l. 16: Richard/William
p. cxliv, l. 15: *delete* 'about 3000'
    l. −3: Fot/For

Text
p. 15, l. 4: *add* '[Crew]' *after* 'Wal-grave'
p. 44, l. 6: *add* asterisk *after* 'Palace'
p. 56, l. −4: *add* '[Crew]' *after* 'Wal-grave'
p. 85, 12 March, l. 1: rise/ris
p. 207, l. 12: *delete* asterisk

Notes
p. 16, n. 1, l. 4: Henry/Herbert
p. 25, n. 4, l. 2: violonist/violinist
p. 49, n. 4, l. 1: *add* '[Girolamo Franzini],' *before* '*Las*'
p. 54, n. 1, l. 5: Joseph/Joshua (re-current)
p. 70, n. 4, l. 2: Much Munden/Great Munden
p. 80, n. 3, l. 1: n. 6/n. 5
p. 87, n. 1, l. 5: borough/county
p. 105, n. 3: *replace by* 'The 16th-century artillery forts of Walmer, Deal, and Sandown.'
p. 140, n. 4: *add* 'The *Novum Organum;*' *before* 'probably'
p. 183, n. 2, l. 4: 94/203
p. 197: *delete* note *a*
p. 267, n. 4, l. 4: it/she (recurrent)
p. 272, n. 3, l. 3: 1672/1673
p. 314, n. 2: *delete* second sentence
p. 334, l. 6 (St Michel): Mary/Dorothea (recurrent)
    l. 22 (Trice): half/step (recurrent)

VOLUME II

Text
p. 67, 7 April, l. −1: Battnes/Battens
p. 124, l. 3: her/him (MS. 'her')
p. 197, l. 14: *delete* semi-colon
p. 203, l. 2: Therobo/Theorbo
p. 240, 28 December, l. 3: *delete* 'too' (MS. 'into to')

Notes
p. 6, n. 3, l. 5: *delete* 'well'
p. 41, n. 1, l. −1: June/January
p. 43, n. 2: p. 62; 17 December 1665/pp. 62–3 & n.; vii. 32

p. 58, n. 5: James/Benjamin
p. 110, n. 2, l. 2: 4th/2nd
p. 132, n. 1, l. 3: 72/74
p. 137, n. 2, l. 1: Kt/cr. bt 1662
p. 146, n. 1: *delete* note
p. 160, n. 3, l. 1: sailed ... 1662/in July returned from W. Africa
p. 165, n. 1, l. 3: Chapeton/Chapoton
p. 192, n. 5: Josias/James
p. 198, n. 3: George/?Richard
    n. 4, last line: Committee/Corporation
p. 204, n. 1, l. 6: Yarrington/Yarranton

p. 217, n. 1, l. 3: Pepys/Sandwich

p. 239, n. 4: *replace by* 'This is said to be the first known instance of a record of a Marian apparition. The saint was St Gregory Thaumaturgus (c. 213–c. 270): F. L. Cross, *Oxf. Dict. Christian Church* (Oxf. 1974), p. 601.'

VOLUME III

Text

p. 3, 5 January, l. 3: beef./beef,

p. 64, l. −10: Warren/Batten (MS. 'Warren')

p. 78, l. −5: Lue[ll]in/Luein

p. 83, last line: me,/met

p. 105, l. 2: form/from

p. 120, 25 June, l. 6: ships/shops

p. 158, l. 1: *add* superior 1 after 'perticularly'

p. 171, l. 17: Sandwiches/Sandwich (MS. 'Sandwiches')

p. 174, 23 August, l. 1: words/works

p. 194, l. 2: γχ/ούχ

p. 228, 19 October, l. 7: by/be

p. 237, l. 8: jealouses/jealousys

p. 243, l. 8: should not/should (MS. 'should not')

p. 285, l. 12: for/from (MS. 'for') 17 December, l. 4: if/it

p. 300, l. 4: *delete* comma *after* 'Gauden '

Notes

p. 9, n. 3, l. 3: *delete* 'blown'

p. 14, n. 3, l. 6: five/c. fifty

p. 15, n. 2, l. 1: Huntingdon/Dover

p. 30, n. 3, last line: 216/214

p. 44, n. 2, l. 1: Olwin/Oliver

p. 52, n. 1, l. 5: 1686/1676

p. 85, n. 1, l. 2: 1682/1681

p. 113, n. 3, l. 8: 10 July 1664/vii. 359

& n. 3

p. 142, n. 3, l. 8: 13 February 1665 & n./above, p. 137 & n. 3

p. 159, n. 2: *replace by* 'Millicent, of Barham, Cambs., was said to be "the best extemporary fool" at James's court: A. Weldon, *Court . . . of James I* (1650), p. 92. James's monopolies had been notorious'.

p. 173, n. 1, ll, 1–2: i. 222 & n. 1/ii. 179 & n. 1

p. 194, n. 1, ll. 1–4: *Replace by* 'Dr R. Luckett writes: Pepys is loosely paraphrasing, or inaccurately recalling, Epictetus (*Encheiridion* I. i): τῶν ὄντων τὰ μέν ἐστιν ἐφ᾽ ἡμῖν, τὰ δὲ οὐκ ἐφ᾽ ᾽ἡμῖν ('Of things, some are in our power, others are not'). He accidentally writes οὐχ for οὐκ (he intended τὰ ἐφ᾽ ἡμῖν καὶ τὰ οὐκ ἐφ᾽ ημῖν); the slip is a natural one given the extensive use of ligatures in the seventeenth century. That it was a consequence of accident rather than ignorance is demonstrated by his correct rendering of οὐκ at iv. 16.'

p. 221, n. 1: 205/204 & n. 2

p. 232, n. 1, ll. 1–2: below, 15 October 1666 & n./above, ii. 195, n. 3

p. 235, n. 3, l. 3: some/two

p. 270, n. 4, l. 2: 1708/1713

p. 303, n. 2, l. 2: 221/222

VOLUME IV

Text

p. 16, l. 3: ἐφ ηυῖῦ/ἐκ ηυῖν

p. 61, 28 February, l. 4.: Batten/ Warren (MS. 'Batten')

p. 75, l. −4: *repunctuate* sees, and saith,

p. 98, l. 3: *add* '[?plain]' *after* 'most'

p. 118, l. −5: wood/woo'd

p. 133, l. 7: up,/up [to]

p. 144, l. −5: over/*over*

p. 145, l. 9: leade/gold (MS. 'leade')

p. 155, l. 3: fist/first

p. 298, 4 September, l. −5: place and/ placed at (MS. 'place and')

p. 366, l. 13: Lord it/Lord in

p. 367, l. −2: *add* '[him]' *after* 'have'

p. 369, l. 7: Hear/Here

p. 380, l. −2: rooms/room

p. 386, last line: *transpose* 'I pray' *to* beginning of l. 1 p.389

p. 405, 5 December, l. 3: *repunctuate* 'Allen home to dinner,'

p. 409, l. −1: *repunctuate* 'and I,'

p. 428, l. 3: this/these (MS. 'this')
p. 436, 29 December, l. 12: not/nor (MS. 'not')

Notes

p. 17, n. 1: *delete* note
p. 20, n. 2, l. 1: 7/6
p. 25, n. 1, ll. 3–4: Sir William Berkeley/Sir Charles Berkeley, jun.
p. 37, n. 3: *add* ',1660' *after* 'borough'
p. 41, n. 5, l. 4: St Jago/Santiago
p. 73, n. 1, l. 10: Solebay/Lowestoft
p. 75, n. 3, l. 6: 68/61
p. 91, n. 1: *replace by* 'The stempiece was the main vertical timber of the bow'.
p. 95, n. 3, l. —5: during the Interregnum/in the 1620s
p. 105, n. 2, l. —1: 1663/1652
p. 119, n. 2, l. 5: Sturtlow/Stirtloe
p. 126, n. 2, l. 12: not/nor
p. 159, n. 4: *transpose to* p. 160 as n. 1
p. 164, n. 2: milk/cold milk
p. 187, n. 3, l. 1: *add* 'eldest' *before* 'sons'
p. 210, n. 1: *add* '*Recte* manslaughter.' *before* 'See'
p. 235, n. 2: *replace* last sentence *by* 'PL 1075(11).'

p. 255, n. 1, last line: *Varii Sectiones/ Variæ Lectiones*
p. 304, n. 1, l. 8: 419/421
p. 308, n. 1: *replace* first sentence *by* 'Near Kettering, Northants.'
p. 312, n. 2: Huntingdon/Brampton
p. 319, n. 1: Hart St/Seething Lane
p. 320, n. 2: *delete* second sentence
p. 322, n. 1, ll. 10–11: *delete* 'and N. America'
p. 349, n. 1, ll. 5–6: *delete* 'appears . . . She'
p. 354, n. 1, l. 1: James/Benjamin
p. 363, n. 1, l. 2: 437/439
p. 372, n. 3, l. 2: exluded/extruded
p. 382, n. 3, l. 2: *replace* 'App. B, pp. 440–1' *by* 'pp. 387–8'
p. 423, n. 1: *replace by* 'Cf. B. J. Whiting, *Proverbs, sentences &c.* (Camb. Mass. 1968), item F635. The verse, in various forms, was in current use within living memory.'
p. 424, n. 2: 402/404
    n. 3: 412/421
p. 435, n. 1: 393, n. 1/395, n. 2
p. 441, n. 2: *replace* 'Calabrian . . . Excelsior' *by* 'and *sal prunellæ*, with three ounces of Calabrian manna (dried sap of *Fraxinus ornus L.*)'

VOLUME V

Text

p. 7, last line: *add* '[her]' after 'commend'
p. 16, 15 January, para. 4, l. 1: with/that
p. 283, l. —6: *repunctuate* 'angry, . . . plain;'

Notes

p. 8, n. 2, ll. —3 & —2: The year date should be '1659/60'
p. 42, n. 2: *replace by* 'See above, iii. 17 & n. 1'
p. 53, n. 3, ll. 1–2: *replace by* 'At Tooting Bec (C. A. F. Meekings, ed., *Surrey Hearth Tax 1664*, 1942, p. 86).'
p. 56, n. 4: 405/407
p. 63, n. 1, l. 7: 1660/1661
p. 73, n. 5: *delete* 'trotting'
p. 116, n. 1, col. 1, l. —8: 24 May 1669/

December 1672
p. 117, n. 4, ll. 6–7: *delete* 'and . . . will'
p. 170, n. 3, l. 4: French/Spaniards
p. 184, n. 2, l. 2: *delete* 'groomporter'
p. 189, n. 2: *replace by* 'Drawing the outline for the mould of a ship. Cf. PL2910.'
p. 190, n. 1, l. —1: hat/that
p. 237, n. 3, l. 2: *add* 'and arithmetic' *after* 'penmanship'
    n. 4, l. 2: ll. 146–73/ll. 1461–3
p. 244, n. 2, l. —1: quarrel with his father/disgrace at court
p. 281, n. 1, l. 1: *delete* 'Sir'
p. 289, n. 2, ll. —5 to —2: *delete* 'Pepys . . . 162'
p. 316, n. 2: *replace by* 'Now the New Armouries'
p. 321, n. 3, l. 4: Holmes's/Nicholls's

p. 342, n. 1: Christopher Cisner/David Primerose
n. 2: *delete* queries
p. 346, n. 3, l. 11: November/

December
p. 353, n. 1, l. 4: Allin's/Holmes's
p. 361, n. 1, ll. 13–14: both . . . 1680/ who died in 1680 and 1689

VOLUME VI

Text
p. 125, 12 June, l. 4: sleeve-bands/ sleeve-hands
p. 135, 23 June, l. −3: *add*, 'did give him' *after* 'Albimarle'; *delete* note *b*
p. 162, 19 July, l. 3: Falconer/Falconbridge

Notes
p. 24, n. 2, l. −1: *Office/Board*
p. 37, n. 2, l. 1: Harvey/Hervey (recurrent)
p. 41, n. 2: Charlotte/Lady Charlotte
p. 53, n. 5: v. 269 & n. 2/v. 323 & n. 2
p. 95, n. 2, l. 2: 32/34
n. 4: *delete* second sentence

p. 100, n. 5: iii. 17 & n. 2/iv. 379 n. 6: n. 1/n. 2
p. 101, n. 1, l. 5: son Samuel/cousin John
p. 102, n. 6: Wanstead/Walthamstow
p. 126, n. 1, l. 5: son/grandson
p. 149, n. 2: n. 1/n. 2
p. 152, n. 2, ll. 2–3: *delete* 'whom . . . Cambridge'
p. 160, n. 1, ll. 4–5: probably . . . Romford/St Peter's, South Weald
p. 163, n. 4: *alter to* 'were London merchants'
p. 166, n. 1: Greenwich tradesman/ Westminster draper
p. 279, n. 2, l. 3: *delete* 'iron'
p. 280, n. 1, l. 3: 255, n. 1/254, n. 2

VOLUME VII

Text
p. 44, l. 4: How/Hewer (MS. 'WH')
p. 107, l. −9: in/is (MS. 'in')
p. 150, l. −2: Ball/Bell (MS. 'Ball')
p. 183, l. 13: *repunctuate* 'work, so is'
p. 229, l. 11: him/it (MS. 'him')

Notes
p. 41, n. 2, l. 1: John/Edward, son of John
l. 3: *delete* 'of the same name'
p. 54, n. 1, l. 3: lieutenants/rivals
p. 94, n. 6, l. 7: Herts./Hants.
p. 108, n. 4: p. 93, n. 1/p. 44, n. 2
p. 111, n. 2: iv./v.
p. 114, n. 3, l. 10: 1655/1665
p. 115, n. 2: n. 3/n. 4
p. 132, n. 3, l.−3: 220–1/385 & n. 2
p. 145, n. 7, l. 1: John/Samuel
p. 154, n. 3, l. 5: elder brother/cousin
p. 225, n. 2: Weilings/Wielings

p. 229, n. 3, l. 2: Koenders/Coenders
p. 243, n. 3, l. 3: possibly Edmond/ probably William
p. 245, n. 4, l. 4: 1662–6/1662–83
p. 271, n. 2: *alter to* 'Barbara Sheldon'
p. 290, n. 2, l. −1: 1641/?1652
p. 309, n. 1, last line: 4/3
p. 341, n. 2: *add* 'The Queen's birthday was in fact on 15 November: see below.'
p. 346, n. 1, l. 5: 1667/November 1666
p. 352, n. 5: *replace by* 'Clerk-Comptroller of the Green Cloth'
p. 375, n. 2, l. 6: Henry/William
p. 383, n. 3: *replace by* 'John Ashburnham, Groom of the Bedchamber'.
p. 385, n. 2, last line: 245 & n. 5/132 & n. 3
p. 386, n. 3, l. 5: 1654/1652
p. 391, n. 1, ll. 8–9: Henley, Som./ Bramshill, Hants.
p. 403, n. 3, l. −1: George/Charles

VOLUME VIII

Text

p. 27, l. −5: Ball/Hall (MS. 'Ball')
p. 29, l. −1: they ng/they not being
p. 111, l. −5: believe she/believes he
p. 215, 15 May, l. 13: Cholmely/ Chichely (MS. 'Ch.')
p. 239, l. 2: [?coach]/[water]
p. 270, l. 5: foretell/[did] foretell
p. 345, ll. 11 & 12: *add* comma *after* 'pretty'; *delete* comma *after* 'fast'
p. 495, l. 4: *add* comma *after* 'series'
p. 564, l. 12: Edwd/Richard (MS. 'Edwd')

Notes

p. 19, n. 2: Peter/John
p. 37, n. 2: John/James
p. 45, n. 1, l. 2: n. 3/n. 1
p. 56, n. 6: *replace by* 'Vicenzo Albrici'
p. 73, 20 February, l. 14: *repunctuate* 'closet, all our business lack of money'
p. 85, n. 3, l. −1: the borough/ Cambridge borough
p. 131, n. 1: *replace by* 'Sir William Turner.'
p. 144, n. 3, l. 3: n. 3/n. 4
p. 154, n. 2, l. 2: 1664/1665
p. 171, n. 5, l. 2: 15/13
p. 179, n. 2: *add* at beginning 'The New Armouries:'
p. 205, n. 2, l. 2: purchase/acquisition
p. 218, n. 3, l. 6: 1880/1884
p. 236, n. 2, l. −3: *Works/Writings*
p. 241, n. 1, ll. 1–3: had been a fellow . . . Cambridge/had presumably been a private tutor to Brookes
p. 257, n. 5: *replace by* 'The defences of

Gravesend.'
p. 265, n. 1, l. 8: *delete* 'the Presbyterian'
p. 267, n. 2: *replace by* 'Thomas Wilson, newly appointed storekeeper at Chatham.'
p. 269, n. 1: n. 2/n. 1
p. 275, n. 3: *replace by* 'Cf. below, ix. 500 & n. 1.'
n. 4: n. 4/n. 5
p. 330, n. 5, l. 2: 3rd/1st
p. 347, n. 1: n. 5/n. 7
p. 367, n. 2: a lieutenant . . . *Royal Charles*/captain of a frigate
p. 377, n. 2: [n.]4/n. 3
p. 381, n. 2: *replace by* 'In the High St.'
p. 384, n. 1, l. 2: Ferdinand III/ Leopold I
p. 418, n. 1: n. 4/n. 3
n. 3, l. −1: *delete* 'Sir'
p. 421, n. 3: *delete* note
p. 425, n. 3: who became messenger . . . 1670/Groom of the Privy Chamber from 1660
p. 446, n. 6: *preface by* '?'
p. 464, n. 1: n. 1/n. 2
p. 469, n. 1, l. 8: 1603/1626
p. 505, n. 2, l. 1: 1553/1552
p. 511, n. 3, l. −2: 1660/1666
p. 515, n. 4: 514 & n. 1/513 & n. 2
p. 526, n. 4, l. 3: Charles I/Charles II
p. 538, n. 3: Robert/John
p. 557, n. 2: n. 2/n. 4 *add* '(E)'
p. 582, n. 2, l. 2: *delete* '(Batten's son-in-law)'
p. 585, n. 6: *replace* second sentence *by* 'Ensum had died in 1666 . . . Jackson'

VOLUME IX

Text

p. 12, l. −2: house/office (MS. 'house')
p. 78, l. −1: *add* comma *after* 'at it'
p. 148, last line: Aldersgate/Aldgate
p. 154, l. −9: House/[?Gate-]house
p. 158, l. 10: *delete* comma *after* 'coaches'

p. 180, l. −9: to/to [do]
p. 201, l. −2: bands/hands
p. 410, 8 January, ll. 13–14: no great/ great (MS. 'no great')
p. 411, 10 January, l. 1: *add* comma *after* 'Accidentally'
p. 429, 28 January, l. 1: afternoon/

morning (MS. 'afternoon')
p. 468, l. −1: Maids/Maid
p. 480, l. 15: Chancer/Chancery
p. 520, 15 April, l. 5: Aldersgate/
Aldgate
p. 531, 22 Apr. 1669, l. 6: given/give
p. 554, l. −9: the Bishop make himself/
the Bishop (MS. 'the Bishop make
himself')

Notes
p. 6, n. 1: discharged/dismissed
p. 83, n. 1, ll. 2, 4: 1666/1667
p. 108, n. 2, l. 4: n. 1/n. 2
p. 117, n. 3: Eliezer/Eliezer Jenkins
p. 147, n. 2: David/Daniel
p. 157, n. 2, ll. 5–6: Sir William . . .
Yorks./the late Ald. Robert Lowther
of London
p. 161, n. 2: *replace by* 'Mary Ham-
mon, Sir John Mennes's sister.'
p. 163, n. 5: *replace by* 'Of prize
goods.'
p. 184, n. 1: *delete* note
p. 207, n. 3: *delete* 'at Aubrey's
house'
p. 215, n. 3, ll. 1–3: *replace* final
sentence *by* 'Probably Viscountess

Lambart (d. 1649) an Irish acquain-
of Penn's. I owe this suggestion to
J. Ferris.'
p. 231, n. 2: n. 2/n. 1
p. 238, n. 4: 1620/1621
p. 241, n. 1: *replace by* 'All the Avebury
stones and most of those at Stonehenge were of local sarsen.'
p. 293, n. 1, l. 11: ib./id.
p. 341, n. 1, last line: 67, n. 3/64–5
p. 347, n. 1, l. 4: 1662/1661
p. 383, n. 3: 1659/?1652
p. 416, n. 1, ll. 4–5: first President/
first pre-Charter President
p. 430, n. 1, l. 1: Jennings/Jennens
n. 3, l. 2: Philip/Henry
p. 441, n. 4, l. 4: n. 4/n. 3
p. 460, n. 5, l. 5: *add* 'W. Chappell
and' *before* 'J. W. Ebsworth'
p. 506, n. 1, l. 11: 1633/1660
p. 507, n. 3: Charles . . . London/
Thomas Foulkes, Groom of the
Buckhounds

Select Glossary
BALLET: *delete* 'broadside'
CAUDLE: *add* 'made with wine'

ACKNOWLEDGEMENTS, VOLUMES I TO IX

It is with deep regret that I have to record the death in 1975 of my co-editor, the late Professor William Matthews. It therefore falls to me at this point to acknowledge the debt to the large number of institutions and individuals who have assisted in the publication of the volumes of text since 1970, in addition to those whose names appear in the list of acknowledgements published in volume I:

To Magdalene College, the Trustees of the Leverhulme Foundation and the Goldsmiths' Company, for financial help without which it could not have been done.

To the late Prof. Edward Wilson of Cambridge for his translations of Pepys's Spanish; and to Esmond de Beer, Richard Ollard and MacDonald Emslie for help with the proofs.

To the archivists who have extended me every courtesy on my visits to their collections – at the Admiralty; the Berkshire County Record Office; the city of Bristol; Christ Church, Oxford; Eton College; the Goldsmiths' Company; Gray's Inn; Guildhall, London; the House of Lords; Huntingdon Borough and Huntingdonshire County Record Offices; the Mercers' Company; the Middle Temple; the National Maritime Museum; the North Yorkshire County Record Office; the University of Cambridge; the Dr Williams Library; Messrs Williams & Glyn; and the parish priests in charge of the parochial records at Brampton, Huntingdon, and St Olave's, Hart St.

To the officials I have consulted by letter – of the Victoria and Albert Museum; the Rijksmuseum, Amsterdam; the London Survey Committee of the Greater London Council; the Royal Geographical Society; the College of Heralds; the county record offices of Hertfordshire, Kent and Norfolk; the town libraries of Brentford and Chiswick, of Deal, Dover, Lambeth, Norwich, Portsmouth, Rochester, Shrewsbury, Walthamstow, Wandsworth and Woolwich; the county library of Wiltshire; the William Andrews Clark Library, Los Angeles; the Huntington Library, San Marino; St Paul's School; Westminster School and Canterbury Cathedral.

To the following for information on particular points – P. J. Adams, Dr S. O. Agrell, Lee Ash, Prof. V. Barbour, R. A. Barker, J. Berryman, M. F. Bond, Prof. W. H. Bond, Dr D. S. Brewer, Dr G. L. Broderick, Dr R. A. Brown, Prof. D. Chandaman, I. A. Crawford, Mrs P. E. Cunnington, J. Daniels, the late Prof. Alun Davies, G. Devey, Prof. G. Donaldson, Prof. K. Downes, Prof. J. D. Fage, C. Farthing, Dr P. J. Fitzpatrick, Dr D. Foxon, Miss D. Gifford, Mrs P. Glanville, the late

Prof. D. V. Glass, Dr J. Gmitro, G. H. Gollin, Sir J. Graham, Dr G. S. Graham-Smith, Rev. D. N. Griffiths, Dr R. Gwynn, Prof. J. R. Hale, Dr G. Hammersley, Miss F. Harman, C. E. Hart, Prof. R. Hatton, A. M. Hawker, Prof. H. T. Heath, R. L. Helps, P. Heselton, J. E. Hobbs, Miss C. Hole, Lord Hylton, Dr C. Imber, the late Sir G. Isham, Dr D. Johnson, Rev. M. O. W. Johnson, Dr C. H. Josten, Prof. H. A. Kaufman, Miss L. Kirk, Prof. E. H. Kossmann, Prof. W. A. Lamont, Dr P. Laslett, R. E. Latham, Prof. R. Leslie, B. Lillywhite, W. Lockwood, Sir R. Mackworth-Young, Dr G. C. R. Morris, the late Dr. A. N. L. Munby, Rev. Prof. G. F. Nuttall, J. C. T. Oates, Lt-Col. C. D. L. Pepys, R. L. Percival, J. Porteous, the late Maj.-Gen. M. W. Prynne, W. J. Rasbridge, M. Richardson-Bunbury, Dr P. Rickard, C. A. Rivington, Prof. C. Robbins, G. Roper, Dr V. A. Rowe, Dr I. Roy, the late J. Saltmarsh, Miss M. L. Savell, D. Scott, Dr A. Sharp, Maj.-Gen. H. B. Sitwell, R. S. Smailes, Prof. T. R. Smith, Sir R. Somerville, G. D. Squibb, P. Strong, Sir J. Summerson, Prof. G. H. Turnbull, Mrs S. Tyacke, Sir A. Wagner, Prof. R. R. Walcott, H. M. Walton, Rev. J. Watson, J. J. Wells, the late Prof. D. Whitelock, Dr T. D. Whittet, C. J. Whitwood, Col. F. B. Wiener, J. Wilson, Cmdr H. B. Wise, Prof. A. H. Woolrych, and Brig. P. Young.

And finally to the friends and correspondents who have commented on the volumes as they appeared and offered suggestions for their improvement – particularly John Ferris, J. J. van Herpen, Richard Luckett, Dr J. C. Mitchell, R. G. Pascoe, Dr T. D. Rogers and Capt. A. B. Sainsbury.

Robert Latham